RIGHT CONDUCT
Theories and Applications
SECOND EDITION

Edited by

MICHAEL D. BAYLES

Florida State University
Tallahassee, Florida

AND

KENNETH HENLEY

Florida International University
The State University of Florida at Miami

RANDOM HOUSE · NEW YORK

Second Edition

98765432

Copyright © 1983, 1989 by Random House, Inc.

LIBRARY OF CONGRESS
Library of Congress Cataloging-in-Publication Data

Right conduct : theories and applications / edited by
  Michael D. Bayles and Kenneth Henley.–2nd ed.
    p.   cm.
  Includes bibliographies.
  ISBN 0-394-38060-6
  1. Ethics.   2. Social ethics.   I. Bayles, Michael D.
  II. Henley, Kenneth.
  BJ1012.R49   1988   88-15864
  170–dc19   CIP

Manufactured in the United States of America

Cover Credit: "Mourning Athene," Acropolis Museum, Athens.
Cover Design by Lisa Polenberg.

Preface

*M*any ethical issues confront contemporary society. In response to this, over the last two decades or so, many philosophers have returned to an examination of ethical problems. Enrollments in ethics courses have increased, and various courses on specialized topics—bioethics, business ethics, professional ethics—have developed. Yet the majority of students still take only one general course in ethics. This book has been designed to acquaint introductory students with ethical theory as well as to present to them various approaches to interesting topics of practical concern.

Our primary principle in editing this book has been to emphasize the relationship of theory to practice. This principle has significantly influenced the structure of the text. First, we have focused exclusively on theories of conduct and have omitted material dealing primarily with metaethics, such as the meaning of the word "good" or such questions as "Why be moral?" Second, the applications have been chosen to illustrate different theoretical approaches to debatable issues. Some topics have been omitted because they do not readily exhibit the variety of theoretical approaches. Others, such as racism, have been omitted because no philosopher today seriously argues for racism.

Part I sets out six basic ethical theories: natural law, natural rights, Kantianism, contractarianism, and utilitarianism, both act and rule. Classical and contemporary sources are used to illustrate both historical origins and modern formulations of theories. This part should be studied before the student goes on to Part II, which deals with applications.

In Part II, the selections have been chosen to illustrate the different theoretical approaches presented in Part I; each of the three selections in a chapter illustrates a theory from a chapter in Part I. Although many authors of the selections do not fully subscribe to the views they have been chosen to illustrate, their selections exhibit an argument form of a particular type of theory. There is nothing sacrosanct about the order of the chapters in this part. An instructor can use them in any order he or she wishes. Each chapter stands independently.

This text arose from our dissatisfaction with the materials that we had each previously used in teaching ethics. Despite the fact that natural law and natural-rights arguments figure prominently in discussions of contemporary issues, it has been difficult to obtain class materials representing them. We have also found that many students need considerable assistance in understanding selections and are often unable to take satisfactory notes in class. They need concise expositions that they can examine repeatedly. Consequently, we have provided rather extensive introductions to each chapter setting out the major problems and views. In these introductions, we have striven to be objective and impartial, not favoring one theory over another. We have also tried to choose materials of differing levels of difficulty. Our experience indicates that students have most difficulty with abstract considerations of theory, and the chapters on applications should help increase understanding of theories by providing an opportunity for a more detailed consideration of particular aspects of them. As a basis for testing views and classroom discussion, we have provided a brief case at the beginning of each chapter on applications.

In preparing this edition, we have omitted and added various readings and topics to make them more interesting and current. We received the advice of four anonymous reviewers who had used the book. Although it was impossible to accommodate all their suggestions, the book is undoubtedly better for their help. Finally, we wish to thank Delores Jenkins, John Settle, and Garrett Maass for their bibliographical and library assistance.

Contents

RIGHT CONDUCT

Theories and Applications

General Introduction: The Importance and Possibility of Ethics

Moral claims abound in everyday life. Each of us demands that others do what is right toward us, and we make moral judgments of others: "He was unfair." "He cheated me." "What he did to me wasn't right." People also judge their own conduct, and sometimes guide their conduct accordingly: "I can't do anything that dishonest." "I ought to show a little kindness in this situation." And people show their moral beliefs in what they regret doing or failing to do.

Reasoning in support of such judgments also occurs frequently, both in discussions between people and within the reflections of a person thinking alone. Moral concepts are used to categorize actions, persons, and institutions. These concepts range from the richly substantive (courage, kindness, cruelty, honesty, loyalty) through the abstract (fairness, justice) to the most abstract and general (duty, obligation, what is right, what ought to be done). Ordinary moral reasoning often consists in considering whether one of the more substantive concepts applies to a particular course of action. "Would it be dishonest for me to do that?" "Let me explain why I think your action was inconsiderate." The goal is an adequate and fair description, avoiding the bias of a self-interested and partial viewpoint. It is only a short step from this rejection of bias to the emergence of a general moral principle of impartiality, such as the Golden Rule: "Do unto others as you would have them do unto you." And so ordinary moral reasoning leads naturally into the search for underlying principles general enough to bring order and coherence to moral thought. This search is one aspect of the area of philosophy called *ethics*.

A *normative ethical theory* is a principle (or a set of principles) that can be used to decide what morally ought to be done, along with the supporting reasons for such a principle. Principles are general guidelines for right conduct. The principles in ethical theories are very general, so that they will apply to every situation one encounters. The Golden Rule is a good example of a principle with this level of generality; from it one

1

can work out more specific principles or rules for truth telling, killing, and so on. The injunction "Do not lie" is also general, but there are many ethical problems it does not cover, such as those concerning killing.

The reasoning supporting a principle must be understood in order to apply that principle intelligently to practical moral problems. For example, without understanding the point of the Golden Rule, someone might think it means that since he or she wants rock-and-roll albums for Christmas, he or she should give everyone else rock-and-roll albums. Since there are competing theories of right conduct, the reasoning for each theory tries to show why its principles are correct. Such reasoning, however, will probably fail to convince everyone. Ethical theories are at least as controversial as are practical moral problems.

The Study of Ethics   Why then should one study theories of right conduct? Since there is controversy over theory, why not confront moral problems directly without separate treatment of theory? Some people go so far as to say that theories only serve to rationalize moral views that really stem from other sources (such as childhood training or religious beliefs).

Indeed, theories can be used to justify beliefs already held—and, perhaps, this is to some extent inevitable. Almost all theories try to justify some central ethical beliefs, such as the wrongness of torturing people for pleasure. But there is a difference between mere rationalization, with the goal of rigidly keeping all one's beliefs, and justification of central beliefs, with the goal of making one's beliefs consistent and rational. Consistency will almost always require changes in some less central particular belief. For example, if one believes that women should be treated as equal to men, one may have to abandon a belief that it is permissible to exclude girls from Little League baseball teams. But even if many beliefs remain untouched, a given ethical theory should not necessarily be considered mere rationalization. After all, many of the moral beliefs commonly taught to children are rationally justifiable. And it would make little sense to suggest that most very central moral beliefs are *mistaken.* What would it be like to discover that intentional cruelty, murder, rape, lying, and stealing are all morally acceptable? Any theory that would lead to such conclusions is incorrect, simply because these conclusions are unacceptable. It might make sense to suggest that all our talk about morality is a sham, but that is a different matter; if morality is an illusion, then no moral beliefs can be either mistaken or correct.

So one should expect that most of one's central moral beliefs will survive examination of the theories in this text. The changes and additions that theory can make to a person's moral beliefs come mainly in the area of difficult or new cases. One of the chief benefits of studying ethical theory is that one learns to think clearly and systematically when confronted with cases about which one's moral beliefs may be shaky or even unformed. Ethical theory will uncover the principles implicit in most of one's central moral beliefs and so enable one to think clearly and consistently. And because they are general, theoretical principles can be applied to new problems (for instance, those created by changing social conditions or advances in technology).

Another important benefit of ethical theory is an increased ability to understand and respect the viewpoints of others. Once one comes to see the principles and concepts that underlie other views, moral disagreement is less likely to lead to accusations of bad intentions. The abortion controversy is a good illustration of the need for understanding the theoretical basis of moral disagreement. Each side accuses the other of bad faith but does not bother to investigate the differing theory of right conduct that would make sense of the opposing view. The study of ethical theory makes it possible to see how a reasonable and well-intentioned person can hold a moral view different from one's own.

But the most important benefit of studying ethics is the increased ability to reason about moral questions. Without some way of bringing order and coherence to moral thought, positions taken on difficult moral issues will seem unreasoned. Ethical theory does not replace the use of more substantive concepts (such as kindness and honesty) with abstract and general principles. Rather, the structure of principles found in a normative theory connects the particular substantive standards—usually kindness and honesty fit together, and both are justified by the Golden Rule, or by whatever fundamental principle the normative theory proposes. But the same structure of principles can be used to resolve conflicts when substantive standards pull in opposite directions—in special circumstances, it may be very unkind to be honest. Ethical theory seeks to refine and extend ordinary moral reasoning. However, skeptical doubts lead some to deny the possibility of ethical theory.

Moral Skepticism Can human beings know moral truths? Are there moral truths at all? The moral skeptic denies the possibility of knowledge about morality. There is no fact of the matter where moral values are concerned, asserts the skeptic. Skepticism can be developed in many different ways, but the key element is always the denial that moral judgments can be sufficiently supported by reasons. Usually the moral skeptic draws a contrast between morality and science, granting that scientific propositions can be sufficiently supported by reasons. Indeed, this contrast with science has often motivated the attack on the possibility of moral knowledge.

Should a contrast with science lead to skepticism about morality? Undoubtedly there are differences between scientific and moral judgments. An important difference is the distinction between "is" and "ought"; scientific judgments concern what *is* the case (what in fact happens), while moral judgments concern what *ought* to be done. However, it does not follow that moral judgments cannot be sufficiently supported by reasons, though it does follow that what counts as supporting a judgment with reasons will differ in important ways in science and morality. For instance, rejecting a scientific hypothesis that implies a prediction that turns out to be false shows good reasoning. Since moral judgments do not entail any predictions of what will in fact happen, there is no direct analog in moral reasoning of this kind of falsification of a judgment.

But there are also similarities between reasoning in science and in ethics. In both areas, reasoning proceeds by seeking to understand the particular instance by reference to general features it shares with other particular instances. Both seek to rise above bias and prejudice and to achieve an understanding free of the accidental features of personal circumstance. There is reason to doubt that moral thought can achieve these goals as completely as science; even so, sharing these goals connects rationality in science and ethics.

The moral skeptic cannot be conclusively refuted. However, skepticism is clearly not justified merely by the contrast between science and ethics and the distinction between "is" and "ought." To decide whether to embrace skepticism, it is necessary to examine moral reasoning in detail. Ethical theories that claim to offer a rational basis for moral judgment must be rejected by the skeptic, and surely it is unreasonable to reject these theories without detailed examination. Involvement in the search for an acceptable ethical theory must precede any serious consideration of skepticism as a live option. Even if all proposed ethical theories were examined and rejected for good reasons, moral thought at a less theoretical level might sometimes count as sufficiently supported by reasons, and so a full skepticism about morality might be unjustified.

Relativism   Skeptical doubts about establishing moral principles have led some people toward moral relativism. The relativist joins with the skeptic in denying that moral judgments can be supported by reasons that establish their truth for all rational and objective thinkers. But the relativist then denies that this standard of universal rationality is appropriate for morality. Morality is relative, and so skepticism can be avoided by confining each moral judgment to its relativized framework, for within that particular framework there can be sufficient support by reasons. This view that rational justification is relativized to a framework is called *metaethical relativism,* and there are as many varieties as there are ways of specifying the frameworks within which moral reasoning is confined. Rational justification of moral judgments may be relativized to the society or culture, or to the religious tradition within which the judgments are made, or to the individual person making the judgments.

Metaethical relativism must be distinguished from other forms of relativism about morality. *Descriptive relativism* is the view that fundamental moral beliefs do in fact differ, for instance, from society to society, or from person to person. There is more room for dispute about descriptive relativism than might first be thought, for describing the moral beliefs found in very different cultures is often problematic, and it is also difficult to disentangle differences in nonmoral beliefs from differences in moral beliefs. For instance, do supporters of apartheid in South Africa have different fundamental moral beliefs from opponents, or do both sides share the same fundamental moral beliefs and reach differing conclusions because of disagreements about facts (such as the capacity of black South Africans to participate fully in political life)? Much will depend on what is meant by calling a moral belief "fundamental." If "fundamental" is removed from the definition of descriptive relativism, then everyone will agree that this form of relativism is true—for obviously there are differences in moral beliefs. But such a weakened descriptive relativism is uninteresting, since people have differing beliefs about all sorts of topics, not just about morality.

Despite its problems, descriptive relativism in its strong form might be true—*fundamental* moral beliefs might differ, either from society to society or at the level of individuals. What would follow from this? Metaethical relativism would not follow, for though fundamental beliefs differed, there might be good reasons to reject one fundamental belief and affirm the other. Descriptive relativism in itself does not touch on the question of the truth or the rational acceptability of the differing fundamental moral beliefs. There are fairly fundamental differences in nonmoral beliefs; for instance, some deny that human beings evolved from other forms of life. Few conclude from such nonmoral disagreements that one view is as good as another. The metaethical relativist asserts that moral matters are different, for there is no evidence that can resolve fundamental moral disputes. Once again the contrast between science and ethics and the distinction between "is" and "ought" are used to call in question the possibility of supporting moral judgments with reasons, though now it is only fundamental moral judgments about which skeptical doubts are raised. The metaethical relativist deserves the same response as the skeptic. It is unreasonable to reject ahead of time the possibility that ethical theory can offer reasons sufficient to support some fundamental moral judgments and to reject others. The task of theoretical inquiry is of heightened importance if descriptive relativism is true.

Let us examine some forms of metaethical relativism more closely, beginning with *individual relativism.* This view relativizes moral reasoning to the system of beliefs of the individual. A particular moral judgment about an action, for instance, will count as true or rationally acceptable if it follows from (or at least is consistent with) more general and fundamental moral beliefs held by the individual making the judgment and as long as any factual claims involved in the judgment are true. It is important to note that this form of metaethical relativism allows room for a great deal of ordinary moral reasoning and serious thinking about moral issues, for it is never easy to achieve consistency even within one's own system of beliefs. Nor should an individual relativist ignore ethical theories, such as those presented in this book, for the study of theories often raises issues of consistency in one's own system of beliefs, and may help in achieving greater consistency. In applying his or her moral beliefs, an individual relativist needs to know the relevant facts, since his or her particular judgment on the issue will be false if his or her own moral commitments would have led to a different judgment given a correct view of the facts. Individual relativists can even engage in serious moral reasoning with others, as long as the parties to the discussion share at least some relevant fundamental moral beliefs.

If individual relativism is true, then there can be no reasoning concerning fundamental moral beliefs, and the individual can only express his or her commitment when asked to give reasons for these beliefs. There is also no possible reason why the relativist should not change his or her fundamental beliefs. Remaining committed or switching will be equally arbitrary. It is this arbitrariness that most ethical theorists seek to avoid.

Social relativism confines moral reasoning to the system of beliefs of the society. This view makes the most sense when applied to fairly isolated and well-defined cultures with clear and publicly recognized sets of customs and rules; in such cases, it is often clear what counts as a moral belief "of the society," and even somewhat clear which beliefs count as fundamental. Social relativism can make sense of reasoning that goes on within the framework of social belief, for there will be questions of consistency and questions of fact. The parallel with individual relativism is easy, for in many customary, isolated cultures social relativism and individual relativism will amount to the same thing. Each individual will be committed to the fundamental beliefs of his or her culture. These fundamental beliefs will be arbitrary, but this problem may go unnoticed in societies that are extremely isolated.

It is different when social relativism is applied to modern, less isolated societies. What counts as a society? Is the United States *one* society, or are various geographical areas or ethnicities separate societies? Or should moral reasoning be relativized to a larger society—perhaps the industrialized democratic West? Can someone be in more than one society? Even if "society" can be defined, it may still be unclear what the moral beliefs of the society are, for there is no agreement within any modern society about many moral issues, and even fundamental moral disagreement seems to exist. Will a majority be sufficient? Why should the minority accept the judgment of the majority? Even if it is clear what the fundamental moral commitments of the society are, these will seem arbitrary. No reasons are possible to support the society's fundamental moral beliefs, according to social relativism. Unlike isolated, customary societies, there is always internal moral debate and external challenge in the modern world. Arbitrariness will not go unnoticed. A natural response is to attempt to give reasons for the fundamental moral beliefs of the society, or to attempt to change those beliefs to others that are better supported by reasons. But this means abandoning social relativism.

Religious relativism can be set out either as a form of social relativism, with the religious group as the society, or as a form of individual relativism, with the individual's religious beliefs seen as fundamental to his moral reasoning. Either account leads to the same difficulty for the relativist; in the end, religious commitments will seem arbitrary. And in a modern, pluralistic society the religious relativist cannot ignore this problem. Why not switch to a different set of religious commitments, or to a nonreligious viewpoint? All options will be equally arbitrary. Why should it be assumed that there can be no reasoning concerning fundamental beliefs within a religious ethics? Many philosophers and theologians have insisted that there can be rational grounds for fundamental moral beliefs within a religious perspective.

All of these forms of metaethical relativism place severe restrictions on the role of reasoning in moral discourse. According to metaethical relativism, moral judgments will be made across individual, social, or religious boundaries. For instance, opponents of apartheid can make the moral judgment that the policies of the South African government are wrong, even if the opponents trace this judgment back to fundamental beliefs not shared by those they criticize. (This judgment will be true relative to its framework, assuming no mistakes in intermediate reasoning or concerning facts.) However, this boundary-crossing judgment cannot be supported by reasoning in a dialogue with those who disagree. But the relativist view is more radical than this picture suggests. If they think clearly, the opponents of apartheid will *themselves* see their own fundamental moral beliefs as unsupported by reasoning. The impossibility of boundary-crossing reasons is merely a reflection of this lack of reasons within the boundaries.

Metaethical relativism, like the skepticism that fuels it, cannot be conclusively refuted. But there is a crude form of relativism that can be as thoroughly refuted as anything in philosophy. *Normative relativism* is the view that each person ought to act in conformity to the moral beliefs of the society, or in conformity to his or her own individual moral beliefs, or to some other relativized standard. This is a normative ethical theory, since it states a principle for deciding what morally ought to be done. The normative relativist will become inconsistent if he or she offers for his or her view any of the reasons given to support metaethical relativism. For if metaethical relativism were true, there could be no nonrelative moral standpoint, outside of particular systems of belief, and such a standpoint is needed in order to justify the normative moral principle asserted in normative relativism. Is the truth of the relativist principle of right conduct itself a relative truth? If it is relative, then to what framework is it relative? If it is not relative, then asserting it is inconsistent with skepticism about fundamental moral judgments.

Divine Command Theory   In seeking a nonrelativist ethical theory, some religious thinkers have turned to the *divine command theory*. Unlike religious relativism, this theory claims that there is only one acceptable moral framework: right conduct is obedience to the commands of God. The intent of the view is nonrelativist, for it is assumed that the commands of God are determinate and that some beliefs about God's commands are in fact correct, and other beliefs are incorrect.

The divine command theory maintains its distinctness only if it resists religious relativism on one side and reason-giving ethical theories on the other side. Not every believer in divine commands is a proponent of the divine command theory of morality. For instance, Saint Thomas Aquinas (see Chapter 1) combined belief in a divine lawgiver with a natural law theory of morality, rather than a divine command theory. In his view, the moral law can be discovered by human reason, beginning with a fundamental principle that is itself required by rationality. And God's command that we do what is morally right is in content based on the same reasons that independent human reason can discern. Whenever divine commands are seen as based on the rightness of the conduct, some other normative ethical theory (not the divine command theory) accounts for the conduct being right. Even some utilitarians (see Chapter 3) believed in a divine lawgiver who commands that we do what is right.

A distinct divine command theory must deny that human reasoning is sufficient to discover what is morally right. This view asserts that conduct is morally right because God commands it, not that God commands conduct because it is morally right. From the perspective of reason, God's commands are arbitrary. And so the divine command theory fails to cure that final arbitrariness that many people find unacceptable in relativism. Obedience to such arbitrary decrees seems to imply that human rationality is of no practical use, though the theist must see this rationality as a gift from God.

According to a distinct divine command theory, how could God's commands be ascertained? Since from the human perspective divine commands are arbitrary, only revelation from God could establish the content of morality. So there will be many different views of what God commands, and no way to judge between them (except by showing that one claim to revelation is true through miracles and other evidence, an appeal that all revealed religions make). The objectivity found at the level of theory disappears then in practice, leaving the same breakdown in moral reasoning as that found in relativism. It can be of no use to appeal to the arbitrary will of God when disagreement exists concerning both what the divine will is and whether there is a God at all. Such disagreement exists in all modern societies.

Egoism   Another attempt to avoid relativism is *ethical egoism.* This is the normative theory that each person ought to do what is consistent with self-interest. The advantages of egoism are obvious. The standard of self-interest offers determinate and clear guidance in a broad range of circumstances (though perhaps not in all). In addition, this fundamental normative principle is easily seen as itself rational, since practical rationality includes seeking the best means to achieve a given end. Egoism thus seems an improvement over relativist and divine command theories, which must affirm arbitrary fundamental commitments. And, finally, the egoist normative principle connects to motivations that human beings in fact have; people are motivated by self-interest, at least sometimes.

It is important to distinguish normative ethical egoism from *psychological egoism,* the view that people always act only from self-interest. The

normative ethical theory is about what people *ought* to do, while the
psychological theory is about what in fact happens in human life. In
Fifteen Sermons Preached at the Rolls Chapel, the eighteenth-century British
moral philosopher Joseph Butler made two devastating points against
psychological egoism. First, psychological egoism involves an unhelpful
and confusing verbal maneuver; human passions and desires such as
resentment, love, hate, and jealousy are redescribed in the language of
self-interest. Psychological egoists will insist on calling every motivation
self-interested, merely because it is their *own* desires and passions that
motivate people. People who in a resentful rage insult their employer
are said to be motivated by their own self-interest (as seen from their
momentary viewpoint). But a more perspicuous description is that they
are motivated by resentment and anger. Probably they do not calculate
self-interest at all (not even short-term self-interest from their momentary perspective), and if they do calculate self-interest then it fails to
motivate them. Of course, it is *their own* passions that motivate them, but
it is confusing to describe that fact using the language of self-interest.

Butler's second point is that the concept of self-interest is empty
unless it is filled in by reference to desires and interests directed toward
things and states of affairs (for instance, a desire for ice cream or for
affection from others). To calculate self-interest is to engage in rational
reflection upon harmonization of the passions and maximization of the
satisfaction of the particular desires and interests one has. Self-interest is
thus a *second-order* motivation, directed toward the *first-order* interests and
desires. Human experience indicates that there are first-order malevolent desires (such as wanting someone not to succeed in a job simply
because one dislikes him) and first-order altruistic desires (such as a
parent wanting a child's pain to be relieved simply out of love). Psychological egoism is conceptually muddled.

Rejecting psychological egoism does not, however, lead to a rejection of ethical egoism. The normative theory of egoism can now be seen
as providing a genuinely evaluative standard, for if not all human conduct is self-interested, one can actually use the standard of self-interest
to decide what to do. (If psychological egoism were true, then no normative ethical theory, including ethical egoism, would be of any interest.
For then moral deliberation could make no difference to anyone's actions.) Normative ethical egoism accepts Butler's distinction between
the second-order concept of self-interest and the concept of first-order
particular desires. The normative egoist principle is thus a principle of
practical rationality—only conduct that is consistent with self-interest is
fully rational, and one ought to do what is fully rational. By this standard,
many things people do are foolish and thus wrong. It is important to see
that according to this theory altruistic conduct is not in itself irrational,
for in many cases acting on particular altruistic desires will be consistent
with self-interest. And since the normative egoist accepts Butler's point
about first- and second-order motivations, it will not be correct to describe such altruistic actions as self-interested, even though they are

consistent with self-interest. Of course, acting on an altruistic desire may in particular circumstances not be consistent with self-interest, but then the same is true of acting on spiteful or malevolent desires. Self-interest must be distinguished from selfishness, which is an absence of first-order altruistic desires and motivations (such as those arising within friendship or love). Acting on the egoist normative principle is not the same thing as acting selfishly, for a life of selfishness might not be as satisfying as one with genuine unselfish attachments. And the normative egoist does not claim that the only rational *motive* for action is self-interest; from the viewpoint of self-interest, it will often be better that actions be spontaneous and directly motivated by the particular desire, rather than dependent on a calculation of self-interest. Self-interest becomes a motive only when conflicting desires or the perception of risk leads to rational reflection about what conduct will maximize long-term satisfaction of the whole set of desires.

When clarified, normative ethical egoism is an individualistic version of *consequentialism* (see below). Egoism denies that the interests of others have any direct moral claim on us, though the particular altruistic desires of a person will lead to some concern for *some* other people (and perhaps even a weak concern for other people in general). This extreme restriction of morally relevant interests seems inconsistent with the central concepts built into moral language. Moral judgment seems to be concerned with the social and the interpersonal; the viewpoint of morality seems to rule out normative egoism, for the moral concepts and moral principles have a kind of umpire's role, connected to the need to resolve conflicting interests between people, not merely within the self. Normative egoism cannot do the job that moral principles are designed to do. This is reflected in the limited role of the egoist principle even on an egoist's own view. It would be inconsistent for an egoist to propose the egoist principle as the public ethical standard for evaluating conduct, for it would be in his or her own interest if other people adopted some nonegoist standard. The egoist can then secretly use consistency with self-interest as his or her own standard of rational conduct. If a moral principle must function as a public standard, then the egoist principle is not a principle of morality.

So it is helpful to think of egoism as a theory of rational conduct, but not as a theory of what is morally right. Egoism attacks the rationality and coherence of most moral thought, rather than attempting to bring order to it in the manner of less radical theories. Egoism is an adequate theory of rational conduct only if ordinary moral thought is irrational in taking a broader viewpoint than the individual's. But it seems inevitable that an intelligent social species with interpersonal conflicts will develop concepts and principles that express a social viewpoint.

Setting Aside Obstacles   It is now reasonable to set aside the above obstacles to theoretical inquiry in ethics. Some of these can be set aside on strong grounds; normative relativism and psychological egoism are conceptually confused. The other impediments can be set aside provisionally. The reasons supporting skepticism and metaethical relativism are not as strong as they first seemed. The divine command theory is not really an improvement over relativism. Normative egoism places severe limits on the kinds of concepts human beings can rationally use in social life. Theoretical inquiry might provide a normative account that is not egoistic and that is rationally acceptable in its fundamental principles (and thus is not a form of skepticism, metaethical relativism, or divine command theory). If the project of theoretical inquiry completely fails to bring order and coherence to moral thought, then it would be reasonable to revive these alternatives and consider them more seriously.

Law, Morality, and Personal Ideals In both theoretical inquiry and applied ethics, it is important to distinguish between moral questions and legal questions. Moral questions concern what people morally ought to do. Legal questions concern what is required or allowed by the laws of a particular jurisdiction. Often there will be both a legal and a moral obligation to do or not do something (for instance, child abuse is both legally and morally wrong). But there are many moral obligations that are not legal obligations, and vice versa. There are even cases in which the requirements of law are so at odds with moral principle that there is a moral obligation to violate the law; for instance, in South Africa it might be morally obligatory to violate some of the apartheid laws. But even in cases where legal and moral obligations coincide, there is still a distinction between the two. Legal obligation is rooted in the institutions of the formal legal system (legislature, courts, penal institutions); moral obligation is rooted in concepts and principles that people use in everyday life to evaluate conduct as right or wrong, fair or unfair, considerate or inconsiderate, and so forth. Moral concepts and principles cover a much wider and more finely detailed range of human life than the more formal set of legal concepts, backed by the machinery of the state and the courts.

There are moral questions *about* law. For instance, it is a moral question whether the apartheid laws are just or unjust. And there is great controversy concerning the moral evaluation of the legal right to terminate pregnancy. Moral questions can be raised about the property, inheritance, and tax laws of a particular jurisdiction—are all people treated with equal justice by the particular provisions of the laws? In raising such questions, careful distinctions need to be made between the various issues involved. Someone might think that a particular course of conduct is good or even *morally* obligatory, but still think that it is morally wrong to coerce people to act in that way through the machinery of the legal system. And it should be kept in mind that in evaluating law there are nonmoral issues, such as the need for coherence with the whole body of laws. The question of what the law ideally should be often has a moral dimension, but it has other dimensions as well.

Moral questions must also be distinguished from questions concerning personal ideals. A person might think that he or she should devote his or her career to helping the poor, but not make the moral judgment that everyone in similar circumstances ought to do likewise. Personal ideals such as this are sometimes connected to moral concepts and values, so in such cases they are in a sense personal moral commitments; but the self-imposed ideal is seen as going beyond what right conduct requires. There are also personal ideals built upon nonmoral standards of excellence (for instance, a commitment to aesthetic standards). Nonmoral personal ideals lie outside the scope of normative ethics. Normative ethical theories develop principles of right conduct that cannot be violated without blame (unless the person was somehow not fully responsible or in some other way excused). The reasoning for principles of right conduct might also make sense of some personal moral ideals—for instance, as extensions of moral values beyond what is obligatory—but that is not the point of the normative principles themselves.

Moral Concepts   Several concepts are central to moral thought and are used by all ethical theories. The concept of *value* ("the good" and "the bad") plays a role in much moral thought. Competing ethical theories often have differing views of what is *intrinsically good,* that is, what is good in itself. Intrinsic goods are contrasted with *instrumental goods,* which are valued only because they are instrumental in bringing about other goods. For instance, happiness is often considered an intrinsic good; and everyone considers a visit to the dentist instrumentally good rather than intrinsically good. Some theories set up a plurality of intrinsic goods (for instance, human life, friendship, knowledge). Other theories insist that there is only one kind of intrinsic good (for instance, pleasure). The difference between a plurality of goods and only one intrinsic good is important. In thinking about a moral problem, one might want to compare the amount of intrinsic good produced by alternative actions. If several different values are at stake, comparing goods is like adding apples and rivers. Only a theory with *one* intrinsic value can treat the comparison as a matter of simple arithmetic.

Theories of right conduct are theories of what one morally ought to do. It is possible to make subtle distinctions between a moral obligation and a moral duty, but here no distinction will be made. The contrary of doing what one ought to do is to do something morally wrong. Both the concept of obligation and that of moral wrong can be defined by the concept of the morally permitted. Most human actions are neither obligatory nor wrong, since both doing the actions and not doing them is permissible. A moral *wrong* is that which is not permitted; a moral *obligation* is something that it is not permitted to leave undone. Not all moral thinking concerns obligation; for instance, moral thinking that concentrates on questions of character and the virtues often proceeds without explicit use of the concept of obligation. One might consider it morally praiseworthy to risk one's own life in order to save someone else, but this need not be considered obligatory.

Another fundamental concept is the concept of a *right,* understood in the sense of such phrases as "human rights" and "civil rights." A right is a valid claim or entitlement that a person can make to restrict the conduct of others in their dealings with him or her. If there are no other conflicting moral considerations, it is obligatory to respect an individual's rights. However, moral problems often involve conflicts between individuals, each of whom has a right that deserves some respect. One important purpose of ethical theories is to help resolve such conflicts of rights, as well as conflicts of rights with other moral considerations.

Some people distinguish between *negative* and *positive* rights. Most commonly recognized rights are negative, requiring only that others not interfere with the right holder's life, conduct, or property. Thus the "right to life" is usually understood as the right not to be killed, rather than the right to be provided with the means to continue to live. If there is a positive right to life, then much more direct help to the needy is morally obligatory than is ordinarily supposed. The extent of positive rights is one of the most controversial questions in ethical theory.

Ethical Theories   Each ethical theory includes an account of value, obligation, and rights. However, these concepts are not of equal importance for each theory. Some theories derive obligations and rights from values; other theories establish rights and obligations independent of values. Most of these latter theories take rights as fundamental.

Theories that base obligations and rights on values are called *teleological* (from *telos,* meaning "goal," or "end"). The values are the end, and conduct is evaluated in terms of these ends. The simplest form of teleological theory is the evaluation of conduct as a means to an end. Theories of this sort, such as utilitarianism (see Chapter 3), are *consequentialist.* That is, they evaluate conduct as right or wrong depending solely upon the value of the consequences of the conduct. However, not all teleological theories are consequentialist. In evaluating conduct as right or wrong, some consider intentions and motives as well as consequences. And teleological theories that recognize many basic values will not be consequentialist, since comparing the value of the consequences of alternative actions is not always possible. Natural-law theory (see Chapter 1) is an example of a teleological theory that is not consequentialist.

Those theories that do not base all obligations and rights upon values are called *deontological* theories. Deontological comes from the Greek word *deon,* "that which is binding." The concept of obligation or duty is thus central for deontologists, but not all deontological theories take duty as primary. For example, natural-rights theory (see Chapter 1) takes rights as fundamental and establishes obligations or duties on the basis of rights. Other theories, such as Kant's (see Chapter 2), do not establish all duties on the basis of rights. The contractarian theory (see Chapter 2) is also a deontological theory.

These classifications are useful only insofar as they help indicate the general structure of the theory. One must then consider the principles and the reasons supporting them. Part I provides a detailed examination of the theories. Part II considers the application of the theories to particular moral problems. In examining the applications one should keep in mind that different people using the same theory can come to different conclusions, because they differ as to interpretation of the facts or because the theories give reasons to support different resolutions of problems. Thus, in examining the applications of theories, one should also consider what light the application sheds on the theory and how it might be applied to yet other problems.

part I

THEORIES

chapter *1*

Natural Law and Natural Rights

INTRODUCTION

Two Kinds of Law: Prescriptive and Descriptive   People live together in societies. Within each society there are social rules that regulate
conduct. Informal customs and formal laws are used to fit individuals into
the life of the social group. Children learn these rules as they grow up.
Violations are punished either informally or through such formal institutions as courts. These customs and laws are *prescriptive,* prescribing or
commanding how people ought to act.

There is quite a different concept of law used both in everyday life
and in science. Scientific laws are *descriptive,* describing what does in fact
happen under certain conditions. The laws of gravity are examples of
descriptive laws. And in everyday life, people use less precise "laws" to
explain what happens to them. (For instance, "People who haven't had
enough sleep are irritable.") Descriptive laws do not say what ought to
happen.

Prescriptive and descriptive laws seem very different. Yet it is possible to attempt to connect them. The term *natural law* is used in ethics
to mean a set of prescriptive rules of conduct rather than the causal,
scientific laws that describe natural processes. Why then is the word
"natural" used? These prescriptive laws are called natural because they
are not prescribed within some particular society for the regulation of
its own social life. "Natural" is thus contrasted to "conventional." Unlike the prescriptive laws of particular societies, the natural law is considered binding upon all human beings simply because they are human
beings. And natural rights are also attributed to people regardless of
the particular society to which they belong. In the arguments for the
theory of natural law and the theory of natural rights, there is an attempt to show that the facts of human nature determine the basic prescriptive laws that all human beings ought to follow. The facts of
human nature are described in descriptive laws, so in these theories
prescriptive laws of conduct are based upon descriptive laws of human
nature.

17

Nature and Convention   The theory of natural law and the theory of natural rights both provide an account of right conduct that is *naturalist;* the rightness of an action is determined by reference to nature rather than to convention, custom, or preferences. The nature determining right conduct is human nature, which is the same for all human beings regardless of social conventions. Cultural differences are merely imposed upon an underlying set of characteristics that constitute humanity. These unchanging characteristics can be distinguished from what is culturally relative by methods of rational inquiry. Although reason is considered the distinguishing mark of humanity, there are other natural characteristics of human beings that are essential in accounting for the distinction between right and wrong in human conduct. Reason is the governing element in human nature, but in its control of right conduct, reason must take into account other elements of complex human nature, such as sexuality and the emotions.

NATURAL LAW

Greek, Roman, and Judaeo-Christian Origins   The ancient Greek philosopher Aristotle (384 B.C.–322 B.C.) gave an account of the nature of human beings that has continued to influence the theory of natural law ever since. The central concept is that each kind of thing has a goal or purpose (in Greek, *telos*). According to this teleological viewpoint, it is the goal of each thing to be or act in accordance with the distinctive characteristics of its kind. The whole history of natural law in ethics stresses that actions are directed toward goals. In the *Nichomachean Ethics,* Aristotle identifies rationality as the distinctive characteristic of human nature, and thus rational activity as the proper (because natural) mode of living for human beings:

> Living is something shared by man even with plants, whereas we are after something specific. Therefore, we must rule out nutritive living, life as growth. Next comes perception; but this too is shared—in this case by horses, cows, and all animals. We are left with a life concerned with action, belonging to the rational part of man.[1]

And yet Aristotle also accepts the reality of human emotional and bodily needs. Rationality is not the only genuinely human characteristic. Right conduct aims at a truly human happiness, a happiness found in activity that expresses our distinctive rationality. But to this active life of reason must be added sufficient external goods (friends, health, family, money, and so on) to meet our equally human emotional and bodily needs.

After Aristotle, the school of philosophers called the Stoics continued to develop a natural-law theory of ethics. The Stoic school began in ancient Athens in about 300 B.C. and achieved great popularity several hundred years later during the late period of the Roman Republic and during the Roman Empire. The Stoic principle of right conduct was that one ought to follow nature rather than convention or custom. This principle, however, did not mean that human beings should pursue every whim or act on every desire. On the contrary, since the Stoics shared Aristotle's view that rationality is distinctive to human nature, following nature meant following reason.

The main difference between the Stoics and Aristotle concerned the value of external goods, for the Stoics denied Aristotle's view that a life cannot be called happy without such external goods as friends, health, family, and sufficient wealth. The Stoic view derived from a more extreme emphasis upon rationality and a disvaluing of human emotions. Thus, the Stoics offered a less biological form of naturalism, placing human beings in a radically different category from other natural things.

The Stoics stressed the distinction between the varying conventions, customs, and laws of particular societies and the unchanging rule of reason in conduct. This distinction was fleshed out in the Stoic ideal of the cosmopolitan, the citizen of the world, who is guided by nature and reason. The cosmopolitan recognizes all human beings as fellow citizens. During the empire, Roman jurists, who needed to work out a system of law dealing with persons who did not share the same customs and national laws, used the Stoic conception of the natural law binding all human beings together in a rational commonwealth. The Stoics and Roman jurists claimed that persons of differing cultures can be obligated to respect each other only if there is a natural law deriving from rationality itself.

The idea of a natural law had also developed in Jewish thought. Reflection upon the Jewish scriptures led to a distinction between cultic and noncultic commandments. Cultic rules concerned only Jews, and could be known only through revelation; rules concerning worship, the Sabbath, and diet were cultic. The noncultic commandments were discernible by human reason and binding upon Jew and Gentile alike; the prohibition of murder, for instance, was noncultic. Although Christian doctrine taught a different set of cultic rules, the distinction between cultic rules and rules binding on all was maintained by Christian philosophers.

The Roman conception of a rational law binding those of differing cultures appealed to the Judaeo-Christian world as well. The Judaeo-Christian conception of the equality of all found kinship in the Stoic ideal of the citizenship of all humanity. Judaeo-Christian philosophers were also attracted to Stoicism because of its insistence on humanity's special dignity and freedom. Saint Thomas Aquinas (1224–1274) gave the theory of natural law its classic expression, bringing together its Aristotelian, Stoic, and Judaeo-Christian elements.

Basic Human Goods The natural abilities and inclinations of human beings are the basis of natural-law theory, for they determine what is good. The fundamental principle of right conduct is that good is to be done and promoted and evil is to be avoided. Of course, this principle is an empty and unhelpful truism without the specification of what is good and what is evil. This specification is found in the natural inclinations and abilities of all human beings. What is understood as constituting a good human life varies from society to society and even from person to person, but that variation lies within a set of limits determined by human nature. Human flourishing occurs in a life in which the inclinations basic to human nature are rationally pursued (with some success) and humanly important abilities are put to active use. What thwarts this flourishing is an evil. The constitutive elements of human flourishing are the universal human goods.

The universal human goods are: life itself, health, procreation and rearing of the young, knowledge, and relationships with other human beings in society and in friendship. Within each of these basic goods lie more specific goods, such as the good of a particular friendship. Cultural differences often mask the underlying identity of the universal human goods that exist in all human societies. A comparison with the diversity of human languages may help. Despite the huge differences found among human languages, it can be argued that there are universal characteristics—a universal grammar—deeply buried under the surface variations.[2] Even if there is no such universal grammar, the concept of one makes sense. The concept of universal human goods makes the same kind of sense, and it need not be discarded merely because of the context of cultural diversity within which these goods are pursued (for instance, the fact that family structure varies from society to society).

Teleological but Not Consequentialist   A theory is *teleological* if it considers right conduct to be determined by the goal or purpose of the conduct. As already explained in the section dealing with the historical origins of natural law, a teleological view of both human nature and human conduct is central to the theory of natural law. The fundamental principle of natural law is clearly teleological: good is to be done and promoted and evil to be avoided.

However, the basic human goods are considered *incommensurable,* that is, they cannot be measured using a common unit, and so they cannot be traded off one for another. For example, the good of friendship cannot be compared on a common scale with the good of knowledge. And since according to natural law, each individual human life is seen as uniquely valuable, one human life cannot be weighed against another. This incommensurability of basic values is extremely important in natural law. If one basic good could be traded off in order to promote another, the teleological structure of natural law would lead to consequentialism. *Consequentialism* is the view that right conduct is that conduct that has the best consequences, all things considered. Consequentialist theories are all teleological, for they consider right conduct to be directed toward the goal of maximizing value. But not all teleological theories are consequentialist, since if values are incommensurable, the concept of the "best consequences" is senseless. To evaluate alternative sets of consequences, one needs a unit of comparison; but if there are many basic values, then no such unit can exist. It is not possible to "maximize value" if incommensurable values are in question.

Absolute Prohibitions   Since natural law is not consequentialist, it is possible for there to be moral prohibitions which are absolute, that is, which forbid some kinds of action *whatever the consequences.* "Do not kill the innocent" is a precept based upon respect for the unique value of each human life, and it forbids killing the innocent no matter what the consequences. Each life is incommensurably valuable, so one life may not be taken in order to save another. The precept against killing the innocent is grounded teleologically, since it is derived from the fundamental principle to avoid evil, along with the distinctive natural-law view of the incommensurable value of each human life.

Intention as the Key to Moral Evaluation   In evaluating conduct, the theory of natural law considers the intention or aim of various courses of conduct. The role of intention in moral evaluation prevents natural law from judging an action solely by its consequences, as does the incommensurability of the basic human goods. The intention is determined by what the person performing the conduct wills, either as a means to a further end or as an end in itself. Thus, all intentional killing of innocent human beings is prohibited, even if the death of the innocent person is willed only as a means to some further good (for instance, saving the lives of five other innocent people). Morally speaking, an action is identified in terms of the intention of the person acting. An external view of an action, therefore, will often fail to distinguish between cases that are morally quite different.

Double Effect   The fact that moral differences can exist between externally similar actions has led to the principle of *double effect;* under certain circumstances one may rightly perform an action that has, besides the effect desired either as a means or an end, a second effect that could not rightly be willed as a means or an end. This principle helps distinguish heroic self-sacrifice from suicide. A soldier jumping on a grenade to save his comrades does not will his own death either as a means or an end, although he foresees that he may die. (If the grenade does not explode, the soldier's intentions have not been thwarted—for he intended to protect others rather than to kill himself, nor did he intend his own death as a means of protecting others.)

The Virtues   The rejection of external viewpoints also connects with the emphasis on the virtues found in the tradition of natural law. A virtue is an excellent trait of character that disposes the person to feel and act in certain characteristic ways. For the virtuous person, the demands of the natural law are at the same time demands of his or her own internal dispositions, not mere external impositions. The content of the virtues is given by reason, but the emotional and affective life acquires a dispositional structure in the person who has become habituated to the life of virtue. The traditional list of the main virtues, going back to Plato and Aristotle, is: prudence (practical wisdom), temperance (self-control), fortitude (courage), and justice. Justice is the virtue that concerns obligations in the sphere of external actions. A just person will be internally disposed to render each what is due or deserved.

Justice and the Social Nature of Human Beings   The theory of natural law views human beings as by nature social. This view, held by Aristotle, the Stoics, and St. Thomas Aquinas, holds that natural human sociality underlies the requirements of justice and equity. Thus, the laws of states are valid only if they are instituted by the public authority for the common good. State laws may require conduct in addition to that required by natural law, but a requirement by the public authority that citizens violate natural law is not a valid law.

And so there is a *jurisprudential* theory of natural law, which concerns itself with the validity of the laws of states. This theory developed out of the legal thought of the Stoics and Roman jurists, who saw a universal core of natural law within the laws of all civilized nations. The jurisprudential theory of natural law received new attention after World War II, for it offered a way to conceptualize the extreme case of the Nazi revisions of the German legal system.[3] A natural-law theorist would judge many Nazi revisions of the law as invalid—mere orders backed by force, rather than laws deserving at least some respect. The case of the Nazis is interesting not only from the perspective of jurisprudence. Those who understand justice as determined solely by actual convention or agreement in a particular society must confront the implication that *morally speaking* the Nazis acted within the requirements of justice. This implication will lead most people to abandon such social relativism.

Deriving Values from Facts   The main philosophical difficulty with the theory of natural law is that it seems to derive value judgments from nonevaluative, merely factual claims about the nature of human beings. Deriving claims about what ought to be done from claims about what is the case has been called the *naturalistic fallacy.*[4] Why should people act in accordance with their nature, even if there were agreement about what nature is? Could it not equally be said that human beings ought to strive to *overcome* human nature? Furthermore, there seem to be many elements in human nature other than those designated by natural-law theorists as the basis of right conduct. For instance, there is good reason to believe that human beings have some innate aggressive tendencies, and yet few would have us follow nature in this respect.

Two interrelated questions present themselves here: (1) How can one logically derive value judgments from any factual claims at all? and (2) How can one consistently choose only some aspects of human nature as the basis of value? The response of the natural-law theorists is the same on both issues. They believe it is possible to derive values from facts and to distinguish some aspects of humanity as the basis of value, because the question of right conduct arises only for a being who is capable of rational choice.

Human beings have many aspects, but not all aspects of humanity have an equal place in rational deliberations concerning right conduct. Some natural inclinations must be resisted in order to make a life in which people's deepest needs (the universal human goods) are met. For instance, aggression must be curbed in favor of friendship and the preservation of life in society—not because sociality is natural to humanity and aggression not natural, but because the natural place of aggression in human life must be subordinate to sociality. Value judgments are grounded in what is valuable for human beings given what they are; this is a complex matter involving relationships of subordination among the many natural aspects of human beings. It is natural to avoid pain, but it is against reason (and so against human nature) to avoid pain at the expense of health (for instance, by not going to the dentist). All voluntary actions aim at some perceived good, and it is the job of reason to weigh the importance of competing goods in the light of an understanding of the incommensurable universal human goods necessary for a good human life.

It is the teleological structure of voluntary action that provides the bridge between fact and value. If all voluntary action aims at some perceived good, then voluntary action *ought* to promote the actual good and avoid the actual evil. The shift from what is in fact the case to what ought to be the case is accomplished by reason. After all, it would be irrational not to will what is actually good rather than what is a mere apparent or limited good. Most people do consider irrational those who knowingly avoid pain at the expense of health, for they rationally judge health as the more basic good. The same judgment usually is made of the person whose aggressiveness deprives him or her of the deep human satisfaction of friendship.

Still, the derivation of values from facts is not an exercise in pure logic. It is not a logical contradiction to embrace a life of aggression at the expense of friendship. Using the word "irrational" to criticize someone for choosing less than a fully human life is to incorporate into that term standards that go beyond mere consistency into the realm of value judgments.

Even if *some* value judgments may be justified by appeal to the actual good of human beings, a full and detailed natural-law theory of right conduct could not be given such a foundation. There are relatively few uncontroversial cases of the distinction between apparent or limited good and actual good. The case of not going to the dentist in order to avoid pain is clear-cut but rare. And such uncontroversial matters are not likely to play a crucial role in genuine moral problems. As Bernard Williams has argued, an understanding of human nature serves to "delimit the possible content of what could be regarded as a morality," but a full account of right conduct cannot be derived directly from an understanding of human nature.[5]

Human Nature and God   There are some who object to natural-law theory on quite different grounds. Existentialists, some Marxists, and some other contemporary philosophers reject the view that there is such a thing as "human nature" in the relevant sense. Human beings, they claim, continually make and remake their nature as they live in society; humanity is malleable and moldable, and people should not limit their actions in either personal or political life by any doctrine of an unchanging human nature. The natural-law idea that the function of human beings is rational activity is rejected, for human beings, they assert, cannot be said to have a function or purpose. To speak of such a function is to conceive of human beings as if they were artifacts or tools, like chairs and hammers. And so the existentialist Jean-Paul Sartre writes: "If God does not exist, there is at least one being in whom existence precedes essence, a being who exists before he can be defined by any concept. . . . Thus, there is no human nature, since there is no God to conceive it. . . . Man is nothing else but what he makes himself."[6] Thus each human being is responsible for deciding, through his or her plans and actions, what "human nature" will be.

However, the conception of human nature found in natural-law theory does not necessarily require a fundamental belief in a Creator who made human beings to serve a function, as a manufacturer makes a hammer to serve a function. Natural-law theory began in Aristotle without a background belief in a Creator. Although the development of Judaeo-Christian natural law presupposed a Creator, the conception of humanity as having an essential nature can perhaps be given an entirely naturalistic, scientific interpretation. The guiding idea of natural law is that there are central abilities and inclinations that set limits to what will count as human flourishing. This might be true whether or not a Creator exists.

NATURAL RIGHTS

Break with an Earlier View   The modern theory of natural rights arose in the seventeenth century and made a definite break with the natural-law tradition out of which it grew. Natural-law theorists had insisted that human beings are social by nature. The defenders of natural rights denied this natural sociality, insisting that the liberty of the individual is the primary moral characteristic of humanity. This individual liberty is understood as natural, since it is independent of the laws and customs of particular societies. The laws of states derive their legitimacy from the agreement or consent of free individuals. The political and social philosophy of natural rights thus requires some version of a freely entered social contract in order to justify any authority over individuals.

Primacy of Individual Rights   *Individual rights* are primary within this theory; each person has a natural right to life, liberty, and justly acquired property. The theory of natural rights is not teleological. Rather, natural-rights theory is *deontological*—that is, it does not derive rights and obligations from the promotion of value. Right conduct is conduct that respects the boundaries of each person's rights, regardless of whether through that conduct good is promoted and evil avoided. Each person has the right to live as he or she chooses (as long as an equal right is left to others), so there are no duties to self within natural-rights theory. (John Locke condemned suicide not as a violation of a duty to self, but rather as a violation of God's property right in the individual's life.) This differentiates it in an important way from the theory of natural law, which places great moral stress upon an individual's duty to lead a fully human life.

Natural-rights theory is essentially negative in its view of morality; *not* violating the rights of others is all that is required. And those rights are for the most part negative rights; for instance, the natural right to life is not the right to be provided the means to live but only the right not to be killed. Apart from special relationships (such as parenthood), there is no duty to help others, only a duty not to harm others. Helping others is perhaps admirable, but it is not strictly obligatory.

Minimal Government   This ethical minimalism—requiring the least possible of people—is matched by a minimalist account of the legitimate functions of government. Government exists to protect the prior natural rights of individuals and cannot legitimately coerce individuals to aid one another. Both ethical and governmental minimalism derive from the fundamental natural-rights principle that right conduct respects the rights of others, construing those rights as rights to noninterference. An absolute value is placed upon individual freedom, regardless of the uses to which that freedom is put. And it would be incorrect to say that the natural-rights theorist seeks to produce the most freedom, for the rights of one individual may not be violated in order to produce more respect for the rights of others. According to the tenets of natural-rights theory, there is not even a teleology of freedom.

Self-Interested Rationality   Natural-rights theorists paint a picture of humanity as self-interested and rational. Self-interest is often understood as primarily an interest in self-preservation and secondarily as an interest in the pursuit of happiness, or the satisfaction of desire. It is humanity's rationality and self-interest, rather than any other distinct aspects of human nature, that explain the pursuit of knowledge and even the choice of life in society, for these are viewed as rationally necessary means to promote self-interest.

Influence on the Constitution and Popular Morality   The natural-rights theorists influenced the founders of the United States. Consequently, there is an emphasis upon individual liberty and the limitation of governmental authority in the Constitution of the United States, especially in the first ten amendments, or the Bill of Rights. In the Declaration of Independence, Thomas Jefferson expressed both the individualist conception of rights and the more traditional background of natural law that was thought to justify this conception of liberty: "We hold these truths to be self-evident, that all men are created equal; that they are endowed by their Creator with certain inalienable rights; that among these, are life, liberty, and the pursuit of happiness. That, to secure these rights, governments are instituted among men, deriving their just powers from the consent of the governed."

The natural right to liberty sets limits to all legitimate interference with the individual (whether governmental or social). A modern corollary to this is the *right to privacy*, which has become central to contemporary natural-rights theory. This idea of the "right to be left alone" has evolved within United States constitutional law (for instance, the constitutional right to terminate pregnancy as determined in *Roe* v. *Wade* is based upon it), but it is also appealed to informally in much current moral debate. It is common to hear controversial conduct defended on the grounds that as long as no one else is harmed, the conduct is the "business" only of those engaged in it. This view that self-regarding conduct (directly affecting only those consenting to it) ought to be free from not only government interference but even from the interference of moral disapproval by society is the equivalent in popular moral thought of the more technical legal concept of the right of privacy.[7]

Readings Saint Thomas Aquinas explains the concept of a virtue, connecting virtue with the distinctive feature of human nature, rationality. The four main virtues are then set out. The definition of law is given, and natural law explained as a special mode of rational participation. The fundamental principle of right conduct is formulated and then filled in by reference to the basic natural inclinations of human beings. Moral precepts are traced to reason. An account of precepts concerning relations with other human beings in society is given. (The account of precepts concerning relations with God is omitted.) Another passage explains the way in which particular cases lead to exceptions to secondary principles that are expressed in general terms. Aquinas considers additions to natural law necessary for the human law of particular societies. But first principles can never be deleted or changed.

Germain Grisez and Russell Shaw give a contemporary version of the theory of natural law. The principle of right conduct is that one must remain open to all fundamental human goods (or purposes). Grisez and Shaw then explain eight virtues or "modes of responsibility" that follow from that principle: commitment to a harmonious set of values, impartiality, benevolence, detachment, fidelity, efficiency, duties deriving from social roles, and the absolute prohibition of directly acting against one of the fundamental human goods. In a passage not printed below, the fundamental human goods are given as: life, play, aesthetic experience, speculative knowledge, integrity, authenticity, friendship, and religion.

The selections from John Locke set out the natural-rights conception of human beings as equal in liberty in the state of nature, with natural rights to life, liberty, and property. Locke explains how property is acquired in a state of nature (by mixing one's labor with the object) and also discusses how the introduction of money allows the just acquisition of wealth beyond what can be used and thus allows for economic inequality without violation of natural rights. He then explains the origin of government as a means of protecting life and property and the limitations on governmental authority due to the natural rights of individuals, from whose consent government derives all legitimacy.

The selection from Robert Nozick offers his account of the "entitlement theory" of justice in property. This theory traces justice in property to a series of events conferring title rather than to any supposed just pattern of distribution. According to Nozick, everyone has a moral right to dispose of property as he or she chooses.

Notes

[1] Aristotle, *Nichomachean Ethics,* book 1, chap. 7, in *The Philosophy of Aristotle,* trans. A. E. Wardman, ed. R. Bambrough (New York: New American Library, 1963), p. 293.

[2] See especially Noam Chomsky, *Language and Mind* (New York: Harcourt, Brace & World, 1968), pp. 69–85.

[3] See Lon Fuller, "Positivism and Fidelity to Law—A Reply to Professor Hart," *Harvard Law Review* 71 (1958): 630–672.

[4] The phrase derives from George E. Moore, *Principia Ethica* (Cambridge: Cambridge University Press, 1903). For a clear discussion of the naturalistic fallacy, see William Frankena, "The Naturalistic Fallacy," *Mind,* 48 (1939): 464–477.

[5] Bernard Williams, *Morality: An Introduction to Ethics* (New York: Harper & Row, 1972), p. 66. In discussing Aristotle's emphasis on rationality as the "distinguishing mark of man," Williams offers a valuable defense of the place of the emotions in human life. This point is also relevant to Kant's ethics, with its Stoic emphasis on rationality beyond that found in Aristotle.

[6] Jean-Paul Sartre, "Existentialism," in *Existentialism and Human Emotions,* trans. B. Frechtman (New York: Philosophical Library, 1957), p. 15.

[7] The utilitarian John Stuart Mill wrote a classic defense of the principle that self-regarding conduct ought to be free from interference by society, either through law or the informal coercion of moral opinion; he claimed, however, that his argument appealed only to utility and not to any doctrine of natural rights. Nevertheless, Mill's *On Liberty* belongs within the tradition of John Locke and individual rights.

Bibliography on Natural Law and Natural Rights

Natural Law

Aquinas, St. Thomas. *Basic Writings of Saint Thomas Aquinas.* 2 vols. Edited by Anton C. Pegis. New York: Random House, 1945. The "Treatise on Virtue" and the "Treatise on Law" from the *Summa Theologica* are found in the second volume.

Copleston, Frederick C. *Aquinas.* Baltimore, Md.: Penguin Books, 1955. Chapter 5.

Donagan, Alan. *The Theory of Morality.* Chicago, Ill.: University of Chicago Press, 1977. (For the Stoic, Christian, and Jewish understanding of morality, see pages 1–9; for a discussion of Aquinas and Kant on the fundamental moral principle, see pages 57–66.)

Finnis, John. *Natural Law and Natural Rights.* New York: Oxford University Press, 1980.

Flippen, Douglas. "Natural Law and Natural Inclinations," *The New Scholasticism* 60 (1986): 284–316.

Foot, Philippa. "Utilitarianism and the Virtues," *Proceedings and Addresses of the American Philosophical Association* 57 (1983): 273–283.

————. *Virtues and Vices.* Berkeley: University of California Press, 1978.

Grisez, Germain G. "The First Principle of Practical Reason: A Commentary on the *Summa Theologica,* 1–2, Question 94, Article 2," *Natural Law Forum* (now *The American Journal of Jurisprudence*) 10 (1965): 168–201.

Hittinger, Russell. *A Critique of the New Natural Law Theory.* Notre Dame, Ind.: University of Notre Dame Press, 1987.

MacIntyre, Alasdair. *After Virtue.* Notre Dame, Indiana: University of Notre Dame Press, 1981. See especially Chapters 12–15.

McInerny, Ralph. *Ethica Thomistica: The Moral Philosophy of Thomas Aquinas.* Washington, D.C.: The Catholic University of America Press, 1982.

"Natural Law." *The Encyclopedia of Philosophy.* New York: Macmillan, 1967. Vol. 5, pp. 450–454.

O'Connor, D. J. *Aquinas and Natural Law.* London: Macmillan, 1968.

Simon, Yves R. *The Tradition of Natural Law: A Philosopher's Reflections.* New York: Fordham University Press, 1965.

Williams, Bernard. *Ethics and the Limits of Philosophy.* Cambridge, Mass.: Harvard University Press, 1985. See especially Chapter 3.

Natural Rights

Andrew, Edward. *Shylock's Rights: A History of Lockean Doctrine.* Toronto: University of Toronto Press, 1987.

Arthur, John. "Resource Acquisition and Harm," *Canadian Journal of Philosophy* 17 (1987): 337–348.

Christman, John. "Can Ownership Be Justified By Natural Rights?," *Philosophy and Public Affairs* 15 (1986): 156–177.

Epstein, Richard A. *Takings: Private Property and the Power of Eminent Domain.* Cambridge, Mass.: Harvard University Press, 1985.

Hart, Herbert L. A. "Are There Any Natural Rights?" *Philosophical Review* 64 (1955): 175–191.

Hayek, Frederick A. *The Constitution of Liberty.* Chicago, Ill.: University of Chicago Press, 1960.

————. *Law, Legislation, and Liberty.* Vol. 1. *Rules and Order.* Chicago, Ill.: University of Chicago Press, 1973.

Ingram, Peter. "Natural Rights: A Reappraisal," *Journal of Value Inquiry* 15 (1981): 3–18.

Locke, John. *The Second Treatise of Government.* Several editions.

Machan, Tibor R., ed. *The Libertarian Reader.* Totowa, N.J.: Rowman and Littlefield, 1982.

Mack, Eric. "In Defense of 'Unbridled' Freedom of Contract," *American Journal of Economics and Sociology* 40 (1981): 1–15.

Neumann, Michael. "Side-Constraint Morality," *Canadian Journal of Philosophy* 12 (1982): 131–143.

Nozick, Robert. *Anarchy, State, and Utopia.* New York: Basic Books, 1974.

Paul, Jeffrey, ed. *Reading Nozick.* Totowa, N.J.: Rowman and Littlefield, 1981.

Schochet, Gordon, ed. *Life, Liberty, and Property: Essays on Locke's Political Ideas.* Belmont, Calif.: Wadsworth, 1971.

SAINT THOMAS AQUINAS
THE VIRTUES AND NATURAL LAW

NATURE, REASON, AND THE VIRTUES

Now the virtue of a thing consists in its being well disposed in a manner befitting its nature. . . . But it must be observed that the nature of a thing is chiefly the form from which that thing derives its species. Now man derives his species from his rational soul, and consequently whatever is contrary to the order of reason is, properly speaking, contrary to the nature of man, as man; while whatever is in accord with reason is in accord with the nature of man, as man. . . . Therefore human virtue, which makes a man good, and his work good, is in accord with man's nature in so far as it accords with his reason; while vice is contrary to man's nature in so far as it is contrary to the order of reason. . . . There is a twofold nature in man, rational and sensitive. . . . Now the presence of vices and sins in man is owing to the fact that he follows the inclination of his sensitive nature against the order of his reason.[1]

Human virtue is a habit perfecting man for the purpose of acting well. Now in man there are but two principles of human actions, viz., the intellect or reason and the appetite. . . . Consequently every human virtue must needs be a perfection of one of these principles. Accordingly, if it perfects man's speculative or practical intellect in order that his action may be good, it will be an intellectual virtue; whereas if it perfects his appetite, it will be a moral virtue. . . . Prudence [practical wisdom] is essentially an intellectual virtue. But considered on the part of its matter, it has something in common with the moral virtues, for it is right reason about things to be done. . . . It is in this sense that it is reckoned with the moral virtues.[2]

Now in order that a choice be good, two things are required. First, that the intention be directed to a due end; and this is done by moral virtue, which inclines the appetitive power to the good that is in accord with reason, which is a due end. Secondly, that man choose rightly those things which are means to the end; and this he cannot do unless his reason counsel, judge and command rightly, which is the function of prudence [practical wisdom] and the virtues annexed to it. . . . Therefore there can be no moral virtue without prudence [practical wisdom], and consequently neither can there be without understanding. For it is by the virtue of understanding that we know naturally known principles both in speculative and in practical matters.[3]

For the formal principle of the virtue of which we speak now is the good as defined by reason. This good can be considered in two ways. First, as existing in the consideration itself of reason, and thus we have

From St. Thomas Aquinas, *Summa Theologica*, I–II, in *Basic Writings of Saint Thomas Aquinas,* ed. Anton C. Pegis (New York: Random House, 1945), vol. 2, selected passages as noted. By permission of the A. C. Pegis Estate.

one principal virtue called *prudence* [practical wisdom]. Secondly, according as the reason puts its order into something else, and this either into operations [external actions], and then we have *justice,* or into passions, and then we need two virtues. For the need of putting the order of reason into the passions is due to their thwarting reason; and this occurs in two ways. First, when the passions incite to something against reason, and then they need a curb, which we thus call *temperance;* secondly, when the passions withdraw us from following the dictate of reason, *e.g.,* through fear of danger or toil, and then man needs to be strengthened for that which reason dictates, lest he turn back, and to this end there is *fortitude.* ⁴

THE STRUCTURE OF NATURAL LAW

Law is nothing else than an ordinance of reason for the common good, promulgated by him who has the care of the community. . . . The natural law is promulgated by the very fact that God instilled it into man's mind so as to be known by him naturally.⁵

. . . Law, being a rule and measure, can be in a person in two ways: in one way, as in him that rules and measures; in another way, as in that which is ruled and measured, since a thing is ruled and measured in so far as it partakes of the rule or measure. Therefore, since all things subject to divine providence are ruled and measured by the eternal law . . . it is evident that all things partake in some way in the eternal law, in so far as, namely, from its being imprinted on them, they derive their respective inclinations to their proper acts and ends. Now among all others, the rational creature is subject to divine providence in a more excellent way, in so far as it itself partakes of a share of providence, by being provident both for itself and for others. Therefore it has a share of the eternal reason, whereby it has a natural inclination to its proper act and end; and this participation of the eternal law in the rational creature is called the natural law.⁶

. . . The precepts of the natural law are to the practical reason what the first principles of demonstrations are to the speculative reason, because both are self-evident principles. Now a thing is said to be self-evident in two ways: first, in itself; secondly, in relation to us. Any proposition is said to be self-evident in itself, if its predicate is contained in the notion of the subject; even though it may happen that to one who does not know the definition of the subject, such a proposition is not self-evident. For instance, this proposition, *Man is a rational being,* is, in its very nature, self-evident, since he who says *man,* says *a rational being;* and yet to one who does not know what a man is, this proposition is not self-evident. . . . Now as *being* is the first thing that falls under the apprehension absolutely, so *good* is the first thing that falls under the apprehension of the practical reason, which is directed to action (since every agent acts for an end, which has the nature of good). Consequently, the first principle in the practical reason is one founded on the nature of good, viz., that *good is that which all things seek after.* Hence this is the first precept of law, that *good is to be done and promoted, and evil is to be avoided.* All other precepts of the natural law are based upon this; so that all the things which the practical reason naturally apprehends as man's good belong to the precepts of the natural law under the form of things to be done or avoided.

Since, however, good has the nature of an end, and evil, the nature of the contrary, hence it is that all those things to which man has a natural inclination are naturally apprehended by reason as being good, and consequently as objects of pursuit, and their contraries as evil, and objects of avoidance. Therefore, the order of the precepts of natural law is according to the order of natural inclinations. For there is in man, first of all, an inclination to good in accordance with the nature which he has in common with all substances, inasmuch, namely, as every substance seeks the preservation of its own being, according to its nature; and by reason of this inclination, whatever is a means to preserving human life, and of warding off its obstacles, belongs to the natural law. Secondly, there is in man an inclination to things that pertain to him more specially, according to that nature which he has in common with other animals; and in virtue of this inclination, those things are said to belong to the natural law *which nature has taught all animals,* such as sexual intercourse, the education of offspring and so forth. Thirdly, there is in man an inclination to do good according to the nature of his reason, which nature is proper to him. Thus man has a natural inclination to know the truth about God, and to live in society; and in this respect, whatever pertains to this inclination belongs to the natural law: *e.g.,* to shun ignorance, to avoid offending those among whom one has to live, and other things regarding the above inclination.[7]

MORAL PRECEPTS DERIVED FROM NATURAL REASON

It is . . . evident that since the moral precepts are about matters which concern good morals; and since good morals are such as are in accord with reason; and since every judgment of human reason must needs be derived in some way from natural reason, it follows, of necessity, that all the moral precepts belong to the law of nature, but not all in the same way. For there are certain things which the natural reason of every man, of its own accord and at once, judges to be done or not to be done: *e.g., Honor thy father and thy mother,* and, *Thou shalt not kill, Thou shalt not steal* (*Exod.* xx. 12, 13, 15): and these belong to the law of nature absolutely. And there are certain things which, after a more careful consideration, wise men deem obligatory. Such belong to the law of nature, yet so that they need to be inculcated, the wiser teaching the less wise: *e.g., Rise up before the hoary head, and honor the person of the aged man* (*Levit.* xix. 32), and the like.[8]

That a man should not do harm to anyone is an immediate dictate of his natural reason, and therefore the precepts of the decalogue that forbid the doing of harm are binding on all men. But it is not an immediate dictate of the natural reason that a man should do one thing in return for another, unless he happen to be indebted to someone. Now a son's debt to his father is so evident that one cannot get away from it by denying it; for the father is the principle of generation and being, and also of upbringing and teaching.[9]

To his neighbors a man behaves himself well both in particular and in general: in particular, as to those to whom he is indebted, by paying his debts: and in this sense is to be taken the commandment about honoring one's parents; in general, as to all men, by doing harm to none, either by deed, or by word, or by thought. By deed, harm is done to one's neighbor, sometimes in his person, *i.e.,* as to his personal existence, and this is forbidden by the words, *Thou shalt not kill;* sometimes in a person united to him, as to the propagation of offspring, and this is prohibited by the words, *Thou shalt not commit adultery;* sometimes in his possessions, which are directed to both the aforesaid, and with regard to this it is said, *Thou shalt not steal.* Harm done by word is forbidden when it is said, *Thou shalt not bear false witness against thy neighbor;* and harm done by thought is forbidden in the words, *Thou shalt not covet.* [10]

SECONDARY PRINCIPLES NOT ALWAYS APPLICABLE

As we have stated above, to the natural law belong those things to which man is inclined naturally; and among these it is proper to man to be inclined to act according to reason. Now it belongs to the reason to proceed from what is common to what is proper [specific] as is stated in [Aristotle's] *Physics* i. The speculative reason, however, is differently situated, in this matter, from the practical reason. For, since the speculative reason is concerned chiefly with necessary things, which cannot be otherwise than they are, its proper [specific] conclusions, like the universal principles, contain the truth without fail. The practical reason, on the other hand, is concerned with contingent matters, which is the domain of human actions; and, consequently, although there is necessity in the common principles, the more we descend towards the particular, the more frequently we encounter defects. Accordingly, then, in speculative matters truth is the same in all men, both as to principles and as to conclusions; although truth is not known to all as regards the conclusions, but only as regards the principles. . . . But in matters of action, truth or practical rectitude is not the same for all as to what is particular, but only as to common principles; and where there is the same rectitude in relation to particulars, it is not equally known to all. . . . Thus, it is right and true for all to act according to reason, and from this principle it follows, as a proper [specific] conclusion, that goods entrusted to another should be restored to their owner. Now this is true for the majority of cases. But it may happen in a particular case that it would be injurious, and therefore unreasonable, to restore goods held in trust; for instance, if they are claimed for the purpose of fighting against one's country. And this principle will be found to fail the more, according as we descend further towards the particular, *e.g.*, if one were to say that goods held in trust should be restored with such and such guarantee, or in such and such a way; because the greater the number of conditions added, the greater the number of ways in which the principle may fail, so that it be not right to restore or not to restore.[11]

A change in the natural law may be understood in two ways. First, by way of addition. In this sense, nothing hinders the natural law from being changed, since many things for the benefit of human life have been added over and above the natural law, both by the divine law and by human laws. Secondly, a change in the natural law may be understood by way of subtraction, so that what previously was according to the natural law, ceases to be so. In this sense, the natural law is altogether unchangeable in its first principles. But in its secondary principles, which, as we have said, are certain detailed proximate conclusions drawn from the first principles, the natural law is not changed so that what it prescribes be not right in most cases. But it may be changed in some particular cases of rare occurrence, through some special causes hindering the observance of such precepts, as was stated above.[12]

Notes

[1] *Summa Theologica,* I–II, Q. 71, Art. 2, in *Basic Writings of Saint Thomas Aquinas,* ed. Anton C. Pegis (New York: Random House, 1945), vol. 2, pp. 561–562.

[2] *S. Th.,* I–II, Q. 58, Art. 3, ibid., p. 444.

[3] *S. Th.,* I–II, Q. 58, Art. 4, ibid., p. 446.

[4] *S. Th.,* I–II, Q. 61, Art. 2, ibid., p. 468.

[5] *S. Th.,* I–II, Q. 90, Art. 4, ibid., p. 747.

[6] *S. Th.,* I–II, Q. 91, Art. 2, ibid., pp. 749–750.

[7] *S. Th.,* I–II, Q. 94, Art. 2, ibid., pp. 774–775.

[8] *S. Th.,* I–II, Q. 100, Art. 1, ibid., p. 828.

[9] *S. Th.,* I–II, Q. 100, Art. 5, ibid., p. 837.

[10] *S. Th.,* I–II, Q. 100, Art. 5, ibid., p. 835.

[11] *S. Th.,* I–II, Q. 94, Art. 4, ibid., p. 777–778.

[12] *S. Th.,* I–II, Q. 94, Art. 5, ibid., p. 779.

GERMAIN GRISEZ AND RUSSELL SHAW
A CONTEMPORARY ACCOUNT OF THE VIRTUOUS LIFE

CHOICE—EXCLUSIVISTIC AND INCLUSIVISTIC

. . . One way of choosing can be called "exclusive" or, better perhaps, "exclusivistic." It may be objected that all choice is exclusivistic, since

From Germain Grisez and Russell Shaw, *Beyond The New Morality: The Responsibilities of Freedom* (Notre Dame, Ind.: University of Notre Dame Press, 1974), pp. 88, 90–91, 108–114, 118–121, 128–133. Copyright 1974, University of Notre Dame Press, Notre Dame, Indiana 46556.

in choosing one thing an individual naturally excludes the things not chosen.

While this is certainly the case, it ignores the fact that there are two radically different attitudes which one can bring to choosing. In making a choice among alternatives one can do so in such a way—and with such an attitude—that those things which are not chosen are also not positively rejected, or one's attitude can be such that the alternatives not chosen *are* rejected. The second way of choosing—with an attitude that positively rejects the alternatives not chosen—is exclusivistic choice. . . .

But it is also possible to choose with an inclusive—or, better, an inclusivistic—attitude. This means simply that while choosing one alternative out of two or more, one continues to respect the values present in the alternatives that were not chosen. A person who chooses in this way in effect acknowledges his own limitations—no one can be or do everything—but he does not shift the blame, as it were, onto the options-not-chosen by denying their value. . . .

We ought always to choose inclusivistically. For consistent inclusivism in choice is in fact the criterion of moral goodness we have been seeking, whereas moral evil consists in choosing exclusivistically. Indeed, it can be said that no one chooses precisely to do *what is morally wrong;* one rather makes choices *in a way* that is morally wrong—in an exclusivistic manner.

This is so because, upon reflection, it becomes apparent that inclusivistic choice corresponds to . . . the meaning of the moral "ought"—the fullest possible realization of ourselves as free. When we choose inclusivistically we remain open to further self-realization even in directions we have not chosen. Even though we have chosen X—instead of Y or Z—we continue to acknowledge the good that is in Y and Z and, in doing so, we remain open to the possibility of realizing that good, given different circumstances. We have not closed off growth in any area of life (which is to say, growth in ourselves).

By contrast, because it involves an attitude which denies the value of that which is not chosen, exclusivistic choice not only prevents self-realization in these directions here and now but tends to block it permanently by creating a mind-set which denies the goodness that is there. . . .

MODES OF RESPONSIBILITY

. . . If one's attitude toward all the fundamental human purposes were open and inclusivistic (the basic criterion of moral goodness), he would not live for passing satisfactions or for specific future objectives. He would instead commit himself to the realization of basic purposes with which he could identify to such an extent that the free actions by which he realized them would in fact constitute him as the person he was.

Furthermore, he would make a number of such commitments—large, third-level actions like marrying or engaging in a profession. And, further still, he would strive to make his commitments consistent with one another, so that they formed a harmonious framework for his life. This, then, is the first mode of responsibility: consistent commitment to a harmonious set of purposes or values.

Negatively, this mode of responsibility rules out a certain kind of premoral spontaneity, in which a man in effect puts himself at the service of a desire or inclination which is not harmonized with the rest of his fundamental life-purposes. Many people do in fact spend a great part of their lives in the service of such goals—pleasure, wealth, status, and so forth—which do not represent rational commitments but instead originated as mere wants or cravings. Such unreflective, slavish activity has nothing to do with a free, self-determined life.

At the same time there is a place for spontaneity within morality. For the individual who has integrated his commitments into a consistent pattern, spontaneous action within this pattern becomes almost second nature. But spontaneity in this case will be in line with one's commitments rather than something that precedes commitment. From the perspective of this mode of responsibility, immorality consists in using one's mature powers in the service of infantile goals, while morality means organizing one's life around basic commitments and acting within the pattern one has created by this organization.

A second mode of responsibility is that if one has an open and inclusivistic attitude toward all the fundamental human purposes, he will at all times take into account all of the goods, and will, furthermore, do so not merely as they apply to himself but as they apply to all other men. He will not regard himself as a special case, demanding concessions and special treatment he is unwilling to grant to others. He will regularly ask himself questions such as "How would I like it if somebody did this to me?" and "What would happen if everybody acted as I wish to act?"

It is no secret that this moral rule is violated frequently in ordinary experience. Violations are especially common on the part of people who have undergone a change in their state of life and no longer remember how things looked "on the other side." How many parents, one wonders, inflict injustices on their children which they, as children suffering the same injustices at the hands of *their* parents, vowed never to be guilty of in adult life?

A third mode of responsibility, also involving relationships with others, might be described simply as openness: willingness to help others, desire to see them develop and perfect themselves by realizing to the fullest the goods of which they are capable. A person with this attitude is not defensive or selfish about protecting his own position of excellence or superiority in relation to others.

A striking example is provided by the good teacher who genuinely rejoices in seeing his students progress in their particular discipline or skill, even if the students come in time to outshine the teacher. A man with this attitude will also accept and take satisfaction in the ways in which other people are different from him; he will not demand that everyone mirror his tastes and enthusiasms.

Morality, from the viewpoint of this mode of responsibility, is often expressed in willingness to accept responsibility for the needs of another even where there is no structured relationship with the other which compels one to do so. Conversely, immorality is apparent in the actions of persons who feel no responsibility for others with whom they come into contact in unstructured relationships (e.g., the driver who does not stop or send help back to a stranded motorist). To insist on having a clear-cut duty before doing what is necessary to help someone else reflects an immoral attitude.

DETACHMENT AND FIDELITY

"Detachment" is the word which characterizes a fourth mode of responsibility. Its contrary is manifested by people who are so oriented toward one purpose that its frustration or loss is a shattering experience which drains their lives of meaning. Someone with a morally good attitude, an openness to all human goods, will not be so totally destroyed by the loss of any one good, no matter how genuinely painful the loss may be. . . .

A person with a religious turn of mind may object at this point that what has just been said cannot apply to loving God above all else—something to which every man ought to be totally dedicated, and dedicated above everything else. This is true, so long as one keeps in mind that God is not an aspect of the human personality, that God transcends all human goods, and that, properly understood, love of God implies love of all human goods; implies, in other words, precisely the morally good attitude we have been attempting to describe. However, it *is* possible to overidentify with and overcommit oneself to the human good of religion, in which case the aberration in question is what is called "religious fanaticism."

The fifth mode of responsibility complements detachment. While prepared to accept the loss of particular satisfactions and achievements without regarding this as a final loss of his personhood, a man should nevertheless remain committed to his ideals. He should, in other words, practice fidelity. A person with such an attitude will persist in seeking to realize realistically realizable purposes; by contrast, a person with an immoral attitude will tend to give up rather easily upon encountering problems and obstacles.

Fidelity or stability in commitment to purposes is not the same thing as mere constancy, much less rigidity. It implies continuing effort to explore new ways of better serving the purposes to which one is committed. Furthermore, it involves refusal to narrow down a human good to those particular expressions of it with which one happens to be familiar. A creative and open approach to living is not only consistent with but essential to genuine fidelity. . . .

Detachment on the one hand and fidelity on the other balance each other in the life of an individual. They enable a man to strike a mean between the immoral extremes of fanaticism and noninvolvement. They also rule out an attitude of unwillingness to attempt difficult things and thereby risk failure.

Morality does not require one to take needless risks or to be unrealistic about circumstances, including one's own abilities, and the consequent chances of failing in an undertaking. But a person with a morally good attitude will be inclined to push beyond what he and others have already accomplished and to take reasonable chances in the process, aware that many good and important things in life will never be done except by people who are willing to run the risk of failing in the attempt to do them.

PURSUIT OF LIMITED OBJECTIVES

Under the sixth mode of responsibility one will seek specific ends which contribute to realization of the broader, deeper purposes to which he has dedicated his life. The pursuit of specific objectives which can be attained by definite, limited means should always be included within the framework of our basic self-constitution.

This may seem a surprising thing to say in view of the many occasions on which we have up to now criticized the pursuit of limited objectives. The point of this criticism, however, has been that it is wrong to limit one's morality, and one's life, merely to this. But, provided life is grounded upon and built around commitment to a consistent set of purposes, it is not only good sense but one's responsibility to, as it were, put flesh on the bones of these commitments by pursuing limited ends which further their realization. . . .

Where, morally speaking, efficiency is possible, it is a virtue, although it is no virtue if it means achieving a limited objective at the expense of violating some basic good. Waste and inefficiency, by contrast, are signs of vice, although it is no vice to be judged "inefficient" in the pursuit of an objective when "efficiency" would require the violation of fundamental human goods.

Thus a nation might be judged inefficient in defending itself against aggression, even to the point of allowing itself to be overrun and conquered. But there would be nothing immoral about such inefficiency—it would in fact reflect an entirely moral attitude—if the efficiency in question came down in cold fact to repelling the aggression by merciless bombing of the potential invader's civilian population.

The modes of responsibility, as the last example suggested, apply not only to individuals but also to communities in their common action. In other words, they hold not only for men singly but for men collectively.

Each mode of responsibility has a social as well as an individual dimension. . . .

COMMUNITIES AND DUTIES

Each of us has a variety of social roles arising from membership in various communities, and each of these social roles carries with it a variety of duties. To see why these duties normally are real *moral* responsibilities (why, that is, they concern good and evil and why they involve our self-determination) it is necessary to bear in mind what constitutes a genuine community.

A crowd of people brought together by accident or force—by something extrinsic to the members of the group—is not a community. . . . A community is characterized by shared commitment on the part of its members to the realization of some fundamental human purpose or purposes and by structures and activity appropriate to bringing this about.

In many respects a family is a model community. Its members are joined by ties of blood and mutual dependence, to be sure, but also by a joint commitment to common purposes of a very basic and intimate sort. Where such a commitment is lacking, a particular family may exist as a socioeconomic unit—as a kind of convenient arrangement—but it is not a genuine "community" as the word is understood and used here.

Definite structures and activity are required for the realization of the purposes which constitute a community. Institutions are necessary to articulate the purposes to which the community members are committed. All this in turn gives rise to various roles—what one might call "job descriptions"—for the different community members. Within the family, for instance, "father" refers to one role, "mother" to another, "eldest son" to a third, and so on.

The fulfillment of these roles will require that the persons filling them act in certain ways. These required ways of acting are duties, and a duty may be defined as something one has a responsibility for doing or not doing by virtue of one's role in a particular community. Just as we all have many social roles, so we have many duties: as a student, as a citizen, as a family member, as an employer or employee, and so on.

A community cannot function efficiently if its members do not live up to their roles and fulfill their duties. But true as this is, it is not this which makes duties genuine moral responsibilities. The aspect of moral responsibility enters in, rather, because of the fact that the members of a community are engaged in a joint . . . action seeking the realization of a fundamental human purpose or purposes.

A community member who does not fulfill his role and live up to his duties is in effect seeking to enjoy participation in the common good for which the community is organized without putting into it what is required of him if the community is to continue to realize the good for which it exists. He is trying to get something for nothing, to enjoy a free ride, at the expense of the other community members. Moreover, he is undermining the community at its roots by refusing to do his part to realize its purposes. If enough members behave in this way, the result, sooner or later, will be the collapse of the community and the end of the possibility that *this* community will realize its constituting purposes. . . .

Having said this, however, it is necessary to add two important qualifications. First, our duties as community members are real moral responsibilities only if the community itself is a genuine one. Second, when duties conflict with one another—as they sometimes do—our moral responsibility is limited to fulfilling only one of the conflicting duties, but deciding which one is not at all easy. . . .

A pure community in which there are no elements of injustice and exploitation is a very rare thing. Indeed, it is doubtful whether such a phenomenon ever does exist in our imperfect world. Certainly, the large-scale societies of which we are all members are not pure communities. They have aspects of genuine community, but they have less attractive aspects as well. And our duties as members of such a society are true moral responsibilities only when they arise from the community aspect of the society rather than from its unjust and exploitative aspects.

Nations, including the United States, are such societies, partly community and partly a highly complex structure to facilitate self-interest and exploitation. To say this is not to engage in breast-beating or viewing with alarm; it is simply to state the evident fact of the matter. . . .

ETHICAL ABSOLUTES

Are there ethical absolutes? Are there principles which should never be violated and therefore things which should never be done, regardless of circumstances and consequences?

Most people, almost instinctively, would answer Yes, and would then go on to cite some action which they feel should never be performed: purposely to torture a small child, for instance. Yet for many ethical theorists in our times the answer is No. For them there are no ethical absolutes and therefore no actions which can flatly be ruled out as being beyond the pale of acceptable human behavior. . . .

Our eighth mode of responsibility states unequivocally that there are such actions. It may be put quite simply: it is never right to act directly against one of the fundamental human goods. But while it is easy enough to state this principle, it is more difficult to show what it means. The question is far removed from idle speculation, however. Indeed, it is one of the most burning ethical issues of our times, an issue of far-reaching practical ramifications for individual and social life.

DUTIES AND RESPONSIBILITIES

In our discussion of duties we saw that many of our moral responsibilities arise from duties (which in turn arise from our structured social relationships with other people). Such responsibilities have true moral force, but they are not absolute. This is evident in the fact that they can and sometimes do conflict with one another. A man's responsibilities arising from his duties as a husband may sometimes come into conflict with his responsibilities as an employee. Both sets of duties are real, but in a particular situation an individual may not be able to respond to both.

In such a case a person must fulfill one set of duties and neglect the other. Provided he is being honest about the facts and his response to the facts, he can do so with a clear conscience, in the knowledge that these duties, while real, are not absolute responsibilities and, where circumstances require, can be neglected in favor of other, equally pressing duties.

However, there are other responsibilities which do not arise from duties and which are not conditional but absolute. They are founded instead on the implications of the ideal of openness to all the goods constitutive of the human person. Openness to the human goods is the basis of a right moral attitude.

In acting directly against any one of them we make that against which we act a means to an ulterior end. But the goods that go to make up personhood are themselves the ends of human action, and as such they should not be treated as if they were mere means to other ends. Because each of these goods is, as we have seen, the supreme good in its own way, no one of them can be subordinated to another as a means to an end. Thus the minimum requirement for a morally correct attitude (and action) is simultaneous respect for all the basic goods: respect which means in practice refusing to violate any fundamental good in order to achieve another.

The seven modes of responsibility we have examined previously are positive: they tell us what to do. But this eighth mode is negative. It tells us what we ought *not* to do. It is not correct to suppose that all morality is summed up in prohibitions ("thou shalt not"), even though it is sometimes caricatured that way. But it is also a mistake to overlook the extremely strong binding force of this negative mode of responsibility: one should never act directly against any of the fundamental human goods.

It is essential to remember that these goods are what human life and human action are all about. The goods are not abstractions existing "out there" beyond us and other people. Rather, as we experience them, the goods are aspects of human persons, ourselves or others, aspects which either already exist in actuality or have the potential of being realized. Thus, to act directly against one of the fundamental goods is to violate an actual or possible aspect of the personhood of a real person or persons: to violate "life," for example, means violating somebody's life. This amounts to using a human person as a means to an end.

ARE THERE INALIENABLE RIGHTS?

Critics of the view that there are ethical absolutes sometimes refer to them disparagingly as "legalistic absolutes." Rhetoric aside, the implication is that this position exalts law (legalism) at the expense of the person. Yet the defense of ethical absolutes, properly understood, does not mean assigning primacy to bloodless law over flesh-and-blood persons. On the contrary, it constitutes a defense of the person and his inalienable rights.

If there are no absolute responsibilities, there are no inalienable rights. If it were true that any action, no matter what, is permitted in certain circumstances, then no good intrinsic to the person would be safe from invasion and suppression provided the justifying circumstances existed. In such a case it would always be possible to conceive of circumstances in which the person could be sacrificed to the attainment of ulterior ends.

Instead of being the norm and source from which other things receive their value, the human person would become simply one more item or commodity with a relative value, inviolable only up to the point at which it became expedient to violate him in order to achieve some objective. It would then make no sense at all to speak of the "infinite value" of the human person. Far from being infinite, the value of a person would be quite specific and quantifiable, something to be weighed calculatingly in the balance against other values.

Often it is assumed that this sort of weighing of human goods (and human persons) is possible. This assumption enters in, tacitly in many instances, as a result of confusion between the fundamental goods constitutive of the person, which are always open-ended and never fully defined (because one can never say that one of these goods has been totally realized and exhausted by oneself or others), and a specific objective which is never completely identical with the person.

Typically, an individual with such an attitude will think along the following lines: Two lives are better than one; therefore if two innocent lives can be saved by sacrificing one innocent life, it is entirely right and proper to sacrifice the one life in order to save the two.

An example dramatizes this attitude. In wartime a military commander is confronted with a group of prisoners who possess important information about the enemy's plans. He needs the information in order to prevent loss of life among his own men, but the prisoners will not tell him what he wants to know. In order to compel the prisoners to talk, he has one of them executed as an example to the others and thereby frightens the survivors into divulging the desired information. Thus, by taking one life he has saved other lives, and according to the principle that two lives are better than one (or twenty better than two, or two thousand better than twenty, and so on) his action is not only expedient but morally right.

One arrives at a very different judgment, however, if human life is regarded not as a concrete, specific, essentially quantifiable object but as a good in which each person participates but which none exhausts or sums up in himself. In such a view of reality it is simply not possible to make the sort of calculation which weighs lives against each other (my life is more valuable than John's life, John's life is more valuable than

Ed's and Tom's combined, etc.) and thus determines whose life shall be respected and whose sacrificed. The value of life, each human life, is incalculable, not in any merely poetic sense but simply because it is something not susceptible to calculation, measurement, weighing, and balancing.

Traditionally this point has been expressed by the statement that the end does not justify the means. This is simply a way of saying that the direct violation of any good intrinsic to the person cannot be justified by the good result which such a violation will bring about. What is extrinsic to human persons may be used for the good of persons, but what is intrinsic to persons has a kind of sacredness and may not be violated.

JOHN LOCKE
NATURAL RIGHTS AND CIVIL SOCIETY

OF THE STATE OF NATURE

4. To understand political power aright, and derive it from its original, we must consider what estate all men are naturally in, and that is, a state of perfect freedom to order their actions, and dispose of their possessions and persons as they think fit, within the bounds of the law of Nature, without asking leave or depending upon the will of any other man.

A state also of equality, wherein all the power and jurisdiction is reciprocal, no one having more than another, there being nothing more evident than that creatures of the same species and rank, promiscuously born to all the same advantages of Nature, and the use of the same faculties, should also be equal one amongst another, without subordination or subjection, unless the lord and master of them all should, by any manifest declaration of his will, set one above another, and confer on him, by an evident and clear appointment, an undoubted right to dominion and sovereignty. . . .

6. But though this be a state of liberty, yet it is not a state of licence; though man in that state have an uncontrollable liberty to dispose of his person or possessions, yet he has not liberty to destroy himself, or so much as any creature in his possession, but where some nobler use than its bare preservation calls for it. The state of Nature has a law of Nature to govern it, which obliges every one, and reason, which is that law, teaches all mankind who will but consult it, that being all equal and independent, no one ought to harm another in his life, health, liberty or possessions; for men being all the workmanship of one omnipotent and infinitely wise Maker; all the servants of one sovereign Master, sent into the world by His order and about His business; they are His property,

From John Locke, *Two Treatises of Government* (1690).

whose workmanship they are made to last during His, not one another's pleasure. And, being furnished with like faculties, sharing all in one community of Nature, there cannot be supposed any such subordination among us that may authorise us to destroy one another, as if we were made for one another's uses, as the inferior ranks of creatures are for ours. Every one as he is bound to preserve himself, and not to quit his station willfully, so by the like reason, when his own preservation comes not in competition, ought he as much as he can to preserve the rest of mankind, and not unless it be to do justice on an offender, take away or impair the life, or what tends to the preservation of the life, the liberty, health, limb, or goods of another.

7. And that all men may be restrained from invading others' rights, and from doing hurt to one another, and the law of Nature be observed, which willeth the peace and preservation of all mankind, the execution of the law of Nature is in that state put into every man's hands, whereby every one has a right to punish the transgressors of that law to such a degree as may hinder its violation. For the law of Nature would, as all other laws that concern men in this world, be in vain if there were nobody that in the state of Nature had a power to execute that law, and thereby preserve the innocent and restrain offenders; and if any one in the state of Nature may punish another for any evil he has done, every one may do so. For in that state of perfect equality, where naturally there is no superiority or jurisdiction of one over another, what any may do in prosecution of that law, every one must needs have a right to do. . . .

14. It is often asked as a mighty objection, where are, or ever were, there any men in such a state of Nature? To which it may suffice as an answer at present, that since all princes and rulers of "independent" governments all through the world are in a state of Nature, it is plain the world never was, nor never will be, without numbers of men in that state. I have named all governors of "independent" communities, whether they are, or are not, in league with others; for it is not every compact that puts an end to the state of Nature between men, but only this one of agreeing together mutually to enter into one community, and make one body politic; other promises and compacts men may make one with another, and yet still be in the state of Nature. The promises and bargains for truck, etc., between the two men in Soldania, in or between a Swiss and an Indian, in the woods of America, are binding to them, though they are perfectly in a state of Nature in reference to one another for truth, and keeping of faith belongs to men as men, and not as members of society. . . .

OF PROPERTY

27. Though the earth and all inferior creatures be common to all men, yet every man has a "property" in his own "person." This nobody has

any right to but himself. The "labour" of his body and the "work" of his hands, we may say, are properly his. Whatsoever, then, he removes out of the state that Nature hath provided and left it in, he hath mixed his labour with it, and joined to it something that is his own, and thereby makes it his property. It being by him removed from the common state Nature placed it in, it hath by this labour something annexed to it that excludes the common right of other men. For this "labour" being the unquestionable property of the labourer, no man but he can have a right to what that is once joined to, at least where there is enough, and as good left in common for others.

28. He that is nourished by the acorns he picked up under an oak, or the apples he gathered from the trees in the wood, has certainly appropriated them to himself. Nobody can deny but the nourishment is his. I ask, then, when did they begin to be his? when digested? or when he ate? or when he boiled? or when he brought them home? or when he picked them up? And it is plain, if the first gathering made them not his, nothing else could. That labour put a distinction between them and common. That added something to them more than Nature, the common mother of all, had done, and so they became his private right. And will any one say he had no right to those acorns or apples he thus appropriated because he had not the consent of all mankind to make them his? Was it a robbery thus to assume to himself what belonged to all in common? If such a consent as that was necessary, man had starved, notwithstanding the plenty God had given him. We see in commons, which remain so by compact, that it is the taking any part of what is common, and removing it out of the state Nature leaves it in, which begins the property, without which the common is of no use. And the taking of this or that part does not depend on the express consent of all the commoners. Thus, the grass my horse has bit, the turfs my servant has cut, and the ore I have digged in any place, where I have a right to them in common with others, become my property without the assignation or consent of anybody. The labour that was mine, removing them out of that common state they were in, hath fixed my property in them. . . .

31. It will, perhaps, be objected to this, that if gathering the acorns or other fruits of the earth, etc., makes a right to them, then any one may engross as much as he will. To which I answer, Not so. The same law of Nature that does by this means give us property, does also bound that property too. "God has given us all things richly." Is the voice of reason confirmed by inspiration? But how far has He given it us—"to enjoy"? As much as any one can make use of to any advantage of life before it spoils, so much he may by his labour fix a property in. Whatever is beyond this is more than his share, and belongs to others. Nothing was made by God for man to spoil or destroy. And thus considering the plenty of natural provisions there was a long time in the world, and the few spenders, and to how small a part of that provision the industry of one man could extend itself and engross it to the prejudice of others, especially keeping within the bounds set by reason of what might serve

for his use, there could be then little room for quarrels or contentions about property so established. . . .

46. The greatest part of things really useful to the life of man, and such as the necessity of subsisting made the first commoners of the world look after—as it doth the Americans now—are generally things of short duration, such as—if they are not consumed by use—will decay and perish of themselves. Gold, silver, and diamonds are things that fancy or agreement hath put the value on, more than real use and the necessary support of life. Now of those good things which Nature hath provided in common, every one hath a right (as hath been said) to as much as he could use, and had a property in all he could effect with his labour; all that his industry could extend to, to alter from the state Nature had put it in, was his. He that gathered a hundred bushels of acorns or apples had thereby a property in them; they were his goods as soon as gathered. He was only to look that he used them before they spoiled, else he took more than his share, and robbed others. And, indeed, it was a foolish thing, as well as dishonest, to hoard up more than he could make use of. If he gave away a part to anybody else, so that it perished not uselessly in his possession, these he also made use of. And if he also bartered away plums that would have rotted in a week, for nuts that would last good for his eating a whole year, he did no injury; he wasted not the common stock; destroyed no part of the portion of goods that belonged to others, so long as nothing perished uselessly in his hands. Again, if he would give his nuts for a piece of metal, pleased with its colour, or exchange his sheep for shells, or wool for a sparkling pebble or a diamond, and keep those by him all his life, he invaded not the right of others; he might heap up as much of these durable things as he pleased; the exceeding of the bounds of his just property not lying in the largeness of his possession, but the perishing of anything uselessly in it.

47. And thus came in the use of money; some lasting thing that men might keep without spoiling, and that, by mutual consent, men would take in exchange for the truly useful but perishable supports of life.

48. And as different degrees of industry were apt to give men possessions in different proportions, so this invention of money gave them the opportunity to continue and enlarge them. . . .

50. But since gold and silver, being little useful to the life of man, in proportion to food, raiment, and carriage, has its value only from the consent of men—whereof labour yet makes in great part the measure—it is plain that the consent of men have agreed to a disproportionate and unequal possession of the earth—I mean out of the bounds of society and compact; for in governments the laws regulate it; they having, by consent, found out and agreed in a way how a man may, rightfully and without injury, possess more than he himself can make use of by receiving gold and silver, which may continue long in a man's possession without decaying for the overplus, and agreeing those metals should have a value. . . .

OF POLITICAL OR CIVIL SOCIETY

87. Man being born, as has been proved, with a title to perfect freedom and an uncontrolled enjoyment of all the rights and privileges of the law of Nature, equally with any other man, or number of men in the world, hath by nature a power not only to preserve his property—that is, his life, liberty, and estate, against the injuries and attempts of other men, but to judge of and punish the breaches of that law in others, as he is persuaded the offence deserves, even with death itself, in crimes where the heinousness of the fact, in his opinion, requires it. But because no political society can be, nor subsist, without having in itself the power to preserve the property, and in order thereunto punish the offences of all those of that society, there, and there only, is political society where every one of the members hath quitted this natural power, resigned it up into the hands of the community in all cases that exclude him not from appealing for protection to the law established by it. And thus all private judgment of every particular member being excluded, the community comes to be umpire, and by understanding indifferent rules and men authorised by the community for their execution, decides all the differences that may happen between any members of that society concerning any matter of right, and punishes those offences which any member hath committed against the society with such penalties as the law has established; whereby it is easy to discern who are, and are not, in political society together. Those who are united into one body, and have a common established law and judicature to appeal to, with authority to decide controversies between them and punish offenders, are in civil society one with another; but those who have no such common appeal, I mean on earth, are still in the state of Nature, each being where there is no other, judge for himself and executioner; which is, as I have before showed it, the perfect state of Nature. . . .

95. MEN being, as has been said, by nature all free, equal, and independent, no one can be put out of this estate and subjected to the political power of another without his own consent, which is done by agreeing with other men, to join and unite into a community for their comfortable, safe, and peaceable living, one amongst another, in a secure enjoyment of their properties, and a greater security against any that are not of it. This any number of men may do, because it injures not the freedom of the rest; they are left, as they were, in the liberty of the state of Nature. When any number of men have so consented to make one community or government, they are thereby presently incorporated, and make one body politic, wherein the majority have a right to act and conclude the rest.

96. For, when any number of men have, by the consent of every individual, made a community, they have thereby made that community one body, with a power to act as one body, which is only by the will and determination of the majority. For that which acts any community, being

only the consent of the individuals of it, and it being one body, must move one way, it is necessary the body should move that way whither the greater force carries it, which is the consent of the majority, or else it is impossible it should act or continue one body, one community, which the consent of every individual that united into it agreed that it should; and so every one is bound by that consent to be concluded by the majority. And therefore we see that in assemblies empowered to act by positive laws where no number is set by that positive law which empowers them, the act of the majority passes for the act of the whole, and of course determines as having, by the law of Nature and reason, the power of the whole. . . .

99. Whosoever, therefore, out of a state of Nature unite into a community, must be understood to give up all the power necessary to the ends for which they unite into society to the majority of the community, unless they expressly agreed in any number greater than the majority. And this is done by barely agreeing to unite into one political society, which is all the compact that is, or needs be, between the individuals that enter into or make up a commonwealth. And thus, that which begins and actually constitutes any political society is nothing but the consent of any number of freemen capable of majority, to unite and incorporate into such a society. And this is that, and that only, which did or could give beginning to any lawful government in the world. . . .

OF THE EXTENT OF THE LEGISLATIVE POWER

135. Though the legislative, whether placed in one or more, whether it be always in being or only by intervals, though it be the supreme power in every commonwealth, yet, first, it is not, nor can possibly be, absolutely arbitrary over the lives and fortunes of the people. For it being but the joint power of every member of the society given up to that person or assembly which is legislator, it can be no more than those persons had in a state of Nature before they entered into society, and gave it up to the community. For nobody can transfer to another more power than he has in himself, and nobody has an absolute arbitrary power over himself, or over any other, to destroy his own life, or take away the life or property of another. A man, as has been proved, cannot subject himself to the arbitrary power of another; and having, in the state of Nature, no arbitrary power over the life, liberty, or possession of another, but only so much as the law of Nature gave him for the preservation of himself and the rest of mankind, this is all he doth, or can give up to the commonwealth, and by it to the legislative power, so that the legislative can have no more than this. Their power in the utmost bounds of it is limited to the public good of the society. It is a power that hath no other end but preservation, and therefore can never have a right to destroy, enslave, or designedly to impoverish the subjects; the obligations of the law of Nature cease not in society, but only in many cases

are drawn closer, and have, by human laws, known penalties annexed to them to enforce their observation. Thus the law of Nature stands as an eternal rule to all men, legislators as well as others. The rules that they make for other men's actions must, as well as their own and other men's actions, be conformable to the law of Nature—*i.e.,* to the will of God, of which that is a declaration, and the fundamental law of Nature being the preservation of mankind, no human sanction can be good or valid against it.

136. Secondly, the legislative or supreme authority cannot assume to itself a power to rule by extemporary arbitrary decrees, but is bound to dispense justice and decide the rights of the subject by promulgated standing laws, and known authorised judges. For the law of Nature being unwritten, and so nowhere to be found but in the minds of men, they who, through passion or interest, shall miscite or misapply it, cannot so easily be convinced of their mistake where there is no established judge; and so it serves not as it aught, to determine the rights and fence the properties of those that live under it, especially where every one is judge, interpreter, and executioner of it too, and that in his own case; and he that has right on his side, having ordinarily but his own single strength, hath not force enough to defend himself from injuries or punish delinquents. To avoid these inconveniences which disorder men's properties in the state of Nature, men unite into societies that they may have the united strength of the whole society to secure and defend their properties, and may have standing rules to bound it by which every one may know what is his. To this end it is that men give up all their natural power to the society they enter into, and the community put the legislative power into such hands as they think fit, with this trust, that they shall be governed by declared laws, or else their peace, quiet, and property will still be at the same uncertainty as it was in the state of Nature. . . .

138. Thirdly, the supreme power cannot take from any man any part of his property without his own consent. For the preservation of property being the end of government, and that for which men enter into society, it necessarily supposes and requires that the people should have property, without which they must be supposed to lose that by entering into society which was the end for which they entered into it; too gross an absurdity for any man to own. Men, therefore, in society having property, they have such a right to the goods, which by the law of the community are theirs, that nobody hath a right to take them, or any part of them, from them without their own consent; without this they have no property at all. For I have truly no property in that which another can by right take from me when he pleases against my consent. Hence it is a mistake to think that the supreme or legislative power of any commonwealth can do what it will, and dispose of the estates of the subject arbitrarily, or take any part of them at pleasure. This is not much to be feared in governments where the legislative consists wholly or in part in

assemblies which are variable, whose members upon the dissolution of the assembly are subjects under the common laws of their country, equally with the rest. But in governments where the legislative is in one lasting assembly, always in being, or in one man as in absolute monarchies, there is danger still, that they will think themselves to have a distinct interest from the rest of the community, and so will be apt to increase their own riches and power by taking what they think fit from the people. For a man's property is not at all secure, though there be good and equitable laws to set the bounds of it between him and his fellow-subjects, if he who commands those subjects have power to take from any private man what part he pleases of his property, and use and dispose of it as he thinks good.

ROBERT NOZICK
DISTRIBUTIVE JUSTICE

THE ENTITLEMENT THEORY

The subject of justice in holdings consists of three major topics. The first is the *original acquisition of holdings,* the appropriation of unheld things. This includes the issues of how unheld things may come to be held, the process, or processes, by which unheld things may come to be held, the things that may come to be held by these processes, the extent of what comes to be held by a particular process, and so on. We shall refer to the complicated truth about this topic, which we shall not formulate here, as the principle of justice in acquisition. The second topic concerns the *transfer of holdings* from one person to another. By what processes may a person transfer holdings to another? How may a person acquire a holding from another who holds it? Under this topic come general descriptions of voluntary exchange, and gift and (on the other hand) fraud, as well as reference to particular conventional details fixed upon in a given society. The complicated truth about this subject (with place-holders for conventional details) we shall call the principle of justice in transfer. (And we shall suppose it also includes principles governing how a person may divest himself of a holding, passing it into an unheld state.)

If the world were wholly just, the following inductive definition would exhaustively cover the subject of justice in holdings.

1. A person who acquires a holding in accordance with the principle of justice in acquisition is entitled to that holding.

2.   A person who acquires a holding in accordance with the principle of justice in transfer, from someone else entitled to the holding, is entitled to the holding.

3.   No one is entitled to a holding except by (repeated) applications of 1 and 2.

The complete principle of distributive justice would say simply that a distribution is just if everyone is entitled to the holdings they possess under the distribution.

A distribution is just if it arises from another just distribution by legitimate means. The legitimate means of moving from one distribution to another are specified by the principle of justice in transfer. The legitimate first "moves" are specified by the principle of justice in acquisition.[1] Whatever arises from a just situation by just steps is itself just. The means of change specified by the principle of justice in transfer preserve justice. As correct rules of inference are truth-preserving, and any conclusion deduced via repeated application of such rules from only true premises is itself true, so the means of transition from one situation to another specified by the principle of justice in transfer are justice-preserving, and any situation actually arising from repeated transitions in accordance with the principle from a just situation is itself just. The parallel between justice-preserving transformations and truth-preserving transformations illuminates where it fails as well as where it holds. That a conclusion could have been deduced by truth-preserving means from premises that are true suffices to show its truth. That from a just situation a situation *could* have arisen via justice-preserving means does *not* suffice to show its justice. The fact that a thief's victims voluntarily *could* have presented him with gifts does not entitle the thief to his ill-gotten gains. Justice in holdings is historical; it depends upon what actually has happened. We shall return to this point later.

Not all actual situations are generated in accordance with the two principles of justice in holdings: the principle of justice in acquisition and the principle of justice in transfer. Some people steal from others, or defraud them, or enslave them, seizing their product and preventing them from living as they choose, or forcibly exclude others from competing in exchanges. None of these are permissible modes of transition from one situation to another. And some persons acquire holdings by means not sanctioned by the principle of justice in acquisition. The existence of past injustice (previous violations of the first two principles of justice in holdings) raises the third major topic under justice in holdings: the rectification of injustice in holdings. If past injustice has shaped present holdings in various ways, some identifiable and some not, what now, if anything, ought to be done to rectify these injustices? What obligations do the performers of injustice have toward those whose position is worse than it would have been had the injustice not been done? Or, than it would have been had compensation been paid promptly? How, if at all, do things change if the beneficiaries and those made worse off are not the direct parties in the act of injustice, but, for example, their descendants? Is an injustice done to someone whose holding was itself based upon an unrectified injustice? How far back must one go in wiping clean the historical slate of injustices? What may victims of injustice permissibly do in order to rectify the injustices being done to them, including the many injustices done by persons acting through their government? I do not know of a thorough or theoretically sophisticated treatment of such issues.[2] Idealizing greatly, let us suppose theoretical investigation will produce a principle of rectification. This principle uses historical information about previous situations and injustices done in them (as defined by the first two principles of justice and rights against interference), and information about the actual course of events that flowed from these injustices, until the present, and it yields a description (or descriptions) of holdings in the society. The principle of rectification presumably will make use of its best estimate of subjunctive information about what would have occurred (or a probability distribution over what might have occurred, using the expected value) if the injustice had not taken place. If the actual description of holdings turns out not to be one of the descriptions yielded by the principle, then one of the descriptions yielded must be realized.

The general outlines of the theory of justice in holdings are that the holdings of a person are just if he is entitled to them by the principles of justice in acquisition and transfer, or by the principle of rectification of injustice (as specified by the first two principles). If each person's holdings are just, then the total set (distribution) of holdings is just. To turn these general outlines into a specific theory we would have to specify the details of each of the three principles of justice in holdings: the principle of acquisition of holdings, the principle of transfer of holdings, and the principle of rectification of violations of the first two principles. I shall not attempt that task here. . . .

HISTORICAL PRINCIPLES AND END-RESULT PRINCIPLES

The general outlines of the entitlement theory illuminate the nature and defects of other conceptions of distributive justice. The entitlement theory of justice in distribution is *historical;* whether a distribution is just depends upon how it came about. In contrast, *current time-slice principles* of justice hold that the justice of a distribution is determined by how things are distributed (who has what) as judged by some *structural* principle(s) of just distribution. A utilitarian who judges between any two distributions by seeing which has the greater sum of utility and, if the sums tie, applies some fixed equality criterion to choose the more equal distribution, would hold a current time-slice principle of justice.

As would someone who had a fixed schedule of trade-offs between the sum of happiness and equality. According to a current time-slice principle, all that needs to be looked at, in judging the justice of a distribution, is who ends up with what; in comparing any two distributions one need look only at the matrix presenting the distributions. No further information need be fed into a principle of justice. It is a consequence of such principles of justice that any two structurally identical distributions are equally just. (Two distributions are structurally identical if they present the same profile, but perhaps have different persons occupying the particular slots. My having ten and your having five, and my having five and your having ten are structurally identical distributions.) Welfare economics is the theory of current time-slice principles of justice. The subject is conceived as operating on matrices representing only current information about distribution. This, as well as some of the usual conditions (for example, the choice of distribution is invariant under relabeling of columns), guarantees that welfare economics will be a current time-slice theory, with all of its inadequacies.

Most persons do not accept current time-slice principles as constituting the whole story about distributive shares. They think it relevant in assessing the justice of a situation to consider not only the distribution it embodies, but also how that distribution came about. If some persons are in prison for murder or war crimes, we do not say that to assess the justice of the distribution in the society we must look only at what this person has, and that person has, and that person has, . . . at the current time. We think it relevant to ask whether someone did something so that he *deserved* to be punished, deserved to have a lower share. Most will agree to the relevance of further information with regard to punishments and penalties. Consider also desired things. One traditional socialist view is that workers are entitled to the product and full fruits of their labor; they have earned it; a distribution is unjust if it does not give the workers what they are entitled to. Such entitlements are based upon some past history. No socialist holding this view would find it comforting to be told that because the actual distribution *A* happens to coincide structurally with the one he desires *D*, *A* therefore is no less just than *D*; it differs only in that the "parasitic" owners of capital receive under *A* what the workers are entitled to under *D*; and the workers receive under *A* what the owners are entitled to under *D*; namely very little. This socialist rightly, in my view, holds onto the notions of earning, producing, entitlement, desert, and so forth, and he rejects current time-slice principles that look only to the structure of the resulting set of holdings. (The set of holdings resulting from what? Isn't it implausible that how holdings are produced and come to exist has no effect at all on who should hold what?) His mistake lies in his view of what entitlements arise out of what sorts of productive processes.

We construe the position we discuss too narrowly by speaking of *current* time-slice principles. Nothing is changed if structural principles operate upon a time sequence of current time-slice profiles and, for example, give someone more now to counterbalance the less he has had earlier. A utilitarian or an egalitarian or any mixture of the two over time will inherit the difficulties of his more myopic comrades. He is not helped by the fact that *some* of the information others consider relevant in assessing a distribution is reflected, unrecoverably, in past matrices. Henceforth, we shall refer to such unhistorical principles of distributive justice, including the current time-slice principles, as *end-result principles* or *end-state principles.*

In contrast to end-result principles of justice, *historical principles* of justice hold that past circumstances or actions of people can create differential entitlements or differential deserts to things. An injustice can be worked by moving from one distribution to another structurally identical one, for the second, in profile the same, may violate people's entitlements or deserts; it may not fit the actual history.

PATTERNING

The entitlement principles of justice in holdings that we have sketched are historical principles of justice. To better understand their precise character, we shall distinguish them from another subclass of the historical principles. Consider, as an example, the principle of distribution according to moral merit. This principle requires that total distributive shares vary directly with moral merit; no person should have a greater share than anyone whose moral merit is greater. (If moral merit could be not merely ordered but measured on an interval or ratio scale, stronger principles could be formulated.) Or consider the principle that results by substituting "usefulness to society" for "moral merit" in the previous principle. Or instead of "distribute according to moral merit," or "distribute according to usefulness to society," we might consider "distribute according to the weighted sum of moral merit, usefulness to society, and need," with the weights of the different dimensions equal. Let us call a principle of distribution *patterned* if it specifies that a distribution is to vary along with some natural dimension, weighted sum of natural dimensions, or lexicographic ordering of natural dimensions. And let us say a distribution is patterned if it accords with some patterned principle. (I speak of natural dimensions, admittedly without a general criterion for them, because for any set of holdings some artificial dimensions can be gimmicked up to vary along with the distribution of the set.) The principle of distribution in accordance with moral merit is a patterned historical principle, which specifies a patterned distribution. "Distribute according to I.Q." is a patterned principle that looks to information not contained in distributional matrices. It is not historical, however, in that it does not look to any past actions creating differential entitlements to evaluate a distribution; it requires only distributional matrices whose columns are labeled by I.Q. scores. The distribution in a society, however, may be composed of such simple patterned distributions, without itself being simply patterned. Different sectors may operate different patterns, or some combination of patterns may operate in different proportions across a society. A distribution composed in this manner, from a small number of patterned distributions, we also shall term "patterned." And we extend the use of "pattern" to include the overall designs put forth by combinations of end-state principles.

Almost every suggested principle of distributive justice is patterned: to each according to his moral merit, or needs, or marginal product, or how hard he tries, or the weighted sum of the foregoing, and so on. The principle of entitlement we have sketched is *not* patterned. There is no one natural dimension or weighted sum or combination of a small number of natural dimensions that yields the distributions generated in accordance with the principle of entitlement. The set of holdings that results when some persons receive their marginal products, others win at gambling, others receive a share of their mate's income, others receive gifts from foundations, others receive interest on loans, other receive gifts from admirers, others receive returns on investment, others make for themselves much of what they have, others find things, and so on, will not be patterned. Heavy strands of patterns will run through it; significant portions of the variance in holdings will be accounted for by pattern-variables. If most people most of the time choose to transfer some of their entitlements to others only in exchange for something from them, then a large part of what many people hold will vary with what they held that others wanted. More details are provided by the theory of marginal productivity. But gifts to relatives, charitable donations, bequests to children, and the like, are not best conceived, in the first instance, in this manner. Ignoring the strands of pattern, let us suppose for the moment that a distribution actually arrived at by the operation of the principle of entitlement is random with respect to any pattern. Though the resulting set of holdings will be unpatterned, it will not be incomprehensible, for it can be seen as arising from the operation of a small number of principles. These principles specify how an initial distribution may arise (the principle of acquisition of holdings) and how distributions may be transformed into others (the principle of transfer of holdings). The process whereby the set of holdings is generated will be intelligible, though the set of holdings itself that results from this process will be unpatterned.

The writings of F. A. Hayek focus less than is usually done upon what patterning distributive justice requires. Hayek argues that we cannot know enough about each person's situation to distribute to each according to his moral merit (but would justice demand we do so if we did have this knowledge?); and he goes on to say, "our objection is against all attempts to impress upon society a deliberately chosen pattern of distribution, whether it be an order of equality or of inequality."[3] However, Hayek concludes that in a free society there will be distribution in accordance with value rather than moral merit; that is, in accordance with the perceived value of a person's actions and services to others. Despite his rejection of a patterned conception of distributive justice, Hayek himself suggests a pattern he thinks justifiable: distribution in accordance with the perceived benefits given to others, leaving room for the complaint that a free society does not realize exactly this pattern. Stating this patterned strand of a free capitalist society more precisely, we get "To each according to how much he benefits others who have the resources for benefiting those who benefit them." This will seem arbitrary unless some acceptable initial set of holdings is specified, or unless it is held that the operation of the system over time washes out any significant effects from the initial set of holdings. As an example of the latter, if almost anyone would have bought a car from Henry Ford, the supposition that it was an arbitrary matter who held the money then (and so bought) would not place Henry Ford's earnings under a cloud. In any event, *his* coming to hold it is not arbitrary. Distribution according to benefits to others *is* a major patterned strand in a free capitalist society, as Hayek correctly points out, but it is only a strand and does not constitute the whole pattern of a system of entitlements (namely, inheritance, gifts for arbitrary reasons, charity, and so on) or a standard that one should insist a society fit. Will people tolerate for long a system yielding distributions that they believe are unpatterned? No doubt people will not long accept a distribution they believe is *unjust.* People want their society to be and to look just. But must the look of justice reside in a resulting pattern rather than in the underlying generating principles? We are in no position to conclude that the inhabitants of a society embodying an entitlement conception of justice in holdings will find it unacceptable. Still, it must be granted that were people's reasons for transferring some of their holdings to others always irrational or arbitrary, we would find this disturbing. (Suppose people always determined what holdings they would transfer, and to whom, by using a random device.) We feel more comfortable upholding the justice of an entitlement system if most of the transfers under it are done for reasons. This does not mean necessarily that all deserve what holdings they receive. It means only that there is a purpose or point to someone's transferring a holding to one person rather than to another; that usually we can see what the transferrer thinks he's gaining, what cause he thinks he's serving, what goals he thinks he's helping to achieve, and so forth. Since in a capitalist society people often transfer holdings to others in accordance with how much they perceive these others benefiting them, the fabric constituted by the individual transactions and transfers is largely reasonable and intelligible. (Gifts to loved ones, bequests to children, charity to the needy also are nonarbitrary components of the fabric.) In stressing the large strand of distribution in accordance with benefit to others, Hayek shows the point of many transfers, and so shows that the system of transfer of entitlements is not just spinning its gears aimlessly. The system of entitlements is defensible when constituted by the individual aims of individual transactions. No overarching aim is needed, no distributional pattern is required.

To think that the task of a theory of distributive justice is to fill in the blank in "to each according to his ———" is to be predisposed to search for a pattern; and the separate treatment of "from each according to his ———" treats production and distribution as two separate and independent issues. On an entitlement view these are *not* two separate questions. Whoever makes something, having bought or contracted for all other held resources used in the process (transferring some of his holdings for these cooperating factors), is entitled to it. The situation is *not* one of something's getting made, and there being an open question of who is to get it. Things come into the world already attached to people having entitlements over them. From the point of view of the historical entitlement conception of justice in holdings, those who start afresh to complete "to each according to his ———" treat objects as if they appeared from nowhere, out of nothing. A complete theory of justice might cover this limit case as well; perhaps here is a use for the usual conceptions of distributive justice.

So entrenched are maxims of the usual form that perhaps we should present the entitlement conception as a competitor. Ignoring acquisition and rectification, we might say:

> From each according to what he chooses to do, to each according to what he makes for himself (perhaps with the contracted aid of others) and what others choose to do for him and choose to give him of what they've been given previously (under this maxim) and haven't yet expended or transferred.

This, the discerning reader will have noticed, has its defects as a slogan. So as a summary and great simplification (and not as a maxim with any independent meaning) we have:

> *From each as they choose, to each as they are chosen.*

Notes

[1]Applications of the principle of justice in acquisition may also occur as part of the move from one distribution to another. You may find an unheld thing now and appropri-

ate it. Acquisitions also are to be understood as included when, to simplify, I speak only of transitions by transfers.

²See, however, the useful book by Boris Bittker, *The Case for Black Reparations* (New York: Random House, 1973).

³F.A. Hayek, *The Constitution of Liberty* (Chicago: University of Chicago Press, 1960), p. 87.

chapter 2

Kant and Contractarianism

INTRODUCTION

KANT

Rationality as the Key to Morality The natural-law account of right conduct emphasized rationality as the distinguishing characteristic of humanity. But other distinct features were also considered morally relevant. For instance, the social nature of human beings was understood as the natural basis of the requirements of justice. The seventeenth-century natural-rights theorists, however, emphasized a more individualist and self-interested rationality as the key to right conduct. Immanuel Kant (1724–1804) shared with the modern natural-rights theorists this narrowing of the basis of right conduct to rationality alone, but he differed from them in an insistence that self-interest, too, must be excluded as a component of the rationality that determines right conduct.

In Kant the emphasis upon disinterested rationality frees ethical theory at its most abstract level from any connection with human beings as specific biological species. Right conduct has the same basis for all rational beings, whether human, extraterrestrial, or even angelic. It is in applying the fundamental principle of right conduct to cases that one must take into account the specifics of human nature. At this level of application to cases, Kant often argues just as the natural-law theorists did. This traditional part of Kant has had little influence, but Kant's more innovative attempt to free basic ethical theory from any relation to specific human nature has been tremendously influential.

The Rational Self as the Source of Morality Kant's basic ethical theory is characterized by an emphasis upon rationality as the source of moral law. Kant traces the basic forms of scientific thought back to the operation of the mind of the knower rather than to an external reality independent of the knower. To interpret the world in terms of cause and effect was thus a necessity grounded in the rational faculties of the interpreter. Kant could then trace moral judgments back to that same rationality of the interpreter; on the one hand, one must interpret the world causally in order to know and to understand it, while on the other hand, in order to act at all, one must interpret one's own actions as freely chosen. Kant finds the key to morality in this necessary presupposition of freedom by every rational being who acts. There are two ways of looking at human conduct, each determined by its context. Within the context of scientific inquiry, human conduct is a part of the natural order of causal laws; within the context of practical reasoning (deciding what one will do), human conduct is under self-imposed "laws of freedom," which are derived from the rational will (also called "practical reason" by Kant).

Autonomy *Autonomy* (from the Greek words *autos,* meaning "self," and *nomos,* meaning "law") is the self-legislative characteristic of rational agents, by virtue of which they are free. For Kant, autonomy (and so freedom) is not the same thing as mere subjective and arbitrary personal decision. The *nomic* ("lawlike") aspect of autonomy is central in Kant's account of both free action and right conduct. Autonomy requires that the merely personal and arbitrary be subordinated to the requirements of reason, which are the same for all rational beings. It is by virtue of this impersonality and regularity that free agents bring a moral order to their actions comparable to the causal order in the realm of nature.

Many followers of Kant, however, emphasize not the nomic aspect of autonomy but its other aspect, the *self,* which is seen as governing the actions of free rational agents rather than anything external. But this view of autonomy is really no more than *self-determination*—that is, the ability and right of rational agents to make choices in their own lives. Such contemporary proponents of autonomy are using Kantian language to express what is essentially an individualistic, natural-rights viewpoint. There is nothing individualistic about Kant's conception of autonomy, for the order that each individual rationally imposes on conduct is understood by him as unvarying from person to person.

For Kant freedom from external determination is no more important than is freedom from internal determination by any aspect of the self other than reason. Kant did not count as autonomous actions those resulting from the agent's own desires if they are uncontrolled by reason. According to Kant, not only can an agent lack autonomy by submitting himself blindly to external authority, he can lack autonomy by becoming a slave to his own passions. This attitude is indicative of a great Stoic influence on Kant.

Hypothetical Versus Categorical Imperatives What is the order that reason imposes on conduct? Kant distinguishes between two kinds of rational control over conduct. The first kind is the rationality of choosing the best available means to achieve one's goals. The rational conclusion that given a certain goal or end one *ought* to adopt certain means is called a *hypothetical imperative* by Kant. The imperative, or command, to adopt the means holds good only on the hypothesis that one has the goal. To Kant happiness is the only goal that all people *must* have. General rules, which he calls "counsels of prudence," ordinarily tend to promote happiness, but the means to happiness are indeterminate. Most goals, however, Kant understands as *contingent,* that is, some people have the goal and some do not. Hypothetical imperatives called "rules of skill" outline determinate means to contingent ends.

Suppose, for instance, that an obese person goes to a physician and, after ruling out other causes of obesity, the physician prescribes that the patient ought to eat less if he wants to lose weight. The patient wants to lose weight and acts rationally by following the imperative. The patient will then lose weight. Suppose also that the patient thinks that losing weight will substantially contribute to his happiness. But after losing weight there may, in fact, be no gain in happiness, even though it was reasonable to think that there would be. In Kant's view, happiness is a goal for which we inevitably strive, but the recipe for success cannot be surely given even by well-informed, rational deliberation.

There are thus no universal and certain hypothetical imperatives, for either the goals are contingent or the means are uncertain. Nevertheless, Kant thought that there are imperatives prescribed by reason universally and with certainty. These imperatives bring order to conduct in an entirely different way than do hypothetical imperatives. It is through this second kind of rational control over conduct, these *categorical imperatives,* that the agent becomes aware of his freedom from his own desires and passions. An imperative prescribes conduct categorically if the prescription holds good without any hypothesis about the goals or ends of the agent. Not even happiness may be presupposed as a goal by a categorical imperative.

What does reason command categorically? Many philosophers would answer, "Nothing." The eighteenth-century British philosopher David Hume insisted that "reason is, and ought only to be the slave of the passions, and can never pretend to any other office than to serve and obey them."[1] In other words, Hume was denying that there can be categorical imperatives. But Kant thought that the rationality of each person imposes on his conduct a requirement independent of the particular desires, passions, and feelings that he happens to have. These inclinations are the basis of hypothetical imperatives, having happiness as their final goal. But apart from these contingent inclinations, reason demands categorically (without any "if" clause, whether explicit or implicit) that each person bring order to his or her conduct through obedience to universal principles.

Universality is the formal characteristic of law—whether laws of cause and effect, laws of states, or moral law. Form is here contrasted with content. In this understanding, the laws of Newtonian physics and the laws against murder have entirely different contents or topics, but both are universal in form, covering all occurrences of a certain kind. Universality—the form of law—is all that remains for reason to com-

tion came to be common, no one would trust anyone enough to make a loan. The immoral agent wants to make a special exception for himself, while unable to will that the same conduct be generally adopted. The immoral agent is a kind of parasite upon the general practice of right conduct. But it is irrational to think that what is permissible for one person is not permissible for all.

A maxim that proposes a violation of imperfect duty cannot be universalized, for although its universal adoption can be consistently described, the agent cannot will such universal adoption without a conflict. Thus, it is impossible to will that no one should help others, for the agent would be depriving him- or herself of possible aid. For Kant, finite rational beings necessarily have their own happiness as a goal. To universalize the maxim not to help others, an agent would have to abandon the goal of his or her own happiness, for there are possible circumstances in which he or she would need the help of others. Consideration of the likelihood of ever needing the help of others is irrelevant. The argument depends upon the structure of rationality in beings with needs and desires, rather than upon the calculations of self-interest of the particular person who is deliberating.

A Kantian Decision Procedure The elements of Kant's theory can be put together as a decision procedure. The first step is to formulate the maxim, describing the primary intention of the proposed conduct. Irrelevant descriptive details should not be included in the maxim. For instance, if someone is considering cheating a friend in order to make money, it is clearly irrelevant to this project that the friend happens to be blond. (Even excluding irrelevant details, it seems that more than one maxim applies to any particular action. See below for a discussion of this difficulty.)

The second step is to universalize the maxim. Since the maxim expresses the intention of the agent, its subject is the personal pronoun "I." To universalize, the maxim is modified so that the subject is not the individual, but rather *everyone.* The maxim "I will cheat in order to make money" is universalized as the principle "Everyone will cheat in order to make money."

The third step is to test the universal principle for consistency in conception. Is it possible for everyone to act according to the principle, or would contradictions result? Attempt to imagine the principle as a universal law of nature to see whether it would be self-defeating: in a world where everyone automatically acted according to the principle, could such conduct actually serve the purpose of the principle? If the principle could not be a law of nature, then the proposed conduct violates a perfect duty and the decision procedure ends. If the principle could be a law of nature, a fourth step is necessary.

The fourth step is to test the universal principle for conflict in will. Given the agent's own desire for happiness, could the universal principle be willed sincerely? If there is a conflict in will, then the proposed conduct violates an imperfect duty. If there is no conflict, then the conduct is morally permissible.

Difficulties with the Theory   One major difficulty with Kant's theory is that it provides no standard for deciding *what* maxim the agent must test for universality. The intention of the agent can be described correctly in many different ways and at many different levels of generality or specificity. For instance, "I will tell a lie in order to protect an innocent human life" is a universalizable maxim. It would not be self-defeating if everyone lied in order to save innocent human lives, for such lies would be rare and trust would still be general. But for Kant the maxim of *all* lying was a highly general description of intention, such as "I will tell a lie in order to achieve my ends." This maxim cannot be universalized, so Kant considered all lying wrong.

There is a comparable problem with the formula of respect for persons. If someone lies to a would-be murderer, does he treat the other as a mere means and thereby fail to respect him as a person? Understood as simply lying in order to get one's own way, it would be natural to speak of manipulation in this case. But if one describes the action as lying in order to prevent another from murdering, it is more natural to understand the deception as a way of showing respect for both the personhood of the intended victim and that of the would-be murderer.[10] Neither the test of universalization nor the test of respect for persons can provide a clear reason for choosing a highly general description of intention.

Perhaps Kant's theory of right conduct loses its intended rigor because of this multiplicity of possible maxims to describe the agent's intentions. But Kant was more concerned with the integrity of the agent as a conscious, rational being than with fine distinctions in difficult cases—although he does argue many such cases with a certainty that fails to convince. The ideas of universalizability and of respect for persons as ends in themselves work better as an account of goodness of will, for who can doubt the blameworthiness of a conscious intent to make an exception in one's own favor, or to treat a person as a mere tool?

Kant thinks that a full account of right conduct can be generated from these ideas when they are accompanied by an understanding of human life. Although this may not be possible, his ideas are still instructive. Why should there not remain difficult, even irresolvable, cases even if the fundamental principle of right conduct is understood? Most immoral conduct results not from ignorance of the right in difficult cases but from selfishness, confusion, and self-deception. Kant combats these sources of immorality with his insistence on clarity of intention and motive and through the ideas of universality and impartiality.

The Dignity of Persons   Impartiality and clarity of intention and motive seem uncontroversial elements in an account of right conduct. What makes Kant distinct? Kant places a special emphasis on the absolute value of persons as ends in themselves, and this is very controversial. In the natural-law tradition, each human life is incommensurably valuable, and this value attaches to the life as a whole rather than solely to the rationality of the person. For Kant, persons have a special dignity deriving solely from their rationality and the freedom that this rationality brings. Thus Kant is not a consequentialist; he recognizes the existence of incommensurable values as does the natural-law theorist. The value of persons as rational, free agents is not merely incommensurable, but it is so great that the dignity of persons is the only unconditional value. Kant differs from the natural-law tradition by his radical separation of the rational self from other aspects of the self. It is thus possible for a Kantian to say that a living human being no longer has the distinctive dignity of a person if, for instance, he has suffered severe and irreparable brain damage. However, in arguing cases, Kant himself tends to support traditional natural-law positions that do not separate the value of rationality and the value of human life.

Structure of the Theory   Kant is not a teleologist; he does not base right conduct on the promotion of value. There are, however, teleological components within Kant's theory. The imperfect duties, for instance, require that one promote certain values (the perfection of the self and the happiness of others). But the pursuit of these obligatory ends is itself limited by the perfect duties, so that even here conduct is not evaluated solely in terms of the promotion of a good end. Thus Kant's theory is deontological, for right conduct is not derived from the promotion of good ends. The basic structure of his theory is similar to that of the theory of natural rights. But while natural-rights theory places absolute value on the liberty of the individual, Kant places absolute value on the freedom that rationality makes possible. Kant thus can make sense of the idea of duties to self; natural-rights theory has no conceptual room for anything but duties to others. And underneath the basic deontological structure, Kant includes imperfect duties both to self and others; these imperfect duties are positive, requiring the promotion of good ends beyond anything found in such contemporary natural-rights theorists as Nozick.

CONTRACTARIANISM

The Connection with Kant   Many recent philosophers have been influenced by the Kantian idea of universal moral principles requiring respect for persons as ends in themselves. The contemporary American philosopher John Rawls, for instance, has developed an account of justice that has roots in Locke, Rousseau, and Kant. The guiding idea behind this account is the social contract in a form similar to that underlying the fifth formulation of Kant's categorical imperative: "Every rational being must act as if he, by his maxims, were at all times a legislative member in the universal realm of ends." In this formula Kant uses the conception of the social contract found in Jean-Jacques Rousseau (1712–

1778), although he interprets it in his own distinctive way.[11] Kant's understanding of the social contract is entirely conceptual. It does not involve any question of the historical origin of societies in positing an initial contract; nor, in its recognition of social obligations, is there any question of actual contractual undertakings by individuals. So Kant's formulation includes the all-important phrase "as if." The "universal realm of ends" consists of an imaginary community of all rational beings ("ends in themselves") who are establishing rules of right conduct that will bind each and all.

The Original Position and the Veil of Ignorance

John Rawls has made this Kantian version of contract more determinate by describing the equivalent of the realm of ends in terms of an *original position,* the state of nature found in Locke and Rousseau. Within the original position, the parties to the social contract deliberate about the rules of right conduct that will be strictly followed once they enter society. The imaginative assumption of strict compliance is equivalent to the Kantian requirement that the rules be universal. In his important book *A Theory of Justice,* Rawls indicates that a contractarian account can be given of almost all principles of right conduct, although he works out in detail only the specific principles determining the justice of the basic structure of society.

The original position is a hypothetical, imaginary situation meant to embody basic constraints on arguments for moral principles. These constraints are Kantian for the most part. They are equality; impartiality; not taking advantage of accidental features of one's particular situation; and the assumption of the generality, universality, and publicity of the principles that are to be justified. Impartiality and equality are ensured imaginatively by the *veil of ignorance* that hides from the persons in the original position all particular facts about themselves. Each person is ignorant of his own place in society (social and economic), ignorant of his own particular talents and abilities, indeed ignorant of everything that can distinguish one person from another in the particular society into which he will enter. But each person in the original position does know the general principles of social theory and human psychology. In order to justify more specific principles, the contractors will know general facts about their particular society (such as the level of technology), but for the justification of the basic principles of justice these facts, too, will be hidden behind the veil of ignorance.

Self-Interest and Primary Goods

Another important feature of the original position is the assumption that each person is motivated by self-interest, giving no consideration to the interests of others. This assumption imparts an un-Kantian flavor to Rawls, but given the veil of ignorance there is no real self-interest at work, even in the original position. Behind the veil of ignorance one cannot distinguish between one's own interests and the interests of others. The motivational assumption of self-interest is an imaginative way of capturing Kant's insight that the structure of rationality for finite beings (with needs and desires) includes the necessary goal of happiness.

And so Rawls justifies principles of right conduct by imagining an original position of equality in which rational persons, ignorant of all particular information about themselves but informed about general facts, decide upon the principles that will be publicly acknowledged and strictly followed in the society they will form. In deciding these principles, each person seeks to further his or her own interests. Rawls specifies the interests to be furthered: rights and liberties, powers and opportunities, income and wealth, and self-respect. Rawls chooses these *primary goods* on the ground that "these goods normally have a use whatever a person's rational plan of life."[12]

Rawls considers self-respect the most important of the primary goods. This accords with his view that the original position captures the Kantian idea of respect for persons as ends in themselves. The veil of ignorance makes it impossible to promote one's own self-respect without promoting everyone's self-respect, and so promoting self-respect is the same as promoting respect for persons.

The Two Principles of Justice Rawls argues in great detail that rational contractors in the original position of equality would agree upon two principles of justice for the basic structure of society. The first principle states that "each person is to have an equal right to the most extensive total system of equal basic liberties compatible with a similar system of liberty for all." According to the second principle, "social and economic inequalities are to be arranged so that they are both: (a) to the greatest benefit of the least advantaged . . . , and (b) attached to offices and positions open to all under conditions of fair equality of opportunity."[13]

These two principles are ranked in order of priority, so that the first principle has complete priority over the second: equal basic liberties cannot be sacrificed as a means to secure social and economic goals.[14] (Further details of the two principles are omitted here.)

In a complete contractarian account of right conduct, the veil of ignorance would be gradually lifted, allowing more and more facts to be known by the contractors. Contractors must know all general facts morally relevant to deciding between alternative principles, however specific the topic of those principles. The only facts that can never enter into a contractarian solution of a moral problem are facts that allow contractors to identify their own particular interests as individuals or members of a class, for this knowledge would destroy the original position as an imaginative model of Kantian impartiality.

Readings The selection from Kant's *Foundations of the Metaphysics of Morals* gives an extensive analysis of rational principles of conduct, both hypothetical and categorical. The foundational principle of right conduct, the categorical imperative, is then formulated in several versions and applied to examples.

The selection from Onora O'Neill explores various conceptions of not using others merely as means and develops a distinctively Kantian view based on the idea of possible consent by the other person to the underlying intention of the action. She then turns to the positive side of Kant's formula of respect for persons, arguing that it requires that the particular capacities of individuals be considered in order to treat them with respect and beneficence.

The selection by John Rawls is from the introductory sections of *A Theory of Justice*. In it, he outlines the general idea of contractarianism and the original position. He also briefly explains the two principles of justice.

Notes

[1]David Hume, *A Treatise of Human Nature*, ed. L. A. Selby-Bigge (Oxford: Clarendon Press, 1888), p. 415.

[2]Immanuel Kant, *Foundations of the Metaphysics of Morals*, trans. Lewis White Beck (Indianapolis, Ind.: Bobbs-Merrill, 1959), p. 9.

[3]Kant himself numbered these formulations so that there are only three, counting the second as a version of the first and the fifth as a version of the fourth.

[4]Kant, *Foundations*, p. 39.

[5]Ibid.

[6]Ibid., p. 47.

[7]Ibid., p. 52.

[8]Ibid., p. 57.

[9]H. J. Paton, *The Categorical Imperative* (New York: Harper & Row, 1967), p. 172.

[10]For Kant's rigorist rejection of all lying, see "Concerning the Common Saying: This May Be True in Theory but Does Not Apply in Practice," in *The Philosophy of Kant*, trans. Carl J. Friedrich (New York: Modern Library, 1949).

[11]For Rousseau's influence on Kant, see Ernst Cassirer, *Rousseau, Kant, and Goethe* (New York: Harper & Row, 1963).

[12]John Rawls, *A Theory of Justice* (Cambridge, Mass.: Harvard University Press, 1971), p. 62.

[13]Ibid., p. 302.

[14]Ibid., p. 63.

Bibliography on Kant and Contractarianism

Aune, Bruce. *Kant's Theory of Morals*. Princeton, N.J.: Princeton University Press, 1979.

Barry, Brian. *The Liberal Theory of Justice: A Critical Examination of the Principal Doctrines in* A Theory of Justice *by John Rawls*. Oxford: Clarendon Press, 1973.

Blocker, H. Gene, ed. *John Rawls' Theory of Social Justice*. Cambridge: Cambridge University Press, 1979.

Daniels, Norman, ed. *Reading Rawls*. New York: Basic Books, 1975.

Donagan, Alan. *The Theory of Morality*. Chicago, Ill.: University of Chicago Press, 1977.

Gewirth, Alan. *Reason and Morality*. Chicago, Ill.: University of Chicago Press, 1978.

Gregor, Mary J. *Laws of Freedom: A Study of Kant's Method of Applying the Categorical Imperative in the* Metaphysik der Sitten. Oxford: Basil Blackwell, 1963.

Hill, Thomas. "Humanity as an End in Itself." *Ethics* 91 (1980–1981): 84–99.

Kant, Immanuel. *Foundations of the Metaphysics of Morals: With Critical Essays.* Translated by Lewis White Beck. Edited by Robert Paul Wolff. Indianapolis, Ind.: Bobbs-Merrill, 1959.

―――. *The Doctrine of Virtue.* Translated by Mary J. Gregor. Philadelphia, Pa.: University of Pennsylvania Press, 1964.

―――. *The Metaphysical Elements of Justice.* Translated by John Ladd. Indianapolis, Ind.: Bobbs-Merrill, 1965.

Korsgaard, Christine M. "Kant's Formula of Universal Law." *Pacific Philosophical Quarterly* 66 (1985): 24–47.

Martin, Rex. *Rawls and Rights.* Lawrence, Kansas: University Press of Kansas, 1985.

Murphy, Jeffrie G. *Kant: The Philosophy of Right.* London: Macmillan, 1970.

Nell, Onora (now O'Neill, Onora). *Acting on Principle: An Essay on Kantian Ethics.* New York: Columbia University Press, 1975.

O'Neill, Onora. "Kant after Virtue." *Inquiry* 26 (1983): 387–405.

Paton, H. J. *The Categorical Imperative.* New York: Harper & Row, 1967.

Rawls, John. *A Theory of Justice.* Cambridge, Mass.: Harvard University Press, 1971.

Richards, David A. J. *A Theory of Reasons for Action.* Oxford: Clarendon Press, 1971.

Wolff, Robert Paul. *Understanding Rawls.* Princeton, N.J.: Princeton University Press, 1977.

IMMANUEL KANT
THE CATEGORICAL IMPERATIVE

IMPERATIVES COMMAND EITHER HYPOTHETICALLY OR CATEGORICALLY

All imperatives command either hypothetically or categorically. The former present the practical necessity of a possible action as a means to achieving something else which one desires (or which one may possibly desire). The categorical imperative would be one which presented an action as of itself objectively necessary, without regard to any other end.

Since every practical law presents a possible action as good and thus as necessary for a subject practically determinable by reason, all imperatives are formulas of the determination of action which is necessary by the principle of a will which is in any way good. If the action is good only as a means to something else, the imperative is hypothetical; but if it is thought of as good in itself, and hence as necessary in a will which of itself conforms to reason as the principle of this will, the imperative is categorical.

The imperative thus says what action possible to me would be good, and it presents the practical rule in relation to a will which does not forthwith perform an action simply because it is good, in part because the subject does not always know that the action is good and in part (when he does know it) because his maxims can still be opposed to the objective principles of practical reason.

The hypothetical imperative, therefore, says only that the action is good to some purpose, possible or actual. In the [415] former case it is a problematical, in the latter an assertorical, practical principle. The categorical imperative, which declares the action to be of itself objectively necessary without making any reference to a purpose, i.e., without having any other end, holds as an apodictical (practical) principle.

HYPOTHETICAL IMPERATIVES: SKILL

We can think of that which is possible through the mere powers of some rational being as a possible purpose of any will. As a consequence, the principles of action, in so far as they are thought of as necessary to attain a possible purpose which can be achieved by them, are in reality infinitely numerous. All sciences have some practical part which consists of problems of some end which is possible for us and of imperatives as to how it can be reached. These can therefore generally be called imperatives of skill. Whether the end is reasonable and good is not in question at all, for the question is only of what must be done in order to attain it. The precepts to be followed by a physician in order to cure his patient and by a poisoner in order to bring about certain death are of equal value in so far as each does that which will perfectly accomplish his purpose. Since in early youth we do not know what ends may occur to us in the course of life, parents seek to let their children learn a great many things and provide for skill in the use of means to all sorts of arbitrary ends among which they cannot determine whether any one of them may later become an actual purpose of their pupil, though it is possible that he may some day have it as his actual purpose. And this anxiety is so great that they commonly neglect to form and correct their judgment on the worth of things which they may make their ends.

HYPOTHETICAL IMPERATIVES: PRUDENCE

There is one end, however, which we may presuppose as actual in all rational beings so far as imperatives apply to them, i.e., so far as they are dependent beings; there is one purpose not only which they *can* have but which we can presuppose that they all *do* have by a necessity of nature. This purpose is happiness. The hypothetical imperative which represents the practical necessity of action as means to the promotion of happiness is an assertorical imperative. We may not expound it as merely necessary to an uncertain and a merely possible purpose, but as necessary to a purpose which we can a priori and with assurance assume for everyone [416] because it belongs to his essence. Skill in the choice of means to one's own highest welfare can be called prudence[1] in the narrowest sense. Thus the imperative which refers to the choice of means to one's own happiness, i.e., the precept of prudence, is still only hypothetical; the action is not absolutely commanded but commanded only as a means to another end.

THE CATEGORICAL IMPERATIVE DIFFERS FROM SKILL AND PRUDENCE

Finally, there is one imperative which directly commands a certain conduct without making its condition some purpose to be reached by it. This imperative is categorical. It concerns not the material of the action and its intended result but the form and the principle from which it results. What is essentially good in it consists in the intention, the result being what it may. This imperative may be called the imperative of morality.

Volition according to these three principles is plainly distinguished by dissimilarity in the constraint to which they subject the will. In order to clarify this dissimilarity, I believe that they are most suitably named if one says that they are either rules of skill, counsels of prudence, or commands (laws) of morality, respectively. For law alone implies the concept of an unconditional and objective and hence universally valid necessity, and commands are laws which must be obeyed, even against inclination. Counsels do indeed involve necessity, but a necessity that can hold only under a subjectively contingent condition, i.e., whether this or that man counts this or that as part of his happiness; but the categorical imperative, on the other hand, is restricted by no condition. As absolutely, though practically, necessary it can be called a command in the strict sense. We could also call the first imperative technical (belonging to art), the second pragmatic[2] (belonging to well [417] fare), and the third moral (belonging to free conduct as such, i.e., to morals).

RULES OF SKILL AND COUNSELS OF PRUDENCE NOT PUZZLING

The question now arises: how are all these imperatives possible? This question does not require an answer as to how the action which the imperative commands can be performed but merely as to how the constraint of the will, which the imperative expresses in the problem, can be conceived. How an imperative of skill is possible requires no particular discussion. Whoever wills the end, so far as reason has decisive influence on his action, wills also the indispensably necessary means to it that lie in his power. This proposition, in what concerns the will, is analytical; for, in willing an object as my effect, my causality as an acting cause, i.e., the use of the means, is already thought, and the imperative derives the concept of necessary actions to this end from the concept of willing this end. Synthetical propositions undoubtedly are necessary in determining the means to a proposed end, but they do not concern the ground, the act of the will, but only the way to make the object real. Mathematics teaches, by synthetical propositions only, that in order to

bisect a line according to an infallible principle I must make two inter-
secting arcs from each of its extremities; but if I know the proposed result
can be obtained only by such an action, then it is an analytical proposition
that, if I fully will the effect, I must also will the action necessary to
produce it. For it is one and the same thing to conceive of something as
an effect which is in a certain way possible through me and to conceive
of myself as acting in this way.

If it were only easy to give a definite concept of happiness, the
imperatives of prudence would completely correspond to those of skill
and would be likewise analytical. For it could be said in this case as well
as in the former that whoever [418] wills the end wills also (necessarily
according to reason) the only means to it which are in his power. But
it is a misfortune that the concept of happiness is so indefinite that,
although each person wishes to attain it, he can never definitely and
self-consistently state what it is he really wishes and wills. The reason for
this is that all elements which belong to the concept of happiness are
empirical, i.e., they must be taken from experience, while for the idea
of happiness an absolute whole, a maximum, of well-being is needed in
my present and in every future condition. Now it is impossible even for
a most clear-sighted and most capable but finite being to form here a
definite concept of that which he really wills. If he wills riches, how much
anxiety, envy, and intrigue might he not thereby draw upon his shoulders! If he wills much knowledge and vision, perhaps it might become
only an eye that much sharper to show him as more dreadful the evils
which are now hidden from him and which are yet unavoidable, or to
burden his desires—which already sufficiently engage him—with even
more needs! If he wills a long life, who guarantees that it will not be long
misery? If he wills at least health, how often has not the discomfort of
the body restrained him from excesses into which perfect health would
have led him? In short, he is not capable, on any principle and with
complete certainty, of ascertaining what would make him truly happy;
omniscience would be needed for this. He cannot, therefore, act according to definite principles so as to be happy, but only according to empirical counsels, e.g., those of diet, economy, courtesy, restraint, etc., which
are shown by experience best to promote welfare on the average. Hence
the imperatives of prudence cannot, in the strict sense, command, i.e.,
present actions objectively as practically necessary; thus they are to be
taken as counsels *(consilia)* rather than as commands *(praecepta)* of reason,
and the task of determining infallibly and universally what action will
promote the happiness of a rational being is completely unsolvable.
There can be no imperative which would, in the strict sense, command
us to do what makes for happiness, because happiness is an ideal not of
reason but of imagination, depending only on empirical grounds which
one would expect in vain to determine an [419] action through which
the totality of consequences—which is in fact infinite—could be
achieved. Assuming that the means to happiness could be infallibly
stated, this imperative of prudence would be an analytical proposition,

for it differs from the imperative of skill only in that its end is given, while in the latter case it is merely possible. Since both, however, only command the means to that which one presupposes, the imperative which commands the willing of the means to him who wills the end is in both cases analytical. There is, consequently, no difficulty in seeing the possibility of such an imperative.

CATEGORICAL IMPERATIVE IS A PRIORI (NOT DERIVED FROM EXPERIENCE)

To see how the imperative of morality is possible is, then, without doubt the only question needing an answer. It is not hypothetical, and thus the objectively conceived necessity cannot be supported by any presupposition, as was the case with the hypothetical imperatives. But it must not be overlooked that it cannot be shown by any example (i.e., it cannot be empirically shown) whether or not there is such an imperative; it is rather to be suspected that all imperatives which appear to be categorical may yet be hypothetical, but in a hidden way. For instance, when it is said, "Thou shalt not make a false promise," we assume that the necessity of this avoidance is not a mere counsel for the sake of escaping some other evil, so that it would read, "Thou shalt not make a false promise so that, if it comes to light, thou ruinest thy credit"; we assume rather that an action of this kind must be regarded as of itself bad and that the imperative of the prohibition is categorical. But we cannot show with certainty by any example that the will is here determined by the law alone without any other incentives, even though this appears to be the case. For it is always possible that secret fear of disgrace, and perhaps also obscure apprehension of other dangers, may have had an influence on the will. Who can prove by experience the non-existence of a cause when experience shows us only that we do not perceive the cause? But in such a case the so-called moral imperative, which as such appears to be categorical and unconditional, would be actually only a pragmatic precept which makes us attentive to our own advantage and teaches us to consider it.

Thus we shall have to investigate purely a priori the possibility of a categorical imperative, for we do not have the [420] advantage that experience would give us the reality of this imperative, so that the [demonstration of its] possibility would be necessary only for its explanation and not for its establishment. In the meantime, this much may at least be seen: the categorical imperative alone can be taken as a practical *law,* while all the others may be called principles of the will but not laws. This is because what is necessary merely for the attainment of an arbitrary purpose can be regarded as itself contingent, and we get rid of the precept once we give up the purpose, whereas the unconditional command leaves the will no freedom to choose the opposite. Thus it alone implies the necessity which we require of a law.

Secondly, in the case of the categorical imperative or law of morality, the cause of difficulty in discerning its possibility is very weighty. This imperative is an a priori synthetical practical proposition,[3] and, since to discern the possibility of propositions of this sort is so difficult in theoretical knowledge, it may well be gathered that it will be no less difficult in the practical.

In attacking this problem, we will first inquire whether the mere concept of a categorical imperative does not also furnish the formula containing the proposition which alonè can be a categorical imperative. For even when we know the formula of the imperative, to learn how such an absolute law is possible will require difficult and special labors which we shall postpone to the last section.

FORMULA OF UNIVERSAL LAW

If I think of a hypothetical imperative as such, I do not know what it will contain until the condition is stated [under which it is an imperative]. But if I think of a categorical imperative, I know immediately what it contains. For since the imperative contains besides the law only the necessity [421] that the maxim[4] should accord with this law, while the law contains no condition to which it is restricted, there is nothing remaining in it except the universality of law as such to which the maxim of the action should conform; and in effect this conformity alone is represented as necessary by the imperative.

There is, therefore, only one categorical imperative. It is: Act only according to that maxim by which you can at the same time will that it should become a universal law.

Now if all imperatives of duty can be derived from this one imperative as a principle, we can at least show what we understand by the concept of duty and what it means, even though it remain undecided whether that which is called duty is an empty concept or not.

FORMULA OF UNIVERSAL LAW OF NATURE & EXAMPLES

The universality of law according to which effects are produced constitutes what is properly called nature in the most general sense (as to form), i.e., the existence of things so far as it is determined by universal laws. [By analogy], then, the universal imperative of duty can be expressed as follows: Act as though the maxim of your action were by your will to become a universal law of nature.

We shall now enumerate some duties, adopting the usual division of them into duties to ourselves and to others and into perfect and imperfect duties.[5]

1. A man who is reduced to despair by a series of evils feels a weariness with life but is still in possession of his reason [422] sufficiently to ask whether it would not be contrary to his duty to himself to take his own life. Now he asks whether the maxim of his action could become a universal law of nature. His maxim, however, is: For love of myself,

I make it my principle to shorten my life when by a longer duration it threatens more evil than satisfaction. But it is questionable whether this principle of self-love could become a universal law of nature. One immediately sees a contradiction in a system of nature whose law would be to destroy life by the feeling whose special office is to impel the improvement of life. In this case it would not exist as nature; hence that maxim cannot obtain as a law of nature, and thus it wholly contradicts the supreme principle of all duty.

2. Another man finds himself forced by need to borrow money. He well knows that he will not be able to repay it, but he also sees that nothing will be loaned him if he does not firmly promise to repay it at a certain time. He desires to make such a promise, but he has enough conscience to ask himself whether it is not improper and opposed to duty to relieve his distress in such a way. Now, assuming he does decide to do so, the maxim of his action would be as follows: When I believe myself to be in need of money, I will borrow money and promise to repay it, although I know I shall never do so. Now this principle of self-love or of his own benefit may very well be compatible with his whole future welfare, but the question is whether it is right. He changes the pretension of self-love into a universal law and then puts the question: How would it be if my maxim became a universal law? He immediately sees that it could never hold as a universal law of nature and be consistent with itself; rather it must necessarily contradict itself. For the universality of a law which says that anyone who believes himself to be in need could promise what he pleased with the intention of not fulfilling it would make the promise itself and the end to be accomplished by it impossible; no one would believe what was promised to him but would only laugh at any such assertion as vain pretense.

3. A third finds in himself a talent which could, by means of some cultivation, make him in many respects a useful [423] man. But he finds himself in comfortable circumstances and prefers indulgence in pleasure to troubling himself with broadening and improving his fortunate natural gifts. Now, however, let him ask whether his maxim of neglecting his gifts, besides agreeing with his propensity to idle amusement, agrees also with what is called duty. He sees that a system of nature could indeed exist in accordance with such a law, even though man (like the inhabitants of the South Sea Islands) should let his talents rust and resolve to devote his life merely to idleness, indulgence, and propagation—in a word, to pleasure. But he cannot possibly will that this should become a universal law of nature or that it should be implanted in us by a natural instinct. For, as a rational being, he necessarily wills that all his faculties should be developed, inasmuch as they are given to him for all sorts of possible purposes.

4. A fourth man, for whom things are going well, sees that others (whom he could help) have to struggle with great hardships, and he asks, "What concern of mine is it? Let each one be as happy as heaven wills,

or as he can make himself; I will not take anything from him or even envy him; but to his welfare or to his assistance in time of need I have no desire to contribute." If such a way of thinking were a universal law of nature, certainly the human race could exist, and without doubt even better than in a state where everyone talks of sympathy and good will, or even exerts himself occasionally to practice them while, on the other hand, he cheats when he can and betrays or otherwise violates the rights of man. Now although it is possible that a universal law of nature according to that maxim could exist, it is nevertheless impossible to will that such a principle should hold everywhere as a law of nature. For a will which resolved this would conflict with itself, since instances can often arise in which he would need the love and sympathy of others, and in which he would have robbed himself, by such a law of nature springing from his own will, of all hope of the aid he desires.

UNIVERSALIZING: CONTRADICTION IN CONCEPTION, CONFLICT IN WILL

The foregoing are a few of the many actual duties, or at least of duties we hold to be actual, whose derivation from the one stated principle is clear. We must be able to will that [424] a maxim of our action become a universal law; this is the canon of the moral estimation of our action generally. Some actions are of such a nature that their maxim cannot even be *thought* as a universal law of nature without contradiction, far from it being possible that one could will that it should be such. In others this internal impossibility is not found, though it is still impossible to *will* that their maxim should be raised to the universality of a law of nature, because such a will would contradict itself. We easily see that the former maxim conflicts with the stricter or narrower (imprescriptible) duty, the latter with broader (meritorious) duty. Thus all duties, so far as the kind of obligation (not the object of their action) is concerned, have been completely exhibited by these examples in their dependence on the one principle.

When we observe ourselves in any transgression of a duty, we find that we do not actually will that our maxim should become a universal law. That is impossible for us; rather, the contrary of this maxim should remain as a law generally, and we only take the liberty of making an exception to it for ourselves or for the sake of our inclination, and for this one occasion. Consequently, if we weighed everything from one and the same standpoint, namely, reason, we would come upon a contradiction in our own will, viz., that a certain principle is objectively necessary as a universal law and yet subjectively does not hold universally but rather admits exceptions. However, since we regard our action at one time from the point of view of a will wholly conformable to reason and then from that of a will affected by inclinations, there is actually no contradiction, but rather an opposition of inclination to the precept of reason *(antagonismus)*. In this the universality of the principle *(universalitas)* is changed into mere generality *(generalitas)*, whereby the practical principle of reason meets the maxim halfway. Although this cannot be justified in our own impartial judgment, it does show that we actually acknowledge the validity of the categorical imperative and allow ourselves (with all respect to it) only a few exceptions which seem to us to be unimportant and forced upon us.

We have thus at least established that if duty is a concept [425] which is to have significance and actual legislation for our actions, it can be expressed only in categorical imperatives and not at all in hypothetical ones. For every application of it we have also clearly exhibited the content of the categorical imperative which must contain the principle of all duty (if there is such). This is itself very much. But we are not yet advanced far enough to prove a priori that that kind of imperative really exists, that there is a practical law which of itself commands absolutely and without any incentives, and that obedience to this law is duty.

BASIS IN RATIONALITY AS SUCH

With a view to attaining this, it is extremely important to remember that we must not let ourselves think that the reality of this principle can be derived from the particular constitution of human nature. For duty is practical unconditional necessity of action; it must, therefore, hold for all rational beings (to which alone an imperative can apply), and only for that reason can it be a law for all human wills. Whatever is derived from the particular natural situation of man as such, or from certain feelings and propensities, or even from a particular tendency of the human reason which might not hold necessarily for the will of every rational being (if such a tendency is possible), can give a maxim valid for us but not a law; that is, it can give a subjective principle by which we might act only if we have the propensity and inclination, but not an objective principle by which we would be directed to act even if all our propensity, inclination, and natural tendency were opposed to it. This is so far the case that the sublimity and intrinsic worth of the command is the better shown in a duty the fewer subjective causes there are for it and the more there are against it; the latter do not weaken the constraint of the law or diminish its validity. . . .

The question then is: Is it a necessary law for all rational beings that they should always judge their actions by such maxims as they themselves could will to serve as universal laws? If it is such a law, it must be connected (wholly a priori) with the concept of the will of a rational being as such. But in order to discover this connection we must, however reluctantly, take a step into metaphysics, although into a region of it different from speculative philosophy, i.e., into metaphysics of morals. In a practical philosophy it is not a question of assuming grounds for what happens but of assuming laws of what ought to happen even though it may never happen—that is to say, objective, practical laws. Hence in practical philosophy we need not inquire into the reasons why [427] something pleases or displeases, how the pleasure of mere feeling differs from taste, and whether this is distinct from a general satisfaction of reason. Nor need we ask on what the feeling of pleasure or displeasure rests, how desires and inclinations arise, and how, finally, maxims arise from desires and inclination under the co-operation of reason. For all these matters belong to an empirical psychology, which would be the second part of physics if we consider it as philosophy of nature so far as it rests on empirical laws. But here it is a question of objectively practical laws and thus of the relation of a will to itself so far as it determines itself only by reason; for everything which has a relation to the empirical automatically falls away, because if reason of itself alone determines conduct it must necessarily do so a priori. The possibility of reason thus determining conduct must now be investigated.

RELATIVE ENDS ARE CONDITIONED BY DESIRES

The will is thought of as a faculty of determining itself to action in accordance with the conception of certain laws. Such a faculty can be found only in rational beings. That which serves the will as the objective ground of its self-determination is an end, and, if it is given by reason alone, it must hold alike for all rational beings. On the other hand, that which contains the ground of the possibility of the action, whose result is an end, is called the means. The subjective ground of desire is the incentive, while the objective ground of volition is the motive. Thus arises the distinction between subjective ends, which rest on incentives, and objective ends, which depend on motives valid for every rational being. Practical principles are formal when they disregard all subjective ends; they are material when they have subjective ends, and thus certain incentives, as their basis. The ends which a rational being arbitrarily proposes to himself as consequences of his action are material ends and are without exception only relative, for only their relation to a particularly constituted faculty of desire in the subject gives them their worth. And this worth cannot, therefore, afford any universal principles for all rational beings or valid and necessary principles for every volition. That is, they cannot give rise to any practical laws. [428] All these relative ends, therefore, are grounds for hypothetical imperatives only.

RATIONAL BEINGS AS ENDS IN THEMSELVES

But suppose that there were something the existence of which in itself had absolute worth, something which, as an end in itself, could be a ground of definite laws. In it and only in it could lie the ground of a possible categorical imperative, i.e., of a practical law.

Now, I say, man and, in general, every rational being exists as an end in himself and not merely as a means to be arbitrarily used by this or that will. In all his actions, whether they are directed to himself or to other rational beings, he must always be regarded at the same time as an end. All objects of inclinations have only a conditional worth, for if the inclinations and the needs founded on them did not exist, their object would be without worth. The inclinations themselves as the sources of needs, however, are so lacking in absolute worth that the universal wish of every rational being must be indeed to free himself completely from them. Therefore, the worth of any objects to be obtained by our actions is at all times conditional. Beings whose existence does not depend on our will but on nature, if they are not rational beings, have only a relative worth as means and are therefore called "things"; on the other hand, rational beings are designated "persons" because their nature indicates that they are ends in themselves, i.e., things which may not be used merely as means. Such a being is thus an object of respect and, so far, restricts all [arbitrary] choice. Such beings are not merely subjective ends whose existence as a result of our action has a worth for us, but are objective ends, i.e., beings whose existence in itself is an end. Such an end is one for which no other end can be substituted, to which these beings should serve merely as means. For, without them, nothing of absolute worth could be found, and if all worth is conditional and thus contingent, no supreme practical principle for reason could be found anywhere.

FORMULA OF THE END IN ITSELF (RESPECT FOR PERSONS) AND EXAMPLES

Thus if there is to be a supreme practical principle and a categorical imperative for the human will, it must be one that forms an objective principle of the will from the conception of that which is necessarily an end for everyone because it is an end in itself. Hence this objective principle can serve [429] as a universal practical law. The ground of this principle is: rational nature exists as an end in itself. Man necessarily thinks of his own existence in this way; thus far it is a subjective principle of human actions. Also every other rational being thinks of his existence by means of the same rational ground which holds also for myself;[6] thus it is at the same time an objective principle from which, as supreme practical ground, it must be possible to derive all laws of the will. The practical imperative, therefore, is the following: Act so that you treat humanity, whether in your own person or in that of another, always as an end and never as a means only. Let us now see whether this can be achieved.

To return to our previous examples:

First, according to the concept of necessary duty to one's self, he who contemplates suicide will ask himself whether his action can be consistent with the idea of humanity as an end in itself. If, in order to escape from burdensome circumstances, he destroys himself, he uses a person merely as a means to maintain a tolerable condition up to the end of life. Man, however, is not a thing, and thus not something to be used merely as a means; he must always be regarded in all his actions as an end in himself. Therefore, I cannot dispose of man in my own person so as to mutilate, corrupt, or kill him. (It belongs to ethics proper to define more accurately this basic principle so as to avoid all misunderstanding, e.g., as to the amputation of limbs in order to preserve myself, or to exposing my life to danger in order to save it; I must, therefore, omit them here.)

Second, as concerns necessary or obligatory duties to others, he who intends a deceitful promise to others sees immediately that he intends to use another man merely as a means, without the latter containing the end in himself at the same time. For he whom I want to use for my own purposes by means of such a promise cannot possibly assent to my mode of acting [430] against him and cannot contain the end of this action in himself. This conflict against the principle of other men is even clearer if we cite examples of attacks on their freedom and property. For then it is clear that he who transgresses the rights of men intends to make use of the persons of others merely as a means, without considering that, as rational beings, they must always be esteemed at the same time as ends, i.e., only as beings who must be able to contain in themselves the end of the very same action.[7]

Third, with regard to contingent (meritorious) duty to one's self, it is not sufficient that the action not conflict with humanity in our person as an end in itself; it must also harmonize with it. Now in humanity there are capacities for greater perfection which belong to the end of nature with respect to humanity in our own person; to neglect these might perhaps be consistent with the preservation of humanity as an end in itself but not with the furtherance of that end.

Fourth, with regard to meritorious duty to others, the natural end which all men have is their own happiness. Humanity might indeed exist if no one contributed to the happiness of others, provided he did not intentionally detract from it; but this harmony with humanity as an end in itself is only negative rather than positive if everyone does not also endeavor, so far as he can, to further the ends of others. For the ends of any person, who is an end in himself, must as far as possible also be my end, if that conception of an end in itself is to have its full effect on me. . . .

Notes

[1]The word "prudence" may be taken in two senses, and it may bear the name of prudence with reference to things of the world and private prudence. The former sense means the skill of a man in having an influence on others so as to use them for his own purposes. The latter is the ability to unite all these purposes to his own lasting advantage. The worth of the first is finally reduced to the latter, and of one who is prudent in the

former sense but not in the latter we might better say that he is clever and cunning yet, on the whole, imprudent.

[2]It seems to me that the proper meaning of the word "pragmatic" could be most accurately defined in this way. For sanctions which properly flow not from the law of states as necessary statutes but from provision for the general welfare are called pragmatic. A history is pragmatically composed when it teaches prudence, i.e., instructs the world how it could provide for its interest better than, or at least as well as, has been done in the past.

[3]I connect a priori, and hence necessarily, the action with the will without supposing as a condition that there is any inclination [to the action] (though I do so only objectively, i.e., under the idea of a reason which would have complete power over all subjective motives). This is, therefore, a practical proposition which does not analytically derive the willing of an action from some other volition already presupposed (for we do not have such a perfect will); it rather connects it directly with the concept of the will of a rational being as something which is not contained within it.

[4]A maxim is the subjective principle of acting and must be distinguished from the objective principle, i.e., the practical law. The former contains the practical rule which reason determines according to the conditions of the subject (often its ignorance or inclinations) and is thus the principle according to which the subject acts. The law, on the other hand, is the objective principle valid for every rational being, and the principle by which it ought to act, i.e., an imperative.

[5]It must be noted here that I reserve the division of duties for a future *Metaphysics of Morals* and that the division here stands as only an arbitrary one (chosen in order to arrange my examples). For the rest, by a perfect duty I here understand a duty which permits no exception in the interest of inclination; thus I have not merely outer but also inner perfect duties. This runs contrary to the usage adopted in the schools, but I am not disposed to defend it here because it is all one to my purpose whether this is conceded or not.

[6]Here I present this proposition as a postulate, but in the last section grounds for it will be found.

[7]Let it not be thought that the banal *"quod tibi non vis fieri, etc.,"* ["What you do not want done to you, etc.," the Golden Rule—eds.] could here serve as guide or principle, for it is only derived from the principle and is restricted by various limitations. It cannot be a universal law, because it contains the ground neither of duties to one's self nor of the benevolent duties to others (for many a man would gladly consent that others should not benefit him, provided only that he might be excused from showing benevolence to them). Nor does it contain the ground of obligatory duties to another, for the criminal would argue on this ground against the judge who sentences him. And so on.

ONORA O'NEILL
TREATING OTHERS AS PERSONS

Much of Kant's ethics is distant from the ordinary moral consciousness of our day. But one pair of Kantian notions is still widely current. Few moral criticisms strike deeper than the allegation that somebody has used

Onora O'Neill, "Between Consenting Adults," *Philosophy and Public Affairs*, vol. 14, no. 3 (Summer 1985). Copyright © 1985 by Princeton University Press. Reprinted with permission of Princeton University Press.

another; and few ideals gain more praise than that of treating others as persons.

But this consensus is often shallow, since there is little agreement about what it takes to use others in morally problematic ways or to treat them as persons. . . . On the interpretations I offer the two ideals are distinct, though related. Merely not to be used is not enough for being treated as a person. Making another into a tool or instrument in my project is one way of failing to treat that other as a person: but only one way. . . . I shall not explore Kant's thoughts about using oneself and treating oneself as a person. I shall try only to make plausible a certain understanding of what it is to use others and to treat them as persons. . . .

THE PERSONAL TOUCH

One view of treating another as a person rather than using him or her is that it demands a certain tone and manner. If we show indifference to others, we do not treat them as persons; if our interactions are personal in tone, whether sympathetic or hostile, we treat them as persons. . . .

If this is what it is to treat others as persons and not to use them, neither notion can be fundamental for moral or political thought. We are familiar with uses of others which are cloaked by an involved and concerned manner. A planned seduction of someone less experienced treats him or her as means even when charmingly done. Employers who take paternalistic interest in employees' lives may yet both use them and fail to treat them as persons. Yet relationships without a personal tone may neither use others nor fail to treat them as persons. . . .

ACTUAL CONSENT

A deeper and historically more important understanding of the idea of treating others as persons sees their consent to actions which affect them as morally significant. On this view it is morally objectionable to treat others in ways to which they do not consent. To do so treats another as a thing or tool, which cannot, so does not, consent to the ways in which it is used; so fails to treat others as persons, who can choose, so may withhold consent from actions which affect them. . . .

This liberal understanding of avoiding using others and of treating them as persons encounters difficulties of various sorts when we consider what consent is.

An initial difficulty is that it is unclear what constitutes consent. In legal and institutional contexts the criteria are supposedly clearest. Here formal procedures supposedly show who consents to which actions by which others. But here too presumptions of consent are defeasible. . . .

Where formal procedures are lacking, the problem of determining what has been consented to is greater. Various debates about express and tacit consent reflect these difficulties. But the real problem here is not that consent is sometimes given in ways that are implicit rather than explicit, but that it is unclear where consent—even the most explicit consent—stops. . . .

A second range of difficulties arises when the consent given does not match the activities it supposedly legitimates. Marxist critics of capitalist economic forms suggest that workers do not consent to their employment despite its outwardly contractual form. For workers, unlike capitalists, cannot (at least in "ideal" capitalism) choose to be without work, on pain of starvation. Hence the outward contractual form masks an underlying coercion. Workers choose between employers (in boom times) and cannot choose or consent to nonemployment. Analogously, women in most societies hitherto have not really consented to their restricted life possibilities. A choice between marriage partners does not show that the married life has been chosen. . . .

A third range of difficulties with taking actual consent as pivotal for treating others as persons emerges when abilities to consent and dissent are impaired. Discussions in medical ethics show how hard it is to ensure that the consent that patients provide to their treatment is genuine. . . .

It is not only when we are subjects or employees or patients that we have a partial understanding of ways in which others propose to act toward us and an incomplete ability to make decisions for ourselves. Others' apparent consent, even their apparently informed consent, may *standardly* be insufficient to show that we treat them as persons when we interact with them. The problems of the defeasibility and indeterminacy of consent, of ideological distortions and self-deception, and of impaired capacities to consent, are all forms of one underlying problem. . . . When we consent to another's proposals we consent, even when "fully" informed, only to some specific formulation of what the other has it in mind to do. We may remain ignorant of further, perhaps equally pertinent, accounts of what is proposed, including some to which we would not consent. ("I didn't know I was letting myself in for that!" we may protest.) Even when further descriptions are inferable from the one consented to, the inference may not be made; and often we cannot infer which determinate action will enact some proposal. If we want to give an account of genuine, morally significant, consent, we need to explain *which* aspects of actions must be consented to if nobody is to be used or treated as less than a person. An account of genuine consent must then show how the morally significant aspects of plans, proposals, and intentions are picked out as candidates for consent.

HYPOTHETICAL CONSENT

Before considering how this might be done, I shall look at an account of treating others as persons which doesn't require us to know what they consent to. This strategy explains treating others as persons not in terms of the consent actually given, but in terms of the hypothetical consent fully rational beings would give to the same proposal. The strategy has obvious merits.

One merit is that it suggests that at least sometimes actual consent is not morally decisive, even if well informed. Hence it allows for our strong intuitions that even a consensus may be iniquitous or irrelevant (perhaps it reflects false consciousness), and that not everything done between consenting adults treats the other as a person. This approach also deals readily with cases of impaired capacities to consent. Since it appeals to capacities that are standardly lacking, there is, in a way, no difference in its approach to those in "the maturity of their faculties" and to those more gravely impaired. By the standards of full rationality we are all impaired. But we can always ask whether the fully rational would consent.

But these merits are the acceptable face of a serious deficiency in this strategy. If treating others as persons requires only hypothetical rational consent, we may . . . find ourselves overriding the actual dissent of others, coercing them in the name of higher and more rational selves who would consent to what is proposed. It seems implausible that treating others as persons should even sometimes be a matter of overriding what others as we know them actually choose.

Other difficulties with this strategy arise from the varied conceptions of rationality invoked. Many conceptions of rationality presuppose a given set of desires. If these are the actual desires of the consenter, appeal to hypothetical consent will not overcome the worry that a consensus may be iniquitous or reflect local ideology. Yet if there is no appeal to the consenter's actual desires, but only to some hypothetical set of rationally structured desires, then the theory may be too weak to determine what would rationally be consented to. Given that there are many rationally structured sets of hypothetical desires, rational structure alone cannot determine what would rationally be consented to. . . .

The appeal of hypothetical consent criteria of treating others as persons is to overcome the limitations of actual consent criteria by endowing hypothetical agents with cognitive capacities that extend their understanding of what is proposed. But it is just not clear how far the insight of even the ideally rational reaches. Do they, for example, have a more determinate insight into proposals addressed to them than do those who make the proposals? What do they make of internally incoherent proposals? Which aspects of others' proposals are pivotal for the consent or dissent of the fully rational? A convincing account of hypothetical rational consent has to explain *which* aspects of others' actions must be hypothetically consented to if those actions are not to use others or fail to treat them as persons. This approach cannot exempt us from the need to discover the morally significant aspects of plans, proposals, and intentions that are candidates for consent.

SIGNIFICANT AND SPURIOUS CONSENT

If the notion of consent is to help explicate what it is to treat others as persons, we need an account of genuine, morally significant consent, and to distinguish this from spurious or morally trivial consent. Three preliminary points seem to me significant.

First, morally significant consent cannot be consent to all aspects of another's proposals which may affect me. Any complicated action will be done under many descriptions; but most of these will be without moral significance. Morally significant consent will, I suggest, be consent to the deeper or more fundamental aspects of another's proposals. . . .

Second, if another's consent is to be morally significant, it must indeed be his or her consent. To treat others as persons we must allow them *the possibility either to consent to or to dissent from what is proposed.* The initiator of action can ensure this; but the consenting cannot be up to him or her. The morally significant aspect of treating others as persons may lie in making their consent or dissent *possible,* rather than in what they actually consent to or would hypothetically consent to if fully rational. A requirement that we ensure that others have this possibility cuts deep whenever they will be much affected by what we propose. . . .

Third, we need to understand what makes genuine consent to the more fundamental aspects of action possible. But there is no guarantee that any one set of requirements makes genuine consent possible in all circumstances. There may be some necessary conditions, whose absence always makes genuine consent or dissent impossible, and other conditions which are needed to make consent possible only in some circumstances. It is plausible to think that when we act in ways that would *always* preclude genuine consent or dissent, we will have used others. For example, if we coerce or deceive others, their dissent, and so their genuine consent, is in principle ruled out. Here we do indeed use others, treating them as mere props or tools in our own projects. Even the most autonomous cannot genuinely consent to proposals about which they are deceived or with which they are compelled to comply. Even if a proposal would have been welcomed, and coercion or deception is otiose, its enforcement or surreptitious imposition precludes consent.

In other cases a proposal for action may not in principle preclude consent and dissent, but the particular others affected may be unable to dissent from it, or genuinely to consent to it. A full understanding of treating others as persons should, I suggest, take some account of the particularities of persons. It must allow that we take seriously the possibility of dissent and consent for others who, far from being abstractly autonomous beings, have their particular cognitive limitations and partial autonomy, which affect their abilities to dissent and to consent variously in varying circumstances. We are concerned not only to be treated as a person—any person—but to some extent as the particular persons we are. We are not merely possibly consenting adults, but particular friends, colleagues, clients, rivals, relations, lovers, neighbors; we have each of us a particular history, character, set of abilities and weaknesses, interests and desires. Even when others do not deceive or coerce us, or treat us in any way as tools, we may yet feel that they do not treat us as persons either. There is some point to the thought that being treated as a person needs a personal touch. Not being used may be enough for being treated as a person when our particular identity and specific character are irrelevant, for example in commercial or other transactions with anonymous members of the public. (Even here we may think standards of courtesy must be met.) Still, in public contexts not being used may be the major part of being treated as a person: for if consent and dissent are in principle possible, we can refuse the opportunities, offers, or activities that do not suit us. But where we have specific relations with particular others, being treated as a person may require far more. It may demand that we treat others not impersonally, but to some extent as the persons they are.

POSSIBLE CONSENT: A KANTIAN READING

A shift of focus to possible consent has deep implications. When we see morally required actions as those to which others either actually or hypothetically consent, we implicitly view morality as closely connected to desires. Another's actual consent will usually reflect his or her wants or preferences; and standard modern views of hypothetical consent construe it in terms of actual preferences on which a rational ordering is hypothetically imposed. Yet it seems implausible that treating others as persons can be of *prime* moral importance if it amounts only to avoiding what they don't want or wouldn't rationally want. In a moral theory in which wants are basic, the notion of treating others as persons carries no independent weight. In Kantian terms we might say that the notion of a person doesn't matter in a heteronomous moral theory. If wants or rationalized preferences are morally fundamental, consent is of derivative concern. It is only within moral theories for beings who can sometimes act independently of desires—who are to that extent autonomous—that the notion of consent carries independent weight. In such theories it is important that consent be possible for others, but of less concern whether what they consent to is what they want.

An account of using others and treating them as persons which starts from the notions of possible consent and dissent reveals the Kantian origins of these notions. The Kantian texts also provide suggestions for explicating, elaborating, and differentiating the two notions.[1]

Kant's theory of action sees each act as done on a *maxim,* an underlying principle (often, but not necessarily, an agent's fundamental intention) used to guide and orchestrate more specific, ancillary aspects of action. The Formula of the End in Itself enjoins action on maxims that treat humanity whether in your own person or in the person of any other never simply as a means, but always at the same time as an end (*Groundwork*, p. 429).

Here there are two separate aspects to treating others as persons: the maxim must not use them (negatively) as mere means, but must also (positively) treat them as ends in themselves (cf. ibid., p. 430).

Kant describes the first sort of failure as action on maxims to which no other could possibly consent, and the second as pursuit of ends another cannot share. He writes of such a case:

The man whom I seek to use for my purposes by such a (false) promise cannot possibly agree with my way of behaving to him, and so cannot himself share the end of action (ibid., p. 429).

The failure is dual: the victim of deceit *cannot agree* to the initiator's maxim, so is used, and *a fortiori cannot share* the initiator's end, so is not treated as a person. Similarly with a maxim of coercion: victims cannot agree with a coercer's fundamental principle or maxim (which denies them the choice between consent and dissent), and further cannot share a coercer's ends. (Victims may *want* the same ends as their coercers; but that is not the same as sharing those ends, for one who is coerced, even if pointlessly, is not pursuing, nor therefore sharing, ends at all.) Those who are either deceived or coerced are then *both* used *and* not treated as persons.

It does not follow from this that nothing done in acting on a maxim of deception or coercion can be agreed to or shared by those deceived or coerced. On the contrary, deception standardly works by revealing subsidiary intentions or aspects of action, which misleadingly point to some underlying maxim to which consent can be given. Deception only works when the underlying intention or proposal is kept obscure. The deceiver's actual maxim therefore cannot be consented to. A maxim of coercion does not have to be obscure—it may be brutally plain—but clearly denies victims the choice between consent and dissent.

While the boundaries of coercive action are often unclear, we can agree on central cases involving physical force, dire and credible threats and institutionalized forms of domination such as slavery. But here too victims can and do consent to many of the coercer's subsidiary intentions. It is always hard to know when "going along with" what is coercively proposed becomes collaboration with the coercer. . . . And it is hard to tell just when an ostensibly deceived party becomes a conniving party. But while such complexities make judgment of actual cases hard, they don't alter the point that a maxim of deception or coercion treats another as mere means and not as a person, even if the victim becomes so involved in the initiator's action that we judge that he or she has become a collaborator or accessory.

The second part of Kant's account of treating others as persons urges us not merely not to use them as means, but to treat them as "ends in themselves." By this he doesn't mean that others should be our goals or purposes. Only what we aim for, including what we desire, can be a goal or purpose. This sort of subjective end depends on us for its existence. Others who exist independently of our action can't be subjective ends, but only ends in themselves. Ends in themselves may provide us with grounds of action not by being the *aim* or *effect* of action, but by constituting *limits* to our actions (*Groundwork,* p. 428). Others may limit my action by being autonomous beings whose maxims guide their projects and activities to their varied ends. To respect a limit of this sort cannot be thought of on a spatial analogy of avoiding certain areas, for the varying activities of others take place in the world that we share, and not in discrete spatial capsules (as libertarians might prefer). Not to treat others as mere means introduces minimal, but indispensable, requirements for coordinating action in a world shared by autonomous beings, namely that nobody act in ways others cannot possibly consent to, so in principle precluding their autonomous action. To treat others as ends may also require action when dissent is in principle possible, but those who are actually involved have limited capacities to dissent.

The negative requirement of not using others can be stated in some (no doubt incomplete) abstraction from the particular features of other rational beings ("the problem of justice can be solved even for a 'nation of devils' " [*Kant's Political Writings,* p. 112]), but we can give only an indeterminate account of the "positive" requirements for treating others as ends in themselves. Whenever treating others as persons goes beyond not using them, we must take into account "humanity in their person," i.e., their *particular* capacities for rational and autonomous action. This can be done with vacuous ease for abstractly rational beings. But human beings, while they are creatures of reason rather than instinct, are yet only limitedly rational beings, of whose capacities for autonomous action we can give no determinate account in the abstract. Hence the only abstract account we can give of the "positive" maxims on which we must act in treating other men and women as persons are very general policies. But these "wide" duties to share others' ends (and develop talents) can have determinate implications in particular contexts.

The "positive" aspects of treating others as ends in themselves require action on maxims of sharing others' ends. It is not enough when we deal with other human beings (as opposed to abstract rational beings) to act on maxims with which they can possibly agree, whatever their ends. It is also necessary to adopt maxims which "endeavour to further the ends of others" (*Groundwork,* p. 430). To treat human beings as persons, rather than as "ideal" rational beings, we must not only not use them, but must take their particular capacities for autonomy and rationality into account. Since other humans have varied ends, are precariously autonomous and rational, and far from self-sufficient in other ways, sharing even some of their ends may make varied demands. Kant claims that these demands can be grouped under the headings of respect and love (or beneficence). He repeatedly uses physical metaphors to express the ways in which these two sorts of demands differ:

> The principle of *mutual love* admonishes men constantly to *come nearer* to each other; that of the *respect* which they owe each other to keep themselves at a *distance* from one another (*The Doctrine of Virtue,* p. 447).

Policies of respect must recognize that others' maxims and projects are *their* maxims and projects. They must avoid merely taking over or achieving the aims of these maxims and projects, and allow others the "space" in which to pursue them for themselves. Respect for others requires, Kant thinks, that we avoid contempt, mockery, disdain, detraction, and the like and that we show others recognition (ibid., pp. 461–68). Policies of practical love or beneficence require us to recognize the needs particular others have for assistance in acting on their maxims and achieving their ends. Love requires us to adopt maxims of "active practical benevolence (beneficence) which consists in making another's happiness my own" (ibid., p. 451). To do this is to make the other's ends, whose achievement would constitute his or her happiness, in part my own. Such beneficence includes assistance to others, generosity, active sympathy, and conciliatoriness and the avoidance of envy and malicious joy (ibid., pp. 451–60).

However, the Kantian conception of beneficence is from the start antipaternalistic. The duty to seek others' happiness is always a duty to promote and share others' ends *without* taking them over, rather than a duty to provide determinate goods and services or to meet others' needs, or to see that their ends are achieved. Beneficence of this sort presupposes others who are at least partly autonomous and have their own ends. The tension between beneficence and treating others as persons, which is central to many discussions of paternalism, is absent from Kant's account:

> I cannot do good to anyone according to *my* conception of happiness (except to young children and the insane) but only according to that of the one I intend to benefit (ibid., p. 453).

What remains is, as Kant indicates, the unavoidable tension between love and respect. We experience it every time we try to work out how to share others' ends without taking them over.[2] It is a tension that has no general solution, but can be resolved in particular contexts. Kant's wide duties specify no rules of action for all rational beings, for the ways in which sharing others' ends can perhaps be exemplified would differ wholly for other sorts of rational beings (imagine beings who are psychologically impervious to one another, or less dependent on the physical world than we are), and will in any case differ greatly for human beings with varied ends.

The overall picture which this reading of the Formula of the End in Itself generates is that a morally worthy life must be based on maxims of justice (including noncoercion and nondeceit), of respect, and of love. Such a life neither uses others (by acting on maxims which preempt consent or dissent), nor fails to share others' ends (by acting on maxims which either disregard or take over those ends or lend them no support). In each case it is our *fundamental* proposals, principles, or basic intentions that must meet these conditions. We neither do nor can make it possible for others, even for others closely affected, to consent to or dissent from *every* aspect (or even every intentional aspect) of what we propose; nor can we lead lives in which we at all times help all others achieve all their ends. Justice and respect vary with circumstances, and beneficence is in addition unavoidably selective. Nevertheless there are occasions when action of a specific sort is required: there are contexts and relationships to others in which to do nothing would be sufficient evidence that the underlying maxim or principle is unjust or lacking in respect or non-beneficent. Although love and beneficence are unavoidably selective, this does not mean that when we act on these maxims we can neglect all the central projects of lives with which ours are closely involved. . . .

Notes

[1] References to Kantian texts will be parenthetical, using the following editions: *Groundwork,* trans. H. J. Paton, as *The Moral Law* (London: Hutchinson), 1953, Prussian Academy pagination; *The Doctrine of Virtue,* trans. M. Gregor (New York: Harper & Row), 1964, Prussian Academy pagination; "Perpetual Peace" in *Kant's Political Writings,* ed. Hans Reiss, trans H. B. Nisbet (Cambridge: Cambridge University Press, 1971).

[2] But what will count as a good resolution? One guideline might be this: the underlying principle of action should be one that subordinates sharing ends to leaving another with ends that can be shared. Hence only nonfundamental failures of respect may be part of loving action (e.g., presuming to make a minor arrangement or commitment for another which he or she will likely want made . . .); but where lack of respect is fundamental the supposedly loving action will cease to be so.

JOHN RAWLS
A CONTRACTARIAN THEORY OF JUSTICE

THE MAIN IDEA OF THE THEORY OF JUSTICE

My aim is to present a conception of justice which generalizes and carries to a higher level of abstraction the familiar theory of the social contract

Reprinted by permission of the publishers from pp. 11–15, 17, and 60–65 of *A Theory of Justice* by John Rawls. Cambridge, Mass.: Harvard University Press, Copyright © 1971 by the President and Fellows of Harvard College.

as found, say, in Locke, Rousseau, and Kant.[1] In order to do this we are not to think of the original contract as one to enter a particular society or to set up a particular form of government. Rather, the guiding idea is that the principles of justice for the basic structure of society are the object of the original agreement. They are the principles that free and rational persons concerned to further their own interests would accept in an initial position of equality as defining the fundamental terms of their association. These principles are to regulate all further agreements; they specify the kinds of social cooperation that can be entered into and the forms of government that can be established. This way of regarding the principles of justice I shall call justice as fairness.

Thus we are to imagine that those who engage in social cooperation choose together, in one joint act, the principles which are to assign basic rights and duties and to determine the division of social benefits. Men are to decide in advance how they are to regulate their claims against one another and what is to be the foundation charter of their society. Just as each person must decide by rational reflection what constitutes his good, that is, the system of ends which it is rational for him to pursue, so a group of persons must decide once and for all what is to count among them as just and unjust. The choice which rational men would make in this hypothetical situation of equal liberty, assuming for the present that this choice problem has a solution, determines the principles of justice.

In justice as fairness the original position of equality corresponds to the state of nature in the traditional theory of the social contract. This original position is not, of course, thought of as an actual historical state of affairs, much less as a primitive condition of culture. It is understood as a purely hypothetical situation characterized so as to lead to a certain conception of justice.[2] Among the essential features of this situation is that no one knows his place in society, his class position or social status, nor does any one know his fortune in the distribution of natural assets and abilities, his intelligence, strength, and the like. I shall even assume that the parties do not know their conceptions of the good or their special psychological propensities. The principles of justice are chosen behind a veil of ignorance. This ensures that no one is advantaged or disadvantaged in the choice of principles by the outcome of natural chance or the contingency of social circumstances. Since all are similarly situated and no one is able to design principles to favor his particular condition, the principles of justice are the result of a fair agreement or bargain. For given the circumstances of the original position, the symmetry of everyone's relations to each other, this initial situation is fair between individuals as moral persons, that is, as rational beings with their own ends and capable, I shall assume, of a sense of justice. The original position is, one might say, the appropriate initial status quo, and thus the fundamental agreements reached in it are fair. This explains the propriety of the name "justice as fairness": it conveys the idea that the principles of justice are agreed to in an initial situation that is fair. The name does not mean that the concepts of justice and fairness are the same, any more than the phrase "poetry as metaphor" means that the concepts of poetry and metaphor are the same.

Justice as fairness begins, as I have said, with one of the most general of all choices which persons might make together, namely, with the choice of the first principles of a conception of justice which is to regulate all subsequent criticism and reform of institutions. Then, having chosen a conception of justice, we can suppose that they are to choose a constitution and a legislature to enact laws, and so on, all in accordance with the principles of justice initially agreed upon. Our social situation is just if it is such that by this sequence of hypothetical agreements we would have contracted into the general system of rules which defines it. Moreover, assuming that the original position does determine a set of principles (that is, that a particular conception of justice would be chosen), it will then be true that whenever social institutions satisfy these principles those engaged in them can say to one another that they are cooperating on terms to which they would agree if they were free and equal persons whose relations with respect to one another were fair. They could all view their arrangements as meeting the stipulations which they would acknowledge in an initial situation that embodies widely accepted and reasonable constraints on the choice of principles. The general recognition of this fact would provide the basis for a public acceptance of the corresponding principles of justice. No society can, of course, be a scheme of cooperation which men enter voluntarily in a literal sense; each person finds himself placed at birth in some particular position in some particular society, and the nature of this position materially affects his life prospects. Yet a society satisfying the principles of justice as fairness comes as close as a society can to being a voluntary scheme, for it meets the principles which free and equal persons would assent to under circumstances that are fair. In this sense its members are autonomous and the obligations they recognize self-imposed.

One feature of justice as fairness is to think of the parties in the initial situation as rational and mutually disinterested. This does not mean that the parties are egoists, that is, individuals with only certain kinds of interests, say in wealth, prestige, and domination. But they are conceived as not taking an interest in one another's interests. They are to presume that even their spiritual aims may be opposed, in the way that the aims of those of different religions may be opposed. Moreover, the concept of rationality must be interpreted as far as possible in the narrow sense, standard in economic theory, of taking the most effective means to given ends. I shall modify this concept to some extent . . . but one must try to avoid introducing into it any controversial ethical elements. The initial situation must be characterized by stipulations that are widely accepted.

In working out the conception of justice as fairness one main task clearly is to determine which principles of justice would be chosen in the original position. To do this we must describe this situation in some detail and formulate with care the problem of choice which it presents. These matters I shall take up in the immediately succeeding chapters. It may be observed, however, that once the principles of justice are thought of as arising from an original agreement in a situation of equality, it is an open question whether the principle of utility would be acknowledged. Offhand it hardly seems likely that persons who view themselves as equals, entitled to press their claims upon one another, would agree to a principle which may require lesser life prospects for some simply for the sake of a greater sum of advantages enjoyed by others. Since each desires to protect his interests, his capacity to advance his conception of the good, no one has a reason to acquiesce in an enduring loss for himself in order to bring about a greater net balance of satisfaction. In the absence of strong and lasting benevolent impulses, a rational man would not accept a basic structure merely because it maximized the algebraic sum of advantages irrespective of its permanent effects on his own basic rights and interests. Thus it seems that the principle of utility is incompatible with the conception of social cooperation among equals for mutual advantage. It appears to be inconsistent with the idea of reciprocity implicit in the notion of a well-ordered society. Or, at any rate, so I shall argue.

I shall maintain instead that the persons in the initial situation would choose two rather different principles: the first requires equality in the assignment of basic rights and duties, while the second holds that social and economic inequalities, for example inequalities of wealth and authority, are just only if they result in compensating benefits for everyone, and in particular for the least advantaged members of society. These principles rule out justifying institutions on the grounds that the hardships of some are offset by a greater good in the aggregate. It may be expedient but it is not just that some should have less in order that others may prosper. But there is no injustice in the greater benefits earned by a few provided that the situation of persons not so fortunate is thereby improved. The intuitive idea is that since everyone's well-being depends upon a scheme of cooperation without which no one could have a satisfactory life, the division of advantages should be such as to draw forth the willing cooperation of everyone taking part in it, including those less well situated. Yet this can be expected only if reasonable terms are proposed. The two principles mentioned seem to be a fair agreement on the basis of which those better endowed, or more fortunate in their social position, neither of which we can be said to deserve, could expect the willing cooperation of others when some workable scheme is a necessary condition of the welfare of all.[3] Once we decide to look for a conception of justice that nullifies the accidents of natural endowment and the contingencies of social circumstances as counters in quest for political and economic advantage, we are led to these principles. They express the result of leaving aside those aspects of the social world that seem arbitrary from a moral point of view. . . .

A final remark. Justice as fairness is not a complete contract theory. For it is clear that the contractarian idea can be extended to the choice of more or less an entire ethical system, that is, to a system including principles for all the virtues and not only for justice. Now for the most part I shall consider only principles of justice and others closely related to them; I make no attempt to discuss the virtues in a systematic way. Obviously if justice as fairness succeeds reasonably well, a next step would be to study the more general view suggested by the name "rightness as fairness." But even this wider theory fails to embrace all moral relationships, since it would seem to include only our relations with other persons and to leave out of account how we are to conduct ourselves toward animals and the rest of nature. I do not contend that the contract notion offers a way to approach these questions which are certainly of the first importance; and I shall have to put them aside. We must recognize the limited scope of justice as fairness and of the general type of view that it exemplifies. How far its conclusions must be revised once these other matters are understood cannot be decided in advance. . . .

TWO PRINCIPLES OF JUSTICE

I shall now state in a provisional form the two principles of justice that I believe would be chosen in the original position. In this section I wish to make only the most general comments, and therefore the first formulation of these principles is tentative. As we go on I shall run through several formulations and approximate step by step the final statement to be given much later. I believe that doing this allows the exposition to proceed in a natural way.

The first statement of the two principles reads as follows.

> First: each person is to have an equal right to the most extensive basic liberty compatible with a similar liberty for others.
>
> Second: social and economic inequalities are to be arranged so that they are both (a) reasonably expected to be to everyone's advantage, and (b) attached to positions and offices open to all. . . .

By way of general comment, these principles primarily apply, as I have said, to the basic structure of society. They are to govern the assignment of rights and duties and to regulate the distribution of social and economic advantages. As their formulation suggests, these principles presuppose that the social structure can be divided into two more or less distinct parts, the first principle applying to the one, the second to the other. They distinguish between those aspects of the social system that define and secure the equal liberties of citizenship and those that specify and establish social and economic inequalities. The basic liberties of citizens are, roughly speaking, political liberty (the right to vote and to be eligible for public office) together with freedom of speech and assembly; liberty of conscience and freedom of thought; freedom of the person along with the right to hold (personal) property; and freedom from arbitrary arrest and seizure as defined by the concept of the rule of law. These liberties are all required to be equal by the first principle, since citizens of a just society are to have the same basic rights.

The second principle applies, in the first approximation, to the distribution of income and wealth and to the design of organizations that make use of differences in authority and responsibility, or chains of command. While the distribution of wealth and income need not be equal, it must be to everyone's advantage, and at the same time, positions of authority and offices of command must be accessible to all. One applies the second principle by holding positions open, and then, subject to this constraint, arranges social and economic inequalities so that everyone benefits.

These principles are to be arranged in a serial order with the first principle prior to the second. This ordering means that a departure from the institutions of equal liberty required by the first principle cannot be justified by, or compensated for, by greater social and economic advantages. The distribution of wealth and income, and the hierarchies of authority, must be consistent with both the liberties of equal citizenship and equality of opportunity.

It is clear that these principles are rather specific in their content, and their acceptance rests on certain assumptions that I must eventually try to explain and justify. A theory of justice depends upon a theory of society in ways that will become evident as we proceed. For the present, it should be observed that the two principles (and this holds for all formulations) are a special case of a more general conception of justice that can be expressed as follows.

> All social values—liberty and opportunity, income and wealth, and the bases of self-respect—are to be distributed equally unless an unequal distribution of any, or all, of these values is to everyone's advantage.

Injustice, then, is simply inequalities that are not to the benefit of all. Of course, this conception is extremely vague and requires interpretation.

As a first step, suppose that the basic structure of society distributes certain primary goods, that is, things that every rational man is presumed to want. These goods normally have a use whatever a person's rational plan of life. For simplicity, assume that the chief primary goods at the disposition of society are rights and liberties, powers and opportunities, income and wealth. (Later on in Part Three the primary good of self-respect has a central place.) These are the social primary goods. Other primary goods such as health and vigor, intelligence and imagination, are natural goods; although their possession is influenced by the basic structure, they are not so directly under its control. Imagine, then, a hypothetical initial arrangement in which all the social primary goods are equally distributed: everyone has similar rights and duties, and income and wealth are evenly shared. This state of affairs provides a benchmark for judging improvements. If certain inequalities of wealth and organizational powers would make everyone better off than in this hypothetical starting situation, then they accord with the general conception.

Now it is possible, at least theoretically, that by giving up some of their fundamental liberties men are sufficiently compensated by the resulting social and economic gains. The general conception of justice imposes no restrictions on what sort of inequalities are permissible; it only requires that everyone's position be improved. We need not suppose anything so drastic as consenting to a condition of slavery. Imagine instead that men forego certain political rights when the economic returns are significant and their capacity to influence the course of policy by the exercise of these rights would be marginal in any case. It is this kind of exchange which the two principles as stated rule out; being arranged in serial order they do not permit exchanges between basic liberties and economic and social gains. The serial ordering of principles expresses an underlying preference among primary social goods. When this preference is rational so likewise is the choice of these principles in this order.

In developing justice as fairness I shall, for the most part, leave aside the general conception of justice and examine instead the special case of the two principles in serial order. The advantage of this procedure is that from the first the matter of priorities is recognized and an effort made to find principles to deal with it. One is led to attend throughout to the conditions under which the acknowledgment of the absolute weight of liberty with respect to social and economic advantages, as defined by the lexical order of the two principles, would be reasonable. Offhand, this ranking appears extreme and too special a case to be of much interest; but there is more justification for it than would appear at first sight. Or at any rate, so I shall maintain. . . . Furthermore, the distinction between fundamental rights and liberties and economic and social benefits marks a difference among primary social goods that one should try to exploit. It suggests an important division in the social system. Of course, the distinctions drawn and the ordering proposed are bound to be at best only approximations. There are surely circumstances in which they fail. But it is essential to depict clearly the main lines of a reasonable conception of justice; and under many conditions anyway, the two principles in serial order may serve well enough. When necessary we can fall back on the more general conception.

The fact that the two principles apply to institutions has certain consequences. Several points illustrate this. First of all, the rights and liberties referred to by these principles are those which are defined by the public rules of the basic structure. Whether men are free is determined by the rights and duties established by the major institutions of society. Liberty is a certain pattern of social forms. The first principle simply requires that certain sorts of rules, those defining basic liberties, apply to everyone equally and that they allow the most extensive liberty compatible with a like liberty for all. The only reason for circumscribing the rights defining liberty and making men's freedom less extensive than it might otherwise be is that these equal rights as institutionally defined would interfere with one another.

Another thing to bear in mind is that when principles mention persons, or require that everyone gain from an inequality, the reference is to representative persons holding the various social positions, or offices, or whatever, established by the basic structure. Thus in applying the second principle I assume that it is possible to assign an expectation of well-being to representative individuals holding these positions. This expectation indicates their life prospects as viewed from their social station. In general, the expectations of representative persons depend upon the distribution of rights and duties throughout the basic structure. When this changes, expectations change. I assume, then, that expectations are connected: by raising the prospects of the representative man in one position we presumably increase or decrease the prospects of representative men in other positions. Since it applies to institutional forms, the second principle (or rather the first part of it) refers to the expectations of representative individuals. As I shall discuss below, neither principle applies to distributions of particular goods to particular individuals who may be identified by their proper names. The situation where someone is considering how to allocate certain commodities to needy persons who are known to him is not within the scope of the principles. They are meant to regulate basic institutional arrangements. We must not assume that there is much similarity from the standpoint of justice between an administrative allotment of goods to specific persons and the appropriate design of society. Our common sense intuitions for the former may be a poor guide to the latter.

Now the second principle insists that each person benefit from permissible inequalities in the basic structure. This means that it must be reasonable for each relevant representative man defined by this structure, when he views it as a going concern, to prefer his prospects with the inequality to his prospects without it. One is not allowed to justify differences in income or organizational powers on the ground that the disadvantages of those in one position are outweighed by the greater advantages of those in another. Much less can infringements of liberty be counterbalanced in this way. Applied to the basic structure, the principle of utility would have us maximize the sum of expectations of representative men (weighted by the number of persons they represent, on the classical view); and this would permit us to compensate for the losses of some by the gains of others. Instead, the two principles require that everyone benefit from economic and social inequalities. It is obvious, however, that there are indefinitely many ways in which all may be advantaged when the initial arrangement of equality is taken as a bench-mark. How then are we to choose among these possibilities? The princi-ples must be specified so that they yield a determinate conclusion. I now turn to this problem.

Notes

[1] As the text suggests, I shall regard Locke's *Second Treatise of Government,* Rousseau's *The Social Contract,* and Kant's ethical works beginning with *The Foundations of the Metaphysics of Morals* as definitive of the contract tradition. For all of its greatness, Hobbes's *Leviathan* raises special problems. A general historical survey is provided by J. W. Gough, *The Social Contract,* 2nd ed. (Oxford, The Clarendon Press, 1957), and Otto Gierke, *Natural Law and the Theory of Society,* trans. with an introduction by Ernest Barker (Cambridge, The University Press, 1934). A presentation of the contract view as primarily an ethical theory is to be found in G. R. Grice, *The Grounds of Moral Judgment* (Cambridge, The University Press, 1967)

[2] Kant is clear that the original agreement is hypothetical. See *The Metaphysics of Morals,* pt. I *(Rechtslehre),* especially §§ 47, 52; and pt. II of the essay "Concerning the Common Saying: This May Be True in Theory but It Does Not Apply in Practice," in *Kant's Political Writings,* ed. Hans Reiss and trans. by H. B. Nisbet (Cambridge, The University Press, 1970), pp. 73–87. See Georges Vlachos, *La Pensée politique de Kant* (Paris, Presses Universitaires de France, 1962), pp. 326–335; and J. G. Murphy, *Kant: The Philosophy of Right* (London, Macmillan, 1970), pp. 109–112, 133–136, for a further discussion.

[3] For the formulation of this intuitive idea I am indebted to Allan Gibbard.

chapter *3*

Utilitarianism

INTRODUCTION

At approximately the same time Kant was developing his theory of ethics, the English philosopher Jeremy Bentham (1748–1832) was formulating his theory of utilitarianism. Although philosophers before Bentham, especially David Hume, had developed theories with utilitarian aspects, he was the first to provide a systematic formulation of the view much as it is discussed today. Bentham's primary statement of utilitarianism is presented in his book *The Principles of Morals and Legislation* first published in 1789. As the book's title indicates, the theory has a political as well as a personal orientation.

Although working out its details is often difficult, part of utilitarianism's attraction is the simplicity of its central idea. According to the utilitarian, the rightness and wrongness of conduct depends solely on its consequences; thus it is a consequentialist theory. The criterion of ethical conduct is to produce as great a balance of good over bad as possible. Happiness is the only intrinsic good, and unhappiness the only intrinsic bad. Each person's happiness is as important as is anyone else's. Conduct is right or wrong depending on whether it produces as much *net utility* (the balance of happiness over unhappiness) as anything else that could be done.

Bentham and his close friend James Mill sought to educate a successor to lead the ethical and political movement that they started in the early nineteenth century. They developed a very strict educational plan for James Mill's oldest son, John Stuart. From about the age of three, John was trained to be the intellectual leader of the utilitarian movement. Bentham and the elder Mill were quite successful, and John Stuart Mill (1806–1873) became the leading philosopher in Great Britain, making significant contributions to logic, metaphysics, ethics, political philosophy, and economics.

The impact of utilitarian ideas in the nineteenth century was great. Utilitarianism significantly influenced the British penal and electoral reforms of that century. But though these were important achievements,

99

the reforms did not improve the lot of the average person as much as Bentham and the Mills had hoped they would.

At the beginning of the twentieth century, George E. Moore severely attacked utilitarianism by rejecting the view of Bentham and Mill that the sole end of ethics is happiness or pleasure.[1] Moore, however, still held that the rightness and wrongness of conduct depends on its consequences. During the 1930s even that aspect of utilitarian theory was severely criticized by W. David Ross.[2] In many ways, however, utilitarian ideas were still alive and significantly affected society through their incorporation into legal and economic thought.

Since the 1950s philosophers have had a renewed interest in utilitarian theory. One reason for this increased interest is the distinction, never made explicit by Bentham or Mill, between two types of utilitarianism. One version of the theory—*act utilitarianism*—directly determines the rightness and wrongness of conduct by considering the utility of particular acts. The other version—*rule utilitarianism*—indirectly determines the rightness and wrongness of conduct by judging acts by their conformity to rules and judging rules by their utility.

Act Utilitarianism The following is a representative act-utilitarian principle:

> An act is permissible if, and only if, its net utility is at least as great as that of any alternative act the agent could perform in the situation.

The crucial concept involved is that of net utility, usually simply termed utility. The net utility of an act is the sum of its good (positive) and bad (negative) consequences. Bentham and Mill considered pleasure (happiness) to be the only intrinsic good and pain (unhappiness) the only intrinsic evil. Other theorists, such as Moore, expand this understanding, believing that things other than pleasure and pain are also intrinsically good and bad. Most contemporary utilitarians consider the satisfaction of interests or preferences to be that which is intrinsically good and their frustration to be that which is intrinsically bad. The following discussion refers to happiness and unhappiness as intrinsically good and bad, leaving open whether they are to be equated with pleasure and pain, satisfaction and frustration, or something else.

Determining the net utility of an act requires three steps. First, one sums all the happiness that will be caused by the act. Second, one sums all the unhappiness that will be caused by the act. Third, one in effect subtracts the unhappiness from the happiness. This result is the net utility, which is negative if the act will produce more unhappiness than happiness and positive if the consequences are vice versa.

This concept of utility requires that one can mathematically compare the happiness and unhappiness of different people, or, as it is said, make mathematical comparisons of interpersonal utility. To sum up the happiness of an act, say, Fred's eating ice cream or Sharon's earning a bachelor's degree, produces, one must be able to assign standard units of happiness to it. One must also be able to assign the same standard units to unhappiness. There are two problems involved. First, it might not always be possible to assign definite units to the pleasure a person gets through the performance of a particular action. For example, it might not be possible to figure out exactly how many units of happiness Fred gets from eating ice cream, as compared to playing tennis. Second, even if one could do that for each person, there is no way to be certain that the units assigned for Fred are the same as those assigned for Sharon. A number of philosophers and economists have struggled to develop a system of making mathematical comparisons, but as yet no one has provided a generally accepted method for so doing.

To determine which act or acts are morally permissible in a situation, one must go through the following three steps. (1) One must determine all the alternative acts that could be performed. People learning to reason in a utilitarian manner often forget to consider all the available alternatives. For example, suppose one is trying to decide whether to study or to go to a movie. There are not just two alternatives available. One could also, perhaps, study for a while and then go to the movie when one is tired, take a shorter break by watching a half-hour television show, go for a walk, or commit suicide. Some of these actions, such as committing suicide, are not plausibly going to produce as much utility as others and can practically be ignored. (2) As described previously, one must determine the net utility of each of the alternative acts. (3) One determines which acts have at least as much net utility as any of the others. Any of these acts will be morally permissible. If one act has more net utility than any other, then it is obligatory and no other act is permissible. In some situations, it will be discovered that none of the acts has a positive net utility. The act-utilitarian principle does not imply that they are all wrong; it simply implies that the one(s) with the least balance of unhappiness over happiness is (are) permissible. In short, if all acts will on balance cause net unhappiness, or disutility, then act utilitarianism implies that one should do what will cause the least net unhappiness.

A few points should be noted about act-utilitarian theory. It differs from Kantian theory in that only the consequences of actions are considered relevant to determining their rightness, whereas Kant and others believe that something other than the utility of consequences is morally relevant. Also, although it shares some characteristics with egoism, it differs from egoism by considering the happiness and unhappiness of everyone equally. An egoist is concerned only with the consequences for himself, but a utilitarian does not consider the consequences for himself to be of any more importance than are the consequences for others. Nor does the act-utilitarian principle state that one should aim for "the greatest happiness of the greatest number," a conception that does not make sense in some situations. Suppose one act will affect five people and produce a net utility of ten units and the only alternative act will affect ten persons and produce a net utility of five units. The second act will produce happiness for more people, but the first one will produce more happiness overall. Seeking the greatest happiness for the greatest number does not tell one what to do in this situation. Such a formulation tries to maximize two independent variables—happiness and number of people—at the same time, something that is not always possible.

Three widely influential criticisms of act utilitarianism should be considered here. The first criticism pertains to promise keeping. According to act utilitarianism, one has an obligation to keep a promise if and only if no other act has as much utility as keeping it does. (If another act has the same net utility, then keeping the promise is permissible but not obligatory.) Suppose one has borrowed money from a friend and promised to repay it. After a couple of weeks one earns enough money to repay the friend, but funds are being collected for famine relief in a particularly desperate country. Assume that, everything considered, giving the money to famine relief would have more net utility than would repaying the friend. According to act utilitarianism, it is not permissible to repay the friend; instead, one has an obligation to give it to famine relief (assuming no other alternative has as much net utility as that act does). But, the critics claim, one is obligated to repay one's friend. Therefore, act utilitarianism is not a correct principle.

Short of abandoning or modifying the theory, the act utilitarian can give two different replies to this type of criticism. He or she can claim that when one examines the situation in detail, repaying one's friend does have greater net utility, for one must consider the extra disappointment breaking one's promise will cause the friend, the bad example it will set, and the bad effect it will have on one's character. Usually repaying one's friend will have more net utility. In some cases, however, even if all these factors are taken into account, giving to famine relief might have greater utility. If so, act utilitarianism implies that one is obligated to break the promise. At this point, the utilitarian can simply reply that it is mistaken to think that it would be wrong to break the promise.

The critics claim that the promise-keeping example shows that something other than consequences is relevant to determining the rightness of conduct. One should keep one's promise because one made it. The promise was something made in the past and is not a matter of the future consequences of promise keeping. The obligation to keep promises, they claim, is a "backward-looking" obligation, and act utilitarianism cannot account for such considerations because it is solely "forward looking." Other commonsense obligations, such as gratitude, are also backward looking.

The second criticism of act utilitarianism pertains to justice. Suppose the finance minister of a country is trying to decide between two economic policies. Policy A will produce tremendous economic growth, but most of the benefits will accrue to the upper 30 percent of the population. Policy B will produce much less economic growth, but the benefits will be more widely and evenly distributed. Further suppose that policy A will produce more net utility than policy B. Assuming that no other policy has as much net utility as A, according to act utilitarianism, the finance minister has an obligation to choose policy A; it would be wrong to choose policy B. According to the critics, since one is not obligated to make the rich richer, act utilitarianism must be incorrect.

An act utilitarian can try to argue on the facts that policy B will have more net utility than policy A. In general, dollar for dollar, economic benefits to the poor produce more happiness than economic benefits to the rich, because they provide goods more essential for happiness. Nonetheless, if policy A would produce many more goods for the wealthy 30 percent of the population than would policy B, it will still have more net utility. Alternately, the act utilitarian can simply accept the implications and defend the moral correctness of policy A. Of course, one can also abandon or try to revise the theory.

The underlying difficulty brought out by this example is that act utilitarianism does not consider the distribution of utility, only its amount. It thus, according to critics, ignores the important consideration of equality of distribution. Although utilitarians count the happiness of each person equally, a greater amount of happiness for one person outweighs a lesser amount of unhappiness for another, no matter how happy the first person already is or how unhappy the second person already is.

The third criticism of act utilitarianism pertains to cooperative conduct and, in particular, to what are called *maximizing conditions*. [3] These are situations in which most people need to act the same way to obtain great utility, but most utility will be achieved if a few people do not act that way. Say, for instance, that due to an energy shortage, the government has asked everyone to lower their thermostat to sixty-five degrees. Now June, a cold-blooded act utilitarian, reasons as follows. If everyone lowers the thermostat to sixty-five, more energy will be saved than needs to be. As I am very cold-blooded, chilly temperatures cause me more unhappiness than they do other people. If I keep my thermostat at seventy-two degrees, I will not encourage others to do so because I live alone and no one will know. Consequently, it is permissible for me to leave my thermostat at seventy-two degrees, because it will give me happiness and will not cause anyone else unhappiness. The critics have two objections to this form of act-utilitarian reasoning. First, it is unfair for June to leave her thermostat at seventy-two degrees when everyone else must turn theirs down. Second, suppose that everyone reasoned as June does. Then everyone would leave the thermostat at seventy-two degrees; no energy would be saved; and an economic or energy disaster (no heat at all) would occur.

Utilitarians can argue that their theory does not imply that it is permissible for everyone to leave the thermostat at seventy-two degrees.

Only cold-blooded persons can do so. Alternately, they can accept the implications and say that it is permissible for everyone to do so, unless the government adopts a policy (such as fines or higher energy prices) making it more attractive for persons to turn down their thermostats. The critics, however, claim that the example shows that utilitarianism ignores considerations of fairness.

Rule Utilitarianism   The following is a formulation of a general rule-utilitarian principle:

> An act is permissible if, and only if, it is not prohibited by a rule to which conformance would have at least as much net utility as conformance to any other rule applicable to the situation.

By this principle, often called *primitive rule utilitarianism,* an act is not evaluated as right or wrong by directly considering its utility but by considering whether it is prohibited by a rule. An act prohibited by a relevant rule is wrong. The chief difficulty with this theory, many critics claim, is that it produces the same results as act utilitarianism. For example, consider promise keeping. Conforming to a rule that it is always wrong to break promises would not have as much utility as conforming to one that allowed exceptions. When would it be most useful to allow exceptions? Whenever more utility would result from breaking a promise than in keeping it. Thus, it seems the most useful rule would be, "It is wrong to break promises except when doing so has as much utility as does keeping them." Although some philosophers argue that primitive rule utilitarianism does not always give the same results as act utilitarianism, it would be likely to have the same results as does act utilitarianism, if applied in the objectionable cases considered in the preceding section.

However, if one considers the utility of accepting rules, otherwise known as *acceptance utility,* rather than of conforming to them, one does not get the same results as with act utilitarianism. In the use of acceptance utility, one does not assume that people will always conform to the rules; one can allow for people not always doing what, in a reflective moment, they would think is right.

A major problem with primitive rule utilitarianism is that it evaluates the utility of one rule at a time, although different rules might conflict in any given situation. Also, while it is always possible to work out a rule for a particular situation, one may end up with so many rules that it would be difficult to remember them all. Consequently, it is usually better to consider the utility of different sets of rules, or moral codes. A useful code would be composed of rather simple rules, including a rule or two explaining what to do in the event of rule conflict. Nonetheless, in most cases one will only have to consider differences between codes having different rules applicable to the kind of situation one is confronted with.

A rule-utilitarian principle making allowances for these considerations can be formulated as follows:

> An act is permissible if, and only if, it is not prohibited by a set of rules the acceptance of which would have at least as much net utility as the acceptance of any other set.

Actually, the steps in rule-utilitarian reasoning are quite similar to those in act-utilitarian reasoning. (1) One must determine the relevant codes. As noted above, one need not consider every code, only those having different rules applicable to the type of situation confronted (keeping promises, showing gratitude, distributing goods, and so on). Usually then, one can simply consider alternative rules applicable to the type of situation. As with act utilitarianism, a common failing is a lack of imagination in considering alternative rules. For example, with regard to promise keeping, the choice is not simply between the two rules "Never break promises" or "Never break promises unless more net utility will result from doing so." One should consider relevant rules with other exceptive clauses, such as "Never break promises unless they were coerced, or if breaking them can save a life." (2) One must determine the net utility of the acceptance of each of the various relevant rules, or sets of rules. (3) One picks a rule, or set of rules, the acceptance of which has at least as much net utility as the acceptance of any other. (4) One must ask whether this rule, or set of rules, prohibits the act in question. If so, it is wrong; if not, it is permissible.

Perhaps the strongest argument for rule utilitarianism is that while it retains the concern for the utility of conduct, it avoids some of the objectionable implications of act utilitarianism. Consider the example of breaking a promise to repay a loan in order to give the money to famine relief. A rule that "It is wrong to break promises unless doing so will produce more net utility" would probably not have as much net acceptance utility as another rule. If people were permitted to break promises whenever they happened to think more net utility would result, because of bias or improper calculations of utility they would break promises much of the time. Consequently, rules with more precise exceptions are better. Nor is it likely that a rule that permitted breaking promises to repay loans in order to give to famine relief would have as much acceptance utility as a rule that did not. Famines occur rather frequently. In many cases, people who loaned money could not rely on getting their money back. Consequently, they might be less inclined to loan money, and few people would be able to borrow. Moreover, a code with high acceptance utility would probably include other rules specifically providing for famine relief, so there would be no need to include such an exception in a rule about promise keeping. Consequently, the rule utilitarian would likely infer that it would be wrong to break the promise made in the example.

Now consider the example of leaving the thermostat at seventy-two degrees. Suppose the rule stated that it is wrong not to lower one's thermostat to sixty-five degrees unless one is cold-blooded. The acceptance utility of such a rule is apt to be much less than that of a rule without that exceptive condition. As stated, the rule leaves too much leeway for people to make exceptions in their own favor. Quite likely, so many people would decide that they were cold-blooded and, therefore, free to keep the heat up that most of the utility of lowering thermostats would be lost. This is not to say that a rule with as high an acceptance utility as any other would not contain some exceptions. Exceptions, for instance, might be admitted for people who are very sick, or for the elderly.

Rule utilitarianism does not, however, diverge from act utilitarianism in the example of justice and economic policy. The choice between policies is in effect a choice between two rules. By hypothesis, policy A, in which most benefits go to the rich, has the higher utility. The resentment of the poor resulting from its primarily benefiting the rich might decrease its utility, but if most of the people accepted the high-growth policy, then resentment would be minimized. People do not resent policies they approve of. Thus, rule utilitarianism, like act utilitarianism, is concerned only with the amount of utility, *not* with its distribution.

Two criticisms of rule utilitarianism should be mentioned. The first is the act utilitarians' charge that rule utilitarians are guilty of *superstitious rule worship.* Their argument is simple. Like us, they say, rule utilitarians claim to be interested in promoting happiness, yet their theory prescribes different acts from ours. Our theory prescribes the acts that produce as much utility as possible; rule utilitarianism does not. In short, rule utilitarians do not permit breaking rules even when they admit there may be more utility in breaking than in following them. Why then do they follow the rules? Because of superstitious rule worship.

The second criticism usually comes from nonutilitarians.[4] Rule utilitarianism holds that one should follow those rules that would have as much utility as possible *if* they were accepted. But suppose the rules are not in fact accepted. Rule utilitarianism would still imply that one should follow the rules, whether acceptance is hypothetical or real. Sometimes this will lead a person to make a useless sacrifice. Consider again the energy shortage. Suppose the legislature has failed to act, but as high a net utility as possible would result if everyone accepted the rule to lower thermostats to sixty-five degrees, unless they were seriously ill or over seventy years of age. The vast majority of people do not accept the rule, therefore, do not lower their thermostats, and energy shortages occur. Meanwhile, rule utilitarians have turned their thermostats down to sixty-five degrees. Why? Because it is required by the rule that *would* have as much utility as possible *if* it were accepted. The result is that the rule utilitarians make a useless sacrifice. They are chilly when others are warm, and when the energy runs out, their heat will be shut off just like everyone else's. This is a ridiculous consequence, of course. Moreover, the useless sacrifices need not be made by rule utilitarians; their actions can lead to sacrifices by others. For example, suppose the government does not have a social security system, but some rule utilitarians conclude that such a system would be best. Consequently, instead of caring for their parents when they are old as everyone else in the society does, they simply make an "extra" contribution to the government in the amount they calculated they would have to pay under a social security system. Their parents receive nothing; they have made a useless sacrifice.

When faced with these objections, rule utilitarians can claim that in fact their theory does not have the objectionable implications. Alternately, they can accept the implications and suggest that our beliefs should be reformed. As a last resort, they can abandon or modify their theory.

Readings The selection from John Stuart Mill provides his statement of utilitarianism and his argument for it. Mill believes that he can justify acceptance of utilitarianism if he can show that happiness and only happiness is intrinsically good. His argument, however, is frequently said to contain a number of logical fallacies. A distinguishing aspect of his theory is the suggestion that some kinds of pleasure are preferable to others. The more preferable ones he calls higher and believes to be chiefly intellectual. In this respect, he differs markedly from Bentham who considered all pleasures to be on a par.

The selection by J. J. C. Smart is a contemporary statement and defense of act utilitarianism. He distinguishes between evaluating actions and persons and comments on the problem of cooperation. Omitted here is his account of how utilities can be compared. The selection concludes with some comments about applying act utilitarianism.

The last selection by Richard Brandt is a statement of rule utilitarianism. He discusses some puzzles and problems of rule utilitarianism. Among them is whether different moral codes might be appropriate for different subgroups in society, such as lawyers and doctors. He concludes with some comments about utilitarianism and equality.

Notes

[1]*Principia Ethica* (Cambridge: Cambridge University Press, 1903).

[2]W. David Ross, *The Right and the Good* (Oxford: Clarendon Press, 1930) and *Foundations of Ethics* (Oxford: Clarendon Press, 1939).

[3]David Lyons, *Forms and Limits of Utilitarianism* (Oxford: Clarendon Press, 1965), pp. 128–131.

[4]See B. J. Diggs, "A Comment on 'Some Merits of One Form of Rule-Utilitarianism,'" in *Readings in Contemporary Ethical Theory,* ed. Kenneth Pahel and Marvin Schiller (Englewood Cliffs, N.J.: Prentice-Hall, 1970), pp. 307–317.

Bibliography on Utilitarianism

Bentham, Jeremy. *An Introduction to the Principles of Morals and Legislation.* 1789. Several editions.

Brandt, Richard B. *A Theory of the Good and the Right.* Oxford: Clarendon Press, 1979.

———. "Utilitarianism and Moral Rights." *Canadian Journal of Philosophy* 14 (1984): 1–20.

Hare, R. M. *Moral Thinking: Its Levels, Method and Point.* Oxford: Clarendon Press, 1981.

Harsanyi, John C. "Does Reason Tell Us What Moral Code to Follow and, Indeed, to Follow Any Moral Code at All?" *Ethics* 96 (1985): 42–55.

Mill, John Stuart. *Utilitarianism with Critical Essays.* Edited by Samuel Gorovitz. Indianapolis, Ind.: Bobbs-Merrill, 1971.

Miller, Harlan B., and Williams, William H., eds. *The Limits of Utilitarianism.* Minneapolis: University of Minnesota Press, 1982.

Rachels, James. *The Elements of Moral Philosophy.* New York: Random House, 1986. Chapters 7–8.

Regan, Donald H. *Utilitarianism and Co-operation.* Oxford: Clarendon Press, 1980.

Sen, Amartya, and Williams, Bernard, eds. *Utilitarianism and Beyond.* Cambridge: Cambridge University Press, 1982.

Sidgwick, Henry. *The Methods of Ethics.* 7th ed. London: Macmillan, 1907. Book IV.

Smart, J. J. C., and Williams, Bernard. *Utilitarianism: For and Against.* Cambridge: Cambridge University Press, 1973.

JOHN STUART MILL
UTILITARIANISM

CHAPTER II WHAT UTILITARIANISM IS

. . . The creed which accepts as the foundation of morals, Utility, or the Greatest Happiness Principle, holds that actions are right in proportion as they tend to promote happiness, wrong as they tend to produce the reverse of happiness. By happiness is intended pleasure, and the absence of pain; by unhappiness, pain, and the privation of pleasure. To give a clear view of the moral standard set up by the theory, much more requires to be said; in particular, what things it includes in the ideas of pain and pleasure; and to what extent this is left an open question. But these supplementary explanations do not affect the theory of life on which this theory of morality is grounded—namely, that pleasure, and freedom from pain, are the only things desirable as ends; and that all desirable things (which are as numerous in the utilitarian as in any other scheme) are desirable either for the pleasure inherent in themselves, or as means to the promotion of pleasure and the prevention of pain.

Now, such a theory of life excites in many minds, and among them in some of the most estimable in feeling and purpose, inveterate dislike. To suppose that life has (as they express it) no higher end than pleasure—no better and nobler object of desire and pursuit—they designate

From John Stuart Mill, *Utilitarianism* (1861).

as utterly mean and grovelling; as a doctrine worthy only of swine, to whom the followers of Epicurus were, at a very early period, contemptuously likened; and modern holders of the doctrine are occasionally made the subject of equally polite comparisons by its German, French, and English assailants.

When thus attacked, the Epicureans have always answered, that it is not they, but their accusers, who represent human nature in a degrading light; since the accusation supposes human beings to be capable of no pleasures except those of which swine are capable. If this supposition were true, the charge could not be gainsaid, but would then be no longer an imputation; for if the sources of pleasure were precisely the same to human beings and to swine, the rule of life which is good enough for the one would be good enough for the other. The comparison of the Epicurean life to that of beasts is felt as degrading, precisely because a beast's pleasures do not satisfy a human being's conception of happiness. Human beings have faculties more elevated than the animal appetites, and when once made conscious of them, do not regard anything as happiness which does not include their gratification. I do not, indeed, consider the Epicureans to have been by any means faultless in drawing out their scheme of consequences from the utilitarian principle. To do this in any sufficient manner, many Stoic, as well as Christian elements require to be included. But there is no known Epicurean theory of life which does not assign to the pleasures of the intellect, of the feelings and imagination, and of the moral sentiments, a much higher value as pleasures than to those of mere sensation. It must be admitted, however, that utilitarian writers in general have placed the superiority of mental over bodily pleasures chiefly in the greater permanency, safety, uncostliness, etc., of the former—that is, in their circumstantial advantages rather than in their intrinsic nature. And on all these points utilitarians have fully proved their case; but they might have taken the other, and, as it may be called, higher ground, with entire consistency. It is quite compatible with the principle of utility to recognise the fact, that some *kinds* of pleasure are more desirable and more valuable than others. It would be absurd that while, in estimating all other things, quality is considered as well as quantity, the estimation of pleasures should be supposed to depend on quantity alone.

If I am asked, what I mean by difference of quality in pleasures, or what makes one pleasure more valuable than another, merely as a pleasure, except its being greater in amount, there is but one possible answer. Of two pleasures, if there be one to which all or almost all who have experience of both give a decided preference, irrespective of any feeling of moral obligation to prefer it, that is the more desirable pleasure. If one of the two is, by those who are competently acquainted with both, placed so far above the other that they prefer it, even though knowing it to be attended with a greater amount of discontent, and would not resign it for any quantity of the other pleasure which their nature is capable of, we are justified in ascribing to the preferred enjoyment a superiority in quality, so far out-weighing quantity as to render it, in comparison, of small account.

Now it is an unquestionable fact that those who are equally acquainted with, and equally capable of appreciating and enjoying, both, do give a most marked preference to the manner of existence which employs their higher faculties. Few human creatures would consent to be changed into any of the lower animals, for a promise of the fullest allowance of a beast's pleasures; no intelligent human being would consent to be a fool, no instructed person would be an ignoramus, no person of feeling and conscience would be selfish and base, even though they should be persuaded that the fool, the dunce, or the rascal is better satisfied with his lot than they are with theirs. They would not resign what they possess more than he for the most complete satisfaction of all the desires which they have in common with him. If they ever fancy they would, it is only in cases of unhappiness so extreme, that to escape from it they would exchange their lot for almost any other, however undesirable in their own eyes. A being of higher faculties requires more to make him happy, is capable probably of more acute suffering, and certainly accessible to it at more points, than one of an inferior type; but in spite of these liabilities, he can never really wish to sink into what he feels to be a lower grade of existence. We may give what explanation we please of this unwillingness; we may attribute it to pride, a name which is given indiscriminately to some of the most and to some of the least estimable feelings of which mankind are capable: we may refer it to the love of liberty and personal independence, an appeal to which was with the Stoics one of the most effective means for the inculcation of it; to the love of power, or to the love of excitement, both of which do really enter into and contribute to it: but its most appropriate appellation is a sense of dignity, which all human beings possess in one form or another, and in some, though by no means in exact, proportion to their higher faculties, and which is so essential a part of the happiness of those in whom it is strong, that nothing which conflicts with it could be, otherwise than momentarily, an object of desire to them. Whoever supposes that this preference takes place at a sacrifice of happiness—that the superior being, in anything like equal circumstances, is not happier than the inferior—confounds the two very different ideas, of happiness, and content. It is indisputable that the being whose capacities of enjoyment are low, has the greatest chance of having them fully satisfied; and a highly endowed being will always feel that any happiness which he can look for, as the world is constituted, is imperfect. But he can learn to bear its imperfections, if they are at all bearable; and they will not make him envy the being who is indeed unconscious of the imperfections, but only because he feels not at all the good which those imperfections qualify. It is better to be a human being dissatisfied than a pig satisfied; better to be Socrates dissatisfied than a fool satisfied. And if the fool, or the pig, are of a different opinion, it is because they only know their own side of the question. The other party to the comparison knows both sides.

It may be objected, that many who are capable of the higher pleasures, occasionally, under the influence of temptation, postpone them to the lower. But this is quite compatible with a full appreciation of the intrinsic superiority of the higher. Men often, from infirmity of character, make their election for the nearer good, though they know it to be the less valuable; and this no less when the choice is between two bodily pleasures, than when it is between bodily and mental. They pursue sensual indulgences to the injury of health, though perfectly aware that health is the greater good. It may be further objected, that many who begin with youthful enthusiasm for everything noble, as they advance in years sink into indolence and selfishness. But I do not believe that those who undergo this very common change, voluntarily choose the lower description of pleasures in preference to the higher. I believe that before they devote themselves exclusively to the one, they have already become incapable of the other. Capacity for the nobler feelings is in most natures a very tender plant, easily killed, not only by hostile influences, but by mere want of sustenance; and in the majority of young persons it speedily dies away if the occupations to which their position in life has devoted them, and the society into which it has thrown them, are not favourable to keeping that higher capacity in exercise. Men lose their high aspirations as they lose their intellectual tastes, because they have not time or opportunity for indulging them; and they addict themselves to inferior pleasures, not because they deliberately prefer them, but because they are either the only ones to which they have access, or the only ones which they are any longer capable of enjoying. It may be questioned whether any one who has remained equally susceptible to both classes of pleasures, ever knowingly and calmly preferred the lower; though many, in all ages, have broken down in an ineffectual attempt to combine both.

From this verdict of the only competent judges, I apprehend there can be no appeal. On a question which is the best worth having of two pleasures, or which of two modes of existence is the most grateful to the feelings, apart from its moral attributes and from its consequences, the judgment of those who are qualified by knowledge of both, or, if they differ, that of the majority among them, must be admitted as final. And there needs be the less hesitation to accept this judgment respecting the quality of pleasures, since there is no other tribunal to be referred to even on the question of quantity. What means are there of determining which is the acutest of two pains, or the intensest of two pleasurable sensations, except the general suffrage of those who are familiar with both? Neither pains nor pleasures are homogeneous, and pain is always heterogeneous with pleasure. What is there to decide whether a particular pleasure is worth purchasing at the cost of a particular pain, except the feelings and judgment of the experienced? When, therefore, those feelings and judgment declare the pleasures derived from the higher faculties to be preferable *in kind,* apart from the question of intensity, to those of which the animal nature, disjoined from the higher faculties, is susceptible, they are entitled on this subject to the same regard.

I have dwelt on this point, as being a necessary part of a perfectly just conception of Utility or Happiness, considered as the directive rule of human conduct. But it is by no means an indispensable condition to the acceptance of the utilitarian standard; for that standard is not the agent's own greatest happiness, but the greatest amount of happiness altogether; and if it may possibly be doubted whether a noble character is always the happier for its nobleness, there can be no doubt that it makes other people happier, and that the world in general is immensely a gainer by it. Utilitarianism, therefore, could only attain its end by the general cultivation of nobleness of character, even if each individual were only benefited by the nobleness of others, and his own, so far as happiness is concerned, were a sheer deduction from the benefit. But the bare enunciation of such an absurdity as this last, renders refutation superfluous.

According to the Greatest Happiness Principle, as above explained, the ultimate end, with reference to and for the sake of which all other things are desirable (whether we are considering our own good or that of other people), is an existence exempt as far as possible from pain, and as rich as possible in enjoyments, both in point of quantity and quality; the test of quality, and the rule for measuring it against quantity, being the preference felt by those who in their opportunities of experience, to which must be added their habits of self-consciousness and self-observation, are best furnished with the means of comparison. This, being, according to the utilitarian opinion, the end of human action, is necessarily also the standard of morality; which may accordingly be defined, the rules and precepts for human conduct, by the observance of which an existence such as has been described might be, to the greatest extent possible, secured to all mankind; and not to them only, but, so far as the nature of things admits, to the whole sentient creation. . . .

The objectors to utilitarianism cannot always be charged with representing it in a discreditable light. On the contrary, those among them who entertain anything like a just idea of its disinterested character, sometimes find fault with its standard as being too high for humanity. They say it is exacting too much to require that people shall always act from the inducement of promoting the general interests of society. But this is to mistake the very meaning of a standard of morals, and confound the rule of action with the motive of it. It is the business of ethics to tell us what are our duties, or by what test we may know them; but no system of ethics requires that the sole motive of all we do shall be a feeling of duty; on the contrary, ninety-nine hundredths of all our actions are done from other motives, and rightly so done, if the rule of duty does not condemn them. It is the more unjust to utiliarianism that this particular misapprehension should be made a ground of objection to it, inasmuch as utilitarian moralists have gone beyond almost all others in affirming that the motive has nothing to do with the morality of the action, though much with the worth of the agent. He who saves a fellow-creature from drowning does what is morally right, whether his motive be duty, or the hope of being paid for his trouble; he who betrays the friend that trusts him, is guilty of a crime, even if his object be to serve another friend to whom he is under greater obligation. But to speak only of actions done from the motive of duty, and in direct obedience to principle: it is a misapprehension of the utilitarian mode of thought, to conceive it as implying that people should fix their minds upon so wide a generality as the world, or society at large. The great majority of good actions are intended not for the benefit of the world, but for that of individuals, of which the good of the world is made up; and the thoughts of the most virtuous man need not on these occasions travel beyond the particular persons concerned, except so far as is necessary to assure himself that in benefiting them he is not violating the rights, that is, the legitimate and authorised expectations, of any one else. The multiplication of happiness is, according to the utilitarian ethics, the object of virtue: the occasions on which any person (except one in a thousand) has it in his power to do this on an extended scale, in other words to be a public benefactor, are but exceptional; and on these occasions alone is he called on to consider public utility; in every other case, private utility, the interest or happiness of some few persons, is all he has to attend to. Those alone the influence of whose actions extends to society in general, need concern themselves habitually about so large an object. In the case of abstinences indeed—of things which people forbear to do from moral considerations, though the consequences in the particular case might be beneficial—it would be unworthy of an intelligent agent not to be consciously aware that the action is of a class which, if practised generally, would be generally injurious, and that this is the ground of the obligation to abstain from it. The amount of regard for the public interest implied in this recognition, is no greater than is demanded by every system of morals, for they all enjoin to abstain from whatever is manifestly pernicious to society. . . .

CHAPTER IV   OF WHAT SORT OF PROOF THE PRINCIPLE OF UTILITY IS SUSCEPTIBLE

It has already been remarked, that questions of ultimate ends do not admit of proof, in the ordinary acceptation of the term. To be incapable of proof by reasoning is common to all first principles; to the first premises of our knowledge, as well as to those of our conduct. But the former, being matters of fact, may be the subject of a direct appeal to the faculties which judge of fact—namely, our senses, and our internal consciousness. Can an appeal be made to the same faculties on questions of practical ends? Or by what other faculty is cognisance taken of them?

Questions about ends are, in other words, questions what things are desirable. The utilitarian doctrine is, that happiness is desirable, and the only thing desirable, as an end; all other things being only desirable as means to that end. What ought to be required of this doctrine—what conditions is it requisite that the doctrine should fulfil—to make good its claim to be believed?

The only proof capable of being given that an object is visible, is that people actually see it. The only proof that a sound is audible, is that people hear it: and so of the other sources of our experience. In like manner, I apprehend, the sole evidence it is possible to produce that anything is desirable, is that people do actually desire it. If the end which the utilitarian doctrine proposes to itself were not, in theory and in practice, acknowledged to be an end, nothing could ever convince any person that it was so. No reason can be given why the general happiness is desirable, except that each person, so far as he believes it to be attainable, desires his own happiness. This, however, being a fact, we have not only all the proof which the case admits of, but all which it is possible to require, that happiness is a good: that each person's happiness is a good to that person, and the general happiness, therefore, a good to the aggregate of all persons. Happiness has made out its title as *one* of the ends of conduct, and consequently one of the criteria of morality.

But it has not, by this alone, proved itself to be the sole criterion. To do that, it would seem, by the same rule, necessary to show, not only that people desire happiness, but that they never desire anything else. . . .

We have now, then, an answer to the question, of what sort of proof the principle of utility is susceptible. If the opinion which I have now stated is psychologically true—if human nature is so constituted as to desire nothing which is not either a part of happiness or a means of happiness, we can have no other proof, and we require no other, that these are the only things desirable. If so, happiness is the sole end of human action, and the promotion of it the test by which to judge of all human conduct; from whence it necessarily follows that it must be the criterion of morality, since a part is included in the whole.

And now to decide whether this is really so; whether mankind do desire nothing for itself but that which is a pleasure to them, or of which the absence is a pain; we have evidently arrived at a question of fact and experience, dependent, like all similar questions, upon evidence. It can only be determined by practised self-consciousness and self-observation, assisted by observation of others. I believe that these sources of evidence, impartially consulted, will declare that desiring a thing and finding it pleasant, aversion to it and thinking of it as painful, are phenomena entirely inseparable, or rather two parts of the same phenomenon; in strictness of language, two different modes of naming the same psychological fact: that to think of an object as desirable (unless for the sake of its consequences), and to think of it as pleasant, are one and the same thing; and that to desire anything, except in proportion as the idea of it is pleasant, is a physical and metaphysical impossibility.

J. J. C. SMART
UTILITARIANISM AND ITS APPLICATIONS

HEDONISTIC ACT UTILITARIANISM

I shall take the paradigm of utilitarianism to be hedonistic act utilitarianism, a theory that has come down to us through Jeremy Bentham[1] and Henry Sidgwick[2]. (There has been some controversy as to how far J. S. Mill's *Utilitarianism* fits this paradigm.[3]) According to this paradigm, what it is right to do on any occasion is to maximize the total happiness (now and at all future times) of all sentient creatures, whether humans, other animals, or extraterrestrials (should we ever have to do with these last). The theory has an obvious appeal. What could be better than to maximize happiness? Any theory that was not equivalent to hedonistic act utilitarianism would imply that on occasion one should make the world less happy than it would otherwise be. By concentrating on consequences of actions the theory contrasts with theories that assess the rightness of actions by their motives (e.g. whether they arise out of respect for persons) or by whether they are in conformity with particular but nevertheless ethically ultimate rules ('Keep promises,' 'Tell the truth,' and so on) or by whether they are in accordance with essential human nature (whatever that is). The theory also contrasts with theories that say that there are basic human rights, since giving a person his or her rights need not always maximize total happiness. Similarly it contrasts with theories that stress fairness or equal distribution of happiness. This is not to say of course that a hedonistic act utilitarian, in a capacity as legislator, may not enact a system of *legal* rights or of equal distribution (not of happiness but, for example, of money). The setting up of such a *legal* system may well lead to maximization of happiness.

The hedonistic act utilitarian principle, as stated above, is a criterion of right action. Utilitarianism needs to give us more than that: it needs to give us a method of ethical decision. At first sight it might be thought that the method would simply be to try to do on any occasion the act that most probably satisfies the criterion. However the most probably maximizing act may be one that gives a smaller probability of very great disaster. There is something wrong therefore with this idea. What the utilitarian should do is to maximize *expected utility*. . . .

The need to consider choices between infinite future courses of the universe might be thought to make utilitarianism impracticable. However it is plausible that the expected ethical consequences of our actions usually diminish rapidly to zero like ripples in a pond. Whether Jim

From Joseph P. DeMarco and Richard M. Fox, eds., *New Directions in Ethics: The Challenge of Applied Ethics* (New York: Routledge & Kegan Paul, 1986), pp. 24–30, 36–41. Reprinted with permission.

marries Mary or Martha it will probably not affect the general happiness a thousand years hence. Or if it does, the probability of it mattering one way is balanced by the probability of it mattering the other way. In some cases, the relevant consequences of actions have values that do not diminish rapidly to zero, but this need not prevent utilitarian comparisons. Assuming that each future generation, even if these went on to infinity (not that this is really possible), would be on the whole happy rather than unhappy, it is clear that it would maximize utility to avoid destroying all life on earth.

As I construe it, hedonistic act utilitarianism is a *normative* theory. It is not an account of our common ethical beliefs, since it may well conflict with them, nor is it put forward as an explanation of them. Indeed if the theory did not conflict in some measure with ordinarily accepted ethical ideas there would be little practical importance in putting it forward.[4] Since hedonistic utilitarianism is put forward as a normative theory, the proponent of it must resist supposed refutations of it that depend on its conflict with common sense reactions.

UTILITARIANISM AND MOTIVES FOR ACTIONS

Hedonistic act utilitarianism says that the right action is the one that maximizes total happiness. By 'happiness' here is meant a sum of pleasures. (Unhappiness is negative happiness and displeasure is negative pleasure. I prefer to say 'displeasure' rather than 'pain,' since 'pain' is ambiguous. In one sense of these words pleasure and pain are not opposites. An itch or a feeling of loneliness can be unpleasant, but neither is a pain.) Utilitarianism as defined in terms of maximization of pleasure is a case of ethical hedonism. Ethical hedonism is a doctrine of how we ought to act and must not be confused with psychological hedonism, which is a doctrine about how we in fact act. According to psychological hedonism, which is false, we always act for the sake of our own pleasure. . . . I take the utilitarian principle to be the expression of an *overriding* desire or attitude (of benevolence), and this is not incompatible with the existence of subordinate desires, which in some cases may even conflict with the overriding one.[5] Our overriding attitude is what predominates 'in a cool hour,' to use Bishop Butler's expression,[6] and by which we act in such a way as to strengthen or weaken subordinate desires.

As a utilitarian, therefore, I appeal to the motive of generalized benevolence, and hope that if the theory can be stated lucidly it will appeal to those who have generalized benevolence as an overriding attitude. This may enable already benevolent persons to exercise their benevolence with clearer heads in the light of a definite ethical theory. Nevertheless the utilitarian will not suppose that his overriding attitude ought always or even generally be made the motive for action.[7] Happiness mainly comes from satisfying all sorts of more humdrum desires. Furthermore there are motives such as family affection, loyalty to an institution, and so on that can be more powerful in affecting action, and provided that on the whole they tend in the right direction then on utilitarian grounds the utilitarian will encourage actions from these motives. As Sidgwick remarked, universal benevolence is not the only right or the best motive for action. Similarly, it is not possible or even desirable, to be calculating consequences all the time, and a utilitarian will normally act according to common sense rules, such as to keep promises, so long as they tend towards the maximization of happiness. On the other hand suppose that rules conflict, or for some other reason the utilitarian does think it worth while to calculate consequences. In such a case if the utilitarian has good reason to believe that on the particular occasion in question conformity to these rules will not maximize happiness, then he or she will ignore the rules: he or she will take these as mere rules of thumb.[8]

This attitude conflicts with so-called 'rule utilitarianism' according to which we do not judge actions directly by consequences, but by their conformity with rules, these rules being judged by the consequences of everyone obeying them being better than the consequences of everyone obeying some alternative rule. 'Rule utilitarianism' is contrasted with 'act utilitarianism'. The act utilitarian will object that if he or she knows that in a particular case disobeying a generally optimific rule will maximize happiness, it would be sheer rule worship to obey the rule.[9]

An act utilitarian, on his or her own principles, will not want to think as a utilitarian all the time. Moreover he or she will have a genuine worry about whether it is right to try to persuade the general public to become utilitarians. It may be that this would merely weaken people's propensities to act in accordance with ordinary morality without making them utilitarians so that the end result would be that they would behave in a *less* utilitarian manner. It might be that even if they tried to act in a utilitarian manner they would fail to do so because of lack of skill in calculating consequences, or because of incorrect empirical beliefs. There can be something elitist about act utilitarianism. (Though I am not one of those who believe 'elitist' to be a naughty word!) In the context of nineteenth-century society Sidgwick was probably right in urging extreme tact in a utilitarian's relations with common sense morality. In the context of the late twentieth century, when there is danger of the ultimate catastrophe of nuclear annihilation, not to mention huge problems of overpopulation and famine, I am inclined to think that on utilitarian grounds a utilitarian should try to get utilitarian thinking adopted very widely. Common-sense rules may now give less of an approximation to utilitarian conduct than they used to do, at least in certain overwhelmingly important areas of application. Moreover, as Onora O'Neill has suggested to me, the early Benthamite utilitarians were felt to provide a progressive and reforming critique of existing institutions, at a time when political and economic institutions were inappropriate to an emerging industrial and social order. Unclarities about what happiness was and how to maximize it were less crucial than they have often seemed to non-utilitarian philosophers.

A utilitarian will assess the goodness or badness of dispositions and motives for actions by the utility of praise or blame of the actions. Utility of an action may not correspond exactly or at all with the utility of praise or blame of it.[10] Failure to observe this distinction may cause people to overestimate the clash between common sense ethics and utilitarianism. Thus common sense says that it is not wrong to omit to do supererogatory actions, while a utilitarian cannot admit the notion of supererogation, because nothing can be better than to maximize. However he or she can admit to a distinction between acts that are wrong but for which an agent ought not to be blamed or punished and acts that are wrong and for which an agent ought to be blamed or punished. A mother may do a wrong act misguidedly but from affection for her child. To blame her might weaken affectionate feelings in the mother and in others. Another example comes from a recent proposal by Michael Slote to modify consequentialism by replacing maximization by 'satisficing', that is, bringing about a certain level of good results.[11] Surely, the utilitarian will say, if one has a choice between satisficing and maximizing one ought to maximize.[12] Nevertheless one may often advise others or decide oneself to aim only at satisficing. Trying to maximize may be too much of a strain and the agent may give up the effort and instead act either from impulse or from conventional rules. It may therefore be useful for the agent to praise satisficers and not blame them for not maximizing. I therefore suspect that the appeal of the satisficing theory, at least for some people, may come from confusing questions of the rightness or wrongness of actions with questions of praise or blame of them. Of course satisficing is more in accordance with utilitarianism if it is taken as an economic doctrine. It is always better to have more happiness rather than less, but there is a level of wealth above which an increase produces no significant increase in happiness, or may even produce a decrease in happiness.

CO-OPERATION

Situations of the type of the well-known Prisoner's Dilemma (except for all participants being actuated by universal benevolence instead of self-interest) provide some difficulty for act utilitarianism. Consider the following simplified case. Suppose that there is an important university committee with 100 eligible participants, all of whom, if they attend, will be sure to vote beneficially on an important issue, which is such that it is important that most of the eligible participants attend. If one of the members is an act utilitarian he or she may reason that most members will behave conventionally, as they have been brought up to do, and will turn up. As he or she has valuable other work to get on with, he or she will go on to deduce that the best outcome will be achieved if he or she stays away. But what if all the 100 are act utilitarians? Perhaps there will

not even be a quorum and the consequences will be very bad. . . . I am
. . . now attracted to the 'co-operative utilitarianism' recently put forward
by Donald Regan. This theory is in the *spirit* of act utilitarianism and is
quite different from rule utilitarianism. Indeed it reduces to act utilitarianism in those cases (which are very common) in which the agent does
not need to co-operate with other agents.

(In such cases he or she may very well depend on the predictable
behavior of other agents, as when travelling by aeroplane one depends
on the actions of the pilot, without of course co-operating in actually
flying the aeroplane.)

Regan's theory, expounded in his important book, *Utilitarianism and
Co-operation,* [13] is roughly that in a situation requiring co-operation, each
agent should co-operate with other co-operators so as to maximize utility.[14] The behavior of non-co-operators will be an empirical fact to be
taken into account like any other. The difficulty arises from a sort of
circularity in the co-operative situation. Without going into Regan's own
subtle and complex analysis, let me merely remark that we could think
of a group of co-operating agents who behave according to Regan's
principles as a single supra-personal agent which behaves in a simply act
utilitarian way.[15] After all, different parts of a single brain co-operate
with one another, and it need not be objectionably metaphysical to think
of a group of co-operating brains (not necessarily in causal interaction
with one another) as a single spatially scattered super-brain. In cases in
which co-operation is not needed, as when a rescuer dives into a river,
with no other helper in the vicinity, the supra-personal agent will reduce
to a single personal one and the theory will reduce to ordinary act
utilitarianism.[16] . . .

Utilitarian thinking has practical importance (assuming that it is
adopted) in so far as it differs from common sense and traditional moral
thinking. An important respect in which this is so is that utilitarianism
leaves no room for ordinary moral notions of justice and of rights. This
does not mean, however, that a utilitarian may not support legal and
customary rules of justice and of rights. He or she may hold that such
rules, enforceable either legally or by pressure of public opinion, may
be extremely useful. Indeed the utilitarian may endeavor to modify these
legal and customary institutions in the cause of utility, if he or she thinks
that they need modifying. Jeremy Bentham did much to reform the
English legal system, by continually asking of its rules and traditions
'What's the use of it?' . . .

Utilitarianism leads to a different political philosophy from those of
two influential writers, John Rawls[17] and Robert Nozick.[18] In connection with Rawls I mention the fact that he bases his theory on the
principle of 'maximin'.[19] Out of various alternative actions, each with
various possible outcomes, the maximin strategy is to choose the one
with the most favorable worst possible outcome. In contrast, a utilitarian
will maximize expected utility. A utilitarian will also disagree with

Rawls's 'difference principle'—the principle of doing only that which will make the worst off person in a society better off. This can conflict with maximizing total expected utility. As for Nozick, in the preface to his *Anarchy, State and Utopia* [20] he baldly asserts 'Individuals have rights,' which takes a utilitarian's breath away, as the utilitarian will certainly not accept this axiom, and will therefore be unwilling to accept the recommendations that Nozick draws from it in the book, some of which conclusions the utilitarian will reject as inimical to the general happiness.

Utilitarianism is particularly favourable to the present expansion of concern for non-human animals. Indeed, Jeremy Bentham expressed the matter very well when he said, 'The question is not, Can they reason? nor Can they talk? but Can they suffer?'[21]

Sidgwick argued that conventional moral rules have grown up and survived, for the most part but not completely, because of their utility. However, we now live in a much more dangerous and quickly changing world than Sidgwick did, mainly because of the pace of technological change. A terrible instance of this is the rapid increase in the sophistication and destructiveness of military weapons. Developments in biology, with the possible application of techniques such as genetic engineering to humans, will obviously give rise to awesome and unprecedented decisions of social choice—if indeed decisions are made and the situation does not simply develop in an uncontrolled way. Furthermore, consider the problems connected with the population explosion (itself a product of medical and sanitary technology). It is likely therefore that useful as conventional ethical principles have been in the past, they may in the future sometimes be counter-productive. A striking example of this is the obvious inapplicability of the so-called Protestant work ethic to an age of automation and robotics.

Notes

[1] Jeremy Bentham, *The Principles of Morals and Legislation.*

[2] Henry Sidgwick, *The Methods of Ethics,* 7th edition (Indianapolis: Hackett Publishing Company, 1981).

[3] Some of Mill's remarks have led some critics to ascribe to him the view of rule utilitarianism that one should obey rules, though these rules are assessed by the utility of general obedience to these rules. There is also doubt as to how far Mill should be regarded as a hedonist.

[4] Cf. Sidgwick, op. cit., p. 425. Sidgwick did also hold that utilitarian estimates of consequences do to a considerable extent explain the survival of common sense moral rules, and also explain the admitted limitations and need for qualification of these rules. (See p. 425 again.)

[5] See my paper 'Benevolence as an Over-Riding Attitude', *Australasian Journal of Philosophy* 55 (1977), 127–135.

[6] See Joseph Butler, *Sermon XI,* paragraph 20. In *Fifteen Sermons and A Dissertation on the Nature of Virtue,* with Introduction, Analyses and Notes by W. R. Matthews (London: Bell, 1953).

[7]Sidgwick, op. cit., p. 413 and pp. 432 ff.

[8]R. M. Hare does not like this talk of rules of thumb, but nevertheless I have a good deal of respect for his theory of two levels of moral thinking, as expounded in his *Moral Thinking* (Oxford: Clarendon Press, 1981).

[9]Cf. my paper 'Extreme and Restricted Utilitarianism', in Philippa Foot (ed.), *Theories of Ethics* (Oxford University Press, 1967). As I discovered more recently, similar objections (to Paley's form of rule utilitarianism) were put into the mouth of a hypothetical 'sophistical' utilitarian opponent by the eighteenth century anti-utilitarian moralist, Thomas Green. See the extract from Thomas Green's *An Examination of the Leading Principle in the New System of Morals* in D.H. Monro (ed.), *A Guide to the British Moralists* (London: Fontana, 1972), pp. 198–203, especially p. 201.

[10]See Sidgwick, op. cit., pp. 428–429.

[11]See the symposium between Michael Slote and Philip Pettit, 'Satisficing Consequentialism'. *Aristotelian Society,* supp. vol. 58 (1984). Slote is a pluralist consequentialist, not a hedonistic utilitarian. His notion of satisficing is a modification of a proposal in economics by H.A. Simon. See references in Pettit, op. cit., p. 166 footnote.

[12]Compare Philip Pettit's somewhat similar comments, ibid.

[13]Donald Regan, *Utilitarianism and Co-operation* (Oxford: Clarendon Press, 1980). Indeed on p. 198 Regan rather generously suggests that in my discussion of the mixed strategy method I was 'in a hazy fashion and in a specific sort of case' groping for the co-operative utilitarian theory. I think that I was probably even more confused than this suggests.

[14]Ibid., p. 11.

[15]See B.C. Postow, 'Generalized Act Utilitarianism', *Analysis* 37 (1977), 49–52.

[16]Each co-operative utilitarian has to identify the class of people with whom he or she is to co-operate. Could this empirical information be used by him or her to reason in a purely act utilitarian way? (As in David Lewis, 'Utilitarianism and Truthfulness', *Australasian Journal of Philosophy* 50 (1972), 17–19). This seems to work in the 2-person case, but in the case of *n* persons, for large *n,* each may think that he or she can do more good by acting differently, since there will still be sufficient co-operation. But if *each* reasons this way there will *not* be sufficient co-operators. So after all there does seem to be an important difference between co-operative utilitarianism and act utilitarianism. (On the importance of the many person case *cf.* Derek Parfit, *Reasons and Persons* (Oxford: Clarendon Press, 1984), p. 59 at bottom.)

[17]John Rawls, *A Theory of Justice* (Harvard University Press, 1971).

[18]Robert Nozick, *Anarchy, State and Utopia* (Oxford: Blackwells, 1974).

[19]John Harsanyi in effect anticipated Rawls's method of deducing an ethical system from what a group of self-interested persons in an 'original position' would decide should be the rules. (I see little merit in this method, and I do not see what an original position, in which I am not and never have been, has to do with the price of fish. I prefer to found ethics directly on a sentiment of generalized benevolence.) However, Harsanyi reasonably rejected 'maximin' and used expected utility instead. As he has pointed out, one would not take an aeroplane trip if one were to use maximin! (There is a small probability of the plane crashing.) Using expected utility instead of maximin, Harsanyi deduced a form of rule utilitarianism, very different from Rawls's non-utilitarian system. See J.C. Harsanyi, 'Cardinal Utility in Welfare Economics and in the Theory of Risk Taking', *Journal of Political Economy* 61 (1953), 434–435, 'Cardinal Welfare, Individualistic Ethics, and Interpersonal Comparisons of Utility', *Journal of Political Economy* 63 (1955), 309–321, and 'Can the Maximin Principle Serve as a Basis for Morality?' in Harsanyi's book *Essays on Ethics, Social Behaviour and Scientific Explanation* (Dordrecht-Holland: D. Reidel,

1976). This last paper contains a postscript replying to some objections in John Rawls, 'Some Reasons for the Maximin Criterion,' *American Economic Review* 64 (1974), 141–146.

[20]Op. cit.

[21]See the long footnote to paragraph 4 of Section 1 of Chapter XVII of Jeremy Bentham's *Principles of Morals and Legislation.* See also Peter Singer's criticisms of 'speciesism' in his *Animal Liberation* (New York: Random House, 1975). Concern for non-humans should also extend to extra-terrestrials, should we come across such.

RICHARD B. BRANDT
THE REAL AND ALLEGED PROBLEMS OF UTILITARIANISM

Everybody believes that some actions, or types of action, are morally right or wrong; or that it is a person's moral obligation to do, or to avoid doing, these actions. Many philosophers, however, have wanted to introduce some order into this chaos of opinions, and have sought to find a small number of fundamental principles of right and wrong from which all justified moral beliefs can be deduced, given relevant factual information. A few philosophers—among them Immanuel Kant, with his famous "categorical imperative," and recently John Rawls, with his emphasis on justice—have thought that we can make do with just one fundamental principle. The oldest of such one-principle theories, which has shown vitality and appeal for philosophers for thousands of years, is utilitarianism, the view that the benefit or harm done by an act, or class of actions, or prohibition of an act-type, determines whether it is wrong or right morally. If acts of incest or homosexual contact or deceit are wrong, for example, it is because the acts or practice or traits of character they involve have impact for good or ill, happiness or unhappiness.

Unfortunately from the point of view of simplicity, there are different kinds of utilitarianism. One of them is "act-utilitarianism"—the thesis that a particular act is right if, and only if, no other act the agent could perform at the time would have, or probably would have (on the agent's evidence), better consequences. Such important philosophers as G. E. Moore, Henry Sidgwick, and Bertrand Russell advocated this view at about the turn of the century. A second form, which is older and probably more influential among philosophers at present, is "rule-utilitarianism"; its thesis is roughly that an act is morally right if, and only if, it would be as beneficial to have a moral code permitting that act as to have any moral code that is similar but prohibits the act. There are other types of utilitarianism, but these two seem most important now. . . .

Philosophers who criticize utilitarianism usually center their fire on the first form of the theory (act-utilitarianism). Unfortunately they often

From *Hastings Center Report* 13, 2 (April 1983): 37–43. Reproduced by permission. © The Hastings Center.

imply, if not state, that this criticism disposes of utilitarianism in all its forms. This is a mistake. Adherents of rule-utilitarianism are themselves quite critical of act-utilitarianism, although the theories are fairly closely related, especially when evaluation of a long-range public policy is the issue.

In what follows I shall discuss rule-utilitarianism, since it seems to me more plausible. The choice is not eccentric; despite the number of thoughtful advocates today of act-utilitarianism I believe most philosophers who advocate utilitarianism today are in the rule-utilitarian camp. Another reason for concentrating on rule-utilitarianism is that some of its problems have not received comparable attention.

WHAT IS RULE-UTILITARIANISM?

. . . However, rule-utilitarianism as a theory of *action*—not of right laws—goes back at least as far as Richard Cumberland in 1672. Bishop Berkeley, in his *Passive Obedience* (1712), was the first to distinguish clearly between the two forms of utilitarianism, and he opted for the second. More specifically, he asserted that we are not morally bound to do whatever we believe will produce most good or happiness, but we are morally bound to follow certain moral laws, prohibiting or enjoining certain types of action—these being God's laws as identified by revelation or natural reason. These laws have been selected by God because, in his benevolence, he wants the happiness of mankind and knows that following these laws will maximize it. God, incidentally, also lets it be known that it will not be to the long-range interest of anyone to infringe his laws; so the theory provides motivation to do what is right. Now, if the part about God is deleted from Berkeley's view, what remains is the skeleton of much the kind of rule-utilitarianism I wish to discuss. This is the view roughly held by J. S. Mill; we of course have to flesh out the account a bit.

First, we have to think of the morality of a society: that is, of people in the society mostly sharing certain aversions to or desires for (partly as a matter of innate or learned benevolence, but partly as a result of a process of motivational learning we need not try to specify) certain types of actions. These presumably will include aversions to hurting others, telling lies, and breaking promises. But there are also learned dispositions to experience guilt in case we act contrary to these aversions, and disapproval of others when they act contrary. We also admire others who do what we say is above and beyond the call of duty. Further, we disapprove of, and are averse to, various kinds of acts in different degrees: we would not commit murder and we disapprove intensely of anyone who does (without excuse); we also don't like it very much when a person brushes off a request for a match, but our disapproval is slight, and we feel only mild aversion to doing the same thing. Consciences are also equipped with a system of excuses; we don't feel guilty, or at least don't disapprove so vigorously of others, if we believe infractions are the result of certain conditions, say, ignorance, insanity, extreme fear, and so on.

This motivational description of conscience may not be appealing, but most of it appears in Mill's third chapter, and to some extent in the fifth chapter, of *Utilitarianism*. To my mind that *is* conscience, and the morality of a society is nothing more than the consciences of its members; or, if you like, the conscience of the average person.

If this is what a morality—or moral code—is, what is a "rule-utilitarian"? A rule-utilitarian thinks that right actions are the kind permitted by the moral code optimal for the society of which the agent is a member. An optimal code is one designed to maximize welfare or what is good (thus, utility). This leaves open the possibility that a particular right act by itself may not maximize benefit.

This definition does not imply anything about what a utilitarian means by "right" or "optimal," or about how a utilitarian will justify the main thesis. Utilitarians need not have any particular account of the meaning of these terms, and they need not offer any particular justification of their thesis; they can simply advocate the utilitarian principle.

On the rule-utilitarian view, then, to find what is morally right or wrong we need to find which actions would be permitted by a moral system that is "optimal" for the agent's society.

THE FIRST REAL PUZZLE

The last phrase in this definition raises the first "problem" or "puzzle" I wish to discuss—for an agent's society will comprise various subgroups, and it could be that the moral code optimal for one may not be optimal for others. For instance, perhaps the moral code comprising the consciences of physicians and lawyers should be more clearly articulated in certain areas than the moral code of the general public. There is no reason to burden the general public with, say, aversion to refusing to treat patients who cannot pay, or breaches of confidentiality. Remember that we have to include the learning-costs in a cost-benefit analysis of a moral system. That being so, perhaps the rule-utilitarian must recognize special moralities for groups like physicians who, unlike the general public, meet certain problems regularly and need to respond to them intuitively without long inference from general principles. Similarly, it is possible that the morality optimal for children is not the morality optimal for adults. Rule-utilitarians, then, may be free to think that the moral codes justified for physicians, lawyers, children, bishops, and university students will differ. The identification of such possible special codes is part of the subject matter of "professional ethics."

This conception raises a difficult question that I shall not try to answer. Could the optimal moral code for a physician or a politician or an army officer direct a person to do something incompatible with what the optimal code for the general public would prescribe for the same situation? Presumably we *do* think that the optimal code for one society might lead to behavior incompatible with behavior required by the optimal code for another society. If that is possible, what is the really right thing to do when these codes conflict? For a rule-utilitarian who thinks that the actions of governments may be morally right or wrong, there is a related question. Must we talk of an "optimal moral code" for governments? Can we think of governments as quasi-persons, and talk of an optimal conscience for them? Or may we talk not of the acts of governments being right or wrong, but only of the morally right or wrong acts of office-holders or politicians? Rule-utilitarians should think more about this. . . .

THE SECOND PUZZLE

The rule-utilitarian, then, says that right action is action permitted by the moral code for society that would maximize net-benefit or utility. But what is meant to count as benefit or utility? The traditional answer has been: pleasure, hedonic tone (positive or negative), or happiness. So said Bentham, Mill, and the earlier theological utilitarians. Now many philosophers argue that this is not what we should try to maximize, and that anyone who thinks this way is taking a crude view of human nature. What then should we add? J. L. Mackie suggests in *Ethics: Inventing Right and Wrong* (1977): "Liberty of thought and discussion, thought and discussion themselves, understanding of all sorts of things, including ourselves and other human beings, a self-reliant, enterprising, and experimental spirit and way of life, artistic creation and craftmanship of any sort, the enjoyment and appreciation of beauty, and general participatory self-government both in smaller institutions and in the determination of large scale social policies and laws" (p. 150). He says this in criticism of utilitarianism of all kinds. Is utilitarianism in all its forms committed to a hopelessly narrow view of what is good?

There is no *logical* connection between either act- or rule-utilitarianism and hedonism, and none between a deontological ethics and non-hedonism. True, the utilitarian says we are to identify right action by appeal to maximizing net benefit or utility, but he leaves the definition of these terms open. Indeed, one can say: we should maximize what is intrinsically good, and go on to say, as "ideal utilitarians" like Moore and Rashdall did, that various states of affairs quite different from pleasure are intrinsically good—say, knowledge, virtue, and friendship. One could then say, as these ideal utilitarians did, that the right action is fixed by maximizing the intrinsically good, and then propose that one can make justified comparative judgments about the intrinsic worth of knowledge, virtue, and the like so as to determine, roughly, when the good is being maximized.

However, this heterogeneity of intrinsic goods should surely be avoided, if possible. For different persons, with different intuitions about how intrinsically good some of these things are, can come out in very different places in their estimates of the total goodness that one action or moral code is likely to produce, as compared with another. So philosophers have wanted to find a view that does not rely so much on intuitions. This is one consideration that makes hedonism attractive; for the hedonist holds that only one sort of thing is good in itself, so the question of which code or action maximizes the good can be reduced to a factual question of how much enjoyment is produced. But there is another theory that avoids both reliance on intuitions and the alleged narrowness of the hedonist view. This is the view that "utility" is to be defined not in terms of pleasure, but of *satisfaction of desires or interest.* Whereas the hedonist says state of affairs X is better than state of affairs Y if it contains more pleasure, the desire-satisfactionist says X is better than Y if there is more preference for X over Y than for Y over X. This last sounds a bit complex, but many people who have observed betting behavior think that cardinal numbers can be assigned to a person's desires: if so, then, if the strengths among different persons' desires can be compared and we can determine how many people prefer X over Y (or Y over X) and by how much, we have a way to aggregate preferences of a society. So, ideally (just as does the traditional hedonist view, assuming pleasures can be measured) the interest-satisfaction theory provides a way to identify which policy or behavior would maximize desire-satisfaction.

Thus hedonism and the desire theory have emerged as leading contenders for a conception of utility suited for a simple maximizing theory of right and wrong conduct—simple in the sense that essentially there is only one sort of thing that is good in itself. The second theory is probably more popular today, for one or more of three reasons. First, it allows many things to be good—anything wanted for itself. Second, it seems easier to measure the strength of desires than an amount of pleasure. Third, the desire theory may seem more democratic; it goes on the basis of what people actually want, not on the basis of what will give them happiness—we are not to deny people what they want just because we think it will make them happier in the long run.[1]

From a practical point of view, the two theories are not all that different, since there is a close relation between desire and pleasure. People want to attain pleasant states and avoid unpleasant ones, other things being equal. Further, other things being equal, getting what one wants is pleasant and not getting it is unpleasant. So there is a close connection between desire and pleasure, but the implications of the two theories are not identical. . . .

I don't think we really want to maximize satisfaction of desire in general. People desire all sorts of things that it is idiotic to desire. At most we should want to maximize the satisfaction of those desires that people *would* have if they were fully informed about everything that might make them change their desires. Call this the "informed desire" theory. Even so, I doubt that we want to maximize desire-satisfaction as such; mostly we are concerned to help people get what they want because we think it will make them happy, whereas not getting it will sadden or frustrate them. There is a further complicated point that I cannot develop. People's desires are continually changing. So which desires should one try to satisfy at any time? Only the unchanging desires? The desires the person has now but won't have later? Desires the person will have at the time he is to get what he now wants? It is very difficult to find any convincing formulation.

The utilitarian, then, has to decide upon his conception of the "utility" which, when maximized, is the test of right and wrong. He ought to think more about this choice. But the charge that the utilitarian is committed to a crude or narrow view of what is good seems manifestly mistaken. . . .

THE THIRD PUZZLE

For the sake of simplicity let us assume from here on that we are opting for a hedonist conception of "utility." Let us think of pleasure as being measurable, so that the basic unit is a "hedon-moment"—an experience, for one minute, with a pleasure level of plus one. We shall speak of "hedon-moments" having a negative value when the pleasure level is negative. An experience for one minute with a hedonic tone of level plus two would be two hedon-moments, just as an experience for two minutes with hedonic tone or level plus one. And so on.

Given these concepts, we might say that moral system A produces more utility than moral system B if and only if the net balance of hedon-moments from getting A current in the society and keeping it there would be, or would probably be, greater than the net balance from getting B into place and keeping it there. When a system A is more satisfactory in this sense than any other system, we can say that A is the optimal moral system, and that its content fixes which acts are morally right or wrong. . . .

THE FIRST ALLEGED PROBLEM

I now take leave of puzzles, thought about which might lead us to some refinements of rule-utilitarianism, and turn to just plain objections that have been raised against rule-utilitarianism in any form. The ones I shall discuss are related, and together they may be viewed as variations on a charge of Utopianism.

In order to appraise these objections, I must expand still more the conception of an "optimal" moral code. The term does not refer to a set of rules that would do most good if everyone conformed to them all the time. The meaning is more complex. Recall that "a moral code" is a set of desires or aversions directed at certain types of acts, and the disposition to feel guilty about not conforming to these desires or aversions, as

well as to disapprove of such failure to conform on the part of others
when they have no excuse. Now these dispositions may vary both in their
intensity, and in their prevalence in a given society. The more intense
and widespread an aversion to a certain sort of behavior, the less frequent the behavior is apt to be. But the more intense and widespread,
the greater the cost of teaching the rule and keeping it alive, the greater
the burden on the individual, and so on.

The "optimality" of a moral code encompasses both the benefits of
reduced objectionable behavior and the long-term cost. So the moral
code optimal for a given society is that whole system, with a given degree
of average intensity, and spread among the population, for each of its
components, that comes out best in a cost-benefit analysis. Needless to
say, like the law, the optimal moral code normally will not produce 100
percent compliance with all its rules; that would be too costly. It may do
so in small homogeneous populations: physical violence is unheard of on
the Hopi reservation. But mostly not. According to our conception, the
rule-utilitarian believes that an act is prima facie obligatory if and only
if (and to the degree that) such an optimal code would build in some
degree of moral aversion to not performing it.

The first objection to this view is that it would be harmful for some
people to live according to the optimal code, in a society where the
optimal code is not widespread, for so doing could be either pointless
or injurious. For instance, the optimal moral code might call for no one
ever to carry a lethal weapon, whereas living by such a code would not
be a good idea, these critics say, in a society where most persons are
trigger-happy gun-carrying demons. Furthermore, it is especially incoherent for a utilitarian to advocate behaving in such a counterproductive
way; his basic thesis is that utility is the point of morality, but here the
rule-utilitarian seems to be advocating behavior that is likely to be harmful.

There is an adequate reply to this objection: it has not been shown
that such harmful requirements would ever appear in an optimal moral
code. In the gun-carrying society, an optimal moral code would surely
give directions to be prepared to defend one's self and one's family, but
of course to defend only. The rule might be: "Never carry a gun when
it can be done at no personal risk; otherwise carry a gun but use it only
in self-defense." (An actual moral code would rarely include injunctions
as specific as this but it might, if a rule were aimed at meeting a specific
problem about which more abstract principles were not much help.) An
optimal moral code may not always provide for doing the very best
possible thing in every situation; morality is a blunt instrument, like the
law. But no proof has been offered that an optimal code would prescribe
doing seriously harmful things as a result of the optimal moral code not
being widely accepted in the society. True, an optimal code might well
tell one to keep a promise when few others are doing so, and this might
do little immediate good; but at least it would be a step in building a
convention of promise-keeping. . . .

TWO FINAL ALLEGED PROBLEMS

Thus far I have said nothing about two rocks upon which many philosophers think utilitarianism in all its forms must necessarily founder: the moral demand for economic equality, and the moral requirement for legal punishment only where and to the extent it is deserved. Philosophical critics of utilitarianism suppose that there are here certain well-founded moral injunctions about both distributive and retributive justice and that these are inconsistent with the implications of utilitarianism in all its forms.

I shall limit my comments to the first charge, which strikes me as the more serious, but what I say about the first can in principle be transposed to a discussion about the second.

If we look at present legislation regarding the welfare of the poor or underprivileged in the United States, we find aid to dependent children, the food stamp program, a limited program of negative income tax, a Medicaid program to take care of the health of those who are less well off, and an assistance program for the aged, the blind, and the disabled. How is all this paid for? Mostly out of general funds: from a progressive income tax on those who are more well off. Now I do not suggest that this system is perfect; far from it. But every one of the provisions of the system—which after all is a system for the redistribution of income—can be defended on utilitarian grounds. The utilitarian justification for all this is that a dollar taken in taxes from the wealthy would have done the wealthy far less good than the same dollar spent providing food stamps, medical care, and so on for the poor or handicapped. All this the utilitarian can defend, and it is easy to see that application of the utilitarian criterion for optimal institutions moves in the direction of economic equality for all.

True, utilitarians do not take equality as an end in itself; the move in the direction of equality is advocated only because maximizing the general welfare can be attained only by more equality. Utilitarians also do not favor taking steps that would diminish the general welfare just for the sake of equality—for instance, perhaps, giving a great deal of extra income to a disabled person in order to make up for a natural disability. (Neither, incidentally, as far as I can see, does Rawls's theory.) But when we see how far a utilitarian theory does take us toward economic equality, we can well wonder how much farther the critics of utilitarianism would like to go. How large a percentage of the gross national product would they want diverted for the achievement of more equality than the utilitarian would ask for, and exactly how would they want it distributed? I suggest that when we reflect on how much economic equality we want in society, we shall not think that the implications of utilitarianism fall short. Many attacks on utilitarianism suppose that we are in a position to distribute happiness, not money, and it is said that a utilitarian must be oblivious of any inequalities in happiness, however great, so long as the maximum amount of happiness has been produced. But this charge, while true, ignores the fact that the utilitarian theory does provide against severe deprivation of happiness, as in the case of a disabled person, on the ground that such provision is the best investment of national resources. As far as I can see, the response of the utilitarian to the charge of an unsatisfactory theory of distributive justice comes off very well.

Notes

[1] Actually, one could argue with some force that Mill, who is supposed to be a hedonist, was straddling the two. For he takes the odd view that virtue and wealth are *parts* of happiness. He has often been accused of confusion here, and doubtless he was confused. What he had good reason for saying was only that people *want* things like money and virtue, and may be made unhappy by not obtaining them. Could he have confused being desired and being pleasant? On a later page he seems to confirm such a confusion by saying that "desiring a thing and finding it pleasant . . . are two different modes of naming the same psychological fact" (*Utilitarianism*, Ch. 4).

part II

APPLICATIONS

chapter *4*

*A*bortion

INTRODUCTION

Is it morally permissible to obtain an abortion? Is abortion ever a violation of the moral rights of the fetus? Should abortion be legally prohibited? Is the choice of obtaining an abortion ever the expression of a morally blameworthy trait of character (for instance, selfishness)? These are only some of the many distinct normative questions concerning abortion. An argument advanced in answer to one question may also have implications for the answer to another, but these implications are seldom as obvious as might at first appear. This chapter will concentrate on the first two questions and the relationship between them. But the third question deserves some attention initially, if only to clarify the boundaries of the dispute.

The Legal Question   The current public debate concerning abortion is largely the result of changes in the law in the United States and in Canada. In *Roe* v. *Wade* (1973) the Supreme Court of the United States ruled that the right of privacy includes a right to terminate pregnancy; this right, however, is not absolute; after the first three months of pregnancy, states may regulate abortion to safeguard the health of the pregnant woman and to maintain medical standards, and, during the final three months of pregnancy, states may protect fetal life, though not at the expense of the life or health of the mother.[1] Legal abortions are obtainable in many other nations. In 1988 the Canadian Supreme Court struck down the federal law that had allowed abortion only to preserve the physical or mental health of the pregnant woman. The court ruled that such restrictions on the freedom of pregnant women violate the Charter of Rights and Freedoms. The legislature has the power under the Canadian constitution to adopt new legislation specifically excluding the application of the Charter, or it can pass legislation conforming to the court's interpretation of the Charter. In the United States, the legislature cannot by statute change the present legal situation. Those seeking a change press for anti-abortion appointments to the Supreme Court, or for the adoption of a constitutional amendment either to allow the states to prohibit abortion by statute, or, more directly, to give constitutional protection to the rights of human fetuses. Many are now asking whether there should be a return to prohibition of abortion in the criminal law.

Many of those seeking criminalization of abortion base their demand for the illegality of abortion on the claim that abortion is morally wrong. In its strongest form, the view states that, morally, abortion is the killing of the innocent and thus the moral equivalent of murder. Weaker versions claim only that abortion violates the moral rights of the fetus and that the criminal law should give legal protection to those moral rights. Assuming for the moment that under some conditions abortion is a violation of the moral rights of the fetus, does it follow that abortion should be illegal under those conditions?

Even the natural-law theorists restrict the legitimate scope of law to a class of wrongs less extensive than the whole class of moral wrongs. Saint Thomas Aquinas, for instance, holds that "human laws do not forbid all vices . . . but only the more grievous vices . . . , and chiefly those that are injurious to others, without the prohibition of which human society could not be maintained."[2] But, argue some of the proponents of criminalization, abortion is the killing of an innocent human being (or, at least, a serious violation of the moral rights of the fetus), and this is a clear-cut case of the *kind* of wrong that should also be illegal. The law exists, it is argued, to protect individuals against infringements of their basic rights. Baruch Brody, for instance, has argued that it is not consistent to hold that abortion is the moral equivalent of murder while opposing recriminalization.[3]

If abortion is understood as a serious violation of the moral rights of the fetus, then it may be said to be a crime with a "victim," as opposed to such victimless crimes as homosexual acts between consenting adults. When victimless moral wrongs are at issue, there is a strong argument that the moral views of some should not be forced upon all through the coercion of the law. But whether the fetus can properly be considered a victim is debatable and is an important part of the moral dispute. It is this peculiarity that makes the legal question about abortion so difficult to extricate from the moral questions surrounding it.

The Supreme Court attempted to extricate itself from the moral controversy by denying that the judiciary could resolve the issue of when human life begins if physicians, theologians, and philosophers were unable to reach a consensus. The Court then turned to legal precedent, arguing that the law has never recognized the unborn as persons in the whole sense. Daniel Callahan has argued that the Court first announced its unwillingness to intervene where there was no consensus, and then, in fact, decided the matter by denying fetuses full legal personhood.[4]

But perhaps there is some sense in the Supreme Court's apparent inconsistency. It can be argued that, however unclearly, the Court did keep separate the questions of the moral status and the legal status of the unborn. The Court may be interpreted as claiming that the judiciary may not set aside the precedents of the law in order to take sides in a moral or theological dispute. Although *Roe* v. *Wade* broke new legal ground, it did not deviate from settled law in holding that the unborn are not legal persons in the whole sense. Indeed, statutes prohibiting abortion would not have existed if the unborn had been protected, as full legal persons, by the laws against homicide. The novelty of *Roe* v. *Wade* is its extension of the right of privacy to the choice to obtain an abortion, an extension that could not have been made if the law recognized the unborn as full legal persons.

A comparable argument could be made that since there is moral disagreement about the status of the unborn, there should not be a constitutional amendment making the unborn full legal persons. It can be claimed that in a pluralistic, democratic society, the Constitution itself must not become partisan concerning disputed moral and religious issues. But this argument has less force than the Court's, since it is one function of amendments to the Constitution to change basic law. Even such changes, however, can be judged by standards of consistency with the most fundamental principles embedded in the Constitution.

And so it may be possible to hold simultaneously that abortion is a serious violation of the moral rights of the fetus and yet not seek recriminalization of abortion within a pluralistic, democratic society. However, the contrary view has not been clearly refuted. It remains possible to argue with Brody that pluralism is no argument for allowing the moral equivalent of murder.

Is abortion the killing of an innocent human being? Is it a violation of the moral rights of the fetus? These questions could be definitively answered *only* if the fundamental dispute between competing ethical theories were resolved—something that has yet to be done.

Natural Law   According to natural-law theory, it is always wrong to kill the innocent intentionally. Each human life is incommensurably valuable, and so it is always wrong to act on the intention to kill an innocent human being, either as a means to a further end or as an end in itself.

But is a fetus an innocent human being in the relevant sense? It is clear that in the natural-law view the unborn are included in the moral category of human beings from the moment of conception. To be human in the morally relevant sense is to be a member of a natural kind differentiated by rationality from other natural kinds. From conception, the new organism is an individual member of such a rational species. (Although no other rational species is known, if a rational species other than *Homo sapiens* were discovered, the same view would be taken of them.) The fetus has not yet developed his rationality, but the newborn infant has also not developed his rationality. Nevertheless, from the perspective of natural law both fetus and newborn infant are human beings in the moral sense.

Are the unborn *innocent* in the relevant sense? This is a much more difficult question to answer within the theory of natural law. Certainly most fetuses are innocent, in all senses, but it can be argued that if the woman's life is endangered by continuing the pregnancy, the fetus is not materially innocent. In self-defense, it is permissible to kill not only an aggressor (who is formally culpable) but also someone formally innocent (for instance, an insane person) whose actions *in fact* constitute a mortal threat. If the fetus whose continued growth threatens the life of the mother is morally like such a nonresponsible insane person, then abortions to protect the life of the pregnant woman can be justified even within the terms of natural-law theory.

If this comparison is rejected (as in current official Roman Catholic teaching), then direct abortion will be considered wrong even in order to save the life of the pregnant woman. Only "indirect" abortions will be justifiable—for instance, the removal of a cancerous uterus. In such cases the doctrine of double effect is used to argue that the action causes the death of the innocent fetus only as an unintended side effect. The intention is to save the woman's life by removing her cancerous uterus; it is incidental that there is a fetus there, and the operation would have had to be performed even if the woman had not been pregnant.

Natural-law theory thus prohibits all direct abortion, or, if the fetus is considered materially not innocent when endangering the woman's life, all direct abortion except to save the pregnant woman's life. Within natural-law theory an argument may be made that a fetus conceived as a result of rape is not materially innocent; but since the woman's life is not endangered, the appeal to the rightfulness of self-defense will be more strained than it would be in the case of an actual danger to life.

Natural Rights   It is more difficult to apply the theory of natural rights to abortion. The fundamental natural-rights principle is that one ought to respect the individual rights of others. Since natural law appeals to the precept that each human life is an incommensurable good that may not be destroyed, there is no need for natural-law theorists to settle the question of whether the fetus has rights (though rights are usually ascribed to the fetus from conception, nothing depends upon this ascription).[5] But natural-rights theorists cannot avoid this question.

Much of the debate in the United States about the morality of abortion has centered on the question of whether the fetus has rights (and at what stage of development it has those rights), for the natural-rights approach is central to both legal and moral thought in the United States. If the fetus is not a moral person in the whole sense, just as it is not a legal person in the whole sense, then the pregnant woman's right to obtain an abortion will be vindicated from the viewpoint of natural rights. Even though natural-rights theory *may* recognize some rights of nonpersons (for instance, the right of animals not to be treated cruelly), the individual rights of persons are *always* morally crucial. The woman's right to live her life as she chooses can be limited only by conflicting rights of other persons with the same claim to liberty. If the fetus (at whatever stage) has no such claim or right, then the woman has every right to choose not to carry the fetus full-term.

An even stronger argument for the woman's right to choose has been made by Judith Jarvis Thomson.[6] She has argued that even if the fetus is a person with a right to life, the woman may still, in some circumstances, have the right to choose not to carry it full-term. Thomson compares carrying a fetus to cases of rendering aid (as in the Parable of the Good Samaritan). Within the morality of respect for individual rights, no one has a duty to provide others with aid at any major risk, or even inconvenience, to himself or herself. The right to life is not the right to be provided with what is needed in order to live. The only duties one has to provide for others at serious expense to oneself are duties that result from deliberate assumptions of responsibility; for instance, choosing to rear a child creates such a duty. And so in cases of rape, the woman has no duty to provide the fetus with the use of her womb, even if the fetus is a person with a right to life, for the woman has clearly assumed no such responsibility. And Thomson argues that the woman has no special responsibility for the fetus if she has taken *reasonable* precautions against conception and yet becomes pregnant. Thomson's argument is rooted within the ethical minimalism of the natural-rights tradition. When coupled with her view that the fetus is *not* a person, at least in the early stages of development (and so may be aborted even if the woman is responsible for becoming pregnant), Thomson's natural-rights argument constitutes a forceful defense of the woman's moral right to choose whether to terminate pregnancy.

Kant   Is the fetus a person? This question is important both to natural-rights theory and to a Kantian approach. In Kant's view, there are no direct moral duties to nonpersons. (Our duty not to treat animals cruelly is indirect, for it is justified by the tendency of cruelty to animals to lead to mistreatment of persons.) According both to natural-rights theory and to Kant, freedom and rationality are criteria of personhood. The question then is whether the *potential* for rationality is sufficient for personhood, since neither the fetus nor the infant is actively rational. It would be morally incomprehensible to hold an infant (or a fetus) responsible for anything at all. Does this show that from a Kantian viewpoint, the infant and the fetus are not moral persons?

Kant himself would not have drawn this conclusion, for in applying his theory to cases he usually follows traditional views. Within the compass of Christian morality, infanticide is viewed as murder. And so Kant would not consider active rationality essential to personhood. If the infant can be a person without active rationality, then so can the fetus. It is possible then to be a Kantian and to oppose abortion as a failure to respect the humanity of the fetus as an end in itself.[7]

However, a neo-Kantian approach *can* insist on the criterion of active rationality (or some other stringent criterion) and, therefore, judge the fetus a nonperson. The argument is that the respect owed to persons derives from their status as autonomous, rational beings with goals and values of their own. But a fetus cannot be an object of such respect, for it has no autonomy and no goals. Such stringent criteria for personhood will clearly imply that infants also are nonpersons.

Could a natural-rights theorist or a neo-Kantian consider viability, the ability of the fetus to survive outside of the mother's womb, the point at which the fetus becomes a person? From the Kantian point of view, viability is morally irrelevant, for the rational faculties of the fetus remain merely potential before and after viability. From the natural-rights viewpoint, however, viability may be seen as morally significant, since at the point of viability the new human being can be protected without requiring the woman to give up her own right to live as she chooses. However, this would argue not against the woman's right to terminate but rather for the protection of the viable fetus if pregnancy is terminated.

Contractarianism   The contractarian answer to the moral question of abortion might seem to depend upon whether fetuses are viewed as parties to the contract by which principles of right conduct are determined. Since the contractors are viewed as engaging in rational deliberation, fetuses (and infants) are probably not contractors. However, John Rawls specifies the contractors as "heads of families . . . having a desire to further the welfare of their nearest descendants."[8] Although the parties must themselves be actively rational, they will take into account the welfare of future persons. The neo-Kantian stringency of the criterion of active rationality is thus qualified, but in a way that makes difficult the application of the theory to the abortion issue. The welfare of descendants could be promoted, arguably, by a principle that permitted pregnant women to choose abortion if the quality of life of the child would be minimal (for instance, in the case of birth defects and, perhaps, that of *unwanted* children). When one adds to this concern for the welfare of future persons the self-interest of the contractors (who do not know whether they are men or women), a contractarian approach to abortion will seem very similar to a rule-utilitarian approach.

Rule Utilitarianism   The rule utilitarian seeks to adopt a general rule the acceptance of which will have at least as much net utility as the acceptance of any other rule. (See Chapter 3 for alternative formulations of rule utilitarianism.) Net utility is the balance of happiness over unhappiness resulting as the consequence of accepting the rule. Applied to abortion, this form of rule utilitarianism leads to a permissive view. An early abortion surely causes no unhappiness to the fetus and satisfies the desire of the pregnant woman to free herself of the pregnancy. A moral rule permitting women to choose early abortion seems unproblematic from this viewpoint. Even if there are occasionally desires that are frustrated (for instance, an aspiring father's desire for a child), it is a reasonable general rule that the most intense interests at issue are those of the pregnant woman herself. The future child's own happiness is threatened by any moral rule that requires a woman to continue a pregnancy against her own better judgment. Occasionally, a fetus may be aborted that would have produced more happiness (either in its own life or by benefiting others) than the sum of unhappiness that would have resulted from continuing the pregnancy against the woman's wishes. But generally, better consequences will result from allowing the woman to choose.

In the case of late abortions, the rule-utilitarian argument becomes less clear. At viability, an aborted child is in danger of suffering impaired health if it survives. A moral rule restricting abortions roughly from the time of viability might be justified by the risk to the happiness of the viable child from impaired health, combined with the increased emotional damage risked by the woman (who may not realize until afterward what her own response will be to late abortion).

Act Utilitarianism   An act-utilitarian approach to abortion must consider all facets of each individual case. The pregnant woman's own interests are quite important, but *all* consequences must be considered. Although the *actual* net utility of a particular action determines its rightness, from the viewpoint of a person deliberating whether to abort, the *foreseeable* consequences are all-important. In most cases, it will not be possible to form any reasonable opinion about the future happiness of the potential child; the main exception is where, because of a genetic defect or other known circumstances, the child has a less than normal chance at a decent life. If the woman wants an early abortion, then the *foreseeable* consequences of abortion for her are positive. And so in many cases an act utilitarian will arrive at the moral decision to terminate pregnancy, for the *foreseeable* consequences will be a net gain in happiness.

Abortion after viability, of course, raises new questions and new foreseeable risks. For the act utilitarian, late abortions will probably be justified less frequently than would be early abortions, though there will certainly be cases in which even very late abortion will be accepted as justifiable.

Readings   The selection from Alan Donagan presents the natural-law view that moral duties are owed to human beings from conception. Donagan's ethical theory is Kantian, but he also consciously grounds his thought in Aquinas. This selection is clearly within the natural law tradition.

The essay by R. M. Hare argues that Kantian universalization requires that in general (in ordinary cases) pregnancies ought not to be terminated. But on Hare's view, in some circumstances abortion will be universalizable and so morally right. Many contemporary Kantians use the test of universalization in this flexible manner, allowing detailed descriptions of circumstances to be included in the maxim that is being tested. As Hare notes, his version of universalization is not in conflict with utilitarianism.

The selection from Laura Purdy and Michael Tooley offers a utilitarian defense of the woman's right to choose abortion. After explaining the benefits of allowing abortion, they argue that the fetus has no right to life since it lacks the capacity for self-consciousness.

Notes

[1]*Roe* v. *Wade,* 410 U.S. 113, 93 S. Ct. 705 (1973).

[2]St. Thomas Aquinas, *Summa Theologica,* I–II, Q. 96, trans. Anton Pegis, *The Basic Writings of Saint Thomas Aquinas* (New York: Random House, 1945).

[3]Baruch Brody, *Abortion and the Sanctity of Human Life* (Cambridge, Mass.: MIT Press, 1975), chap. 3.

[4]Daniel Callahan, "Abortion: The New Ruling," in *The Problem of Abortion,* ed. Joel Feinberg (Belmont, Calif.: Wadsworth, 1973), p. 195.

[5]See John Finnis, "The Rights and Wrongs of Abortion," *Philosophy and Public Affairs* 2 (1973): 117–145.

[6]Judith Jarvis Thomson, "A Defense of Abortion," *Philosophy and Public Affairs* 1 (1971): 47–66.

[7]In the first selection below, Alan Donagan presents a traditional natural-law view of the moral status of the fetus within a theoretical framework grounded in both Aquinas and Kant.

[8]John Rawls, *A Theory of Justice* (Cambridge, Mass.: Harvard University Press, 1971), p. 128.

Bibliography on Abortion

Brody, Baruch. *Abortion and the Sanctity of Human Life: A Philosophical View.* Cambridge, Mass.: MIT Press, 1975.

Callahan, Daniel. *Abortion: Law, Choice, and Morality.* New York: Macmillan, 1970.

———. "How Technology is Reframing the Abortion Debate." *Hastings Center Report* 16 (1986): 33–42.

Davis, Michael. "Foetuses, Famous Violinists, and the Right to Continued Aid." *Philosophical Quarterly* 33 (1983): 259–278.

Davis, Nancy. "Abortion and Self-Defense." *Philosophy and Public Affairs* 13 (1984): 175–207.

Devine, Philip E. *The Ethics of Homicide.* Ithaca, N.Y.: Cornell University Press, 1978. Chapter 3.

———. "Relativism, Abortion, and Tolerance." *Philosophy and Phenomenological Research* 48 (1987): 131–138.

Feinberg, Joel. "Abortion." In *Matters of Life and Death,* 2d ed. edited by Tom Regan. New York: Random House, 1986.

———, ed. *The Problem of Abortion,* 2d ed. Belmont, Calif.: Wadsworth, 1983.

Finnis, John. "The Rights and Wrongs of Abortion: A Reply to Judith Thomson." *Philosophy and Public Affairs* 2 (1973): 117–145.

Foot, Philippa. "The Problem of Abortion and the Doctrine of the Double Effect." *Oxford Review,* no. 5 (1967).

Garry, Ann. "Abortion: Models of Responsibility." *Law and Philosophy* 2 (1983): 371–396.

Gensler, Harry J. "A Kantian Argument Against Abortion." *Philosophical Studies* 49 (1986): 83–98.

Grisez, Germain G. *Abortion: The Myths, the Realities and the Arguments.* New York: Corpus Books, 1970.

Hare, R. M. "Abortion and the Golden Rule." *Philosophy and Public Affairs* 4 (1975): 201–222.

Manier, Edward, Liu, William, and Solomon, David, eds. *Abortion.* Notre Dame, Ind.: University of Notre Dame Press, 1977.

Noonan, John T., Jr. *A Private Choice.* New York: Free Press, 1979.

————, ed. *The Morality of Abortion: Legal and Historical Perspectives.* Cambridge, Mass.: Harvard University Press, 1970.

Perkins, Robert L., ed. *Abortion.* Cambridge, Mass.: Schenkman, 1975.

Ramsey, Paul. "The Morality of Abortion." In *Moral Problems,* edited by James Rachels. New York: Harper & Row, 1975.

Roth, Paul A. "Personhood, Property Rights, and the Permissibility of Abortion." *Law and Philosophy* 2 (1983): 163–191.

Strasser, Mark. "Dependence, Reliance and Abortion." *Philosophical Quarterly* 35 (1985): 73–82.

Sumner, L. W. *Abortion and Moral Theory.* Princeton, N.J.: Princeton University Press, 1981.

Thomson, Judith Jarvis. "A Defense of Abortion." *Philosophy and Public Affairs* 1 (1971): 47–66.

————. "Rights and Deaths." *Philosophy and Public Affairs* 2 (1973): 146–159.

Tooley, Michael. "Abortion and Infanticide." *Philosophy and Public Affairs* 2 (1972): 37–65.

————. *Abortion and Infanticide.* Oxford: Clarendon Press, 1983.

Problem Case
The Untimely Pregnancy

Jane Doe is a lawyer, devoted to her career. She is also married, and she and her husband John plan eventually to have a child. They plan to share responsibility for rearing the child, each giving up some time and energy that would have gone into their careers; neither of them is yet ready to make these changes. Also, Jane wants to be more established in her career before the interruptions caused by the final stages of pregnancy and childbirth.

Jane and John have also decided to share responsibility for contraception. During a period of switching from one method to another, Jane discovers that she is pregnant. Jane has always supported the legal right of women to terminate pregnancy. But she has not previously given much thought to the moral question whether abortion is right—and if so, under what conditions. Her present situation does not lead her to doubt her commitment to maintaining the legal right to choose abortion. But she now sees clearly that she must answer the moral question.

What considerations should Jane take into account as she decides whether it would be morally right to terminate her pregnancy? Does she have a *moral* right to do as she wishes? Does the fetus have any moral rights? Would a decision to terminate the pregnancy be a decision to end an individual human life? Ought Jane to give moral weight to her husband's wishes? Would it make a moral difference if it were determined that the fetus carries a genetic defect or disease?

ALAN DONAGAN

A NATURAL LAW ACCOUNT OF THE MORAL STATUS OF THE FETUS

In investigating duties to others, it is convenient to begin with those that can arise between one man and another independently of any institution with which either may be associated. By an institution, following John Searle, I understand any system of constitutive rules according to which anything of a certain kind, in situations of a certain kind, is counted as something of a certain kind.[1] The most familiar institutions, like those of civil society, such as parliament and the legal system, invest certain official positions with certain rights, duties, and immunities; specify certain kinds of action as impermissible and others as permissible; and provide for the adjudication of whether the rules have been violated, and for the imposition of penalties if they have.[2] . . .

The first set of noninstitutional duties to others to be considered are those having to do with force and violence. Since respect for human beings as rational creatures entails, in general, treating every normal adult as responsible for the conduct of his own affairs, to interfere by force with anybody else's conduct of his life, unless there is a special and adequate reason, is not to respect him as a rational creature. The principle may therefore be laid down that *it is impermissible for anybody at will to use force upon another.*

Not all human beings are normal, however, and not all are adult. The insane, who cannot wholly take care of themselves, must be looked after; and, if it is necessary for their well-being, may be constrained to do various things they would not do if they had their own way. The question of how far a man's insanity gives those charged with looking after him the right of coercion is a difficult one, which I shall not pursue. The general principle, however, is clear: since a madman is a rational creature whose reason is impaired, he is entitled to the respect due to a normal rational creature except to the extent that the impairment of his reason makes it necessary to prevent him from harming himself or others, and to bring him to undergo treatment which it is reasonable to think may benefit him, provided that it is neither cruel nor offensive.

Reprinted from Alan Donagan, *The Theory of Morality,* © 1977 by the University of Chicago (Chicago, Ill.: University of Chicago Press, 1977), pp. 81–83, 164–165, and 168–171, by permission of The University of Chicago Press.

Children also are rational creatures, whose reason is in process of development. Although it must be recognized that the power of normal children to look after themselves is constantly growing, while they remain children they are not fully capable of doing so: and, in a measure as they are not, those in charge of them may forcibly prevent them from harming themselves or others, and may compel them to submit to education reasonably thought to be of benefit to them.

The question of when a given human being's life as an individual begins is of great importance in the Hebrew-Christian system. The duties of human beings to others are duties to them as human beings, that is, as rational creatures of a certain kind. The forms which may be taken by the fundamental moral duty of respect for a rational creature as such will vary with the degree to which that creature is actually in possession of the reason a mature creature of that kind would normally possess; but such variations in no way annul the duty. In simpler ages, it was practically sufficient to treat duties to others as beginning with their birth. However, as medical knowledge has grown, and as techniques have been developed by which the unborn can be both benefited and injured, the theoretical issue cannot be set aside on the ground of practical unimportance.

The question of when the life of a human being begins is a biological one, since human beings are rational *animals;* and biology answers it simply and unequivocally: a human life begins at conception, when the new being receives the genetic code.[3] Although a zygote does not, even when made visible through a microscope, look like a human being, and although adult human beings cannot have the kind of relations with it that they can have to other adults, or even to children, its status as a rational creature is in no way compromised. Attempts to deny the humanity of zygotes, by declaring that humanity begins at birth, or at viability (that is, at the point when an unborn child, extruded from the womb, could be kept alive) are scientifically obscurantist. An eight-month-old premature baby is biologically less mature than an eight-and-three-quarter-month-old unborn one; and viability has no biological significance. Whether an unborn child is viable or not depends on the state of medical technology. It is reasonable to forecast that, in a century or so, a zygote will be viable.

It follows that the principle *it is impermissible for anybody at will to use force upon another* applies to adult and child alike, to born and unborn. However, just as it is legitimate to use force on children for purposes for which it would not be legitimate to use it on adults, so very difficult questions are raised about the extent to which it is legitimate to use force upon an unborn child. . . .

. . . Now it is at least possible to argue that, in some societies at least, unless the forbidden methods of limiting families are resorted to, in some cases individual parents, in others society at large, will not be able to discharge the duty owed to children who will be born. Such problems are fittingly described as "Malthusian," after T. R. Malthus, whose *Essay on the Principle of Population as it Affects the Future Emprovement of Society* (1st. ed., 1798) first persuasively presented the hypothesis that population always tends to outrun the growth of production.[4] . . .

Finally, it should be mentioned that a further possible solution of Malthusian problems would be effected if the recent revival of the pagan doctrine that abortion is permissible could be reconciled with common morality. Two distinct lines of argument have been offered.

The first is that procuring an abortion does not, as was traditionally believed, violate the rights of a human child. This is sometimes asserted on the ground that a foetus is not a human being at all. But that is forced. It would be superfluous to rehearse the argument, neatly summed up in a brilliant if occasionally perverse paper by Roger Wertheimer, for the conclusion that "fertilization . . . [is] a non-arbitrary point marking the inception of a particular object, a human being."[5] It is difficult, in view of modern scientific biology, to maintain that, although a newborn child, or a twenty-weeks-old unborn one, is a human being, a zygote is not.

Yet it is tautological to assert that the relations between a nonviable foetus and the world are different from those of a viable one or of a newborn child: namely, that the nonviable foetus can only survive in its mother's womb. And it has been argued that it has no absolute right to be there; and that the mother, under certain circumstances, has the right to have her womb evacuated. Judith Jarvis Thomson has put the matter thus:

> If a set of parents . . . have taken all reasonable precautions against having a child, they do not simply by virtue of their biological relationship to the child who comes into existence have a special responsibility for it. They may wish to assume responsibility for it, or they may not wish to. And . . . if assuming responsibility for it would require large sacrifices, then they may refuse.[6]

As she recognizes, it may be objected that the parents of an unborn child brought into existence, although unintentionally, by their joint voluntary action, stand to it in a relation utterly different from that in which they would stand to a child left on their doorstep, or from that in which either would stand to another human being whose bloodstream had, without permission, been surgically connected with either of theirs, and who would die if the connection were broken.

That what matters here is not "simply . . . their biological relationship" is shown by the related case of a woman who has conceived as a result of rape. Here the unborn child has not been brought into existence by any voluntary action of hers. And so, in my opinion, for her to refuse to have it in her womb would not fail to respect it as a rational creature. Although the child is formally innocent, it is an involuntary intruder whom the mother may have removed from her body, even should that cause its death, without violating the prohibition of causing the death of the materially innocent. . . . Of course, she would have no right to object to its being reared in an artificial womb, if that were possible, as presumably one day it will be. And it would be a supererogatory act of great nobility for her to choose to give birth to it, out of reverence for its innocent humanity.

Accordingly, as Mary Anne Warren has acknowledged in a strong and original defence of abortion, if a foetus is human, and if moral duties are owed to human beings as such, then Thomson's argument "can provide a clear and persuasive defence of a woman's right to obtain an abortion only with respect to those cases in which the woman is in no way responsible for her pregnancy."[7] If the absolute right of a pregnant woman to procure an abortion is to be sustained, it must be on the ground that a human being is not, as such, owed moral duties. That is the foundation of the second line of argument for the permissibility of abortion.

In Warren's version, that line is as follows.[8] Only "full-fledged members of the moral community" have moral rights. A being becomes such a full-fledged member by virtue of being a person, not by virtue of being a member of the species *homo sapiens,* or of any other species of rational animal. The characteristics that make for personhood are: consciousness, developed reason, self-motivated activity, the power to communicate messages of an indefinite variety of types, and self-awareness. Hence "highly-advanced, self-aware robots or computers, should such be developed," would be persons, as would "intelligent inhabitants of other worlds." Unborn human children, human infants, and senile human dotards, would not—nor would their counterparts among nonterrestrial rational animals.

This argument implies that moral rights are acquired and lost according as one comes to be capable of certain sorts of mental activity, or ceases to be. To be a person, in Warren's sense, is not the nature of any being, but a stage through which some beings pass. And the concept of that stage varies with those who conceive it, despite Warren's belief that it "is very nearly universal (to people)"[9]—that is, to persons. Michael Tooley, her ally in maintaining that moral rights go with personhood and not with membership of a rational species, let the cat out of the bag when he defined a person as a being having "a (serious) moral right to life."[10] Tooley himself would grant this right to any organism that possesses the concept of a self as a continuing subject of experiences and other mental states, and that believes itself to be such a continuing entity.[11] Hence his persons are not identical with Warren's. But that is the nature of our contemporary concept of personhood: it is a do-it-yourself kit for constructing a "moral community" to your own taste.

Yet within the concepts of traditional morality, could not the core of positions like Warren's and Tooley's be preserved without recourse to the factitious concept of personhood? A being whose actions are subject to moral judgment must be a full rational agent; and is not full rational agency a stage through which rational animals pass? Why then, should not traditional morality be revised by recognizing only beings in a state of full rational agency as proper objects of moral duties, and possessors of moral rights?

Although it has been asserted that the dispute between those who take moral rights to go with a state ("personhood," or full moral agency, or what you will), and those who take them to go with membership of a rational species, probably cannot be settled objectively,[12] there nevertheless seems to be an objective ground for settling it.

Duties owed to any being arise out of the respect that is owed to it. Let it, then, be provisionally conceded that, in the first instance, respect is recognized as owed to beings by virtue of a state they are in: say, that of rational agency. If there are beings who reach that state by a process of development natural to normal members of their species, given normal nurture, must not respect logically be accorded to them, whether they have yet reached that state or not? The principle underlying this reasoning is: if respect is owed to beings because they are in a certain state, it is owed to whatever, by its very nature, develops into that state. To reject this principle would be arbitrary, if indeed it would be intelligible. What could be made of somebody who professed to rate the state of rational agency as of supreme value, but who regarded as expendable any rational creature whose powers were as yet undeveloped?

Since it would be arbitrary to accord the respect that generates moral duties to beings in a state of developed rationality, while refusing it to beings who naturally develop into that state, there is a fundamental moral difference between a member of the species *homo sapiens,* or of any other species of rational animal there may be in the universe, and a cat or a sparrow.[13] "Ye are of more value than many sparrows" even when your natural development is at the foetal stage.

Abortion is therefore not a possible solution of Malthusian problems within common morality.[14]

Notes

[1]John R. Searle, *Speech Acts: An Essay in the Philosophy of Language* (Cambridge: Cambridge University Press, 1969), pp. 51–52.

[2]John Rawls, *A Theory of Justice* (Cambridge, Mass.: Harvard University Press, 1971), p. 55.

[3]Cf. John T. Noonan, Jr., ed. *The Morality of Abortion* (Cambridge, Mass.: Harvard University Press, 1970), pp. 51–59.

[4]Donagan then considers various methods of controlling population. He rejects infanticide and sterilization, for they are prohibited by precepts of Hebrew-Christian morality—precepts derivable from the fundamental principle of respect for every human being as a rational creature. Donagan defends artificial contraception, however, arguing that it is legitimate. Eds.

[5]Roger Wertheimer, "Understanding the Abortion Argument," *Philosophy and Public Affairs* 1 (1971): p. 81. Cf. Paul Ramsey, in Noonan, *The Morality of Abortion,* pp. 64–79. For a serious argument for a later (but still prenatal) beginning, see Lawrence Becker, "Human Being: The Boundaries of the Concept," *Philosophy and Public Affairs* 4 (1974–1975): 334–359.

[6]Judith Jarvis Thomson, "A Defense of Abortion," *Philosophy and Public Affairs* 1 (1971), p. 65.

[7]Mary Anne Warren, "On the Moral and Legal Status of Abortion," *The Monist* 57 (1973), p. 50.

[8]Ibid., p. 56.

[9]Ibid., p. 56.

[10]Michael Tooley, "Abortion and Infanticide," *Philosophy and Public Affairs* 2 (1972), p. 40

[11]Ibid., p. 44.

[12]Warren, p. 56.

[13]Contrary to Tooley's repeated assertion (Tooley, pp. 51, 55). With regret, I have forborne examining Tooley's celebrated argument for it, which I think mistaken.

[14]I have expressed no opinion upon whether abortion, when morally impermissible, should be a criminal offence. However, I incline to think that there may be circumstances in which the wrongful taking of life ought not to be prohibited by criminal law. The institution of duelling is evil, and leads to the wrongful taking of life; but there have been states of popular mores in which it would have done more harm than good legally to prohibit duelling. The present state of our mores with respect to abortion may be of such a kind.

R. M. HARE

A KANTIAN APPROACH TO ABORTION[1]

The position of somebody wondering whether to have an abortion is usually too wretched for it to be decent for a philosopher to try to make her decision depend on the definitions of words that could in principle have several different definitions. So let us start by putting to rest the question 'Is the foetus a person?', which has occupied so many pages in discussions of this problem. It leads straight to a dead end, and we would best avoid it. We know what a foetus is, in the sense that if anybody were to ask whether an object before us or even inside us was a human foetus, there would be no difficulty in principle in determining whether it was. For the same sort of reason, we know how to determine some of the properties the foetus has. We know, for example, that it has the *potentiality* of becoming a human adult—that is, that *if* the pregnancy comes to term, it will have turned into a baby, and if the baby survives it will turn into an adult more or less like us.

There are some things of the same ordinary sort about which we cannot be so certain, but which do not present great problems. For example, we do not know for certain whether foetuses, at any rate at a late stage of pregnancy, may not have some rudimentary conscious experiences, including experiences of suffering. It is fairly certain that at earlier stages, before their nervous systems have become at all developed, they do not have such experiences. So let us avoid this question by supposing, either that the abortion in question would be at such an early stage of pregnancy, or, if later, that it could be done without causing pain to the foetus (e.g. by anaesthesia).

As I said, there seems to be no difficulty in principle in deciding *these* facts about the foetus. They are facts which may be, and I think are, morally relevant when we are deciding what it is all right to do to the foetus. But what about the question whether the foetus is a *person*? How would we answer that? We have to see that it is not the same kind of question at all as the question 'Will the foetus, if the pregnancy continues and the child survives, turn into a human adult like us, or into, say, a horse?'. The reason is that it is uncertain what we *mean* by 'person', whereas it is not uncertain what we mean by 'horse', or 'human adult'. We all know how to tell whether something is a horse or a human adult. But we do not know how to tell whether the foetus is a person. To that extent the term 'person' is unclear.

The main trouble is that 'person', and other words like 'human being' which have been used in this dispute, all have several different meanings. There is a clear sense in which a foetus is *not* a person. It is altogether too different from the things which we instantly recognize as people. If the notice in the elevator says it may not carry more than six persons, a pregnant woman is still allowed to have five adult companions in the elevator.

At the opposite extreme, there is a sense in which it is a necessary condition for something's being called a person that it has the rights which persons have, or that the duties are owed to it which we owe to persons. Obviously, if the foetus were a person in that sense, it would have the rights that other persons have, and to kill it would be murder. But for that very reason, if having the rights is a qualification for being called a person, then we cannot know whether the foetus is a person without *first* deciding whether the foetus has the rights. But that was the question we started with. So it is obviously no use trying to settle that question by asking whether the foetus is a person; we shan't know whether it is, in the required sense, until we have already decided the question about its rights.

There are going to be a lot of senses of 'person' besides these, or in between these, and there will not be room even to list them all. It should be clear already that most of the disputes about this allegedly crucial question of whether the foetus is a person are going to be a waste of time and can never get anywhere.

How do people get into this impasse? The cause is this: they have some excellent firm principles about murder and about liberty, and in this difficult case of abortion it looks as if the principles conflict. If one forbids the abortion, one infringes the liberty of the mother; if one allows it, one is allowing murder. So people take sides for one principle or the other, call themselves 'pro-life' or 'pro-choice', and stop thinking. They even start bombing one another.

We start with these good firm simple principles about life and liberty (though we do not know how to formulate them clearly and explicitly), and then they come into conflict. If we terminate a pregnancy, we are offending against the principle requiring us to preserve life. If we stop women terminating their pregnancies, we are offending against the other principle requiring us to preserve liberty or choice. The right thing to do in this predicament is to think some more and try to formulate the principles exactly and apply them to this case, and see whether we can find forms of them that do *not* conflict with each other. That indeed is what people are trying to do when they argue about whether the foetus is a person. For if there were a sense in which the foetus is *not* a person, the conflict might be resolved; in killing the foetus, one would not be committing a murder, because killing is not murder unless it is the killing of people. And so we could observe the principle about liberty by letting the foetus be killed, without breaking the principle about murder.

As we saw, this manoeuvre does not do any good, because the word 'person' is indeterminate; taken one way, we can say that it is all right to kill the foetus because it is not a person (in the sense of occupying one person's place in the elevator); but the side that does not think the foetus ought to be killed was not using the word in that sense. It was using it in the sense in which to be a person is to be a possessor of the rights that ordinary persons have. And we are not in a position to say whether the foetus is a person in *that* sense. This is a moral, not a factual question, and we cannot answer it until we have settled the prior question of whether we have the duties to the foetus that we have to ordinary adults, i.e. whether the foetus has the same rights as adults have.

So what ought we to do, instead of disputing endlessly about whether the foetus is a person? My advice is that we forget about the word 'person', and ask instead about the properties of the foetus that might be reasons why we ought not to kill it—properties in the ordinary factual sense in which we can *determine* whether or not it has them. It may be that the word 'person' stands for some combination of these properties, or ambiguously for more than one possible set of them. In that case, if we can isolate a set of ordinary properties of the foetus which together constitute a reason why we ought not to let it be killed, we might sum up this set of properties by saying that the foetus is a person. But, for the reasons I have given, we should be able to do this only *after* first answering the moral question. The word 'person' would not have helped in the argument; it would at most be a convenient way of summarizing its conclusion. The real work would have been done in identifying the ordinary properties of the foetus which made us want to say (if that was what we did want to say) that it ought not to be killed. The hard part of the moral thinking is that involved in this identification of the ordinary properties which are the reasons for or against killing the foetus.

What then are these ordinary properties? One is that, if the foetus suffered while being killed, then that would be *a* reason for not inflicting this suffering on it, though there could be reasons on the other side. But we can ignore this property if we confine ourselves, as I have proposed, to cases where we can be sure it will not suffer.

What other properties of the foetus, besides its capacity for suffering which we have now discounted, could give us reasons for not killing it? I cannot think of any besides the foetus's potentiality, already mentioned, of turning into someone like us. Here is an example that will illustrate why I cannot think of any. Suppose that in the case of a given pregnancy we can be absolutely certain that for reasons beyond anybody's control the foetus will not survive. It has, say, some recognizable disease from which foetuses never recover. Let us suppose additionally that, if we did kill the foetus, we could do so painlessly, say by using an anaesthetic. In such a case is there any reason for not killing the foetus if there are other grounds for killing it (say the health of the mother)? This case illustrates rather well what is wrong with what I shall call the absolutist pro-life position. It also illustrates the difference between foetuses and ordinary human persons. In the case of an ordinary person who you were certain would die in a month, there *would* be reasons for not killing that person. It would disappoint hopes of what he or she might have done in the remaining month; the process of killing might cause fear; it might cause sorrow to others; the terminally ill patient might be deprived of the chance of ordering his financial affairs for the benefit of his family, or even reconciling himself and them to his impending death. There could be reasons, all the same, on the other side, such as the suffering he would undergo if his life were prolonged. None of these reasons applies to the foetus. The foetus does not have *now,* at the present moment, properties which are reasons for not killing it, given that it will die in any case before it acquires those properties which ordinary human adults and even children have, and which are our reasons for not killing *them.* A foetus before it has achieved sentience does not *currently* possess any properties that could be morally relevant to its treatment and which are not possessed equally by oysters and earthworms.

If we are to find reasons for not killing the foetus, we must look for some properties which it does not have now, but which it *will* have later if it survives. Philosophers call these *potential* properties, and argue about whether the potentiality that the foetus has of turning into someone like us is morally relevant to what we may or may not do to the foetus now. The case that I have just described shows that defenders of the foetus, if they are going to make good their defence, have nothing else that they can rely on *except* the foetus's potentiality. But I shall be arguing in a moment, against the views of many philosophers like Michael Tooley,[2] that potentiality does provide a powerful weapon with which to defend the foetus *in normal cases.*

In order to set up this argument I shall have to do a little ethical theory, though I will try to make as light work of it as I can. The ethical theory I am going to use is of a more or less Kantian sort.[3] I am also going, for reasons which I hope will become clear in a moment, to make a time-switch into the past. Suppose that it is not this girl now who is deciding whether or not to have an abortion, but some other girl in the past. Suppose, for example, it was my own mother deciding whether or not to terminate the pregnancy which actually resulted in *me.* In that case, am I going to say that it is morally quite all right for her to have an abortion?

Please note that the question is *not* 'What *would* I say if I were speaking to her at that time?'. Nor is it 'What *would* I say now if I did not exist?'. I have deliberately formulated the question in such a way as to avoid the difficulties with those other questions. The question is, 'What *do* I (a presently existing person) now say about this past situation?'.

I will draw attention to an obvious reason why I might not like to say that it was all right for her to have an abortion. It is a reason which might be outweighed by other reasons, but it is at least *a* reason. The reason is that if she had had an abortion, I would not now have existed. Let us suppose that I am able to reach back in time and give instructions to my mother as to what she should do. Suppose, even, that she is able to ask me questions about what she ought to do. In order to get into a position in which I can communicate with her at that time, I shall have to penetrate some noumenal world outside time (this is really getting very Kantian) and have access to her in that past time. This of course raises deep philosophical problems, into which I am not going to go. But just suppose I can do it. What shall I say to her?

I am sure I shall not say 'Carry on, have the abortion; it's all the same to me'. Because my existence now is valuable to me, I shall not, other things being equal, will (to use another Kantian term) that she should have the abortion, thereby depriving me of the possibility of existence. I value my existence, not for its own sake, but for the sake of the nice things that happen to me, which couldn't happen if I did not exist. There is a sentence in the Anglican Prayer Book in which we thank God for our creation, preservation and all the blessings of this life.[4] If there were no blessings but only curses, then we could not thank him for our creation either; but he has been good enough to arrange things otherwise for most of us. The fact that we can thank him for our creation does not show that mere existence in itself is a good; but it does show that it is a good at least as a means to the other good things that those who exist can have. Therefore, faced with the possibility of either existing now or not existing now, the normally happy person will tell his mother not to have the abortion. And therefore, all things being equal (if, for example, *she* is not going to die if the pregnancy is not terminated), he will say that she ought not to have it.

I put the whole dialogue in the past, because of an argument which is sometimes used by philosophers who write about this question. They say that *potential* people or *merely possible* people do not have any rights, and we cannot have any duties to them. But in the case I described we were talking about an actual person, namely myself. I am asking myself, as an actual person, to prescribe as to what ought to have been done at a time in the past when my mother was contemplating having an abortion. Potential people do not come into this argument.

However, it is a part of ethical theory that is accepted by almost all moral philosophers, that if one makes a moral judgment about any case or situation, one has, in consistency, to make the same moral judgment about any other case which resembles it in all its non-moral particulars. For example, if it is all right for one person to do something (call him *A*), it must be all right for anybody else to do the same thing in exactly the same situation. By 'the same situation', I mean the same in all respects, and these include the properties of the people in it. So I am not saying that if it is all right for *A* to tickle *B* when *B* likes being tickled, it must be all right for *B* to tickle *A* who hates being tickled. What I am saying is that if the circumstances and all the properties, including the wishes, of the people are the same, the moral judgment has to be the same.

In applying this theoretical doctrine, which, as I said, is accepted by nearly all moral philosophers, at least all who understand what the doctrine is (some have denied it through *not* understanding it) we have to apply it to hypothetical cases as well as to actual ones. If it *was* wrong for my mother to have an abortion, then it *would be* wrong for any other mother to have an abortion in exactly the same circumstances, and therefore would now be wrong for the girl we started with to have an abortion, if the circumstances were the same. And this, in general, is the prima facie case for being against abortion, as most of us are *in general*. By that I mean that most of us, if asked whether it just does not matter in the least whether people have abortions or not, would say that we think that in most cases it does matter; most pregnancies ought to be allowed to continue; those who want to legalize abortion want to do so because that will leave the decision to the individuals concerned in *special* cases where there are strong grounds for termination. Nobody thinks that *no* abortions matter, except those who do not care whether the human race survives or not, or who even want it not to survive.

The reason why most of us think that *all things being equal* pregnancies should not be terminated, is that we think that on the whole they are likely to result in people being born who will in the course of their lives be glad to have been born. There is of course a problem about having too many people: if there were so many people, and the results of over-population made them so unhappy, that they wished they had not been born, that would be different; but I am assuming that this is not the case, yet. I shall be returning to this point.

However, reverting for a moment to the dialogue between myself in the present and my mother in the past, there is one other thing that I *might* think I could say. We have considered two things I might say, namely 'Do not have the abortion' and 'You ought to have the abortion'. What I said was that I would not say 'You ought to have the abortion', because this would be a prescription to her to have the abortion, and I do not want that. So, if those were the only two things I could say, I would choose the first, 'Do not have the abortion', and rule out the second 'You ought to have the abortion'. But a third thing I might say is 'I do not say you ought to have an abortion; but I do not claim, either, that you ought not to have it; of course I want you not to have it, because otherwise I shall not exist; so I still go on saying, so far as I am concerned "Do not have it". But if you ask me whether it is the case, morally speaking, that you ought not to have it, I would not go so far as that. You will not be doing wrong if you have it, but please do not'.

This possibility, though important, raises difficulties which are really too great for me to deal with here. If I am trying to give my mother positive moral guidance, I shall be confined to the two answers, 'You ought' and 'You ought not'; and, if this is so then, because I prefer to be existing now, I shall not say 'You ought', and shall therefore have to say 'You ought not'.[5]

There is, then, a reason for accepting the *general* principle which forbids abortions in ordinary cases. The question is, then, whether we ought to allow any exceptions to this principle, and whether they ought to extend further than the exceptions that can be made to the principle that we should not kill adults. Let us ask what are the reasons for having the latter principle. We have looked at some of them already. Nearly all of us want not to be killed, and want not to live in fear of being killed. So, when faced with a choice between a universal prohibition on killing people and a universal license to kill them, we would choose the former. But most of us do not want to have to choose between these stark alternatives; we want to make *some* exceptions to the principle forbidding killing people, of which killing in self-defence is an obvious one, and killing in war or as a penalty for murder are more controversial. If we are speaking, as we are, of a general principle to be inculcated in children when we bring them up, and protected by the law, the principle has to be fairly simple and cannot contain too many complicated exceptions. So we allow killing in self-defence and perhaps in these other cases, but try to keep the prohibition as simple as we can. This is in the interests of workability.

It is sometimes said that if one allows exceptions to such simple principles one will be inserting the thin end of a wedge, or starting down a slippery slope. This is indeed sometimes the case; but sometimes it is not. Whether it is, will depend on whether there is a clear stopping-place on the slope where we can dig in our heels. And sometimes there is. When it was decided in the United States to allow cars to turn right at a red light after stopping, did anybody say 'You are starting down a slippery slope: if you let people turn right on a red light, then you will have breached the absolute ban on crossing a red light, and people will soon begin crossing it when they want to go straight ahead or turn left'?. People realized that it was quite easy to distinguish the cases in which it was now to be legal to cross the red light from those in which it was still to be forbidden. So the slope was not slippery.

Similarly, nobody says that we ought to forbid killing *even* in self-defence, because if you allow that, people will start killing for other reasons too. In this case, there is a real difficulty in deciding what counts as self-defence, and no doubt there are volumes of cases in the criminal law in which this has had to be sorted out. But even so (even though, that is, the slope is a little bit slippery) we do allow killing in self-defence, and the slope has not in practice proved *too* slippery.

In principle, we could do the same for abortion. The argument is sometimes used that if we allow the killing of foetuses, people will soon be killing adults *ad lib.* I cannot see much force in this argument. In many countries the killing of foetuses has been legalized under certain conditions, and in others it has never been illegal. I know of no evidence that this has led to a greater incidence of ordinary murder.

Although the slope from killing foetuses to killing adults is not slippery, there *is* a slippery slope from killing foetuses under certain conditions to killing them under other conditions. This is because it is rather difficult to delimit precisely in law the conditions under which abortion is allowable. Expressions like 'congenital defect' and 'the health of the mother' are capable of being stretched. However, whether we think it is dangerous that this slope is slippery will depend on what view we take about the general question of what abortions should be allowed, and who should make the decision. For example, *if* we took the view that abortion should be allowed freely and the mother should decide, we should not mind the law being stretched in this way. I do not myself take so extreme a view; but I do not think it bad that the law has been stretched a bit, as it has been in different ways in different countries.

But at any rate the slope from killing foetuses to killing adults is not slippery. So we can reasonably ask whether it would be all right to allow an exception, in the case of foetuses, to the general ban on killing. How would we decide such a question? The general ban on killing has a point, as we saw earlier, namely that people want not to be killed. But does this point extend to foetuses? *They* do not want not to be killed.

I have argued that most people prefer not *to have been* killed when they were foetuses; and that this gives us a general reason for having a principle that we ought not to kill foetuses. But here we have to be rather careful. The general preference for existence over non-existence does not justify the principle that we ought to bring into existence all the people we *could* bring into existence. If we tried to do that, there would obviously be too many people, and perhaps a majority of those people would wish that we had *not* brought them into existence, thus destroying the premiss of our argument. So evidently any principle that we are likely to accept is going to allow some limitation of the population, if only by the use of the methods approved by the Pope.

However we limit the population, it is going to result in some people not being born who *could* have been born. We have to ask next, 'Is there any reason for giving precedence to some of these people over others?' Notice that the argument used earlier in defence of the foetus does not provide any such reason. Suppose that if this girl does not have a baby now she will have one in a year's time, but that she will not have that other baby if she has one now. Each of these people, if born, will, we hope, have reason to be thankful that he or she was born; but, other things being equal, neither will have any *more* reason for being thankful than the other has. So, given that we are going to limit the population, does it make any difference *which* of the possible people is born, and which gets excluded? The argument used so far does not provide any reason for saying that it makes a difference.

There are certainly factors which could make a difference. If, for example, the mother is not at present married but hopes to be soon, this might mean that the present foetus, if born, will not have such a good start in life as the other would. Or, to take a case which points in the opposite direction: if the mother is thirty-five years old, there is a reason for having a child in the next five years. The reason is that if she postpones having it until she is forty, the chance of the child being born with Down's syndrome is greater. So there can be reasons for choosing to have a child later rather than now, or the reverse. But we have so far not been able to discover any general reason for giving precedence to the child that this foetus would turn into over other possible future children, given that one or another of them is going to be born.

Are there any strong reasons for preferring the child that this foetus would turn into? The feeling many people have that it should have precedence may be due to a false analogy between foetuses and adults. Certainly it would be wrong to kill an adult in order to replace him or her with some other person who might be born. This is because the existing adult has desires (above all the desire to live) which will be frustrated if he is killed. That is the reason why we have the general ban on killing adults. And this applies even to young children. Whether it applies to neonates, who do not have the desire to live, is a controversial question which there is no room to discuss here. It certainly applies to children from a very early age. But it clearly does not apply to foetuses; so at any rate *that* reason for saying that foetuses ought not to be killed lacks force.

At this point it will be claimed that the argument so far provides no reason for forbidding abortions that does not apply equally to contraception or even to abstinence. I think that this is right. So far we have no such reason. Perhaps reasons can be found, but they are relatively weak ones. Abortion is a more tricky procedure medically than contraception. But there are contraceptive methods which are really abortifacients, because, when used before or during copulation, they kill the zygote (perhaps by preventing implantation) after it has been formed. There is no clear reason for distinguishing such methods from the kind which prevents the formation of zygotes. Again, the feeling that there is a difference is due to a false analogy.

There is also the consideration that normally the foetus attracts feelings of affection on the part of the mother and perhaps others—feelings which do not yet attach to a possible future child that she might have. To kill the foetus, even if the mother herself desires this all things considered, is bound to wound those feelings. She might feel that it would have been better to have used contraception.

There is also what might be called the 'bird in the hand' argument. The foetus is *there,* and will turn into an adult if it survives; future conceptions and births are more problematical. However, given that there is likely to be a child that will be born, if not to this family, then to some other family, and so occupy the place in the demography that this child would occupy, that does not seem a very strong argument.

If, as already argued, abortions are in general wrong, but allowable in particular cases, what such exceptions ought the law to allow, and who should have the task of deciding when to perform an abortion? The general principle is that, if there are interests affected by a decision, then since we have to treat people as ends, those interests should be protected impartially; and this is most likely to happen if those who have the interests have a say in the decision, or, if they are not in a position to have a say, are in some way represented, and if the greater interests have the greater say. This is likely to result in the maximal and impartial protection of the interests. Those who like to speak about rights (and I see no harm in that) can speak equally well of the protection of their rights. But interests will do for the present argument.

Obviously the mother has a very great interest in the outcome. That is the justification for the claim that the mother ought to have the only say; and this would indeed be so if there were no other interests affected. But there *are* other interests, and we must consider them. The father has an interest—certainly a smaller one than the mother, but not negligible. The person into whom the foetus would turn if not aborted has an interest—a very great one. But this interest may be counterbalanced by those of other children who might be born thereafter, if the family is in any case to be limited. Certainly, if it is known that this foetus is seriously defective (the mother say, had rubella) but she could have a normal child later, the interest of that normal child is much greater than that of the defective child that would be born from this pregnancy.

There is also the interest of doctors, surgeons and nurses who may be called upon to perform the abortion. If ever we have an abortifacient pill that can be bought at pharmacies and used at any stage in early pregnancy, that would cut out the doctors; but I think it unlikely that such a pill will be developed soon which could safely be sold without prescription. So for the moment we have to consider the interest of the doctor who is being asked to act against his conscience—and this *is* an interest, even if the conscience is misguided.

The question of who should decide whether to allow an abortion is the question of how best to be fair to all these interests. The mother's interest is preponderant but not the sole one. What the best procedure is depends on a lot of factors which I am not able to assess with confidence. But I am inclined to think that there are procedures now followed in some countries which have worked well in practice and have done reasonable justice between the interests affected. In any case, that is what we should be aiming at.

Notes

[1] I have tried in this paper to improve the argument in my 'Abortion and the Golden Rule', *Philosophy and Public Affairs* 4 (1975): 201–22. There are, however, some important points in that earlier paper which are not here repeated.

[2] Michael Tooley, 'Abortion and Infanticide', *Philosophy and Public Affairs* 2 (1972): 37–65, revised in Joel Feinberg, ed., *The Problem of Abortion* (Belmont, Calif.: Wadsworth, 1973).

[3] The theory can also be put into a utilitarian form, and I have often so put it. The idea that Kantianism and utilitarianism are irreconcilable is the result of attempts by modern deontologists to borrow Kant's authority for their own intuitionist positions; but they seldom document their claims about Kant, and it could in fact be shown that a properly formulated utilitarianism and a properly formulated Kantianism need not conflict. For hints, see references to Kant in index to my *Moral Thinking* (Oxford: Oxford University Press, 1981), and my 'Punishment and Retributive Justice', *Philosophical Topics* 14 (1986): p. 219.

[4] *Book of Common Prayer* (old and new versions), the General Thanksgiving.

[5] I deal at length with this problem in my *Moral Thinking,* pp. 182 ff.

LAURA PURDY AND MICHAEL TOOLEY
IS ABORTION MURDER?

This essay deals with the morality of abortion. We shall argue that abortion is morally unobjectionable, and that society benefits if abortion is available on demand. We begin by setting out a preliminary case in support of the practice of abortion. . . . We conclude by considering what

From Laura Purdy and Michael Tooley, "Is Abortion Murder?" *Abortion: Pro and Con,* edited by Robert L. Perkins (Cambridge, Mass.: Schenkman, 1974), pp. 129–136, 144–148. Reprinted by permission.

properties something needs in order to have a serious right to life, and we show that a human fetus does not possess those properties. Thus since there is no moral objection to abortion, the practice must be viewed as both permissible and desirable, in the light of the advantages outlined in the first section of our paper.

PRELIMINARY CONSIDERATIONS IN SUPPORT OF ABORTION

One way of approaching the abortion question is to envision two possible societies, one where strict anti-abortion laws are in force, the other where abortion is unrestricted. In imagining these two societies, we suppose that all other factors are the same, and that the societies otherwise resemble the United States in their social arrangements.

To flesh out these images, we must make some empirical assumptions, which philosophers are no more qualified to evaluate than is the ordinary educated individual, since it is not the main business of philosophy to ascertain facts. However, such assumptions cannot be avoided in moral and political philosophy, unless one is uninterested in the outcomes of various courses of action. About the facts relevant to the issues discussed in this section there is room for disagreement, for we are dependent upon sciences that are as yet incomplete and upon common sense. But while the accuracy of the following pictures is contingent upon future investigation, the major features of the pictures seem plausible, in the light of present knowledge and theory.

The first society is much like that which has existed in the United States up until the present, where abortion has been generally unavailable, either because of restrictive legislation or because of de facto unobtainability. The second society is very different. In it, abortion is freely available. We contend that, as a result, individuals in that society suffer less unhappiness than those in the first society.

Let us consider, in concrete terms, why this is the case. First of all, men and women in our second world can enjoy sex more, since anxiety regarding contraceptive failure will no longer exist. Moreover, pregnancies can be timed so that no child is neglected, reducing stress on all concerned. As a result, couples can plan on temporary or permanent childlessness when necessary or desirable to achieve life goals. In addition, if pregnancy threatens the health—either physical or mental—of the mother, or of other parties, or unduly strains the marriage, it can be safely terminated. Last, and most important perhaps, illegal abortions, now a significant factor in the maternal death rate, can be replaced by legal abortions, thus saving the lives of very many women.

That abortion on demand would reduce frustration and unhappiness among the young is equally evident. When abortion is readily available we can prevent the birth of babies who would otherwise enter the world with gross physical or mental abnormalities and who would face short and unhappy lives. We can also ensure that only wanted children will be born. Since parents who sincerely desire a child are more apt to provide for its physical, intellectual, and emotional needs, it is probable that children will be better cared for than at present. This change should be especially significant in light of our growing awareness of the problem of child abuse.

It also seems reasonable to believe that members of society who do not belong to families availing themselves of abortion will benefit. It is generally frustrated and unhappy individuals who turn to crime, violent or otherwise. Happy people, if not necessarily constructive citizens, are at least not destructive ones. Thus readily available abortions, by eliminating sources of frustration and unhappiness, should improve the social environment for everyone. Secondly, abortion, by making childbearing completely voluntary, will help keep the population in check. The importance of this with respect to education and the environment, and thus the impact upon the general quality of life, need not be labored.

It seems reasonable to conclude then, on the basis of our present knowledge, that the second society will be much happier than the first. At this point two questions arise. The first is empirical: "Is abortion on demand in fact the *best* way to satisfy the needs and desires of members of society? Mightn't some third type of society be superior to both of the possibilities we have so far considered, as measured in terms of the happiness of its members?" The second is moral: "Even if members of the second society are on the whole happier than members of the first, does it follow that the second society is morally preferable to the first? Are there not other factors that should be taken into account, such as the rights of the unborn, that tell in favor of the first society?" . . .

The issue, then, is this. May there not be alternative social arrangements, not involving abortion, that would result in even greater happiness? Those who are wary of the practice of abortion on demand sometimes suggest that the same ends can be achieved as follows. First, society should ensure that everyone has access to safe and completely reliable methods of contraception. Secondly, there should be legislation to cope with the social welfare problems that are created or aggravated by unwanted or defective children.

This alternative presupposes the existence of a foolproof contraceptive having no undesirable side effects. At present no such device exists. It is true that if a perfect method of contraception were developed, it would dissolve much of the abortion problem. However, at least two problems would remain. First, pregnancy, even though initially desired, sometimes has a serious negative effect upon the mother or other people. We will still need abortion to handle cases of this sort. Secondly, some fetuses turn out to be grossly deformed, or otherwise seriously defective. If abortion is not available, what is likely to happen to such defective children? Proper care is expensive, and if the societies we are envisaging do resemble the present day United States, then we know that to do the job adequately will be thought to impose too great a sacrifice upon parents and taxpayers. This fact cannot be swept under the rug; it must enter any realistic assessment of the available options. As the real alternative to abortion here, the defective person will face life in an uncaring environment, where physical needs will be only barely met, and where emotional needs will generally go unfulfilled. Only if drastic changes in social legislation were to occur would such individuals have the opportunity to lead a protected life and to develop fully their potentialities. Thus it is not possible to achieve, by contraception and social legislation, all of the benefits that can be realized by abortion.

We must now consider two important objections to our position. The first is that in evaluating the happiness of society, one should take into account the happiness of the fetus, and we have failed to do this. We have considered only the happiness of other members of society. So that, while abortion may increase the happiness of these other members, it certainly does not satisfy the fetus's desires and so contribute to its happiness.

Our response to this is that it is a mistake to attribute to a fetus a significant range of desires. A fetus may have a few very rudimentary desires, such as a desire not to feel pain, but it is incapable of having most of the desires that adult humans can have.

How can we support this claim that a fetus is capable of having only very elementary desires? Perhaps the place to start is by drawing a distinction between having a desire for some state, and being programmed to act so as to increase the likelihood that the state in question will be attained. Thus, imagine a machine constructed so that when its batteries run down, it searches for an electrical outlet to recharge its batteries. The machine is programmed to behave in ways that tend to bring about certain states, but one could not literally speak of the machine having a *desire* to recharge its batteries. Similarly, imagine a more complex machine that can "recognize" certain situations as threats to its survival, and take action that decreases the likelihood of its being destroyed. Even if such a machine were capable of a wide range of complex and effective survival behavior, it would not make sense to speak of it having a desire for continued existence. Moreover, all plant behavior and that of lower animals provide other examples in which there is complex programmed behavior directed toward some goal, but where the organism has no corresponding desire.

What, then, is required before one can attribute desires to something? Our view is that first, it is not possible to attribute desires to something unless it is capable of *consciousness*. So if a machine is not conscious, one cannot attribute any desires to it, no matter how sophisticated its behavior. Second, the *specific* desires a thing can have are limited by the concepts it possesses. The justification for this claim is as follows. The fundamental way of describing a given desire is as a desire that a certain proposition be true. But one cannot desire that a certain proposition be true unless one understands it, and since one cannot understand it without possessing the concepts involved in it, it follows that the desires one can have are limited by the concepts one possesses.

A slightly different way of developing this point is this: if something is to have any desires at all, it must possess consciousness. But to have a specific desire it is not enough to be conscious and to be disposed to bring about certain states. The migration of birds, for example, enables them to achieve a certain end, and it certainly seems likely that they are to some extent conscious. Yet it is implausible to attribute to them a desire for those states that their migratory behavior makes possible. What is needed is a specific connection between consciousness and the goal towards which the behavior is directed. One speaks of a desire only where the organism is capable of recognizing that its behavior is directed towards certain ends: where the organism is incapable of being aware of the object of its behavior, one does not attribute the corresponding desire to it. To be aware of a certain state as the aim of one's behavior presupposes that one possesses concepts that can be employed to characterize that state.

Given this account of the conditions an organism must satisfy if it is to have desires, the justification for our claim that a fetus has at best extremely simple desires should be clear. In the early stages of the development of a human organism it has no mental life at all, i.e., no consciousness, and hence no desires. At later stages, it is reasonable to think that the fetus has some sensations, but its mental life is still very limited. Thus if one compares, say, a human fetus with a chimpanzee fetus, there are no grounds for holding that the mental life of the former is significantly richer than that of the latter. This means that one should not attribute desires to a human fetus which one would be unwilling to attribute to a chimpanzee fetus. The upshot is that one cannot consistently object to abortion in the case of humans, on the grounds that the destruction of the fetus violates some desires that the fetus has, unless one would also object to abortion in the case of chimpanzees.

Moreover, there seem to be no grounds for attributing complex desires to fetuses, human or otherwise. In particular, it seems absurd to attribute to any fetus a desire for continued existence, since to have such a desire it would have to have a conception of what it is to be a continuing subject of experiences and other mental states.

Are there any desires that a fetus has which might be violated by abortion? It appears reasonable to say that fetuses can feel pleasure and pain. Thus abortion might violate a fetus's desire to avoid pain. As it is certainly undesirable to inflict suffering upon any living organism, abortion should be carried out so as to inflict as little pain as possible upon the fetus. If this is done, we do not think that the fetus has any desires that are violated by abortion.

To sum up, our response to the first objection is this: we certainly agree that in choosing policies and institutions, one should take into account everyone affected. So in particular, if the fetus had desires which were adversely affected by abortion, it would be unfair not to take those desires into account. But we have argued that, as a matter of fact, the fetus is incapable of having desires that will go unsatisfied if it is destroyed, providing that action is carried out painlessly.

This brings us to the second objection. It involves the suggestion that while the consequences of isolated acts of abortion do benefit society, this would not be true if abortion were to become a *generally accepted practice*. It is precisely the latter issue that one is interested in.

It has often been suggested that general acceptance of abortion would have disastrous consequences; however, no convincing evidence has been offered in support of this contention. Antiabortionists usually attempt to sway unreflective people with vague claims that abortion will lead to the "denigration of humanity," or to an "erosion of respect for the sanctity of life." Such emotion-laden appeals are in the same intellectual category as politicians' rhetoric about patriotism and the family. Both are designed to encourage unthinking acceptance of a position that would fare ill if exposed to impartial, rational scrutiny.

It is possible, however, to divest the claim of its illicit emotional appeal. When this is done, the underlying suggestion appears to be that if one permits the killing of some humans, viz., fetuses, then respect for human life will decrease, so that other classes of humans, such as the handicapped and the elderly, become candidates for elimination. But this conclusion rests upon intellectual and moral confusion. Specifically, it rests upon a failure to get clear about the conditions something must satisfy if it is to have a serious right to life. To advocate abortion is *not* to suggest that one allow violations of one's moral principles when it happens to be socially convenient. The proabortionist's position is that the *fundamental* principle involved here is that it is seriously wrong to kill, not human beings, but *persons*. If it is seriously wrong to kill a human being it is *because* he is a person, not because he is a human being. And our contention is that fetuses are not persons, but only *potential* persons. Once one realizes that it is persons who have a right to life, and that abortion is morally unobjectionable because fetuses are not persons, there is no danger that one will conclude that it is morally acceptable to kill other humans, such as handicapped and elderly ones, who are persons. When the moral principles relevant to abortion are clear, it is apparent that general acceptance of the practice should not have any undesirable consequences of the sort envisioned by the antiabortionist.

This completes our defense of the claim that where abortion is viewed as morally permissible and is available on demand, people are happier than they would otherwise be. We can now proceed to consider the views of those who hold that abortion should be prohibited even if it is the case that to do so will result in significant frustration and unhappiness. Most antiabortionists feel that there are moral considerations involved in the issue of abortion that far outweigh considerations of human happiness. In view of what is at stake, this is not a claim to be lightly advanced. By lobbying for the prohibition of abortion, the antiabortionist is in effect assuming responsibility for the consequences of those actions. As we have emphasized above, these consequences are deeply disturbing. If antiabortionists prohibit abortion, they will be responsible for untold human misery. They will be responsible for lessened enjoyment of sex; for frustration caused by inconvenient pregnancies and childbearing; for ill health, either physical or mental, of mothers or other persons; for deaths of women resulting from pregnancies and illegal abortions; for child abuse; for crimes committed by frustrated or improperly socialized individuals; and for the stunted life of everyone if overpopulation seriously curbs our freedoms or lowers the quality of life. The ardent antiabortionist must shoulder the burden of responsibility for these things since, had he acted otherwise, they would not have existed. What considerations, then, can the antiabortionist point to that outweigh the suffering produced by the prohibition of abortion?

In reply to the accusation that the responsibility for this catalogue of woes lies on his shoulders, the antiabortionist will argue that these evils are necessary in order to avoid a much greater evil. Fetuses have a right to life. They have a right to be born and to have the opportunity to become adults. To destroy them by abortion is seriously wrong, and in comparison with it the miseries enumerated above pale into insignificance. Fetuses are human beings, and to kill a human being is murder. . . .

WHEN DOES AN ORGANISM HAVE A RIGHT TO LIFE?

. . . Our view is as follows: an organism can have a right to life only if it now possesses, or possessed at some time in the past, the capacity to have a desire for continued existence. An organism cannot satisfy this requirement unless it is a person, that is, a continuing subject of experiences and other mental states, and unless it has the capacity for self-consciousness—where an organism is self-conscious only if it recognizes that it is itself a person.

The basis for our contention is the claim that there is a conceptual connection between, on the one hand, the rights an individual can have and the circumstances under which they can be violated, and, on the other, the desires he can have. A right is something that can be violated and, in general, to violate an individual's right to something is to frustrate the corresponding desire. Suppose, for example, that someone owns a car. Then you are under a *prima facie* obligation not to take it from him. However, the obligation is not unconditional: if he does not care whether you drive off with his car, then *prima facie* you do not violate his right by doing so.

A precise formulation of the conceptual connection in question would require considerable care. The most important point is that violation of an individual's right to something does not always involve thwarting a *present* desire, that is, a desire that exists at the same time as the action that violates the right. Sometimes the violation of a right involves thwarting a *past* desire. The most dramatic illustration is provided by the rights of dead persons, since here the individual whose right is being transgressed no longer exists. A more common example is that of people who are temporarily unconscious. When a person is unconscious, he does not have any desires. Yet his rights can certainly be infringed upon. This presents no problem when one takes past desires into account. The reason that it is wrong to kill a temporarily unconscious adult is that in the period before he became unconscious, he had a desire to go on living—a desire which it is possible to satisfy.

Violation of an individual's right may also involve frustrating a *future* desire. The most vivid example of this is the case of rights of future generations. Most people would hold that for those living today to use up all of the world's resources would violate the rights of future individuals. Here, as in the case of the rights of a dead person, the violation of an individual's rights occurs at a time when the individual does not even exist.

However, it is very important to notice that what is relevant are the desires that individuals will *actually have* at some time in the future. The desires that individuals would have *if* they were to exist at certain times at which, as a matter of fact, they will not exist, are not relevant. . . . Rights of future generations provide . . . an example. Suppose we know with certainty that no future generation will ever exist. Then there is no objection to using up the world's resources now. But if one were obliged to take into account the desires future individuals would have if they were to exist, it would be wrong to use up the world's resources.

A complete account of the connection between rights and desires would also have to take into consideration unusual cases, where an individual is in an emotionally unbalanced state, or where a person's desires have been affected by lack of relevant information, or by his being subjected to abnormal physiological or psychological factors. We shall ignore these, and confine ourselves to paradigm cases of violations of an individual's rights. When this is done, we can say that first, an individual cannot have a right to something unless there can be actions that would violate it. Second, an action cannot violate an individual's right to something unless it wrongs him by depriving him of the thing in question. And thirdly, an action can wrong an individual by depriving him of something only if it violates his desire for that thing. The desire is generally a present desire, but it may be a past or future desire. It follows that a person cannot have a right to something unless he is at some time capable of having the corresponding desire.

Let us now apply this to the case of the right to life. The expression "right to life" misleads one into thinking that the right concerns the continued existence of a biological organism. The following example shows that this interpretation is inadequate. Suppose that we could completely reprogram an adult human so that it has (apparent) memories, beliefs, desires, and personality traits radically different from those associated with it before the reprogramming. (Billy Graham is reprogrammed as a replica of Bertrand Russell.) In such a case, however beneficial the change might be, it is true that *someone* has been destroyed, that someone's right to life has been violated, even though no biological organism has been killed. So the right to life cannot be construed as merely the right of a biological organism to continue to exist.

How then can the right in question be more accurately described? A natural suggestion is that the expression "right to life" refers to the right of a person—a subject of experiences and other mental states—to continue to exist. However, this interpretation begs the question against certain possible positions. It might be that while persons have a right to continue to exist, so do other things that are only potentially persons. A right to life on this view would be either the right of a person to continue to exist or the right of something that is only potentially a person to become a person.

We concluded above that something cannot have a specific right unless it is capable at some time of having the corresponding desire. It follows from this together with the more accurate analysis of the right to life that something cannot have a right to life unless it is capable at some time either of having a desire to continue to exist as a person, or of having a desire to become a person. If something has not been capable of having either of these desires in the past, and is not now capable, then if it is now destroyed, it will never have possessed the capacity in question. Hence an organism cannot have a right to life unless it is now capable, or was capable at some time in the past, of having a desire to continue to exist as a person or a desire to become a person.

But recall now the discussion of desires [above]. We showed that one's desires are limited by the concepts one possesses. Therefore one cannot have a desire to continue to exist as a person or a desire to become a person unless one has the concept of a person. The question we must now ask is whether something that is not itself a person could have the concept of such an entity. It seems plausible to hold that it could not. This means that something that is not a person cannot have a desire to become a person. Hence the right to life is confined to persons.

This brings us to our final requirement: an organism cannot have a right to life unless it is capable of self-consciousness, where an organism is self-conscious only if it recognizes that it is itself a continuing subject of experiences and other mental states. To justify this requirement, let us ask whether a person can fail to recognize that it is a person. If the answer were negative, it would follow from the requirement just established that an organism cannot have a right to life unless it possesses self-consciousness.

It is unclear, however, that something necessarily possesses self-consciousness if it is a person. Perhaps a person might fail to notice this fact about himself. Even if this is possible, it seems reasonable to believe that if something is a person, then it is *ipso facto capable* of acquiring the concept of a person, and of recognizing that it is itself a person. Thus even if something can have a right to life without having been self-conscious, it appears that it cannot have such a right without ever having possessed the capacity for self-consciousness.

Thus, the psychological characteristics that bestow a right to life upon an organism are these: it must be a person, capable of self-consciousness, of envisaging a future for itself, and of having desires about its own future states. . . .

The issue of abortion thus ceases to be puzzling. A human fetus does not have a right to life because it does not have the capacity for self-consciousness: it cannot conceive of itself as a continuing subject of experiences; it cannot envisage a future for itself, nor have desires about such a future. A fetus is not a person, but only a potential person. Hence there is no moral objection to abortion. To prohibit it is to inflict unjustified suffering and death upon society.

chapter 5

Euthanasia

INTRODUCTION

Historically, the term *euthanasia* referred to an easy or good death. But it was also often used to mean the active killing of a person for that person's own good, especially to relieve suffering. The definition of the term has now been extended to include the withdrawal or withholding of life-prolonging medical treatment. The latter is frequently called *passive* euthanasia and the former *active* euthanasia. Euthanasia is distinguished from other types of killing by its motive, namely, a concern for the good of the "victim." A murderer intends harm to the victim, but one who commits euthanasia wishes to end another's life because one thinks that the person would be better off dead.

A couple of factors have made euthanasia a recent topic of wide concern. One factor is that people now die from different causes than they did in the past. The causes of death have changed radically during this century. In the United States in 1900 infectious diseases accounted for 60 percent of nonfetal deaths, excluding accidents and suicide; due to the development of vaccines, antibiotics, and better sterilization procedures in 1970 they accounted for fewer than 5 percent.[1] People are much more likely to die in old age of such chronic illnesses as cancer. With these chronic, debilitating diseases, death may come only at the end of a long, painful, and demoralizing process. A second factor is the development of medical technology. With artificial respirators, dialysis, and other technology, people—both adults and children—can now be kept alive when formerly they would have died.

Euthanasia can be accomplished in several ways and in different circumstances. These must be kept distinct, because some people believe they are ethically different. Besides distinguishing between active and passive euthanasia, one can also distinguish between euthanasia that is voluntary and euthanasia that is not. If the victim is rationally competent and voluntarily requests or consents to euthanasia, then it is voluntary; otherwise it is not. However, one also must distinguish between the two forms of euthanasia that are not voluntary. In *involuntary euthanasia,* the

167

victim is rationally competent and is not asked or refuses to consent; in *nonvoluntary euthanasia,* the victim is not rationally competent to make a choice. Thus one can speak of six types of euthanasia: (1) voluntary passive euthanasia; (2) voluntary active euthanasia; (3) involuntary passive euthanasia; (4) involuntary active euthanasia; (5) nonvoluntary passive euthanasia; and (6) nonvoluntary active euthanasia. It is possible, for each type of euthanasia, to hold that some or all instances are wrong, permissible, or obligatory. The following discussion focuses on the first two types and then briefly considers the types of euthanasia that are not voluntary.

Voluntary Passive Euthanasia   In voluntary passive euthanasia, it is assumed that the victim is rationally competent and consents to or requests being allowed to die by the withholding or withdrawal of life-prolonging treatment. Each of the theories will judge the acceptability or inacceptability of this conduct according to its own tenets. The central premise of a *natural-law* view is that life is a basic good. This premise derives from Aquinas's view that all beings act toward self-preservation, which shows that life is a good.[2] Any act directly contrary to the good of human life is wrong. If one chooses to act on a proposal or plan that intentionally includes someone's death, the act is wrong. One can intend a death either directly as an end, as in the murdering of one's enemy, or as a means, as in killing oneself to avoid pain.

Since intending a person's death is wrong, whether one actively brings about the death or fails to prevent death is irrelevant. Seen this way, if one fails to provide intravenous fluids to a person so that he or she dies of dehydration, one has intended that person's death and acted wrongly. But although it is wrong to intentionally bring about someone's death, one need not do everything possible to keep oneself or another alive. If the means necessary to preserve life are unduly burdensome, one need not use them. For example, during the Middle Ages, if persons were advised to move from the seashore to the mountains for their health, they were not ethically required to do so. In refusing or withholding means of prolonging life that are burdensome, one is not intending death. One's intention is simply to avoid an excessive burden rather than to bring about death, for one's intention also will be fulfilled if the person lives. Today, when the permissibility of omitting burdensome means is considered, the terms ordinary and extraordinary means are often used. *Ordinary means* are those that do not impose a sufficient burden to make the failure to use them permissible. *Extraordinary means* are all those that are not ordinary, that are so burdensome that withholding them is permissible. In contemporary medical practice, for example, artificial respirators and heart transplants are understood as extraordinary means, whereas antibiotics for pneumonia or intravenous fluids to prevent dehydration are ordinary means.

To sum up, according to natural-law theory, allowing someone to die is wrong if the intention includes that person's death either as an end or as a means. Extraordinary means of prolonging life need not be employed, provided the intention is merely to avoid their burden rather than to bring about death.

The fundamental premise of a *natural-rights* position is that everyone has a right to life. Traditionally, the right to life is understood as the right not to be killed by others. It has not encompassed positive acts by one person to prolong another's life, as for example, by saving someone from drowning. Consequently, withholding or withdrawing life-prolonging treatment does not violate the right to life and so is permissible.

The *Kantian* tradition is not clear about the permissibility of allowing a person to die. Although Kant clearly holds that suicide is wrong, many commentators believe that his theory does not imply suicide is always wrong. Even if suicide is wrong, it does not follow that refusing life-prolonging treatment is wrong. It probably depends on the reason a person refuses the treatment. Even though Kant believed suicide is wrong, he did not think it necessarily wrong to place oneself in a position in which death would almost certainly result. He, therefore, found it acceptable to die to save one's country, or even to kill oneself if one might be a danger to others, as for example, if one contracted incurable rabies.[3] Kant rejected suicide because it destroys the subject of morality, which is the rational will.[4] Refusing treatment that would incapacitate one's reason would not destroy but preserve the rational will and so seems permissible according to Kant's own rationale.

A *contractarian* view would almost certainly permit compliance with a person's rational, voluntary request to be allowed to die. Rational contractors would presumably choose a system incorporating a maximum liberty compatible with the assurance of a like liberty for others. The liberty to choose one's medical treatment is an application of the basic freedom of bodily integrity protected by the laws of assault and battery. Individual liberties, however, may be limited to better secure the overall system of liberty. A contractor might fear that the liberty to decide for oneself whether treatment should be withheld could be threatened by the withholding of treatment in cases when the victim did not voluntarily consent. Although this consideration might lead contractors to permit the withholding of treatment only under stringent conditions to guarantee the voluntariness and rationality of consent, it would not lead them to forbid the withholding of treatment on a voluntary request.

Finally, *utilitarianism* generally permits people to die voluntarily. Consenting victims have judged that their prolonged lives would be miserable, so withholding treatment and allowing them to die avoids misery and, as far as the victims are concerned, has more utility than prolonging their lives. However, act utilitarians might decide that, in some cases, continued life-prolonging treatment, despite the victim's request to be allowed to die, would be permissible or even obligatory. They might argue that although competent, the victim was mistaken in his or her perception of the utility of prolonging his or her life. They might also argue that the benefits to others would outweigh the continued suffering of the victim. For example, experiments on the victim might help prevent the occurrence of the disease in others or help develop the means to alleviate their suffering.

Voluntary Active Euthanasia   While theories that do not permit allowing persons to die voluntarily are unlikely to permit them to be killed, theories that do permit voluntary passive euthanasia may not permit active euthanasia. Whereas *natural-law* views usually will permit a person to die by the omission of extraordinary treatment, almost all active killing is forbidden. (In killing, one usually chooses a plan that intends death.) Nonetheless, some conduct that will cause death is permissible. Many natural-law theorists adopt the doctrine of double effect. The doctrine of double effect holds that an action having both a good and bad effect is permissible if (1) the bad effect is not intended as a means or as an end; and (2) the good effect outweighs the bad.[5] Condition 1 is the crucial one, for it guarantees that death is not intended. The doctrine of double effect gives little scope for euthanasia. Although it permits, for example, giving drugs to alleviate pain even if side effects were to shorten a person's life, it does not justify injecting a lethal dose of morphine.

The central question asked in the *natural-rights* tradition is whether the right not to be killed can be waived. One must distinguish between the inalienability of a right and its unwaivability. Consider the property right to one's car, which includes a right that others not use it. One may waive that right for particular people, for example, by letting a friend use it for an afternoon. However, one retains one's property right to the car. One alienates one's right to the car if one sells it and thus surrenders one's entire right to it. An inalienable right not to be killed could thus still be waivable. In one natural-rights view, which is basically that of John Locke, one cannot waive one's right not to be killed, because life is a gift from God and people are, in effect, God's property. Curiously, in this view, the right to life really is already alienated, inasmuch as it is God's right rather than one's own. If one considers individuals the full possessors of their right to life, then the right can be waived and voluntary active killing is permissible.

A *Kantian* view of active killing depends on whether Kant is correct about suicide. If suicide is wrong, then with a few possible exceptions noted earlier, active euthanasia is wrong. By the universal law of nature test, one could not rationally will a universal maxim that one be killed. Consequently, no one else could will a universal law permitting him or her to kill the victim, for were that person in the victim's position, he or she could not rationally will the universal law. Similarly, by the doctrine of ends, if one would not be treating oneself as an end in willing one's death, neither would someone else. In short, active euthanasia always depends on whether it is permissible that the individual will he or she be killed.

A very prevalent justification for active killing stems from the Kantian tradition. It emphasizes the autonomy (self-determination) of rational agents. To respect that autonomy, competent persons must be free to choose life or death. As it is permissible for competent persons to exercise their autonomy to choose death, it is also permissible for another to kill them if they rationally and voluntarily choose it. This argument does not, however, establish that medical personnel or anyone else has an obligation to kill a person who so requests it.

Although *contractarians* would certainly hold a principle generally forbidding the killing of others, they might allow an exception if the person rationally and voluntarily requested to be killed. To allow for such a death might maximize liberty and benefit people suffering intolerable conditions who might thus be classified as among the least advantaged persons. Contractors would insist that the person voluntarily request that he or she be killed, for otherwise a significant freedom would be infringed. Moreover, they would require that, allowing for people's differing conceptions of a good life, the decision be rational. One would want to be protected from decisions one might make in an irrational state of mind or perhaps even from irrational decisions made when in a normal state of mind. How, precisely, another person is to decide whether one's decision is rational, given one's conception of the good, is not completely clear. Contractors would wish to balance assurance that the decision was rational with the claim to freedom, but no clear, explicit formula for so doing is evident.

Finally, *utilitarian* theory implies that no intrinsic moral difference exists between actively killing and allowing to die. Here it clearly and sharply differs from the natural-law tradition. The latter emphasizes whether death is intended, but for the utilitarian the intention makes no difference as long as the utility of the consequences is the same. Indeed, in some cases, utilitarian considerations clearly favor active killing. If, for instance, allowing a person to die will result in great pain during the lengthy process of dying, then painless killing is preferable. Generally, to decide whether the dying process will be so painful as to render actively killing a person preferable, one should be guided by the patient's wishes. If patients request only that they be allowed to die, then they have decided that the process of dying will not be so bad as to render active killing more useful for them. Sometimes a utilitarian might decide that a person is mistaken as to which method will have the highest utility for her or him. Rule utilitarians might differ from act utilitarians, for they might believe that accepting a rule against killing with an exception permitting actively killing people on their request would have worse consequences than not allowing that exception. It might significantly decrease people's respect for life and thus lead to other undesirable consequences. However, few rule utilitarians would be so persuaded by this argument as to forbid active euthanasia, although they might have fairly stringent conditions as to the circumstances in which it is permissible.

Involuntary and Nonvoluntary Euthanasia   If voluntary euthanasia is prohibited by a theory so, of course, is euthanasia that is not
voluntary. For some theories, voluntariness is crucial to the permissibility of euthanasia. In *natural-law* theory, however, the voluntariness of
euthanasia is irrelevant to its permissibility. As it is the intention of
causing death rather than its voluntariness that is crucial, it can be permissible to cause or to allow someone to die who cannot consent to it.
Extraordinary treatment may be withheld from, or medicines shortening
life as a side effect may be administered to, incompetent adults or infants
and perhaps even competent persons who refuse to consent, although it
is difficult to conceive of an acceptable example of the latter.

In the *natural-rights* tradition, involuntary active euthanasia is always
wrong. The right not to be killed is certainly violated if the victim does
not consent, no matter what the reason. The only possible exception to
the wrongness of active involuntary euthanasia would be if the person
were a threat to someone else's life, even innocently so.[6] However, in
that case, the reason for the killing would be self-defense, not the well-
being of the victim, so it would not even be appropriately classified as
euthanasia. As no right to life-prolonging treatment exists, withholding
it is permissible whether the person is incompetent or is competent and
requests its continuation.

Likewise, in the *Kantian* tradition involuntary euthanasia of competent persons is wrong. If a competent patient wills treatment, one could
not will withholding it were one in the patient's condition. The permissibility of nonvoluntary euthanasia is somewhat more difficult to determine. The problem is that the Kantian view is not clear about the status
that should be accorded to nonrational persons. Morality is founded on,
and holds for, rational wills. In one interpretation, all human beings have
an underlying rational self, so they must all be treated as ends. In another
interpretation, only beings manifesting rationality must be treated as
ends. The former position seems to be the better interpretation of Kant.
According to it, nonvoluntary euthanasia is permissible if, and only if,
a rational person in the victim's position could consistently will his death.
Finally, the neo-Kantian argument from autonomy for voluntary euthanasia cannot be extended to support involuntary euthanasia, for such
euthanasia clearly denies a person's autonomy. Nor can nonvoluntary
euthanasia with substituted consent be considered an exercise of the
victim's autonomy, even if it respects the victim's expressed wishes before becoming incompetent.

Although *contractarians* emphasize the importance of voluntariness
for the permissibility of euthanasia, they might permit some euthanasia
that is not voluntary. Contractarians would not agree to involuntary
euthanasia, for it permits someone to end another's life against his or her
will. However, they might well agree to a principle permitting nonvoluntary euthanasia. For example, contractarians would have no reason
to prohibit euthanasia of the irreversibly comatose. If comatose, people
have no opportunity to enjoy the primary goods or to achieve their

conception of the good. Generalizing from this, contractors would probably agree to nonvoluntary euthanasia for anyone incapable of significantly achieving any plausible conception of the good.

Finally, although *utilitarians* have good reason to be cautious about euthanasia that is not voluntary, they do not prohibit it in all cases. Act and rule utilitarians usually will differ in their thinking about involuntary euthanasia. In either view, the fact that a person wants to live is evidence of the utility to him or her of continued life. However, the utility of continued life to the individual must be weighed against its utility to others. Suppose that in order to live a few more weeks, someone wants a very expensive treatment, for example, an artificial heart costing $200,000. The cost, and other burdens, on relatives and others might outweigh the utility to the patient. Accepting a rule limiting the amount of resources persons could consume in prolonging their lives might have more utility than accepting a rule without such a limit, so a rule utilitarian might agree to this limit. But an act utilitarian might go further. Suppose a person's continued life would be a financial and emotional strain on his or her family, and if he or she died his or her kidneys and eyes could be transplanted to others. The utility to others of euthanasia might well outweigh the utility of continued life to the person. Rule utilitarians probably would not accept a rule permitting euthanasia in such cases. If a rule permitting involuntary euthanasia were accepted, then everyone would be afraid that should they become seriously ill a physician or someone else might judge that there would be more utility in their dying. A rule prohibiting euthanasia in such situations would produce less unhappiness and so more utility, everything considered.

Act utilitarians would permit nonvoluntary euthanasia whenever its utility was greater than that of the person's continued life. The first and most important consideration would be the happiness the victim might expect from continued life. If the person was likely to suffer great pain and never recover, then life would have net disutility for him or her. If the person were likely to recover and have an enjoyable life, or have an enjoyable life even if he or she did not fully recover, then life would have net utility for him or her and euthanasia could be justified only if the benefits to others from his or her death outweighed those to the person from continued life. For the reasons given above, a rule utilitarian would probably limit the permissibility of nonvoluntary euthanasia to situations in which continued life would have net disutility for the victim.

Readings   The selection from Germain Grisez and Joseph Boyle, Jr., represents the natural-law tradition. They argue that every act of killing is wrong but that not every deadly deed is killing. Active euthanasia as a form of killing is wrong regardless of its voluntariness. Allowing a person to die, as long as it involves acting on a proposal encompassing a person's death as an end or as a means, is also wrong. Although they do not use the doctrine of double effect, according to their theory, it is permissible to provide medicines that might shorten life, if the proposal one acts on does not include the person's death as a means or as an end.

Finally, they distinguish between ordinary and extraordinary means and argue that it is permissible to refuse or not to provide treatment by extraordinary means.

David Richards analyzes the right to life and its limits on the basis of an "autonomy-based interpretation of treating persons as equals." By this, he means that equality is due persons because of their capacity to evaluate critically and to alter their first-order desires.[7] Protection of persons as equals requires the recognition of human rights both morally and legally. Thus, his recognition of human rights is based on the Kantian tradition. In the material included here, he analyzes the right to life by the principles of nonmaleficence, mutual aid, and paternalism. These principles do not prohibit euthanasia if persons voluntarily and rationally choose it.

In the final selection, James Rachels examines the argument that euthanasia for persons suffering from intractable pain is an act of mercy. He notes that this argument stems from utilitarianism, but that traditional utilitarianism faces some difficulties. He thus modifies the utilitarian conception of happiness as pleasure and the absence of pain to promoting people's interests. Finally, he notes that almost any plausible theory will have to consider the consequences of actions on people's interests and, to that extent, recognize the argument from mercy.

Notes

[1]U. S. Department of Commerce, Bureau of the Census, *Historical Statistics of the United States,* Bicentennial Edition (Washington, D.C.: U. S. Government Printing Office, 1975), vol. 1, p. 58.

[2]St. Thomas Aquinas, *Summa Theologica,* trans. Anton Pegis, *The Basic Writings of Saint Thomas Aquinas* (New York: Random House, 1945), I–II, Question 94, Article 2.

[3]Immanuel Kant, *The Doctrine of Virtue,* trans. Mary J. Gregor (New York: Harper & Row, 1964), p. 86; Akademie, p. 423.

[4]Ibid., p. 85; Akademie, pp. 422–423.

[5]Edwin F. Healey, S.J., *Medical Ethics* (Chicago, Ill.: Loyola University Press, 1956), p. 98; Norman St. John-Stevas, *Life, Death, and the Law* (Cleveland, O.: World, Meridian Books, 1961), p. 190; John C. Ford, S.J., "The Morality of Obliteration Bombing," in *War and Morality,* ed. Richard A. Wasserstrom (Belmont, Calif.: Wadsworth, 1970), p. 26.

[6]Robert Nozick, *Anarchy, State, and Utopia* (New York: Basic Books, 1974), pp. 34–35.

[7]David A. J. Richards, *Sex, Drugs, Death, and the Law* (Totowa, N. J.: Rowman and Littlefield, 1982), pp. 8–10.

Bibliography on Euthanasia

Bayles, Michael D. *Reproductive Ethics.* Englewood Cliffs, N.J.: Prentice-Hall, 1984. Chapter 5.

Feinberg, Joel. *Harm to Self.* New York: Oxford University Press, 1986. Chapter 27.

————. "Voluntary Euthanasia and the Inalienable Right to Life." *Philosophy & Public Affairs* 7 (1978): 93–123.

Glover, Jonathan. *Causing Death and Saving Lives.* New York: Penguin, 1977.

Keyserlingk, Edward W. *Sanctity of Life or Quality of Life.* Protection of Life Series. Ottawa: Law Reform Commission of Canada, 1979.

Kipnis, Kenneth, and Williamson, Gailyn M. "Nontreatment Decisions for Severely Compromised Newborns." *Ethics* 95 (1984): 90–111.

Kluge, Eike-Henner W. *The Ethics of Deliberate Death.* Port Washington, N.Y.: Kennikat Press, 1981.

Kohl, Marvin. *The Morality of Killing.* New York: Humanities Press, 1974.

————, ed. *Beneficent Euthanasia.* Buffalo, N.Y.: Prometheus Books, 1975.

Kuhse, Helga, and Singer, Peter. *Should the Baby Live?* Oxford: Oxford University Press, 1985.

Ladd, John, ed. *Ethical Issues Relating to Life and Death.* New York: Oxford University Press, 1979.

President's Commission for the Study of Ethical Problems in Medicine and Biomedical and Behavioral Research. *Deciding to Forego Life-Sustaining Treatment.* Washington, D.C.: U.S. Government Printing Office, 1983.

Rachels, James. *The End of Life: Euthanasia and Morality.* Oxford: Oxford University Press, 1986.

————. "Euthanasia." In *Matters of Life and Death,* edited by Tom Regan, 2d ed., pp. 35–76. New York: Random House, 1986.

Steinbock, Bonnie, ed. *Killing and Letting Die.* Englewood Cliffs, N.J.: Prentice-Hall, 1980.

VanDeVeer, Donald. "Whither Baby Doe?" In *Matters of Life and Death,* edited by Tom Regan, 2d ed., pp. 213–255. New York: Random House, 1986.

Veatch, Robert M. *Death, Dying and the Biological Revolution.* New Haven: Yale University Press, 1976.

Problem Case
Allowing Dad to Die?

Stan and Lorraine have a serious and fateful decision to make, namely, whether to remove their father from the respirator and allow him to die. Since Dad and their mother were divorced a number of years ago, and Dad's second marriage also ended in divorce, the decision falls on Stan and Lorraine.

Dad has just had his second severe heart attack. Apparently his heart had stopped for some time before being resuscitated, and there was significant brain damage. The doctors say that although it is too early to tell for sure just how much mental ability he will have, they are confident that he will have a significant deficit but, barring another heart attack, he could live for a good while. They say that they have seen people in worse shape pull through and lead minimal but pleasant lives. Currently, Dad is stabilized and on a respirator.

A few years ago Dad made a Living Will specifying that should he not be likely to recover from physical or mental disability, he not be kept alive by artificial means or heroic measures. Dad's personal doctor has been called and informed the hospital physicians about the Living Will. If they ignore the Living Will, nothing can be done to them, so they say they will be guided by the family's wishes.

What should Stan and Lorraine tell the doctors? Why? Suppose Dad had not made a Living Will (or the state does not provide for them) but has said that when his time comes, he wants to go peacefully. Would that make a difference to what Stan and Lorraine should do? To what the doctors should do?

GERMAIN GRISEZ AND JOSEPH M. BOYLE, JR.
EUTHANASIA

THE MORALITY OF KILLING: GENERAL CONSIDERATIONS

In the strict sense one kills a person when, having considered bringing about a person's death as something one could do, one commits oneself to doing it by adopting this proposal instead of some alternative and by undertaking to execute it. By definition killing in the strict sense is an action contrary to the good of life. The adoption of a proposal to bring about someone's death is incompatible with respect for this good. Thus every act which is an act of killing in the strict sense is immoral. No additional circumstance or condition can remove this immorality.

This definition and moral characterization of killing in the strict sense make no distinction between intent to kill, attempt to kill, and the consummation of the undertaking by successful execution. These distinctions, which are legally significant, are morally irrelevant. If one commits oneself to realizing a certain state of affairs, by the commitment one constitutes oneself as a certain type of person. If one commits oneself to killing a person, one constitutes oneself a murderer. This remains true even if one is prevented from attempting to execute one's purpose—for example, if someone else kills the intended victim first. Even more obviously it remains true if one attempts to execute one's purpose but fails—for example, if one shoots to kill but misses the intended victim.

Although everything which is an act of killing in the strict sense is immoral, not every deadly deed is an act of killing in this sense. . . . Some deadly deeds carry out a consciously projected design, but the performance is not the execution of a proposal adopted by the actor's choice to bring about the death of a human individual. . . . In what follows we call this type of performance a "deadly deed" to distinguish it from a killing in the strict sense.

From Germain Grisez and Joseph M. Boyle, Jr., *Life and Death with Liberty and Justice: A Contribution to the Euthanasia Debate* (Notre Dame, Ind.: University of Notre Dame Press, 1979), pp. 393–394, 412–419. Copyright 1979, University of Notre Dame Press, Notre Dame, Indiana 46556.

Finally, there are other cases of causing death, such as some killing in self-defense, which are neither killing in the strict sense nor deadly deeds as here defined. The proposal adopted or the consciously projected design carried out by persons defending themselves might not extend beyond incapacitating the attacker, but this can result in the attacker's death if the only available and adequate means to incapacitate the attacker also will result in mortal wounds.

Deadly deeds and death-causing behavior which are not killing in the strict sense might or might not be immoral. The fact that killing in the strict sense always is immoral does not mean that other acts which result in someone's death are morally acceptable or less immoral than killing in the strict sense. What is distinctive about deadly deeds and death-causing behavior is that their morality is not settled by the kinds of acts they are, whereas the morality of killing in the strict sense is settled by the kind of act it is.

Of course, ordinary language, which heavily relies upon observable behavior in classifying acts, does not embody the distinctions we have made. Thus, to evaluate the morality of various classes of acts which result in death, we begin from the ordinary conceptions of these acts which are described by ordinary language and then apply our analysis to the morally significant distinctions in the subject matter.

It is worth noticing that our approach here would be quite impossible in the law, where actions must be determined by factors about which evidence is possible. But morality is not primarily a matter of making judgments about actions, still less a matter of one person judging the actions of another. Rather, morality is a matter of shaping one's own life toward its fullness. Hence, distinctions which individuals can respect or ignore in the hidden depths of their own consciences can be extremely important to morality, although totally unrealistic as instruments of social control, and so wholly irrelevant to the law. . . .

ACTIVE EUTHANASIA: VOLUNTARY AND NONVOLUNTARY

Considering matters from a moral point of view and from the side of the one whose life is to be ended, voluntary euthanasia is not significantly different from other cases of suicide. The proposal is to bring about death as a means to ending suffering. This proposal, if adopted and executed, is an instance of killing in the strict sense. It can never be morally justified.

Of course, a person who is in severe pain and who seeks death to escape it is likely to have mitigated responsibility or even to be drawn into acceptance without a deliberate choice, just as is the case with others whose suffering drives them to a deadly deed against themselves.

However, if an individual plans to seek euthanasia and arranges for it well in advance of the time of suffering, then the possibility that the demand for death is not an expression of deliberate choice is greatly lessened. The conditions which from the point of view of proponents of euthanasia are optimum for making a decision about the matter are precisely the conditions in which the decision is likely to be a morally unjustifiable act of killing in the strict sense.

Considering voluntary euthanasia from the point of view of the person who would carry out the killing, matters seem no better from a moral viewpoint. The performance can hardly fail to be an execution of a deliberate choice; the one carrying out the killing can hardly be driven to it, nor can anyone in the present culture accept the duty unquestioningly.

Of course, when a family member kills a relative under the present legal conditions, there is considerable likelihood that pressures of emotion are an important factor, and there is a possibility that no act of killing is done. But we are now thinking of the moral responsibility of someone who would carry out requested euthanasia if the practice were legalized, through acting by deliberate choice and perhaps in a professional capacity.

It might be objected that not everyone believes that human life itself is a basic good. Perhaps this belief is sincere. In such a case individuals seeking euthanasia and those providing this service would be doing nothing immoral by deliberate choice, for they would be acting upon a sincere belief, even if this belief is mistaken. After all, people are responsible, not for what they actually do, but for what they sincerely believe they are doing. How can one consider immoral the acts of those who seek or provide beneficent euthanasia in acting upon the conviction that human life is merely an instrumental good?

Our first response to this objection is that we are concerned here, not to judge anyone, but only to clarify sound guidelines for morally responsible deliberation and choice. We have argued . . . against the instrumentalist view of human life. If it is false, then those who shape their lives on this false assumption at the least are seriously mistaken about a matter of basic human concern. This mistake can hardly fail to lead to serious consequences for their attitudes and behavior toward other persons in many instances in which life is at stake.

But a further response to this objection is needed. The insight that human life is a basic good of persons is not a matter of empirical fact; it is a principle of practical reasoning. This principle underlies large areas of everyone's rational behavior. It is not easy to be mistaken about the inherent goodness of life, its inviolability, its worthiness of respect in every instance without exception. Somewhere there must be moral responsibility for a bias which hides and distorts so fundamental a truth.

This responsibility might be in an individual's own previous immoral choices. The opinion that life is not a basic good which deserves respect might be an effect of personal rationalization. Then again there is a tendency for this false opinion to attain the status of a climate of opinion by the formation of a social or cultural bias against human life. Here those who form opinion, shape the law, provide what ought to be scholarly reflection upon morality, and so on are the morally responsible agents of the moral blindness of others.

Nonvoluntary euthanasia also clearly proposes death as a treatment of choice. The act hardly can fail to be killing in the strict sense. And in addition to the violation of the good of life, the rights of those to be killed also will be violated—for example, by denial to them of equal protection of the laws. Nonvoluntary euthanasia would violate both life and justice.

On our analysis abortion is a subclass of nonvoluntary euthanasia. It is especially complicated, since in the case of abortion there are instances in which the child's death results from some act which is not itself the execution of a proposal that the child should die. In cases in which the retarded, the insane, the senile, or others would be terminated by nonvoluntary euthanasia it is difficult to think of circumstances in which their deaths would be caused otherwise than by the carrying out of the proposal that they should die, on the rationalization that their lives are not worth living and that they will be better off dead.

It will be objected that some who carried out nonvoluntary euthanasia—or who now promote it—might be motivated by genuine sympathy for others. We do not deny this possibility, although we suspect that the movement for euthanasia would have little political power were it not also motivated by the desire to get rid of the burden of unwanted people.

The important point is that sympathy, like other emotions, can lead to grossly immoral acts. Not all immorality is explicit egoism and self-indulgence. By sympathy one is identified with another psychologically, just as by patriotism one is identified with one's country, by racism with one's race, and so on. These emotions are morally neutral in themselves. They do permit one, however, to act immorally while to seem not to act out of self-interest. Sympathy together with a fanatical attachment to the good of avoiding pain and suffering can lead to grossly immoral violations of the good of life and rights of others in the ultimate form of paternalism: the killing of people for their own good.

Like all forms of paternalism, beneficent euthanasia would involve the arrogant presumption that one can determine on the basis of one's own scheme of values what is best for others who might well not share that scheme. And like all forms of paternalism which become institutionalized, beneficent euthanasia could easily become a mask for intentional injustices toward those whose lives were "kindly" extinguished—extinguished in the interests of others or society at large.

OMISSIONS, KILLING, AND LETTING DIE

The preceding treatment has been concerned with instances in which people bring about death by an outward performance. We now turn to a consideration of cases in which individuals refuse treatment for themselves or others, or withhold treatment, or fail or neglect to give it. To apply the moral theory which we articulated . . . to such cases we must first say something about omissions.

If people act when they carry out a proposal which they have adopted by choice, certain cases of outward nonperformance must count as human actions. One can adopt a proposal and carry it out by deliberately not causing or preventing something which one could cause or prevent. One's choice not to cause or prevent something can be a way of realizing a state of affairs one considers somehow desirable. For example, one might adopt the proposal to protest against a government policy permitting the use of public funds for abortion by not paying certain taxes. In this case one aims to realize a desired state of affairs by means of nonconformance with the demands of the law. The nonconformance need involve no outward performance at all.

Omissions of this type—those in which one undertakes to realize a proposed state of affairs by not causing or preventing something—are very important for understanding the morality of withholding treatment from dying patients, refusing treatment proposed for oneself, and in general letting people die.

On the analysis of this sort of omission which we just now stated it clearly is possible to kill in the strict sense by deliberately letting someone die. If one adopts the proposal to bring about a person's death and realizes this proposal by not behaving as one otherwise would behave, then one is committed to the state of affairs which includes the person's death. This commitment, although carried out by a nonperformance, is morally speaking an act of killing. It involves the adoption and execution of a proposal contrary to the basic good of human life. Thus, any case in which one chooses the proposal that a person die and on this basis allows the person to die is necessarily immoral.

For example, if a child is born suffering from various defects and if the physicians and parents decide that the child, the family, and society will all be better off if the burdens entailed by the child's continued life are forestalled by its death, and if they therefore adopt the proposal not to perform a simple operation, which otherwise would be done, so that the child will die, then the parents and physicians morally speaking kill the child—"kill" in the strict sense clarified at the beginning of this chapter. The fact that there is no blood spilled, no poison injected, that the death certificate can honestly show that the child has died from complications arising from its defective condition—none of this is morally relevant. The moral act is no different from any other moral act of murder.

The same thing will be true in every instance in which a judgment is made that someone—whether oneself or another—would be better off dead, the proposal to bring about death by not causing or preventing something is considered and adopted, and this proposal is executed by outward nonperformance of behavior which one otherwise might have attempted.

Moreover, it must be noticed that hastening death is bringing about death; no one lives forever, and so all killing merely hastens death. The essential factor from a moral point of view is, not whether a person killed already is dying, but whether one's performance or omission executes a proposal that one bring about the state of affairs which includes the person's being dead when one thinks that otherwise they might be alive.

It is worth noting that one's adopting a proposal to bring about a person's death does not require that one regard the person's death as desirable in itself, or that one will be pleased when it occurs. One might regret that a patient is suffering from a painful and mortal disease; one might wish that a retarded, insane, or senile person were normal and vigorously healthy. One might feel deep compassion for the person to be killed; one might be very reluctant to kill the person; one might feel very sad when the person dies. Nevertheless, if one adopts a proposal to hasten death—for example, by injecting an overdose of opiates—one does an act of killing in the strict sense. The commitment contrary to the good of life is made, although it is made in a situation in which alternatives lack much of their ordinary appeal, and although it is made with great sadness and executed with great regret.

This point is not too difficult to grasp in cases of action which involves an outward performance. But the same thing is just as true when the proposed method of killing is by not causing or preventing something. The murderous quality of an omission can more easily be overlooked or rationalized, however, due to confusion between the adoption of the proposal and the emotional situation and wishes which accompany the adoption of the proposal.

One killing by omission in a case of this sort both wants and does not want dead the person who is to be killed. The wanting is the voluntary adoption of the proposal that the person be dead; this is what is morally determinative. The not-wanting is in the wishes that things might be otherwise, the feeling of sadness and so forth with which the chosen means to the desired good—for example, release from suffering—are brought about.[1] . . .

NONTREATMENT AND REFUSAL OF TREATMENT

The fundamental point about these omissions is that one can omit to do some good or prevent some evil without adopting any proposal which either is opposed to the good or embraces (as means) the evil whose occurrence one accepts. This possibility is most obviously instantiated when one must forgo doing a certain good or preventing a certain evil because one has a duty, incompatible with doing the good or preventing the evil, to do some other good or prevent some other evil.

For example, in an emergency situation in which many people are seriously injured and the medical resources—including time and personnel—are limited, those making decisions must choose to treat some and put off the treatment of others, perhaps with fatal consequences to those not treated first. The nontreatment of those who are not treated is deliberate; even their deaths might be foreseen as an inevitable consequence and knowingly accepted when the decision to treat others is made. Yet plainly the nontreatment of those who are not treated need involve no proposal that these people should die or die more quickly than they otherwise would. Provided there is no partiality or other breach of faith with those not treated, the execution of a proposal to save others does not embrace the death of those who die, and no immorality is done.

In the preceding example there is a certain lack of choice, in that the situation itself prohibits one from treating everyone. There are other situations in which someone forgoes doing something good because of the opportunity to do something else which also is good but incompatible with the adoption and execution of the first proposal. This situation arises whenever there is a choice between alternatives, any of which can be adopted without moral fault. It can arise in a specific case in which one and only one alternative would involve acting to save a person's life.

For example, physicians can refuse to accept additional patients, even though they know that their refusal will lead to a patient's earlier death, without proposing that the patient die. Physicians might simply be choosing to limit their practice at a level which permits them to take reasonable care of their children's personal needs, of their own health, their religious duties, and other legitimate concerns.

Obviously there are limits. Physicians who refuse occasionally to interrupt their recreation to tend to a severe medical emergency might not be in violation of medical ethics or any specific duty, but any person with a proper level of dedication will be generous with time and talents in the service of others, and all who are fair-minded will do to others as they would wish others to do to them and to their own loved ones. In other words, the golden rule sets a very important moral limit beyond which an upright person will not go in omitting to serve the needs of others. To violate this limit is just as immoral—and can show just as vicious a disposition—as to violate the good of life by killing in the strict sense.

There is another type of reason for forgoing doing good which involves no disrespect for the good which would be realized by the action. One might notice that doing the action good in itself will in fact bring about many undesirable consequences. And one might choose not to adopt the proposal to do the good in order to avoid accepting these various bad consequences. This situation is exemplified in a very important way in many instances in which potentially life-prolonging treatment is refused, withheld, or withdrawn—even in the case of a patient who is not dying—because of the expected disadvantages of accepting, carrying out, or continuing treatment.

In chapter nine we have articulated grounds on which someone might reasonably consider treatment undesirable: if the treatment is experimental or risky, if it would be painful or otherwise experienced negatively, if it would interfere with activities or experiences the patient might otherwise enjoy, if it would conflict with some moral or religious principle to which the patient adheres, if it would be psychologically repugnant to the patient, or if the financial or other impact of the treatment upon other persons would constitute a compelling reason to refuse treatment.

The moral legitimacy of refusing treatment in some cases on some such grounds certainly was part of what Pius XII was indicating by his famous distinction between ordinary and extraordinary means of treatment. The Pope defined "extraordinary means" as ones which involve a "great burden," and he allowed that one could morally forgo the use of extraordinary means.[2]

The conception of extraordinary means clearly is abused, however, when the proposal is to bring about death by the omission of treatment, and the difficulties of the treatment are pointed to by way of rationalizing the murderous act. If it is decided that a person would be better off dead and that treatment which would be given to another will be withheld because of the poor quality of the life to be preserved, then the focus in decision is not upon the means and its disadvantageous consequences. Rather, what is feared is that the means would be effective, that life would be preserved, and that the life itself and its consequences would be a burden.

Moreover, even when treatment is refused, withheld, or withdrawn because of an objection to the means—and without the adopting of a proposal to bring about death—there still can be a serious moral failing.

A person who refuses lifesaving or life-prolonging treatment, not on a suicidal proposal but because of great repugnance for the treatment itself, might have an obligation to maintain life longer in order to fulfill duties toward others.

For example, someone on dialysis might wish to give up the treatment because of the difficulties it involves, and some persons in this situation could discontinue treatment and accept death without moral fault. But a parent with children in need of continued care, a professional person with grave responsibilities, and many other persons who can prolong their lives at considerable sacrifice to themselves are morally bound to do so, even by this extraordinary means, because they have accepted duties which others are entitled to have fulfilled, and persons who love the goods as one ought will faithfully fulfill duties toward others at considerable cost to themselves.

Similarly, if one refuses, withholds, or withdraws lifesaving or life-prolonging treatment for another because of the grave burdens entailed by such treatment, the burdens must be grave indeed. This is especially clear in cases in which the patient is not dying—for example, cases of defective infants. One must be quite sure, at the least, that with no suicidal proposal one would in the patient's place not wish the treatment. Otherwise, one accepts moral responsibility for a very grave wrong toward the patient. . . .

Again, people can omit treatment as part of a project to cause death without becoming morally guilty of killing in the strict sense because the project is not the proposal upon which they act. Consider, for instance, the situation of nurses who are trained—perhaps too strictly—to follow the orders of physicians. If parents and physicians conspire in the killing of a defective infant by starving it to death, and if the physicians order that neither food nor fluids are to be given the infant, a nurse might not think of disobeying. In such cases nurses do not make themselves parties to the conspiracy. Their fault, if fault it is, is in their too uncritical acceptance of the domination of their own proper sphere of activity by physicians, even when physicians no longer act in the interest of the patient and in the service of life.

Notes

[1]See Gerald Hughes, "Killing and Letting Die," *The Month* 236 (1975): 43–44.
[2]Pius XII, "The Prolongation of Life," *The Pope Speaks* 4 (1957–1958): 395–396 (*AAS,* 49 [1957], pp. 1027–1033 at 1030).

DAVID A. J. RICHARDS
MORAL PRINCIPLES CONSTITUTIVE OF THE RIGHT TO LIFE

For purposes of the present analysis of the moral right to life, let us stipulate a common denominator of the idea of rights as such, whether moral rights or legal rights—those enforceable by the civil or criminal law. Having a right implies at least the justifiability of coercion, in some form, in protecting certain kinds of choice from incursion by others, whether the individual has the additional liberty of choosing whether these rights shall be enforced, for example, contracts in the civil law, or whether he does not have that choice, for example, rights to personal safety in the criminal law.[1] In the moral sphere, such justifiability of coercion would be crucially defined by moral principles of obligation and duty, which by definition justify coercion in their enforcement. Accordingly, the delineation of the moral structure of the right to life requires analysis of the pertinent moral principles of obligation and duty that justify coercion in the protection of life. We shall focus here on the relevant aspects of three such principles: nonmaleficence, mutual aid, and paternalism. . . .

From David A. J. Richards, *Sex, Drugs, Death and the Law* (Totowa, N.J.: Rowman and Littlefield, 1982), pp. 217–227. Reprinted with permission.

1. THE PRINCIPLE OF NONMALEFICENCE. The principles of natural duty are those principles, justifying coercion in their enforcement, that would be agreed to or universalized, consistent with the autonomy-based interpretation of treating persons as equals, as an effective public morality governing the relations of persons *simpliciter,* whatever their institutional relations to one another. Foremost among these principles is the principle of nonmaleficence,[2] which, for our present purposes, we may construe in terms of the requirement not intentionally, knowingly, or negligently to inflict harms on other persons except in cases of necessary and proportional self-defense or in certain extreme cases of just necessity or extreme duress. Since our present concern is with the broad implications of this principle for the right to life, which it in part defines, let us focus here on the moral basis of the prohibition of harm.

Let us begin with the idea of personhood, or rational autonomy, in terms of which treatment as equals, from the human rights perspective, is defined. . . . Personhood is defined in terms of certain higher-order capacities, developed or undeveloped, that enable persons critically to reflect on and revise the form of their lives in terms of arguments and evidence to which they freely and rationally assent. The exercise of these capacities is shown when people adopt plans of living in terms of various forms of evaluative criteria—: sometimes principles of rational choice whereby they define and pursue their system of ends in a way designed to satisfy all or a great number of them in an harmonious and complementary way over their life cycle, sometimes personal ideals of excellence in which they invest their rational self-esteem, and sometimes in terms of ethical principles either of minimal decency or superogatory heroism or beneficence. From the perspective of an autonomy-based ethics, divergent and quite disparate plans of life may be reasonably affirmed and pursued on such terms; the notion of rationality, in terms of which persons often evaluate and revise their lives, yields a neutral theory of the good which is compatible with enormous diversity and idiosyncrasy of life design. Consistent with this diversity and idiosyncrasy, however, are certain things which we may assume all rational persons want as typical conditions of whatever else they want. For purposes of his theory of distributive justice, Rawls calls these "general goods" and focuses on wealth, status, property, etc., as examples. For purposes of our present focus on the natural duties, we may identify as such goods the typical rational interest of persons, as conditions of pursuing whatever else they want, in basic integrity and control of their bodies, persons, and lives and thus in security from forms of interference with this integrity, including injury, pointless cruelty, and most forms of killing.

The principle of nonmaleficence would be agreed to or universalized, consistent with the autonomy-based interpretation of treating persons as equals, because it secures the fundamental interest of personal integrity in terms of a prohibition that does not typically require persons to sacrifice substantial interests. Substantial interests are not sacrificed because the pursuit of persons' substantial interests does not indispensably require acts forbidden by the principle, or at least does not typically do so. Forms of self-defense and the like are expressly exempt from the principle because they do not clearly observe this or similar conditions.[3]

The principle of nonmaleficence, consistent with its moral basis in protecting personal integrity on fair terms to all persons who both benefit from the principle and bear the burden of observing it, is defined in terms of the prohibition of harms, which is in turn defined in terms of the frustration of the rational interests of persons as conditions of whatever else they want. It is important to see and give weight to the place that *harm,* so understood, plays in properly interpreting its requirements. Not all forms of pain are forbidden by the principle, for some kinds of pain infliction do not violate the rational interests of persons and thus are not harms. Consider, for example, the pain of self-knowledge that good education or therapy may indispensably involve. The infliction of such pain, guided by wise experience, is no harm; indeed it is often among the greater benefits one person can do for another.

Correspondingly, the principle does not forbid killing as such, but forbids those killings which are harms. Clearly, most killings of persons are harms in the sense to which we can give a sensible interpretation, namely that persons typically have a rational interest in living which killing frustrates. Epicurus, in a famous conundrum, challenged the intuition that one's death could be an evil:

> So death, the most terrifying of ills, is nothing to us, since so long as we exist, death is not with us; but when death comes, then we do not exist. It does not then concern either the living or the dead, since for the former it is not, and the latter are no more.[4]

Surely this paradox falsely supposes that the evil of death must, to be sensible, be contemporal with life as such, which would render the concept senseless and incoherent, but it is a mistake to identify the evil of death with some absence of good in living. The rational self-interest of persons in life is not in life as such, but in the kinds of plans and aspirations of the person which life makes possible. Such plans and aspirations are independent of our actually living, for their success or failure may be known only long after our deaths. And during our lives, such plans and aspirations are our reasons for living; indeed, death is an evil, where it is an evil, because it cuts off those still vital plans in which we have centered our selves.

It must follow that there are some cases in which killing or ending one's life will not be a harm, namely, where a person has a rational interest in dying. We can illustrate this idea not merely in terms of specific examples, such as the terminally ill cancer patient, in terrible pain and demanding death, but in terms of a general characterization of cases, namely, those in which the person's plans, assessed and subject to revision in terms of standards and arguments to which he or she gives free and rational assent, are better satisfied by death than by continued life. From the point of view of the neutral theory of the good, fundamental to the autonomy-based interpretation of treating persons as equals, these matters must be assessed in terms of the individual person's coherent system of rational ends, plans, and projects. From this perspective, there are cases of both altruistic and egoistic motivation in which certain persons more reasonably secure their rational ends by death than by continued life. We have no difficulty in understanding the reasonableness of such actions in cases of heroism or saintly beneficence, when death is embraced as the necessary means to do great goods for others and death thus realizes a personal vision of fulfillment whose ideals cannot be met better. Comparable cases exist in which, for persons with certain coherent and rationally affirmed plans of life in certain circumstances, death may be reasonably justified in terms of better realizing the ends of their life plan. For example, a person for whom the pain of terminal illness has no redemptive meaning, for whom the illness frustrates all the projects of life in which the person centers life's meaning, for whom death is, in any event, highly probable, and for whom pointless pain and physical decline affirmatively violate ideals of personal integrity and control, may find in present death more rationality and meaning than in prolonged life. Even outside such contexts as terminal illness, present death may be a reasonable course for persons who find in continued life the frustration of all the significant aims and projects in which, as persons with freedom and full rationality, they define themselves and in which the choice of death may, as an expression of dignified self-determination, better realize their ideals of living than a senseless life of self-contempt. In Ibsen's *Ghosts,* when Mrs. Alving is asked by her son Oswald to kill him when his incurable idiocy comes on him again, Oswald's voluntary choice appears rational in terms of his preference for death rather than a life spent in dependent idiocy and childishness.[5] The sense in which Oswald rationally wishes death must be interpreted in terms of his individual desire for personal competence and autonomy which is, for him, the sine qua non of satisfying all other desires he may have. His rational ends are better secured by being killed intentionally by another, and thus ending all desire, rather than by continuing life with the frustration of his basic personal ideals of competence. Perhaps, as Seneca argued,[6] for some persons such a course would be similarly reasonable when facing the prospect of senility.

If death in such cases cannot be regarded as harmful, such forms of killing cannot be properly regarded as within the scope of the principle of nonmaleficence. But, consistent with our discussion of these cases, we must underline the limited nature of the exemption of these cases from the principle of nonmaleficence, namely, that the infliction of death is not a case of harm when the individual person voluntarily requests such death, or can reasonably be shown would request it, *and* the request appears rational in terms of the system of rational ends that the person would, with full freedom and rationality, affirm. Fundamental to the autonomy-based interpretation of treating persons as equals is the idea that the rational self-determination of the person is ethically fundamental and cannot be parsed in terms of some more basic moral element like pleasure or pain. A main objection of this perspective to utilitarianism is that utilitarianism, in its obsessive focus on pleasure as such, dissolves moral personality into utilitarian aggregates ignoring the *ethically* crucial fact that *persons* experience pleasure and that pleasure has significance and weight only in the context of the life that a person chooses to lead. Accordingly, the human rights perspective, which focuses on treating *persons* as equals, gives no fundamental weight to pleasure or pain as such; rather, it secures to persons, on fair terms to all, respect for higher-order capacities of personal dignity, whereby persons may define for themselves the weight that pleasure will play in their design of life. In the context of the present discussion of nonmaleficence, we see the dramatic implications of this perspective in concrete terms: forms of killing are not exempt from nonmaleficence on any basis of a net of pain over pleasure or evil over good, however measured, in the life of the person, let alone the surrounding persons. Many people whose lives contain more misery and pain than pleasure find in such lives robust and sustaining meaning and find death wholly irrational, certainly nothing they would voluntarily request. From the perspective of human rights, killing them is as violative of nonmaleficence as killing the most flourishing hedonist. Properly exempt from nonmaleficence are only those cases of killing that express the underlying values of human rights—voluntary choice *and* rational self-definition.[7]

It is important to understand the significant constraints that this account imposes on exempt forms of killing: if a person is capable of voluntary consent, such consent must always be secured; if such consent is impossible, it must be determined reasonably that it would be given in such circumstances. Even voluntary consent, however, does not suffice. In addition, it must be clear that the form of death is one that appears rational in terms of the system of ends that the person would, with full freedom and rationality, affirm. We shall return to this point when we examine the principle of paternalism.

Again in contrast to utilitarianism, this account puts sharp constraints on killing in cases where persons are incapable of consent, for example, young children and the defective. We begin with the thought that all creatures are persons who have the capacities, developed or undeveloped, to be persons with some capacity for self-critical reflection on their lives. Aside from certain extreme cases,[8] most young children and defectives are persons in this sense: they have these capacities in some form. It is difficult to see how killing them could be justified as an exemption from nonmaleficence. In the case of those who have been mature adults, but who are now incapable of consent, for example, the comatose, we may reasonably infer the nature of their consent from those who have known them intimately. But in the case of those who have been incapable of consent, it appears difficult to give a defensible sense to either imputed consent on their behalf or to the idea that they would rationally consent to die. The point is not merely the obvious one of just suspicion of the independent judgment of those who consent on their behalf, who may have strong interests to free themselves from such dependents; but at a deeper level, how can a person who has lived as a mature adult justly enter into the personal world of a child or defective who has never been a mature adult? There is no injustice in asking the intimate of a mature adult now incapable of consent what that person, if still capable of consent, would wish to be done if he knew he would be in his present situation; we regard the reasonably ascertained wishes of a mature adult as authoritative in such cases. But there is no moral symmetry between this case and that of a person who has never been capable of rational consent. A person, while capable of rational consent, certainly has authority to determine what shall happen to her or him when lacking such capacity, but there is no comparable moral author-ity—at least over decisions to die—of mature adults for those who have never been capable of consent. To permit this inference would allow persons to decide this issue on irrelevant grounds, supposing the choice to be what they—with the ideals of personal independence of a mature adult—would want if they knew they would become a child or defective, like Ibsen's Oswald. But of course the child or defective lacks these ideals, and justly may center her or his life in other sensible ways; which the adult cannot conceive.[9] Without reasonable access to the consent of these persons or insight into their system of ends, there is little reason to infer an exemption from nonmaleficence.

2. THE PRINCIPLE OF MUTUAL AID. Another set of facts, relevant to the formulation of another principle of natural duty that bears on the right to life, relates to forms of assistance and aid which, at only slight cost to oneself, one person may render to another in saving the other from grave forms of harm. Consistent with the autonomy-based interpretation of treating persons as equals, persons would agree to or universalize this principle, enforceable by coercion if necessary, because in this way they will guard against the possibility that they themselves may end up in such a position of requiring assistance from other persons, where they would wish such assistance to be given.

It is important to see that the agreement on the principle of mutual aid arises from the consideration of a certain circumscribed set of circum-stances and not all possible circumstances of aid. In other words, the principle is concerned only with aid, given at slight personal cost, that secures a great good to the person aided. . . .

Mutual aid, in contrast to beneficence, requires aid only where rendering the aid is of little cost to the person who aids: a person may save another from drowning by merely putting out her hand or throwing out a lifebelt. This feature explains how the principle could be agreed to as one of duty, justifying coercion and defining correlative rights: persons would only agree to or universalize such a principle, as one of duty, if they knew it did not require a person to sacrifice life and limb to save another. Of course, acts of heroism, saving persons at such risks, are morally admirable on the ground of the principle of beneficence. But we are here concerned not with the moral ideals of saints and heroes, but with the human rights that are properly enforceable by law. The principle of mutual aid defines a natural duty which, properly understood and limited, imposes such enforceable rights.

For purposes of our present analysis, we should note that the operative concept in the principle of mutual aid, as in that of nonmaleficence, is harm—here, relieving likely harms. Again consistent with the underlying values of equal concern and respect for autonomy, harm must be interpreted in terms of the rational interests of the person. Thus, in line with our previous discussion of death as harm, in the absence of reason to believe that a person both wants death and such death is reasonable in terms of a rational life plan, the opportunity to save from death would be governed by the principle of mutual aid.

In order to assess the concrete implications of this principle, consider that mutual aid appears to be a fundamental ethical principle underlying medical care. Medical professionals, by training and self-conception, are in a position to render forms of life-saving aid. In addition, because they are well paid and define their lives in terms of rendering such aid, often, it will be of little cost for them to render aid. Indeed, there may be some gain. In consequence, the requirements of mutual aid apply to such professionals more extensively than they do to ordinary people. If this is so, it appears that different moral principles relevant to the right to life have different scopes of application. Whereas the principle of nonmaleficence appears broadly to apply to all persons equally, the principle of mutual aid appears to have more extensive applications to some persons than to others. Most cases of mutual aid involve saving from harms which no one, including the person aided, would dispute were harms calling for relief; but some cases are disputed.

3. THE PRINCIPLE OF JUST PATERNALISM. . . . The autonomy-based interpretation of treating persons as equals would clearly justify a natural duty defined by a principle of paternalism and explain its proper scope and limits. From the point of view of agreement to or universalization of basic principles of natural duty consistent with this perspective, persons would be concerned with the fact that human beings are subject to certain kinds of irrationalities with severe consequences, including irreparable harms. They accordingly would agree to an insurance principle requiring interference, if at little cost to the agent, to preserve

persons from certain serious irrationalities in the event they might occur to them. There are two critical constraints on the scope of such a principle.

First, the relevant idea of irrationality itself cannot violate basic constraints of the autonomy-based interpretations of treating persons as equals: the neutral theory of the good, expressed by Rawls as ignorance of specific identity, and reliance only on facts capable of empirical validation. For this purpose, the idea of rationality must be defined relative to the person's system of ends which, in turn, are determined by the person's appetites, desires, capacities, and aspirations. Principles of rational choice require the most coherent and satisfying plan for accommodating the person's projects over time. Accordingly, only those acts are irrational that frustrate the person's own system of ends.

Second, within the class of irrationalities so defined, paternalistic considerations would properly come into play only when the irrationality was severe and systematic, that is, due to undeveloped or impaired capacities or lack of opportunity to exercise such capacities, *and* a serious, permanent impairment of interests was in prospect.

When we consider the application of these paternalistic considerations to decisions to die, we immediately see that the second constraint is satisfied: death is, typically, an irreparable harm, indeed the most irreparable of harms. Accordingly, decisions to die are a natural object of paternalistic concern. Indeed, in the absence of any specific knowledge of the situation or life history of a person about to inflict death on himself, the general presumption that death is a harm would appear to warrant paternalistic interference. In such contexts, one's possibly mistaken interference may only lead to postponement, which is certainly preferable to not interfering and discovering that the death in question was clearly irrational.

On the other hand, as we earlier observed, there are surely some deaths that are not harms that are both voluntarily embraced and consonant with a rational plan of life, which is, with freedom and rationality, affirmed. In such cases, the first constraint of just paternalism is not satisfied, and assuming a potential interferer has knowledge that a person's prospective death is of such a kind, one would lack any moral title to interfere.

If medical care often is governed by mutual aid, in some cases paternalism as well comes into play. Consider a case where the medical professional's conception of the good of the patient is inconsistent with the patient's conception, so that we do not have a clear case of proper mutual aid. In such controversies, arguments of paternalism naturally come into play: may the professional interfere for the patient's own good? Surely the conditions of just paternalism are, at least arguably, present: the interference is often at little cost to the professional, and the patient appears irrationally to decline medical services that may alone save his life. If the state of the law is that patients in all such cases have an absolute right to decline medical treatment, the law cannot be justified by the principles here articulated, for such rejection may be clearly irrational in terms of the patient's own rational life plan and thus the proper object of paternalistic interference.

On the other hand, it would be grotesquely wrong for the state to compel any person, other things being equal, to have medical treatment, even if necessary to save life, when the person conscientiously rejects such treatment as inconsistent with a life plan that he rationally and freely affirms. To defend such interference on the ground of the universal value of life is the essence of unjust paternalism, smuggling into the content of irrationality, which defines the scope of just paternalism, majoritarian ideologies which are no more neutral than the religious ideologies they despise—for example, that of a Jehovah's Witness. Complications are introduced when dependent children and the like are introduced into the picture, either in the form of dependents of the person who prefers death or as the person who allegedly prefers death. These are cases in which other factors are relevant. Absent such factors, however, paternalism is clearly unjust.

Notes

[1] See D. Richards, *A Theory of Reasons for Action* 99–106 (1971).

[2] For a general discussion of this principle, see D. Richards, *Reasons for Action*, pp. 176–185. See also T. Beauchamp and J. Childress, *Principles of Biomedical Ethics* 97–134 (1979).

[3] In self-defense contexts, the agent would be harmed unless harm were used in defense. . . . In cases of just necessity, harm is inflicted only as a way of fairly avoiding greater harm. . . . In duress, the agent is threatened with harm which a reasonable person cannot resist.

[4] Epicurus, "Letter to Monoeceus," in *The Stoic and Epicurean Philosophers* 31 (W. Oates ed. 1940).

[5] The example is taken from D. Richards, *Reasons for Action*, pp. 178–179.

[6] Seneca observes:

I will not relinquish old age if it leaves my better part intact. But if it begins to shake my mind, if it destroys its faculties one by one, if it leaves me not life but breath, I will depart from the putrid or tottering edifice. I will not escape by death from disease so long as it may be healed, and leaves my mind unimpaired. I will not raise my hand against myself on account of pain, for so to die is to be conquered. But if I know that I must suffer without hope of relief, I will depart, not through fear of pain itself, but because it prevents all for which I would live.

H. Fedden, *Suicide: A Social and Historical Study* 178 (1938) (quoting Seneca).

[7] The infliction of pain, as opposed to killing, may be justified in certain cases without a voluntary consent requirement. D. Richards, *Reasons for Action*, p. 180.

[8] An example of such extremes is human creatures born without brains, a condition

characterized medically as anencephaly. See J. Warkany, *Congenital Malformations* 189–199 (1971).

⁹The supposition appears to be that the child or defective is a former mature adult now in the child's or defective's body and tortured by the perception of present degradation of previous talents and competence. But, of course, in this case, unlike the case of Oswald and the like, there is no such previous person against whom the perception may be ethically checked.

JAMES RACHELS
THE MORALITY OF EUTHANASIA

AN ABSOLUTE RULE?

The late Franz Ingelfinger, who was editor of the *New England Journal of Medicine,* observed that

> This is the heyday of the ethicist in medicine. He delineates the rights of patients, of experimental subjects, of fetuses, of mothers, of animals, and even of doctors. (And what a far cry it is from the days when medical 'ethics' consisted of condemning economic improprieties such as fee splitting and advertising!) With impeccable logic—once certain basic assumptions are granted—and with graceful prose, the ethicist develops his arguments. . . . Yet his precepts are essentially the products of armchair exercise and remain abstract and idealistic until they have been tested in the laboratory of experience.[1]

One problem with such armchair exercises, he complained, is that in spite of the impeccable logic and the graceful prose, the result is often an absolutist ethic that is unsatisfactory when applied to particular cases, and that is therefore of little use to the practising physician. Unlike some absolutist philosophers (and theologians), 'the practitioner appears to prefer the principles of individualism. As there are few atheists in fox holes, there tend to be few absolutists at the bedside.'

Dr Ingelfinger was right to be suspicious of absolute rules. However, despite his picture of the flexible physician, there are some rules that doctors do tend to regard as absolute. One such rule is the prohibition of mercy-killing. From the time of Hippocrates, whose oath has doctors pledge 'not to give a deadly drug', they have held firm to this absolute 'at the bedside' as well as in the seminar room. The 'principles of individualism' have made little headway against it.

Are the doctors right? . . .

. . . We will be concerned with the morality of killing in what we might call the 'standard case' of euthanasia—that is, the case of the suffering terminal patient who, while rational, requests to be killed as an alternative to a slow, lingering death. Moreover, we will be concerned with the morality of *individual acts* of killing in such cases: considered separately, are they morally wrong? This is slightly different from asking whether euthanasia ought to be illegal, in the way that questions of individual morality are often different from questions of social policy. . . .

THE ARGUMENT FROM MERCY

The most common argument in support of euthanasia is one that we may call 'the argument from mercy'. It is an exceptionally simple argument, at least in its main idea, which makes one uncomplicated point. Terminal patients sometimes suffer pain so horrible that it can hardly be comprehended by those who have not actually experienced it. Their suffering can be so terrible that we do not like even to read about it or think about it; we recoil even from its description. The argument from mercy says: euthanasia is justified because it puts an end to *that.*

The great Irish satirist Jonathan Swift took eight years to die while, in the words of Joseph Fletcher, 'His mind crumbled to pieces.'[2] At times the pain in his blinded eyes was so intense he had to be restrained from tearing them out. Knives and other potential instruments of suicide were kept from him. For the last three years of his life, he could do nothing but drool; and when he finally died it was only after convulsions that lasted thirty-six hours.

Swift died in 1745. Since then, doctors have learned how to eliminate much of the pain that accompanies terminal illness, but the victory has been far from complete. Here is a more recent example.

Stewart Alsop was a respected journalist who died in 1975 of a rare form of cancer. Before he died, he wrote movingly of his experiences as a terminal patient. Although he had not thought much about euthanasia before, he came to approve of it after sharing a room briefly with someone he called Jack:

The third night that I roomed with Jack in our tiny double room in the solid-tumor ward of the cancer clinic of the National Institutes of Health in Bethesda, Md., a terrible thought occurred to me.

Jack had a melanoma in his belly, a malignant solid tumor that the doctors guessed was about the size of a softball. The cancer had started a few months before with a small tumor in his left shoulder, and there had been several operations since. The doctors planned to remove the softball-sized tumor, but they knew Jack would soon die. The cancer had metastasized—it had spread beyond control.

Jack was good-looking, about 28, and brave. He was in constant pain, and his doctor had prescribed an intravenous shot of a synthetic opiate—a pain-killer, or analgesic—every four hours. His wife spent many of the daylight hours with him, and she would sit or lie on his bed and pat him all over, as one pats a child, only more methodically, and this seemed to help control the pain. But at night, when his pretty wife had left (wives cannot stay overnight at the NIH clinic) and darkness fell, the pain would attack without pity.

At the prescribed hour, a nurse would give Jack a shot of the synthetic analgesic, and this would control the pain for perhaps two hours or a bit more. Then he would begin to moan, or whimper, very low, as though he didn't want to wake me. Then he would begin to howl, like a dog.

When this happened, either he or I would ring for a nurse, and ask for a pain-killer. She would give him some codeine or the like by mouth, but it never did any real good—it affected him no more than half an aspirin might affect a man who had just broken his arm. Always the nurse would explain as encouragingly as she could that there was not long to go before the next intravenous shot—'Only about 50 minutes now.' And always poor Jack's whimpers and howls would become more loud and frequent until at last the blessed relief came.

The third night of this routine, the terrible thought occurred to me. 'If Jack were a dog,' I thought, 'what would be done with him?' The answer was obvious: the pound, and chloroform. No human being with a spark of pity could let a living thing suffer so, to no good end.[3]

I have discussed this case with some physicians who were indignant that Jack was not given larger doses of the pain-killing drug more often. They suggest that modern medicine can deal better with this type of pain. But it is worth noting that the NIH clinic is one of the best-equipped modern facilities we have; it is not as though Jack's suffering was caused by neglect in some backward rural hospital. Few of us could expect better care, were we in Jack's position. Moreover, the moral issue regarding euthanasia is not affected by whether more could have been done for Jack. The moral issue is whether mercy-killing is permissible *if* it is the only alternative to this kind of torment. We may readily grant that in any particular case where suffering can be eliminated, the argument for euthanasia will be weaker. But we will still need to know what is morally permissible in those cases in which, for whatever reason, suffering cannot, or will not, be eliminated.

I have quoted Alsop at length not for the sake of indulging in gory details but to give a clear idea of the kind of suffering we are talking about. We should not gloss over these facts with euphemistic language, or squeamishly avert our eyes from them. For only by keeping them firmly and vividly in mind can we appreciate the full force of the argument from mercy: if a person prefers—and even begs for—death as an alternative to lingering on *in this kind of torment,* only to die anyway after a while, then surely it is not immoral to help this person die sooner. As Alsop put it, 'No human being with a spark of pity could let a living thing suffer so, to no good end.'

UTILITARIANISM

The basic idea of the argument from mercy is clear enough; but how is it to be developed into a rigorous argument? Among philosophers, the utilitarians attempted to do this. They held that actions should be judged right or wrong according to whether they cause happiness or misery; and they argued that when judged by this standard, euthanasia turns out to be morally acceptable. The classic utilitarian version of the argument may be elaborated like this:

1. Any action is morally right if it serves to increase the amount of happiness in the world or to decrease the amount of misery. Conversely, an action is morally wrong if it serves to decrease happiness or increase misery.

2. Killing a hopelessly ill patient, who is suffering great pain, at his own request, would decrease the amount of misery in the world.

3. Therefore, such an action would be morally right.

The first premise of this argument states the principle of utility, the basic utilitarian assumption. Today most philosophers think this principle is unacceptable, because they think the promotion of happiness and the avoidance of misery are not the *only* morally important things. To take one example: People *might* be happier if there were no freedom of religion; for, if everyone adhered to the same religious beliefs, there would be greater harmony among people. There would be no unhappiness caused by Jewish girls marrying Catholic boys; the religious element of conflicts such as in Northern Ireland would be removed; and so forth. Moreover, if people were brainwashed well enough, no one would mind not having freedom of choice. Thus happiness might be increased. But, the argument continues, even if happiness *could* be increased in this way, it would be wrong to do so, because people should be allowed to make their own choices. Therefore, the argument concludes, the principle of utility is unacceptable.

There is a related difficulty for utilitarianism, which connects more directly with euthanasia. Suppose a person is leading a miserable life—full of more unhappiness than happiness—but does not want to die. This person thinks a miserable life is better than none at all. Now I assume we would all agree that this person should not be killed; that would be plain, unjustifiable murder. Yet it *would* decrease the amount of misery in the world if we killed him—and so it is hard to see how, on strictly utilitarian grounds, it could be wrong. Again, the principle of utility seems to be an inadequate guide for determining right and wrong.

Such arguments have led many philosophers to reject this moral theory. Yet contemporary utilitarians have an easy answer. In the first place, in so far as euthanasia is concerned, the classical utilitarian argument retains considerable force, even if it is faulty. For even if the promotion of happiness and the avoidance of misery are not the *only* morally important things, they are still very important. So, when an action would decrease misery, that is *a* very strong reason in its favour. The utilitarian argument in favour of euthanasia might therefore be decisive, even if the general complaints about the principle of utility are sound.

Moreover, utilitarianism may also be defended against the general complaints. Classical utilitarianism, as set out by Bentham and Mill, is a combination of three ideas. The first is that actions are to be judged right or wrong entirely according to their *consequences*. Nothing else matters— actions are not good or bad 'in themselves', and moral 'rules' have no independent importance. Right actions are, simply, the ones that have the best results. The second idea is that good and evil are to be measured in terms of happiness and unhappiness—nothing else is ultimately valuable. Material goods, art and ideas, friendship, and so on, are good only *because* they contribute to happiness. Thus, right actions are said to be those that produce the most happiness, or prevent the most misery. Third, and finally, classical utilitarianism includes the idea of equality— each individual's happiness is counted as equally important.

The difficulties we noted for utilitarianism all may be traced to its narrow identification of good and evil with happiness and unhappiness. . . . All that is necessary to save it, therefore, is to adopt a broader conception of individual welfare. The basic idea of the theory is that actions are right or wrong as they increase or decrease welfare. So, suppose we substitute a better conception of welfare: rather than speaking of maximizing *happiness,* let us speak of maximizing *interests*—let the principle of utility say that actions are right if they satisfy as many interests as possible. Such a broader principle will still be 'utilitarian' in that it still sees the rightness of actions as consisting in their effects on the welfare of the creatures affected by them. But the new principle avoids the problems that plagued the old one: if it is in a person's best interests to have freedom of choice in religion, or in choosing to remain alive, then the principle will not countenance taking away that freedom or that life. Armed with this better version of the principle of utility, we may then offer this improved argument concerning euthanasia:

1.   If an action promotes the best interests of everyone concerned, then that action is morally acceptable.

2.   In at least some cases, euthanasia promotes the best interests of everyone concerned.

3.   Therefore, in at least some cases euthanasia is morally acceptable.

It would have been in everyone's best interests if euthanasia had been employed in the case of Stewart Alsop's room-mate Jack. First, and most important, it would have been in Jack's own interests, since it would have provided him with an easier death, without additional pain. Moreover, it would have been best for his wife. Her misery, helplessly watching him suffer, was second only to his. Third, the hospital staff's interests would have been served, since if Jack's dying had not been prolonged, they could have turned their attention to other patients whom they could have helped. Fourth, other patients would have benefited since medical resources would no longer have been used in the sad, pointless maintenance of Jack's physical existence. Finally, if Jack himself requested to be killed, the act would not have violated his rights. Considering all this, how can euthanasia be wrong?

Two additional comments are necessary before we leave the argument from mercy. First, I have discussed the utilitarians in connection with this argument, but one does not have to accept a general utilitarian theory of ethics to find it persuasive. There are other possible theories that one might prefer. However, no matter what ethical theory one accepts, the consequences of one's actions—whether they do or do not promote people's interests, or cause happiness or misery—must be among the matters considered important. An ethical theory that did *not* have an important place for this would have no credibility at all. And, to the extent that these matters *are* seen as important, the argument from mercy will be compelling.

Second, it should be noted that the argument does *not* imply that euthanasia is justified *whenever* a patient says he can no longer endure pain. Suppose the doctor, or the family, knows that the painful condition can be cured, and that the patient's request to die is only a temporary irrational reaction, which he will later repudiate. It is entirely reasonable for them to take this into account, and to refuse the irrational request. The argument from mercy does not say otherwise; in such circumstances euthanasia would not promote his best interests, and would hardly be 'merciful' at all. This should not be taken to mean, however, that such requests are always irrational, or that pain always destroys a patient's ability to make sensible choices. Sadly, some requests to die, in circumstances such as those of Stewart Alsop's room-mate, are all too rational.

Notes

[1]Franz J. Ingelfinger, "Bedside Ethics for the Hopeless Case," *New England Journal of Medicine,* Vol. 289 (1973), p. 914.

[2]Joseph Fletcher, *Morals and Medicine* (Boston, 1960), p. 174.

[3]Stewart Alsop, "The Right to Die With Dignity," *Good Housekeeping,* August 1974, pp. 69, 130.

chapter 6

*P*unishment and the Death Penalty

INTRODUCTION

During the last three decades, punishment has been a topic of much philosophical and public discussion. One reason for this interest has been the movement in the English-speaking world toward elimination of the death penalty. In 1965 the British Parliament abolished the death penalty for a trial period of five years. At the end of that time, it was permanently eliminated. In 1972 the U.S. Supreme Court declared unconstitutional the death penalty provisions of the Georgia state law and by implication those of most other states.[1] In 1976 the Canadian Parliament abolished the death penalty, although controversy still surrounds the issue, with various groups arguing for its reimposition. That same year the U.S. Supreme Court refused to declare all use of the death penalty to be unconstitutionally cruel and unusual punishment.[2] The Court left the issue up to the state legislatures, which may, but need not, impose the death penalty. As of 1987, thirty-six states had death penalty statutes.

The issue of the death penalty is part of a larger controversy surrounding criminal punishment. During the late 1960s and early 1970s, as the crime rate in the United States increased rapidly, views of punishment and imprisonment changed. In the early 1960s rehabilitation was the dominant ideal. Many people claimed that criminals were suffering from psychological problems and that effective psychological therapy would rehabilitate them. But as the results of various experiments in group therapy for criminals came in, many people became disillusioned with rehabilitation. Community treatment then became popular. Imprisonment, it was argued, does not deter criminals; indeed, many persons become more criminal as a result of their imprisonment. Treating people in local communities, it was thought, would be both cheaper and more effective in preventing future crime. Subsequently, some have become disillusioned with community treatment because it did not decrease the rate of offenders who committed further crimes. The trend in the 1980s has been to return to the imposition of a fixed punishment for crimes.

199

This confusion about punishment is not due simply to a lack of empirical evidence about what works best but also stems from disagreement about what punishment is to accomplish. It is at this point that the ethical principles of just punishment become involved.

The ethics of punishment involves a number of issues. (1) What is the definition of punishment? How is punishment different from compulsory treatment? Is, for example, compulsory treatment for heroin or alcohol dependency punishment, or is it a form of treatment akin to compulsory inoculation against communicable diseases? (2) What is the justifying aim of punishment? Punishment involves the imposition of such undesirable conditions as death, physical pain (flogging), or deprivation of liberty, which normally it is ethically wrong to impose on others. Consequently, punishment requires some aim that will ethically justify it. (3) Who should be punished? Should the insane and young teenagers be punished, or should they be excused from punishment due to their mental disability or age? (4) How much should people be punished for various criminal acts? In particular, should the death penalty ever be imposed? This chapter focuses on issues (2) and (4). A theory of the justifying aim of punishment usually will also have implications for issues (3) and (4).

The Aim of Punishment   Interestingly, despite the variety of ethical theories, views of punishment tend to reduce to two, with some mixed views. One view is *retributivism,* that wrongdoing deserves punishment in proportion to the wrong done. The other view is *deterrence,* that in order to deter wrongdoing punishment may be justified. These two views are most explicit in Kantian and utilitarian theory, but one should also understand why other ethical theories tend to one or the other of these views of the justifying aim of punishment.

Aquinas's *natural-law* theory combines both retributivist and deterence considerations. Principles of natural law prescribe that humans live in society and avoid conduct detrimental to the good of society.[3] Justice is a habit of rendering each person his due.[4] Good things are due to those who act rightly, and evil things to those who act wrongly.[5] Some people are prone to wrongful conduct, and human punishment serves to deter them from it and thus to protect others. As habits are developed by doing, punishment can also enable the wrongdoers to become habituated to acting rightly.[6] The aim of human (as opposed to divine) punishment is to deter people from wronging others in society.

According to *natural-rights* theory, the aim of punishment is to protect people's rights.[7] In the state of nature, each person has the right to punish a transgression of the natural rights of anyone. This system of punishment is unsatisfactory, because there is no settled law, no impartial judge to decide disputes, and no assured power to impose punishment. Consequently, people form a civil society and establish a government to remedy these defects of the state of nature.[8] Although the aim of punishment is to protect rights, its imposition appears to deprive the wrongdoer of his or her natural rights. It is not immediately clear whose rights should prevail. John Locke resolved this puzzle by the *doctrine of forfeiture,* which states that in commiting wrongs, wrongdoers in effect declare war on society and thus forfeit their rights.[9]

The natural-rights theory essentially adopts a deterrence view of punishment. As the aim of punishment is to protect the rights of others, to be justified punishment must deter the wrongdoer and others from future crimes. A problem with the natural-rights approach is the doctrine of forfeiture. Do wrongdoers forfeit all their rights? Modern practice implies that they do not; criminals have rights, for example, to fair trials and not to be tortured. But if only specific rights are forfeited, how can one tell which right or rights are forfeited by the commission of a particular crime?

Kant's theory generates a strong form of retributivism. Deterrence is clearly ruled out as a justification of punishment, because it involves using a person as a mere means to the good of others. Justice and the law of the state are confined to duties for which legislation is possible.[10] Duties that require a particular motive are excluded, because legislation can concern only external conduct. The law of justice is to "act externally in such a way that the free use of your will is compatible with the freedom of everyone according to universal law."[11] Coercion to enforce duties of justice is justifiable, because it counteracts their violation. Consequently, state laws may prescribe coercive punishment. The principle of equality, however, is necessary for the imposition of punishment, for otherwise one person would be treated worse than another; no one could will such a universal law. Equality requires the principle of *lex talionis,* an eye for an eye and a tooth for a tooth.

Kant's retributive theory of punishment involves two principles: (1) justice requires that punishment be imposed if, and only if, a person has committed a wrong; and (2) the punishment must be equal to the wrong. Kant's theory is a strong form of retributivism, because justice requires that wrongdoers be punished and any consideration of the good that might come from punishment is excluded. The most serious objection to Kant's theory is that it requires punishment even when no good will result. In such cases, punishment appears to cause pointless suffering.

A *contractarian* theory of punishment is apt to present a weak form of retributivism.[12] Contractors will support a system of legal justice for approximately the same reasons Locke thought the state was justified. Thus, a system of legal justice will be expected to decide disputes impartially and to enforce those fundamental principles of justice that are so important that everyone benefits by their enforcement. The principle of liberty entails that punishment be imposed only if the defendant could have avoided committing the crime. Without that limitation, the liberty of people would be restricted, for they would be punished for unavoidable conduct. To secure maximum liberty, contractors would also prohibit punishing the innocent. As the aim of punishment is to enforce principles of justice, contractors would require punishment to be proportional to the wrong done, understood as the importance of the duty violated and the culpability of the wrongdoer. Finally, as contractors wish as much freedom and as little suffering as possible, they would accept a principle of effectiveness and economy of punishment. Only the smallest punishment needed to ensure compliance with duties should be imposed.

This view is called *weak retributivism* for several reasons. First, unlike Kant's view, it does not require that wrongdoers be punished. The doing of a wrong only makes punishment permissible; punishment of an innocent person is not permissible. Second, instead of requiring that punishment be equal to the wrong done, it requires only that punishment be proportional to the wrong done. Third, by the principle of effectiveness and economy it leaves room for considerations of the good that punishment might do. This last feature is crucial. The first two considerations would not justify punishment, for the permissibility of punishment fails to provide a reason for punishing. It is permissible for the reader to go to a movie, but the permissibility of so doing does not provide a reason for doing it. The principle of effectiveness and economy provides a reason to impose punishment, namely, to deter wrongdoing.

Weak retributivism takes deterrence to be the justifying aim of punishment, but restricts pursuit of that aim by other principles of justice. It thus avoids imposing punishment when no good will result. Although the principle of proportionality seems more flexible than Kant's principle of *lex talionis,* there are problems with it. The principle of proportionality requires that both crimes and punishments be ranked from the most serious to the least serious. However, it is not clear how one can thus rank crimes. Supposedly, one should consider both the harm done and the mental state in which the person acted, whether, for instance, he acted with intention or only with disregard of a serious risk of harm. But how can these two items be put together? Is intentionally beating a person (battery) more or less serious than killing a person by disregarding a serious risk of death (manslaughter)?

Even if one can combine harm done and mental states to rank crimes, the principle of proportionality does not specify how the ranking of crimes is to be mapped onto the ranking of punishments. Should the penalty for the most serious crime be the death penalty, imprisonment for natural life, life imprisonment with possibility of parole, or imprisonment for a definite time? So long as lesser crimes receive lesser punishments, the principle of proportionality is satisfied. The principle of economy, however, does imply that one impose the smallest penalty that will deter.

The importance of these restrictions of justice on pursuit of deterrence, no matter how difficult they are to formulate, becomes clear when one examines a pure deterrence view, such as that held by act utilitarians.

Act utilitarianism justifies punishment (as it does any other act) if, and only if, its net utility is at least as great as that of any alternative act the agent could perform in the situation. Generally, as punishment itself is unpleasant, it cannot be justified unless the prevention of crime will avoid greater unhappiness. Bentham put the point concisely when he wrote, "All punishment in itself is evil. Upon the principle of utility, if it ought at all to be admitted, it ought only to be admitted in as far as it promises to exclude some greater evil."[13]

Utilitarians usually recognize three (and sometimes four) ways in which punishment can prevent greater unhappiness. First, punishment can be a specific deterrent, that is, deter the person punished from committing crimes in the future. Second, punishment can serve as a general deterrent, that is, deter other persons from committing crimes for fear of being similarly punished. Third, punishment can serve to incapacitate the person punished and thus prevent him or her from committing other crimes. While they are imprisoned, for example, criminals will not be able to commit most crimes. Fourth, punishment can serve to reform a criminal so that he or she will not want to commit crimes in the future. This consideration differs from specific deterrence only by the motive—fear, or lack of desire—a punished person has for refraining from future crime.

The principle of utility implies several restrictions on punishment. Punishment should not be imposed if it would involve more unhappiness than it would prevent. Nor should it be imposed if it would not deter; for example, if the harm were caused by accident. Neither the offender nor others can be deterred from causing harm by accident. Furthermore, the punishment ought to be as light as possible, while still assuring the prevention of future unhappiness. A greater punishment than necessary would have less net utility. Sometimes a lesser punishment should be imposed even if it would result in more crime, because the unhappiness avoided by using the lesser punishment will be greater than that which would be caused by a few more crimes. Finally, punishments that are more severe should be reserved for more serious crimes. Were all crimes to be punished in the same way, people would have no reason to commit less rather than more serious crimes.

The act-utilitarian deterrence view confronts a number of objections. Perhaps the most serious is that it might justify punishing an innocent person. Critics have imagined various situations in which punishing an innocent person might have more net utility than not punishing him. For example, suppose the police have been unable to apprehend the perpetrator of a rash of crimes and other people are now committing similar crimes because they think they can get away with them. Much crime might be prevented if some innocent person were to be tried, convicted, and punished for the original crimes. Similarly, a prosecutor might have evidence that a particular defendant is innocent of the crime with which he or she is charged but know that he or she is guilty of other crimes for which he or she cannot be convicted. Suppressing the evidence and allowing the person to be convicted of the crime of which he or she is innocent might have more net utility than not doing so. Another objection is that utilitarianism might justify too severe a punishment. Alcohol-impaired drivers cause more deaths than do murderers. A punishment of life imprisonment for vehicular homicide while drunk might save many lives and be justified according to a utilitarian theory, although critics would find the punishment too harsh.

Utilitarians, of course, reply to these objections as they do to others (see Chapter 3) by denying that their theory has these implications or by maintaining that conventional views are incorrect. Still, the objections show why many people think the principles of retributivism are important. They exclude punishing the innocent and retain some proportionality between the punishment and the crime.

Punishment is one area in which *rule utilitarianism* is often thought to be a significant improvement over act utilitarianism. Rule utilitarianism shares act utilitarianism's emphasis on deterrence and incapacitation. However, acceptance of a rule that would permit the punishment of innocent people or would allow a punishment disproportionate to the crime would probably not have as much utility as acceptance of one that did not permit so punishing. Acceptance of rules permitting such punishment would cause people to fear that they might be framed or punished excessively. Moreover, punishment might lose much of its deterrent effect, because citizens often would not know whether the person punished had indeed committed the crime charged or had been framed. Although some critics of rule utilitarianism argue that it would not prohibit absolutely all punishment of the innocent,[14] most critics recognize that it would do so except in the most extreme cases. Rule utilitarianism, however, might support very severe punishment for such crimes as vehicular homicide while drunk.

The Death Penalty   Arguments about the death penalty concern the amount or kind of punishment appropriate for particular crimes. For *natural-law* and *natural-rights* theories, a particular problem with the death penalty stems from their emphasis on the injunction not to kill and the right to life. Aquinas's natural-law theory leaves room for one to adopt either a retributivist or deterrence view in determining the appropriate amount of punishment. The natural law prescribes only that wrongdoers be punished, not the amount of punishment appropriate to each crime.[15] Natural-law theorists might adopt a retributivist view that what is due a wrongdoer should be equal to the wrong done, thereby justifying, for example, the death penalty for murder. Or, they might adopt a deterrence view that state punishment is to protect society and to enable people to live together. Aquinas appears to have adopted a form of deterrence. He argued for the permissibility of the death penalty by an analogy with surgery in which a part of the body is removed to protect the rest. Likewise, Aquinas claimed, the state may order the execution of a person who is dangerous to the community.[16] For Locke, the forfeiture of rights legitimates the death penalty. Since the criminal forfeits his or her right to life, the death penalty is permissible. However, as the aim of punishment is to protect rights, one must ask whether the death penalty is a more effective deterrent than would be life imprisonment.

Only the strong *Kantian* retributivist view requires the death penalty. If one person deliberately kills another without justification or excuse, then the only equal punishment is death. Kant's retributivism does not clearly require the death penalty for crimes other than homicide. The death penalty, for instance, does not seem to be an equal punishment for kidnapping in which the victim is released unharmed. In such a case, imprisonment would seem to be the most appropriate punishment, since it implies a loss of liberty equal to that committed in kidnapping. Nor does the death penalty appear appropriate for rape. The crime of rape, however, points out a severe difficulty with Kant's principle, because, for most crimes, one cannot inflict an equal punishment on the wrongdoer. For example, theft is often committed by poor people, who lack sufficient property for it to be possible to deprive them of an amount equal to what they stole, although one might require them to work to compensate the victims. This is one of the chief reasons for preferring the principle of proportionality to that of equality *(lex talionis)*.

Insofar as the weak retributivism of the *contractarian* view rests on deterrence, its justification of the death penalty depends on whether it is an effective and economical deterrent. Although it does not necessarily exclude the death penalty,[17] contractarianism does provide the basis for one strong argument against it. The weak retributivist view prohibits punishment of the innocent. In the imperfect justice of criminal trials, innocent persons have been mistakenly convicted of capital crimes. If the death penalty is imposed, no opportunity exists later to rectify the mistake. If, however, life imprisonment is imposed and the conviction is later discovered to have been mistaken, the person can be released. Although a person cannot have time spent in prison returned to him or her, he or she can be compensated and thus avoid the full punishment that was to be imposed. Many people, therefore, argue that the death penalty should be abolished in order to avoid, as far as possible, irrevocably punishing the innocent.

The whole argument about the death penalty for *utilitarians* rests on its deterrent effect. If it is a significantly stronger deterrent than life imprisonment, it is justified. But even a deterrence view will not justify the death penalty whenever it is a greater deterrent than would be life imprisonment. Suppose that for every 100 executions only 1 murder is prevented that would not be prevented by life imprisonment. Then with the death penalty 100 lives would be lost and 1 saved, which is a net loss

of 99 lives. However, it does not follow that for a utilitarian to justify
the death penalty at least one murder must be prevented for each execution. The increased unhappiness from practice of the death penalty is the
difference between the unhappiness of execution and that of life in
prison. This difference is probably not as great as that between life and
death for an innocent victim. Consequently, according to a utilitarian
theory, the lives of those convicted of serious crimes might not weigh
as heavily as those of potential victims.

It should now be clear why contemporary debate over the death
penalty focuses on its deterrent effect versus that of life imprisonment.
Only the strong Kantian retributivist view makes this irrelevant. As far
as most theories are concerned, to be justified, the death penalty must
deter more crime than would life imprisonment. Whether it does so is
an empirical question that is not easily settled. Obtaining evidence
about the relative deterrent effects of the death penalty and life imprisonment faces a number of problems. First, one cannot directly determine how many crimes are prevented by the death penalty or by life
imprisonment. Second, one cannot determine how many, if any, crimes
occurred because criminals were not deterred by life imprisonment,
but would have been by the death penalty. Third, the death penalty
was not suddenly eliminated in any country or state but more or less
withered away. The rate and number of executions declined for years
before it was abolished. Moreover, it may take years before its absence
is fully absorbed by society. Even if it did deter, the crime rate might
not change immediately after its abolition. So one cannot simply compare crime rates before and after abolition. Fourth, the evidence and
statistics gathered generally have focused on the death penalty as punishment for homicide. However, the effectiveness of the death penalty
might vary for different types of murders. People who commit un-
premeditated murder are probably less likely to be deterred by the
death penalty than are others.

Finally, one other argument about the death penalty has been prevalent. In practice, critics argue, the death penalty is imposed unfairly.
More poor and minority people receive the death penalty than do mid-
dle- and upper-class white people. The death penalty should be abolished, in this view, because it is unfairly applied. Defenders of the death
penalty reply that this problem is not specific to the death penalty, but
endemic to the entire criminal justice system. The remedy, they suggest,
is to make the whole criminal justice system more impartial, not to
remove the death penalty.

Readings   In the first selection, Thomas Hurka sets out a contemporary natural-rights approach to punishment. Unlike Locke, he does not
rely on criminals forfeiting their rights. Instead, he claims that all natural
rights can be derived from a natural right to the most extensive liberty
compatible with a like liberty of others. The right to liberty justifies
making and carrying out threats of punishment if others violate rights.

However, one cannot threaten to infringe more important rights of others to protect less important ones, and one cannot infringe more important rights of others if infringing less important ones will suffice. These conditions imply that capital punishment can be justified only for murder and only if no less severe punishment will equally deter people from murder.

The selection from Kant provides his account of the strong retributivist view. Kant argues for the *lex (jus) talionis* as the only appropriate principle and as one that requires the imposition of punishment. The categorical imperative justifies an action only if everyone can will the universal law it implies, yet it seems no criminal could will his own punishment. Kant argues that the criminal does not will his own punishment. Rather his rational self *(homo noumenon)* wills the system of laws that involves the punishment that is imposed on his sensible self *(homo phaenonmenon)*. As rational persons, even criminals are able to *will* the law by which they are punished, although as persons with desires, they do not *desire* their punishment.

In the final selection, Jonathan Glover presents a utilitarian view of capital punishment. He rejects both a retributivist and an absolutist approach. An absolutist approach opposes capital punishment in all circumstances. However, it depends on what Glover calls the "acts and omissions doctrine." This doctrine holds that in some contexts an omission or failure to perform an act is morally less bad than performing an act, even if the utility of their consequences is the same.[18] Contrary to what is suggested above, Glover contends that executing a murderer has less utility than the death of an innocent murder victim. The reader should consider which argument is the appropriate one for a utilitarian or whether they can be combined in some manner. In the end, Glover opposes capital punishment because it has not been shown to be a more effective deterrent than a lesser punishment.

Notes

[1]*Furman* v. *Georgia,* 408 U.S. 238 (1972).

[2]*Gregg* v. *Georgia,* 428 U.S. 153 (1976).

[3]*Summa Theologica,* 1–11, Q. 94, a. 2.

[4]Ibid., 11–11, Q. 58, a. 1.

[5]*Summa Contra Gentiles,* Chap. 145, 4.

[6]*Summa Theologica,* 1–11. Q. 95, a. 1.

[7]John Locke, *Second Treatise of Government,* Chap. 2, sec. 7.

[8]Ibid., Chap. 9, secs. 124–126.

[9]Ibid., Chap. 4, sec. 23; Chap. 15, sec. 172.

[10]Immanuel Kant, *Metaphysical Elements of Justice,* trans. John Ladd (Indianapolis, Ind.: Bobbs-Merrill, 1965), p. 45; Akademie, p. 239.

[11]Ibid., p. 34; Akademie, p. 231.

[12]See David A. J. Richards, *The Moral Criticism of Law* (Encino, Calif.: Dickenson, 1977), pp. 235–246.

[13]Jeremy Bentham, *An Introduction to the Principles of Morals and Legislation* (New York: Hafner, 1948), p. 170 (Chap. 13, 2).

[14]See Alan Donagan, "Is There a Credible Form of Utilitarianism?" in *Contemporary Utilitarianism,* ed. Michael D. Bayles (Garden City, N.Y.: Doubleday, Anchor Books, 1968), pp. 187–202.

[15]*Summa Theologica,* 1–11, Q. 95, a. 2.

[16]Ibid., 11–11, Q. 64, a. 2; *Summa Contra Gentiles,* Chap. 146, 5.

[17]Richards, *Moral Criticism of Law,*, p. 254.

[18]Jonathan Gover, *Causing Death and Saving Lives* (Harmondsworth, England: Penguin Books, 1977), p. 92.

Bibliography on Punishment and the Death Penalty

Bayles, Michael D. *Principles of Law: A Normative Analysis.* Dordrecht: D. Reidel, 1987. Sections 6.1, 6.4.

Bedau, Hugo Adam. "Capital Punishment." In *Matters of Life and Death,* 2d ed., edited by Tom Regan, pp. 175–212. New York: Random House, 1986.

————. "*Gregg* v. *Georgia* and the 'New' Death Penalty." *Criminal Justice Ethics* 4 (1985): 3–17.

————, ed. *The Death Penalty in America,* 3rd ed. New York: Oxford University Press, 1982.

Berger, Raoul. *Death Penalties.* Cambridge: Harvard University Press, 1982.

————. "Death Penalties and Hugo Bedau: A Crusading Philosopher Goes Overboard." *Ohio State Law Journal* 45 (1984): 863–881.

Berns, Walter. *For Capital Punishment.* New York: Basic Books, 1979.

Black, Charles L. *Capital Punishment: The Inevitability of Caprice and Mistake,* 2d ed. New York: Norton, 1980.

Davis, Michael. "How to Make the Punishment Fit the Crime." *Ethics* 93 (1983): 726–752.

"Death Penalty Symposium." *U. C. Davis Law Review* 18 (1985): 865–1480.

Ezorsky, Gertrude, ed. *Philosophical Perspectives on Punishment.* Albany, N.Y.: SUNY Press, 1972.

Furman v. *Georgia,* 408 U.S. 238 (1972).

Greenberg, Jack. "Against the American System of Capital Punishment." *Harvard Law Review* 99 (1986): 1670–1680.

Gregg v. *Georgia,* 428 U.S. 153 (1976).

Hart, Herbert L. A. *Punishment and Responsibility.* New York: Oxford University Press, 1968.

Nathanson, Stephen. "Does It Matter If the Death Penalty Is Arbitrarily Administered?" *Philosophy & Public Affairs* 14 (1985): 149–164.

Rabkin, Jeremy. "Justice and Judicial Hand-Wringing: The Death Penalty Since 'Gregg'." *Criminal Justice Ethics* 4 (1985): 18–29.

Reiman, Jeffrey H. "Justice, Civilization, and the Death Penalty: Answering Van Den Haag." *Philosophy & Public Affairs* 14 (1985): 115–148.

Richards, David A. J. *The Moral Criticism of Law.* Encino, Calif.: Dickenson, 1977. Chapter 6.

Van Den Haag, Ernest. "Refuting Reiman and Nathanson." *Philosophy and Public Affairs* 14 (1985): 165–176.

————. "The Ultimate Punishment: A Defense." *Harvard Law Review* 99 (1986): 1662–1669.

————, and Conrad, John P. *The Death Penalty: A Debate.* New York: Plenum Press, 1983.

Wasserstrom, Richard. "Capital Punishment as Punishment: Some Theoretical Issues and Objections." *Midwest Studies in Philosophy* 7 (1982): 473–502.

Zimring, Franklin E., and Hawkins, Gordon. *Capital Punishment and the American Agenda.* Cambridge: Cambridge University Press, 1987.

Problem Case

A Jury Faces the Death Penalty

This is the first time Fred and Sue have ever served on a jury. Everyone at work laughed at their being called for jury duty and teased them about having it easy for a week. However, it is now anything but easy. The defendant, George, is a large, brutal-looking black man in his late twenties. He was charged with first-degree murder, and the evidence of his guilt was clear.

About 12:35 A.M. on February 21, George entered a convenience store where only one person was working, a twenty-two-year-old white woman. He apparently pulled a knife and forced her to close the store. He then forced her into the back room, where he raped her and then slit her throat, practically decapitating her. The medical evidence showed that she had had intercourse shortly before her death, and the semen was of the same blood type as George's. Traces of dried semen were also found on George's clothing. Apparently, he had also beat her during the attack, because the body had two cracked ribs and a broken nose. He took all the money from the cash register and made off on foot. He did not get far. A routine police patrol noted that the store was closed early, investigated, and radioed in a report. George was caught a few blocks away with the knife and money on him. Tests showed traces of the clerk's blood on the knife.

Having convicted George and heard further testimony, the jury is now deliberating whether the death penalty should be imposed. The prosecutor argued that there are several aggravating factors. Not only was the murder deliberate, unnecessary, and brutal, it was committed during the course of a felony. Moreover, George has previously been convicted and served time for armed robbery. The defense claimed that George has little education, being a high school dropout, and his I.Q. places him just above the retarded category. George is a cocaine addict and committed the robbery to support his habit. Moreover, George was considered a model prisoner during his previous sentence. George is not, the defense claimed, an unreformable murderer; given his age, he could live a decent life in prison. The defense lawyer asked that George's life be spared.

If you were Fred or Sue, would you vote for or against the death penalty for George? Why or why not? Does the fact that he is black and the victim was white make any difference?

THOMAS HURKA
RIGHTS AND CAPITAL PUNISHMENT

Discussions of the morality of capital punishment, and indeed discussions of the morality of punishment in general, usually assume that there are two possible justifications of punishment, a deterrence justification associated with utilitarianism and other consequentialist moral theories, and a retributive justification associated with deontological moral theories. But now that rights-based theories are attracting the increasing attention of moral philosophers it is worth asking whether these theories may not employ a different justification of punishment, with different consequences for the morality of particular forms of punishment. I will argue that rights theories do employ a different justification of punishment, and that this justification combines many of the attractive features of the deterrence and retributive justifications while avoiding their unattractive features. In particular, I will argue that the rights-based justification has more attractive consequences for the morality of capital punishment than either the deterrence or retributive justifications.

Rights-based moral theories hold that persons have certain natural rights, and the fact that these rights are natural is often expressed by saying that persons would possess them "in the state of nature". Among the rights which persons are usually said to possess in the state of nature is the right to punish those who violate the rights of others. In Section 7 of the *Second Treatise* Locke says that the state of nature has a Law of Nature to govern it, and that "every one has a right to punish the transgressors of the Law to such a Degree, as may hinder its Violation."[1] Nozick too includes a right to punish among those he grants in *Anarchy, State, and Utopia,* quoting Locke's description of this right with approval, and devoting an entire section to a discussion of "the right of all to punish".[2] . . .

The right to punish which persons have in the state of nature is not a primitive right, but derives from another more general right which they possess. Whenever persons in the state of nature have a natural right they also have the right to *enforce* that right, that is, the right to use coercion against other persons to prevent them from violating it.[3] The most familiar form of coercion is the use of force, and persons in the state of nature therefore have the right to use force to defend themselves against would-be violators of their rights, and also to defend third parties. But this right of self- (and other-) defence is not the only enforcement right which they possess. The making of threats is also a form of coercion, and persons in the state of nature therefore also have the right to threaten others with certain harms if they succeed in violating their rights, or succeed in violating the rights of third parties. It is from this second enforcement-right that the right to punish derives. If persons in

From Thomas Hurka, "Rights and Capital Punishment," *Dialogue* 21 (1982): 647–656, 657, 659–660. Reprinted by permission.

the state of nature have the right to threaten others with harms if they succeed in violating rights, then they surely also have the right to inflict these harms on them once the relevant rights have been violated. But this is just what the right to punish is: a right to inflict harms on persons who have successfully violated the rights of others. . . .

This justification of enforcement rights . . . applies to the right to make and carry out threats which lies behind the right to punish. When we threaten a person with harms if he successfully violates rights we do not remove from him the liberty of violating rights as such. But we do remove from him the more complex liberty of violating rights and not having those harms inflicted on him afterwards. If he does not have the right to exercise the simple liberty he does not have the right to exercise the more complex one either, and in giving other persons the right to remove the more complex liberty from him a libertarian rights theory is once again extending the scope of their right to liberty without in any way detracting from his.

Because it derives the right to punish from a right to make certain threats, the rights-based justification has two attractive consequences which also follow from the retributive justification. The first is that it is never permissible to punish persons who have not violated, or who have not been found by reliable proceedings to have violated, the rights of other persons. Guilt, in other words, is a necessary condition of the permissibility of punishment on the rights-based view. The reasoning leading up to this consequence should be fairly evident. The right to use coercion to prevent others from violating rights only entitles us to make a very specific threat, namely the threat to inflict certain harms on them if they actually succeed in violating rights, and we could not claim to be carrying out this threat if we inflicted harms on someone whom we did not have reliable reasons to think had violated rights. This first consequence also follows from the retributive justification, but it is a well-known objection to the deterrence justification that no such consequence follows from it. Critics of the deterrence justification often point out that it could license the framing and "punishment" of an innocent man if this would be sufficiently effective in deterring future crimes. The rights-based justification is not open to this objection for it holds, along with the retributive justification, that guilt is always a necessary condition of the permissibility of punishment. The second consequence is that it is never permissible to punish persons for rights violations unless our intention to punish persons for those violations has been publicly announced in the past. The reasoning leading up to this consequence should also be evident. If punishment is only permissible because it is the carrying out of a permissible threat, then it is only permissible when that threat has actually been made. Punishments for the violation of secret laws, or for the violation of retroactive laws, are never permissible on the rights-based view, though we can easily imagine circumstances in which they would be permissible and even required on the deterrence view, and perhaps even on some retributive views as well.

The rights-based justification, then, has some attractive consequences in common with the retributive justification for the question when punishment is permissible. But when it turns to the question how much punishment is permissible, or how severe a punishment is permissible, it has some consequences in common with the retributive justification and some in common with the deterrence justification. The important thing to realize here is that the enforcement rights which persons have in the state of nature are not unqualified. They are subject to at least two qualifications, and these qualifications place limits on the severity of the punishments which they may inflict in the state of nature, and which their governments may inflict in civil society. . . .

Let us begin by imagining the following case. One person X is trying to violate a fairly unimportant right of another person Y, say, the right not to be tickled,[4] and Y is considering how to prevent this. Y is not nearly as strong as X, so he cannot hope to stop X just by resisting him physically. Nor will any threat of Y's deter X. But Y does have in his hands a pistol with which he can kill X. If killing X is the only way Y can prevent X from violating his right not to be tickled, is it permissible for Y to use his pistol? Locke seems to have thought it is permissible, for in Section 19 of the *Second Treatise* he says, "a *Thief*, whom I cannot harm but by appeal to the Law, for having stolen all that I am worth, I may kill, when he sets on me to rob me, but of my Horse or Coat." But Nozick thinks it is not permissible,[5] and I think most of us would agree with him. We would insist that there is an upper limit on the amount of coercion persons can use to enforce their rights, and that this limit is lower the less important the rights are which they are enforcing. For Y to kill X just to prevent him from tickling him is for Y quite clearly to overstep a limit which is, in the case of a very unimportant right like the right not to be tickled, very low indeed.

Reflection on this case suggests what I will call an *upper limit* qualification on persons' enforcement rights. The most natural way for a rights theory to express this qualification is as follows. Although Y's right to enforce his right to φ entitles him to act in ways which would otherwise involve violating some rights of X's, it does not entitle him to act in ways which would otherwise involve violating any rights of X's which are more important than his own right to φ. In the course of enforcing his right to φ Y can act in ways which would otherwise involve violating X's right to φ, or any rights of X's which are less important than his right to φ. So if X is trying to kill him Y can kill X in self-defence, or assault him or tie him up. But he cannot act in ways which would otherwise involve violating any rights of X's which are more important than his right to φ. For an important right like the right to life this will not be much of a restriction but for other less important rights it will be. For a very unimportant right like the right not to be tickled, for instance, the upper limit qualification will rule out anything more than the very smallest amount of coercion to enforce it.

Now let us imagine another case. X is attacking Y with the intention of killing him, and Y is considering how to prevent this. He has in one hand a pistol, with which he can kill X, and in the other hand a tranquilizer gun, with which he can sedate X long enough to make his escape but with which he will not do X any permanent damage. The two weapons will be equally effective in repelling X's attack and Y knows this. Is it permissible for Y to use his pistol and kill X? Although Y's killing X would not violate the upper limit qualification I think most of us would agree that it is not permissible. We would insist that there is another limitation on the amount of coercion Y can use to enforce his rights, one which requires him never to use more than the minimum amount of coercion necessary to prevent the violation of his rights. In this case Y's killing X would involve more than the minimum amount of coercion, for he can also use the tranquilizer gun on X, and killing him is therefore impermissible.

This second case suggests another qualification on persons' enforcement rights, one which I will call a *minimum necessary* qualification, and which it is most natural for a rights theory to express as follows. Although Y's right to enforce his right to φ sometimes entitles him to act in ways which would otherwise involve violating X's right to ψ, it only does so when it is not possible for Y to prevent the violation of his right to φ just as effectively by acting in ways which would otherwise involve violating only rights of X's which are less important than his right to ψ. (If it is possible for Y to prevent the violation of his right to φ by acting in ways which would not otherwise involve violating any of X's rights, e.g. by running away, this qualification requires him to run away.) The minimum necessary qualification, and the upper limit qualification as well, can be given a somewhat tidier formulation if we make the following terminological stipulation. Let us say that when Y exercises his enforcement rights against X he always *infringes* some rights of X's, but he does not always *violate* those rights, for not all rights infringements are morally forbidden. Then the upper limit and minimum necessary qualifications can be read as imposing the following two conditions on permissible infringements of the rights of others:

> Y's right to enforce his right to φ (or the right to φ of a third party) only permits him to infringe X's right to ψ if
> (i) X's right to ψ is not more important than Y's right to φ (or the third party's right to φ); and
> (ii) it is not possible for Y to prevent the violation of his right to φ (or the third party's right to φ) just as effectively by infringing only rights of X's which are less important than his right to ψ.[6]

In discussing the upper limit and minimum necessary qualifications I have made extensive use of the notion of the *importance* of a natural right, and there will no doubt be questions about exactly what this notion involves. In speaking of the importance of a right I have intended in the first place to speak of something intuitive. We all have, I trust, an intuitive sense that the right to life is more important than the right not to be physically assaulted, which is in turn more important than the right not to be tickled. But the notion can also be given a formal representation in a libertarian rights theory of the kind we have been discussing. If every right is an instance of the right to liberty, then it seems natural to say that one right is more important than another whenever it is a right to a more extensive liberty than the other. And although comparing the extent of some liberties raises obvious difficulties the following should once again be uncontroversial. If one liberty contains another as a proper part, so that exercising the second liberty always involves exercising the first, but exercising the first liberty does not always involve exercising the second, then the first liberty is more extensive than the second. The ranking procedure which these two suggestions yield is perhaps most usefully put as follows: one right is more important than another whenever violating the first right always involves violating the second, but violating the second right does not always involve violating the first (an example: the right to buy property in Canada is more important than the right to buy property in Alberta because preventing a person from buying property in Canada always involves preventing him from buying it in Alberta, but preventing him from buying it in Alberta does not always involve preventing him from buying it in Canada). This ranking procedure does not generate anything like a complete ordering over rights. It only generates a partial ordering, but the ordering is not so partial as to be useless. It has, for instance, some clear results about a number of rights that are important for questions about self-defence. It holds that the right not to be both tied up and beaten is more important than the right simply not to be tied up, that the right not to have both arms broken is more important than the right not to have one's left arm broken, and that the right not to have property valued at $100 destroyed is more important than the right not to have property valued at $1 destroyed. It also has some clear results about a number of rights that are important for questions about punishment. It holds that the right not to be imprisoned for ten years is more important than the right not to be imprisoned for five years, and that the right not to be fined $100 is more important than the right not to be fined $1. Most importantly for our concerns, however, it has clear results about the right which is most centrally involved in questions about capital punishment, namely the right to life. On a libertarian view the right to life is the right to exercise the liberty of choosing life over death, and imposes on others the duty not to remove that liberty, as they would do if they forcibly chose death for us. But this means that the right to life has to be the most important natural right there is. Choosing life is choosing to exercise all the liberties we do exercise when we are alive, while choosing death is choosing to exercise no further liberties at all. A person who removes the liberty of choosing life from us is therefore removing all our other liberties from us. In violating our right to life he is violating all our other rights as well, for he is leaving us in a position where we can never exercise those rights again. Although the proper part ranking procedure has clear results in these areas it does not have clear results in certain others. It does not say anything determinate about the relative importance of property rights and rights not to be physically assaulted, for instance, or of property rights and rights not to be imprisoned. These gaps in the ordering it generates weaken but they do not prevent the operation of the upper limit and minimum necessary qualifications. If property rights and rights not to be physically assaulted are unranked with respect to each other then neither is more important than the other, and persons may if necessary use force against others to prevent them from destroying their property, and destroy others' property to prevent them from assaulting them. Far from being an unwanted result this is one which I think we ought to welcome, for our intuitions seem to support the view that in most cases these two forms of self-defence are, if necessary, permissible. . . .

Having discussed the upper limit and minimum necessary qualifications in a general way let us now see what their implications are for questions about punishment. The qualifications place limits on the severity of the punishments which persons are permitted to inflict in the state of nature, and which their governments are permitted to inflict in civil society. It follows from the upper limit qualification that they are never permitted to inflict punishments which infringe rights that are more important than the ones which the offender has violated, and which they are therefore enforcing. And it follows from the minimum necessary qualification that they are never permitted to inflict punishments which infringe rights that are more important than is necessary to prevent further violations of the right which they are enforcing. If two punishments will be equally effective in deterring violations of this right, they have a duty to impose the less severe punishment; and if no punishments will be effective in deterring violations, they have a duty to impose no punishment at all. Something like this last consequence was accepted by Locke, and the fact that it was suggests that, while Locke may not have accepted the upper limit qualification, he did accept the minimum necessary qualification on enforcement rights. When Locke says in Section 7 of the *Second Treatise* that persons have the right to enforce the Law of Nature he says they have the "right to punish the transgressors of that Law *to such a degree, as may hinder its violation*" (my emphasis). . . .

What are the consequences of the rights-based justification for the special case of capital punishment? Capital punishment infringes the right to life of a criminal, and the right to life is the most important right there is. This means that, given the upper limit qualification, the rights-based justification will only allow capital punishment to be imposed on persons who have violated the right to life of another, that is, it will only allow capital punishment to be imposed for the crime of murder. At the same time, however, given the minimum necessary qualification, the rights-based justification will only allow capital punishment to be imposed for the crime of murder if there is no other less severe punishment which is equally effective at deterring murder. Extensive criminological studies have failed to produce any evidence that capital punishment is a more effective deterrent to murder than life imprisonment, and the rights-based justification will therefore hold that, until such evidence is produced, the imposition of capital punishment for any crime at all is impermissible.[7] This is in my view an attractive consequence, and it is one which also follows from the deterrence justification. But it is not bought at the cost of the many unattractive consequences of the deterrence justification. Many of us believe that if capital punishment is not an effective deterrent to murder then it ought not to be imposed. But we would not want this view to commit us to the simple deterrence justification, with all the unattractive consequences which that justification has. We would not want it to commit us to the view that capital punishment could be a permissible or even a required punishment for shoplifting, and we would not want it to commit us to the view that it could be permissible or even required to frame and "punish" an innocent man. The rights-based justification allows us to give some weight to the question of deterrence in assessing the morality of capital punishment, without giving it the overwhelming weight which it has in the deterrence justification.

Perhaps the distinctive consequences of the rights-based justification for the morality of capital punishment can best be summarized as follows. Assuming that a retributive calculus will find capital punishment a "fitting" punishment for the crime of murder, the retributive justification holds that it is a necessary and sufficient condition for the permissibility (and even requiredness) of imposing capital punishment on a person that he be guilty of murder. The rights-based justification agrees that this is a necessary condition but denies that it is sufficient; for a punishment to be permissible, it maintains, it must have some independent deterrent effect. The deterrence justification, by contrast, holds that it is a necessary and sufficient condition for the permissibility (and even requiredness) of imposing capital punishment on a person that this punishment have some independent deterrent effect. The rights-based justification once again agrees that this is a necessary condition but denies that it is sufficient; for a punishment to be permissible the person who undergoes it must be guilty of a crime, and guilty of a crime which violated rights at least as important as those which his punishment will infringe. In the rights-based justification conditions which are individually both necessary and sufficient in the deterrence and retributive justifications are made individually necessary but only jointly sufficient, and for this reason the rights-based justification can be said to combine the attractive features of the other two justifications while avoiding their unattractive features.

Notes

1John Locke, *Two Treatises of Government,* ed. Peter Laslett, 2nd ed. (New York: Cambridge University Press, 1967).

2Robert Nozick, *Anarchy, State, and Utopia* (New York: Basic Books, 1974), 10, 137–142.

3On this see H. L. A. Hart, "Are There Any Natural Rights?" *Philosophical Review* 64 (1955), 175–191.

4Those who do not believe there is a right not to be tickled as such can imagine that X is trying to violate all the (fairly unimportant) rights that he would violate if he tickled Y without his consent.

5*Anarchy, State, and Utopia,* 62–63.

6Analogues of these two qualifications as they apply to self-defence are recognized in the legal systems of Canada, Britain, and the United States, though they are not recognized in Germany or the Soviet Union. For a helpful survey see George P. Fletcher, *Rethinking Criminal Law* (Boston: Little, Brown, 1978), 855–875.

7As is often pointed out, the studies have not produced evidence that capital punishment is *not* a deterrent to murder either. But the onus of proof in this question is surely on the defenders of capital punishment to show that it is.

IMMANUEL KANT

THE RIGHT TO PUNISH

The right to punish contained in the penal law [*das Strafrecht*] is the right that the magistrate has to inflict pain on a subject in consequence of his having committed a crime. It follows that the suzerain of the state cannot himself be punished; we can only remove ourselves from his jurisdiction. A transgression of the public law that makes him who commits it unfit to be a citizen is called either simply a crime *(crimen)* or a public crime *(crimen publicum).* [If, however, we call it a public crime, then we can use the term "crime" generically to include both private and public crimes.]1 The first (a private crime) is brought before a civil court, and the second (a public crime), before a criminal court. Embezzlement, that is, misappropriation of money or wares entrusted in commerce, and fraud in buying and selling, if perpetrated before the eyes of the party who suffers, are private crimes. On the other hand, counterfeiting money or bills of exchange, theft, robbery, and similar acts are public crimes, because through them the commonwealth and not just a single individual is exposed to danger. These crimes may be divided into those of a base character *(indolis abjectae)* and those of a violent character *(indolis violentae).*

Judicial punishment (poena forensis) is entirely distinct from natural punishment *(poena naturalis).* In natural punishment, vice punishes itself, and this fact is not taken into consideration by the legislator. Judicial

From Immanuel Kant, *The Metaphysical Elements of Justice: Part I of the Metaphysics of Morals,* trans. John Ladd (Indianapolis, Ind.: Bobbs-Merrill, 1965), pp. 99–106. Reprinted by permission.

punishment can never be used merely as a means to promote some other good for the criminal himself or for civil society, but instead it must in all cases be imposed on him only on the ground that he has committed a crime; for a human being can never be manipulated merely as a means to the purposes of someone else and can never be confused with the objects of the Law of things [*Sachenrecht*]. His innate personality [that is, his right as a person] protects him against such treatment, even though he may indeed be condemned to lose his civil personality. He must first be found to be deserving of punishment before any consideration is given to the utility of this punishment for himself or for his fellow citizens. The law concerning punishment is a categorical imperative, and woe to him who rummages around in the winding paths of a theory of happiness looking for some advantage to be gained by releasing the criminal from punishment or by reducing the amount of it—in keeping with the Pharisaic motto: "It is better that one man should die than that the whole people should perish." If legal justice perishes, then it is no longer worthwhile for men to remain alive on this earth. If this is so, what should one think of the proposal to permit a criminal who has been condemned to death to remain alive, if, after consenting to allow dangerous experiments to be made on him, he happily survives such experiments and if doctors thereby obtain new information that benefits the community? Any court of justice would repudiate such a proposal with scorn if it were suggested by a medical college, for [legal] justice ceases to be justice if it can be bought for a price.

What kind and what degree of punishment does public legal justice adopt as its principle and standard? None other than the principle of equality (illustrated by the pointer on the scales of justice), that is, the principle of not treating one side more favorably than the other. Accordingly, any undeserved evil that you inflict on someone else among the people is one that you do to yourself. If you vilify him, you vilify yourself; if you steal from him, you steal from yourself; if you kill him, you kill yourself. Only the Law of retribution (*jus talionis*) can determine exactly the kind and degree of punishment; it must be well understood, however, that this determination [must be made] in the chambers of a court of justice (and not in your private judgment). All other standards fluctuate back and forth and, because extraneous considerations are mixed with them, they cannot be compatible with the principle of pure and strict legal justice.

Now, it might seem that the existence of class distinctions would not allow for the [application of the] retributive principle of returning like for like. Nevertheless, even though these class distinctions may not make it possible to apply this principle to the letter, it can still always remain applicable in its effects if regard is had to the special sensibilities of the higher classes. Thus, for example, the imposition of a fine for a verbal injury has no proportionality to the original injury, for someone who has a good deal of money can easily afford to make insults whenever he wishes. On the other hand, the humiliation of the pride of such an offender comes much closer to equaling an injury done to the honor of the person offended; thus the judgment and Law might require the offender, not only to make a public apology to the offended person, but also at the same time to kiss his hand, even though he be socially inferior. Similarly, if a man of a higher class has violently attacked an innocent citizen who is socially inferior to him, he may be condemned, not only to apologize, but to undergo solitary and painful confinement, because by this means, in addition to the discomfort suffered, the pride of the offender will be painfully affected, and thus his humiliation will compensate for the offense as like for like.

But what is meant by the statement: "If you steal from him, you steal from yourself"? Inasmuch as someone steals, he makes the ownership of everyone else insecure, and hence he robs himself (in accordance with the Law of retribution) of the security of any possible ownership. He has nothing and can also acquire nothing, but he still wants to live, and this is not possible unless others provide him with nourishment. But, because the state will not support him gratis, he must let the state have his labor at any kind of work it may wish to use him for (convict labor), and so he becomes a slave, either for a certain period of time or indefinitely, as the case may be.

If, however, he has committed a murder, he must die. In this case, there is no substitute that will satisfy the requirements of legal justice. There is no sameness of kind between death and remaining alive even under the most miserable conditions, and consequently there is also no equality between the crime and the retribution unless the criminal is judicially condemned and put to death. But the death of the criminal must be kept entirely free of any maltreatment that would make an abomination of the humanity residing in the person suffering it. Even if a civil society were to dissolve itself by common agreement of all its members (for example, if the people inhabiting an island decided to separate and disperse themselves around the world), the last murderer remaining in prison must first be executed, so that everyone will duly receive what his actions are worth and so that the bloodguilt thereof will not be fixed on the people because they failed to insist on carrying out the punishment; for if they fail to do so, they may be regarded as accomplices in this public violation of legal justice.

Furthermore, it is possible for punishment to be equal in accordance with the strict Law of retribution only if the judge pronounces the death sentence. This is clear because only in this way will the death sentence be pronounced on all criminals in proportion to their inner viciousness (even if the crime involved is not murder, but some other crime against the state that can be expiated only by death). To illustrate this point, let us consider a situation, like the last Scottish rebellion, in which the participants are motivated by varying purposes, just as in that rebellion some believed that they were only fulfilling their obligations to the house of Stuart (like Balmerino and others),[2] and others, in contrast, were pursuing their own private interests. Suppose that the highest court were to pronounce as follows: Each person shall have the freedom to choose between death and penal servitude. I say that a man of honor would choose death and that the knave would choose servitude. This is implied by the nature of human character, because the first recognizes something that he prizes more highly than life itself, namely, honor, whereas the second thinks that a life covered with disgrace is still better than not being alive at all *(animam praeferre pudori).* [3] The first is without doubt less deserving of punishment than the other, and so, if they are both condemned to die, they will be punished exactly in proportion [to their inner viciousness]; the first will be punished mildly in terms of his kind of sensibility, and the second will be punished severely in terms of his kind of sensibility. On the other hand, if both were condemned to penal servitude, the first would be punished too severely and the second too mildly for their baseness. Thus, even in sentences imposed on a number of criminals united in a plot, the best equalizer before the bar of public legal justice is death.

It may also be pointed out that no one has ever heard of anyone condemned to death on account of murder who complained that he was getting too much [punishment] and therefore was being treated unjustly; everyone would laugh in his face if he were to make such a statement. Indeed, otherwise we would have to assume that, although the treatment accorded the criminal is not unjust according to the law, the legislative authority still is not authorized to decree this kind of punishment and that, if it does so, it comes into contradiction with itself.

Anyone who is a murderer—that is, has committed a murder, commanded one, or taken part in one—must suffer death. This is what [legal] justice as the Idea of the judicial authority wills in accordance with universal laws that are grounded a priori. The number of accomplices *(correi)* in such a deed might, however, be so large that the state would soon approach the condition of having no more subjects if it were to rid itself of these criminals, and this would lead to its dissolution and a return to the state of nature, which is much worse, because it would be a state of affairs without any external legal justice whatsoever. Since a sovereign will want to avoid such consequences and, above all, will want to avoid adversely affecting the feelings of the people by the spectacle of such butchery, he must have it within his power in case of necessity *(casus necessitatis)* to assume the role of judge and to pronounce a judgment that, instead of imposing the death penalty on the criminals, assigns some other punishment that will make the preservation of the mass of the people possible, such as, for example, deportation. Such a course of action would not come under a public law, but would be an executive decree [*Machtspruch*], that is, an act based on the right of majesty, which, as an act of reprieve can be exercised only in individual cases.

In opposition to this view, the Marquis of Beccaria,[4] moved by sympathetic sentimentality and an affectation of humanitarianism, has asserted that all capital punishment is illegitimate. He argues that it could not be contained in the original civil contract, inasmuch as this would imply that every one of the people has agreed to forfeit his life if he murders another (of the people); but such an agreement would be impossible, for no one can dispose of his own life.

No one suffers punishment because he has willed the punishment, but because he has willed a punishable action. If what happens to someone is also willed by him, it cannot be a punishment. Accordingly, it is impossible to will to be punished. To say, "I will to be punished if I murder someone," can mean nothing more than, "I submit myself along with everyone else to those laws which, if there are any criminals among the people, will naturally include penal laws." In my role as colegislator making the penal law, I cannot be the same person who, as subject, is punished by the law; for, as a subject who is also a criminal, I cannot have a voice in legislation. (The legislator is holy.) When, therefore, I enact a penal law against myself as a criminal it is the pure juridical legislative reason *(homo noumenon)* in me that submits myself to the penal law as a person capable of committing a crime, that is, as another person *(homo phaenomenon)* along with all the others in the civil union who submit themselves to this law. In other words, it is not the people (considered as individuals) who dictate the death penalty, but the court (public legal justice); that is, someone other than the criminal. The social contract does not include the promise to permit oneself to be punished and thus to dispose of oneself and of one's life, because, if the only ground that authorizes the punishment of an evildoer were a promise that expresses his willingness to be punished, then it would have to be left up to him to find himself liable to punishment, and the criminal would be his own judge. The chief error contained in this sophistry . . . consists in the confusion of the criminal's own judgment (which one must necessarily attribute to his reason) that he must forfeit his life with a resolution of the Will to take his own life. The result is that the execution of the Law and the adjudication thereof are represented as united in the same person.

Notes

[1][Natorp and Cassirer agree that there is something wrong with the sentence following this one. Either a sentence has been omitted or the sentence in question has been misplaced. Kant's meaning is, however, perfectly clear, and I have inserted a sentence to provide the transition.]

[2][Arthur Elphinstone, Sixth Baron Balmerino (1688–1746), participated in the Jacobite rebellion that attempted to put Prince Charles Edward Stuart on the British throne. He was captured, tried, found guilty, and beheaded. He is said to have acted throughout with great constancy and courage.]

[3]["To prefer life to honor"—Juvenal, *Satire* 8. 83.] . . .

[4][Cesare Bonesana, Marquis di Beccaria (1738–1794), Italian publicist. His *Dei delitti e delle pene* (1764) (*On Crimes and Punishments,* trans. Henry Paolucci, "The Library of

Liberal Arts," No. 107 [New York: The Liberal Arts Press, 1963]) was widely read and had great influence on the reform of the penal codes of various European states.]

JONATHAN GLOVER
EXECUTION

The debate about capital punishment for murder is, emotionally at least, dominated by two absolutist views. On the retributive view, the murderer must be given the punishment he deserves, which is death. On the other view, analogous to pacifism about war, there is in principle no possibility of justifying capital punishment: in execution there is only 'the unspeakable wrongness of cutting a life short when it is in full tide'. Supporters of these two approaches agree only in rejecting the serpent-windings of utilitarianism.

Let us look first at the retributive view. According to retributivism in its purest form, the aim of punishment is quite independent of any beneficial social consequences it may have. To quote Kant again:

> Even if a Civil Society resolved to dissolve itself with the consent of all its members—as might be supposed in the case of a people inhabiting an island resolving to separate and scatter themselves throughout the whole world—the last Murderer lying in the prison ought to be executed before the resolution was carried out. This ought to be done in order that everyone may realize the desert of his deeds, and that blood-guiltiness may not remain upon the people; for otherwise they might all be regarded as participators in the murder as a public violation of justice.

This view of punishment, according to which it has a value independent of its contribution to reducing the crime rate, is open to the objection that acting on it leads to what many consider to be pointless suffering. To impose suffering or deprivation on someone, or to take his life, is something that those of us who are not retributivists think needs very strong justification in terms of benefits, either to the person concerned or to other people. The retributivist has to say either that the claims of justice can make it right to harm someone where no one benefits, or else to cite the curiously metaphysical 'benefits' of justice being done, such as Kant's concern that we should have 'blood-guiltiness' removed. I have no way of refuting these positions, as they seem to involve no clear intellectual mistake. I do not expect to win the agreement of those who hold them, and I am simply presupposing the other view, that there is already enough misery in the world, and that adding to it requires a justification in terms of non-metaphysical benefits to people.

This is not to rule out retributive moral principles perhaps playing a limiting role in a general theory of punishment. There is a lot to be said for the retributive restrictions that *only* those who deserve punishment should receive it and that they should never get more punishment than they deserve. (The case for this, which at least partly rests on utilitarian considerations, has been powerfully argued by H.L.A. Hart.)[1] But the approach to be adopted here rules out using retributive considerations to justify any punishment not already justifiable in terms of social benefits. In particular it rules out the argument that capital punishment can be justified, whether or not it reduces the crime rate, because the criminal deserves it.

This approach also has the effect of casting doubt on another way of defending capital punishment, which was forthrightly expressed by Lord Denning: 'The ultimate justification of any punishment is not that it is a deterrent, but that it is the emphatic denunciation by the community of a crime: and from this point of view, there are some murders which, in the present state of public opinion, demand the most emphatic denunciation of all, namely the death penalty.'[2] The question here is whether the point of the denunciation is to reduce the murder rate, in which case this turns out after all to be a utilitarian justification, or whether denunciation is an end in itself. If it is an end in itself, it starts to look like the retributive view in disguise, and should be rejected for the same reasons.

If we reject retribution for its own sake as a justification for capital punishment, we are left with two alternative general approaches to the question. One is an absolute rejection in principle of any possibility of capital punishment being justified. . . . The other is the rather more messy approach, broadly utilitarian in character, of weighing up likely social costs and benefits.

1 THE ABSOLUTIST REJECTION OF CAPITAL PUNISHMENT

To some people, it is impossible to justify the act of killing a fellow human being. They are absolute pacifists about war and are likely to think of capital punishment as 'judicial murder'. They will sympathize with Beccaria's question: 'Is it not absurd that the laws which detest and punish homicide, in order to prevent murder, publicly commit murder themselves?'

The test of whether an opponent of capital punishment adopts this absolutist position is whether he would still oppose it if it could be shown to save many more lives than it cost: if, say, every execution deterred a dozen potential murderers. The absolutist, unlike the utilitarian opponent of the death penalty, would be unmoved by any such evidence. This question brings out the links between the absolutist position and the acts and omissions doctrine. For those of us who reject the acts and omissions doctrine, the deaths we fail to prevent have to be given weight, as well as the deaths we cause by execution. So those of us who do not accept the acts and omissions doctrine cannot be absolutist opponents of capital punishment.

There is a variant on the absolutist position which at first sight seems not to presuppose the acts and omissions doctrine. On this view, while saving a potential murder victim is in itself as important as not killing a murderer, there is something so cruel about the kind of death involved in capital punishment that this rules out the possibility of its being justified. Those of us who reject the acts and omissions doctrine have to allow that sometimes there can be side-effects associated with an act of killing, but not with failure to save a life, which can be sufficiently bad to make a substantial moral difference between the two. When this view is taken of the cruelty of the death penalty, it is not usually the actual method of execution which is objected to, though this can seem important, as in the case where international pressure on General Franco led him to substitute shooting for the garrotte. What seems peculiarly cruel and horrible about capital punishment is that the condemned man has the period of waiting, knowing how and when he is to be killed. Many of us would rather die suddenly than linger for weeks or months knowing we were fatally ill, and the condemned man's position is several degrees worse than that of the person given a few months to live by doctors. He has the additional horror of knowing exactly when he will die, and of knowing that his death will be in a ritualized killing by other people, symbolizing his ultimate rejection by the members of his community. The whole of his life may seem to have a different and horrible meaning when he sees it leading up to this end.

For reasons of this kind, capital punishment can plausibly be claimed to fall under the United States constitution's ban on 'cruel and unusual punishments', so long as the word 'unusual' is not interpreted too strictly. The same reasons make the death penalty a plausible candidate for falling under a rather similar ethical ban, which has been expressed by H. L. A. Hart: 'There are many different ways in which we think it morally incumbent on us to *qualify* or *limit* the pursuit of the utilitarian goal by methods of punishment. Some punishments are ruled out as too barbarous to use *whatever their social utility*'[3] (final italics mine). Because of the extreme cruelty of capital punishment, many of us would, if forced to make a choice between two horrors, prefer to be suddenly murdered rather than be sentenced to death and executed. This is what makes it seem reasonable to say that the absolutist rejection of the death penalty need not rest on the acts and omissions doctrine.

But this appearance is illusory. The special awfulness of capital punishment may make an execution even more undesirable than a murder (though many would disagree on the grounds that this is outweighed by the desirability that the guilty rather than the innocent should die). Even if we accept that an execution is worse than an average murder, it does not follow from this that capital punishment is too barbarous to use *whatever its social utility.* For supposing a single execution deterred many murders? Or suppose that some of the murders deterred would themselves have been as cruel as an execution? When we think of the suffering imposed in a famous kidnapping case, where the mother received her son's ear through the post, we may feel uncertain even that capital punishment is more cruel than some 'lesser' crimes than murder. The view that some kinds of suffering are too great to impose, whatever their social utility, rules out the possibility of justifying them, however much more suffering they would prevent. And this does presuppose the acts and omissions doctrine, and so excludes some of us even from this version of absolutism.

2 A UTILITARIAN APPROACH

It is often supposed that the utilitarian alternative to absolutism is simply one of adopting an unqualified maximizing policy. On such a view, the death penalty would be justified if, and only if, it was reasonable to think the number of lives saved exceeded the number of executions. (The question of what to do where the numbers exactly balance presupposes a fineness of measurement that is unattainable in these matters.) On any utilitarian view, numbers of lives saved must be a very important consideration. But there are various special features that justify the substantial qualification of a maximizing policy.

The special horror of the period of waiting for execution may not justify the absolutist rejection of the death penalty, but it is a powerful reason for thinking that an execution may normally cause more misery than a murder, and so for thinking that, if capital punishment is to be justified, it must do better than break even when lives saved through deterrence are compared with lives taken by the executioner.

This view is reinforced when we think of some of the other side-effects of the death penalty. It must be appalling to be told that your husband, wife or child has been murdered, but this is surely less bad than the experience of waiting a month or two for your husband, wife or child to be executed. And those who think that the suffering of the murderer himself matters less than that of an innocent victim will perhaps not be prepared to extend this view to the suffering of the murderer's parents, wife and children.

There is also the possibility of mistakenly executing an innocent man, something which it is very probable happened in the case of Timothy Evans. The German Federal Ministry of Justice is quoted in the Council of Europe's report on *The Death Penalty in European Countries* as saying that in the hundred years to 1953, there were twenty-seven death sentences 'now established or presumed' to be miscarriages of justice. This point is often used as an argument against capital punishment, but what is often not noticed is that its force must depend on the special horrors of execution as compared with other forms of death, including being murdered. For the victim of murder is innocent too, and he also has no form of redress. It is only the (surely correct) assumption that an innocent man faces something much worse in execution than in murder that gives this argument its claim to prominence in this debate. For, otherwise, the rare cases of innocent men being executed would be completely overshadowed by the numbers of innocent men being murdered. (Unless, of course, the acts and omissions doctrine is again at work here, for execution is something that we, as a community, *do,* while a higher murder rate is something we at most *allow.*)

The death penalty also has harmful effects on people other than the condemned man and his family. For most normal people, to be professionally involved with executions, whether as judge, prison warder or chaplain, or executioner, must be highly disturbing. Arthur Koestler quotes the case of the executioner Ellis, who attempted suicide a few weeks after he executed a sick woman 'whose insides fell out before she vanished through the trap'.[4] (Though the chances must be very small of the experience of Mr. Pierrepoint, who describes in his autobiography how he had to execute a friend with whom he often sang duets in a pub.[5]) And there are wider effects on society at large. When there is capital punishment, we are all involved in the horrible business of a long-premeditated killing, and most of us will to some degree share in the emotional response George Orwell had so strongly when he had to be present. It cannot be good for children at school to know that there is an execution at the prison down the road. And there is another bad effect, drily stated in the *Report of the Royal Commission on Capital Punishment:* 'No doubt the ambition that prompts an average of five applications a week for the post of hangman, and the craving that draws a crowd to the prison where a notorious murderer is being executed, reveal psychological qualities that no state would wish to foster in its citizens.'

Capital punishment is also likely to operate erratically. Some murderers are likely to go free because the death penalty makes juries less likely to convict. (Charles Dickens, in a newspaper article quoted in the 1868 Commons debate, gave the example of a forgery case, where a jury found a £10 note to be worth 39 shillings, in order to save the forger's life.) There are also great problems in operating a reprieve system without arbitrariness, say, in deciding whether being pregnant or having a young baby should qualify a woman for a reprieve.

Finally, there is the drawback that the retention or re-introduction of capital punishment contributes to a tradition of cruel and horrible punishment which we might hope would wither away. Nowadays we never think of disembowelling people or chopping off their hands as a punishment. Even if these punishments would be specially effective in deterring some very serious crimes, they are not regarded as a real possibility. To many of us, it seems that the utilitarian benefits from this situation outweigh the loss of any deterrent power they might have if re-introduced for some repulsive crime like kidnapping. And the longer we leave capital punishment in abeyance, the more its use will seem as out of the question as the no more cruel punishment of mutilation. (At this point, I come near to Hart's view that some punishments are too barbarous to use whatever their social utility. The difference is that I think that arguments for and against a punishment should be based on social utility, but that a widespread view that some things are unthinkable is itself of great social utility.)

For these reasons, a properly thought-out utilitarianism does not enjoin an unqualified policy of seeking the minimum loss of life, as the no trade-off view does. Capital punishment has its own special cruelties and horrors, which change the whole position. In order to be justified, it must be shown, with good evidence, that it has a deterrent effect not obtainable by less awful means, and one which is quite substantial rather than marginal.

3 DETERRENCE AND MURDER

The arguments over whether capital punishment deters murder more effectively than less drastic methods are of two kinds: statistical and intuitive. The statistical arguments are based on various kinds of comparisons of murder rates. Rates are compared before and after abolition in a country, and, where possible, further comparisons are made with rates after reintroduction of capital punishment. Rates are compared in neighbouring countries, or neighbouring states of the U.S.A., with and without the death penalty. I am not a statistician and have no special competence to discuss the issue, but will merely purvey the received opinion of those who have looked into the matter. Those who have studied the figures are agreed that there is no striking correlation between the absence of capital punishment and any alteration in the curve of the murder rate. Having agreed on this point, they then fall into two schools. On one view, we can conclude that capital punishment is not a greater deterrent to murder than the prison sentences that are substituted for it. On the other, more cautious, view, we can only conclude that we do not know that capital punishment is a deterrent. I shall not attempt to choose between these interpretations. For, given that capital punishment is justified only where there is good evidence that it is a substantial deterrent, either interpretation fails to support the case for it.

If the statistical evidence were conclusive that capital punishment did not deter more than milder punishments, this would leave no room for any further discussion. But, since the statistical evidence may be inconclusive, many people feel there is room left for intuitive arguments. Some of these deserve examination. The intuitive case was forcefully stated in 1864 by Sir James Fitzjames Stephen:[6]

No other punishment deters men so effectually from committing crimes as the punishment of death. This is one of those propositions which it is difficult to prove, simply because they are in themselves more obvious than any proof can make them. It is possible to display ingenuity in arguing against it, but that is all. The whole experience of mankind is in the other direction. The threat of instant death is the one to which resort has always been made when there was an absolute necessity for producing some result. . . . No one goes to certain inevitable death except by compulsion. Put the matter the other way. Was there ever yet a criminal who, when sentenced to death and brought out to die, would refuse the offer of a commutation of his sentence for the severest secondary punishment? Surely not. Why is this? It can only be because. 'All that a man has will he give for his life.' In any secondary punishment, however terrible, there is hope; but death is death; its terrors cannot be described more forcibly.

These claims turn out when scrutinized to be much more speculative and doubtful than they at first sight appear.

The first doubt arises when Stephen talks of 'certain inevitable death'. The Royal Commission, in their *Report,* after quoting the passage from Stephen above, quote figures to show that, in the fifty years from 1900 to 1949, there was in England and Wales one execution for every twelve murders known to the police. In Scotland in the same period there was less than one execution for every twenty-five murders known to the police. Supporters of Stephen's view could supplement their case by advocating more death sentences and fewer reprieves, or by optimistic speculations about better police detection or greater willingness of juries to convict. But the reality of capital punishment as it was in these countries, unmodified by such recommendations and speculations, was not one where the potential murderer faced certain, inevitable death. This may incline us to modify Stephen's estimate of its deterrent effect, unless we buttress his view with the further speculation that a fair number of potential murderers falsely believed that what they would face was certain, inevitable death.

The second doubt concerns Stephen's talk of 'the threat of instant death'. The reality again does not quite fit this. By the time the police conclude their investigation, the case is brought to trial, and verdict and sentence are followed by appeal, petition for reprieve and then execution, many months have probably elapsed, and when this time factor is added to the low probability of the murderers being executed, the picture looks very different. For we often have a time bias, being less affected by threats of future catastrophes than by threats of instant ones. The certainty of immediate death is one thing; it is another thing merely to increase one's chances of death in the future. Unless this were so, no one would smoke or take on such high-risk jobs as diving in the North Sea.

There is another doubt when Stephen very plausibly says that virtually all criminals would prefer life imprisonment to execution. The difficulty is over whether this entitles us to conclude that it is therefore a more effective deterrent. For there is the possibility that, compared with the long term of imprisonment that is the alternative, capital punishment is what may appropriately be called an 'overkill'. It may be that, for those who will be deterred by threat of punishment, a long prison sentence is sufficient deterrent. I am not suggesting that this is so, but simply that it is an open question whether a worse alternative here generates any additional deterrent effect. The answer is *not* intuitively obvious.

Stephen's case rests on the speculative psychological assumptions that capital punishment is not an overkill compared with a prison sentence; and that its additional deterrent effect is not obliterated by time bias, nor by the low probability of execution, nor by a combination of these factors. Or else it must be assumed that, where the additional deterrent effect would be obliterated by the low probability of death, either on its own or in combination with time bias, the potential murderer thinks the probability is higher than it is. Some of these assumptions may be true, but, when they are brought out into the open, it is by no means obvious that the required combination of them can be relied upon.

Supporters of the death penalty also sometimes use what David A. Conway, in his valuable discussion of this issue, calls 'the best-bet argument'.[7] On this view, since there is no certainty whether or not capital punishment reduces the number of murders, either decision about it involves gambling with lives. It is suggested that it is better to gamble with the lives of murderers than with the lives of their innocent potential victims. This presupposes the attitude, rejected here, that a murder is a greater evil than the execution of a murderer. But, since this attitude probably has overwhelmingly widespread support, it is worth noting that, even if it is accepted, the best-bet argument is unconvincing. This is because, as Conway has pointed out, it overlooks the fact that we are not choosing between the chance of a murderer dying and the chance of a victim dying. In leaving the death penalty, we are opting for the certainty of the murderer dying which we hope will give us a chance of a potential victim being saved. This would look like a good bet only if we thought an execution substantially preferable to a murder and either the statistical evidence or the intuitive arguments made the effectiveness of the death penalty as a deterrent look reasonably likely.

Since the statistical studies do not give any clear indication that capital punishment makes any difference to the number of murders committed, the only chance of its supporters discharging the heavy burden of justification would be if the intuitive arguments were extremely powerful. We might then feel justified in supposing that other factors distorted the murder rate, masking the substantial deterrent effect of capital punishment. The intuitive arguments, presented as the merest platitudes, turn out to be speculative and unobvious. I conclude that the case for capital punishment as a substantial deterrent fails.

Notes

[1]H. L. A. Hart: 'Prolegomenon to the Principles of Punishment', *Proceedings of the Aristotelian Society*, 1959–1960.

[2]Quoted in the *Report of the Royal Commission on Capital Punishment*, 1953.

[3]H. L. A. Hart: 'Murder and the Principles of Punishment', *Northwestern Law Review*, 1958.

[4]Arthur Koestler: *Reflections on Hanging*, London, 1956.

[5]Albert Pierrepoint: *Executioner: Pierrepoint*, London, 1974.

[6]James Fitzjames Stephen: Capital Punishments, *Fraser's Magazine*, 1864.

[7]David A. Conway: 'Capital Punishment and Deterrence', *Philosophy and Public Affairs*, 1974.

chapter 7

Pornography and Censorship

INTRODUCTION

Pornography and censorship raise complex questions of ethics, politics, and law. During the past decade, the governments of the United States, Canada, and Great Britain have each conducted special studies of the problem.[1] However, these reports certainly did not settle the issues.

One source of confusion is the meaning of the terms. "Pornography" is perhaps best used to mean sexually explicit representations (writings, pictures, films, etc.) designed or intended to arouse sexually the reader or observer.[2] In its nonlegal sense, "obscene" is primarily used to express, endorse, or predict offense toward something.[3] Obviously, pornography need not be obscene, for it need not produce offense. Contrarily, things can be obscene and not be pornographic; for example, many people claim that some representations of nonsexual violence are obscene.

The U.S. Attorney General's Commission on Pornography suggested a rough classification of types of pornography. One type is material that portrays violence or threatened violence in a sexually explicit fashion.[4] This is the type many people find most objectionable. A second type is nonviolent but depicts people, mostly women, in a degrading fashion, as being dominated by or subordinate to others, or engaged in sexual acts many people would find humiliating.[5] Finally, there can be sexually explicit portrayals that are neither violent nor degrading, for example, of consenting adults with basically equal roles.[6]

Pornography and obscenity raise a number of distinct issues. First, there is the problem of defining terms, which we have just briefly examined. Second, several ethical issues can be distinguished. One might ask whether the content of pornographic or obscene materials is unethical. If one decides that it is, then one might ask whether it is unethical (wrong) to produce, distribute, or view such materials. One could hold that producing or selling pornographic materials is wrong but that perceiving them is not. Third, one can ask whether the law should be concerned with pornography and obscenity. If so, one must also consider how the law should respond to it.

Legal and Political Background   In the United States, legal obscenity is not speech protected by the freedom of speech clause of the First Amendment to the Constitution. The test of obscenity is "(a) whether 'the average person, applying contemporary community standards,' would find that the work, taken as a whole, appeals to the prurient interest, (b) whether the work depicts or describes, in a patently offensive way, sexual conduct specifically defined by the applicable state law, and (c) whether the work, taken as a whole, lacks serious literary, artistic, political, or scientific value."[7] This test provides some leeway for communities to have their own standards. The Court has provided less protection to pornographic materials with children as subjects.[8] Almost any sexual activity with children in the production of such materials will involve a crime, because children cannot give legal consent to sexual conduct. Consequently, most states prohibit distribution of photographic representations of real children whether or not the material is legally obscene.

At least four different principles might be relevant to legislation against pornography and obscenity. Each of these principles presents a kind of reason for legally controlling conduct. A particular principle need not apply to justify legally restricting conduct; and if a principle does apply, one still might choose to maintain the legal permissibility of the conduct. The principles are as follows: (1) the *harm principle* states that conduct may be restricted if it might cause harm to others; (2) the *offense principle* states that conduct may be restricted if it might offend others; (3) the *paternalist principle* states that conduct may be restricted to prevent persons from harming themselves; and (4) the *legal moralist* principle states that conduct may be restricted if it is immoral. In considering whether the production and distribution of obscene and pornographic materials should be legally restricted, one must first determine which principles are appropriate for legislation and then apply them to obscene and pornographic materials.

Most of the political debate about pornography and obscenity has implicitly assumed that the harm and sometimes offense principles are the only appropriate ones for legislating against pornography. However, what is considered harm often blurs the distinction between the various principles. For example, the Attorney General's commission stated that "to a number of us, the most important harms must be seen in moral terms, and the act of moral condemnation of that which is immoral is not merely important but essential. From this perspective there are acts that need be seen not only as causes of immorality but as manifestations of it."[9] This comment collapses the distinction between the harm and legal moralist principles by claiming that manifestations of immorality are harms.

Given the variety of consequences that people might classify as harms, it is not surprising that people disagree about whether pornography causes harm. On the one hand, the Attorney General's commission found a causal relationship between violent pornography and sexual aggression.[10] It also found that exposure to degrading pornography, by affecting people's attitudes and beliefs, is likely to increase sexual violence and coercion in the population. The members disagreed about the harmfulness of nonviolent, nondegrading pornography, but they did agree that it was little cause for concern if kept from children. On the other hand, the Williams report in Britain did not find a significant relationship between pornography and harm.[11] One significant agreement did result from the studies. The British committee recommended that the printed word not be restricted or prohibited.[12] Although the Attorney General's commission did not agree on a clear rule against prosecution of the printed word, all members agreed that except for material directed at children, it should "be undertaken only with extraordinary caution."[13]

Finally, it is important to keep in mind the various types of legal control of pornography that might be exercised. The Williams report emphasized the difference between prohibition and restriction. It primarily recommended prohibition of materials whose production involves the harm of sexual exploitation and restriction of the public display of other materials offensive to reasonable persons. Prohibition can take two forms. One is prior censorship to prevent the distribution of objectionable material. This method is often used by film censorship boards in Canada and England. In the United States, any such legally imposed censorship would constitute unconstitutional prior restraint. However, television networks do voluntarily censor their own material. The other method of prohibition is simply to make the production or distribution of the material a criminal offense.

Restriction of pornographic materials can involve a variety of approaches. First, public display of pornographic materials, as on billboards or uncovered fronts of magazines in racks, can be made a criminal offense. Second, some cities have zoned pornography shops. Third, Indianapolis and some other cities have attempted to provide so-called "victims" of pornography a right to civil suits for injunctions and damages. However, the Indianapolis ordinance was struck down as unconstitutional.[14] More success in this respect might be possible in Canada under human rights codes.[15] Fourth, government might forbid the use of its facilities for the display or sale of pornographic materials, as on college campuses, or otherwise not support pornography.

Much of the recent argument about pornography has concerned its degrading women by depicting them in subordinate sex roles and endorsing sexual inequality. Some people contend that it defames women and supports sexual discrimination. There are two significant objections to this type of analysis.[16] First, it is unclear whether graphic pornography has any message, any propositional content, that could be defamatory.

Second, even if it does, the producer or distributor need not endorse or support that claim. Any endorsement might be defeated by a disclaimer at the bottom of a picture or the beginning of a film. Television news often shows scenes of violence, but few people take it to be endorsing violence.

Ethical and Political Perspectives   The following discussion concentrates on the ethical and political nature of pornography and its censorship by punishment for production and distribution.

In the traditional *natural-law* view, since sexual intercourse is permissible only within heterosexual marriage, the content of most pornographic materials portraying sexual intercourse will be judged as wrong conduct. Producing and distributing such materials, of course, is also wrong, if it encourages immoral ideas and conduct. One must distinguish the discussion of such conduct from the portrayal of it in an appealing manner. But in the natural-law view, even viewing obscene pornographic materials is apt to be wrongful, because doing so appeals to interests and desires that are wrongful (perhaps unnatural) and should not be satisfied or promoted.

Society is a natural organization of individuals to promote the common good. Classically, promoting the common good has included the morality of the community's members. If pornography and obscenity are immoral, then the state may, subject to other considerations, regulate or prohibit it for the common good. A minimalist natural-law view would only subject the political process and law to certain basic standards of morality that could not be violated. It might permit obscenity and pornography. However, this minimalist view comes close to a natural-rights approach.

A *natural-rights* view holds conduct to be wrong only if it violates the rights of others. Sexual conduct between consenting adults does not violate people's rights and so is not wrongful. This statement will hold if the theory contains a broad natural right to freedom. However, to determine that conduct is not wrong does not settle the issue of its ethical character. Some conduct is not good—is something one ought not to do—even though it is not wrong. Thus, perhaps one should not engage in some sexual conduct even though it does not violate anyone's rights. Also, in the natural-rights view, portrayals of brutality and violence (including nonconsensual sexual conduct) depict wrongful conduct.

But even if content is judged unethical, it does not follow that producing, distributing, and perceiving it are. A natural right to freedom of speech (and press) would likely imply that producing and distributing obscene and pornographic materials are within an individual's rights. Similarly, a right to freedom would allow individuals to perceive such materials. One might hold that a right to freedom allows individuals to view obscene materials in the privacy of their own home, but does not allow their production and dissemination. The Supreme Court, which in interpreting the First Amendment has engaged in reasoning similar to that a natural-rights theorist might use, has held that private possession of obscene materials is a constitutionally protected right to freedom or privacy.[17]

States and governments are not permitted to abridge people's natural rights. Consequently, determining the rights with respect to obscenity and pornography also partly settles the political-legal questions of legislation prohibiting it. If producing and distributing pornography and obscenity are within an individual's natural rights, then the state cannot prohibit those activities unless they violate more important rights of others. If those activities are not within the scope of natural rights, then the state perhaps may prohibit them; it may certainly do so if they violate the rights of others. Public displays of obscenity raise the issue of a natural right not to be offended. If such a right exists, then not only may governments prohibit public displays of obscenity, but failure to do so would permit people's rights to be violated. As the state primarily exists to protect and enforce natural rights, the government should then act against public indecency.

It is not completely clear what a *Kantian* view of pornography entails. By the law of nature formula, portrayals of sexual conduct between consenting adults are likely to be of ethically permissible conduct. As long as the partners are consenting, one could will the conduct to be a universal law of nature, even were the roles reversed. However, as in the natural-rights view, the content of pornography would be immoral if one of the parties did not consent; this applies as well to all violence, not just sexual violence. By the formula of treating humanity as an end, it is less clear that content displaying consensual sexual conduct is ethically permissible. Even though a party consents, one (or both) partners might view the other merely as a means to sexual gratification. However, Kant viewed marriage essentially as a contract for the mutual exclusive use of each other's genitals.[18] Nonmarital relationships for mutual sexual gratification might not be wrong, but be only short-term contracts. If so, then nonmarital relationships between consenting adults would be ethically permissible, for the mutual short-term contract would mean that each person was also treated as an end.

The ethical nature of the content of pornography and obscenity, for a Kantian, probably determines the morality of its production and distribution. Given that the content is unethical, then one could not rationally will its production and distribution nor could one be treating humanity as an end in so doing. Producing and distributing unethical material does not respect humanity, if it encourages people to enjoy unethical conduct. The fact that unethical conduct is merely portrayed does not seem to make a difference.

In the political realm, Kant held that the law should not be concerned with whether people act from respect for the moral law; instead, it should be restricted to behavior. The universal law of justice governing legislation is to "act externally in such a way that free use of your will is compatible with the freedom of everyone according to a universal law."[19] Violations of this principle may be punished. Hence, if the production and distribution of pornography are immoral, they come under the universal law of justice and are an appropriate subject for state prohibition. Indeed, Kant himself obeyed a government edict prohibiting him from publishing further on religion, although some people have noted that he had by then published about everything he had to say.

A *contractarian* approach to pornography, obscenity, and censorship primarily involves the equal-liberties principle. An equal right to the greatest equal liberties compatible with like liberties for all includes the freedom of speech and other forms of communication. The rights involved relate to both the individual as a speaker and as a member of the audience. To preserve equal liberties, captive audiences, for instance, unforewarned passers-by, should not be subjected to obtrusive and unwanted speech. The content of obscenity, appropriately defined, can be seen as unethical, because it involves abuse of bodily or personal functions that are demeaning and disgusting to the person involved.[20] Of course, by this view not all pornography will be judged obscene. But if the depicted act is obscene, this guarantees that its communication is also wrong.[21] Thus, both obscene acts and communications will be understood as having unethical content. They are or depict conduct demeaning and disgusting, because it violates the standards of the individuals involved. Furthermore, purveyors and consumers of pornographic materials might hold standards by which the conduct would not be considered wrong and, therefore, might be expressing a pornographic view of life. Since obscenity can be communicated, it is included in the liberty of free speech. Rational contractors behind the veil of ignorance would not prohibit the communication of ideas involving different standards, because they would not know which standards they might hold. As the principles of justice restrict what the majority may do to protect and promote its standards, the equal-liberty principle implies that obscenity and pornography should not be legally prohibited. This conclusion is subject to two qualifications. First, it does not apply to children; the liberty principle does not apply to them because they lack full rationality.[22] Second, laws may be passed prohibiting public displays of obscenity, for such displays infringe upon each person's liberty of choice as to what will be viewed.[23]

Utilitarians have rarely discussed the ethical as opposed to the political-legal aspect of pornography and obscenity. From a *utilitarian* ethical point of view, it would be wrong to conclude that the content as well as the production and distribution of pornographic and obscene materials are permissible so long as they do not harm anyone. That is not the appropriate *act-utilitarian* test. To be permissible, acts must produce at least as much net utility as any other acts the agents could perform in the given situation. No matter what sexual thrills and delights are expressed by the actors in pornographic films, other conduct might produce more net utility. This conclusion becomes more plausible if one considers the producers and distributors of such materials. Thus, by act-utilitarian reasoning, possibly the content, and probably the production and distribution, of obscene and pornographic materials might be wrong.

This conclusion is less likely to be reached by a *rule utilitarian.* The content of pornographic and obscene materials would be unethical only if they portrayed conduct violating a set of rules the adoption of which would have as much net utility as any other. Such a moral code is unlikely to contain a rule prohibiting consensual sexual conduct (what is the utility in that!). However, it would almost certainly prohibit violence and nonconsensual sexual conduct. Whether it would also contain a rule prohibiting the production and distribution of materials depicting such conduct is another matter. Generally, such a code is unlikely to prohibit conduct unless it causes net disutility; otherwise the psychological, and other, costs required to support the rule would not be worthwhile. Thus, in a rule-utilitarian view, the production and distribution of obscene and pornographic materials are less likely to be wrong than in an act-utilitarian view.

The differences between act and rule utilitarianism usually vanish when one considers the legal prohibition of obscenity and pornography. As the act of legislating creates a rule, in most situations evaluation of the act is tantamount to evaluation of the rule. Historically, most utilitarian discussions of obscenity and pornography legislation derive from John Stuart Mill's *On Liberty.* Mill generally held that only the harm principle provides an acceptable basis for legislation. He rejected the legal moralist principle and accepted paternalism only for children.[24] At one place in the book, he appeared to accept the offense principle for certain public conduct.[25]

Reading The selection by Harry Clor largely represents a natural-law view of the justifiability of legal prohibition of obscenity, including portrayals of violence and death. He argues that all societies have public moral standards concerning the sensual aspects of life. If such standards are essential (and natural?) for societies, then censorship can support them by reducing corrupting influences and upholding authoritative standards. Further, he argues, merely punishing indecency without censorship would require greater penalties than those extant, or society would have to lower its standards.

The selection by Judith DeCew first considers the ethical nature of violent pornography. In a Kantian vein, she contends that the only argument that unconditionally condemns it is that it disregards the worth and dignity of human beings. In a discussion omitted here, she argues that Feinberg's offense principle might prohibit too much. She also thinks that it is too weak a social response. Thus, she considers a principle condemning the support of violent pornography.

In the final selection, Joel Feinberg discusses Mill's view about the legal prohibition of obscenity and pornography. After distinguishing harm from offense, he argues that a restricted offense principle can be used to justify prohibition of public offensive conduct but not books and films, because individuals have a free choice to read or view them.

Notes

[1] U.S. Department of Justice, Attorney General's Commission on Pornography, *Final Report* (July 1986); Special Committee on Pornography and Prostitution, appointed by Minister of Justice of Canada, chaired by Paul Fraser, Q.C., *Pornography and Prostitution Issues Paper* (Ottawa: Minister of Supply and Services Canada, 1983); Bernard Williams, ed., *Obscenity and Film Censorship* (Cambridge: Cambridge University Press, 1981) [the government issued this report in 1979].

[2] Joel Feinberg, *Offense to Others* (New York: Oxford University Press, 1985), p. 127; Williams, *Obscenity,* para. 8.2.

[3] Feinberg, *Offense,* p. 97; Williams, *Obscenity,* para. 8.4.

[4] Attorney General's commission, *Final Report,* p. 323.

[5] Attorney General's commission, *Final Report,* p. 331.

[6] Attorney General's commission, *Final Report,* p. 335.

[7] *Miller* v. *State of California,* 413 U.S. 15, 24 (1973).

[8] *New York* v. *Ferber,* 458 U.S. 747 (1982).

[9] *Final Report,* p. 303.

[10] See generally, *Final Report,* part 2, chap. 5.

[11] Williams, *Obscenity,* chap. 6.

[12] Williams, *Obscenity,* paras. 7.22, 13.4 (6).

[13] Attorney General's commission, *Final Report,* p. 385.

[14] *American Booksellers Ass'n, Inc.* v. *Hudnut,* 598 F. Supp. 1316 (S.D. Ind. 1984), *aff'd,* 771 F.2d 303 (7th Cir. 1985), *aff'd without opinion,* 106 S. Ct. 1172 (1986).

[15] See *Saskatchewan Human Rights Comm'n* v. *Waldo,* 5 Can. Human Rights Rep. secs. 17609–17783 (1985) (Bd. of Inquiry); and more generally, Kathleen A. Lahey, "The Canadian Charter of Rights and Pornography: Toward a Theory of Actual Gender Equality," *New England Law Review* 20 (1984–1985): 677–684.

[16] See Alan Soble, "Pornography: Defamation and the Endorsement of Degradation," *Social Theory and Practice* 11 (1985): 61–87.

[17] *Stanley* v. *Georgia,* 394 U.S. 557 (1969).

[18] Immanuel Kant, *The Philosophy of Law,* trans. W. Hastie (Edinburgh: T. & T. Clark, 1887), p. 110.

[19] Immanuel Kant, *The Metaphysical Elements of Justice,* trans. John Ladd (Indianapolis, Ind.: Bobbs-Merrill, 1965), p. 35; Akademie, p. 231.

[20] David A. J. Richards, *The Moral Criticism of Law* (Encino, Calif.: Dickenson, 1977), p. 61. This book contains an excellent, lengthy contractarian analysis of obscenity and pornography, pp. 56–77.

[21] Ibid., p. 66.

[22] Ibid., p. 72.

[23] Ibid., p. 73.

[24] *On Liberty,* ed. Currin V. Shields (Indianapolis, Ind.: Bobbs-Merrill, 1956), p. 13.

[25] Ibid., p. 119.

Bibliography on Pornography

American Booksellers Ass'n, Inc. v. *Hudnut,* 598 F. Supp. 1316 (S.D. Ind. 1984), *aff'd,* 771 F.2d 303 (7th Cir. 1985), *aff'd without opinion,* 106 Sup. Ct. 1172 (1986).

Burstyn, Varda, ed. *Women Against Censorship.* Vancouver: Douglas & McIntyre, 1985.

Clor, Harry M. *Obscenity and Public Morality: Censorship in a Liberal Society.* Chicago, Ill.: University of Chicago Press, 1969.

Copp, David, and Wendell, Susan, eds. *Pornography and Censorship.* Buffalo: Prometheus Books, 1983.

Dworkin, Andrea. *Pornography: Men Possessing Women.* New York: G. P. Putnam's Sons, 1981.

Dworkin, Ronald. *A Matter of Principle.* Cambridge: Harvard University Press, 1985. Chapter 17.

Feinberg, Joel. *Offense to Others.* New York: Oxford University Press, 1985. Chapters 10–12.

Ferber v. *New York,* 458 U.S. 747 (1982).

Kittay, Eva Feder. "Pornography and the Erotics of Domination." In *Beyond Domination: New Perspectives on Women and Philosophy,* edited by Carol C. Gould, pp. 145–174. Totowa, N.J.: Rowman & Allanheld, 1984.

MacKinnon, Catharine. "Pornography, Civil Rights, and Speech." *Harvard Civil Rights-Civil Liberties Law Review* 20 (1985): 1–70.

Miller v. *State of California,* 413 U.S. 15 (1973).

Richards, David A. J. *The Moral Criticism of Law.* Encino, Calif.: Dickenson, 1977. Pages 56–77.

Smart, Brian. "Offensiveness in the Williams Report." *Philosophy* 59 (1984): 516–22.

Sobel, Alan. *Pornography: Marxism, Feminism, and the Future of Sexuality.* New Haven: Yale University Press, 1986.

Special Committee on Pornography and Prostitution. Appointed by Minister of Justice of Canada, chaired by Paul Fraser, Q.C. *Pornography and Prostitution Issues Paper.* Ottawa: Minister of Supply and Services Canada, 1983.

Symposium on Pornography. *New England Law Review* 20 (1984–1985): 629–777.

Tong, Rosemarie. *Women, Sex and The Law.* Totowa, N.J.: Rowman and Allanheld, 1984. Chapter 1.

U.S. Department of Justice. Attorney General's Commission on Pornography. *Final Report.* July 1986.

Williams, Bernard. *Obscenity and Film Censorship.* Cambridge: Cambridge University Press, 1981.

Problem Case
A Neighborhood Porn Shop

The Fairview homeowner's meeting has been a turbulent one. The difficulty all started innocently enough last spring when construction commenced on a neighborhood shopping center adjacent to the Fairview subdivision. Most people were happy to have it, because it meant a few stores nearby for drugs, video tapes, and pizza. However, the week before last, when it was discovered that one of the tenants of the shopping center was to be an adult book and video tape store, considerable opposition arose. Tonight's meeting has been tumultuous.

Some women denounced the store as a porn shop and claimed that the filth it would distribute defamed and degraded women. Other women, however, claimed that liberated women were as interested in sexual matters as men, that some women they knew watched pornographic movies with their husbands.

Another group declaimed the store as likely to corrupt the children of the neighborhood. Although the owner said he would not permit people under eighteen years of age to buy materials or rent tapes, it was objected that older children would get materials for younger ones. However, some people replied that if parents did not want their children viewing such materials, they should watch their children better.

Other members claimed that the store would attract undesirable people to the area and that property values would fall. Although people might have a right to distribute pornographic materials and to view them in the privacy of their own home, stores purveying the materials should be restricted to downtown business areas. The owner of the shopping center said that had he realized there would be so much opposition, he would not have leased the space to the store. However, the store owner now has a one-year lease, and he cannot be removed without the shopping center paying significant damages.

Several proposals have been made, and it is now time to vote on them. One proposal is to petition the city council to enact a zoning law banning adult book stores from the area. Another is to ask the local prosecutor and police to inspect the store periodically and to prosecute whenever any obscene material is found. A third proposal is to picket the store and to boycott all the stores in the shopping center until the adult shop leaves. Another alternative, of course, is to defeat the proposals and do nothing.

If you were a homeowner in Fairview, how would you vote? Why? Do you have an alternative proposal for the situation that would be better than any of the others? If so, what is it?

HARRY M. CLOR
LAW, VIRTUE, AND SEX

It is often observed that standards of morality and immorality, obscenity and non-obscenity, differ widely from culture to culture. In some societies kissing in public is prohibited, while in others public acts of coitus are performed as religious ceremonies.[1] But, as anthropologist Margaret Mead observes, "every known human society exercises some explicit censorship over behavior relating to the human body, especially as that behavior involves or may involve sex."[2] There is no known society in which matters relating to sex and the human body are left wholly unregulated. And there is no known society in which the regulation of these things is left wholly to individuals or to spontaneous social activity.

The proper treatment of the physical or sensual side of life is a crucial and universal social problem. Says Mead: "Society has two problems—how to keep sex activity out of forbidden channels that will endanger the

From Harry M. Clor, *Obscenity and Public Morality: Censorship in a Liberal Society* (Chicago, Ill.: University of Chicago Press, 1969). Reprinted by permission of the University of Chicago Press. © 1969 by the University of Chicago.

bodies and souls of others or the orderly co-operative processes of social life, *and* how to keep it flowing reliably in those channels where it is necessary if children are to be conceived and reared in homes where father and mother are tied together by the requisite amount of sexual interest"[3] (italics in original).

All human societies deal with these matters in essentially the same way: they establish public moral standards which are made binding on their members. These standards dictate what sexual acts may be performed and with whom; they establish the distinction between physical acts which may be done in public and those which may be done only in private; and they govern to some extent permissible verbal expression about such matters. My point here is twofold: (1) these standards have the character of *public* standards—they are imposed by society as such; and (2) these standards have the character of *moral* standards—violation of them is supposed to be attended by the appropriate feelings of guilt, shame, or disgust.

Why do we need to have public standards of decency? The issues which are the subject of such standards are highly perplexing and disturbing to the great majority of mankind. They concern the control and direction of powerful passions, the determination of the proper relation between the physical, social, and spiritual sides of life, and the moral judgments which are implicit in such terms as "higher" and "lower." No man (or very few) can resolve these problems alone, on the basis of his own private reasoning. Nor can he resolve them on the basis of a spontaneous "free exchange of ideas" with others. Therefore, we will always require some authoritative pronouncements on such subjects as: the proper character of the family, the nature of the marriage bond, the duties and rights of married persons, the human meaning of sex and its relation to love, and the extent to which the human body and its various functions should be revealed or concealed in public. In matters so problematic, men rely upon guidance from the community in which they live. They need public standards.

But why should public moral standards require the support of law? Why can we not rely for their promulgation and maintenance upon society or the community?

Whatever may be the case in primitive communities, in civilized communities "society" is not an autonomous self-regulating entity. Society does not resolve its problems autonomously without authoritative direction. In civilized times it is the political community which most effectively represents the common ends and interests of society, and the political community characteristically acts by means of law. Indeed in the absence of the political community and its laws, it would be most difficult to locate, amid the complex diversities which characterize modern life, anything deserving the name of "the society" or "the community."

Society as such cannot censor morals. Strictly speaking, society as such cannot make decisions and act purposively. Thus, when it is said that "censorship should be the proper activity of the community rather than the law," this can reasonably mean only that the contemporary public opinion should do it, the family should do it, or the church should do it. It is not to be denied that these can be influential agencies promoting moral restraint or ethical training. But are they alone capable of performing the community's civilizing and moralizing functions? And can they perform these functions without the support of law?

If public opinion is to be a moral influence, from whence is public opinion to receive its moral guidance? It is well known that on particular issues—the "issues of the day"—public opinion is often unstable, uncertain, and transitory. Ill-defined feelings and half-formed attitudes tend to become public opinion when positions are taken by influential persons—including statesmen, lawmakers, and judges. The formation of public opinion is profoundly influenced by actions or positions taken in government and by laws—past, present, and prospective.

There is a more stable and more continuous "underlying" public opinion. Such opinion has more than one source, but surely one of its most important sources is to be found in tradition and customs which have been supported by (if not engendered by) the fundamental laws and principles of the country. Continuing public attitudes on many subjects (e.g., the rights of private property) may be traced in this manner to the Constitution and to the attitudes and decisions of such political men as Alexander Hamilton and John Marshall.

I dwell upon these commonplaces only in order to make the point that public opinion cannot be relied upon as if it were a self-dependent moral agent. The long-term or underlying public attitudes are what they are largely because of the context of social and political traditions in which they are formed. The public looks, in part, to the country's customs and laws for ethical and intellectual guidance. If there is now a body of public attitudes in support of moral decency, this must be, to a large extent, because there have been positions taken in the past in support of moral decency—positions resulting in or fostered by law. One may at least wonder what contemporary attitudes on moral matters would be if there had been no such decisions and no such laws.

Like the various public opinions, the family is but a part of civil society and is subject to the influences predominant therein. It would not be reasonable to expect "the home" to produce morally decent children if indecency prevailed in the society around it. The education promoted in the home could not withstand the influence of the surrounding moral environment, nor could the family as an institution avoid the effects of such an environment. For instance, the institution of monogamous marriage as we know it presupposes and requires some commitment to sexual fidelity. This is not to say that any lapse whatever from this commitment must be regarded as a "sin" which destroys a marriage. But, at least, there must be a belief in the obligation of faithfulness and efforts to live up to that obligation, if the family is to have the significance and perform the tasks which traditionally belong to it in our society. If, in the community at large, the commitment to fidelity as a norm were replaced by radical promiscuity, monogamy could not long retain its character. And the new institution, whatever moral training it might provide, could hardly continue to be a teacher of sexual fidelity. The family is not an autonomous social force capable of independently generating and sustaining values.

Traditionally, religious institutions have been such a source of values. For a number of reasons, they no longer have the political stature, the social influence, or the moral authority to perform for the community the civilizing functions which it requires.[4] The churches can teach morality, and they can lend their support to social movements concerned with morality, but they cannot be relied upon as a predominant influence upon character in modern society.

It is quite true that the social agencies under consideration are those most directly concerned with the promotion of virtue or decency. But inquiry shows that their success or failure is dependent upon factors or forces in society at large which they do not control.

The community, then, cannot rely solely upon public opinion, the family, and the church to promulgate and maintain its public morality. These agencies can shape the values which prevail in society, but, to a greater extent, they are shaped by these values.

Therefore, it must be a task of modern government and law to support and promote the public morality upon which a good social life depends. Censorship can serve this end in two ways: (1) by preventing or reducing some of the most corrupt influences and (2) by holding up an authoritative standard for the guidance of opinions and judgment.

Legitimate censorship is not designed to prevent the circulation of all literature which might have an immoral influence. It aims primarily at the most vicious materials. And it seeks, not directly to shape mind and character, but to contain some of those influences in modern society which shape mind and character in harmful ways. The effects of censorship upon these influences are not confined to the specific books or motion pictures which the censor condemns. Its more significant effects are those of deterrence. Publishers are deterred from publishing, and authors from writing, materials which cannot legally be circulated. Thus the results of legal censorship consist not in the confiscation of the relatively few obscene publications which the censor catches, but in the general reduction in the circulation of materials of that kind.

Laws against obscene publications may have a more subtle and, perhaps, more profound consequence. Such laws announce a moral decision of the community arrived at and issued through its official organs. They assert, in effect, that the organized community draws a line between the decent and the indecent, the permissible and the impermissible. Individuals may, of course, step over the line, but they are made aware that the community is committed to a distinction between what is right and what is not. In the long run this awareness must have an effect upon the moral attitudes and values of most people.

The coercive and preventing functions of censorship are thus supplemented by its hortatory and educative functions. Or perhaps it would be more correct to say that the latter are supplemented by the former. Libertarian authors are inclined to speak as if punishment were the heart of all legal censorship. They are inclined to refer to censorship exclusively as "the legal enforcement of morality." But there are some forms of censorship which do not involve criminal proceedings and need not involve any punishment at all. This is the case when the law employs purely administrative or civil proceedings for the condemnation or confiscation of obscene materials. Here the purveyor will receive no legal penalties unless he defies the orders of a court. And when the criminal law is used, punishment and the threat of punishment, while serving as a deterrent to specific acts against morality, are subordinate means to the larger educative ends. By its willingness to punish some violations of its morality, the community indicates that it is serious about that morality. Conceivably, a community could officially promulgate ethical standards without the slightest efforts to use coercion in support of them. It is all too likely that such standards would not be taken with sufficient seriousness by those most in need of guidance. Willingness to use coercion in their support is surely a prime indicator of the significance which society attaches to its various principles and purposes.[5] We do not know of any political community which has relied upon simple promulgation and exhortation for the implementation of its principles.

Laws against obscenity or other forms of vice serve to render community standards authoritative. They can also serve to clarify and define such standards. One need not presuppose that there would be no criteria of decency whatever in the absence of legislation. Individuals and groups do, obviously, have moral attitudes and values which they have not received from government. But attitudes and values which arise in "society" tend often to be vague, over-general, and contradictory. Individuals and social groups do not easily succeed in establishing the precise applications and limits of those general principles they hold in common. These principles, then, seldom constitute a clear and agreed-upon boundary line between decent and indecent activity. The law contributes to the drawing of boundary lines by its definition of such terms as "obscenity." The law thus helps to transform indistinct, indefinite, and personal moral feelings into public standards.

In the absence of public norms thus established, social attitudes (or public opinion) may remain ill-defined, inconclusive, and ineffectual. Or, they may vacillate between extremes of moral indifference and moralistic zealotry. As legal censorship is relaxed, the private standards of many citizens may also be relaxed. Other citizens may be aroused to replace legal censorship with a form of censorship considerably more repressive. Many authors have observed that as legal censorship is restricted the censorship activities of private groups tend often to increase.

And these groups can be far less discriminating in their moral and aesthetic judgments than is the law.

Communal standards, properly formulated, promulgated, and enforced, will inhibit the emergence—and perhaps prevent the ascendancy—of immoderate or unreasonable private standards. A public moral philosophy, supported in part by law, can profoundly affect the dispositions and opinions by which social life is shaped. It can encourage civil or reasonable dispositions and opinions, and it can discourage those which are uncivil or unreasonable.

Can it be truly said that the organized community has no right to be thus concerned with the minds of citizens, with their "inner lives"? And can it be reasonably said that the operations of law must be strictly confined to overt antisocial conduct or to considerations of peace and security?

I have presented arguments showing that the political community cannot be indifferent to the moral values and the moral character of its members and why it cannot rely simply upon nonpolitical institutions to sustain values and character at a moral level consistent with its needs. Public standards are required, and private agencies cannot be confidently relied upon to provide them. In the absence of legal and political support, the capacity of such agencies to provide a communal morality would depend upon the many diverse influences—economic, social, psychological, and intellectual—which make them what they are. If civil society requires certain virtues in its members, it cannot afford to leave this to the determination of fortuitous circumstances and chance influences.

Of course, the law can punish indecent acts. This is the policy recommended to it by opponents of censorship—you may punish wrongful conduct, but you must never do anything involving the slightest degree of coercion to influence men's values or the character of their private lives. But the threat of legal coercion will not sufficiently deter indecent acts when little attention has been given to the conditions which breed indecent men. If the law must restrain immoral conduct, then it cannot be indifferent to the influences which break down moral standards, weakening their hold upon conduct. If political society were to adopt a policy of legal coercion plus moral indifference, if it would seek by coercion to prevent immoral conduct while remaining neutral toward immoral character, two possible results are predictable. The penalties for bad conduct would have to be considerably increased; the coercive functions of the law would have to be made more effective. Or, the categories of punishable acts would have to be considerably reduced; society would have to lower its standards of conduct. If society is interested in the prevention of acts contrary to its moral standards, then it is neither reasonable nor safe to require it to wait until the acts have been done or are about to be done. A community with a large number of vicious citizens will have to control them by force—or the effort to control them will have to be abandoned.

Long before such a state of affairs is reached, the community is deeply interested in the morality of its citizens. Civilized social life requires not only that men observe certain decencies, but also that they believe in them. And political life requires not only that men perform certain duties, but also that they believe in them. The political education of every nation testifies to this communal interest in the minds, dispositions, and beliefs of its citizens.

These considerations are not less compelling when applied to the sensual or the sexual side of life. Every community must devote its attention to the discipline and direction of powerful natural impulses. Every social order must endeavor to give the sensual side of life its due while preventing undue or excessive preoccupation with it. The minds and energies of citizens must be available for the long-range pursuits and higher ends of the community. This requires socially imposed restraints upon the indulgence of the passions and, also, socially imposed standards and values concerning the indulgence of the passions. Since the community cannot be indifferent to what its members do about the physical side of life, it cannot be wholly indifferent to what they feel and believe about it. Censorship of some kind or degree is implicit in these propositions.

Notes

[1] Weston La Barre, "Obscenity: An Anthropological Appraisal," *Law and Contemporary Problems,* 20 (Autumn, 1955): 533–43.

[2] Margaret Mead, "Sex and Censorship in Contemporary Society," *New World Writing* (New York: The New American Library of World Literature, 1953), p. 7.

[3] Ibid., p. 11.

[4] For a substantiation of this proposition presented from a point of view quite different from that of this essay, see Harvey Cox, *The Secular Society* (New York: Macmillan Co., 1965).

[5] H. L. A. Hart reports the following assertions of a nineteenth-century Royal Commission on capital punishment: "The fact that men are hanged for murder is one great reason why murder is considered so dreadful a crime." Hart is not impressed with this proposition, but he does not refute it. See *Law, Liberty and Morality* (New York: Vintage Books, 1966), p. 58.

JUDITH WAGNER DECEW
VIOLENT PORNOGRAPHY

. . . It is difficult to distinguish clearly between what could be classified as erotica or 'softcore' pornography and violent pornography. Erotica, emphasising the sensual or physical aspects of sex, attempts to be appealing to the audience, and need not be incompatible with the values of mutual pleasure, care, and concern for others. . . .

From Judith Wagner DeCew, "Violent Pornography: Censorship, Morality and Social Alternatives," *Journal of Applied Philosophy* 1 (1984): 83–86, 88–94. Reprinted by permission.

. . . Thus I shall mean by violent pornography sexual material which depicts violent, coercive, abusive or non-consensual acts, and which endorses or recommends such behaviour.[1] Given my descriptions, erotica and violent pornography do not exhaust all sexually explicit materials. Nevertheless, without further differentiation, I shall assume we have a general idea of the difference between them. For the rest of this paper I shall focus on the moral status of, and social responses to, violent pornography.

IS VIOLENT PORNOGRAPHY MORALLY WRONG?

Rights Violations

There appear to be a wealth of arguments that violent pornography is morally wrong, derived by applying traditional ethical principles. First, it would be wrong if it involved a serious violation of individual rights. If actors or actresses are abused in any way that fails to protect their rights to privacy or bodily security, for example, then it is difficult to see how the rights of others to have access to the material, or any benefit to consumers, could outweigh such a violation.

However, it is not easy to defend the view that any rights have been violated if the material is written or if the participants are consenting adults. The major problem with the latter is determining the extent to which participants genuinely and knowingly consent or are pressured by other individuals or social forces. It seems clear that in some cases there is virtually no consent, or that consent is not genuine, so individual rights are violated. For example, Linda Lovelace of *Deep Throat* and other pornography models indicate that some participants are sold or coerced by spouses or parents to perform, that physical violence and forced drugs are sometimes used to gain 'consent', and that models who do agree to participate, even in written contracts, often feel trapped when they discover that what happens after signing is beyond their control.[2] Nevertheless, this fails as a general moral argument against *all* violent pornography, for in literary work as well as films, photographs, or plays done by consenting sadists, it is hard to identify any individual rights that are being transgressed. (Note, however, that sado-masochistic pornography may *portray* consensual pleasure, without using sadistic models.)

Treatment of Human Beings

One might rely on the more general statement that violent pornography portrays actions which fail to respect the integrity, worth and dignity of human beings. The claim could be made to show that individual rights are violated, but as such the argument is extremely vague.[3] The claim might be used more successfully as a general moral indictment of violent pornography because it approvingly depicts treatment of human beings in a violent, non-consensual manner which thus fails to respect their worth. As such, it would apply as well to other violent literature, movies, and television shows which portray human life as expendable, violence toward others without cause as acceptable, etc. While some may believe this could adequately justify legal censorship, it is worthwhile to note that it is not and never has been a criminal offence to publish accounts or photographs of harmful or illegal actions. Thus, unless we radically change our views on criminal law, portrayal of violence alone provides no argument for repression of what is displayed or written. Still, it may be plausible to say that such material, including violent pornography, is morally objectionable due to its content: approving depiction of violent, non-consensual treatment of human beings.[4]

Harm to Participants

A third way of arguing that violent pornography is morally wrong involves appealing to the harm (apart from violation of rights) it causes either (a) to the participants, or (b) to others. It is extremely difficult for those of us not part of the pornographic industry to have a clear idea of the extent models in films or photographs, for example, actually suffer pain, or merely act as though they do. However, the pornographic thriller, *Snuff,* banned six years ago, has recently resurfaced on videotape. This film depicts the dismemberment and murder of a woman for the sexual stimulation of male characters and viewers, and it is rumoured that at least one actress actually died during the filming. Pornographic models also relate stories of women having to endure hot candle wax dripped on their breasts, cigarette burns on their bodies, and other pain.[5] Furthermore, it is not difficult to imagine that many participants are exploited in much the same way that prostitutes are exploited by pimps. The exploitation might be physical or psychological. I suspect the analogy is a fair one, and it is substantiated by personal reports.[6] But virtually no research has corroborated the extent and pervasiveness of harm caused to participants to make this a firm moral argument against violent pornography.

Harm to Others

The argument that violent pornography harms others is more diffuse but at least as important and troubling. It is worrisome because it relies on the premise that there is a causal relationship between violent pornography and violence produced in society at large. Yet, as already noted, the studies on the extent to which exposure to pornography leads to crime yield conflicting results. Moreover, most of the empirical studies have not aimed at gaining the type of information necessary for the argument. For example, the Congressional Committee on Obscenity concluded in 1970 that exposure to erotica had "little or no effect" on attitudes toward sexuality or sexual morality, that patterns of sexual behaviour were "not altered substantially by exposure to erotica", and that their data did not show "erotic material is a significant cause of sex crime."[7] But concluding that there is no evidence relating *erotica* to violent attitudes or behaviour does not even address the effects of *violent pornography*. If violent pornography depicts and recommends sexual relations with someone getting hurt involuntarily, and through its approval of such behaviour encourages emulation, then it may well have effects on others.

Given that the President's Commission on the Causes and Prevention of Violence concluded in 1969 that media violence can induce viewers to act aggressively, it is reasonable to infer that analogous results follow for viewers of sexual violence. Some studies done in the last ten years do show that violent pornography is closely linked to violent behaviour. But to have a moral argument against violent pornography based on the harm it inflicts on others, we need studies verifying not merely a *correlation,* but also a *causal relationship* between portrayals of violent pornography and crime. Such information would also provide a strong, though not unproblematic, argument for censorship of violent pornography. However, we still await solid confirming data. And research establishing effects in the world is always difficult because of discrepancies between what people say and what they really believe, and between what they think they will do and what they actually do.[8]

Sexism and Violence

Although there are exceptions, violent pornography is overwhelmingly intended for the gratification of males, and is acknowledged by many to be sexist in the sense that it exploits sexual inequality and enhances a degrading view of women. Women's groups view most violent pornography as bloody, woman-as-victim, horror shows. Irving Kristol says, of pornography in general, that

. . . . there can be no question that pornography is a form of "sexism," as the Women's Liberation Movement calls it, and the instinct of Women's Lib has been unerring in perceiving that, when pornography is perpetrated, it is perpetrated against them, as part of a conspiracy to deprive them of their full humanity.[9]

Others believe that pornography often reflects the worst social conceptions of sexual relations in that many of the scenes depict male dominance over women, females as sexual servants or toys, and male aggression and violence toward women.

It would be ideal if we could argue separately for the immorality of violence and the immorality of sexism. They clearly can be different. Dismemberment is distinguishable from debasement of women. With respect to violence, depictions which encourage it, especially those that lead to violent acts against innocents, must surely be morally wrong. The difficulty arises in establishing a causal relationship between portrayal and physical harm. For sexism, the concern is perhaps more controversial. It is not merely that there is harm to an image of women (whatever that may mean), nor is it easy to identify direct harm to women. The claim is that sexism is morally wrong because it condones, recommends, and perpetuates an immoral view about how women should act and be treated. To the extent that pornography expresses that view or affects behaviour, it is also morally wrong.

Unfortunately it is especially difficult to separate arguments about violent and sexist pornography. Robert Baker and Frederick Elliston have pointed out, for example, strong linguistic evidence that our society connects the concept of sex with the concept of harm, traditionally using male subjects and female objects.[10] Feminist Julia Robbins worries that part of pornography's hateful message is that a "steady diet of [pornographic] images suggests that females will never say no or, at least, never mean it. Men . . . buy the idea that women are there for the taking."[11] "The concern is that violence depicted in a sexual context conveys the message that women *desire* and *enjoy* being treated in an abusive way, or *want* and *need* to be forced to submit. While pornography which is sexist may be wrong independently of any violence, violent pornography which portrays sexism in a dramatic way by condoning and encouraging such acts as rape and battering of women, is worse for intertwined reasons. We cannot usually separate what sexually excites, what is sexist, and what is violent.

Summary

Each of the arguments discussed give some ground for moral complaint against violent pornography. It is noteworthy and initially surprising, however, that the conclusions that violent pornography is morally wrong are generally conditional ones. That is, violent pornography is immoral *when* it depicts sexist attitudes, or *if* it fosters sexist behaviour, or *if* it leads to violent crime, or *if* it exploits or abuses participants psychologically or physically, or *if* it violates an individual's right by involving participation without genuine consent. In each case, concluding that violent pornography is morally wrong depends on accepting one of these conditions which may not always be true.

The only unconditional conclusion that all violent pornography is wrong is based on the claim that every portrayal endorsing and recommending treatment of human beings in a way disregarding their dignity and worth is immoral. Then, given that violent, coercive, abusive or non-consensual treatment of human beings disregards their dignity and worth, all violent pornography is morally wrong.

I think it is reasonable to accept this argument. More generally, I believe it is reasonable to judge violent pornography on its content: it is morally wrong when it enhances a degrading view of women (and men) through an unworthy portrayal of violent, hurtful treatment of human beings, even if it leads to no sexist or violent behaviour in the world. But it has been suggested that more support may be needed to argue that morally objectionable content is sufficient to judge material itself unethical.[12] Anyone who finds such a portrayal misguided or ignorant, but not properly judged morally wrong, or any consequentialist who believes moral right and wrong are determined solely by effects, will be unpersuaded by this argument.

SOCIAL ALTERNATIVES TO CENSORSHIP OF VIOLENT PORNOGRAPHY: TWO APPROACHES

. . . Imagine that a student group on a university campus shows a film which we assume is clearly an instance of violent pornography. Students flock to see it and so such films are shown on a regular basis for the audience and as a fundraiser for other activities. While we may assume the advertisements are innocuous and that the films are clearly avoidable without unreasonable effort, they may have been purchased with funds from students who would not want to attend. Or even if students' funds are not used, each film showing is subsidised by the university as long as it is shown on university property.

Refusing Support and Subsidy

Assuming that violent pornography is morally objectionable, it might be that . . . we should endorse:

(P₂) It is morally wrong for any individual or institution to do anything which supports or subsidises the industry that produces violent pornography.[13]

This principle defends a position much stronger than one advocating avoidance or even boycotting. In the above example, according to (P₂) the individual students are morally wrong to show the movie, even if there is an audience for it and it provides a hefty income, and the university is morally wrong to allow its property to be used to show the film. . . .

However, there are major difficulties with (P₂). First, other examples lead to the worry that (P₂) is too strong. Consider the following: Suppose someone subscribes to a cable television channel to get news and weather information and movies unavailable on commercial television. The station then begins to add pornographic films, including violent ones, late at night to increase its subscriber audience. Imagine also that alternative cable channels with similar benefits (but without the pornographic films) are not available in the geographical areas. Furthermore, the subscriber has no interest in the pornographic films, and never watches them. Nevertheless, aware that they are part of the parcel, is it morally wrong for one to continue subscribing to the channel?

The case can be altered a bit, and become even more puzzling. Suppose on a trip one stays in a hotel with a television which one discovers shows, among other things, violent pornographic films. Even if one does not watch the films, is one morally required to get another room without a television? Or a room without a television showing the pornography? Or move to another hotel to avoid any action which subsidises violent pornography in any way?

Our examples lead us to a second slippery slope problem. How much is morally required of one who finds violent pornography morally wrong for any or all of the reasons discussed above? Must one give up the benefits of cablevision because the station in one's area shows the objectionable films? Must one leave one's hotel room even if it is late at night, one has an early business meeting the next day, and it is a great inconvenience? Must one check out even in the extreme case when no alternative lodging is available? Apparently we must answer yes if we accept (P_2), according to which it is morally wrong to do *anything* which supports or subsidises the industry producing violent pornography.

Second, (P_2) is ambiguous. How are we to interpret it? Is the implicit assumption that the multi-million dollar industry, allegedly linked with organised crime, illicit drugs, and prostitution, is immoral and should not be supported? If so, it seems analogous support and subsidy for the industry producing erotica is also wrong, and thus accepting (P_2) requires defending a position stronger than many are willing to endorse.

Or is the assumption that the industry exploits and violates the rights of models in the production of violently pornographic material? On this reading, (P_2) may again be too broad because it very likely implies acceptance of an analogous principle applying to erotica as well. Also, on this interpretation, the principle appears too weak since it may apply to the production of films, peep shows, posters, etc., but not to books or other written material.

Or is the basis of the objection the only unconditional one, that the content of violent pornography generally portrays, endorses and recommends immoral attitudes and behaviour? If so, then (P_2) is too strong as formulated. Even if the content is unethical, it does not follow that producing, distributing and perceiving it are.[14]

Or is the objection implicit in (P_2) the most worrisome one, that violent pornography has dangerous effects, assuming that this is true and that it can be shown that such pornography is causally related to increases in violent crime, particularly against women? If so, then (P_2) focuses on the effects of the material, which are independent of objections to the industry.

Determining the best response to violent pornography requires getting clearer on what is most objectionable about it. If our objections focus on the *content* of most violent pornography because of the attitudes it portrays and recommends or on the *effects* it has due to the behaviour it incites, rather than its *source* in the industry, then we must reformulate (P_2) to reflect the basis of our moral protest. But then it is less obvious what the moral responsibilities of institutions and individuals are.

Consider again the student film example. If the university decides to ban violent pornographic films on campus on the grounds that it is morally wrong to allow university property to be used to display materials whose *content* is morally objectionable, then we may ask what standard of morality is being used for the judgment. Moreover, if the university does ban the film on campus, then it is clearly making a decision that affects what students may or may not see or hear on campus. Even if the reason for the ban is a moral objection to the content of the film, the effect of the university's action is control over availability of what may be seen or heard. This of course is the essence of censorship, considered contrary to a free society and antithetical to the concept of a university. If there is no harm to others, Mill defended the liberty of tastes and pursuits, even though others think them foolish, perverse or wrong.

Universities have used similar reasoning for permitting speakers such as Professor William Shockley, the Stanford physicist whose theories concerning the genetic transmission of intelligence are considered by many to be false as well as racist. On this view, there should be no restraints on the availability of information or expression, even if it fosters objectionable opinions and attitudes. A public invitation to a speaker does not acknowledge the acceptability of the views. Indeed, heckling and protest are allowed. Furthermore, it is claimed that banning such speakers from campus carries the implicit assumption that students cannot distinguish true from false, or worthy from unworthy, and such banning is thus presumptuous and insulting to the intellectual maturity of the university community. Analogously, allowing violent pornographic films on university property neither condones nor acknowledges their acceptability. A contrary decision to ban the films from campus, if made by the institution and not, for example, by a referendum of the student body, can be viewed as a paternalistic decision in its *least* justifiable form.[15] The university is interfering with a person's liberty, not because the person is physically or psychologically unable to make a thoughtful choice about whether or not to attend, but because the content is thought inappropriate.

In reply, it might be argued that violent pornographic films do not in any identifiable way further the quest for truth. Not all 'expression' is information. Moreover, it can be claimed that the university decision is not a paternalistic one. It is not one that restricts an individual's liberty for his or her *own* good, but does so to take a strong moral stand on the part of the university. The Constitution provides against governmental repression, but a university need not provide a forum for such films. Most compellingly, if the university cannot proscribe use of its property in the case of violent pornography, when can it assert moral leadership, a role often viewed as an essential function of a university?

Limitations on free speech can be justified based on either (a) the content of, or (b) the effect of, the expression. Historically, the courts have found non-content features, such as time, place, volume, and 'clear risk' of danger, to be admissible justifications. But what has consistently been viewed as an illegitimate ground for curbing expression is any reason based on the content or message. Unfortunately, the line between these two types of justification is not easy to draw.[16] With respect to violent pornography it is especially troublesome to distinguish material which endorses and invites objectionable attitudes and behaviour, from that which poses a 'clear risk' of violent actions. Nor is it at all clear how great a threat generates a 'clear risk' of violence.

If a university administration has good reason to fear dangerous effects from allowing violent pornographic films on campus (effects such as increased violence in the dorms), then I believe it has no choice but to refuse to allow the films.[17] However not all deleterious effects are sufficient to justify campus bans. The problem, of course, is determining whether violent and non-violent effects ever exist independently. In my view, barring clear risk of violent behaviour, a university may allow students to show violent pornographic films. While it is difficult to justify violent pornography at a serious workplace, a university can take a strong moral stand on it by issuing public disclaimers, for example, without resorting to campus bans based on arguments normally found unacceptable as grounds for state censorship. Of course a university need not always take a moral stand by issuing public statements rather than taking action. A university can and should refuse funding from racist countries, and limit recruitment on campus by groups that do not admit minorities. But in the case of violent pornography, if the major concern is the *content* of the material, not dangerous *effects,* then the issue is what others may or may not see and hear. It is thus distinguishable from other instances where a university might want to assert moral leadership.

Notes

[1]This is similar to the definition of pornography in the National Lawyer's Guild Resolution on Pornography, passed by the Convention on August 9 1980, except that I have added 'abusive' as explained. I am grateful to Gail Hanlon of Women Against Violence Against Women in Boston for the NLG material and for suggesting the addition, although WAVAW uses 'degrading' instead of 'abusive' for portrayals of self-abuse. Like the NLG, others have used 'pornography' non-neutrally. Gloria Steinem distinguishes erotica and pornography, where the latter involves violence, dominance, and conquest, but she fails to make clear the difference between material which *endorses* the power portrayed and that which does not. Erotica and pornography: a clear and present difference, *Ms.,* 1978. Helen Longino proposes a definition of pornography emphasising the approving quality of the material, but which may be broader than my definition, depending on how one interprets 'degrading' and 'abusive'. She says, "Pornography, then, is verbal or pictorial material which represents or describes sexual behavior that is degrading or abusive to one or more of the participants *in such a way as to endorse the degradation".* Pornography, oppression, and freedom: a closer look, in Lederer, Laura (Ed.) *Take Back the Night* (New York, Bantam Books, 1982) pp. 36–41.

[2]Lovelace, Linda (1980) *Ordeal* (Seacaucus, New Jersey, Citadel Press). Lederer, Laura, Then and now: an interview with a former pornography model, in Lederer, *op. cit.*, pp. 45–59.

[3]This appears to be one type of argument defended by Helen Longino. On her view, portrayals in pornography violate women's rights to respect and against defamation and libel. Longino, *op. cit.*

[4]But see below and note [12].

[5]Laura Lederer, *op. cit.*, (note [2]).

[6]Ibid.

[7]*The Report of the Commission on Obscenity and Pornography* (Bantam Books, 1970). Excerpts reprinted in Gunther, Gerald (1980) *Constitutional Law*, pp. 1355–1356 (The Foundation Press). The Commission was given a $2 million appropriation, but chose to focus on 'erotic' or 'explicit sexual materials'. It is not clear whether the Commission used 'erotica' in the sense I have, but it *is* clear that few materials used in their studies would qualify as violent pornography as I have defined it. Several members of the Commission protested about this and argued that other available studies were ignored or underrated. The minority also accused the majority of being biased, of suppressing evidence, of misrepresentation and misinterpretation of research statistics and conclusions, underscoring how controversial the report was. Feminist critiques describing biases and inadequacies of the Commission's majority report are in Lederer, *op. cit.*, section IV.

[8]Because much of the research on pornography was done before violence pervaded it, studies focusing on violent pornography are still rare. Perhaps the best thus far are by Malamuth and his colleagues, but even these show *correlations* and are not uncontroversial. See Lederer, *op. cit.*, section IV, especially pp. 228–236.

[9]Kristol, Irving (1971) Pornography, obscenity, and the case for censorship, *New York Times Magazine*, March 28, reprinted in Feinberg & Gross (Eds) *Philosophy of Law*, 2nd ed., p. 222 (New York, Wadsworth, 1980).

[10]Baker, Robert & Elliston, Frederick (1975) 'Pricks' and 'chicks': a plea for persons, *Philosophy and Sex*, (Buffalo, New York, Prometheus Books). For example, the active male screws, fucks, bangs, the passive female.

[11]Robbins, Julia (1983) Pornography's hateful message, Letter to the Editor, *Boston Globe*, February 4. Robbins' critique is directed against all pornography, and to that extent is surely an overgeneralisation.

[12]Garry, Ann (1978) Pornography and respect for women, *Social Theory and Practice* 4, pp. 395–421. Reprinted in Bayles & Henley (Eds) *Right Conduct: Theories and Applications* (New York, Random House, Inc., 1983).

[13]S. J. Keyser first suggested this alternative to me. For those like myself, who agree all violent pornography is morally wrong because of its content—portrayal and endorsement of coercive, abusive, non-consensual actions which fail to respect human dignity—it is clear we can recommend moral or legal action against all violent pornography.

Those who do not accept this unconditional argument recognise that conclusions from empirical studies will be generalisations and will not apply to every instance. It is surely possible, however rare, for a violently pornographic book, for example, not to violate any individual rights, promote sexism, or lead to violence. Thus they must determine whether to recommend action against all violent pornography, even if not all produces harmful consequences.

It is likely that they will not know of a particular instance, however, whether it has the morally objectionable features or effects. They may have subjective opinions about the material, and certain cases may seem obviously wrong, but they may yet have no general standard for judging instances of violent pornography and its effects. If this is correct, they may also be justified in recommending action against all violent pornography, recognising that they cannot adequately distinguish that which is unobjectionable. 'Innocent' materials will be sacrified in order to deal with the rest.

14In *Stanley* v. *Georgia,* 394 U.S. 577 (1969), the Supreme Court argued that individual freedom and a right to privacy protect an individual's right to view obscene material in the privacy of his or her home. And it is not at all clear, although it is a serious and important question, that this individual freedom and privacy should be overridden if the material is violent pornography. Thus, criticism of the content does not suffice as criticism of the industry, especially where there is a voluntary audience.

15See Dworkin, Gerald (1971) Paternalism, in: Wasserstrom (Ed.) *Morality and the Law* (Belmont, Cal, Wadsworth Publishing Co., 1971) for a view on when paternalism might be justified, namely when it "enhances for the individual his ability to rationally consider and carry out his own decisions", p. 125.

16For interesting examples and discussion see Scanlon, T.M. 'A theory of freedom of expression', in: Dworkin (Ed.), *Philosophy of Law,* (Oxford University Press, 1977).

17For example, a striking study by Feshbach and Malamuth found that of 53 male students who voluntarily read a passage describing a male student raping a female student after holding a knife to her throat when she refused his offer to walk her to her car, an astounding 51% responded they might act as the rapist did if they were assured they would not be caught! Feshbach, Seymour & Malamuth, Neal (1978) Sex and aggression: proving the link, *Psychology Today,* 12, 6, November, pp. 116–117. Donald Mosher claims that these high percentages are misleading because of the methods used for calculating subjects' agreement with various sentences, in 'Social and psychological effects of violent pornography', presented at Violent Pornography: Legal Censorship or Alternative Community Responses?, a conference at Clark University, April 9 1983. For a summary of other recent results similar to Malamuth's, see 'Sex and violence: pornography hurts', *Science News,* 118, September 13 1980.

JOEL FEINBERG
HARM, OFFENSE, AND OBSCENITY

Whatever else we believe about freedom, most of us believe it is something to be praised, or so luminously a Thing of Value that it is beyond praise. What is it that makes freedom a good thing? Some say that freedom is good in itself quite apart from its consequences. On the other hand, James Fitzjames Stephen wrote that " . . . the question whether liberty is a good or a bad thing appears as irrational as the question whether fire is a good or a bad thing."[1] Freedom, according to Stephen, is good (when it is good) only because of what it does, not because of what it is.

It would be impossible to demonstrate that freedom is good for its own sake, and indeed, this proposition is far from self-evident. Still, Stephen's analogy to fire seems an injustice to freedom. Fire has no constant and virtually invariant effects that tend to make it, on balance,

From Joel Feinberg, *Social Philosophy* (Englewood Cliffs, N.J.: Prentice-Hall, 1973), pp. 20–22, 28–29, 33–34, 41–45. © 1973. Reprinted by permission of Prentice-Hall, Inc., Englewood Cliffs, New Jersey.

a good thing whenever and wherever it occurs, and bad only when its subsequent remoter effects are so evil as to counterbalance its direct and immediate ones. Thus, a fire in one's bed while one is sleeping is dreadful because its effects are evil, but a fire under the pot on the stove is splendid because it makes possible a hot cup of coffee when one wants it. The direct effect of fire in these and all other cases is to oxidize material objects and raise the temperature in its immediate environment; but *these* effects, from the point of view of human interests, and considered just in themselves, are neither good nor bad.

Freedom has seemed to most writers quite different in this respect. When a free man violates his neighbor's interests, then his freedom, having been put to bad use, was, on balance, a bad thing, but unlike the fire in the bed, it was not an unalloyed evil. Whatever the harmful consequences of freedom in a given case, there is always a direct effect on the person of its possessor which must be counted a positive good. Coercion may prevent great evils, and be wholly justified on that account, but it always has its price. Coercion may be on balance a great gain, but its direct effects always, or nearly always, constitute a definite loss. If this is true, there is always a *presumption* in favor of freedom, even though it can in some cases be overridden by more powerful reasons on the other side.

The presumption in favor of freedom is usually said to rest on freedom's essential role in the development of traits of intellect and character which constitute the good of individuals and are centrally important means to the progress of societies. One consensus argument, attributable with minor variations to Von Humboldt, Mill, Hobhouse, and many others, goes roughly as follows. The highest good for man is neither enjoyment nor passive contentment, but rather a dynamic process of growth and self-realization. This can be called "happiness" if we mean by that term what the Greeks did, namely, "The exercise of vital powers along lines of excellence in a life affording them scope."[2] The highest social good is then the greatest possible amount of individual self-realization and (assuming that different persons are inclined by their natures in different ways) the resultant diversity and fullness of life. Self-realization consists in the actualization of certain uniquely human potentialities, the bringing to full development of certain powers and abilities. This in turn requires constant practice in making difficult choices among alternative hypotheses, policies, and actions—and the more difficult the better. John Stuart Mill explained why:

> The human faculties of perception, judgment, discriminative feeling, mental activity, and even moral preference are exercised only in making a choice. He who does anything because it is the custom makes no choice. He gains no practice either in discerning or in desiring what is best. The mental and moral, like the muscular, powers are improved only by being used.[3]

In short, one does not realize what is best in oneself when social pressures to conform to custom lead one mindlessly along. Even more clearly, one's growth will be stunted when one is given no choice in the first place, either because of being kept in ignorance or because one is terrorized by the wielders of bayonets.

Freedom to decide on one's own while fully informed of the facts thus tends to promote the good of the person who exercises it, even if it permits him to make foolish or dangerous mistakes. Mill added to this argument the citation of numerous social benefits that redound indirectly but uniformly to those who grant freedom as well as those who exercise it. We all profit from the fruits of genius, he maintained, and genius, since it often involves doggedness and eccentricity, is likely to flourish only where coercive pressures toward conformity are absent. Moreover, social progress is more likely to occur where there is free criticism of prevailing ways and adventurous experiments in living. Finally, true understanding of human nature requires freedom, since without liberty there will be little diversity, and without diversity *all* aspects of the human condition will be ascribed to fixed nature rather than to the workings of a particular culture.

Such are the grounds for holding that there is always a presumption in favor of freedom, that whenever we are faced with an option between forcing a person to do something and letting him decide on his own whether or not to do it, other things being equal, we should always opt for the latter. If a strong general presumption for freedom has been established, the burden of proof rests on the shoulders of the advocate of coercion, and the philosopher's task will be to state the conditions under which the presumption can be overridden. . . .

The relation of offensiveness to harmfulness can be treated in much the same way as that of hurtfulness to harmfulness. The following points can be made of both:

1.   Some harms do not offend (as some do not hurt).

2.   All offenses (like all hurts) are harms, inasmuch as all men have an interest in not being offended or hurt.

3.   Some offenses (like some hurts) are symptoms or consequences of prior or concurrent harms.

4.   Some offenses (like some hurts) are causes of subsequent harms: in the case of extreme hurt, harm to health; in the case of extreme offense, harm from provoked ill will or violence. These subsequent harms are harms of a different order, i.e., violations of interests other than the interest in not being hurt or offended.

5.   Some offenses, like some hurts, are "harmless," i.e., do not lead to any *further* harm (violations of any interests other than the interest in not being hurt or offended).

6. Although offense and hurt are in themselves harms, they are harms of a relatively trivial kind (unless they are of sufficient magnitude to violate interests in health and peace).

Partly because of points 5 and 6, many writers use the word "harm" in a sense that is much narrower than "the invasion of any interest." In this narrower sense, harm is distinguished from and even contrasted with "mere offense." Some distinguish "harm to one's interests" from "offense to one's feelings" (as if there were no interest in unoffended feelings). This is a permissible, even useful, way of talking, if we agree that offensiveness as such is strictly speaking a kind of harm, but harm of such a trivial kind that it cannot by itself ever counterbalance the direct and immediate harm caused by coercion. One should appreciate how radical the harm principle is when interpreted in the strict and narrow way that excludes mere offensiveness as a relevant sort of harm. Both the British Wolfenden Report and the American Model Penal Code, for example, recognize "harmless" offensiveness as a ground for preventive coercion in some circumstances. . . . For clarity and convenience only, I shall stipulate then that "offensiveness as such" is a proposed ground for coercion distinct from harm of the sort required by the harm principle (narrowly interpreted), so that "the offense principle" can be treated as an independent principle in its own right.

Offensive behavior is such in virtue of its capacity to induce in others any of a large miscellany of mental states that have little in common except that they are unpleasant, uncomfortable, or disliked. These states do not necessarily "hurt," as do sorrow and distress. Rather the relation between them and hurt is analogous to that between physical unpleasantness and pain, for there is also a great miscellany of unpleasant but not painful bodily states—itches, shocks, and discomforts—that have little in common except that they don't hurt but are nevertheless universally disliked. Among the main sorts of "harmless but disliked" *mental* states are irritating sensations (e.g., bad smells, cacophony, clashing colors), disgust, shocked moral sensibilities, and shameful embarrassment. . . .

. . . One might hold that restriction of one person's liberty can be justified:

1. To prevent harm to others, either
   a. injury to individual persons *(The Private Harm Principle)*, or
   b. impairment of institutional practices that are in the public interest *(The Public Harm Principle)*;

2. To prevent offense to others *(The Offense Principle)*;

3. To prevent harm to self *(Legal Paternalism)*;

4. To prevent or punish sin, i.e., to "enforce morality as such" *(Legal Moralism)*;

5. To benefit the self *(Extreme Paternalism);*

6. To benefit others *(The Welfare Principle).*

The liberty-limiting principles on this list are best understood as stating neither necessary nor sufficient conditions for justified coercion, but rather specifications of the *kinds* of reasons that are always relevant or acceptable in support of proposed coercion, even though in a given case they may not be conclusive. Each principle states that interference might be permissible *if* (but not *only if*) a certain condition is satisfied. Hence the principles are not mutually exclusive; it is possible to hold two or more of them at once, even all of them together, and it is possible to deny all of them. Moreover, the principles cannot be construed as stating sufficient conditions for legitimate interference with liberty, for even though the principle is satisfied in a given case, the general presumption against coercion might not be outweighed. The harm principle, for example, does not justify state interference to prevent a tiny bit of inconsequential harm. Prevention of minor harm always counts in favor of proposals (as in a legislature) to restrict liberty, but in a given instance it might not count *enough* to outweigh the general presumption against interference, or it might be outweighed by the prospect of practical difficulties in enforcing the law, excessive costs, and forfeitures of privacy. A liberty-limiting principle states considerations that are always good reasons for coercion, though neither exclusively nor, in every case, decisively good reasons. . . .

Up to this point we have considered the harm and offense principles together in order to determine whether between them they are sufficient to regulate conventional immoralities, or whether they need help from a further independent principle, legal moralism. Morals offenses were treated as essentially private so that the offense principle could not be stretched to apply to them. Obscene literature and pornographic displays would appear to be quite different in this respect. Both are materials deliberately published for the eyes of others, and their existence can bring partisans of the unsupplemented harm principle into direct conflict with those who endorse *both* the harm and offense principles.

In its untechnical, prelegal sense, the word "obscenity" refers to material dealing with nudity, sex, or excretion in an offensive manner. Such material becomes obscene in the legal sense when, because of its offensiveness or for some other reason [this question had best be left open in the definition], it is or ought to be without legal protection. The legal definition then incorporates the everyday sense, and essential to both is the requirement that the material be *offensive.* An item may offend one person and not another. "Obscenity," if it is to avoid this subjective relativity, must involve an interpersonal objective sense of "offensive." Material must be offensive by prevailing community standards that are public and well known, or be such that it is apt to offend virtually everyone.

Not all material that is generally offensive need also be harmful in any sense recognized by the harm principle. It is partly an empirical question whether reading or witnessing obscene material causes social harm; reliable evidence, even of a statistical kind, of causal connections between obscenity and antisocial behavior is extremely hard to find.[4] In the absence of clear and decisive evidence of harmfulness, the American Civil Liberties Union insists that the offensiveness of obscene material cannot be a sufficient ground for its repression:

> . . . the question in a case involving obscenity, just as in every case involving an attempted restriction upon free speech, is whether the words or pictures are used in such circumstances and are of such a nature as to create a clear and present danger that they will bring about a substantial evil that the state has a right to prevent. . . . We believe that under the current state of knowledge, there is grossly insufficient evidence to show that obscenity brings about *any* substantive evil.[5]

The A.C.L.U. argument employs *only* the harm principle among liberty-limiting principles, and treats literature, drama, and painting as forms of expression subject to the same rules as expressions of opinion. In respect to both types of expression, "every act of deciding what should be barred carries with it a danger to the community."[6] The suppression itself is an evil to the author who is squelched. The power to censor and punish involves risks that socially valuable material will be repressed along with the "filth." The overall effect of suppression, the A.C.L.U. concludes, is almost certainly to discourage nonconformist and eccentric expression generally. In order to override these serious risks, there must be in a given case an even more clear and present danger that the obscene material, if not squelched, will cause even greater harm; such countervailing evidence is never forthcoming. (If such evidence were to accumulate, the A.C.L.U. would be perfectly willing to change its position on obscenity.)

The A.C.L.U. stand on obscenity seems clearly to be the position dictated by the unsupplemented harm principle and its corollary, the clear and present danger test. Is there any reason at this point to introduce the offense principle into the discussion? Unhappily, we may be forced to if we are to do justice to all of our particular intuitions in the most harmonious way. Consider an example suggested by Professor Schwartz. By the provisions of the new Model Penal Code, he writes, "a rich homosexual may not use a billboard on Times Square to promulgate to the general populace the techniques and pleasures of sodomy."[7] If the notion of "harm" is restricted to its narrow sense, that is, contrasted with "offense," it will be hard to reconstruct a rationale for this prohibition based on the harm principle. There is unlikely to be evidence that a lurid and obscene public poster in Times Square would create a clear and present danger of injury to those who fail to avert their eyes in time as they come blinking out of the subway stations. Yet it will be surpassingly difficult for even the most dedicated liberal to advocate freedom of expression in a case of this kind. Hence, if we are to justify coercion in this case, we will likely be driven, however reluctantly, to the offense principle.

There is good reason to be "reluctant" to embrace the offense principle until driven to it by an example like the above. People take perfectly genuine offense at many socially useful or harmless activities, from commercial advertisements to inane chatter. Moreover, widespread irrational prejudices can lead people to be disgusted, shocked, even morally repelled by perfectly innocent activities, and we should be loath to permit their groundless repugnance to override the innocence. The offense principle, therefore, must be formulated very precisely and applied in accordance with carefully formulated standards so as not to open the door to wholesale and intuitively unwarranted repression. At the very least we should require that the prohibited conduct or material be of the sort apt to offend almost everybody, and not just some shifting majority or special interest group.

It is instructive to note that a strictly drawn offense principle would not only justify prohibition of conduct and pictured conduct that is in its inherent character repellent, but also conduct and pictured conduct that is inoffensive in itself but offensive in inappropriate circumstances. I have in mind so-called indecencies such as public nudity. One can imagine an advocate of the unsupplemented harm principle arguing against the public nudity prohibition on the grounds that the sight of a naked body does no one any harm, and the state has no right to impose standards of dress or undress on private citizens. How one chooses to dress, after all, is a form of self-expression. If we do not permit the state to bar clashing colors or bizarre hair styles, by what right does it prohibit total undress? Perhaps the sight of naked people could at first lead to riots or other forms of antisocial behavior, but that is precisely the sort of contingency for which we have police. If we don't take away a person's right of free speech for the reason that its exercise may lead others to misbehave, we cannot in consistency deny his right to dress or undress as he chooses for the same reason.

There may be no answering this challenge on its own ground, but the offense principle provides a ready rationale for the nudity prohibition. The sight of nude bodies in public places is for almost everyone acutely *embarrassing*. Part of the explanation no doubt rests on the fact that nudity has an irresistible power to draw the eye and focus the thoughts on matters that are normally repressed. The conflict between these attracting and repressing forces is exciting, upsetting, and anxiety-producing. In some persons it will create at best a kind of painful turmoil, and at worst that experience of exposure to oneself of "peculiarly sensitive, intimate, vulnerable aspects of the self"[8] which is called *shame.* "One's feeling is involuntarily exposed openly in one's face; one is uncovered . . . taken by surprise . . . made a fool of."[9] The result is not mere "offense," but a kind of psychic jolt that in many normal people can be a painful wound. Even those of us who are better able to control our feelings might well resent the *nuisance* of having to do so.

If we are to accept the offense principle as a supplement to the harm principle, we must accept two corollaries which stand in relation to it similarly to the way in which the clear and present danger test stands to the harm principle. The first, the *standard of universality,* has already been touched upon. For the offensiveness (disgust, embarrassment, outraged sensibilities, or shame) to be sufficient to warrant coercion, it should be the reaction that could be expected from almost any person chosen at random from the nation as a whole, regardless of sect, faction, race, age, or sex. The second is the *standard of reasonable avoidability.* No one has a right to protection from the state against offensive experiences if he can effectively avoid those experiences with no unreasonable effort or inconvenience. If a nude person enters a public bus and takes a seat near the front, there may be no effective way for other patrons to avoid intensely shameful embarrassment (or other insupportable feelings) short of leaving the bus, which would be an unreasonable inconvenience. Similarly, obscene remarks over a loudspeaker, homosexual billboards in Times Square, and pornographic handbills thrust into the hands of passing pedestrians all fail to be reasonably avoidable.

On the other hand, the offense principle, properly qualified, can give no warrant to the suppression of *books* on the grounds of obscenity. When printed words hide decorously behind covers of books sitting passively on bookstore shelves, their offensiveness is easily avoided. The contrary view is no doubt encouraged by the common comparison of obscenity with "smut," "filth," or "dirt." This in turn suggests an analogy to nuisance law, which governs cases where certain activities create loud noises or terrible odors offensive to neighbors, and "the courts must weigh the gravity of the nuisance [substitute "offense"] to the neighbors against the social utility [substitute "redeeming social value"] of the defendant's conduct.[10] There is, however, one vitiating disanalogy in this comparison. In the case of "dirty books" the offense is easily avoidable. There is nothing like the evil smell of rancid garbage oozing right out through the covers of a book. When an "obscene" book sits on a shelf, who is there to be offended? Those who want to read it for the sake of erotic stimulation presumably will not be offended (or else they wouldn't read it); and those who choose not to read it will have no experience by which to be offended. If its covers are too decorous, some innocents may browse through it by mistake and be offended by what they find, but they need only close the book to escape the offense. Even this offense, minimal as it is, could be completely avoided by prior consultation of trusted book reviewers. I conclude that there are no sufficient grounds derived either from the harm or offense principles for suppressing obscene literature, unless that ground be the protection of children; but I can think of no reason why restrictions on sales to children cannot work as well for printed materials as they do for cigarettes and whiskey.

Notes

[1] James Fitzjames Stephen, *Liberty, Equality, Fraternity* (London: 1873), p. 48.

[2] See Edith Hamilton, *The Greek Way* (New York: W. W. Norton & Company, Inc., 1942), pp. 35ff.

[3] John Stuart Mill, *On Liberty* (New York: Liberal Arts Press, 1956), p. 71.

[4] There have been some studies made, but the results have been inconclusive. See the *Report of the Federal Commission on Obscenity and Pornography* (New York: Bantam Books, 1970), pp. 169–308.

[5] *Obscenity and Censorship* (Pamphlet published by the American Civil Liberties Union, New York, March, 1963), p. 7.

[6] *Obscenity and Censorship,* p. 4.

[7] Louis B. Schwartz, "Morals Offenses and the Model Penal Code," *Columbia Law Review,* LXIII (1963), 680.

[8] Helen Merrill Lynd, *On Shame and the Search for Identity* (New York: Science Editions, Inc., 1961), p. 33.

[9] Lynd, *On Shame and the Search for Identity,* p. 32.

[10] William L. Prosser, *Handbook of the Law of Torts* (St. Paul, MN: West Publishing, 1955), p. 411.

chapter 8

Controlling Risks: AIDS and Other Dangers

INTRODUCTION

No one can be absolutely safe. Life is full of risks. We drive cars and walk down streets, exposed to danger from the carelessness of others and from our own human lapses. There are even completely unavoidable accidents, the fault of no one. Staying at home isn't absolutely safe either, since household accidents occur frequently.

The presence of risks does not itself pose a moral problem. However, the avoidable imposition of special risks does raise moral issues. Although the roads can never be totally safe, reckless driving and driving while drugged or intoxicated create special and avoidable dangers. A drug-using pilot or alcoholic physician also poses serious risks. And those who pollute the air or water, or knowingly expose others to carcinogens (cancer-causing agents) are creating risks that might be avoidable—though usually at some cost to someone (perhaps to the public at large). Moral problems arise whenever there is an increased risk of harm due to avoidable human actions or arrangements. These moral problems can be divided into two categories: the responsibilities of the persons whose actions create the increased risk, and the responsibilities of others, including the government, who might control or lessen the creation of the increased risk.

Risk-Creating Behavior The person who drives while so intoxicated or drugged that driving is greatly impaired creates a serious risk of causing serious harm. This kind of behavior will be condemned from almost any moral perspective. But suppose that someone must take prescribed medication that impairs driving ability only marginally, so that the likelihood of an accident is increased only slightly (but the potential *harm* from such an unlikely accident is still serious)? And there are many people who know, or should know, that when perfectly clear-headed their driving abilities are not very great, and so their presence on the road creates more risk than the presence of the average driver. Do below-average drivers have a moral duty not to drive, or not to drive except when necessary? Among the morally relevant factors in assessing

risk creation are the probability of the occurrence of harm, the seriousness of the potential harm, the number of people who might be harmed,
and the cost of avoiding the creation of the risk (costs include not only
monetary expenses but also other losses, such as lost opportunities or
restrictions upon available options and ways of life). And perhaps there
also needs to be some sense of comparability to the ordinary, unavoidable risks of life, so that the creation of risks so small as to be within the
ordinary range might not be considered morally significant, even when
the risk is identifiable and avoidable; this might cover cases like the
below-average driver.

Interventions to Control Risks   In addition to the factors relevant
to the individual's moral assessment of his or her own risk-creating
behavior, potential interventions by others raise quite distinctive moral
issues. The most common kinds of intervention come from government
action or indirect government regulation; but nongovernmental institutions acting on their own and even individuals can at times face the
question whether to intervene in order to stop or decrease risks caused
by voluntary behavior of others. The moral question whether and how
to intervene is much more complex than the moral question for the
risk-creator. Clearly intervention will be morally wrong if the behavior
of the risk-creator is morally acceptable. But if the behavior is morally
wrong, it does not follow that even the slightest intervention is justified.
And even when intervention is morally justified, there might be moral
limits to the kind of interventions that are acceptable.

The most important distinctive issues for intervention are conflicts
with the rights of privacy and autonomy of individuals. It might be
possible to lower the risks caused by drunk driving by raising the legal
drinking age to twenty-five, but this would deprive many responsible
people of the right to choose to drink, thus restricting their autonomy.
The recent changes in the legal drinking age had exactly this autonomy-
restricting effect on those between age eighteen and twenty-one. It
might be possible to decrease the risks caused by drug-using hospital
personnel by subjecting all responsible for patient care to random urine
tests, or even blanket tests of everyone on a monthly basis. But this
would be a serious invasion of the privacy of those subjected to the tests.

Privacy and Autonomy   The right of privacy, narrowly conceived,
is the right of individuals to control access to knowledge of their personal
lives and affairs. It has become common, however, to extend the meaning of right to privacy to include a much broader range, so that in some
contexts (such as U.S. constitutional law) the right to privacy covers
much or all of the right to autonomy—the "right to be let alone" and
to make decisions about one's own life.[1] It is sometimes important to
distinguish between privacy and autonomy, especially when dealing with
the moral issues of risk-creation and interventions. If it is clear that a
particular individual intends to expose others to a serious risk of serious
harm, the right to autonomy does not seem relevant—for it is no longer

merely his or her own life about which decisions are being made. But the right to privacy in the narrow sense is still potentially relevant; some interventions would invade the privacy of the individual, and a moral judgment must be made whether such an invasion is justified given the features of the case. In other areas of intervention, autonomy may be at stake and privacy irrelevant. Government regulations of industry to decrease the risk of injury to informed and fully consenting workers, willing to take the risk for the wages, pose a conflict between autonomy and the reduction of risk; but there are not likely to be any issues of privacy in such cases.

AIDS Recently a particular risk has become a focus of attention and even public fear. Acquired immune deficiency syndrome (AIDS) is a devastating illness that leads to a breakdown of the body's defenses against infection and disease. Those who develop the full-blown syndrome are subjected to illness after illness and eventually die. AIDS is caused by a virus known as HIV (or HTLV-III). It is unknown what percentage of those exposed to the virus will develop either full-blown AIDS or less serious symptoms (ARC—AIDS related complex). The period from exposure to the virus until the appearance of symptoms is unusually long—between one and seven years seems common, and no upper limit is known. It is also not known whether everyone exposed to the virus is a potential transmitter of infection to others. But the working assumption of public health officials is that everyone exposed to the virus is a carrier capable of passing on the virus.

Fortunately, the HIV virus is *very* difficult to transmit. It is not transmitted by casual contact, coughing, sneezing, touching, embracing, or sharing such things as drinking glasses or towels. Even such close contact as between mother and child is safe. The only known modes of transmission are sexual intercourse, sharing infected needles (for instance, by drug abusers), transfusion with infected blood or blood products, transmission to fetuses during pregnancy, and blood-to-blood contact in rare accidents occurring in medical care. And so there is no threat to others from the presence of those infected with the virus in school, at work, or in the household. It is only quite specific *behavior* that poses a risk to others. Those who choose to engage in risky behavior can reduce the risk significantly by taking precautions; using condoms decreases the risk of transmission in sexual intercourse, and either using new needles or cleaning needles with diluted bleach decreases the risk for intravenous drug users. Since the introduction of blood testing, the risk of infection from transfusion has become very slight.

Research is still in progress. In June 1988 the common blood tests (including ELISA) detect antibodies, showing exposure to the virus. In rare cases, no antibodies are formed for an undetermined length of time while the virus "hides" inside macrophages, scavenger cells of the immune system, where it reproduces. One of the most important moral questions of intervention is whether there should be mandatory testing for certain groups of people—those seeking marriage licenses, or those admitted to hospitals. There is already mandatory testing in the armed forces. The conflict with the right to privacy is especially intense, for there is reason to fear discriminatory behavior against those who are known to be antibody-positive. Many people believe that even strong legal protection of the confidentiality of test results would not be sufficient to guarantee privacy. There is a further question of privacy: should spouses and sexual partners of those testing positive be informed? While the public at large has nothing to fear from people who test positive, sexual partners are at risk.

The social benefits of mandatory HIV-antibody testing seem more doubtful than for some other testing. If a pilot or police officer uses drugs, there is nothing others can do to protect themselves from the risks created. But antibody-positive people pose no risk to the public at large, and those who choose risky behavior can take precautions. Furthermore, as long as exposure to the virus is largely confined to identifiable high-risk groups—male homosexuals, intravenous drug users, and sexual partners of these groups—almost everyone who might transmit the virus already knows that his or her behavior might pose that danger to others. And most of those who might become infected know that their behavior poses such a risk. In cases of doubt, precautions can be taken; those unwilling to expose themselves even to the small risks remaining can abstain altogether from risky behavior. There are special cases in which a particular person (for instance, a spouse) will be ill-informed, but this will not be significant for large-scale testing programs, nor would such programs be likely to prevent this. And so in the case of AIDS there are not many benefits to be weighed against the right to privacy that mandatory testing would threaten.

Natural Law   Natural-law theorists see each human life as incommensurably valuable and so insist that there is a stringent moral duty not to endanger others and not to neglect protecting one's own life. However, the duty to respect life is seen against a background of natural human sociality and mortality; thus accepting the ordinary risks of human social life does not count as failing to respect life. Even taking fairly serious risks in a career or in recreation or play does not violate the duty to respect life, for human beings are fulfilled only in activity, and such activity will also create risks.[2]

Creating minimal risks to others is also morally acceptable, as long as there is no intention to harm and no negligence, and the probability of harm is comparable to the probability of serious harm inevitable in living together in society. For instance, the private airplane pilot creates a tiny additional risk for those over whom he or she flies, but such exposure to danger is found throughout human social life. However, the imposition of serious risks of creating serious harm to others is normally wrong. There are exceptions, such as creating serious risks to innocents in order to rescue other innocents from death. Here again intention is decisive (and for some theorists the doctrine of double effect); there must also be proportionality between the risks created for others and the value being pursued.

Traditionally natural law has not given great weight to the right of privacy when it conflicts with protecting human life against extraordinary risks. The community is seen as natural, and its protective purpose justifies interventions to prevent serious risks of serious harms, even if that means that individuals have less control over both their lives (less autonomy) and information about their lives (less privacy).

Natural Rights   Contemporary natural rights theory has no room for duties to self, so any risk that is consented to is morally acceptable. (There might, of course, be problems in some contexts about what counts as fully informed and voluntary consent.) Major problems of interpretation of the theory arise when considering the imposition of risks upon nonconsenting people. It seems clear that if harm eventuates, the imposition of the risk constitutes a violation of rights. In some cases, the fear of harm might itself constitute an injury, even if the harm does not eventuate. But suppose there is no knowledge of the risk (so no fear) and no harm occurs; it is unclear whether by itself the imposition of the risk constitutes a violation of rights. And interventions to prevent the imposition of risks are perhaps violations of the individual rights of those restricted—after all, in many cases no harm would have come from their actions.[3] Robert Nozick's suggestion for solving these problems is to allow risky actions as long as there is compensation to those upon whom risks are imposed (or perhaps only to those actually harmed) and to prohibit risky actions by those who cannot afford to compensate others for the risk, but to compensate these people for having restricted their freedom.[4]

Individual autonomy and privacy are primary values for natural-rights theory, so government interventions are particularly hard to justify. Both constitutional law and popular morality in the United States have been influenced by this individualist emphasis upon privacy and personal freedom. Mandatory testing for drug use, for instance, seems a serious invasion of the individual rights of those subjected to such coercive inspection. Even though harms might be prevented by such means, the natural rights approach must discount such a direct teleological concern for results. Indirectly results can be affected by requiring compensation when actual harm occurs; the prospect of owing damages should decrease risky behavior. It might be argued within a natural-rights theory that those creating serious risks have forfeited their privacy rights in regard to the detection of the risks. But this point only justifies at most mandatory testing in cases of individualized suspicion (for instance, someone stopped for erratic driving); it cannot justify programs of mandatory group testing, in which most of the subjects would not have forfeited any rights of privacy. In popular morality, there seems to be more willingness to sacrifice privacy and autonomy when the risky behavior is itself unconventional; thus prohibiting the use of marijuana seems more reasonable to most people than prohibiting alcohol, even though both create risks. But the natural-rights emphasis upon individual autonomy seems to allow no such distinctions based on the popularity of the risky behavior.

Kant Kantian approaches to risk must emphasize the irreplaceable value of each rational being. Even intentional creation of serious risks to oneself poses moral problems for Kant, unless the underlying intention of the action is the fulfillment of some perfect duty. It is not clear whether fulfilling imperfect duties can justify actions known to create a very high degree of risk to life. However these moral problems are resolved in particular cases, a person is never morally free to treat her or his life as of little value.[5] Kant's approach seems more restrictive than the natural-law view, since he gives less weight to natural aspects of humanity other than rationality; Kant does not emphasize the natural sociality of human beings and the inclination to play, both of which involve risks.

The respect due to others as persons rules out any intentional imposition of serious risks, unless the underlying intention is the fulfillment of some *perfect* duty. The question of intervention, however, raises difficulties. Kant himself paid little attention to privacy where the enforcement of perfect duties was in question, and the duty not to impose serious risks on others is clearly a perfect duty. And autonomy for Kant was only the right to do one's duty—not a more general right to be let alone and to make decisions about one's own life. The individual had considerable latitude in fulfilling imperfect duties, and here the state should generally not use coercion. But perfect duties, whether to oneself or to others, left no such latitude and were fully coercible.

But some contemporary philosophers give an account of Kantian autonomy that is more expansive and connect privacy to this expanded idea of autonomy. In this view, privacy must be respected in order to show respect for the autonomous agent who is responsible for his or her own moral principles. The account of privacy and autonomy thus tends in the direction of the natural-rights view; it takes overriding reasons to justify intrusions into the private sphere of the autonomous moral agent, and these grounds must be individualized. Intrusions into the privacy of groups cannot be justified by the good consequences that might be produced.

Contractarianism In the original position, rational contractors do not know their own specific conceptions of the good, and they do not know even the degree of probability attaching to quite different social structures and economic conditions in which they may find themselves on entering society. These features of the original position explain the "maximin" rule's applicability—the contractors are to choose principles that will maximize the primary goods under the worst possible conditions. If the question of principles for risk-creation and intervention were raised within the original position with such a full veil of ignorance, it might seem that very stringent principles against creating even minor risks and very wide powers of intervention to lessen risks would be chosen, since the contractors have been characterized as, in effect, risk-averse. But the contractors do have full knowledge of general facts about human psychology and sociology, so they know that risks are unavoidable in human social life; they also know that human beings are generally interested in activities that create risks both for themselves and for others, and that severe restrictions on such conduct might lead to great unhappiness and lack of fulfillment. So when the topic is not the basic structure of institutions, but rather principles for controlling risks, it is not clear that the contractors will be especially risk-averse. It seems that a principle allowing self-imposed risks (and risks that are consented to) would be adopted, without any restriction as to the seriousness of the risks. Minimal risks imposed on others can be justified because of the need to allow for a full range of human activities. Rational contractors would adopt a stringent moral principle against intentionally imposing serious risks on others, though there would be exceptions in cases where more stringent duties required imposing such risks.

Rawls follows Kant in construing autonomy narrowly; respect for a person as an autonomous agent does not mean accepting that individual's moral views where they conflict with those justified from the perspective of the original position.[6] Thus intervention to prevent imposition of serious risks upon others is fully justified and not a failure to respect the coerced person. However, this would seem clear only where an identifiable action by a particular person (or group) would create a serious risk, and large-scale restrictions on kinds of conduct would not seem justified if only some actions within that category would impose serious risks on others (for instance, banning private airplanes because, despite all attempts to prevent it, one can predict that accidents will happen because there will be drugged, drunk, or inattentive pilots).

In the original position, it seems plausible that privacy would be protected by principles allowing intrusion only on grounds of individualized suspicion that the rights of others are at issue. The contractors do not know whether they are members of a despised minority, subject to harassment by authorities if they have no right to privacy. And privacy is valued by individuals no matter what position they find themselves in within the social structure. Contractarians are then not likely to support broad mandatory drug testing or other interventions that invade the privacy of groups only some of whom are irresponsibly imposing serious risks on others.

Act Utilitarianism Since net utility can often be increased by actions that create risks, an act utilitarian approach will not include a general condemnation of risk-creation. The creation of risks will be wrong only if the consequences of the action are worse than the consequences of some available alternative would have been; and in considering the consequences, the method is to aggregate the satisfactions of interests, so that damage done to one person's interests can be offset by benefits to others. Also, no special weight is given to the protection of human life as such. If a worker prefers a risky job at high pay to a less risky job at lower pay, this tends to show that his interest in money (and the variety of satisfactions that money can buy) is greater than his interest in the greater security for his life that avoiding the risk would provide. An act-utilitarian approach will thus allow for much more risk-taking and much more risk-imposing than other theories. Imposing risks on others will also be justified if it maximizes net utility, and often serious harms and loss of life for a few will be the cost of producing benefits for many more. Thus act utilitarians are not willing to accept the costs in decreased productivity (with resulting decreases in standard of living) that severe government regulation of risk-creating industry would likely bring.

However, where government or other intervention can lessen serious risks without incurring offsetting disadvantages, act utilitarians see no barrier to such intervention. Neither privacy nor autonomy have any separate role in an act-utilitarian account. Thus if drug testing or HIV antibody testing were in fact beneficial on balance (taking all costs and all consequences into account), an act utilitarian would see no moral difficulty in the intrusion into privacy.

Rule Utilitarianism   In choosing rules whose acceptance will maximize satisfactions in the aggregate, the rule utilitarian must take into account the facts of human psychology and the facts of the actual society for which the moral code is intended. Since moderate risk-taking seems psychologically normal and since modern industrial society creates many risks for the public at large, it seems plausible that a utilitarian moral code will be fairly lenient about moderate risks, except where few benefits accrue. There will be no rule against self-imposed risks, for such conduct is an important source of both self-fulfillment and, sometimes, social benefits. (A rule requiring insurance for some kinds of risk-takers might be reasonable, to spare society the costs of aiding them in distress or after injury.) A moral code might include some restrictions on consensual risk-taking by employees, in order to maximize overall satisfaction within a complex technological system where individual actions cannot reflect the needs of society. Imposing serious risks would be prohibited where the risks are immediate and avoidable; this rule would not allow for exceptions simply to maximize utility in the particular case, for then the rule would lose much of its cautionary force, thus decreasing the utility produced by its acceptance. But it seems unlikely that the mere creation of statistical risks for a few would be prohibited if major benefits for many were produced. Rather, there would be a rule requiring compensation for the few actually harmed. As with act utilitarianism, aggregation of satisfaction is the method, and no special weight is given to the protection of human life as such, apart from the preferences people actually have.

A utilitarian moral code for a contemporary industrial society will include rules protecting both privacy and personal autonomy. It is clear that most people in fact value privacy and autonomy, so satisfaction is increased to the extent that these are secured, other things being equal. Also, privacy and autonomy may promote more personal creativity and innovation, thus benefitting the whole society in the long run. But privacy and autonomy are not special for the rule utilitarian—they are only two sources of satisfaction among many. So there would be exception clauses in the rules protecting privacy and autonomy, and not only for cases of individualized suspicion that great risk to others might be created. If great social harms could be avoided only by mandatory group testing, it seems that a rule utilitarian would allow the intrusions.

Readings The selection from Grant Gillett considers the question of medical confidentiality (a stringent and special form of privacy right) of an AIDS diagnosis when the patient refuses to allow his wife to be informed. Gillett's approach has affinities with the natural-law view that moral insight is needed in particular cases where it would be unconscionable to follow generally reliable secondary principles, like the principle of respecting confidentiality. Though more like natural law in method, Gillett also echoes the natural rights view that rights can be forfeited.

The selection by Alan Gewirth considers the risk of cancer, but many of his points could also be applied to the risk of AIDS. The essay is a complex discussion of the right not to have cancer inflicted upon one, the right of informed control, intervening causes, minimal risks and probabilities, and cost-benefit analysis. Throughout, Gewirth advocates a Kantian approach, viewing the lives and health of persons as basic goods not to be measured on the same scale with other goods.

The selection by Gostin, Curran, and Clark sets out the argument that no clear public health benefit is likely to be gained through mandatory case finding using the ELISA test for HIV antibodies. Before the selection included here, they explained that the ELISA test is justified where the results are used in the aggregate and there are no adverse consequences for identified individuals: screening donors of blood, tissue, and organs. They also defended aggregate use of tests in research settings. In the selection, they set out five criteria for assessing mandatory screening. The selection includes two of the six illustrative cases of the application of the criteria. (The ones omitted are screening in the military, at treatment centers for sexually transmitted disease and intravenous drug use, screening of health care patients and staff, and screening in prisons. In each case they find mandatory screening unjustified.) They give an implicitly rule-utilitarian account of confidentiality. Their whole argument aims at protecting the health of the community and is basically utilitarian.

Notes

[1]See Hyman Gross, "Privacy and Autonomy," in *Privacy: Nomos XIII,* ed. J. Roland Pennock and John W. Chapman (New York: Atherton Press, 1971).

[2]See Alan Donagan, *The Theory of Morality* (Chicago: The University of Chicago Press, 1977), pp. 79–80.

[3]Robert Nozick, *Anarchy, State, and Utopia* (New York: Basic Books, 1974), p. 78.

[4]Ibid., pp. 75–82.

[5]Kant considers that even the decision to be vaccinated against smallpox raises difficult moral questions, since it places one's life at risk. See Immanuel Kant, *The Doctrine of Virtue,* trans. Mary J. Gregor (Philadelphia: University of Pennsylvania Press, 1971), pp. 85–87.

[6]John Rawls, *A Theory of Justice* (Cambridge, Mass.: Harvard University Press, 1971), pp. 518–519.

Bibliography on Controlling Risks: AIDS and Other Dangers

"AIDS: The Emerging Ethical Dilemmas." Special Supplement, *Hastings Center Report* 15, No. 4 (Aug., 1985): 1–31.

"AIDS: Public Health and Civil Liberties." Special Supplement, *Hastings Center Report* 16, No. 6 (Dec., 1986): 1–36, see especially Ruth Macklin, "Predicting Dangerousness and the Public Health Response to AIDS," pp. 16–23.

Altham, J. E. J. "The Ethics of Risk." *Proceedings of the Aristotelian Society* 84 (1984): 15–29.

Anderson, Elizabeth. "Values, Risks, and Market Norms." *Philosophy and Public Affairs* 17 (1988): 54–65.

Bayles, Michael D. *Professional Ethics,* second edition. Belmont, Cal.: Wadsworth, 1988, Chapter 5, "Obligations to Third Parties."

———. "The Value of Life." In *Health Care Ethics,* edited by Donald VanDeVeer and Tom Regan. Philadelphia: Temple University Press, 1987.

Caplan, Arthur. "The Right to Privacy When Lives Are at Stake." In *Troubling Problems in Medical Ethics,* edited by Marc Basson, Rachel Lipson, and Doreen Ganos. New York: Liss, 1981.

Coburn, Robert C. "Imposing Risks." *Pacific Philosophical Quarterly* 62 (1981): 240–248.

Dalton, Harlon L., and Burris, Scott, eds. *AIDS and the Law: A Guide for the Public.* New Haven, Conn.: Yale University Press, 1987.

Decew, Judith. "The Scope of Privacy in Law and Ethics." *Law and Philosophy* 5 (1986): 145–173.

Gibson, Mary. *Workers' Rights.* Totowa, N.J.: Rowman and Allanheld, 1983, Chapters 1–3.

Gibson, Mary, ed. *To Breathe Freely: Risk, Consent, and Air.* Totowa, N.J.: Rowman and Allanheld, 1985.

Kamisar, Yale. "Drugs, AIDS and the Threat to Privacy." *The New York Times Magazine,* Sept. 13, 1987, pp. 109–114.

Lackey, Douglas P. "Taking Risks Seriously." *Journal of Philosophy* 83 (1986): 633–640.

Landesman, Sheldon H., and Winston, Morton. "AIDS and a Duty to Protect." *Hastings Center Report* 17 (Feb., 1987): 22–23.

MacLean, Douglas, ed. *Values at Risk.* Totowa, N.J.: Rowman and Allanheld, 1986.

Magnus, Eric von. "Rights and Risks." *Journal of Business Ethics* 2 (1983): 23–26.

Mckerlie, Dennis. "Rights and Risk." *Canadian Journal of Philosophy* 16 (1986): 239–252.

Mohr, Richard D. "AIDS, Gays, and State Coercion." *Bioethics* 1 (1987): 35–50.

Parent, W. A. "Privacy, Morality, and the Law." *Philosophy and Public Affairs* 12 (1983): 269–288.

Pargetter, Robert, and Prior, Elizabeth W. "Discrimination and AIDS." *Social Theory and Practice* 13 (1987): 129–153.

Pennock, J. Roland, and Chapman, John W. *Privacy: Nomos XIII.* New York: Atherton Press, 1971.

Pierce, Christine, and VanDeVeer, Donald, eds. *AIDS: Ethics and Public Policy.* Belmont, Cal.: Wadsworth, 1988.

Rescher, Nicholas. *Risk: A Philosophical Introduction to the Theory of Risk Evaluation and Management.* Lanham, Md.: University Press of America, 1983.

Schoeman, Ferdinand David, ed. *Philosophical Dimensions of Privacy: An Anthology.* Cambridge: Cambridge University Press, 1984.

Shrader-Frechette, Kristin. "Technological Risk and Small Probabilities." *Journal of Business Ethics* 4 (1985): 431–446.

Thomson, Judith Jarvis. *Rights, Restitution, and Risk.* Cambridge, Mass.: Harvard University Press, 1986. See especially "The Right to Privacy" and "Imposing Risks."

Westin, Alan F. *Privacy and Freedom.* New York: Atheneum, 1970.

Problem Case
A Small Risk from the Past

Edward is bisexual. He was never extremely promiscuous, but he had several sexual relationships with men during his early twenties. He also had sexual relationships with women during that period. When he was about twenty-five, the AIDS crisis occurred. At first he stopped having sexual intercourse altogether, with men or women. But then he learned more about the way AIDS is sexually transmitted and about safe sex. He learned that anal intercourse poses the greatest risk and was somewhat reassured, since he had never engaged in that activity. He began once again to have sexual relationships with men, practicing safe sex techniques; he knew that his sexual partners were well informed about the extremely small degree of risk remaining. Edward did not, however, resume sexual relationships with women. The problem was that in a heterosexual relationship it could not be assumed that the woman would know that her partner was in a risk group for AIDS and telling her would be embarrassing and probably end the relationship. Also, safe sex techniques were not as common in heterosexual relations and sometimes using them caused problems.

Then Edward met Elizabeth. He soon realized that he was gradually falling in love. They began to see a lot of each other. Edward stopped having sexual relationships with men. Now Edward saw a problem on the horizon. When, as he hoped, the time came for them to make love, did Elizabeth have a right to know about his past homosexual experiences? Would this end the relationship? Would it be morally acceptable to withhold the information, but use a condom? (But surely if they became long-term lovers Elizabeth would expect him to stop using condoms eventually.) Should he now get tested for the HIV antibody? (He had seen no reason for testing before, since he was practicing safe sex with informed partners. And there is no prescribed treatment for those who are antibody-positive.) If he tested negative, could he then forget about both telling Elizabeth and using condoms? (There is a slight chance of false negatives in the first few months after exposure and in unusual cases for even longer when the virus "hides." But this probably doesn't matter, since he has practiced safe sex for several years. And his last sexual encounter was two months ago, almost outside of the possibility of ordinary false negatives even if he had not practiced safe sex.) If he tested positive, what would his moral duties be then?

John is a friend of both Edward's and Elizabeth's. John knows that Edward has had homosexual relationships and that he is in a special risk group for AIDS. John can see that his friends are getting emotionally involved and suspects that they may become sexually involved. He also knows that Elizabeth is not aware of Edward's bisexuality. Does John have a moral right to tell Elizabeth? Does he have a moral duty to tell her? Does Edward have a moral right to privacy concerning his sexual life? John's knowledge of Edward's homosexual relationships came through shared confidences between close friends. Would it be a violation of confidence to disclose this information?

GRANT GILLETT
AIDS AND CONFIDENTIALITY

Does a doctor confronted by a patient with AIDS have a duty to maintain absolute confidentiality or could that doctor be considered to have some overriding duty to the sexual contacts of the AIDS sufferer? AIDS or Acquired Immune Deficiency Disease is a viral disease transmitted for the most part by sexual contact. It is fatal in the short or long term (i.e. nine months to six years) in those infected people who go on to develop the full-blown form of the disease.

Let us say that a 39 year old man goes to his family doctor with a dry persistent cough which has lasted three or four weeks and a 10 day history of night sweats. He admits that he is bisexually active. He is tested and found to have antibodies to HIV virus (indicating that he is infected with the virus that causes AIDS). In the setting of this clinical picture he must be considered to have the disease. He is told of his condition and also, in the course of a prolonged interview, of the risk to his wife and of the distinct possibility of his children aged one and three years old being left without parents should she contract the disease. He refuses to allow her to be told of his condition. The doctor finally accedes to his demand for absolute confidentiality. After one or two initial illnesses which are successfully combatted he dies some 18 months later. Over the last few weeks of his life he relents on his former demands and allows his wife to be informed of his problem. She is tested and, though asymptomatic, is found to be antibody positive. A year later she

From *Journal of Applied Philosophy*, Vol. 4, no. 1 (1987), pp. 15–20. Reprinted by permission.

goes to the doctor with fever, dry cough and loss of appetite. Distraught on behalf of her children, she bitterly accuses the doctor of having failed her and them by allowing her husband to infect her when steps could have been taken to diminish the risk had she only known the truth.

In this case there is a powerful inclination to say that the wife is justified in her grievance. It seems just plain wrong for her doctor to sit back and allow her to fall victim to a fatal disease because of the wish of her husband. Against this intuition we can mobilise two powerful arguments—one deontological and the other utilitarian (of a rule or restricted utilitarian type).[1]

(i) On a deontological view the practice of medicine will be guided by certain inviolate or absolute rules (not to harm, not to neglect the welfare of one's patients, etc.). Among these will be respect for confidentiality. Faced with this inviolable principle the deontologically inclined physician will not disclose what he has been told in confidence—he will regard the tacit agreement not to disclose his patient's affairs to others as tantamount to a substantive promise which he cannot break. Against this, in the present case, we might urge his *prima facie* duty not to neglect the welfare of his other patient, the young man's wife. His inaction has contributed to her death. In response to this he could both defend the absolute duty to respect confidentiality in general and urge some version of the doctrine of double effect,[2] claiming that his clear duty was to honour his implicit vow of confidentiality but it had the unfortunate effect, which he had foreseen as possible but not intended, that it caused the death of his other patient. One is inclined to offer an intuitive response such as 'No moral duty is so binding that you can hazard another person's life in this manner'. It is a notorious feature of deontological systems that they involve conflicts of duties for which there exists no principled method of resolution.

(ii) A rule-utilitarian doctor can mount a more convincing case. He can observe that confidentiality is a cornerstone of a successful AIDS practice. Lack of confidentiality can cause the irrational victimisation of sufferers by a poorly educated public who are prone to witch-hunts of all kinds. The detection and treatment of AIDS, and the consequent protection of that large group of people who have contacts with the patients being treated depends on the patients who seek medical advice believing that medical confidentiality is inviolate. If confidentiality were seen as a relative duty only, suspended or breached at the discretion of the doctor, then far fewer cases would present for detection and crucial guidance about diminishing risks of spread would not be obtained. This would lead to more people suffering and dying. It may be hard on a few, unfortunate enough to be involved with people like the recalcitrant young husband, but the general welfare can only be served by a compassionate but resolute refusal to abandon sound principles in the face of such cases. Many find this a convincing argument but I will argue that it is superficial in the understanding of moral issues that it espouses.

II

Imagine, in order to soften the way for a rather less neatly argued position, a doctor confronted by a young man who has a scratched face and blood on his shirt and who wants to be checked for VD. In the course of the doctor's taking his history it emerges that he has forcibly raped two women and is worried that the second was a prostitute. He says to the doctor "Of course, I am telling you this in confidence, doc, because I know that you won't rat on me". Producing a knife, he then says, "See, this is the blade that I get them going with". Rather troubled, the doctor takes samples and tells the young man that there is no evidence of VD. He tries to talk his patient into giving himself up for some kind of psychiatric treatment but the young man is adamant. It becomes clear that he has certain delusional and persecutional ideas. Two days later the doctor reads that his patient has been arrested because after leaving the surgery he raped and savagely mutilated a young woman who, as a result, required emergency surgery for multiple wounds and remains in a critical condition.

Here we might well feel that any principle which dictates that it is the moral duty of the doctor to keep silent is wrong—but as yet no principles conflicting with or supplementing those above have been introduced. A possible loophole is introduced by the rapist's sadomasochism and probable psychosis but we need to spell out why this is relevant. In such a case we suspend our normal moral obligations to respect the avowed interests of the patient and claim that he is incompetent to make a responsible and informed assessment of his own interests and so we assume the right to make certain decisions on his behalf. In this case it would probably mean arranging for him to be given psychiatric help and society to be protected from him in the meantime. Notice that he may have demonstrated a 'lucid' and 'intelligent' grasp of his predicament, *vis-à-vis* his own wish to avoid detection but we discern that his instrumental rationality is deployed in service of a deep or moral insanity. His lack of awareness of the enormity of what he is doing to others counts as a sufficient basis to diagnose madness even in the face of astute inferential thought. He is insane because a normal person would never begin from the moral position he occupies and so his rights, including that to medical confidentiality, are suspended. He has moved outside the community of trust, mutual concern and non-malificence in which moral considerations for the preferences of others have their proper place. It is not that one 'contracts in' to such a community,[3] nor that one in any sense volunteers,[4] but rather one is a *de facto* member of it by virtue of possessing those human sensitivities and vulnerabilities which give moral predicates their meaning and importance.[5] Such weight as one claims for one's own personal privileges and moral principles—such as the demand for confidentiality—is derived from a 'form of life' where the interpersonal transactions which define trust, respect, harm, and so on, are in play (it is important that no particular ideological overlay has been grafted on to these). Of the insane rapist we can say that he has excluded himself from that moral community by the very fact of his violation of certain of its most basic tenets and assumptions. He has no right to demand a full place in that structure where morally significant human exchanges are operative because his behaviour and attitudes do not fit the place to which he pretends. We are, of course, not released from a *prima facie* duty to try and help him in his odious predicament but we cannot be expected to accord him the full privileges of a member of the moral community as he persists, for whatever reason, in callously turning his back on the constraints normally operative there (albeit, perhaps, without reflective malevolence in its more usual forms). So, in this case, confidentiality can be suspended for legitimate moral reasons. The mad rapist has moved beyond the pale in terms of normal moral interactions and though we may have a duty to try and restore him to full participation within that order we are also entitled to protect ourselves in the interim at the expense of those considerations that would apply to a normal person. Notice again that the boundaries of our attitudes are not arbitrary or merely conventional but involve our most basic human feelings and reactions to one another.[6]

III

We can now move from a case where insanity weights the decision in a certain direction to a case where the issues are more purely moral. Imagine that a 45-year-old man goes to see his family doctor and is also worried about a sexually transmitted disease. On being questioned he admits, in confidence, not only to intercourse with a series of prostitutes but also to forced sexual intercourse with his daughter. He is confident that she will not tell anyone what is happening because she is too ashamed and scared. After counselling he gives no sign of a wish to change his ways but rather continues to justify himself because of his wife's behaviour. The doctor later hears from the school psychological service that the daughter is showing some potentially serious emotional problems.

Here, it seems to me, we have few compunctions about setting in motion that machinery to deal with child abuse, even though the sole source of our information is what was said, in medical confidence, by the father. The justification we might give for the doctor's actions is illuminating. We are concerned for the actual harm being done to the child, both physical and psychological, and we overturn the father's injunction to confidence in order to prevent further harm being done. In so doing we class the situation as one in which a *prima facie* moral claim can be suspended because of the actions and attitudes involved. I believe that we do so because we implicitly realise that here also the agent has acted in such a way as to put himself beyond the full play of moral consideration and to justify our withholding certain of his moral 'dues'. Confidentiality functions to allow the patient to be honest with the doctor and to put trust in him. Trust is (at least in part) a two-way thing and can only exist between morally sensitive human beings (this, of course, blurs a vast range of distinctions between degrees of sensitivity). A basic element of such moral attitudes is the responsiveness of the agents concerned to the moral features of human interactions. The legitimate expectation that a doctor be trustworthy and faithful to his patient's wishes regardless of the behaviour of that patient is undermined when the patient abuses the relationship so formed in ways which show a lack of these basic human reactions because it is just these reactions which ground the importance of confidentiality in general. Therefore, if the father in this example refuses to accept the enormity of what he is doing to his daughter, he thereby casts doubt upon his standing as a moral agent. Stated baldly, that sounds like an open warrant for moralistic medical paternalism, but I do not think it need be. In asking that his affairs be concealed from others, a person is demanding *either* the right to preserve himself from the harms that might befall him if the facts about his life were generally known, *or* that his sensitivity as an individual be respected and protected. On either count it is inconsistent for him to claim some moral justification for that demand when it is made solely with the aim of allowing him to inflict comparable disregard or harm upon another. By his implicit intention to use a position, which only remains tenable with the collusion of the doctor, callously to harm another individual, the father undermines the moral force of his own appeal. His case is only worsened by the fact that from any moral perspective he would be considered to have a special and protective obligation toward his own offspring.

IV

Implicit within what I have said is a reappraisal of the nature of medical confidentiality. I have argued that it is not to be treated as an absolute duty but is rather to rank among other *prima facie* duties and responsibilities of the doctor-patient relationship. Just as the performance of a lifesaving procedure can be vetoed by the patient's choice to forego treatment, even though it is a doctor's duty to strive for his patient's life, so each of these duties can be negated by certain considerations. One generally attempts to prevent a fatal illness overtaking a patient but in the case of a deformed neonate or an elderly and demented patient often the attempt is not made. In the case of confidentiality, I have claimed that we recognise the right of a patient to preserve his own personal life as inviolate. We accept that patients can and should share with a doctor details which it would not be right to disclose to other people. But we must also recognise that implicit within this recognition is the assumption that the patient is one of us, morally speaking. Our attitude to him and his rights assumes that he is one of or a participant in a community of beings who matter (or are morally interacting individuals like himself to whom the same considerations apply). We could offer a superficial and rather gross systematisation of this assumption in the universalisability test.[7] The patient in the last two cases applies a standard to his own human concerns which he is not prepared to extend to others involved with him in relevant situations. We must therefore regard his moral demands as spurious; we are not at liberty to harm him but we are bound to see that his cynical abuse of the moral code within which he lives does not harm others. At this point it might be objected that we are on a 'slippery slope'. Will any moral transgression suffice to undermine the moral privileges of the patient? I do not think that this extreme conclusion can be supported from what I have said. Williams, remarking on the tendency to slide down 'slippery slopes', observes, "that requires that there should be some motive to move from one step to the next" and "Possible cases are not enough, and the situation must have some other feature which means that those cases have to be confronted."[8] Here we are not in such a position. Doctors in general have a strong tendency to protect their patients and keep their confidences. They require strong moral pressures to contemplate doing otherwise. All I have sought to do is to make explicit the moral justification upon which these exceptions can be seen to rest. I have not spelled out any formal decision-making procedure whereby the right answer will be yielded in each case. Indeed it is possible that whereas grounds and reasons recommending a certain course of action are the lifeblood of moral philosophy, such clearcut principles and derivations are a 'will o' the wisp'.

Now we can return to the AIDS patient. From what I have said it becomes clear that it is only the moral intransigent who forces us to breach confidentiality. In most cases it will be possible to guide the patient into telling those who need to know or allowing them to be told (and where it is possible to so guide him it will be mandatory to involve him in an informed way). In the face of an expressed disregard for the harm being caused to those others concerned, we will be morally correct in abandoning what would otherwise be a binding obligation. We should and do feel the need to preserve and protect the already affected life of the potential victim of his deception and in this feeling we exhibit a sensitivity to moral rectitude. Of course, it is only the active sexual partners of the patient who are at risk and thus it is only to them that we and the patient have a moral duty (in this respect talk of 'society at large' is just rhetoric). If it is the case that sexual activity, as Nagel claims, involves a mutual openness in those who have intercourse,[9] one could plausibly argue that the cynical moral and interpersonal attitudes here evinced undermined the patient's sexual rights (assuming that people have such). The sexual activity of this individual is aberrant or perverted in the important respect that it involves a harmful duplicity toward or deception of his sexual partner. Whereas people may have a right to sexual fulfilment in general, they can hardly be said to have a right to perverted sexual fulfilment; but both Nagel's contentions and this talk of rights are contentious and it is outside my present brief to discuss them.

The doctor's obligation to inform, in the face of an enjoinder to keep his confidence, can, even if I am right, be seen to be restricted to those in actual danger and would in no wise extend to employers, friends or non-sexually interacting relatives of the patient or any other person with an even more peripheral interest. His duty extends only so far as to avert the actual harm that he can reasonably expect to arise from his keeping confidence.

Given the intransigent case, one further desideratum presents itself. I believe that doctors should be open with their patients and that therefore the doctor is bound to share his moral dilemma with the patient and inform him of his intention to breach confidentiality. I think he can legitimately claim a pre-emptive duty to prevent harm befalling his patients and should do so in the case of the abuse of others which the patient intends. It may be the case, with the insane rapist for instance, that the doctor will need to deceive in order to carry out his prevailing duty but this will hardly ever be so, and should, I believe, be regarded as unacceptable in general.

One thorny problem remains—the possible deleterious effect on the detection and treatment of AIDS if confidentiality is seen as only a relative principle in medical practice. Clearly, if the attitude were ever to take root that the medical profession could not be trusted to 'keep their mouths shut' then the feared effect would occur. I believe that where agencies and informal groups were told of the *only* grounds on which confidentiality would be breached and the *only* people who would be informed then this effect would not occur.

It seems to me that the remarkable intensification of one's sensitivity to personal and ethical values that is produced by contact with life-threatening or 'abyss' situations means that the cynical abuse of confidentiality by the patient which I have sought to address is likely to be both rare and transient. The greatest resource available to any of us in 'the valley of the shadow' is the closeness of those who will walk alongside us, and for many that will be a close spiritual and sexual partner. Confidentiality within the mutuality of that relationship rather than interpersonal dishonesty would thus seem to be vital to the welfare not only of the co-respondent but also of the patient himself as he struggles to cope with the disease that has him in its grip. To foster that welfare seems to me to be as close as a doctor can ever come to an absolute duty.

Notes

1John Rawls, "Two Concepts of Rules," *Philosophical Review* 64 (1955): 3–32.
2Jonathan Glover, *Causing Death and Saving Lives* (London: Penguin, 1977).

³As is suggested by John Rawls in *A Theory of Justice* (Cambridge, Mass.: Harvard University Press, 1971).

⁴Philippa Foot, "Morality As a System of Hypothetical Imperatives," in *Virtues and Vices* (Berkeley: University of California Press, 1978).

⁵John McDowell suggests that one imbibes the capacities for such judgements as part of the rule-following in which one acquires language, in "Virtue and Reason," *Monist* 62 (1978): 331–350.

⁶I stress this point in order to distance the considerations that are guiding our judgement in this case from those situations in which an ideological framework has been used to override these very natural human reactions and provide a 'justification' for an inhuman moral code.

⁷R. M. Hare, *Freedom and Reason* (New York: Oxford University Press, 1965).

⁸Bernard Williams, "Which Slopes are Slippery?" in M. Lockwood, ed., *Moral Dilemma in Modern Medicine* (Oxford: Oxford University Press, 1986).

⁹Thomas Nagel, "Sexual Perversion," in *Mortal Questions* (London: Cambridge University Press, 1979).

ALAN GEWIRTH

HUMAN RIGHTS AND THE PREVENTION OF CANCER

Every person has a basic human right not to have cancer inflicted on him by the action of other persons. I shall call this right the RNIC (the Right to the Non-Infliction of Cancer). Since it is a species of the right not to be killed or severely injured, the RNIC is perhaps too obvious to need any justificatory argument. Nevertheless, it raises questions of interpretation that have an important bearing both on the ascription of responsibility and on the requirements of social policy.

Closely related to the RNIC is a further right, which I shall call the right of informed control. Each person has a right to have informed control over the conditions relevant to the possible infliction of cancer on himself. This is also a basic human right not only because of its connection with well-being but also because informed control is a component of freedom, which is a necessary condition of action and of successful action.[1]

I

. . . According to current estimates, 80% to 90% of all cancers are caused by the controllable actions of human beings. In the case of cigarette smoking the victims may be held to inflict the cancer on themselves. But in very many cases, it is other persons who cause the victims to get cancer, and it is to such cases that the RNIC directly applies. . . . The victims include workers in factories producing asbestos and vinyl chloride, consumers of sodium nitrite and various chemical emissions, and very many other workers and consumers. . . .[2]

From *American Philosophical Quarterly* 17 (1980): 117–125. Reprinted by permission.

Serious efforts to prevent these cancers must be determined by the specific principles that underlie the RNIC and the right of informed control. First, if we know which substances are causally related to cancer, then exposure to these substances must be prohibited or carefully regulated. Second, every effort must be made to acquire the relevant knowledge and to publicize the results. Hence a major part of the causal and moral responsibility for inflicting various cancers can be attributed to manufacturers, employers, and sellers of various products who control the situations in which the cancers are caused if these persons are made aware of the causal connections and do nothing to stop the actions and policies, in the industrial processes and in marketing, which lead to the cancerous effects. A secondary responsibility can also be attributed to government officials, ranging from legislators to administrators charged with enforcing already existing laws, if, while having knowledge of these carcinogenic dangers, they do not take adequate steps to prevent them.

The basis of this responsibility is similar to that which applies to other forms of killing. The general prohibition against killing innocent humans extends not only to murder but also to manslaughter and other kinds of homicide, including those that stem from advertently negligent and other actions whose likely or foreseeable outcome is the death of their recipients. The general point is that if someone knows or has good reasons to believe that actions or policies under his control operate to cause cancer in other persons, then if he continues these actions or policies, he is in the position of inflicting cancer on these other persons, and he violates a basic human right: he is both causally and morally responsible for the resulting deaths and other serious harms. I shall refer to this as the *informed control criterion* for attributing responsibility.

This criterion is distinct from the criterion of intentionality. To be responsible for inflicting lethal harms, a person need not intend or desire to produce such harms, either as an end or as a means. It is sufficient if the harms come about as an unintended but foreseeable and controllable effect of what he does. For since he knows or has good reasons to believe that actions or policies under his control will lead to the harms in question, he can control whether the harms will occur, so that it is within his power to prevent or at least lessen the probability of their occurrence by ceasing to engage in these actions. Thus, just as all persons have a right to informed control, so far as possible, over the conditions relevant to their incurring cancer and other serious harms, so the causal and moral responsibility for inflicting cancer can be attributed to persons who have informed control over other persons' suffering the lethal harms of cancer.

There is a problem about the informed control criterion for attributing responsibility. Consider, for example, the case of automobile manufacturers. They know, on the basis of statistics accumulated over many years, that a certain percentage of the cars they make and sell will be involved in highway deaths and crippling injuries. Hence, since the actions and policies of making automobiles are under the manufacturers' control, why can't we say that they too are causally and morally responsible for inflicting these deaths and injuries on the victims and hence violate their basic human rights? . . .

The principle of the intervening action enables us to see the difference between the case of the producers of carcinogens and the cases of the automobile manufacturers. . . . In the latter case, an intervening action Y of other persons occurs between the initial action X and the harms suffered Z. When the automobile manufacturers turn out cars, this does not itself usually cause or explain the suffering of injuries by the drivers and car occupants. There intervenes the reckless car operation of the drivers—their going too fast, not using seat belts, driving while drunk, and so forth, all of which are under the drivers' own direct and informed control. . . .

In the case of the producers of most carcinogens, on the other hand (omitting for now the manufacturers of cigarettes), there is no similar intervening action between their production or marketing activities and the incurring of cancer. The workers, consumers, and other persons affected do not actively and knowingly contribute to their getting cancer in the ways in which the drivers . . . actively and knowingly contribute to the ensuing injuries. To be sure, the workers work and the consumers eat and so forth, and these actions are under their respective control. But such actions are part of the normal course of everyday life; they do not involve new intervening actions that go outside the presumed normal cause-effect sequences on the part of persons who are informed about the carcinogenic properties of the substances they use; hence, their actions do not break or "negative" the causal connection between the exposure to carcinogens and the getting of cancer. It is for this reason that these cancers may correctly be said to be other-inflicted, i.e. inflicted on the victims by other persons, the manufacturers or distributors, who hence are guilty of violating the RNIC, as against the self-inflicted cancers that result from such actions as cigarette smoking, or the self-inflicted injuries that result from reckless car-driving.

It may still be contended that part of the causal and moral responsibility for inflicting cancer on workers and consumers rests with the victims themselves, in that they have at least a prudential obligation to use due caution just as motorists do. There is indeed some merit in this contention; but it is important to note its limits. The contention may be viewed as resting in part on the hoary maxim *caveat emptor.* Since workers and consumers are buyers or takers of offers made by employers, distributors, and so forth, the maxim says that it is these buyers who must exercise proper caution in accepting the offers.

While the maxim has much plausibility as a counsel of prudence, it has serious limitations when viewed morally. We can especially see this if we look at a general point about the moral principle which is at the basis of a civilized society. This is a principle of mutual trust, of mutual respect for certain basic rights: that persons will not, in the normal course of life, knowingly inflict physical harm on one another, that they will abstain from such harms insofar as it is in their power to do so, insofar as they can informedly control their relevant conduct. The normal course of life, in a society like ours, includes hiring persons for work and selling substances for use, including consumption of food and other materials. Hence, when workers agree to work for others and when consumers agree to buy various products, they have a right to assume, on the basis of this moral principle, that the work and the products will not be physically harmful to them in ways beyond their normal ability to control, or at least, if there is knowledge or good reason to believe that the products are harmful, as in the case of cigarettes, that full knowledge and publicity will be given to this fact. Failing this knowledge and publicity, the primary responsibility for inflicting cancer on workers and buyers, and thereby violating a basic human right, rests with the employers and producers, since it is they who knowingly offer the conditions of work and the products for sale. What is especially serious about this infliction, by contrast with cases to which the principle of the intervening action applies, is that there is not the same opportunity on the part of the victims to control, with relevant knowledge, the causal factors that proximately impose the cancerous harms on them, so that their own right of informed control is violated.

The most direct requirement that the RNIC lays on the responsible agents is simply that they cease and desist from these lethal policies. This requirement must be enforced by the state because of the pervasiveness and seriousness of the harms in question, especially where the actual or potential victims lack the power and the knowledge to enforce the requirement themselves, and because the voluntary cooperation of the agents in stopping such infliction cannot be assumed. Whether this enforcement takes the form of an outright ban on the use of certain substances or the setting of standards that specify the levels at which various potential carcinogens may be used, in either case there must be appropriate sanctions or penalties for the violators. In addition, sufficient information must be made available so that all persons potentially affected may be able to help to control the conditions that affect them so severely. Thus both the state and the various employers, manufacturers, and distributors are the respondents of the RNIC, and their correlative duties have to an eminent degree the moral seriousness and coercibility that go with all basic human rights.

II

I have thus far presented the RNIC as an absolute right not to have cancer inflicted on one by the action of other persons. I now want to look more closely at the respects in which it is indeed absolute.

To say that someone has an absolute right to have or do something

X means that his having or doing X cannot justifiably be overridden by any other considerations, so that there is a completely exceptionless prohibition on all other persons against interfering with the right-holder's having or doing X. . . .

There appear, however, to be ways of overriding the RNIC. . . . These ways may seem to lead to the conclusion that the prohibition against inflicting cancer on other persons should be *prima facie* and probabilistic rather than absolute and apodictic.

We may distinguish two areas of such probabilism. The first bears on the cause-effect relation between exposure to various substances and the incurring of cancer. It will be recalled that in explicating the RNIC I said that if someone "knows or has good reasons to believe" that actions or policies under his control operate to produce cancer in other persons, then he is in the position of inflicting cancer on these other persons. The question now is: when can someone be said to know or to have good reasons to believe that his actions inflict cancer?

The difficulty here is that the causal relation in question seems to be one of degree. Some substances, such as β-naphthylamine and asbestos, have a very high ability to induce cancer. But with other substances the ability and the correlative risk, as determined on a statistical frequency basis, are much lower. There is a currently unresolved controversy on this question of degrees. One view holds that there is a threshold of dosage of carcinogens, below which they do not induce cancers; the other view holds that there is no such threshold, in that any amount of a carcinogen, no matter how small, may lead to cancerous tumors. This latter view is reflected in the Delaney clause that deals with food additives: "no additive shall be deemed safe if it is found to induce cancer when ingested by man or animal, or if it is found, after tests which are appropriate for the evaluation of the safety of food additives, to induce cancer in man or animal. . . ."[3] Here, then, use of the additives in question is strictly prohibited without regard to the degree of risk to humans at any level of use, and without regard to possible benefits.

The merits of such a blanket prohibition, in the case of other substances as well as food additives, are clear. So long as it is not known which particular workers in the various potentially lethal occupations will get cancer and which not, and similarly which consumers of the various suspect food additives and other substances, the only completely safe course would seem to be a blanket prohibition of the respective exposures. To the objection that such absolutism would entail prohibiting the use of automobiles and of many other modern conveniences, since these too carry the risk of death, the reply is, as before, that automobiles do not usually become harmful apart from the controllable, variable actions of the persons who use them, so that they do not pose the risk of death from external causes, i.e. causes external to their users, in the way that carcinogens do.

On the alternate view of the threshold controversy, it is maintained that just as automobiles may be made safer by a variety of devices that are within the power of their makers and users, so too the risks of getting cancer from various substances may be reduced by lowering the degree of exposure to them. For example, even in the case of vinyl chloride, an exposure standard of one part per million is thought to render it relatively even if not absolutely safe for the workers who are exposed to it, especially by contrast with the previous unregulated concentration of 200 to 5,000 parts per million.

I have two conclusions on this issue, one firm, the other tentative. The firm conclusion is that, in keeping with the right of informed control, it is necessary to try to reduce further the ignorance reflected in the varying probabilities of the cause-effect relations involved in carcinogenesis. For this purpose, intensive research must be pursued, within the limits of safety to humans, to ascertain the more specific causal variables, so that we understand more fully just which substances, at what levels of exposure, carry what risks of cancer to which persons. And the results of this research must be fully disseminated and used both in manufacturing and marketing operations and in appropriate legislation.

My more tentative conclusion is that, in contrast to construing the RNIC as an absolute right against even the slightest risk of cancer, a sliding scale may be introduced. Whether the use of or exposure to some substance should be prohibited should depend on the degree to which it poses the risk of cancer, as shown by bioassays and epidemiological studies. If the risks are very slight, so that, for example, use of the substance increases the chance of getting cancer from 1 in 10,000 to 2 in 10,000, or if the risk can be made very slight by drastically reducing the level of exposure, as in the case just cited of vinyl chloride, and if no substitutes are available, then use of it may be permitted, subject to stringent safeguards.

Does this conclusion entail that the RNIC is not an absolute right? The answer depends on how the word "inflict" is construed. If "inflict" is viewed solely as causal, with no reference to moral responsibility of the agent, then there is a sense in which the tentative conclusion I have reached would remove the absoluteness of the RNIC. For while the conclusion does not say that there may be exceptions to the prohibition against actually inflicting cancer, it does say that certain minimal risks of inducing cancer may be allowed, or that the risk of cancer may be increased so long as the level attained is still very low in the way just indicated.

The case is otherwise, however, if the RNIC's prohibition against inflicting cancer is viewed in the light of the ascription of moral responsibility. Since the RNIC is a strict right, it entails that persons strictly ought to refrain from inflicting cancer on other persons. Now this "ought," like other moral "oughts" addressed to agents, is limited by the possibility of informed control, and hence of knowing the likelihood of one's actions causing such infliction. For insofar as "ought" implies "can," to say that A ought not to do X implies that he can refrain from doing X and also that he can have the knowledge needed for such refraining. Thus, the extent of the RNIC's requirement and of the moral responsibility that stems from violating it is likewise limited by this possibility of knowledge.

In this context of moral responsibility, then, the RNIC is to be construed as entailing: Don't inflict cancer on other persons so far as you can know or have good reason to believe that any of your actions will constitute or produce such infliction, and don't increase the risk of cancer for other persons beyond the minimal level just indicated. On this construal, the RNIC remains an absolute right even where it allows certain minimal risks of persons' getting cancer as a result of the actions of other persons. For the latter are morally responsible only if they can know or can have good reasons for believing that their action will lead to other persons' getting cancer. Where they do not and cannot have such knowledge, the informed control criterion for ascribing responsibility does not apply, nor, usually, does the intentionality criterion. . . .

III

Let us now turn to a second area of probabilism that may be invoked to mitigate the absoluteness of the RNIC's prohibition against inflicting cancer, and that has been implicitly present in my preceding discussion. This area bears not on the varying probabilities of the cause-effect relations themselves in the production of cancer, but rather on a weighing of certain values in reaction to those probabilities. The weighing in question is concerned with the relation between the benefits obtained by prohibiting carcinogenic exposures and the costs of such prohibitions; or alternatively with the relation between the benefits obtained by accepting certain risks of cancer and the costs of accepting those risks. It is here a matter of the cost-benefit analysis dearly beloved of economists, which is simply the contemporary version of the pleasure-pain calculus long pursued by utilitarians.

In view of the extreme importance for human well-being of preventing cancer, and the human right to the non-infliction of cancer, how can the avoidance of such infliction be legitimately subjected to a cost-benefit analysis whereby its benefits are weighed against various costs? The better to understand this question, let us compare the problem of preventing cancer with such a situation as where coal miners are trapped in a mine by an explosion. So long as there is any hope of rescuing the miners, all possible means are used to effect a rescue. Except where other human lives are at stake, questions of cost are deemed irrelevant, and so too is the number of miners; lesser efforts would not be made to rescue one miner than to rescue fifty, except insofar as less equipment might be needed to rescue the one. The basis of such unlimited effort to save human lives is that the right of an innocent person to continue to live is normally regarded as absolute, being limited only by the right to life of other persons, and human life is considered to be priceless, in the literal sense of being without price: it is incommensurable with, cannot be measured in terms of, money or any other material goods that might be needed to preserve the life or lives that are endangered.

There are obvious dissimilarities between such a situation and the prevention of cancer. In the former case the lethal danger is actual and immediate, not potential and remote; it is a danger to determinate individuals, not to some general percentage or statistical frequency out of a much larger, less determinate population; and the life-saving operations that are called for are similarly determinate and immediate. Partly because of these differences and partly for other reasons, economists and others have engaged in the cost-benefit analyses mentioned before. There is, after all, time for calculation, and the calculation bears especially on how much, from among the total values both of the individuals directly concerned and of society at large, it is worth spending in order to avoid the risks of cancer and other lethal harms.

To see how such cost-benefit analyses are even minimally plausible in this context, we may note that many kinds of human decisions involve at least implicit views as to the monetary value of human life. Examples are when someone takes out a life insurance policy, when society takes or fails to take measures to improve automobile safety, and when a court awards money damages to a family one of whose members has been killed through someone else's fault. Morally repugnant as it may be, then, putting a specific money evaluation on human life seems to be a feature of at least some segments of individual and social decision-making.

Accepting for the present at least the possibility of such a procedure, we may ask how the money value of a human life is to be estimated. Economists have answered this question in different ways, but the way that is most favoured is based on the familiar idea of a Pareto improvement.[4] According to this, one allocation of resources is an improvement over another if it involves at least one person's being made better off while no person is made worse off. The criterion of being made better off consists simply in the preferences of the person concerned, so that if some person prefers allocation X to allocation Y, then he is made better off by X than by Y. And if no person prefers Y to X, then the change from X to Y is a Pareto improvement. Thus if some person A is willing to accept some life-risking situation R on payment to him of a certain sum of money S by another person B who is willing to make this payment, then A's having R and S together is to that extent a Pareto improvement over the situation or allocation where he does not have R and S. On this view, the monetary value of A's life to himself is measured by the minimum sum of money he is willing to accept to compensate for the risk of losing his life in some activity or other.

There is a direct application of this Pareto criterion to the case of cancer, especially as this is incurred by industrial workers in various occupations. According to the criterion, the risk of cancer may be imposed on some worker in some job if he is willing to accept that risk on payment to him of a certain sum of money. Since he prefers a situation where he works at some carcinogenically risky job and hence earns money to a situation where he has no job at all, or since he prefers a carcinogenically riskier job at more pay to a less risky job at less pay, while in each case no one else is made worse off, it follows that the former situation is in each case a Pareto improvement over the latter. Hence, in contrast to the earlier position whereby human life is priceless and the RNIC is an absolute right, according to this new position human life turns out to have a price, and the right to the non-infliction of cancer is now limited not only by unavoidable deficiencies of knowledge but also by the willingness of potential victims to accept financial compensation.

There are, however, serious difficulties with this probabilistic alternative. I shall waive the question of whether the risk of getting cancer can be rationally compensated for by any amount of money or other satisfactions. It might be thought that the RNIC is not affected by such cases, since the risk of cancer is here assumed to be imposed on some person with his consent. But there still remain the questions of whether this consent is informed and unforced. Is each of the persons who chooses among alternatives able to know the degree of risk of the possibly carcinogenic alternative for which compensation is required? In the case of the industrial workers in factories making asbestos, kepone, vinyl chloride, and other lethal substances, they were surely not aware of the risks during the years that elapsed between their initial exposure and the time when some of them came down with cancer. For them, consequently, the Pareto criterion would not apply insofar as it assumes that the persons who express their preferences by their acceptance of compensation for risks are aware of the magnitude of the risks. And even when, as is increasingly the case in recent years, research is pursued into carcinogens and its results are made public, there remains the question of whether complicated statistical calculations can be understood and used by the workers who are most vulnerable to their possibly varying implications. In such circumstances it becomes very difficult to apply the right of informed control.

The Pareto criterion's applicability is also dubious over a wide range of cases because of a difficulty bearing on distributive justice. Since the poorer a person is the greater is the marginal utility for him of a given sum of money, whereas the opposite is true the richer a person is, the poor are willing to accept much greater risks for considerably less money. Thus, in effect, they and their relative poverty are exploited as a way of getting them to do dangerous work far beyond what others will accept. While this is, of course, a very old story, it casts doubt on the economists' model of citizens' sovereignty where workers "voluntarily" accept compensation for risks and thereby show that they consider themselves to be better off than they would be without the risks and the compensation. For many workers are in effect confronted with a forced choice, since the alternative to their taking the risky job with its slightly added compensation is their not having any job at all. Where workers and others do not have the power to ward off such risks by themselves, it is an indispensable function of government to protect such persons from having to make such forced choices, and hence to protect their right both to the non-infliction of cancer and to the non-imposition of serious risks of cancer. This function can be generalized to the more extensive duty of the supportive state to try to provide opportunities and means of knowledge and well-being so as to reduce the vulnerability of poorer persons to such coercive alternatives. In this and other respects, the prevention of other-inflicted cancers merges into more general issues of the distribution of power and wealth in a society.

A quite central difficulty with this application of cost-benefit analysis is that human life or health is not a commodity to be bought, sold, or bid for on the market. Thus the Pareto criterion is mistaken in principle insofar as it assumes that any great risk of death can be compensated for by any amount of money. There are important differences in this regard between engaging in carcinogenic work risks, on the one hand, and buying life insurance, driving cars, or doing aerial acrobatic stunts, on the other. Even though in buying life insurance one implicitly places a certain monetary value on one's life, this is different from undertaking the risk of carcinogenic work for pay. In buying life insurance one recognizes that death is inevitable for everyone sooner or later, and one does not thereby voluntarily incur the serious risk of death. But to undertake the risk of cancer by one's work is not itself inevitable, so that the compensation involves putting a market price on one's life in the context of a controllable, avoidable choice. In addition, the worker in a carcinogenic industry usually does not have the same kind of control over his degree of risk as does the driver of a car or an aerial acrobat. Hence the case for outright prohibition of more than minimal risk in the former case is much stronger than it is with regard to auto driving or aerial acrobatics despite the dangers of death common to these kinds of cases.

A further issue about the economic valuation of human life bears on who does the valuing. It is one thing for a person to put a money value on his own life where he has a relatively unforced choice between alternative ways of life and work. It is another thing for other persons to put this money valuation on his life, as is done when the benefits of making jobs less risky and hence prolonging workers' lives are weighed against alternative uses of public money, such as building new roads or ball parks. In such cases the worker and his life are made economic objects vulnerable to the preferences or choices of other persons rather than of himself. The very possibility of making such choices on such grounds represents a drastic lowering of public morality.

A related criticism must be made of the suggestion that the Pareto criterion should be applied to tax firms or manufacturers so as to encourage them to remove or lower the levels at which their workers are exposed to cancer.[5] For a firm may choose or prefer to pay the tax rather than remove the risk, while passing the tax on to its customers and, under conditions of oligopoly, suffering little or no financial drain. Such payment would be small comfort to the workers who continue to be exposed to the lethal dangers. This taxational incentive approach also has the severe difficulty previously noted, that it makes persons' lives and health matters of bargaining or purchase rather than viewing them as basic goods and rights not subject to such cost-benefit calculation.

IV

Thus far I have been dealing with a view of cancer as inflicted on persons against their will by the direct or indirect actions of other persons. It is to these interpersonal transactions that the RNIC directly applies. As against such other-inflicted cancers, let us briefly consider the lung cancer derived from cigarette smoking as a self-inflicted kind of harm. This distinction between other-inflicted and self-inflicted harms may be contested in the case of cigarettes on the ground that the blandishments of advertisers and, for young people, the models set by their peers constitute externally-caused incentives to smoke, so that the resulting lung cancers are here also other-inflicted. There is indeed some truth to this, especially in the case of the cigarette manufacturers. Since the lethal impact of smoking cannot be controlled by individual smokers in anything like the same degree that motorists can control the dangers of auto driving, cigarette manufacturers bear a much heavier responsibility for the resulting deaths than do auto manufacturers. The principle of the intervening action applies in much lesser degree to the former than to the latter because the actions of making cigarettes easily available and attractive have a much closer causal connection to the ensuing lethal harms, despite the intervention of the victims' choices to smoke.

I shall here assume, however, that the final choice to smoke rests with the individual himself, and that he is capable of withstanding the advertisers' blandishments. The fact remains that his smoking may be morally wrong because he may impose serious burdens on others. If he becomes hospitalized, his family suffers and he uses extremely valuable and costly facilities and services for which he may not be able to pay, or even if he can, he still makes extremely stringent demands on others which his knowing, controllable actions might have prevented. He also violates both an important prudential duty to himself and also a moral duty to himself as a rational person who is aware of the moral requirements of not burdening others.[6]

How, then, should the self-inflicted carcinogenesis of cigarette smoking be dealt with? While outright prohibition is a possibility, it would perhaps be too violative of individual freedom and, as with the 18th Amendment, there would be too many possibilities of abuse and evasion. On the other hand, simply to leave the smoker alone would also be unacceptable because, even if we give up all paternalistic concern for his own well-being, there would still remain the problem of externalities, the costs he imposes on others.

The solution I suggest is that the smoker should be made to bear the full cost of his habit, including its external effects. These could be calculated in terms of the excess medical facilities, support of his dependents, and other costs he imposes on others. This would be an application of the Pareto criterion in that the smoker would have to compensate those who would otherwise bear the costs of his habit. If he chooses to pay this compensation, the outcome is a Pareto improvement, since he prefers his smoking together with paying the extra money for it to going without smoking, while, since other persons are compensated, they are not made worse off.

Why is such a compensation permissible in the smoker's case and not in the case of workers in carcinogenic industries? In each case it is the inflicter of cancer who has to pay. There is, however, a difference between a person paying others in order to inflict cancer on himself and his paying his workers in order to inflict cancer on them. The latter, as we have seen, violates the RNIC while the former does not. There is also a difference between the potential cancer victim's paying others, as in the smoking case, and others' paying him, as in the occupational health case. But there is also a more important difference. The industrial worker who is allowed to take money compensation for working in a high-risk industry is told, in effect, that he must choose between losing his job or livelihood and risking his life to cancer. This is an inadmissible choice. The smoker, on the other hand, is confronted with a choice between saving his life from cancer and saving his money, or, alternatively, between continuing his enjoyment of smoking, thereby risking his own life, and paying a larger sum of money. This choice, whatever its psychological hardship for the smoker, is not of the same order of extreme objective adversity as in the case of the high-risk worker. The initial much greater relative economic vulnerability of the unskilled industrial workers makes a crucial difference.

I conclude, then, that the probabilistic issues of the carcinogenic cause-effect relations and cost-benefit analysis do not materially affect the conclusion drawn earlier. So far as the moral responsibility of agents is concerned, the Right to the Non-Infliction of Cancer is an absolute human right, and it requires the most determined efforts both to ascertain when such infliction is likely to occur and to take all possible steps to prevent it, and thereby to make its respondents fulfill their correlative duties.

Notes

[1] On the grounding of human rights in freedom and well-being as the necessary conditions of human action, see my *Reason and Morality* (Chicago, 1978), pp. 63–103. In chs. 2 and 4, I also explain the distinction between "basic" and other human rights.

[2] Useful recent surveys are Larry Agran, *The Cancer Connection* (Boston, 1977); and *Annals of the New York Academy of Sciences,* vol. 271 (1976): *Occupational Carcinogenesis.* See also the summary of the latter in Phyllis Lehmann, *Cancer and the Worker* (New York, 1977).

[3] *U.S. Code* 21, 348 (c) (3). For this reference and for a valuable discussion of related issues I am indebted to Jerome Cornfield, "Carcinogenic Risk Assessment," *Science,* vol. 198 (18 November 1977), pp. 693–699.

[4] Cf. E. J. Mishan, "Evaluation of Life and Limb: A Theoretical Approach," *Journal of Political Economy,* vol. 79 (1971), pp. 687–705; M. W. Jones-Lee, *The Value of Life: An Economic Analysis* (Chicago, 1976), chs. 1–3.

[5] See Albert L. Nichols and Richard Zeckhauser, "Government Comes to the Workplace: An Assessment of OSHA," *The Public Interest,* no. 49 (Fall 1977), 64 ff.

[6] I have discussed relevant aspects of duties to oneself and prudential virtues in *Reason and Morality, op. cit.,* pp. 242–244, and 333–338.

LAWRENCE O. GOSTIN, WILLIAM J. CURRAN, AND MARY E. CLARK

THE CASE AGAINST COMPULSORY CASEFINDING IN CONTROLLING AIDS

. . . Mandatory screening programs for selected populations are unlikely to achieve any clear public health benefit. Knowledge of seropositivity cannot be used to alleviate a person's infectious condition since there is currently no vaccine for prevention or treatment which cures HIV infection. HIV is unlike venereal disease, where the chain of infection can be broken by simple antibiotic treatment. Thus, even with early information of a person's serological status, medicine cannot alter the cycle of infection. Although knowledge of seropositivity enables a person to seek early treatment with such developing therapies as azidothymidine (AZT), AZT presently is not clinically indicated for asymptomatic HIV carriers. Accordingly, early knowledge of seropositivity does not produce any advantage in enabling the person to seek early treatment. Members of high risk groups who clinically present with signs of immunodeficiency can be tested for HIV antibodies for diagnostic purposes with their informed consent. It is difficult to sustain an argument for compulsory screening of large populations in the hope that some might

From "The Case Against Compulsory Casefinding in Controlling AIDS—Testing, Screening, and Reporting," *American Journal of Law and Medicine* 12 (1987): 7–53. Footnotes have been omitted. Reprinted by permission.

have access to an experimental treatment sooner than they would otherwise by visiting their physician at the first sign of a clinical problem.

In the absence of an effective vaccine or treatment, public health arguments for compulsory screening of large populations must be based upon the premise that widespread serological testing will lead to behavior modification among persons who test positive. The critical unanswered question, however, is whether knowledge of seropositivity influences behavior and in what direction. The appropriate precautions in personal conduct to reduce the spread of HIV are already well-known to most members of high risk groups. The spread of HIV can be reduced only through the willingness of individuals to avoid unsafe intimate sexual and needle sharing behavior. The introduction of compulsory screening may have the reverse effect of causing persons vulnerable to HIV to avoid coming forward for testing, counselling, and treatment.

Given the absence of an established prevention or treatment, and the lack of any evidence that compulsory screening would lead to voluntary changes in behavior, the public health benefit of such a program is likely to be marginal or even counterproductive. Balanced against this marginal public health benefit is the potential for substantial harm to those screened. Each person screened, whether seropositive or not, must submit involuntarily to the taking of a blood sample and the collection of sensitive health care information. Moreover, collection of information creates a demand for its use. Unauthorized disclosure of that information could result in opprobrium among family and friends and discrimination in employment, housing, and insurance. The adverse consequences of screening are serious enough for true positives, even though the great majority are likely to be asymptomatic. In addition, there will be a number of individuals who test positive in the ELISA and supplementary tests, but who do not harbor the virus. The price of screening includes the potential for stigma and discrimination to the false positive population.

Widespread screening has public resource, as well as personal, implications. Screening requires the administration and interpretation of the ELISA together with supplementary procedures. This entails significant expense for the administration of laboratories, test equipment, and personnel. The costs of investing in a screening program must be measured against similar levels of expenditures needed for research, education, and counselling.

The personal and economic costs engendered by a program of compulsory screening are likely to be disproportionate to the marginal public health benefit. The objective of screening is to obtain shifts in behavior and early treatment among groups most vulnerable to HIV infection. This objective can be achieved in a more effective and less restrictive way by a comprehensive voluntary program of public health education and professional testing and counselling services. Those inclined to seek treatment and behavior control are likely to respond to cost free, readily available education and services. Such a voluntary program would achieve the same public health advantages as a mandatory program, but without the significant deteriments of the widespread use of compulsion.

Next, a series of criteria are proposed for assessing the merits of compulsory screening. Then, these criteria are applied, together with the general arguments just made, to specific legislative screening proposals.

PROPOSED CRITERIA FOR ASSESSING MANDATORY POPULATION SCREENING

. . . In this section, we will develop general standards for use in cases where compulsory screening is proposed. No single formula can always determine whether screening of particular populations is appropriate public policy. Yet, attempts to evaluate each proposal without a systematic theory of analysis could reach inconsistent results. Accordingly, general criteria should be applied in each case where screening is proposed. In most cases, a reasoned positive response to each of the following criteria is desirable before concluding that compulsory screening is warranted.

High Reservoir of Infection

Screening necessarily entails a restriction on individuals' rights to privacy; it involves blood sampling and the collection of sensitive information. Screening expends scarce health care resources, including the cost of using professionals to administer the test and laboratory equipment and personnel to analyze results. Moreover, properly conducted screening programs should provide health care information and professional counselling, adding to the cost of the program. Wherever possible, therefore, screening programs should be narrowly targeted to select populations with a potentially high reservoir of infection, such as a program administered in a treatment center for sexually transmitted diseases or for IV drug abuse.

Screening programs in large populations with a predictably low frequency of infection, such as pre-marital screening, have a number of disadvantages: a large number of people will have their privacy unnecessarily invaded; procedures will have to be adopted to keep a large amount of health care data confidential; and a significant amount of scarce resources will be expended. Finally, even the ELISA test loses a great deal of its accuracy when it is applied to a population with a low reservoir of infection. Accordingly, the application of the ELISA test to a general population will create a high ratio of false to true positives.

Significant Risk of Transmission

To establish the effectiveness of a screening program, it is necessary to demonstrate not only a high reservoir of infection, but also a high risk of transmission. Effective screening programs require a setting where transmission of infection is reasonably likely to occur. Screening decisions should be grounded upon the best scientific and epidemiologic evidence relating to transmission of the infection. To date, four primary means of transmission have been clearly established: sexual contact involving the exchange of bodily fluids, intravenous drug administration with contaminated needles, use of contaminated blood or blood products, and in utero or intrapartum transmission or transmission postnatally possibly from ingestion of breast milk. There has been considerable research into the possibility of transmission by other routes such as by casual association or intimate caring and nursing functions undertaken within families and health care settings. There is increasingly strong evidence indicating that the virus is not transmitted through casual contact. Thus, there is no public health justification for screening where the only expected association among the population is casual, such as in school settings. However, where the population (e.g., prostitutes or IV drug users) or the environment in which the population operates (e.g., bathhouses) involves the possible exchange of bodily fluids, the public health justification for screening is stronger.

Effective Use of Test Results

If all persons within a selected population are to be screened, the resulting information must be used effectively to reduce the spread of infection. If the precautions that might be taken cannot reduce transmission, there is no purpose to a screening program. Further, if the proposed action or precautions should be taken whether or not the test is given, the action raises the question whether systematic population screening is needed. For example, if hospitals have adopted or should adopt general safety precautions in handling all specimens whether or not they are infected, the rationale for screening specimens is undermined.

Critical Consequences of Screening Should Not Outweigh Benefits

Screening may have many critical consequences for the individual. Screening programs require the collection of personal information. This information may be disclosed to family, employers, landlords, insurers, and others, possibly resulting in opprobrium and discriminatory action against the infected person. Where public health officials screen populations, the information may be used as a condition precedent to other more intrusive public health actions such as sexual contact tracing or isolation. Screening programs and ensuing intrusive actions may have some effect in reducing HIV transmission. Yet, the personal or social costs of these actions may be disproportionate to their expected benefits. The "critical consequences" criterion involves a judgment as to whether the health benefit of screening outweighs the personal, social, and economic costs for those who test positive.

No Less Restrictive or Intrusive Means

Public health law should protect the health of the community with as few restrictions on the rights of individuals as possible. From an individual perspective, this criterion is important because those subjected to public health actions should be allowed as much freedom as possible without imposing significant costs on the public health. The principle of the least restrictive alternative can also further public health interests. A major strategy in combatting the spread of AIDS is to foster voluntary cooperation, such as through notification of contacts and reduction of high risk behavior. The use of involuntary, highly restrictive measures may deter members of high risk groups from cooperating with public health officials or from attending public health programs, such as clinics for the treatment of sexually transmitted diseases or the treatment of drug or alcohol abuse.

Health care professionals may have difficulty with the principle of the least restrictive alternative because public health measures traditionally have been predicated on the notion that it is best to err on the side of caution. Under this philosophy, public health takes precedence over individual rights, and if a control measure might promote the public health, it should be implemented. But, the principle of the least restrictive alternative is not necessarily inconsistent with this view. It does not require a less effective measure merely because it is less intrusive. It requires a less intrusive measure only if it is equally, or more efficacious.

It would be an error to implement a compulsory screening program until the proposed criteria have been applied to the program. . . .

SCREENING OF SELECTED POPULATIONS: ILLUSTRATIVE CASES

Screening in Schools

United States Public Health Service guidelines on "Education and Foster Care of Children Infected with HTLV-III/LAV" advise against mandatory screening as a condition of school entry. The guidelines recommend that infected school-age children be allowed to attend school and after-school day care programs. This is particularly so where they exhibit no higher risk behavioral patterns or conditions such as abnormal biting, drooling, open sores, or bleeding. Despite these recommendations, a number of jurisdictions have sought to automatically exclude HIV-infected children from school. A concurrent resolution has been proposed in Congress stating that public schools should not permit students with AIDS to attend regular classes and that schools should make alternative arrangements for education. Although the resolution is cast as a way of "respecting the education" of children with AIDS, its impact would be to isolate these children from their peers. Exclusion of children who test positive for HIV antibody is a critical consequence of testing; the merits of such exclusion are examined below.

1. Risk of Transmission in Schools None of the identified high risk behaviors are an inherent part of school activities, and they can be virtually ruled out as means of transmission among younger children. The great majority of children with HIV infection contract the virus from their infected mothers. If evidence emerged that some schools had a high reservoir of infection and that transmission was occurring through shared needles or sexual activities, measures to control these activities could be legally justified. It should be noted that these activities are prohibited already on school grounds.

The Public Health Service conclusion that there is no risk of communication of the virus in a normal school environment is based upon a number of studies of families with an infected member. Studies demonstrate that casual contact within the secretion-rich environment of the family does not cause transmission of HIV. There is also evidence demonstrating the difficulty of transmitting HIV in health care settings. While rare cases of parenteral transmission have occurred, no case of transmission from such causes as open wounds or attending to sanitary needs of patients has been documented.

The potential for viral transmission in schools through child-to-child contact is purely theoretical, supported by not a single documented case. Parental fears have been increased by reports of live virus isolated in tears and saliva. Yet, attempts to isolate HIV in saliva are generally quite unsuccessful. All available evidence points to school children having the most remote possibility of contracting the virus on school grounds.

School children are perceived to be a vulnerable population, and it is understandable that parents would adopt a highly conservative formula for risk management; any lethal risk is unacceptable if it can be prevented by exclusion of the infected child. Yet, negligible risks are part of life and society accepts them. Any social activity entails some small risk such as going to school in a motor vehicle or crossing the street. As long as the risks of an activity are outweighed by the benefits of that activity, society condones the activity.

2. The Critical Consequences of Exclusion from School Balanced against the remote risk entailed in allowing infected children to attend school is the critical consequence of excluding them. Compelling a child to forego the enriching experience of social integration at school is a harsh consequence. Education is a constitutionally protected right. Even if basic education could be provided elsewhere, exclusion denies the child the right to association with his or her peers. In *New York State Association for Retarded Children, Inc.* v. *Carey* (612 F.2d 644, 1979), the Second Circuit Court of Appeals held that exclusion or isolation of students, merely because they have a medical condition (hepatitis B) that may pose a remote risk of transmission, violates section 504 of the Federal Rehabilitation Act of 1983. The court found that such students were "handicapped" within the meaning of the statute and were unlawfully excluded from participation in a federally assisted activity on the basis of that handicap. The *Carey* court stated that even separate educational facilities would discriminate against infected children as such a separation would "limit the extent to which they can participate in school-wide activities such as meals, recesses, and assemblies, and will reinforce the stigma to which these children have already been subjected."

The decision in *Carey* that there was no justification in excluding hepatitis B carriers from school should similarly apply to children with HIV. Since the risk of transmission of hepatitis B is greater than HIV, the rationale for exclusion of children with AIDS is even less apparent. . . .

The exclusion of children with AIDS or HIV infection from school represents a restriction of freedom of association and educational benefit. This deprivation is a high price to exact in exchange for a negligible benefit to public health, and thus violates one of the proposed criteria for screening programs. Therefore, whether viewed from a constitutional or statutory perspective, policies which automatically exclude such children from school are unjustified. . . .

Pre-Marital Screening

Pre-marital screening is one of the most frequently proposed measures in state legislatures. Under such proposals an HIV antibody test would be required prior to the issuance of a marriage license. This is similar to current requirements in many states for a recognized serological test for syphilis; if the test is positive, proof that the infection is not communicable is necessary before the certificate is issued. No state, however, has yet adopted a pre-marital screening program for HIV infection.

Despite the current popularity of pre-marital screening proposals, application of the five criteria indicate that such screening would not be effective in controlling the spread of HIV. Under state legislative proposals, pre-marital screening would be required of all applicants for a marriage license. If implemented in every state, this would require serological testing for approximately 1.7 million couples. In a normal healthy population, approximately four out of every 10,000 people are infected with HIV. Thus, the reservoir of infection among marriage license applicants is likely to be exceedingly low, particularly in states with a low incidence of HIV. Use of the ELISA test on a large population with a low frequency of infection would cause potentially insurmountable problems. The ELISA test is highly accurate when applied within a high risk population, but it would produce a significant number of false positive results when applied to a normal healthy population. Under optimal circumstances, a single ELISA test would be expected to produce at least one or two false positives for every true positive within a healthy population. A confirmatory Western Blot test would sharply reverse the ratio of true to false positives to approximately seventy to one. Yet, when such ratios are applied to a large population, the total number of false positives would be significant.

Pre-marital testing programs present other problems. The state must

fully plan the program and incur the expense of providing the laboratories, test equipment, and personnel necessary for administering and
interpreting the ELISA test, administering a second ELISA and Western
Blot test for all positive testing applicants, and providing the professional
psychological and social work services needed to counsel and support
confirmed positive applicants. A testing program, without competent
laboratory services to ensure accuracy and a full range of counselling and
support services, would fail to meet any valid public health objective.

More important than the economic cost of implementing a system of
pre-marital screening is the personal cost to individual privacy. A pre-
marital screening requirement tests a large population, the majority of
which has not been exposed to HIV. Information concerning those who
test positive, including false positives, will be conveyed to prospective
spouses and kept by public health officials.

The substantial economic and privacy costs incurred in a widespread
program of pre-marital screening may be justified by a strong public
health benefit. The objectives of a pre-marital screening program are to
identify positive-testing individuals and to prevent transmission of the
virus to spouses and offspring. Prevention of transmission may be
achieved either by prohibiting marriage to a positive testing applicant,
or by educating the couple about the dangers of unprotected sex and
childbirth. Before enacting such a proposal, a legislature must determine
whether a pre-marital screening program would achieve this objective
or whether less intrusive measures would be as effective.

Since marriage is not necessary for intercourse or impregnation,
pre-marital screening will not prevent all cases of transmission to the
partners and offspring. Many applicants for marriage will already have
had sexual relations. Further, a pre-marital screening requirement does
not assure any change in future sexual or child-rearing behavior.

Some pre-marital screening proposals would withhold a marriage
license where one party is HIV positive. In the venereal disease context,
the existence of antibiotics to cure the syphilis infection makes pre-
marital screening feasible. Since there is no prevention of or cure for the
HIV infection, however, the legislature could not require a therapeutic
intervention as a condition of approval for the marriage certificate. It
would be contrary to public policy to bar marriage to sero-positive
individuals. Such a proposal would face serious constitutional challenge
because the Supreme Court in *Zablocki* v. *Redhail* (434 U.S. 374, 1978)
reaffirmed that marriage is a fundamental right. The Court stated that if
"a statutory classification significantly interferes with the exercise of a
fundamental right, it cannot be upheld unless it is supported by sufficiently important state interests and is closely tailored to effectuate only
those interests." Courts may not find a tight fit between HIV antibody
screening and a compelling public purpose due to the screening's un-
proven impact on impeding the spread of infection to spouses or offspring.

Two other alternatives could achieve the public health objective in a less intrusive manner. Screening could be offered on a voluntary basis, and the results used solely to inform both partners of their serologic status and to determine the need for counselling. Test results would be kept confidential. Thus, partners could choose to enter the marriage prepared to engage in safe methods of sex and birth control. The other alternative has been passed by the California legislature. California imposes a duty on public health officials to provide full information concerning the risk groups for HIV, the importance of testing, and the need for safer behavior to all marriage license applicants. Legislatures considering this approach should provide free and confidential testing and counselling services as an adjunct to this informational requirement. Members of high risk groups intending to marry could thus be provided with a needed incentive to undergo testing voluntarily. . . .

INDIVIDUAL CONFIDENTIALITY AND PUBLIC HEALTH

The screening of selective populations involves the systematic collection of information about the health status of a class of individuals. Screening creates a conflict between the individual's interest in controlling access to personal information and society's right to know and use this information for public health purposes. The conflict between public health and confidentiality is apparent on two levels. First, knowledge that a person is infectious may create a duty to breach confidentiality in order to protect third parties. Second, reporting statutes require states to collect confidential personal information which they use for epidemiologic purposes to control the spread of infection. Balancing individual and collective rights is the most difficult task of legislators and judges when considering the use of information obtained from screening programs.

Confidentiality

Individuals infected with HIV are concerned with maintaining the confidentiality of their health status. HIV infection is associated with sexual practice and drug use, universally regarded as personal and sensitive activities. Consequently, the process of case identification *per se* triggers a concern of confidentiality. Also, the majority of people infected with HIV in the United States are members of groups subject to persistent prejudice and discrimination. Unauthorized disclosure of a person's serological status can lead to social opprobrium among family and friends, and to loss of employment, housing, and insurance. There is also a wide, constitutionally-protected zone of privacy which extends to intimate personal relationships. There are public health pressures to obtain detailed, sensitive information through medical surveillance and contact tracing, such as intrusive observation and forced disclosure of sexual partners.

Persons at risk of HIV infection, therefore, have strong grounds for desiring personal privacy and confidentiality of medical information. Their cooperation with public health authorities and treatment centers

304 CONTROLLING RISKS: AIDS AND OTHER DANGERS

is dependent upon expectations of confidentiality. Efforts to control the spread of AIDS currently rely upon voluntary restraint of behaviors likely to spread HIV. Therefore, the public health objective should be to influence the behavior of those infected with HIV. Trust in and compliance with public health programs depend upon the maintenance of confidentiality.

Most state public health statutes contain provisions protecting confidentiality. Typically, these provisions apply to venereal or sexually transmitted diseases (STDs) because of the deeply rooted personal values implicated by sexual behavior. Currently, one out of the twelve major jurisdictions studied by the federal government reports AIDS as a sexually transmitted disease; the remaining eleven classify it either as a communicable disease or simply as a reportable disease. This presents a major obstacle since communicable diseases are not generally covered by strong confidentiality statutes. While classifying AIDS as a sexually transmitted disease strengthens the confidentiality protections, it also makes individuals potentially subject to compulsory measures such as quarantine, which are often specifically targeted at such diseases.

Several states have enacted legislation or regulations to protect the confidentiality of HIV antibody test results. There is considerable variation in the confidentiality protection offered within these states. For example, California protects test results from subpoena, while Massachusetts simply requires laboratories to develop unspecified procedures for confidentiality.

A public health confidentiality statute should contain the following elements: a specific requirement that informed consent be given before the release of any information or records relating to known or suspected cases of infection, an exemption protecting the information from subpoena, and a testimonial privilege protecting state and local health officials, private health care professionals, and other holders of information. . . .

CONCLUSION

Every individual who becomes infected with HIV has approximately a 35 percent chance of developing clinical AIDS and ultimately dying of the disease. The protection of uninfected persons is critical. Infected individuals must be identified on a voluntary basis, and a comprehensive program of focused education and counseling is essential. To accomplish this, there must be a fully planned distribution of test sites in areas with high infection rates, and accessible, high quality public education and individual counseling services should be provided. This requires a political commitment of major resources toward prevention and infection control strategies. Yet, the Office of Technological Assessment in February, 1985 noted that "relatively few funds were allocated to public education" (Herdman, Behney, and Milkey, *Review of the Public Health Service's Response to AIDS: A Technical Memorandum,* 1985).

States must also enact statutes to protect the confidentiality of sensitive information obtained during testing, counselling, and contact tracing. Only by establishing a basis of trust in the privacy of public health programs can cooperation from vulnerable groups be fostered.

High quality testing and counselling services can help promote behavior change. Experience with hepatitis B virus, which is transmitted in much the same way as HIV, has demonstrated that voluntary compliance can reduce the spread of the disease. Emerging evidence on AIDS shows significant voluntary alteration of behavior is necessary to reduce the spread of the disease within vulnerable groups. In the absence of evidence that compulsory testing, screening, and reporting alters behavior more effectively than voluntary education and counselling programs, federal and state public health authorities should design their strategies and devote their resources toward voluntary services for groups vulnerable to HIV.

chapter 9

Roles and Careers

INTRODUCTION

Almost everyone needs to work for a living. And the exceptions usually pursue a career anyway. For careers can be a source of satisfaction and self-respect, providing a sense of active participation in the social world and opportunities for developing and applying abilities. Even fairly simple jobs can offer some measure of these rewards, especially if the person approaches the job with enthusiasm and looks for ways to add something more than is strictly required (this may be nothing more complicated than friendliness).

At work, some of people's actions are role-related. It is in doing these role-related actions that the person acts in the capacity of the job. It is often noticed that professionals—teachers, physicians, lawyers, judges, nurses—operate within a role and that distinctive moral concerns are raised by this fact.[1] But every job involves a role. Plumbers, business executives, salespeople, waiters and waitresses, stockbrokers, and cashiers operate within roles as they do their work. It is not the "business" of the cashier to advise the customer that the foods purchased are unhealthy according to the latest diet recommendations. And it is no part of the plumber's role to make aesthetic judgments about the color scheme of the bathroom. If they do these things, they are acting *outside* the work role. Although some people may find such nonrole activity irritating, usually it is tolerated or even welcomed, as long as it is not offensive and does not interfere with the work. People *have* work roles, but they *are* more than merely the player of the role; so it is often appropriate and humanly pleasing for people serving in a work role to do much outside the role.

It would be a different matter, however, if the cashier refused to sell the food to the customer on the grounds that she did not want to be responsible for the high cholesterol levels and bad health that might result. Here the action is role-related, but runs counter to the norms of the role (cashiers are supposed to sell whatever the buyer wants from the store). Is it morally justified to violate the requirements of a work role for the sake of moral principle? Does it matter what the principle is and what is morally at stake in its pursuit?

Professional roles sometimes allow (or require) conduct that seems morally suspect. For instance, a lawyer may have a professional duty to portray an honest witness as a liar. But outside the adversarial context of a trial, it would be unjust to portray an honest person as a liar. Is it morally justified to violate general moral principles for the sake of the requirements of a work role? Does it matter what the role is and what is morally at stake in having that role performed?

Professionals often claim that they know what is best for their clients or patients, and they sometimes act as they see fit without seeking consent from their clients. When consent is formally required (for instance, for a surgical procedure or to accept a plea bargain in a criminal case), the professional may "manufacture consent" by withholding information or subtly shading the information presented; there are many ways to manipulate someone into agreement, given the expertise and knowledge of the professional and the client's dependency and lack of technical knowledge. These are all forms of paternalism—treating clients as like children lacking full autonomy in decision making. Is such paternalism ever justified by the role responsibilities of professionals?[2]

There are also roles outside of work. Family roles seem to be of great moral importance to most people. The role of friend is central to many people's conceptions of themselves and of the good life, and the confidences and relationship of special concern found in friendship have been used to model the lawyer-client relationship.[3] Even when they are not really friends, colleagues often recognize special duties of role toward each other. Many other roles call out for a person's loyalty. Not only are there conflicts between general moral principles and the requirements of a role, there are also conflicts between different roles a person occupies. For instance, a wholesale representative who has over the years come to be a friend of a retailer may want to offer special discounts to his friend "in order to keep his valuable business" for the company, knowing that his friend would remain a customer without such a special deal. Assuming that the discounts are within the upper limit of what really would be offered to keep a client thinking of switching to a competitor, would the wholesale representative be acting properly? Giving special consideration to relatives and friends (and friends of friends) is common in hiring and in choosing whom to do business with. Is this fair to other job applicants and businesspeople? Is it fair to the employer or company, who might get better work or better products and services from some less "connected" provider? And the employer or company might then make more profit.

After all, businesses exist to make money. In *The Republic* Plato made much of the distinction between the craftsman's or professional's role as such, which is always directed toward some good for others, and the money-making role held concurrently.[4] The professions also make much of this distinction in their institutionalized ethics. The side-by-side existence of the professional role and the money-making role can lead to major conflicts for professionals. But for many businesspeople no such conflict of roles is possible—if they are to be called professionals, then their "profession" is making money, either for themselves or for their employers. It seems clear that in the pursuit of profit businesspeople ought not to violate the law or commit gross immoralities. Are there additional moral obligations that business should recognize? Do businesses have some responsibility to promote the general welfare, help solve social problems, and even promote respect for human rights internationally? This is one of the issues in the public debate concerning the involvement of U.S. companies in South Africa.[5]

But things are less tidy than this division between professionals and businesspeople suggests. The job role of an executive or manager is almost always more specific than maximizing profits and often is not concerned with maximizing profits at all. Within the total organization, the job may somehow contribute indirectly to increased profits (for instance, quality control may over the long run create more demand for the product), or the job may actually not even indirectly increase profits, though it may be necessary to doing business (for instance, someone charged with maintaining compliance with government regulations). And many businesses involve pride and a sense of accomplishment as well as profit making. When a small company is taken over by a large conglomerate, there are often worries not only about job security, but also that the conglomerate has no concern for the specific product or service to which the small company is devoted. People often choose their businesses because of interests they have. So it is not impossible for there to be conflicts between the money-making role and the "producer of first-rate widgets" role. Not everyone in business lacks the craftsman's concern to produce good work or the professional's concern for the client's well-being.

These craft and professional roles within businesses can lead to "whistle blowing," as can a more obvious conflict between the role of employees and general moral principles; often both conflicts are present. The whistle blower informs outsiders, usually government agencies or the public, that the company is doing something unacceptable (usually violating some standard or regulation). There have even been whistle blowers in the Defense Department, alerting Congress and the public to unacceptable practices. In private industry, whistle blowing often concerns issues of health and safety, either for workers or consumers. Employers (and sometimes fellow workers) see the whistle blower as disloyal. The problem with criticisms in terms of disloyalty is that there are almost always conflicting loyalties in a person's life, and even within the more limited context of a person's career. What are the limits of morally legitimate loyalty to an employer? When is whistle blowing morally permissible—for instance, is it permissible in the case of technical violations or fiscal irregularities, where no risk to others is created? Is it ever a moral *duty* to blow the whistle?

All of the moral problems raised by career roles require reflection about the place of differentiated social roles within general morality. The various normative ethical theories give differing accounts of the individual's relationship to society and thus differing accounts of the nature of role morality.

Natural Law   A traditional natural-law approach sees differentiated roles as natural to human social life, and sociality as natural to human beings. The division of roles within the family is used as a model for other divisions of responsibility, although no other community or organization is accorded the special position of the family itself. Natural-law approaches will accept a fairly large degree of paternalism within such professions as medicine, as long as the well-being of the client is the genuine aim of the professional. Individual choice is not seen as the only important value, since individuals are naturally members of collectivities and individual autonomy is located within a social setting of interdependency.

Duties of social role within organizations such as corporations cannot be absolute for two reasons. First, there are conflicts between various roles. No general and mechanical account can be given for resolving such conflicts; judgment and moral insight must be used, weighing the moral importance of the roles themselves and the importance of the specific duties within the roles. Second, duties attaching to roles are always governed by the absolute prohibitions against directly attacking goods that are intrinsic to persons. Thus no role can justify such actions as violence against the innocent or deception of others in order to make a profit.

Honest profitmaking within moral bounds is legitimate, but the natural-law theory does not see the rights of private property or contractual rights in isolation from the common good of the larger community. Thus business has a responsibility to society, for it is dependent upon the structures of the legal and social community. A holistic view is taken of career roles and the other social and family roles of the individual—the business executive is also a citizen, neighbor, and family member, and these other roles rightfully affect his or her performance of the career role.

Natural Rights   A natural-rights account insists on an individualist perspective. The model is not the family, but rather the contract. This model aims at explicitness concerning the rights and duties attaching to agreed upon roles, for only then will the role player and others involved be able to preserve their individual liberty. Unilateral understandings or general social expectations are not a fully sufficient basis for role morality. Thus, for instance, a professional has a right to treat a client paternalistically only if it is clear that the *individual client* intends that the professional have such a role.

A natural-rights approach denies that there are very many genuine conflicts between roles. Each role is defined by a specific area of action, which often can be indicated fairly well by time and place. Almost always there will be only one relevant role in a given practical situation. At work the employee is governed by the career role; there is no conflict with family role or the role of citizen, for these roles belong outside the workplace. Of course, the natural-rights view forbids the use of violence or deception in the name of career. But the explicit or implicit contracts under which the career role is assumed cannot justify direct invasions against the rights of those who are not party to the contracts—so career roles viewed contractually never call for violations of the rights of others.

This individualist account limits the social responsibility of business to the negative requirement that individual rights not be directly invaded. Unless the employer clearly intends otherwise, employees owe a strict contractual duty to leave family roles at home and the roles of neighbor and concerned citizen at the office or factory door. Typically, an implicit agreement exists that executives and managers will aim solely to maximize profits. Social responsibility is for off-hours.

Kant   A Kantian approach seeks to steer a middle course between the individualism of natural rights and the more communitarian approach of natural law. Many contemporary Kantians, however, tend to move toward the individualist approach, adopting a conception of autonomy that uses the model of contract exclusively. Kant himself made extensive use of the model of contract, but mainly when dealing with the realm of juridical and legal relations; in his view, the sphere of the ethical was not based on contract, but rather on the special and irreplaceble value of each rational being. Moral duties attached to roles were for Kant more extensive than for the natural-rights tradition, for the imperfect duty of benevolence made demands upon persons even within structured roles, such as those in the professions and in business. Kant himself would have seen nothing wrong with a degree of unilateral professional paternalism, as long as the intention was to promote the well-being of the client in ways that it would be rational for the client to consent to.

Conflicts between roles call for an evaluation of the moral claims of the competing roles. Normally perfect duties are negative: not to deceive, not to use violence except in self-defense, and so forth. But there are some perfect duties that are positive, and they typically attach to roles. The most obvious case is the role of parent, carrying with it positive perfect duties to provide for the child. Career roles could be said to carry positive perfect duties to perform the tasks of the job diligently, but unlike the role of parent, the career role does not itself have a categorical hold on the person. The person is free to abandon the role of business executive, for instance, whenever it creates an otherwise irresolvable and serious conflict with an obligatory role like parent (that is, obligatory once one is a parent—it is not obligatory to *become* a parent) or a conflict with some other optional role that the autonomous moral person considers of more importance in the moral life. The Kantian approach never allows the violation of perfect duties owed to persons as such in the name of the requirements of a role, whether the role is one that can be abandoned or not.

From a Kantian perspective, businesspeople do not cease to be under the demands of the imperfect duty of benevolence even in their work life. But since imperfect duties allow great latitude and discretion for the autonomous moral agent to choose the details of fulfilling the duties, the conscientious person will find ways to do good without failing to fulfill the demands of the job role. The benevolent manager or executive is not free to give the company less than it deserves, even in the name of helping others. The moral agent must struggle to fulfill the perfect duties attached to the job while also acknowledging social responsibility.

Contractarianism   Although Rawls uses a hypothetical social contract to work out his ethical theory, he is not committed to a thoroughly individualist and contractualist model of actual social relations within society. The original position is for Rawls only a way of intuitively representing constraints on moral reasoning. And so, unlike Nozick, Rawls actually emphasizes the values of social concern and solidarity. At the same time, there is in Rawls a Kantian insistence on the fundamental value of individual autonomy and self-respect. So in the original position it seems plausible that the contractors would choose principles requiring full respect for the autonomy of the client in professional roles, though allowing for paternalist actions in special cases where the client is not fully able to participate in decision making.

Rational contractors behind a veil of ignorance could address questions of conflicting roles only in the most abstract terms. Clearly, career roles would be given a subordinate place to stringent negative duties of general morality. But it is not clear what rational contractors would choose as a priority rule between specific career roles and general concern for the promotion of well-being in society. A hint may come from the second principle of justice, which allows for inequalities in wealth and position only if they benefit everyone (or, in the final version of the principle, only if they benefit the least advantaged). If differential roles of authority and wealth are justified only to promote the general welfare, or the welfare of the least advantaged, it would seem reasonable that conflicts of role between career and the role of concerned citizen would be resolved in favor of the role of citizen. Conflicts between more specific roles within the workplace would seem to have no systematic resolution for the contractarian. Only the role of socially responsible citizen can be said to have priority across the board.

Act Utilitarianism   An act-utilitarian account of role differentiation approaches the matter from the perspective of efficiency. Greater aggregate satisfaction may accrue by an individual tending to his or her own responsibilities of role rather than by a system lacking such specific responsibilities. Thus act utilitarians have generally favored arrange-

ments that connect role responsibilities with the interests of those playing the role. Parents should care primarily for their own children rather
than children in general, because this will lead to a greater aggregate
satisfaction of the interests of children. And in careers, individuals
should primarily strive for personal success, because this will lead to
greater productivity and eventually greater aggregate satisfaction of the
preferences of all. An act utilitarian gives no separate weight to autonomy as such, though a person's actual *preference* that she or he be fully
informed and consulted will count along with other preferences. Thus
professionals will act so as to promote the aggregate satisfaction of their
clients, and this will in some cases require acting paternalistically.

An act-utilitarian account of resolving conflicts of role is simple in
outline: perform the duties attached to the role only if in the long run
this maximizes aggregate satisfaction. But because of efficiency considerations, this does not mean that one ought always to perform the duties
attached to the role of concerned citizen, or whatever the most general
role is within the situation. Sometimes, however, the role of concerned
citizen will be given priority by an act utilitarian.

It might at first glance seem that an act utilitarian must insist on the
social responsibility of business. And in some contexts this is indeed the
case. Everything depends on whether in the concrete situation the greatest benefits are to be gained by the expenditure of resources and energy
directly upon furthering such social goals, or whether in the long run
devoting the resources to profit making will be more productive of
aggregate satisfaction. Good intentions and symbolic gestures do not
matter for the act utilitarian, and if actions of "social responsibility" lead
to waste or, even worse, produce unhappiness (for instance, by contributing to increased unemployment), then it was an illusion that the
actions were responsive to social needs. The natural-rights theorist insists
on the employee's duty to maximize profits for the company because the
employee owes the company that effort. The act utilitarian usually insists
on businesspeople sticking to the job of profit making because that is
what usually works best. In some extraordinary situations, an act utilitarian would calculate that aggregate satisfaction could be increased by
breaking the agreement to maximize profits, and then the agreement
itself would carry no moral weight (the losses consequent to breaking
the agreement already having been included in the calculation).

Rule Utilitarianism   A rule-utilitarian approach views institutional
and career roles as part of the background factual situation assumed in
evaluating alternative sets of moral rules. Thus differentiated role responsibilities are taken as provisionally set (though moral rules could
justify working to change some particular aspect of these institutional
arrangements), and the question is what moral rules to accept concerning
the performance of role responsibilities in order to maximize welfare.[6]
In contemporary society, general moral rules requiring respect for autonomous decision making would seem likely to apply to professional-

client relationships (allowing exceptions for those not competent to make decisions). At least in some professional contexts, paternalism leads to less satisfactory results than encouraging active client participation.[7] As with other rules, exceptions would not be allowed in individual cases merely to produce more satisfaction of interests in the particular case.

Conflicts between roles cannot all be resolved by reference to the rules of a utilitarian code, for it seems unlikely that rules relevant to resolving all kinds of role conflict would be included. But some roles are of special moral importance due to their impact on important interests. Family roles are thus the subject of special moral rules in most cultures, and this would likely be so in a utilitarian moral code for contemporary society. Some aspects of career roles (especially in the professions) might also receive such attention. But the responsibilities of most career roles are not particularly important from the viewpoint of a general utilitarian moral code. Where there is a conflict between such *mere* institutional expectations and a role of special importance to the moral code, a rule utilitarian will give priority to the morally special role. Of course, stringent moral rules against such things as violence will apply to actions performed within roles.

A utilitarian moral code will hold business responsible for *direct* promotion of the general welfare only if that will in fact maximize welfare in the long run; this seems unlikely to be the case under actual social conditions in the industrial nations and debatable for other contemporary societies. Thus generally there will be no moral rule directly to maximize aggregate welfare either in private life or in business; welfare will be maximized through acceptance of moral rules that do not directly aim at this end, but rather put limits on what actions are allowed or require specific kinds of actions in certain kinds of situation. Only the negative moral rules (for instance, against violence and deception) are generally relevant to business activity; within those constraints, the business executive is free to fulfill the role assigned by the employer.

Readings The selection from Milton Friedman represents a natural-rights viewpoint. Friedman considers business executives to be under an obligation to conduct business in accordance with the aims of their employers, which will normally be the maximization of profits. Friedman's view is thoroughly individualistic, emphasizing the rights of private property and the contractual freedom of individuals.

Dorothy Emmet explains the way social roles make life more determinate and predictable than would otherwise be the case. She emphasizes the element of Kantian universalization found within role morality. Special attention is given to the need for general and impersonal rules of conduct within the professions. But at the same time, the individual does not escape the final responsibility for autonomous moral judgment.

In the selection by Alex Michalos, the idea of being an agent for someone else is scrutinized. Michalos criticizes the "Loyal Agent's Argu-

ment." This kind of defense for otherwise questionable behavior is often found in business and professional life. Michalos concludes by endorsing an act-utilitarian approach to resolving conflicts between principles.

Notes

[1] A profession is marked by extensive intellectual training and provides an important service in society. Professionals are also usually licensed, organized as a group, and somewhat autonomous in their work. See Michael D. Bayles, *Professional Ethics* (Belmont, Cal.: Wadsworth, 1981), pp. 7–8.

[2] See Bayles, pp. 65–68.

[3] Charles Fried, "The Lawyer As Friend: The Moral Foundations of the Lawyer-Client Relationship," *Yale Law Journal* 85 (1976): 1060–1087.

[4] Plato, *The Republic,* trans. Francis MacDonald Cornford (Oxford: Oxford University Press, 1979), pp. 27–28 (Book I. 345–346), and see the discussion in the selection by Dorothy Emmet included in this chapter.

[5] See the double issue devoted entirely to apartheid, *Philosophical Forum* 18 (1987), no. 2–3 (Winter-Spring), and another entire issue, *Business and Society Review* Spring, 1986, no. 57. Also, see Robert N. McCauley, "The Moral Status of Apartheid: Can the Presence of Foreign Corporations in South Africa Be Morally Justified?" *Canadian Journal of Philosophy* 15 (1985): 565–580. For some sense of the complexity of the consequences of divestiture, see John D. Battersby, "U.S. Goods in South Africa: Little Impact of Divestiture," *New York Times,* July 27, 1987, p. 21, p. 25.

[6] See Richard B. Brandt, *A Theory of the Good and the Right* (Oxford: Oxford University Press, 1979), pp. 176–179.

[7] Bayles, p. 68.

Bibliography on Roles and Careers

Baum, Robert J., and Flores, Albert, eds. *Ethical Problems in Engineering.* Troy, N.Y.: Center for the Study of the Human Dimensions of Science and Technology, Rensselaer Polytechnic Institute, 1978.

Bayles, Michael D. *Professional Ethics,* 2nd. ed. Belmont, Cal.: Wadsworth, 1988.

Beauchamp, Tom L., and Bowie, Norman E., eds. *Ethical Theory and Business.* Englewood Cliffs, N.J.: Prentice-Hall, 1983.

Behrman, Jack N. *Essays on Ethics in Business and the Professions.* Englewood Cliffs, N.J.: Prentice-Hall, 1988.

Braybrooke, David. *Ethics in the World of Business.* Totowa, N.J.: Rowman and Allanheld, 1983.

Buchanan, Allen. "Medical Paternalism." *Philosophy and Public Affairs* 7 (1978): 370–390.

Callahan, Joan C., ed. *Ethical Issues in Professional Life.* Oxford: Oxford University Press, 1988.

Downie, R. S. *Roles and Values: An Introduction to Social Ethics.* London: Methuen, 1971.

Elliston, Frederick. "Civil Disobedience and Whistleblowing: A Comparative Appraisal of Two Forms of Dissent." *Journal of Business Ethics* 1 (1982): 23–28.

Emmet, Dorothy. *Rules, Roles, and Relations.* Boston: Beacon Press, 1966.

Flores, Albert, ed. *Professional Ideals.* Belmont, Cal.: Wadsworth, 1988.

Gert, Bernard, and Culver, Charles M. "Paternalistic Behavior." *Philosophy and Public Affairs* 6 (1976): 45–57.

Goldman, Alan H. *The Moral Foundations of Professional Ethics.* Totowa, N.J.: Rowman and Littlefield, 1980.

Gowans, Christopher W. "Integrity in the Corporation: The Plight of Corporate Product Advocates." *Journal of Business Ethics* 3 (1984): 21–28.

Jackson, J. A., ed. *Role.* Cambridge: Cambridge University Press, 1972.

Jensen, J. Vernon. "Ethical Tension Points in Whistleblowing." *Journal of Business Ethics* 6 (1987): 321–328.

Jones, W. T. "Public Roles, Private Roles, and Differential Moral Assessments of Role Performance." *Ethics* 94 (1984): 603–620.

Kipnis, Kenneth. *Legal Ethics.* Englewood Cliffs, N.J.: Prentice-Hall, 1986.

Lachs, John. " 'I Only Work Here': Mediation and Irresponsibility." In *Ethics, Free Enterprise, and Public Policy,* edited by Richard T. DeGeorge and Joseph A. Pichler, pp. 201–213. New York: Oxford University Press, 1978.

Luban, David, ed. *The Good Lawyer: Lawyers' Roles and Lawyers' Ethics.* Totowa, N.J.: Rowman and Allanheld, 1984.

Lydenberg, Steven D., Marlin, Alice Tepper, and Strub, Sean O'Brien. "Rating America's Corporate Conscience." *Business and Society Review* (Winter 1987): 27–31.

Machan, Tibor R., ed. *Commerce and Morality.* Totowa, N.J.: Rowman and Littlefield, 1988.

Machan, Tibor R., and DenUyl, Douglas. "Recent Work in Business Ethics: A Survey and Critique." *American Philosophical Quarterly* (1987): 107–121.

Masters, Roger D. "Is Contract an Adequate Basis for Medical Ethics?" *Hastings Center Report* 5 (December 1975): 24–28.

May, William F. "Code, Covenant, Contract, or Philanthropy?" *Hastings Center Report* 5 (December 1975): 29–38.

"The Public Duties of the Professions." Special Supplement. *Hastings Center Report* 17, no. 1 (February 1987), pp. 1–20.

Regan, Tom, ed. *Just Business: New Introductory Essays in Business Ethics.* New York: Random House, 1984.

Veatch, Robert M. "Medical Ethics: Professional or Universal?" *Harvard Theological Review* 65 (1972): 531–559.

Wasserstrom, Richard. "Lawyers as Professionals: Some Moral Issues." *Human Rights* 5 (1975): 1–24. Reprinted in *Today's Moral Problems,* 3rd. ed., edited by Richard Wasserstrom. New York: Macmillan, 1985, pp. 274–292.

Werhane, Patricia. *Persons, Rights, and Corporations.* Englewood Cliffs, N.J.: Prentice-Hall, 1985.

Westra, Laura S. "Whose 'Loyal Agent'? Towards an Ethic of Accounting." *Journal of Business Ethics* 5 (1986): 119–128.

Problem Case

The Conscientious Cashier

She was 21 years old and working as a cashier at a supermarket in Dublin, Ireland. The Irish Distributive and Allied Trades Union had called on her and its other members to support a boycott of South African products in order to fight apartheid.

She was a conscientious worker, interested in performing her job well. She was also a conscientious supporter of the union. And, even apart from the union's stance, she took moral issues seriously. She considered herself a citizen not just of Ireland, but of the world. Apartheid was not merely morally flawed, the way so many things were. Apartheid, she thought, was *evil,* comparable to systems of slavery and, to some degree, even comparable to the Nazis. She vowed to do all she could to fight the evil.

A customer came to her cash register with some items. Among them was a can of citrus fruit, clearly marked "Product of South Africa." She refused to ring it up. The management of the supermarket suspended her. Ten of her fellow workers walked out in support.

Was it morally permissible for the cashier to refuse to sell the South African product? Was it her moral *obligation* to refuse? If it is appropriate for business executives or physicians to follow their consciences within career roles, would it be a form of class prejudice not to allow ordinary workers the same privilege? Did management act in a morally acceptable way in suspending her? How far ought one to go in expressing opposition to apartheid? For instance, is it morally acceptable to take a job with a company that sells its products in South Africa? Suppose the company stopped direct marketing in South Africa, but only because it knows that intermediaries will make its products readily available there? (See Annie Street, "Irish Workers Strike a Blow Against Apartheid," *Business and Society Review* (Winter 1986): 46–49.)

MILTON FRIEDMAN
THE SOCIAL RESPONSIBILITY OF BUSINESS IS TO INCREASE ITS PROFITS

When I hear businessmen speak eloquently about the "social responsibilities of business in a free-enterprise system," I am reminded of the wonderful line about the Frenchman who discovered at the age of 70 that he had been speaking prose all his life. The businessmen believe that they are defending free enterprise when they declaim that business is not concerned "merely" with profit but also with promoting desirable "social" ends; that business has a "social conscience" and takes seriously its responsibilities for providing employment, eliminating discrimination, avoiding pollution and whatever else may be the catchwords of the contemporary crop of reformers. In fact they are—or would be if they or anyone else took them seriously—preaching pure and unadulterated socialism. Businessmen who talk this way are unwitting puppets of the intellectual forces that have been undermining the basis of a free society these past decades.

From *The New York Times Magazine,* September 13, 1970. Copyright © 1970 by The New York Times Company. Reprinted by permission.

The discussions of the "social responsibilities of business" are notable for their analytical looseness and lack of rigor. What does it mean to say that "business" has responsibilities? Only people can have responsibilities. A corporation is an artificial person and in this sense may have artificial responsibilities, but "business" as a whole cannot be said to have responsibilities, even in this vague sense. The first step toward clarity in examining the doctrine of the social responsibility of business is to ask precisely what it implies for whom.

Presumably, the individuals who are to be responsible are businessmen, which means individual proprietors or corporate executives. Most of the discussion of social responsibility is directed at corporations, so in what follows I shall mostly neglect the individual proprietor and speak of corporate executives.

In a free-enterprise, private-property system, a corporate executive is an employee of the owners of the business. He has direct responsibility to his employers. That responsibility is to conduct the business in accordance with their desires, which generally will be to make as much money as possible while conforming to the basic rules of the society, both those embodied in law and those embodied in ethical custom. Of course, in some cases his employers may have a different objective. A group of persons might establish a corporation for an eleemosynary purpose—for example, a hospital or a school. The manager of such a corporation will not have money profit as his objective but the rendering of certain services.

In either case, the key point is that, in his capacity as a corporate executive, the manager is the agent of the individuals who own the corporation or establish the eleemosynary institution, and his primary responsibility is to them.

Needless to say, this does not mean that it is easy to judge how well he is performing his task. But at least the criterion of performance is straightforward, and the persons among whom a voluntary contractual arrangement exists are clearly defined.

Of course, the corporate executive is also a person in his own right. As a person, he may have many other responsibilities that he recognizes or assumes voluntarily—to his family, his conscience, his feelings of charity, his church, his clubs, his city, his country. He may feel impelled by these responsibilities to devote part of his income to causes he regards as worthy, to refuse to work for particular corporations, even to leave his job, for example, to join his country's armed forces. If we wish, we may refer to some of these responsibilities as "social responsibilities." But in these respects he is acting as a principal, not an agent; he is spending his own money or time or energy, not the money of his employers or the time or energy he has contracted to devote to their purposes. If these are "social responsibilities," they are the social responsibilities of individuals, not of business.

What does it mean to say that the corporate executive has a "social responsibility" in his capacity as businessman? If this statement is not pure rhetoric, it must mean that he is to act in some way that is not in the interest of his employers. For example, that he is to refrain from increasing the price of the product in order to contribute to the social objective of preventing inflation, even though a price increase would be in the best interests of the corporation. Or that he is to make expenditures on reducing pollution beyond the amount that is in the best interests of the corporation or that is required by law in order to contribute to the social objective of improving the environment. Or that, at the expense of corporate profits, he is to hire "hard-core" unemployed instead of better-qualified available workmen to contribute to the social objective of reducing poverty.

In each of these cases, the corporate executive would be spending someone else's money for a general social interest. Insofar as his actions in accord with his "social responsibility" reduce returns to stockholders, he is spending their money. Insofar as his actions raise the price to customers, he is spending the customers' money. Insofar as his actions lower the wages of some employes, he is spending their money.

The stockholders or the customers or the employes could separately spend their own money on the particular action if they wished to do so. The executive is exercising a distinct "social responsibility," rather than serving as an agent of the stockholders or the customers or the employes, only if he spends the money in a different way than they would have spent it.

But if he does this, he is in effect imposing taxes, on the one hand, and deciding how the tax proceeds shall be spent, on the other.

This process raises political questions on two levels: principle and consequences. On the level of political principle, the imposition of taxes and the expenditure of tax proceeds are governmental functions. We have established elaborate constitutional, parliamentary and judicial provisions to control these functions, to assure that taxes are imposed so far as possible in accordance with the preferences and desires of the public—after all, "taxation without representation" was one of the battle cries of the American Revolution. We have a system of checks and balances to separate the legislative function of imposing taxes and enacting expenditures from the executive function of collecting taxes and administering expenditure programs and from the judicial function of mediating disputes and interpreting the law.

Here the businessman—self-selected or appointed directly or indirectly by stockholders—is to be simultaneously legislator, executive and jurist. He is to decide whom to tax by how much and for what purpose, and he is to spend the proceeds—all this guided only by general exhortations from on high to restrain inflation, improve the environment, fight poverty and so on and on.

The whole justification for permitting the corporate executive to be selected by the stockholders is that the executive is an agent serving the interests of his principal. This justification disappears when the corporate executive imposes taxes and spends the proceeds for "social" purposes. He becomes in effect a public employee, a civil servant, even though he remains in name an employee of a private enterprise. On grounds of political principle, it is intolerable that such civil servants—insofar as their actions in the name of social responsibility are real and not just window-dressing—should be selected as they are now. If they are to be civil servants, then they must be selected through a political process. If they are to impose taxes and make expenditures to foster "social" objectives, then political machinery must be set up to guide the assessment of taxes and to determine through a political process the objectives to be served.

This is the basic reason why the doctrine of "social responsibility" involves the acceptance of the socialist view that political mechanisms, not market mechanisms, are the appropriate way to determine the allocation of scarce resources to alternative uses.

On the grounds of consequences, can the corporate executive in fact discharge his alleged "social responsibilities"? On the one hand, suppose he could get away with spending the stockholders' or customers' or employees' money. How is he to know how to spend it? He is told that he must contribute to fighting inflation. How is he to know what action of his will contribute to that end? He is presumably an expert in running his company—in producing a product or selling it or financing it. But nothing about his selection makes him an expert on inflation. Will his holding down the price of his product reduce inflationary pressure? Or, by leaving more spending power in the hands of his customers, simply divert it elsewhere? Or, by forcing him to produce less because of the lower price, will it simply contribute to shortages? Even if he could answer these questions, how much cost is he justified in imposing on his stockholders, customers and employes for this social purpose? What is his appropriate share and what is the appropriate share of others?

And, whether he wants to or not, can he get away with spending his stockholders', customers' or employes' money? Will not the stockholders fire him? (Either the present ones or those who take over when his actions in the name of social responsibility have reduced the corporation's profits and the price of its stock.) His customers and his employes can desert him for other producers and employers less scrupulous in exercising their social responsibilities.

This facet of "social responsibility" doctrine is brought into sharp relief when the doctrine is used to justify wage restraint by trade unions. The conflict of interest is naked and clear when union officials are asked to subordinate the interest of their members to some more general social purpose. If the union officials try to enforce wage restraint, the consequence is likely to be wildcat strikes, rank-and-file revolts and the emergence of strong competitors for their jobs. We thus have the ironic phenomenon that union leaders—at least in the U.S.—have objected to

Government interference with the market far more consistently and courageously than have business leaders.

The difficulty of exercising "social responsibility" illustrates, of course, the great virtue of private competitive enterprise—it forces people to be responsible for their own actions and makes it difficult for them to "exploit" other people for either selfish or unselfish purposes. They can do good—but only at their own expense.

Many a reader who has followed the argument this far may be tempted to remonstrate that it is all well and good to speak of government's having the responsibility to impose taxes and determine expenditures for such "social" purposes as controlling pollution or training the hard-core unemployed, but that the problems are too urgent to wait on the slow course of political processes, that the exercise of social responsibility by businessmen is a quicker and surer way to solve pressing current problems.

Aside from the question of fact—I share Adam Smith's skepticism about the benefits that can be expected from "those who affected to trade for the public good"—this argument must be rejected on grounds of principle. What it amounts to is an assertion that those who favor the taxes and expenditures in question have failed to persuade a majority of their fellow citizens to be of like mind and that they are seeking to attain by undemocratic procedures what they cannot attain by democratic procedures. In a free society, it is hard for "good" people to do "good," but that is a small price to pay for making it hard for "evil" people to do "evil," especially since one man's good is another's evil.

I have, for simplicity, concentrated on the special case of the corporate executive, except only for the brief digression on trade unions. But precisely the same argument applies to the newer phenomenon of calling upon stockholders to require corporations to exercise social responsibility. . . . In most of these cases, what is in effect involved is some stockholders trying to get other stockholders (or customers or employes) to contribute against their will to "social" causes favored by the activists. Insofar as they succeed, they are again imposing taxes and spending the proceeds.

The situation of the individual proprietor is somewhat different. If he acts to reduce the returns of his enterprise in order to exercise his "social responsibility," he is spending his own money, not someone else's. If he wishes to spend his money on such purposes, that is his right, and I cannot see that there is any objection to his doing so. In the process, he, too, may impose costs on employes and customers. However, because he is far less likely than a large corporation or union to have monopolistic power, any such side effects will tend to be minor.

Of course, in practice the doctrine of social responsibility is frequently a cloak for actions that are justified on other grounds rather than a reason for those actions.

To illustrate, it may well be in the long-run interest of a corporation that is a major employer in a small community to devote resources to providing amenities to that community or to improving its government. That may make it easier to attract desirable employes, it may reduce the wage bill or lessen losses from pilferage and sabotage or have other worthwile effects. Or it may be that, given the laws about the deductibility of corporate charitable contributions, the stockholders can contribute more to charities they favor by having the corporation make the gift than by doing it themselves, since they can in that way contribute an amount that would otherwise have been paid as corporate taxes.

In each of these—and many similar—cases, there is a strong temptation to rationalize these actions as an exercise of "social responsibility." In the present climate of opinion, with its widespread aversion to "capitalism," "profits," the "soulless corporation" and so on, this is one way for a corporation to generate goodwill as a by-product of expenditures that are entirely justified in its own self-interest.

It would be inconsistent of me to call on corporate executives to refrain from this hypocritical window-dressing because it harms the foundations of a free society. That would be to call on them to exercise a "social responsibility"! If our institutions, and the attitudes of the public make it in their self-interest to cloak their actions in this way, I cannot summon much indignation to denounce them. At the same time, I can express admiration for those individual proprietors or owners of closely held corporations or stockholders of more broadly held corporations who disdain such tactics as approaching fraud.

Whether blameworthy or not, the use of the cloak of social responsibility, and the nonsense spoken in its name by influential and prestigious businessmen, does clearly harm the foundations of a free society. I have been impressed time and again by the schizophrenic character of many businessmen. They are capable of being extremely far-sighted and clear-headed in matters that are internal to their businesses. They are incredibly short-sighted and muddle-headed in matters that are outside their businesses but affect the possible survival of business in general. This short-sightedness is strikingly exemplified in the calls from many businessmen for wage and price guidelines or controls or incomes policies. There is nothing that could do more in a brief period to destroy a market system and replace it by a centrally controlled system than effective governmental control of prices and wages.

The short-sightedness is also exemplified in speeches by businessmen on social responsibility. This may gain them kudos in the short run. But it helps to strengthen the already too prevalent view that the pursuit of profits is wicked and immoral and must be curbed and controlled by external forces. Once this view is adopted, the external forces that curb the market will not be the social consciences, however, highly developed, of the pontificating executives; it will be the iron fist of Government bureaucrats. Here, as with price and wage controls, businessmen seem to me to reveal a suicidal impulse.

The political principle that underlies the market mechanism is unanimity. In an ideal free market resting on private property, no individual can coerce any other, all cooperation is voluntary, all parties to such cooperation benefit or they need not participate. There are no "social" values, no "social" responsibilities in any sense other than the shared values and responsibilities of individuals. Society is a collection of individuals and of the various groups they voluntarily form.

The political principle that underlies the political mechanism is conformity. The individual must serve a more general social interest— whether that be determined by a church or a dictator or a majority. The individual may have a vote and a say in what is to be done, but if he is overruled, he must conform. It is appropriate for some to require others to contribute to a general social purpose whether they wish to or not.

Unfortunately, unanimity is not always feasible. There are some respects in which conformity appears unavoidable, so I do not see how one can avoid the use of the political mechanism altogether.

But the doctrine of "social responsibility" taken seriously would extend the scope of the political mechanism to every human activity. It does not differ in philosophy from the most explicitly collectivist doctrine. It differs only by professing to believe that collectivist ends can be attained without collectivist means. That is why, in my book "Capitalism and Freedom," I have called it a "fundamentally subversive doctrine" in a free society, and have said that in such a society, "there is one and only one social responsibility of business—to use its resources and engage in activities designed to increase its profits so long as it stays within the rules of the game, which is to say, engages in open and free competition without deception or fraud."

DOROTHY EMMET
ROLES, PROFESSIONS, AND MORAL RESPONSIBILITY

. . . [There are] very real claims and counterclaims which people's roles make upon them as they interact in actual social life. I have said 'counterclaims' advisedly, since these role obligations are not necessarily harmonious. Hence the difficulty of talking of 'the social system' as though it were unitary and coherent. There is of course an over-all status in membership of the society, and if we are considering a territorial society, there is an overriding legal system, and sometimes, though not always, a common political status of citizenship. At any rate everyone is within the bounds of law and government. Within this, there are constellations of roles, e.g. in family relations and in professional relations, and these

From Dorothy Emmet, *Rules, Roles and Relations* (New York: St. Martin's Press, 1966), pp. 146–148, 152, 154–159, 161–166. Reprinted by permission.

are not necessarily coherent; in fact their obligations can and do conflict. So we can talk about 'a system' in the loose sense of an array of elements all of which are determined by some at least of the other elements. 'Array' here means more than a haphazard assemblage, because of common ties of legal status and membership of the society. But within this only some complexes of the role elements are linked with others; it is not a 'coherent' system in the sense of one in which the mutual determination of elements is complete, every role being related to every other role. The expression 'the social system' should therefore be used with caution with this in mind. . . .

What, considered abstractly, is the superimposition of two fields, or role complexes, may appear to the individual as a painful choice between conflicting claims. A person finds himself in more than one constellation of roles, i.e. in 'multiple roles' and also in tensions between different claims within the same 'role-set'. But in deciding what he ought to do, he will be likely to take into account, even if only to reject, notions of what is expected, e.g. of a son or of a headman. Social morality as well as custom, whether it comes to the individual as obligation or pressure to conform, or as occasion for rebellion and conflict, arises out of the possibility of making distinctions intuitively. . . . It is only in extreme Existentialist literature that people can live just as 'Outsiders' or pure individuals, with no interest but one of contempt for role morality, with no awareness of problems arising out of possible conflicts between their roles, and with no institutional loyalties. The notion of role reflects this complexity in human moral consciousness and in the ways in which people see their social demands, as well as indicating the possibility of abstracting a regular pattern of social interaction. . . .

An Existentialist will see role morality as conforming to an expected type and being guided by rules, and so as sub-personal *'mauvaise foi'.* [1] The metaphor of 'play-acting' can also be invoked, and the dead metaphor in 'hypocrite' revived; it may be said that a person is not acting from his own deep and individual powers of self-expression or responsible decision, but is thinking of how other people see him. This is put very forcibly by Sartre.[2] To accept a role is to evade the responsibility of seeing that one is free not so to act, and of freely deciding what one wants to be. It is to evade freedom by sheltering behind one's social function. This freedom Sartre calls 'contingency': the terrifying realization that there is no need to play this role, or indeed any other in particular, unless one so chooses. . . .

The Existentialist has his point. There is a real temptation to seek security in having a function, especially if it is one that carries 'status' (in the colloquial prestige sense, not the sociological sense, where a status is simply any position in a social structure). But is it not possible to take role and function seriously without absorbing the person in the *persona*? (We shall return to this.) And is Sartre right in saying that 'society demands that a grocer limit himself to his function as a grocer'? There is indeed an epitaph on a tombstone in a Scottish burial-ground which reads 'Here lies the body of Tammas Jones, who was born a man and died a grocer'.[3] But 'society' in general is an abstraction. It can be broken down into numbers of people some of whom meet the grocer *qua* grocer in the role of his customers, others of whom meet him as fellow members of his local church council or bowling club, others as members of his family and his friends. Sartre speaks as if there was one role with which a person can identify himself. In fact 'one man in his time plays many parts', and these not only successive ones.[4] Their obligations may pull him in different directions, and he has to find his own way of dealing with such conflicts. The fact that *different* roles and their obligations press upon the same person makes it impossible to think of him realistically as simply the incumbent of a role, though abstractly he can be so thought of as an element in a Social Structure.

Yet the Existentialist still has a point. It is possible for those who deal with grocers to forget that they are also human beings; hence the need for the protective regulations of Shop Acts, Early Closing Days and the like. Are we left then with an antithesis between role behaviour on the one hand with its legal and moral regulations, which Sartre says evades the full freedom and responsibility of the individual, and on the other hand, a purely personal morality, free, spontaneous, unbound by rules?

The trouble about this antithesis is that it hardly comes to grips with social morality, and whether we like it or not, social morality impinges on our lives most of the time. We had much better recognize and respect the fact that, as Aristotle remarked, he that could live apart from society might be a beast or a god, but not a human being. (Solitary hermits have not been born such; they are also visited occasionally, and they relate themselves to God and the world in prayer.) To live in society means, we have seen, that a certain number of reasonably stable functions and expectations can be depended on. There may be a variety of 'reference groups' in any given society, a choice of the groups whose standards one respects, or in whose eyes one wants to be in good standing. Those who most want to assert their freedom to be a law to themselves and to contract out of established society—Outsiders, Beats or their *avant-garde* successors—soon begin to produce their own codes defining what is in and what is out in their circles. Feiffer in some of his cartoons has satirized the anguish of the Beat who is uncertain where he stands in his nonconformist conformity. We probably all need approval and support from some people at least some of the time. . . . The person who makes a stand on a specific issue is more likely to be effective if he is not known as a professional objector. We all know the stage army of the good, who are brought in to sign protests on every possible issue, and no doubt they form a reference group of great solidarity among themselves.

Both role behaviour and the mutual support of people for one another in their reference groups thus go deep into our everyday lives, and do not merely provide useful abstractions for sociological theory. They may even be bound up with our own awareness of ourselves as agents.

At least this was the view of G. H. Mead, who was probably responsible for introducing the notion of 'role' in its sociological sense.[5] The development of self-consciousness, according to Mead, comes through one's being able to call out responses in oneself as well as in others. So comes a realization of others as related to oneself and oneself to others, and thus their attitudes become internalized in an attitude to oneself. Mead's view of the internalized attitude of a 'generalized Other' has obvious affinities with Freud's Super Ego, but it is less closely bound up with immediate emotional ties with the parents.[6] A person to Mead is built up out of internalized roles, so that 'the expectations of others have thus become the self-expectations of a self-steering person'.[7] Mead does not imply that an individual is nothing but a collection of roles: indeed he repudiates this. He does not deny that an individual may have his own style and character; what he underlines is that this exists and develops through relationships to others. In 'reflexive' role-taking a person learns to see himself through the attitudes of others and to enter imaginatively into their roles. This may produce a 'What will they say?' kind of conscience; it may also go on to become something more objective—the notion of how one might appear to someone not directly involved in the situation, in fact Adam Smith's 'impartial spectator'. This clearly links up with the notion of Universalizability, the possibility of judging what one ought to do in a given situation by not making an exception in one's own favour to what one would judge anyone else similarly placed ought to do. Sartre, indeed, with all his Existentialism, is Kantian enough to allow this. One may not always have a precedent to follow in making a decision, but one is creating a precedent; for in legislating for oneself, he says, one legislates for the whole world.

Role morality represents this impersonal element in morality. In a role one is a person of a certain kind put in a certain kind of relationship, and thus detached from purely personal idiosyncrasy. We shall be concerned later with whether a person can also achieve detachment from his roles; that is another story. Here we are concerned with the character of role morality. As a directive for behaviour in certain kinds of relationship, it is structured by rules; if not by explicit and sanctioned rules, at least by implicit understandings, and maxims, or rules of thumb, as to how such a person would behave in this kind of relationship.

The most articulate case of this, where the rules have been deliberately thought out, is a professional code. A profession, to quote Talcott Parsons, 'is a cluster of occupational roles, that is roles in which the incumbents perform certain functions valued in the society in general, and by these activities, typically earn a living at a full time job. Among occupational role types, the professional is distinguished largely by the independent trusteeship exercised by the incumbents of a class of such roles of an important part of the major cultural tradition of the society.'[8] A profession thus carries with it the notion of a standard of performance; it is not only a way of making a living, but one in which the practitioners have a fiduciary trust to maintain certain standards. These are partly standards of competence, or technical ability in carrying out 'functions valued in the society'. But not only so: professional competence has to be joined with professional integrity. The implications of this in a particular profession have been the concern of professional codes from the Hippocratic Oath (about the 4th century B.C.) onwards. A professional man carries out his function in relation to people who also stand in a particular role relation to him. The relationship carries specific obligations, to be distinguished from those of purely personal morality, or from general obligations to human beings as such. It must be distinguished from these, but it may overlap with them, and in some cases this may produce acute moral problems. Because of these difficulties and potential conflicts, some of the older established professions, notably medicine and the law, have formulated principles of professional conduct to guide their practitioners, and violation of these can be matters of discipline within the profession itself. Conduct prescribed by a professional code encourages such confidence between the professional person and his client as will make it more likely that the function in which they are both interested will be carried out successfully. This is a clear case where a morality cannot be looked on as purely a matter of feeling or convention, since here at any rate it can be given a rational justification in terms of the requirements of the job. An instance is the obligation on doctors and lawyers not to divulge confidential information about their clients' affairs to third parties. The assurance that communications will be respected is necessary to establish confidence between the practitioner and his client. . . . Communications between lawyers and their clients are privileged. The reasons for this were given by Knight-Bruce L.J. (1846). 'Truth, like all other good things, may be loved unwisely—may be pursued too keenly—may cost too much. And surely the meanness and the mischief of prying into a man's confidential consultations with his legal adviser, the general evil of infusing reserve and dissimulation, uneasiness, suspicion and fear into those communications which must take place, and which, unless in a condition of perfect security, must take place uselessly or worse, are too great a price to pay for truth itself.'[9] The relation between the professional person and his client is, however, only one of the role relationships in which he is professionally concerned. His 'role-set' comprises also his relationships to his colleagues, and his relations as a professional person to the lay public. Thus, though a barrister is under an obligation not to divulge communications between himself and his client, he also has a duty to the court and to the cause of justice. While his duty is to put the best interpretation he can on the evidence in the interest of his client, he must not deceive the court by making a statement he knows to be false. Professional ethics as between colleagues are intended as means of maintaining mutual trust and collaboration within the profession. . . .

A professional code can therefore be justified on functional grounds, as promoting the kind of relationship within which a job is most likely to be done effectively. But its importance is not only functional; the behaviour becomes valued on its own account as a matter of professional integrity, and adds to the respect with which a professional person is regarded in the community. This does not mean, however, that every-thing about professional codes is beyond criticism. They are in the nature of the case pre-eminently conservative, in the literal sense as conserving the moral and intellectual tradition of the profession, and also in the sense of being administered by what tends to be a conservative hierar-chy, not always adaptable to new demands and new social conditions. . . . And since professional people are generally interested, in a more or less polite way, in being well paid, it is possible for the public to be cynical about 'professional services'. Nevertheless, it is part of the notion of a profession that payment is for *services* in which the practitioner is concerned with the interests of his clients, and in some professions it is against the code to sue for unpaid fees. Socrates put the point long ago: 'This benefit, then,—the receipt of wages—does not come to a man from his special art. If we are to speak strictly, the physician, as such, produces health; the builder, a house; and then each, in his further capacity of wage-earner, gets his pay. Thus every art has its own function and benefits its proper subject' (*Republic,* 346 d). A profession combines both these 'arts', and the importance of the professions in our society shows that a simple distinction between self-interested and altruistic conduct cannot always be maintained. 'Professional conduct' is so designed as to make the motives of desire for success, of service to others and of personal integrity tend to point in the same direction. This may not be the deepest form of sacrificial morality; nor in a largely competitive society is it one to be despised.

I have said that a professional code is a matter of role morality, to be distinguished from a universal morality of person to person. It is concerned with how one should act in a certain capacity. Yet at the same time we esteem the doctor or teacher who also 'treats people as people' (i.e. with the 'concern' as well as the 'detachment'). This does not mean that the special restraints of the role can be abrogated by entering into a purely personal relation or by mixing one's roles. Thus, it can be part of a code that one should not use professional influence to get one's friend or relative a job where his claims may not be as strong as those of other candidates. This professional disapproval of 'nepotism' may be culture bound to Western society, in that in some other cultures it is said to be a first duty of anyone who gets into a position of influence to look out for the interest of his friends and relatives and fit them out with good jobs. This must surely produce real moral conflicts in the minds of new-comers to responsible positions in some of the newly developing countries. But if we say that the professional tradition against nepotism is culture bound, does this mean that it is purely a relativistic matter of historical development? Or are there good reasons against nepotism, reasons which are an application of the wider principle that one should not adjudicate on a matter in which one has an interest—or if one must do so one should declare one's interest? This in turn is part of the still wider principle that justice should not only be done, but be seen to be done.

This is only one of the ways in which personal demands of friendship and family may come into conflict with the demands of a role morality. The professional person will be subject to all sorts of pressures for time and attention as well as for favour. Here a professional code can help, for instance by enabling him to say that there are some things he is not at liberty to do. Such restrictions, while in one sense limiting his freedom, in another sense can safeguard it, in making it clear that there are some matters about which he is not open to argument. Problems of role morality can also arise where there is a conflict of roles, e.g. that of scientific researcher and of medical practitioner. This is the subject of a code of ethics on experiments on human subjects, both in clinical research while they are undergoing professional treatment, and in non-therapeutic clinical research, which has recently been accepted by the World Medical Association.[10] In the former case, it is stated that 'the doctor can combine clinical research with professional care, the objective being the acquisition of new medical knowledge, only to the extent that clinical research is justified by its therapeutic value for the patient'. If at all possible the doctor should obtain the patient's freely given consent after full explanation. If this is not possible, on account of legal or physical incapacity, the consent of the legal guardian should be obtained. In the latter case, the nature, purpose and risk of clinical research must be explained to the subject, and his free consent obtained. It is also stated that in non-therapeutic research 'the subject of clinical research should be in such a mental, physical and legal state as to be able to exercise fully his power of choice', that at any time he should be free to withdraw permission, and that the investigator should discontinue the research if in his judgment it may prove harmful to the individual.

The code is explicitly based on the assumption that a human subject on whom experiments may be carried out is a *person* with reason and power of choice (a 'subject' indeed, and not an 'object' of experiment); or if, through legal or physical incapacity he cannot exercise these powers, his legal guardian must exercise them on his behalf. Thus, here in contrast with the idea that to apply science to human subjects involves regarding them deterministically, this ethical code for a certain area of scientific experiment is based on an assertion of their right to be treated as capable of rational and responsible decisions. In this way such a code, far from leading to a streamlined and inhuman way of looking on human subjects, can stress mutual responsibility within a professional relationship.

Yet, however much a professional code may give guidance on some matters, there will still be conflicts and pressures where a person is thrown back on his own moral resources, and where to see a solution may call for a high degree of intelligence. . . .

It is surely no evasion of the moral responsibility of the individual to ask that some lines may be laid down for his guidance in some of the more typically recurrent problems and temptations which he will meet in his professional roles. For it is abundantly clear that this will not mean that his own powers of moral judgment need go unexercised.

Notes

[1]"Bad faith"—a kind of false consciousness involving the denial of one's radical freedom and responsibility. The concept is important in the thought of Jean-Paul Sartre and other existentialists, who emphasize the existence of the individual as a free and responsible conscious chooser. Eds.

[2]See *L'Etre et le Néant.* English translation by Hazel E. Barnes, *Being and Nothingness* (London, 1957).

[3]Quoted by W. L. Sperry, *The Ethical Basis of Medical Practice* (London, 1951), p. 41.

[4]As in Jaques' speech: *As You Like It,* Act II, Sc. VII, ll. 139–166.

[5]Cf. *Mind, Self and Society,* edited by C. H. Morris (Chicago, 1934). The highly influential lectures out of which this book was composed had been given from 1904 onwards.

[6]Talcott Parsons similarly, and explicitly, takes a broader view than Freud of the Super Ego, through seeing it as the internalizing of a wider range of social relationships. See 'The Super Ego and the Theory of Social Systems', in *Working Papers in the Theory of Action* (with R. F. Bales and E. A. Shils, New York, 1953).

[7]Gerth and Mills, *Character and Social Structure* (London, 1954), p. 84. This book develops Mead's initial view in terms of contemporary social psychology.

[8]*Essays in Sociological Theory,* revised edition (Free Press, Ill., 1954), p. 372. The papers 'A sociologist looks at the legal profession' and 'The Professions and Social Structure' in this volume are a full and interesting treatment of the notion of a professional role; as is also Chapter X, 'The case of modern medical practice', in Talcott Parsons' *The Social System* (Tavistock Publications, London and New York, 1952).

[9]Pearse *v.* Pearse (1846): I De Gex and Sm. 28, 29. Quoted by Quenton Edwards in 'The Law of Privilege', *Crucible* (Jan. 1964).

[10]The final draft, as accepted by the W.M.A. at Helsinki in June, 1964, and known as the 'Declaration of Helsinki', has been printed in full in the *British Medical Journal,* July 18th, 1964, with a supporting editorial.

ALEX C. MICHALOS
THE LOYAL AGENT'S ARGUMENT

INTRODUCTION

According to the Report of the Special Review Committee of the Board of Directors of Gulf Oil Corporation:

> It is not too much to say that the activity of those Gulf officials involved in making domestic political contributions with corporate funds during the

This essay was written for the Conference on Ethics and Economics at the University of Delaware, Newark, Delaware, November 10–12, 1977. Copyright © 1978 by Alex C. Michalos. Reprinted by permission of the author.

period of approximately fourteen years under review [1960–1974] was shot through with illegality. The activity was generally clandestine and in disregard of federal, as well as a number of state, statutes.[1]

Nevertheless, and more importantly for our purposes, the Committee apparently endorsed the following judgment, which was submitted by their lawyers to the U.S. Securities and Exchange Commission.

> No evidence has been uncovered or disclosed which establishes that any officer, director or employee of Gulf personally profited or benefited by or through any use of corporate funds for contributions, gifts, entertainment or other expenses related to political activity. Further, Gulf has no reason to believe or suspect that *the motive of the employee or officer* involved in such use of corporate funds was anything other than *a desire to act solely in what he considered to be the best interests of Gulf and its shareholders.*[2] [Emphasis added.]

If we accept the views of the Committee and their lawyers, then we have before us an interesting case of individuals performing illegal actions with altruistic motives. What they did was admittedly illegal, but they meant well. They had good intentions, namely, to further "the best interests of Gulf and its shareholders." Furthermore, there is no suggestion in these passages or in the rest of the report that the officials were ordered to commit such acts. They were not ordered. On the contrary, the acts seem to have emerged as practically natural by-products of some employees' zeal in looking after their employer's interests. They are, we might say, the result of overzealous attempts of agents to fulfill their fiducial obligations.

In the following paragraphs I am going to pursue this apparently plausible account of overzealous behavior to its bitter end. That is, I'm going to assume for the sake of argument that there really are reasonable people who would and do perform immoral and illegal actions with altruistic motives, i.e., there are people who would and do perform such actions with reasons that they regard as good in some fairly general sense. It's not to be assumed that they are shrewd enough to see that their own interests lie in the advancement of their employer's or client's interests. They are not, I'm assuming, cleverly egoistic. If anything, they are stupidly altruistic by hypothesis. But that's beside the point now. What I want to do is construct a generalized form of an argument that I imagine would be attractive to such agents, whether or not any of them has or will ever formulate it exactly so. Then I want to try to demolish it once and for all.

THE ARGUMENT

What I will call the Loyal Agent's Argument (LAA) runs as follows:

1. *As a loyal agent of some principal, I ought to serve his interests as he would serve them himself if he had my expertise.*

2. *He would serve his own interests in a thoroughly egoistic way.*
Therefore, as a loyal agent of this principal, I ought to operate in a
thoroughly egoistic way in his behalf.

Some clarification is in order. First, in order to make full use of the
fairly substantial body of legal literature related to the *law of agency,* I
have adopted some of the standard legal jargon. In particular, following
Powell, I'm assuming that *"an agent is a person who is authorised to act for*
a principal and has agreed so to act, and who has power to affect the legal relations
of his principal with a third party."[3] The standard model is an insurance
agent who acts in behalf of an insurance company, his principal, to
negotiate insurance contracts with third parties. More generally, lawyers,
real estate agents, engineers, doctors, dentists, stockbrokers, and the
Gulf Oil zealots may all be regarded as agents of some principal. Although for some purposes one might want to distinguish agents from
employees, such a distinction will not be necessary here. The definition
given above is broad enough to allow us to think of coal miners, Avon
Ladies, zoo attendants, and Ministers of Parliament as agents.

Second, as our definition suggests, there are typically three important
relationships involved in agency transactions, namely, those between
agent and principal, agent and third party, and principal and third party.
The law of agency has plenty to say about each of these relationships,
while LAA is primarily concerned with only the first, the fiducial relation
between agent and principal. It would be a mistake to regard this as mere
oversight. Few of us are immune to the buck-passing syndrome. Most of
us are inclined to try to narrow the range of activities for which we are
prepared to accept responsibility and, at the same time, widen the range
of activities for which we are prepared to accept authority. Notwithstanding the psychological theory of cognitive dissonance, most human
beings seem to have sufficient mental magnanimity to accommodate this
particular pair of incompatible inclinations. Like the insects, we are very
adaptable creatures.

Third, I imagine that someone using an argument like LAA would,
in the first place, be interested in trying to establish the fact that agents
have a moral obligation to operate in a thoroughly egoistic way in their
principals' behalf. If most LAA users in fact are primarily concerned with
establishing their legal obligations, then perhaps what I have to say will
be less interesting than I imagine to most people. Nevertheless, I'm
assuming that the force of "ought" in the first premise and conclusion
is moral rather than legal. For our purposes it doesn't matter what sort
of an ontological analysis one gives to such obligations or what sort of
a moral theory one might want to use to justify one's moral principles.
It only has to be appreciated that LAA is designed to provide a moral
justification for the behavior prescribed in its conclusion.

Fourth, an agent may be regarded as operating in a thoroughly
egoistic way if all his actions are designed to optimize his own interests
and he has no inclination at all to identify the interests of anyone else

with his own. (Throughout the essay I usually let the masculine "he" abbreviate "he or she.") He may very well be a self-confident, self-starting, self-sustaining, and self-controlled individual. These are all commendable personal characteristics. But he must be selfish, self-centered, self-sustaining, and/or self-serving. In conflict situations when there are not enough benefits to satisfy everyone, he will try to see that his own needs are satisfied, whatever happens to the needs of others. He is more interested in being first than in being nice, and he assumes that everyone else is too. He may harbor the suspicion that if everyone behaved as he does, the world's resources would be used in a maximally efficient way and everyone would be materially better off. But these are secondary considerations at best. His first consideration, which he regards as only prudent or smart, is to look out for *Número Uno,* himself.

Fifth, to say that an agent is supposed to operate in a thoroughly egoistic way in behalf of his principal is just to say that the agent is supposed to act as he believes his principal would act if his principal were an egoist. The agent is supposed to conduct the affairs of his principal with the single-minded purpose of optimizing the latter's interests and not yielding them to anyone else's interests.

THE SECOND PREMISE

Now we should be talking the same language. The question is: Is the Loyal Agent's Argument sound? Can its conclusion be established or even well-supported by its premises? I think there are good reasons for giving a negative answer to these questions. Moreover, since the argument has been deliberately formulated in a logically valid form, we may proceed immediately to a closer investigation of the content of its premises.

Let's consider the second premise first. This premise can only be regarded as true of real people *a priori* if one of the assumptions we have made for the sake of argument about human motivation is false. Following the quotations from the Special Review Committee, it was pointed out that the case involved agents who apparently performed illegal actions with altruistic motives. What they did wrong, they did in behalf of Gulf Oil Corporation. Fair enough. However, if it's possible to perform illegal but altruistically motivated acts, it must be possible to perform legal but altruistically motivated acts as well. The very assumption required to give the argument initial plausibility also ensures that its second premise cannot be assumed to be generally true *a priori.* Since some people can perform nonegoistically motivated actions, the second premise of LAA requires some defense. Moreover, broadly speaking there are two directions such a defense might take, and I will consider each in turn.

Granted that users of LAA cannot consistently regard every individual as a thoroughly egoistic operator and hence guarantee the truth of the second premise *a priori,* it is still possible to try to defend this premise as a well-confirmed empirical hypothesis. That is, admitting that there are exceptions, one might still claim that if one acted as if the second premise were true, much more often than not one would be right. This is the sort of line economists have traditionally taken toward their idealized rational economic man. They realize that people are capable of altruistic action, but they figure that the capability is seldom exercised and they design their hypotheses, laws, and theories accordingly.

So far as business is concerned, the egoistic line seems to be translated into profit maximization. According to Goodman, for example:

> The Wall Street rule for persons legally charged with the management of other people's money runs as follows: Invest funds in a company with the aim of gaining the best financial return with the least financial risk for the trust beneficiaries. If you later come to disagree with the company's management, sell the stock.[4]

Similarly, in a cautious version of LAA, Friedman has claimed that:

> In a free-enterprise, private-property system, a corporate executive is an employee of the owners of the business. He has a direct responsibility to his employers. That responsibility is to conduct the business in accordance with their desires, which generally will be to make as much money as possible while conforming to the basic rules of the society, both those embodied in law and those embodied in ethical custom.[5]

Instead of challenging the accuracy of these assessments of the motives of people generally or of businessmen in the marketplace in particular now, I want to grant it straightaway for the sake of the argument. The question is: How does that affect LAA?

As you may have guessed, users of LAA are not much better off than they were. If it's a good bet that the second premise is true, then it's an equally good bet that anyone inclined to defend his actions with LAA is not an altruistic operator. No one can have it both ways. Evidence for the empirical hypothesis that people generally act as egoists is evidence for the truth of the second premise and the falsehood of the alleged altruistic motives of anyone using LAA. In short, the premise is still self-defeating.

CORPORATE PRINCIPALS

Instead of regarding the second premise as an empirical claim about real people and attempting to support it inductively, one might treat it as a logical claim justifiable by an appeal to the definitions of some of its key terms. This looks like a very promising strategy when one considers the fact that many contemporary principals, like Gulf Oil Corporation, for example, are abstract entities. Corporate persons are, after all, nothing but fictional persons invented by people with fairly specific aims. In particular, corporations have been invented to assist in the accumulation of material assets. While they typically accomplish many different tasks, the accumulation of assets is generally regarded as their basic aim. Thus, if one's principal happens to be a corporation, one might reasonably argue that it is by definition thoroughly egoistic. The business of such entities is certainly business, because that is their very reason for being, the very point of inventing them in the first place. So, the second premise of LAA could be substantiated by definitional fiat.

The strength of this approach should not be underestimated. The people who design corporate law are not dummies. "A major goal of corporate law, through many decades," Chirelstein wrote,

> has been the development of equitable restrictions and rules of restraint aimed specifically at defending the financial interests of minority shareholders. In essence, the law contemplates that corporate investment decisions shall be wholly independent of the personal tastes of the company's shareholders—whether majority or minority—and shall be based solely on a presumed universal preference for higher market values per share.[6]

In other words, he claims:

> the chief function of corporate law is to "enable," that is, to furnish a suitable formula within the existing system of fiduciary obligation by which *corporate generosity can be approved as properly self-serving.*[7] [Emphasis added.]

Apparently, then, morally conscientious corporate agents may find themselves facing lawsuits if they assume their principals are not self-serving profit maximizers and act accordingly. Legal niceties aside, there is a thought-provoking moral argument in favor of agents acting as if their principals were just as the designers of corporate law imagine them. That is, if any particular stockholder wants to give his money away or to pursue any aims other than profit maximization, he is free to do so. Investors should be and almost certainly are aware that corporations are designed to make money. If they have other aims, they shouldn't be investing in corporations. If they don't have other aims and they go into corporations with their eyes wide open, then they should appreciate and respect the interests of others who have gone in with them.

In principle the defense of the second premise of LAA on the grounds of the defining characteristic of corporations may be challenged as before. Insofar as corporations are defined as egoistic corporate persons (a rough abbreviated definition, to be sure), a serious question arises concerning the morality of becoming an agent for them—not to mention inventing them in the first place. The evils of unbridled egoism are well known and they aren't mitigated by the fact that the egoist in question is a corporate person. If anything, they are magnified because of the difficulties involved in assigning responsibility and holding corporations liable for their activities. It is demonstrably certain that if everyone only attends to what he perceives as his own interests, a socially self-destructive result may occur. That is the clear message of prisoner's dilemma studies. It's also the message of two kids in a playpen who finally tear the toys apart rather than share them.

As before, it will not help to argue that in developed countries most people work for corporations or they don't work at all. Again, self-preservation is not altruism. To serve an evil master in the interests of survival is not to serve in the interests of altruism, and users of LAA are supposed to be motivated by altruism. On the other hand, insofar as corporations are not defined as egoistic corporate persons and are granted more or less benevolent if not downright altruistic aims, the truth of the second premise of LAA is again open to question. In either case, then, an agent trying to salvage LAA with this sort of definitional defense is bound to find the task self-defeating.

THE FIRST PREMISE

Let's turn now to the first premise of LAA. In a way it's as innocuous as motherhood and apple pie. Every discussion I've read of the duties of agents according to agency law in North America and the United Kingdom has included some form of this premise. For example, Powell says, "An agent has a general duty to act solely for the benefit of his principal in all matters connected with the execution of his authority."[8] *The American Restatement of the Law of Agency* says that "an agent is subject to a duty to his principal to act solely for the benefit of the principal in all matters connected with his agency."[9] According to a standard Canadian textbook on business law, "Good faith requires that the agent place the interest of his principal above all else except the law."[10]

The only trouble with the premise is that its limitations are not clearly built into it. In this respect it is like most moral principles and rules of law. Short of turning every principle and rule into a self-contained treatise, it's impossible to indicate every possible exception. For example, no one should kill anyone, except *maybe* in self-defense, war, capital punishment, euthanasia, abortion, or suicide. Similarly, an agent ought to pursue the interests of his principal with certain exceptions. However, the *American Restatement of the Law of Agency* makes it quite clear that "In no event would it be implied that an agent has a duty to perform acts which . . . are illegal or unethical."[11] Moreover, "In determining whether or not the orders of the principal to the agent are reasonable . . . business or professional ethics . . . are considered."[12] Powell also remarks that agents have no duty "to carry out an illegal act."[13] And in the famous Nuremberg trials the Charter of the International Military Tribunal recognized

> that one who has committed criminal acts may not take refuge in superior orders nor in the doctrine that his crimes were acts of states. These twin

principles working together have heretofore resulted in immunity for practically everyone concerned in the really great crimes against peace and mankind. Those in lower ranks are protected against liability by the orders of their superiors. The superiors were protected because their orders were called acts of the state. Under the Charter, no defence based on either of these doctrines can be entertained.[14]

Thus, there is no doubt at all that the first premise of LAA cannot be regarded as a licence to break the law. No respectable court would permit it. In fact, although the courts have no special jurisdiction over moral law, they have shown no reluctance to condemn immoral acts allegedly performed in the interests of fulfilling fiduciary obligations.

Illegality and immorality aside, the first premise still gives up much more than any sane person should be willing to give up. It virtually gives a principal a licence to use an agent in any way the principal pleases, so long as the agent's activity serves the principal's interest. For example, suppose a life insurance agent agrees to sell State Farm Insurance on commission. It would be ludicrous to assume that the agent has also committed himself to painting houses, washing dogs, or doing anything else that happened to give his principal pleasure. It would also be misleading to describe such an open-ended commitment as an agreement to sell insurance. It would more accurately be described as selling oneself into bondage. Clearly, then, one must assume that the first premise of LAA presupposes some important restrictions that may have nothing to do with any sort of law.

Since they are apparently drawn from and applicable to ordinary affairs and usage, perhaps it would be instructive to mention some of the principles developed in the law of agency to address this problem. You may recall that the definition of an agent that we borrowed from Powell explicitly referred to a person being "authorised to act for a principal." An agent's duties are typically limited to a set of activities over which he is granted authority by his principal. The authority may be expressed verbally or in writing, implied by something expressed or perhaps just assumed as usual in a certain sort of transaction.[15] The last principle (i.e., of "usual authority") would be sufficient to prevent the exploitation of the hypothetical insurance agent in the preceding paragraph.

Besides a carefully developed set of principles related to the granting of authority, the law of agency recognizes some other general duties of agents like the previously considered duty of good faith. For example, an agent is expected to "exercise due care and skill in executing his authority."[16] This obviously serves the interests of all concerned, and there are plenty of principles and precedents available to explain "due care and skill." An agent is generally not authorized to delegate his responsibilities to someone else, although such delegation may be built into a particular contract.[17] He is expected to "keep proper accounts," i.e., accounts that clearly distinguish his principal's assets from his own.[18]

Without some prior agreement with his principal, an agent is usually not permitted to occupy the role of the third party in a transaction in which he is also the agent.[19] It is assumed that in the absence of some agreement, an agent would seek some advantage for himself in the contract between his principal and himself as a third party. This assumption of egoistic motives is illustrated very well in a case from 1874 reported by Smyth and Soberman.

> In *Robinson* v. *Mollett* a client gave a broker an order to buy tallow for him. The broker already held some tallow on his own account, and he simply sent this tallow to his client. The court held that the client did not have to accept or pay for it. There was no evidence that the broker had obtained either the best tallow or the best price for his principal. Indeed, *there is a presumption in these circumstances that the broker would obtain as much personal profit as he could.*[20] [Emphasis added.]

Keeping the preceding guidelines in mind, perhaps some form of LAA can be salvaged by tightening up the first premise. Let's suppose I'm in the advertising business and I want to use LAA by suitably restricting the scope of the first premise thus:

1a. *As a loyal advertising agent of some company, I ought to advertise its products as they would advertise them if they had my expertise.*

That would require a consistent modification of the second premise and conclusion, but we need not worry about that. The question is: Does this reformulated premise 1a escape the kinds of criticism leveled against premise 1?

Certainly not. If the company happens to be run by a bunch of thoroughly unscrupulous thugs, it could be immoral and illegal to advertise their products as they would if they had the agent's expertise. Even if the company is run by fools who really don't know what they make, it could be immoral and illegal to advertise their products as they would if they had the agent's expertise. For example, if the company's directors are smart enough to know that they can make more money selling drugs than they can make selling candy, but dumb enough to think that the candy they make is an effective drug, an agent could hardly be under any obligation to advertise their product as a marvelous new drug, i.e., assuming that the agent was smart enough to know that his employers were only capable of producing candy.

If you think the agent could have such an obligation, what would be its source? Clearly it is not enough to say that the agent is employed by the company. That would be tantamount to appealing to LAA in order to establish a version of its own first premise, i.e., it would be a circular salvaging effort. Something else is required to support premise 1a.

QUESTION-BEGGING AND ACT UTILITARIANISM

At this point a critic may be wondering about the justification of my claim that a knowledgeable agent could hardly be obliged to advertise the product as a marvelous new drug. Why, one might ask, isn't that just begging the question in the opposite direction? Clearly it's not enough to say that the agent has an obligation to tell the truth. After all, he also has an obligation to honor his contracts. By asserting that a loyal agent is not obliged to perform silly, illegal, or immoral acts, I am apparently assuming what must be proved, namely, that the obligation incurred by becoming an agent of another party is not superior to other obligations.

This objection has some merit. Sometimes, as in the case of our hypothetical advertiser, it's impossible to satisfy both of two moral principles. Over a hundred years ago Hegel observed that such situations constitute the essential core of human tragedies. Act utilitarian theorists often regard such anomalies as decisive considerations in support of their position. According to this view, which I accept, moral principles should be regarded as rules of thumb subject to the overriding moral obligation to try to act so as to produce the greatest amount of happiness for the largest number of people. Thus, for example, an act utilitarian would argue that our hypothetical advertiser really has only one moral obligation in the candy case, namely, to refrain from advertising candy as a therapeutic drug. That is his only moral obligation in this case because, of the two options he has (to honor his commitment to serve the interests of his employer or to refrain from spreading false or misleading information), the latter will probably produce the greatest amount of happiness for the largest number of people. From this point of view, then, it is not question-begging to assert that the obligation incurred by becoming an agent of another party is not necessarily superior to other obligations.

Although the act utilitarian procedure for deciding which of two moral principles should be given precedence in conflict situations seems eminently reasonable, it has at least three disadvantages which merit some attention. First, the procedure may encounter insuperable operational problems. Someone must assume the responsibility for determining who is how happy, when, where, and why. More often than not, I think, such assessments can and are made with sufficient accuracy to maintain the viability of the act utilitarian position. For example, there is general agreement that Thalidomide should be banned because its use would produce more harm than happiness. Generally speaking, democracy is based on act utilitarian intuitions. Granted that the practice of democracy never quite lives up to the principle or the promise, it's still preferable to its alternatives.

Second, the procedure may lead to apparently perverse judgments since, for example, the greatest happiness for the greatest number of people might be produced by horrible crimes being committed against an innocent person. I believe this sort of anomaly is logically possible but not very likely. But there are two good reasons for not regarding the objection as fatal for act utilitarianism. In the first place, when one tries to justify one's judgment that another judgment is perverse, one will find that one is roughly back where we started. That is, one will be putting some moral principle against the act utilitarian judgment. But then what does one do when one's principles conflict? Clearly there must be some weighing and balancing of benefits and costs to accommodate particular circumstances. In the second place, though I can't demonstrate it here, I think every moral theory is subject to a perverse-judgment type of criticism. I haven't seen one theory that is not liable to lead to anomalies in some circumstances. That, among other things, is what over 2,000 years of moral philosophy has accomplished.

Finally, one may find the retreat to act utilitarianism disappointing because it seems to create a morally chaotic state of affairs. It seems to substitute spur-of-the-moment for principled action. This is a mistake. As indicated above, act utilitarians use moral principles as first-line principles of action. They are committed to keeping promises, honoring contracts, refraining from cheating, and so on. They believe that more often than not, by following these well-known and respected principles, more good than harm will be produced. They realize, however, that such principles are liable to lead to conflicts and other anomalies that require a finer assessment instrument. They also realize that that instrument, the act utilitarian principle, has its own problems; but they are prepared to tolerate them until something better comes along.

CONCLUSION

The announced aim of this essay was to destroy LAA once and for all. I think that has been done. It is perhaps worthwhile to emphasize that if people use LAA when, as we saw earlier, the real reason for their actions is fear (or job preservation) then they will be circulating a distorted view of the world and decreasing the chances of reform. Thus, in the interests of a clear perception and resolution of social problems related to responsible human agency, LAA deserves the sort of treatment it has received here.

Notes

[1] J. J. McCloy, N. W. Pearson, and B. Matthews, *The Great Oil Spill* (New York: Chelsea House, 1976), p. 31.

[2] *Ibid.*, p. 13.

[3] R. Powell, *The Law of Agency* (London: Sir Isaac Pitman and Sons, Ltd., 1965), p. 7.

[4] W. Goodman, "Stocks Without Sin," *Minneapolis Star and Tribune Co., Inc.* Reprinted in *Ethical Arguments for Analysis,* ed. R. Baum (New York: Holt, Rinehart and Winston, 1975), p. 206.

[5] M. Friedman, "The Social Responsibility of Business Is to Increase Its Profits," *The New York Times Magazine,* September 13, 1970. Reprinted in *Ethical Arguments for Analysis,* ed. R. Baum (New York: Holt, Rinehart and Winston, 1975), p. 205.

[6]M. A. Chirelstein, "Corporate Law Reform," *Social Responsibility and the Business Predicament,* ed. J. W. McKie, (Washington, D.C.: The Brookings Institution, 1974), pp. 73–74.

[7]*Ibid.,* p. 73.

[8]Powell, *The Law of Agency,* p. 312.

[9]Section 387 as quoted in P. I. Blumberg, "Corporate Responsibility and the Employee's Duty of Loyalty and Obedience: A Preliminary Inquiry," *The Corporate Dilemma,* ed. D. Votaw and S. P. Sethi (Englewood Cliffs, N.J.: Prentice-Hall, Inc., 1973), p. 87.

[10]J. E. Smyth and D. A. Soberman, *The Law and Business Administration in Canada* (Toronto: Prentice-Hall of Canada, Ltd., 1968), p. 360.

[11]Section 385 as quoted in Blumberg, "Corporate Responsibility," p. 86.

[12]*Ibid.*

[13]Powell, *The Law of Agency,* p. 302.

[14]R. Jackson, *The Nuremberg Case* as quoted in *Philosophy for a New Generation,* ed. A. K. Bierman and J. A. Gould (New York: The Macmillan Company, 1970), p. 217.

[15]Powell, *The Law of Agency,* pp. 35–119.

[16]*Ibid.,* p. 303.

[17]*Ibid.,* p. 305.

[18]*Ibid.,* p. 321.

[19]*Ibid.,* p. 320.

[20]Smyth and Soberman, *The Law and Business Administration in Canada,* pp. 361–362.

chapter *10*

*F*uture Generations

INTRODUCTION

As the twentieth century draws to a close, several major global problems raise issues about obligations to future generations. Many concerns about the environment do not pertain merely to presently existing people but to effects on those who will live during the middle and late twenty-first century, most of whom do not presently exist. Acid rain is despoiling many lakes and forests in North America and Europe. As time goes by, fewer forests and lakes supporting wildlife will exist. Destruction of the ozone layer might significantly increase the rates of skin cancer of future generations, and increasing global temperatures from the "greenhouse" effect might increase sea levels and lead to flooding in many coastal areas. Some of these potential problems will not become major for a half century to a century from now. One could agree with King Louis XIV of France who, when told that his policies would result in revolution, reputedly said "Après moi, le deluge"—After me, the flood! In short, if the damage will come after one is dead, why worry about it?

A variety of other activities will also have detrimental effects primarily on future generations. The destruction or consumption of nonrenewable resources such as arable land, minerals, and fossil fuels will primarily affect future generations. The storage of radioactive nuclear waste from nuclear power plants will create a hazard for hundreds or thousands of years. The rate of population growth and the ultimate size of global and national populations will significantly affect future per capita available resources. During 1987, the total world population surpassed 5 billion people, and by the turn of the century it is apt to be 6 billion or more. This growth is not evenly distributed, being far greater among the poorer countries of the world. Besides the sheer size of future generations, some people are concerned about the genetic endowment of future generations.[1] The ability to keep alive people with genetic defects from which previously they would have died might contribute to a higher rate of defects in future generations. Pollutants in the environment might also increase the rate of genetic mutations.

341

Whereas obligations to future generations have major significance in the problems just noted, they can also affect choices that do not have their major impact on future generations. For example, if one has a choice between allocating funds to a medical program providing acute care for persons presently ill or for preventive programs, obligations to future generations might tilt the decision in favor of funding preventive programs. "Current policy emphasizes repairing [congenital and genetic] defects after they occur rather than preventing them in the first place. It is an irrational allocation of resources. . . ."[2] Such a claim partly depends on obligations to people who do not presently exist—future generations.

Theoretical Problems   Although many choices facing contemporary society can be significantly affected by obligations to future generations and many people believe effects on future generations are important, obligations to future generations raise many theoretical issues. Indeed, these problems might well be the most significant theoretical development in ethical theory during the last part of this century. They can only be briefly mentioned here.

One problem is the *nonexistence* of future generations. If one grounds obligations on rights, rationality, well-being, or interests and considers them to be characteristics of persons, how can those characteristics exist if the persons do not? If the people do not exist, their rights and interests cannot exist either, so how can one have obligations to respect or further rights or interests of nonexistent people? One might respond that they will exist, and when they do, they will have rights and interests that can be violated and harmed. However, not all people who might exist will exist. For example, you might have one, two, or three or more children. Suppose you decide to have only two. Then your third and subsequent children will not in fact exist. Philosophers often distinguish between (actual) future people, those who will in fact exist, and (merely) possible people, those who might exist but will not. Do obligations to future generations extend only to future people or also to possible people?

A second problem is our *ignorance* of future generations, especially those far distant in time, say, two centuries from now. There are at least two aspects of this ignorance. First, their interests and needs are uncertain. What type of life will they want to live? One might say that although it is uncertain whether they will be interested in philosophy, computer hacking, or mountain climbing, they will certainly want to eat and to be healthy, so environmental contamination will violate their rights or set back their interests. However, perhaps they will not need much arable land, being able to grow food from bacteria and oil or by some other exotic technique. Perhaps carcinogens will not be a problem for them, because they will have cures or vaccinations for cancer. So even if there are obligations to future generations, one does not know what one should provide to fulfill those obligations.[3]

The second aspect of ignorance concerns the effects of present conduct on distant generations. Many actions and social policies have unintended consequences. For example, during the late 1940s and early 1950s some pregnant women were given DES to help prevent premature birth. A generation later the daughters of these women were found to be at risk for cervical cancer. During the late 1940s, DDT was used to kill malaria-carrying mosquitos in Ceylon. The success of the program contributed significantly to rapid population growth, because considerably fewer children died of malaria. These are relatively short-term effects. Effects on people many generations from now also depend primarily on the actions of people existing between now and then. Suppose currently existing people protect the environment, only to have people at the end of the next century destroy it by wars?

Another major aspect of ignorance about the future is worth picking out as a separate problem, namely, ignorance of the *identity* of future people. The identity of people depends on when and by whom they are conceived. You do not know the identity of your unconceived child. Whether it will be male or female will depend on when and with whom you conceive. But so what? Well, some people think that rights and interests belong to individual persons. Right conduct is that which does not violate the rights or set back the interests of particular, identifiable people.[4] If one cannot identify particular people who will exist, then one cannot violate their rights.

More particularly, suppose one holds that an action is wrong if and only if it makes someone worse off. Suppose one has a choice between two actions. If one does action A, person X will exist but have a life of little happiness, but better than not existing. If one performs action B, person Y will exist and have a very happy life. But neither action makes someone worse off! Action A does not make X worse off than if one did B, for if one does B, X will not exist at all. Similarly, if one does A, Y will not be worse off, for Y will not exist. In short, as a result of neither alternative does someone exist who is worse off because of the decision.

A fourth theoretical problem concerns the *size* of future generations. How many people there will be in the mid-twenty-first century partly depends on what people do now. If people now have on average three children, there will be more people then than if people have on average two children. How many resources those people will need to lead decent lives also partly depends on how many there are. Is it better that there be more people who are slightly less happy or fewer people who are more happy? Suppose there can be 10 billion people whose rights are fulfilled, provided that they subsequently decrease the population during the next century to 4 billion. Is that better, worse, or the same as 6 billion people throughout? Most ethical theories have implicitly assumed that the same number of persons (as well as the same persons) exist whichever choice is made, but that need not be the case.

A fifth, and more common problem concerns the *content* of obligations to future generations, if there are any. Is there some minimum quality of life (determined by rights, primary goods, happiness, or whatever) that is owed to all future generations? Or are they owed a quality of life at least equal to the present one, or perhaps even better than at present? In short, what precisely is owed to future generations?

The last theoretical problem is the *weight of obligations* to future generations compared to obligations to currently existing people. Practically, are currently existing people required to make sacrifices for future generations? For example, should many hungry people in Africa be allowed to starve to death, because if they are not even more people will starve to death in the future?[5] In many social decisions, future effects are discounted. For example, suppose a person wins a legal case for damages for loss of future income. The amount of money the person receives is the amount the person would probably have earned decreased by a certain percentage to reflect the interest the person can earn by investing the money now. If, however, one discounts by the usual sort of rate—three to five percent annually—over a century future problems vanish to near nothing. Besides, the further in the future effects are, the less certain they are to occur. Should one discount at all, and if so, how much?

Alternative Solutions   Although little has been written about it, there are probably two keys to a *natural-law* approach to the problem of future generations. One key is the duty to procreate. The function of the natural human sexual inclination is reproduction, because only sexual acts can lead to reproduction. The point of reproduction is the preservation of the species. The reproductive function of adding members to the species and community includes their upbringing and education.

Thomas Aquinas distinguished two types of duties, which can be called "individual" and "collective."[6] *Individual duties* must be fulfilled by each person, whereas *collective duties* fall on a group and each person need not act so long as enough others do so to fulfill the duty. For example, an army needs sentries, but not every soldier need be a sentry so long as enough are. As the purpose of the duty to procreate is the preservation of the species, not everyone needs to have children and even those who do need not have as many as they can.

The second key stems from the social nature of human beings and the good of society. People's individual well-being depends on membership and activity in a good and just society. A good society not only provides for the physical well-being of its members, but also their intellectual and cultural well-being. Consequently, there is a duty to promote a good and just society.

Taking the duties to procreate and to promote a good society together, currently existing people should not only act so as to perpetuate the species, but to perpetuate a good society. If the environment is despoiled, nonrenewable resources are consumed exorbitantly, and the population explodes, people will not be able to live in a good society, perhaps not to live at all. However, the natural-law vision of a good society is not necessarily one of consumer abundance—of a Porsche and pocket TV for each person. Consequently, although a decent level of material well-being is needed, a good society need not be one of conspicuous consumption. Love, friendship, and social cooperation are more important.

To the extent the welfare of future generations rests on limited population size, the natural-law tradition imposes what many people take to be a significant constraint on achieving the well-being of future generations. It basically opposes abortion and artificial contraception (the pill, IUDs, and so on). As the function of sexual activity is reproduction, interfering with the reproductive process to prevent generation is contrary to natural law and wrong.[7] Only the rhythm method, by which intercourse is avoided during the time a woman might conceive, accords with natural law.[8] Of course, abortion is also contrary to natural law (see Chapter 4). Because these are absolute obligations, they cannot be outweighed by considerations for future generations.

The *natural-rights* tradition seems to imply that one must not act so as to violate the rights of future generations. Of course, one must first admit that future generations can have rights. John Locke required that when one originally acquires property in the state of nature, one must leave "enough, and as good" for others.[9] If this is extended to future generations, then one would have to leave them "enough, and as good" natural resources. Other natural rights might also establish obligations to future generations.

There are two possible approaches a natural-rights theorist might use to avoid the problems of nonexistence and identity of future generations. One approach is to make the rights conditional. If and when people exist, they have rights that it is wrong to violate, even by acts performed before they came into existence. Given that people will probably exist in the future, one ought not perform acts now that would prevent those rights being fulfilled. A second approach is to argue that acts that would adversely affect people in the distant future can be traced back to the violations of rights of currently existing people.

The problems of ignorance and content of obligations might be resolved by most natural rights being negative, that is, not to kill, rather than positive, that is, to help preserve life. One can more plausibly know what might kill or otherwise harm future generations than what will benefit them. Moreover, fulfilling negative rights of future generations is less likely to conflict with respecting rights of currently existing people. Nevertheless, a right to procreate[10] might block effective action to control population size and prevent serious shortages in the future. Moreover, some natural-rights theorists argue that positive duties are owned to future generations at least as derivative from a right to life.[11]

Kantian ethics seems likely to have significant implications for obligations to future generations, but they have not been elaborated by many philosophers. Perhaps the most fruitful Kantian approach is by the formula of the law of nature: "Act as though the maxim of your action were by your will to become a universal law of nature."[12] By this test, one must both be able to conceive of the maxim becoming a law of nature on which everyone acts and be able to rationally will it. For a maxim to be a law of nature, the species must be able to continue and the time at which effects occur is irrelevant. Thus, dumping toxic wastes that poison the environment would be condemned, because one cannot conceive of a system of nature with the species surviving were that done.[13] Other practices might involve maxims that one could not will were one a member of a future generation.

In the *contractarian* view, the principles for future generations depend significantly on who the contractors are. They can be either (1) all presently existing people; (2) all who actually exist at some time or other; or (3) all possible people, that is, all those who might exist at some time or other. All possible people include all those who actually exist as well as all those who might have been conceived or born but were not.

If, like Rawls,[14] one assumes that only presently existing people are contractors, then the contractors will not agree to principles concerned with persons in the distant future. While they might have some concern for their children and grandchildren, they will not be concerned with people in the fifth or sixth generations.

If the contractors are all actual persons, including persons who will actually exist in the distant future, they will not agree to principles permitting activities such as pollution and population growth at the expense of future generations. Instead, they will accept principles that permit population growth and other acts potentially deleterious to future generations only as long as economic growth is not hindered and the point has not been reached where the principles of justice with the priority of liberty can be secured. They would have no reason to accept principles allowing environmental deterioration or other negative effects after justice is secured.

The actual-persons view faces a couple of major difficulties.[15] First, as all the contractors know they exist, they have no reason to permit population increase except to fulfill their own desires to have children. Second, it does not seem to make sense to have all actual persons choosing population principles that determine who will exist in the future. One cannot determine who will be a contractor until the contract is made, but the contract cannot be made until one knows who the contractors are. This is the chicken and the egg problem with a vengeance.

If all possible people were contractors, the principle agreed to would probably be to maximize one's chances for receiving some primary goods, which means bringing as many people as possible into existence.[16] The worst-off possible people are those who do not exist, for they do not have any primary goods. Each contractor would wish to have as great a chance as possible to receive primary goods. This requires increasing the chance for existence by bringing as many people as possible into existence.

The *utilitarian* tradition is concerned with maximizing net utility, and it makes no difference whether the utility is now or in the future. At first glance, this might seem to be a good basis for being concerned with the happiness of future generations. However, if utilitarianism is restricted to the happiness of identifiable people, it directly falls foul of the identity problem. No one is made worse off if actions result in different people being born in the future, provided their lives are at least minimally worth living.

The variable size problem is also a major difficulty for utilitarianism, and the difference between act and rule utilitarianism is irrelevant, because the problem concerns the general aim, not how it is to be pursued. Once it is recognized that the size of future generations can vary, two different interpretations of the aim of maximizing net utility are possible. (See Chapter 3 for the meaning of "net utility.") The aim can be either as high a total net utility or as high an average net utility as possible. Total net utility is simply the sum of all the happiness minus the sum of all unhappiness. The average net utility is the total divided by the number of people. When the size of the population is constant, these two versions give the same results, because a change in total net utility produces a corresponding change in the average net utility. When the sizes of populations differ, this correspondence does not hold. For example, a small increase in the total net utility due to the addition of happy people might decrease the average net utility.

The total utilitarian view has a number of intuitively objectionable implications. First, the addition implication is that population size should be increased so long as the happiness from the addition is greater than the unhappiness. For example, a world population of 5 billion people ought to be increased to one of 10 billion people, if each of the 10 billion would have more than half the net utility of each of the 5 billion. This can be repeated and leads to what has been called the repugnant conclusion:

> For any possible population of at least ten billion people, all with a very high quality of life, there must be some much larger imaginable population whose existence, if other things are equal, would be better, even though its members have lives that are barely worth living.[17]

Second, the sacrifice implication is that the happiness of people should be sacrificed if it will increase the total net utility. Two versions of the sacrifice implication exist. One states that the happiness of existing people should be sacrificed if the net utility of the additional people is greater than that lost by existing people. According to the other, the population should be increased even if the additional people have net disutility (are miserable), provided the gain in net utility to existing people is greater than the net disutility of the new people.

The average view avoids the addition implication and the repugnant conclusion of the total view, because, in the example, the average happiness of the much larger population would be less than that of the smaller. However, it has a converse addition implication or mere addition paradox. Suppose additional people would be quite happy but less happy than the average of those presently existing. Then by the average view, it would be wrong to allow the additional people, because the average would be lower. Also, while the average view moderates the sacrifice implications, it does not eliminate them. If the average net utility of additional people is great, then it might offset a decrease in the average net utility of presently existing people. Similarly, the gain in the average net utility of presently existing people can be great enough to offset even an average net disutility of additional people.

Readings The readings in this chapter are more theoretical than in the others on applications, because there are so many difficult theoretical issues to resolve before one can discuss concrete problems. In the first selection, James Hudson supports a rights-based approach to future generations. He responds to the identity problem and another difficulty, namely, that one can avoid violations of rights of future people simply by not procreating them. One of his main points is that one is not responsible for rights violations stemming from the voluntary acts of others. Thus, if one's descendants violate the rights of others, one is not responsible—they are. However, this leaves some problems. In consequence, he argues that people have a right to blameless procreation—to bring children into the world without thereby violating the children's rights because events have been set in motion that will harm them. If others act in ways that will harm future generations, they will also violate the rights of currently existing people to blameless procreation. Although in the end he does not claim to have solved all the problems with a rights theory, he does claim to have narrowed the problem.

David Richards, in the second selection, sets out a contractarian view involving a contract of all actual people. He responds to criticisms of that approach based on the difficulty of knowing who the contractors are. He claims that harm to future generations can be handled similarly to harm to currently existing people. That is, it is wrong to intentionally, knowingly, or negligently cause harm. However, he suggests that the standard of negligence might be higher than for currently existing people; that is, one might have to be even more careful. Finally, he concludes that a minimum necessary condition in the use of nonrenewable resources is to leave enough so that together with the then existing state of technology, future generations have an opportunity equal to that of currently existing people to achieve general goods in life.

In the last selection, Derek Parfit explains the identity problem as it might affect a utilitarian concerned with not making persons worse off. After explaining how the identity of future persons depends on current conduct, he shows how various intuitively objectionable policies will not be worse for anyone. In the end, he claims that the nonidentity of people who will exist on different policies makes no difference to their moral evaluation. However, the principle that supports this result is not a common one. In conclusion, he suggests that even though it is not true that certain policies would not be worse for anyone, it is permissible for people to talk as though it were true, because it is not seriously misleading.

Notes

[1]See, for example, Hardy Jones, "Genetic Endowment and Obligations to Future Generations," *Social Theory and Practice* 4 (1976): 29–46.

[2]Michael D. Bayles, *Reproductive Ethics* (Englewood Cliffs, N.J.: Prentice-Hall, 1984), p. 113; see also Ronald M. Green, "Justice and the Claims of Future Generations," in *Justice and Health Care,* ed. Earl E. Shelp (Dordrecht: D. Reidel, 1981), p. 203.

[3]See Martin P. Golding, "Obligations to Future Generations," *The Monist* 56 (1972): 85–99.

[4]See generally, Bryan G. Norton, "Environmental Ethics and the Rights of Future Generations," *Environmental Ethics* 4 (1982): 319–337; Thomas Schwartz, "Obligations to Posterity," in *Obligations to Future Generations,* ed. R. I. Sikora and Brian Barry (Philadelphia: Temple University Press, 1978), pp. 3–13.

[5]See Garrett Hardin, "Lifeboat Ethics: The Case Against Helping the Poor," *Psychology Today* 8 (September 1974): 38ff.

[6]St. Thomas Aquinas, *Summa Theologica,* II–II, Question 152, Article 1, ad. 1.

[7]Aquinas, *Summa Theologica,* II–II, Question 154, Article 1.

[8]See Pope Paul VI, "Humanae Vitae," in *Philosophy and Sex,* ed. Robert Baker and Frederick Elliston, rev. ed. (Buffalo: Prometheus Books, 1984), pp. 167–184; and G. E. M. Anscombe, "Contraception and Chastity," in *Ethics and Population,* ed. Michael D. Bayles (Cambridge, Mass.: Schenkman, 1976), pp. 134–153.

[9]*Two Treatises of Government,* ed. Peter Laslett, rev. ed. (New York: New American Library, 1963), Book 2, Chapter 5, Section 27, p. 329.

[10]See United Nations, *Report of the International Conference on Population, 1984,* Mexico City, August 6–13, 1984, Recommendation 30.

[11]James P. Sterba, "The Welfare Rights of Distant Peoples and Future Generations," *Social Theory and Practice* 7 (1981): 99–119.

[12]Immanuel Kant, *Foundations of the Metaphysics of Morals with Critical Essays,* trans. Lewis White Beck, ed. Robert Paul Wolff (Indianapolis: Bobbs-Merrill, 1969), p. 45.

[13]Annette Baier, "For the Sake of Future Generations," in *Earthbound: New Introductory Essays in Environmental Ethics,* ed. Tom Regan (New York: Random House, 1984), p. 217.

[14]John Rawls, *A Theory of Justice* (Cambridge, Mass.: Harvard University Press, 1971), pp. 140, 292.

[15]See Brian Barry, "Justice Between Generations," in *Law, Morality and Society: Essays in Honour of H. L. A. Hart,* ed. P. M. S. Hacker and J. Raz (Oxford: Clarendon Press, 1977), p. 281.

[16]Brian Barry, "Rawls on Average and Total Utility: A Comment," *Philosophical Studies* 31 (1977): 322–324.

[17]Derek Parfit, *Reasons and Persons* (Oxford: Oxford University Press, 1984), p. 388.

Bibliography on Future Generations

Baier, Annette. "For the Sake of Future Generations." In *Earthbound: New Introductory Essays in Environmental Ethics,* edited by Tom Regan, pp. 214–246. New York: Random House, 1984.

Bayles, Michael D. *Morality and Population Policy.* University, Ala.: University of Alabama Press, 1980. Chapter 2 and Appendices 1–3.

Bickham, Stephen. "Future Generations and Contemporary Ethical Theory." *Journal of Value Inquiry* 15 (1981): 169–177.

Green, Ronald M. "Justice and the Claims of Future Generations." In *Justice and Health Care,* edited by Earl E. Shelp, pp. 193–211. Dordrecht: D. Reidel, 1981.

Jones, Hardy. "Genetic Endowment and Obligations to Future Generations." *Social Theory and Practice* 4 (1976): 29–46.

Kavka, Gregory. "The Paradox of Future Individuals." *Philosophy and Public Affairs* 11 (1982): 93–112.

MacLean, Douglas, and Brown, Peter G., eds. *Energy and the Future.* Totowa, N.J.: Rowman and Littlefield, 1983.

McMahan, Jefferson. "Problems of Population Theory." *Ethics* 92 (1981): 96–127.

Norton, Bryan G. "Environmental Ethics and the Rights of Future Generations." *Environmental Ethics* 4 (1982): 319–337.

Parfit, Derek. "Comments." *Ethics* 96 (1986): 854–862.

———. *Reasons and Persons.* Oxford: Oxford University Press, 1984. Part 4.

Partridge, Ernest, ed. *Responsibilities to Future Generations: Environmental Ethics.* Buffalo, N.Y.: Prometheus Books, 1981.

Sartorius, Rolf. "Government Regulation and Intergenerational Justice." In *Rights and Regulation: Ethical, Political, and Economic Issues,* edited by Tibor R. Machan and M. Bruce Johnson, pp. 177–201. Cambridge, Mass.: Ballinger, 1983.

Sikora, R. I., and Barry, Brian, eds. *Obligations to Future Generations.* Philadelphia, Pa.: Temple University Press, 1978.

Sterba, James P. "The Welfare Rights of Distant Peoples and Future Generations." *Social Theory and Practice* 7 (1981): 99–119.

Wenz, Peter S. "Ethics, Energy Policy, and Future Generations." *Environmental Ethics* 5 (1983): 195–209.

Woodward, James. "The Non-Identity Problem." *Ethics* 96 (1986): 804–831.

Problem Case
A Strip Mine Worker

Billy Bob drives a truck for a strip mine company, taking the coal from the mine to the plant. He did not sleep well last night, and this morning he and Betty are sitting over coffee. He cannot decide whether or not to go to work today or to call in sick. The Hill County Environmentalist Society is to begin picketing outside the mine today, and the situation might become violent. The HCES claims that the land is too steep to mine, that the county's resources for the future are being destroyed, and that the coal company does not adequately restore the land.

"Perhaps I should call in sick today and see how things go," he says. "Maybe they will settle the dispute, and then I can go back tomorrow."

"But Billy Bob, you know we barely get along now when you work full time. With three kids and another on the way, we can't do without even one day's paycheck," Betty responds. "Besides, if you miss a day, especially now, the company might fire you. Then where would we be?"

"I know," replies Billy Bob, "but I think the society has a point. When I look at those wooded hills, and then see the holes where we have mined, I just wonder what will be left for our kids when they are grown. Besides, they say this coal is high in sulphur and creates air pollution when they burn it. Why can't they get better coal some place else or build more of those nuclear reactors up north?"

"If it weren't for the mine, I don't know where you could find a job. Look at all the money it has brought in. People around here, at least many of them, are a lot better off than they were before the mine opened," Betty responds. "I think you just want to go fishing today."

"No," Billy Bob says, "but I can't help wondering whether we are not hurting our kid's children more than we are helping ourselves. I love these hills; I've hunted and fished in them all my life. Where will my grandchildren fish and hunt?"

"I declare, Billy Bob, sometimes I think you love these hills more than your own children. Besides, what good will it do our grandchildren if we can't feed our children?" And with that, Betty stalks out of the room.

What should Billy Bob do? Should he not cross the picket line? If he doesn't, should he call in sick, or should he tell his boss the truth? More generally, what type of energy source should be used? Deep coal mines cost miners lives through black lung; strip mines destroy the land and the coal often causes more pollution. Oil causes pollution and environmental damage from spills. All fossile fuels increase the carbon dioxide levels in the air and contribute to the greenhouse effect warming the earth. Nuclear power leaves radioactive waste. In short, as all the major sources of energy cause environmental damage and risks to present and future people, how does one go about establishing a morally defensible energy policy?

JAMES L. HUDSON
RIGHTS AND THE FURTHER FUTURE

In recent years philosophers have devoted a good deal of attention to a new kind of moral problem: the evaluation of actions whose key feature is that they produce bad effects in the distant future. No doubt this interest has been stimulated by the public alarums over pollution, resource depletion, and over-population; but whatever one thinks of these specific policy issues, problems of this type have a theoretical interest which is independent of any immediate applications. In analyzing such problems, moral philosophers have found little use for the

From James L. Hudson, "Rights and the Further Future," *Philosophical Studies* 49 (1986): 99–107.
Copyright © 1986 by D. Reidel Publishing Co. Reprinted by permission.

notion of a moral right; the problems have seemed to call instead for some form of consequentialist moral theory. The purpose of this note is to suggest that this dismissal of rights theories of morality has been over-hasty, for such theories possess hitherto unused resources for dealing with such problems. It is not clear that these resources are fully adequate, but for now the issue should be regarded as open.

The case against rights theories has been put forward recently by Jefferson McMahan[1] and Derek Parfit.[2] According to them it would be grossly counterintuitive to deny that agents in the present should often act so as to make people in the distant future better off rather than worse off. But this cannot be because of any rights that the future people have to better treatment. For in many cases the people who would exist if we did the favorable action will be numerically different people (though there may be the same number of them) from those who would exist if we did the unfavorable one.[3] Now observance of someone's rights implies better treatment *of that person,* not the suppression of his very coming-to-be and the possible substitution of another person or persons for him. So the kind of procedure we need in order to evaluate actions with consequences in the distant future will concern itself with *consequences,* but in an *impersonal* way; thus it will not be concerned with *personal rights.*

Further reason for thinking that an appeal to rights could not explain our moral concern for future people comes from the reflection that rights have force only if they are not waived by their possessor. But consider again a present action with consequences which we would normally consider bad for distantly future people. Would those people, looking back at the action from their later vantage point, object to it? If it had not been done, *they* would not have existed. Perhaps other, happier people would have existed in their place; but who is going to insist, as a matter of right, that he be compensated for having come into the world at all, in place of someone who would have been better off than he? He will, instead, automatically waive his right to object to any action which was a necessary condition of his own existence, provided only that his existence is not utterly miserable. Thus the rights which might be thought to protect distantly future people from some of the deleterious consequences of present actions will not actually do so, since they will be automatically waived by their possessors.

Rights theories of morality are thus under serious attack. What response can be made on their behalf?

First, it can simply be denied that the point of a right is to protect certain interests of its possessor. It is closer to the truth to say that rights are for the protection of *possible* interests; that one may have a right to something which is not in fact in his interest (though it might have been). If I have a right to X and yet X is taken from me without my explicit consent, my right has probably been violated even if the taking was in my own best interests, and even if I knew it was so. It is true that implicit or hypothetical consent is sometimes deemed adequate to render this *not* a rights-violation; but it is unclear under what circumstances this is proper. Even though I would have consented to be deprived of X had I been asked, it is still often the case that my being deprived of X *without* being asked *does* violate my right.

A further unclarity is that consent, or the waiver of a right, is normally considered invalid if obtained through coercion; and the concept of coercion is a difficult one. In the case under consideration—in which a person is deemed to have consented to a long-past action which does him present harm, on the grounds that the action was also necessary for his own conception—the individual's position is uncomfortably analogous to that of the traveler confronted with the highwayman's demand: "Your money or your life!" Often when one has a choice between two alternatives, one involving the preservation and the other forfeiture of his own life, he is considered to be choosing under coercion, and his rights-waivers are deemed invalid. And so the validity of any *ex post facto* waiver such as here imagined is at least in doubt.

Still, it is awkward for the rights theorist to be reminded that *at least normally* one observes another's rights by treating him with consideration, not by preventing him from coming into existence in the first place. The rights theorist must deny that this is *always* the case, in order to have a rights-based rationale for our present concern for distantly future people. But then he must deal with the observation that we can always avoid violating the rights of future people by preventing their coming into existence. While present people cannot (for the most part) be killed without violating their rights, it is within our collective power ultimately to *eliminate the violation of rights*—which is the rights-theorist's moral ideal—simply by refraining from procreation.

And can we justify doing any less? Anyone who has a full-blooded conception of rights can be morally certain that his children (if any) will have their rights violated from time to time; they are also likely to violate the rights of others on occasion. These potential rights-violations can be prevented only by having no children. It would seem, then, that the rights-theorist is committed to the collective self-extinction of the class of moral agents.

The best hope for evading this unpalatable conclusion is to draw a distinction between different ways in which a rights-violation can be brought about. Let us say that if I beget or bear a child whose rights are then violated by someone else, *I* am not responsible, even though my procreative action is a necessary condition for the violation, and even if I foresaw that the violation would occur. Someone else is the rights-violator, for *his* action is the *proximate cause* of the violation. Similarly, if my child violates someone's rights it would not be proper to blame *me* simply because I produced him. On this view the rights-theorist's moral imperative is: Do not *yourself* violate anyone's rights. Only actions which directly result in rights-violations are prohibited, not actions which are mere necessary conditions for the violations. In general, one is not obliged at a given time to prevent others from later acting in violation of rights; and in particular, one is not obliged to remain childless.

This explanation (which requires further spelling-out, of course) addresses most of the problem; but there remains a residue untouched. Consider, for instance, an extreme example of an action with bad consequences in the distant future. Suppose we could now gain some slight advantage by using a nuclear technology that would produce hazardous wastes, which could be stored for a long while but which would inevitably escape eventually, causing deaths and sickness from radiation. Once the wastes exist, their escape is literally inevitable, as is the harm they will do. (Clearly the example is artificial; I am not seriously attempting to evaluate any actual nuclear technology.) This sort of effect, when brought about by human action, is considered by the rights-theorist to be a violation of rights; but by hypothesis none of the affected people have as yet been conceived—perhaps not even their parents have been. Is there any moral objection, from the point of view of a rights theory, to our use of this technology? The moral theory tells us not to violate rights; but is our use of this technology in itself a violation of rights?

It seems rather to be a necessary condition of (certain) violations, which is not *sufficient* without *further* actions—namely, acts of procreation—on the part of others. If the technology is adopted and at the same time procreation ceases, no ill effects will ever be felt from the radiation; for by the time it escapes, there will be no people. This kind of case differs from the normal one: ordinarily procreation comes first, followed by the action which violates the created person's rights. Then we can regard the procreative act as blameless, the subsequent act as the violation. But in the present case the order is reversed: *first* the nuclear technology is adopted, and *only then* do the acts of procreation take place which result in deaths and sickness. So long as the facts about the nature of this technology are widely known,[4] the people who produce children under the circumstances have no excuse: *their* action is the proximate cause of the violation of their children's rights, and so *they* have acted wrongly.

So it seems, if we look only at the rights of the children; but the rights-theorist can also appeal to the rights of the parents. And among them he can discern a new human right—hitherto overlooked, but not implausible—namely, the right to *blameless procreation.* Some writers have upheld a simple right to procreate; i.e., to make one's own decisions as to how many children to have, if any. But none have mentioned that, besides the normal forms of coercion which may not legitimately be applied to determine reproductive behavior, there is a sort of *moral* coercion which is equally illegitimate.

This is illustrated by our example of the nuclear technology. Suppose that before the technology is adopted I could have children without thereby violating their rights; but once the technology is adopted, the radiation will adversely affect any children I might have. Then the adoption of this technology deprives me of an ability which I formerly had—the ability *to have children without thereby violating their rights* (i.e., to procreate blamelessly). Here, then, is the objection to adopting this technology: not that it violates the rights of my (potential) children, but that it violates *my* right to blameless procreation.

Note that it would not avail the rights theorist to appeal to the simple right to procreate; on this basis alone no clear condemnation of the use of the nuclear technology will be forthcoming. The act of adopting this technology simply creates a conflict between my children's right not to be assaulted by radiation and my simple right to procreate. Creating such a conflict is not violating a right: situations in which rights conflict do not normally involve any rights-*violations* at all. Instead, the strengths of the competing rights must be weighed against each other; and the weaker must be *overridden* (*not* violated). In the present case the right not to be assaulted by radiation probably must be adjudged stronger than the right to procreate, so the latter must give way before the former. (If, on the contrary, the right to procreate were deemed stronger, then it would remain in full force even after the adoption of the nuclear technology, and would not be *violated* by the latter at all. But the rights-theorist must dismiss this possibility, since he wants to claim that the children's being assaulted by radiation is a *violation,* not merely a *legitimate overriding,* of their rights.)

Perhaps it is preferable to reject the idea of *real* conflicts of rights by conceiving of rights as conditional, each containing the implicit proviso: " . . . provided this does not conflict with the exercise of a stronger right". If so, again, the adoption of the nuclear technology does not violate my (conditional) right to procreate, but (at worst) renders it inoperative by falsifying the proviso. Only the stronger right to *blameless* procreation will give the rights theorist a basis for condemning the adoption of the nuclear technology.

This new right may seem to add to the proliferation of putative rights about which some commentators have complained in recent years. But it actually seems less problematic than many of its fellows. Rights to, e.g., a good diet, a loving and supportive environment, an education, a job, must be conceived as "positive" or "welfare" rights, rights which impose a duty on others not just to refrain from acting upon the rights-possessor in certain ways, but actively to provide him with certain benefits if he lacks them. Such rights are evidently conditional, and not just upon their non-interference with stronger rights: for it might be physically impossible to observe them (there might not be enough food to go around, or enough resources to provide everyone with education). Furthermore, they seem to require some inbuilt qualification to allow for the fact that it may be through one's own reckless or improvident actions that he finds himself without food, universally hated, or otherwise lacking in that to which he allegedly has a right. But the right to blameless procreation can be conceived as a purely negative right—if I am in a position in which I can have children without thereby violating their rights, no one may legitimately force me out of that position. At least for present purposes it need not be added that if I am *not* in that position others are obliged to *put me in it.*

Is this new right a right to *unlimited* blameless procreation, or is it limited to, say, one or two children? In a world choked and suffocating with overpopulation (a hypothetical world, which may or may not be our actual one) would it be plausible to uphold the unlimited version of this right—or even a limited one? I think the unlimited right can be vindicated.

Indeed, in the overpopulated world it may well be that everyone is actually *in a position* to procreate as much as he likes without violating anyone's rights. Since it is hard to see how the rights of bystanders could be violated by the mere production of a new child,[5] let us focus on the rights of the child itself. If there are no welfare rights, or if welfare rights are given a conditional interpretation in which the welfare right to X is just the fact that *if possible* everyone should have X, then the child's rights will not be violated by its conception. For example, conceiving a child that inevitably will starve does not violate its rights if it has no right to food, or if it has only a conditional right and the condition is not met (e.g., because there is a food shortage). This is different from the case of conceiving a child after the nuclear technology has been adopted: in the latter the child will be *assaulted,* and so (it is plausible to suppose) a purely negative right of his is violated.

Perhaps, though, there is a stronger sort of welfare right to food, which *is* violated when parents conceive a child who they know will starve. Still, it is not likely that the parents' procreative act is the proximate cause of the children's starving; for probably there are others who could provide food for the children, even if the parents cannot. If the children nevertheless starve it is these others who have violated the children's welfare right to be fed: the parents are blameless.

But in the absence of such others, and in the presence of strong welfare rights, it is true that people *cannot* procreate blamelessly. They lack the *ability* or *opportunity* to do so. However, this is no basis for denying them the *right* to blameless procreation: the distinction between right and ability or opportunity is fundamental for the understanding of rights. Probably the people came to be unable to procreate blamelessly because their right was violated by someone (e.g., by their parents in conceiving them); although if we introduce "acts of God" or natural disasters as possible proximate causes, we may be able to explain this lack of opportunity without blaming anyone. But in any case let us not confuse right with opportunity. Lack of opportunity may make a right *empty* or *valueless,* but not *non-existent.* Hence the right to blameless procreation need not be qualified by any numerical limitation.

We have discussed the case in which an individual's possible future children would be physically affected by a present action, though he himself would not be; and pointed out that such an action can be viewed as violating one of his rights. Now, because of the nature of this right—the right to blameless procreation—the analysis can be iterated indefinitely, and so applied to cases in which the physical effects are felt only by a more distantly future generation. People in the generation immediately prior to that in which the effects are felt have had one of their rights violated, as has already been explained. But if the action in question occurred before *their* conception, then their parents should not have had *them* (assuming the circumstances were known). For it was already determined beforehand that one of their rights would be violated—namely, the right to blameless procreation. In conceiving them, their parents knowingly caused a violation of their rights, for which the parents must bear the responsibility. But since the parents are thus blameworthy, *their* right to blameless procreation must have been violated. If the action which brought about this situation occurred before *their* conception, their parents ought not to have had *them;* etc. No matter how distant are the consequences, it will still be true that the rights of contemporary people are violated by the same act that would violate the rights of the future people (if there were any). Note that when the physical effects are several generations distant it is even clearer that the right to procreation *simpliciter* does not, while the right to *blameless* procreation does, provide a basis for condemning the action.

In practical cases we would not be sure who would be adversely affected by the radiation, or just when it would escape. This introduces the complicating factor of uncertainty, and raises the question: If I am not sure whether a possible action of mine will violate someone's rights, but believe that the probability is p that it will do so, then how close to unity must p be for the rights theory to forbid my doing the action? This question, though, is beyond the scope of the present note, as are a number of other familiar questions about how a rights theory of morality should be spelled out. Nor have I addressed the difficult general question: which rights are and which are not accompanied by the right to their blameless exercise?

Indeed, my aim has been limited to determining how a rights theory might best cope with the problem of actions affecting the further future. We have seen that, contrary to first appearances, such a theory can forbid certain actions whose negative physical effects occur only in the distant future, on the grounds that they do after all infringe a right of people now living.

There remains of the original problem only this much: that if, contrary to morality, the nuclear technology *is* used and the wastes generated, the rights theory seems to imply that people in the last generation before the radiation escapes should all stop having children, lest they be responsible for the violation of the children's rights. This is not obviously the correct answer, since even if they are condemned to die early from the escaped radiation the children will perhaps have lives that are worth living as a whole. Furthermore, the rights theory might condemn the conception of the children even if the radiation were to produce only sickness, not death: the issue here turns on whether the right not to be sickened by radiation is stronger or weaker than the simple right to procreate. (If stronger, we get an unacceptable conclusion; if weaker, we have no rights-theoretical basis for condemning the adoption of a nuclear technology whose wastes produce only sickness.) Finally, the rights theory seems to condemn the conception of children who would not be affected by the radiation but whose descendants would be. It will do so if the children's right to blameless procreation is considered stronger than the parents' simple right to procreate—as it must be in order to support the rights-theorist's condemnation of the nuclear technology. Clouding these issues is the fact that there are no generally accepted guidelines for weighing rights against each other. But my analysis has at least narrowed the scope of the problem facing the rights-theorist, and indicated the lines along which his defense of his position must proceed.[6]

Notes

[1] J. McMahan, 'Problems of population theory', *Ethics* 92 (1981), pp. 96–127, Section IX.

[2] D. Parfit, *Reasons and Persons* (Oxford, 1984), Part Four, Section 124: 'Why an appeal to rights cannot solve the problem'.

[3] This now-familiar point was first made by Derek Parfit, 'On doing the best for our children', in Michael D. Bayles, ed., *Ethics and Population* (Cambridge, MA, 1976), pp. 100–115.

[4] I assume full information on the part of every agent in the situation; for my purposes ignorance would present an unprofitable complication.

[5] In a fuller analysis the situation of the siblings, if any, would have to be considered explicitly.

[6] This paper was read before the Canadian Philosophical Association, May, 1985. For helpful comments I want to thank the CPA referees, especially Trudy Govier, and my commentator, Thomas Hurka.

DAVID A. J. RICHARDS
CONTRACTARIAN THEORY, INTERGENERATIONAL JUSTICE, AND ENERGY POLICY

Arguments of justice are, I take it, forms of moral argument especially concerned with the distribution of goods and evils among the conflicting claims of persons on them. Qua moral, these arguments define forms of practical reasoning that persons would find reasonable whether they are on the giving or receiving end. Moral reasoning thus

From Douglas MacLean and Peter G. Brown, eds. *Energy and the Future.* Totowa, N.J.: Rowman and Littlefield, 1983. Pp. 132–135, 138–145, 148–150. Reprinted with permission.

conceptually incorporates some significant constraint of reciprocity—what some philosophers would call universalizability and others, role reversibility. . . .

In my judgment, we should introduce at this point the Kantian idea of treating persons as equals.[1] When we engage in moral argument we appeal to forms of practical reasoning whereby we inquire whether putative conduct is one persons would reciprocally accept, whether on the giving or receiving end. In Kantian terms, moral argument invokes our capacity to think critically about our lives and to take personal responsibility for them as beings capable of freedom and reason;[2] we identify others as persons by their having the like capacity; and in reasoning morally and acting accordingly, we treat others in terms of principles we and they would reasonably accept, thus expressing respect for their human dignity.

These remarks are obscure, but sufficient to suggest that the idea of equality relevant to the deeper analysis of the concept of justice is the same idea of equality relevant to moral argument generally. Accordingly, the moral idea of reciprocity, which invokes this idea of equality, is not that of reciprocal actual advantage, but that of treating persons in the way one would oneself reasonably like to be treated.

CONTRACTARIAN THEORY AS AN INTERPRETATION OF MORAL RECIPROCITY

Contractarian theory affords one useful way of organizing these moral ideas in a manner that, consistent with them, yields determinate forms of practical reasoning. For clarity of exposition, I shall first summarize the analytic model and the general form of the principles of justice derivable from it; then we may turn to the proper interpretation of the model for the analysis of intergenerational justice.

The basic analytic model is this:[3] moral principles are those that perfectly rational persons, in a hypothetical "original position" of equal liberty, would agree to as the ultimate standards of conduct applicable at large. Persons in the original position are thought of as ignorant of their specific situations, values, or identities, but as possessing all knowledge of general empirical facts and as holding all reasonable beliefs. . . .

The original position presents a problem of rational choice under uncertainty: rational people in the original position have no way of predicting the probability that they will end up in any given situation of life. If a person agrees to principles of justice that permit deprivations of liberty and subsistence rights and later discovers that he occupies a disadvantaged position, he will, by definition, have no just claim against deprivations that may render his life prospects meager and bitterly servile. To avoid such consequences, the rational strategy in choosing the basic principles of justice would be the conservative "maximin" strategy: one would seek to maximize the minimum condition, so that if a person were born into the worst possible situation of life allowed by the adopted moral principles, he would still be better off than he would be in the worst situation allowed by other principles.

The choice of which fundamental principles of justice to adopt requires consideration of the weight assigned to general goods by those in the original position. "General goods" are those things or conditions that are typically the objects of rational choices or desires as the generalized means to a variety of particular desires. It is natural to classify forms of liberty as general goods. Obviously, various rights and liberties are important generalized means enabling each person to pursue his particular ends, whatever they may be. Liberties of thought and expression (freedom of speech, the press, religion, association), civic rights (impartial administration of civil and criminal law in defense of property and person), political rights (the right to vote and participate in political constitutions), and freedom of physical, economic, and social movement are fundamental in this respect. Similarly, it is natural to identify opportunity, property, and wealth as basic distributive goods.[4]

In the interpretation of these general goods and their relative weights, self-respect or esteem for the autonomy of moral personality occupies a place of special prominence. Autonomy, in this sense, is the capacity of persons to plan and shape their lives in accordance with evidence and arguments to which, as rational and independent beings, they personally assent. The competent exercise of such capacities in the pursuit of one's life plan forms the basis of self-respect, without which one is liable to suffer from despair, apathy, and cynicism.[5] Thus, persons in the original position, each concerned to create favorable conditions for the successful pursuit of his life plan but ignorant of his position in the resulting social order, would agree to regulate access to general goods so as to maximize the possibility that every member of society will be able to achieve self-respect.

An important feature of the contractarian interpretation of moral personality is the assumption of ignorance of specific identity. This assumption ensures that the principles decided on in the original position will be neutral among divergent visions of the good life, for the ignorance of specific identity deprives people of any basis for illegitimately distorting their decisions in favor of their own vision. Such neutrality ensures to people the right to choose their own lives autonomously as free and rational beings.[6]

In such ways, contractarian theory expresses the Kantian idea of equality and reciprocity in terms of those principles that would rationally be agreed to by persons from an original position of equal liberty, and the Kantian idea of autonomy is expressed by the stipulation that the contractors choose under a veil of ignorance, thus depriving them of any way of taking account of any features of themselves other than their personhood. . . .

For Kantian ethics, the morally fundamental issue is the relationship among persons as free and rational agents independent of ethically fortuitous features of one's life; from this perspective, one's generation is as irrelevant as one's race, gender, religion, or the like. Accordingly, the natural contractarian expression of this Kantian thought is a hypothetical contract including all generations.

A REPLY TO SOME PARADOXES

The proposal of a contract including all generations may appear paradoxical on several grounds. Brian Barry has suggested that it is question-begging to include all generations and incoherent to include potential future persons whose very existence may turn on the choices made by earlier generations. Surely, Barry suggests, we should not merely give ethical relevance to persons who happen to get born, for it is not without moral weight that, should the human race end in 500 as opposed to 500,000 years' time, potential persons would not have been born.[7] Derek Parfit has elaborated a form of this argument by suggesting that the idea of a hypothetical contract of all generations depends on an indefensible notion of personal identity.[8] Since present policies will determine who the persons of future generations are and each policy will produce different persons, no coherent sense can be given to making persons better off or worse off in the required way since they will be, ex hypothesi, different persons.

First, there appears to be nothing question-begging in analyzing intergenerational justice in terms of a hypothetical contract among all generations that ever exist. The suggestion is surely an intuitive one that as long as persons exist whose actions affect other persons, these relationships may be appropriately analyzed in terms of what I have called moral reciprocity. While one cannot rule out the end of humankind from modern technology of mass destruction or from some unavoidable disaster, it is not an unreasonable factual assumption . . . that many generations will continue to inhabit and use the scarce resources of our world. The moral imagination that these judgments require is not, in principle, different from that we extend to persons currently existing. Only a hypothetical contract among all generations captures, I believe, the full force of intergenerational justice as obligations to persons in other generations.

Second, that future generations are potential persons does not alter the ethical analysis of our relations to them. Our obligations here are owed not to some mysterious set of Kantian noumena waiting to be born (crying, as in the finale of the Richard Strauss opera, *Die Frau Ohne Schatten,* for life), but to the persons whom we may reasonably expect our actions to affect in the future. That we have obligations to persons who do not currently exist appears to me no more ethically demanding than that we have obligations to people of different races, genders, or nationalities. The failure to take seriously the moral fortuity of one's own generation is, I submit, a failure of moral imagination on a par with systematic forms of immorality like racism or sexism.

Third, the appeal to our intuitions about the immorality of ending the human race seems to me threadbare. The suggestion is that an injustice of some kind would be done to potential persons if the human race were ended, and that the interpretation of the contract as extending to all persons who happen ever to exist fails to express this moral fact. But is this a moral fact? I submit that it is not; indeed, that it rests on the worst kind of philosophical fantasy (deserving Wittgensteinian exorcism), attempting to draw determinate moral judgments from cases that we have difficulty in imagining, namely, what kind of situation would exist in which humans lost interest in giving birth to and training future generations. Insofar as I can give a sense to such fantasies, no obligation of justice appears to be thus violated; at most, arguments of beneficence or of personal ideals might be in order.[9] Certainly, as I have pointed out, persons can sensibly believe themselves to be under moral obligations to have children. On the other hand, surely, people sometimes sensibly suppose themselves to be under moral duties to limit procreation (in the interest, for example, of intergenerational justice) and sometimes not to procreate at all (for example, in the certain knowledge that one's child will be mongoloid or dreadfully deformed).[10] It is within the range of my imagination that humans might sensibly decide as a species not to continue; for example, if their children's future appeared to them to involve an irreversible turn in evolution back to earlier animal forms, humans might reasonably decide to preserve the culture they have, for whatever other rational species might evolve, rather than to permit their inhuman children to destroy all that humankind has contributed. So far from such a decision's violating moral obligations, we might arguably in such circumstances be under moral obligations to the previous generations that created human culture not to procreate. In general, however, we should leaven such fantasy with the reality of more ordinary human experience and remind ourselves that not everything in which we invest our personal ideals and aspirations (including the quality of civilization and its development and perpetuation) is an object of moral obligation, let alone an obligation of justice.[11]

Fourth, the Parfit personal identity thesis fails, I believe, to grapple with the relevant moral perspective. That our choice of a certain policy may lead to one class of persons existing as opposed to another does not disable us from raising and answering the question of how, whoever exists, persons will fare under different policies. If, for example, we aply Rawls's maximin strategy intergenerationally, presumably we would choose that policy that makes the worst-off class best off relative to some sensible index of primary goods, such as adequate nutrition and health. Thus, a range of different policies may, in Parfit's sense, result in different persons, including different persons in the worst-off class. But the maximin strategy sensibly picks that policy where the worst-off class, defined here in terms of the index of malnutrition and health, is better off than under any alternative policy, whether or not the persons are different under alternative policies. The identity of the persons under one policy or another is irrelevant. Whether the policy in question involves energy, population, or eugenics, a reasonable interpretation of moral reciprocity does not require that we think in terms of a particular person, but rather in terms of the more general category—persons who will later exist—so that we can assess how, if we were in that category, we would reasonably want to be treated.

The assessment of such questions is conducted in person-affecting terms in an unexceptionable sense: we assess the ethical implications of alternative policies in terms of their impacts on the persons who will exist as a consequence of those policies. The person-affecting terms here deployed do not make reference to some biological individual, whose personal identity, in Parfit's sense, is supposed to be the same under alternative policies: rather, we make reference to the features of moral personality relevant to ethically assessing the actions in question, namely, whether persons—under a veil of ignorance, including ignorance of biological identity—would agree to principles that better secure certain primary goods than alternative principles in the context of decisions about future generations, whether in the form of energy, population, eugenic, or whatever policy.

SUBSTANTIVE PRINCIPLES OF INTERGENERATIONAL JUSTICE AND ENERGY POLICY

If we interpret intergenerational justice in terms of the hypothetical contract of all generations, how would we assess questions of energy policy? Ethical issues of energy policy subdivide into two categories: current forms of energy use or disposal that may harm future generations in serious ways, and resource base depletion.

Harms inflicted by one generation on later generations would appear to require scrutiny under accepted intratemporal principles of not harming or killing the innocent: for example, criminal prohibitions on intentional or knowing infliction of harm, culpable negligence, and the like. With respect to negligence, to the extent that intergenerational harms are reasonably foreseeable consequences of present conduct, the temporal distance of the harm appears to be morally irrelevant. Indeed, cases of intergenerational negligence may be more morally serious than intratemporal cases.

Negligence, both in the law of crimes[12] and the law of torts,[13] is judged in terms of deviations from a standard of acceptable risk imposition; under this standard, unintentional harms may be judged nonnegligent if the probability and gravity of the harm is not large relative to the corresponding gains from the relevant activity. Many activities in modern life impose actuarially predictable harms of serious kinds (e.g., construction of buildings or tunnels, driving automobiles) but, in view of the gains from such activities, we impose negligence liability only when the probabilities and harms exceed reasonable levels. One crucial feature of nonnegligent reasonableness appears to be an element of fairness: the risks and gains tend to be allocated to the same general classes of persons, who undertake both to reap the benefits and bear the costs of the activity in question.[14] In applying negligence principles intergenerationally the fairness feature is saliently absent: the class of persons who reaps the benefit of the activity (the present generation) is not the class who bears all the costs (future generations). This divergence of benefit and burden, combined with the future generation's lack of any voluntary choice in the matter, appears to make intergenerational cases of foreseeable risk imposition morally more questionable than comparable intratemporal cases, quite independent of any disproportion of benefits and burdens. Harms of such kinds in this context appear to be morally asymmetrical with corresponding benefits, and any cost-benefit analysis that suppresses or ignores this moral feature is flatly unethical.

In view of these morally troubling features of intergenerational risk imposition, the general argument about the uncertainty of the future should not suffice, as it might in the intratemporal case, to discount the severity of irreversible and irreparable harms in view of corresponding benefits. In short, we cannot ethically apply in any straightforward way analogies about negligent risk-imposition in the intratemporal case to the intergenerational case. Several suggestions might be in order. For example, since the benefits are not obviously reaped by future generations, a lower risk of harm imposition than in the intratemporal case might suffice to rule out the policy—whether the damage is from the greenhouse effect, permanent destruction of the natural or cultural environment, or higher incidence of disease or defect. At a minimum, the burden of proof must be placed on the proponents of such policies to show how the risks of such harms have been reduced to a morally tolerable minimum. Even within this minimum, the probable imposition of such harms would appear to require, under traditional tort principles of strict liability for ultra-hazardous or nonreciprocal risks,[15] the existence of some fund for tort compensation to whoever may later suffer. None of these suggestions is intended to define a final answer in these matters, but only to suggest the kind of inquiry that would be ethically proper in defining principles of intergenerational risk imposition.

The question of resource base depletion requires us to consider the question of intergenerational distributive justice. From the point of view of the contract of all generations, the moral issue would crucially focus on the depletion of nonrenewable resources: to what extent, if at all, may one generation irreparably deplete the resource base into which persons will later be born? All the arguments that render the maximin strategy of rational choice suitable in many contexts of intratemporal, intrastate justice appear to apply, a fortiori, to this intertemporal question:[16] the possibility of disaster for later generations is real, making the abundance of earlier generations appear disproportionate; indeed, since the disaster would apply to a whole generation, not (as in the intratemporal case) to a subgroup of the present population, the contractors of all generations would understandably converge on intergenerational principles motivated by making the worse off better off. With respect to the energy resource base, a maximining argument in the original position would tend toward some form of equality principle defined in suitably neutral terms consistent with allowing each generation to define the meaning of its own cultural life.

These considerations explain, I believe, why perceptive analysts of intergenerational justice (Brian Barry and Talbot Page) have converged on a principle of equal opportunity, for a principle of this kind provides a neutral standard of intergenerational justice consistent with treating each generation equally and fairly. . . .

The hypothetical contractors of all generations will best secure their aim, consistent with the veil of ignorance, of the highest lowest by requiring each generation to leave the aggregate resource base as good as they found it, relative to the state of culture and technology and the use thus made of resources for realizing general human goods. Accordingly, the depletion of even a nonrenewable resource will not be ruled out if, concurrent with that depletion, a technology has been developed that will meet the depletion and make available to later generations, consistent with obligations of not imposing irreparable harms, a technology that can secure from depleted resources at least as much (for example, energy) as would have been secured from the original resource. Relative to the state of culture-technology thus developed, the intergenerational requirement of equal opportunity will not have been violated.

This intergenerational principle is, I assume, a minimal requirement of intergenerational decency. Indeed, it may be too low a benchmark. Consider, for example, the failure to adopt a reasonable policy of population control, so that a later generation finds itself with a resource base inheritance that meets the equal opportunity criterion, but is overburdened by a population size that is not its responsibility. Arguably, this would work an intergenerational injustice, for the earlier generation's resource base cum culture-technology fails to meet the demands of a larger population. The equal opportunity criterion may have to be adjusted upward to the extent one generation fails to limit population size responsibly; the earlier generation must leave not merely the same resource base, but a resource base so improved as to do justice to the reasonable and fair expectations of the too large later generation.

Questions of intergenerational justice are, I believe, of a piece, particularly if one accepts, as I do, the Kantian premise that the ultimate ethical unit is the person. For the same reason that the ethical analysis of international justice requires us, at crucial points, to pierce the metaphysical veil of the nation-state and to analyze the effects of interna-

tional distributive policies on the persons in those states, so too intergenerational justice requires us not to stay pitched at the global level of
the generation (which the unqualified principle of equal opportunity
appears to do), but to analyze the cumulative effects of the whole
range of intergenerational policies (such as population growth and
transmission of culture and technology) on persons in each generation.
Accordingly, satisfying equal opportunity at the generational level
may, absent concurrent policies of population control and the like, be
ethically inadequate.

As an ethical minimum, the equal opportunity principle appears to
me to be clearly correct. No generation (and no nation, for that matter)
has an absolute property right to basic resources. The location of a
particular resource in a certain generation (or nation) is completely
ethically fortuitous. Such resources must at the intergenerational and
international level be equitably shared, consistent with like obligations
of equitable sharing of the technology and culture that transform those
resources into human goods.

Notes

[1]The classic Kantian text is *Foundations of the Metaphysics of Morals*, translated by Lewis
W. Beck (New York: Liberal Arts Press, 1959).

[2]Cf. [R. M.] Hare, *Freedom and Reason* [Oxford: Clarendon Press, 1963].

[3]See [John] Rawls, *A Theory of Justice* [Cambridge: Harvard University Press, 1971];
[David A. J.] Richards, *A Theory of Reasons for Action* [Oxford: Clarendon Press, 1971],
pp. 75–91.

[4]See David A. J. Richards, "Equal Opportunity and School Financing: Towards a
Moral Theory of Constitutional Adjudication," in *University of Chicago Law Review* 32
(1973): 41–49.

[5]See Richards, *A Theory of Reasons for Action*, pp. 257, 265–268; R. W. White, *Ego
and Reality in Psychoanalytic Theory* (New York: International Universities Press, 1963).

[6]Ronald Dworkin, *Liberalism*, in *Public and Private Morality*, edited by Stuart Hamp-
shire (Cambridge: Cambridge University Press, 1978), pp. 113–143.

[7]See [Brian] Barry, "Justice Between Generations," [in *Law, Morality and Society*,
edited by P. M. S. Hacker and J. Raz (Oxford: Clarendon Press, 1977)], pp. 281–283.

[8]See Derek Parfit, "Energy Policy and the Further Future: The Identity Problem,"
[reprinted below]; see also Derek Parfit, "Rights, Interests and Possible People," in
Moral Problems in Medicine, edited by Samuel Gorovitz et al. (Englewood Cliffs, N.J.:
Prentice-Hall, 1976), pp. 369–375.

[9]Cf. Jonathan Bennett, "On Maximizing Happiness," in [R. I.] Sikora and [Brian]
Barry, eds., *Obligations to Future Generations* [Philadelphia: Temple University Press,
1978], pp. 61–73.

[10]See Richards, *A Theory of Reasons for Action*, pp. 134–137.

[11]Cf. Bennett, "On Maximizing Happiness."

[12]See W. R. LaFave and A. W. Scott, *Handbook on Criminal Law* (St. Paul, Minn.:
West Publishing Co., 1972), pp. 208–218.

[13]See W. L. Prosser, *Law of Torts* (St. Paul, Minn.: West Publishing Co., 1971), pp.
139–204.

[14]See George P. Fletcher, "Fairness and Utility in Tort Theory," in *Harvard Law Review* 85 (1972): 537.

[15]See Prosser, *Law of Torts,* pp. 505–516; Fletcher, "Fairness and Utility," p. 537.

[16]Cf. Rawls, *A Theory of Justice,* pp. 150–161.

DEREK PARFIT

ENERGY POLICY AND THE FURTHER FUTURE: THE IDENTITY PROBLEM

I have assumed that our acts may have good or bad effects in the further future.[1] Let us now examine this assumption. Consider first

> *The Nuclear Technician:* Some technician lazily chooses not to check some tank in which nuclear wastes are buried. As a result there is a catastrophe two centuries later. Leaked radiation kills and injures thousands of people.

We can plausibly assume that, whether or not this technician checks this tank, the same particular people would be born during the next two centuries. If he had chosen to check the tank, these same people would have later lived, and escaped the catastrophe.

Is it morally relevant that the people whom this technician harms do not yet exist when he makes his choice? I have assumed here that it is not. If we know that some choice either may or will harm future people, this is an objection to this choice even if the people harmed do not yet exist. (I am to blame if I leave a man-trap on my land, which ten years later maims a five-year-old child.)

Consider next

> *The Risky Policy:* Suppose that, as a community, we have a choice between two energy policies. Both would be completely safe for at least two centuries, but one would have certain risks for the further future. If we choose the Risky Policy, the standard of living would be somewhat higher over the next two centuries. We do choose this policy. As a result there is a similar catastrophe two centuries later, which kills and injures thousands of people.

Unlike the Nuclear Technician's choice, our choice between these policies affects who will be later born. This is not obvious, but is on reflection clear.

Our identity in fact depends partly on when we are conceived. This is so on both the main views about this subject. Consider some particular person, such as yourself. You are the nth child of your mother, and you were conceived at time t. According to one view, you could not have

From Douglas MacLean and Peter G. Brown, eds. *Energy and the Future.* Totowa, N.J.: Rowman and Littlefield, 1983. Pp. 166–176, 178. Reprinted with permission.

grown from a different pair of cells. If your mother had conceived her nth child some months earlier or later, that child would *in fact* have grown from a different pair of cells, and so would not have been you.

According to the other main view, you could have grown from different cells, or even had different parents. This would have happened if your actual parents had not conceived a child when they in fact conceived you, and some other couple had conceived an extra child who was sufficiently *like* you, or whose life turned out to be sufficiently like yours. On this other view, that child would have been you. (Suppose that Plato's actual parents never had children, and that some other ancient Greek couple had a child who wrote *The Republic, The Last Days of Socrates,* and so on. On this other view, this child would have been Plato.) Those who take this other view, while believing that you could have grown from a different pair of cells, would admit that this would not *in fact* have happened. On both views, it is in fact true that, if your mother had conceived her nth child in a different month, that child would not have been you, and *you* would never have existed.

It may help to shift to this example. A fourteen-year-old girl decides to have a child. We try to change her mind. We first try to persuade her that, if she has a child now, that will be worse for her. She says that, even if it will be, that is her affair. We then claim that, if she has a child now, that will be worse for her child. If she waits until she is grown up, she will be a better mother, and will be able to give her child a better start in life.

Suppose that this fourteen-year-old rejects our advice. She has a child now, and gives him a poor start in life. Was our claim correct? Would it have been better for him if she had taken our advice? If she had, *he* would never have been born. So her decision was worse for him only if it is against his interests to have been born. Even if this makes sense, it would be true only if his life was so wretched as to be worse than nothing. Assume that this is not so. We must then admit that our claim was false. We may still believe that this girl should have waited. That would have been better for her, and the different child she would have had later would have received a better start in life. But we cannot claim that, in having *this* child, what she did was worse for *him*.

Return now to the choice between our two energy policies. If we choose the Risky Policy, the standard of living will be slightly higher over the next two centuries. This effect implies another. It is not true that, whichever policy we choose, the same particular people will exist two centuries later. Given the effects of two such policies on the details of our lives, it would increasingly over time be true that people married different people. More simply, even in the same marriages, the children would increasingly be conceived at different times. (Thus the British Miners' Strike of 1974, which caused television to close down an hour early, thereby affected the timing of thousands of conceptions.) As we have seen, children conceived at different times would in fact be different children. So the proportion of those later born who would owe their existence to our choice would, like ripples in a pool, steadily grow. We can plausibly assume that, after two centuries, there would no one living who would have been born whichever policy we chose. (It may help to think of this example: how many of us could truly claim, "Even if railways had never been invented, I would still have been born?")

In my imagined case, we choose the Risky Policy. As a result, two centuries later, thousands of people are killed and injured. But if we had chosen the alternative Safe Policy, these particular people would never have existed. Different people would have existed in their place. Is our choice of the Risky Policy worse for anyone?

We can first ask, "Could a life be so bad—so diseased and deprived—that it would not be worth living? Could a life be even worse than this? Could it be worse than nothing, or as we might say 'worth *not* living?' " We need not answer this question. We can suppose that, whether or not lives could be worth not living, this would not be true of the lives of the people killed in the catastrophe. These people's lives would be well worth living. And we can suppose the same of those who mourn for those killed, and those whom the catastrophe disables. (Perhaps, for some of those who suffer most, the rest of their lives would be worth not living. But this would not be true of their lives as a whole.)

We can next ask: "If we cause someone to exist, who will have a life worth living, do we thereby benefit this person?" This is a difficult question. Call it the question whether *causing to exist can benefit.* Since the question is so difficult, I shall discuss the implications of both answers.

Because we chose the Risky Policy, thousands of people are later killed or injured or bereaved. But if we had chosen the Safe Policy these particular people would never have existed. Suppose we do *not* believe that causing to exist can benefit. We should ask, "If particular people live lives that are on the whole well worth living, even though they are struck by some catastrophe, is this worse for these people than if they had never existed?" Our answer must be "no." If we believe that causing to exist *can* benefit, we can say more. Since the people struck by the catastrophe live lives that are well worth living and would never have existed if we had chosen the Safe Policy, our choice of the Risky Policy is not only not worse for these people, it *benefits* them.

Let us now compare our two examples. The Nuclear Technician chooses not to check some tank. We choose the Risky Policy. Both these choices predictably cause catastrophes, which harm thousands of people. These predictable effects both seem bad, providing at least some moral objection to these choices. In the case of the technician, the objection is obvious. His choice is worse for the people who are later harmed. But this is not true of our choice of the Risky Policy. Moreover, when we understand this case, we know that this is not true. We know that, even though our choice may cause such a catastrophe, it will not be worse for anyone who ever lives.

Does this make a moral difference? There are three views. It might make all the difference, or some difference, or no difference. There might be no objection to our choice, or some objection, or the objection may be just as strong.

Some claim

> *Wrongs Require Victims:* Our choice cannot be wrong if we know that it will be worse for no one.

This claim implies that there is no objection to our choice. We may find it hard to deny this claim, or to accept this implication.

I deny that wrongs require victims. If we know that we may cause such a catastrophe, I am sure that there is at least some moral objection to our choice. I am inclined to believe that the objection is just as strong as it would have been if, as in the case of the Nuclear Technician, our choice would be worse for future people. If this is so, it is morally irrelevant that our choice will be worse for no one. This may have important theoretical implications.

Before we pursue the question, it will help to introduce two more examples. We must continue to assume that some people can be worse off than others, in morally significant ways, and by more or less. But we need not assume that these comparisons could be even in principle precise. There may be only rough or partial comparability. By "worse off" we need not mean "less happy." We could be thinking, more narrowly, of the standard of living, or, more broadly, of the quality of life. Since it is the vaguer, I shall use the phrase "the quality of life." And I shall extend the ordinary use of the phrase "worth living." If one of two groups of people would have a lower quality of life, I shall call their lives to this extent "less worth living."

Here is another example:

> *Depletion:* Suppose that, as a community, we must choose whether to deplete or conserve certain kinds of resources. If we choose Depletion, the quality of life over the next two centuries would be slightly higher than it would have been if we had chosen Conservation, but it may later be much lower. Life at this much lower level would, however, still be well worth living. The effects might be shown as in Figure 10.1

This case raises the same problem. If we choose Depletion rather than Conservation, this will lower the quality of life more than two centuries from now. But the particular people who will then be living would never have existed if instead we had chosen Conservation. So our choice of Depletion is not worse for any of these people. But our choice will cause these people to be worse off than the different people who, if we had chosen Conservation, would have later lived. This seems a bad effect, and an objection to our choice, even though it will be worse for no one.

Would the effect be *worse,* having greater moral weight, if it *was*

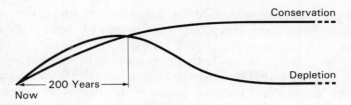

Figure 10.1 Effects of Choice on Future Standard of Living

worse for people? One test of our intuitions may be this. We may remember a time when we were concerned about effects on future generations, but had overlooked my point about personal identity. We may have thought that a policy like Depletion would be against the interests of future people. When we saw that this was false, did we become less concerned about effects on future generations?

I myself did not. But it may help to introduce a different example. Suppose there are two rare conditions X and Y, which cannot be detected without special tests. If a pregnant woman has condition X, this will give to the child she is carrying a certain handicap. A simple treatment would prevent this effect. If a woman has condition Y when she becomes pregnant, this will give to the child she conceives the same particular handicap. Condition Y cannot be treated, but always disappears within two months. Suppose next that we have planned two medical programs, but there are funds for only one; so one must be canceled. In the first program, millions of women would be tested during pregnancy. Those found to have condition X would be treated. In the second program, millions of women would be tested when they intend to try to become pregnant. Those found to have condition Y would be warned to postpone conception for at least two months. We are able to predict that these two programs would achieve results in as many cases. If there is Pregnancy Testing, 1,000 children a year would be born normal rather than handicapped. If there is Pre-Conception Testing, there would each year be born 1,000 normal children, rather than 1,000 different handicapped children. Would these two programs be equally worthwhile?

Let us note carefully what the difference is. As a result of either program, 1,000 couples a year would have a normal rather than a handicapped child. These would be different couples, on the two programs. But since the numbers would be the same, the effects on parents and on other people would be morally equivalent. The only difference lies in the effects on the children. Note next that, in judging these effects, we need have no view about the moral status of a fetus. We can suppose that it would take a year before either kind of testing could begin. When we choose between the two programs, none of the children has yet been conceived. And all of the children will become adults. So we are considering effects, not on present fetuses, but on future people. Assume next that the handicap in question, though it is not trivial, is not so severe as to make life doubtfully worth living. Even if it can be against our interests to have been born, this would not be true of those born with this handicap.

Since we cannot afford both programs, which should we cancel? Under one description, both would have the same effects. Suppose that conditions X and Y are the only causes of this handicap. The incidence is now 2,000 a year. Either program would halve the incidence; the rate would drop to 1,000 a year. The difference is this. If we decide to cancel Pregnancy Testing, those who are later born handicapped would be able to claim, "But for your decision, I would have been normal." Our decision will be worse for all these people. If instead we decide to cancel Pre-Conception Testing, there will later be just as many people who are born with this handicap. But none of these could truly claim, "But for your decision, I would have been normal." But for our decision, they would never have existed; their parents would have later had different children. Since their lives, though handicapped, are still worth living, our decision will not be worse for any of these people.

Does this make a moral difference? Or are the two programs equally worthwhile? Is all that matters morally how many future lives will be normal rather than handicapped? Or does it also matter whether these lives would be lived by the very same people?

I am inclined to judge these programs equally worthwhile. If Pre-Conception Testing would achieve results in a few more cases, I would judge it the better program. This matches my reactions to the questions asked above about our choice of the Risky Policy or of Depletion. There too, I think it would be bad if there would later be a catastrophe, killing and injuring thousands of people, and bad if there would later be a lower quality of life. And I think that it would not be *worse* if the people who later live would themselves have existed if we had chosen the Safe Policy or Conservation. The bad effects would not be worse if they had been, in this way, worse for any particular people.

Let us review the argument so far. If we choose the Risky Policy or Depletion, this may later cause a predictable catastrophe, or a decline in the quality of life. We naturally assume that these would be bad effects, which provide some objection to these two choices. Many think the objection is that our choices will be worse for future people. We have seen that this is false. But does this make a moral difference? There are three possible answers. It might make all the difference, or some difference, or no difference at all. When we see that our choice will be worse for no one, we may decide that there is no objection to this choice, or that there is less objection, or that the objection is just as strong.

I incline to the third answer. And I give this answer in the case of the medical programs. But I know some people who do not share my intuitions. How can we resolve this disagreement? Is there some familiar principle to which we can appeal?

Return to the choice of the Risky Policy, which may cause a catastrophe, harming thousands of people. It may seem irrelevant here that our choice will not be worse for these future people. Can we not deserve blame for causing harm to others, even when our act is not worse for them? Suppose that I choose to drive when drunk, and in the resulting crash cause you to lose a leg. One year later, war breaks out. If you had not lost this leg, you would have been conscripted, and been killed. So my drunken driving saves your life. But I am still morally to blame.

This case reminds us that, in assigning blame, we must consider not actual but predictable effects. I knew that my drunken driving might injure others, but I could not know that it would in fact save your life. This distinction might apply to the choice between our two policies. We know that our choice of the Risky Policy may impose harm on future people. Suppose next that we have overlooked the point about personal identity. We mistakenly believe that, whichever policy we choose, the very same people will later live. We may therefore believe that, if we choose the Risky Policy, this may be worse for future people. If we believe this, our choice can be criticized. We can deserve blame for doing what we *believe* may be worse for others. This criticism stands even if our belief is false—just as I am as much to blame even if my drunken driving will in fact save your life.

Now suppose, however, that we have seen the point about personal identity. We realize that, if we choose the Risky Policy, our choice will *not* be worse for those people whom it later harms. Note that this is not a lucky guess. It is not like predicting that, if I cause you to lose a leg, that will later save you from death in the trenches. We know that, if we choose the Risky Policy, this may impose harms on several future people. But we also know that, if we had chosen the Safe Policy, those particular people would never have been born. Since their lives will be worth living we *know* that our choice will not be worse for them.

If we know this, we cannot be compared to a drunken driver. So how should we be criticized? Can we deserve blame for causing others to be harmed, even when we know that our act will not be worse for them? Suppose we know that the harm we cause will be fully compensated by some benefit. For us to be sure of this, the benefit must clearly outweigh the harm. Consider a surgeon who saves you from blindness, at the cost of giving you a facial scar. In scarring you, this surgeon does you harm. But he knows that his act is not worse for you. Is this enough to justify his decision? Not quite. He must not be infringing your autonomy. But this does not require that you give consent. Suppose that you are unconscious, so that he is forced to choose without consulting you. If he decides to operate, he would here deserve no blame. Though he scars your face, his act is justified. It is enough for him to know that his act will not be worse for you.

If we choose the Risky Policy, this may cause harm to many people. Since these will be future people, whom we cannot now consult, we are not infringing their autonomy. And we know that our choice will not be

worse for them. Have we shown that, in the same way, the objection has
been met?

The case of the surgeon shows only that the objection might be met.
The choice of the Risky Policy has two special features. Why is the
surgeon's act not worse for you? Because it gives you a compensating
benefit. Though he scars your face, he saves you from going blind. Why
is our choice of the Risky Policy not worse for those future people?
Because they will owe their existence to this choice. Is this a compensating benefit? This is a difficult question. But suppose that we answer "no."
Suppose we believe that to receive life, even a life worth living, is not
to be benefited.[2] There is then a special reason why, if we choose the
Risky Policy, this will not be worse for the people who will later live.

Here is the second special feature. If we had chosen the Safe Policy,
different people would have later lived. Let us first set aside this feature.
Let us consider only the people who, given our actual choice, will in fact
later live. These will be the only actual people whom our choice affects.
Should the objection to our choice appeal to the effects on these people?
Because of our choice, they will later suffer certain harms. This seems
to provide an objection. But they owe their existence to this same choice.
Does this remove the objection?

Consider a second case involving a fourteen-year-old girl. If this
second girl has a child now, she will give him a poor start in life. But
suppose she knows that, because she has some illness, she will become
sterile within the next year. Unless she has a child now, she can never
have a child. Suppose that this girl chooses to have a child. Can she be
criticized? She gives her child a poor start in life. But she could not have
given *him* a better start in life, and his life will still be worth living. The
effects on him do not seem to provide an objection. Suppose that she
could also reasonably assume that, if she has this child, this would not
be worse for other people. It would then seem that there is no objection
to this girl's choice—not even one that is overridden by her right to have
a child.

Now return to our earlier case of a fourteen-year-old girl. Like the
second girl, the first girl knows that, if she has a child now, she will give
him a poor start in life. But she could wait for several years and have
another child, who would have a better start in life. She decides not to
wait, and has a child now. If we consider the effects only on her actual
child, they are just like those of the second girl's choice. But the first
girl's choice surely can be criticized. The two choices differ, not in their
effects on the actual children, but in the alternatives. How could the
second girl avoid having a child to whom she would give a poor start
in life? Only by never having a child. That is why her choice seemed not
to be open to criticism. She could reasonably assume that her choice
would not be worse either for her actual child or for other people. In
her case, that seems all we need to know. The first girl's choice has the
same effects on her actual child, and on others. But *this* girl could have
waited, and given some later child a better start in life. This is the

objection to her choice. Her actual child is worse off than some later child would have been.

Return now to the choice between our two social policies. Suppose that we have chosen the Risky Policy. As a result, those who later live suffer certain harms. Is this enough to make our choice open to criticism? I suggest not. Those who later live are like the actual children of the two girls. They owe their existence to our choice, so its effects are not worse for them. The objection must appeal to the alternative.

This restores the second feature that we set aside above. When we chose the Risky Policy, we imposed certain harms on our remote descendants. Were we like the second girl, whose only alternative was to have no descendants? If so, we could not be criticized. But this is not the right comparison. In choosing the Risky Policy, we were like the first girl. If we had chosen the Safe Policy, we would have had different descendants, who would not have suffered such harms.

The objection to our choice cannot appeal only to effects on those people who will later live. It must mention possible effects on the people who, if we had chosen otherwise, would have later lived. The objection must appeal to a claim like this:

(A) It is bad if those who live are worse off than those who might have lived.

We must claim that this is bad even though it will be worse for no one.

(A) is not a familiar principle. So we have not solved the problem that we reached above. Let us remember what that was. If we choose the Risky Policy, or Depletion, this may later cause a catastrophe, or a decline in the quality of life. These seemed bad effects. Many writers claim that, in causing such effects, we would be acting against the interests of future people. Given the point about personal identity, this is not true. But I was inclined to think that this made no moral difference. The objection to these two choices seemed to me just as strong. Several people do not share my intuitions. Some believe that the objections must be weaker. Others believe that they disappear. On their view, our choice cannot be morally criticized if we know that it will be worse for no one. They believe that, as moral agents, we need only be concerned with the effects of our acts on all of the people who are ever actual. We need not consider people who are merely possible—those who never do live but merely might have lived. On this view, the point about identity makes a great moral difference. The effects of our two choices, the predictable catastrophe, and the decline in the quality of life, can be morally totally ignored.

We hoped to resolve this disagreement by appeal to a familiar principle. I suggest now that this cannot be done. To criticize our choice, we must appeal to a claim like (A). And we have yet to explain why (A) should have any weight. To those who reject (A), we do not yet have an adequate reply.

To explain (A), and decide its weight, we would need to go deep into moral theory. And we would need to consider cases where, in the different outcomes of our acts or policies, different numbers of people would exist. This is much too large a task to be attempted here.

I shall therefore end with a practical question. When we are discussing social policies, should we ignore the point about personal identity? Should we allow ourselves to say that a choice like that of the Risky Policy, or of Depletion, might be against the interests of people in the further future? This is not true. Should we pretend that it is? Should we let other people go on thinking that it is?

If you share my intuitions, this seems permissible. We can then use such claims as a convenient form of short-hand. Though the claims are false, we believe that this makes no moral difference. So the claims are not seriously misleading.

Suppose instead that you do not share my intuitions. You believe that, if our choice of Depletion would be worse for no one, this must make a moral difference. It would then be dishonest to conceal the point about identity. But this is what, with your intuitions, I would be tempted to do. I would not *want* people to conclude that we can be less concerned about the more remote effects of our social policies. So I would be tempted to suppress the argument for this conclusion.

Notes

[1] The first third of this section is adapted from my "Future Generations: Further Problems," *Philosophy & Public Affairs* 11, no. 2 (Spring 1982).

[2] Thus we might say: "We are benefited only if the alternative would not have been worse for us." If we had never existed, this would not have been worse for us." These and similar arguments I claim not to be decisive in my "Future Generations." Even if it can be in our interests to have been conceived, most of my later claims would still stand.

chapter *11*

Morality in War

INTRODUCTION

Historical philosophers have defined a state of war as the period of open hostilities or the threat of such.[1] This concept of war is still used in some contexts. For example, despite the absence of fighting, as no peace treaty has been signed, Israel is said still to be at war with some of its neighbors. As the purpose of this chapter is to consider the morality of conduct in war, "war" is used in its more usual sense of hostilities and combat.

There are three central issues concerning morality and war.

1. In what circumstances, if any, is a country justified in going to war? In classical theory, this has been called the issue of *jus ad bellum*—justice of war.

2. What conduct is permissible or prohibited in conducting a war—*jus in bello* (justice in war)?

3. Who can be held responsible for wrongful conduct in going to or fighting a war?

Classical theory tended to ignore this last issue, because people were not held accountable for wrongful conduct relating to war. With the trial of war criminals after World War Two and some soldiers for war crimes in Vietnam, it has become important.

The Charter for the Nuremberg Tribunal at the end of World War Two specified three different types of crimes[2]

1. Crimes against peace involve planning and directing wars of aggression or in violation of international treaties.

2. War crimes consist in violations of laws or customs of war.

3. Crimes against humanity primarily involve inhumane acts, such as extermination, against civilian populations.

377

The expression war crime is often used to cover any or all of these specific crimes.

Justifications for War   Pacifism is the view that war cannot be justified. Some pacifists hold that one is never justified in using force or violence against another; they would not even permit the use of force or violence against a rapist. Other pacifists do not condemn the use of force by police against criminals, but they do reject its use in war.[3] One must distinguish pacifism from conscientious objection. The latter is refusal to participate in a war, in particular, to refuse induction into the armed forces. U.S. law requires that one be opposed to all war, and thus a pacifist, to obtain conscientious objector status.[4] Selective conscientious objection, that is, objection to some but not all wars, is certainly plausible. Indeed, most philosophical theories of justifications for war imply that sometimes war is morally permissible and sometimes it is not, and consequently that sometimes there are sufficient moral reasons for refusing to fight and sometimes not.

Classical just war theory stems from St. Thomas Aquinas. He held that there are three conditions for a just war.[5] First, it must be by the decision of a ruler with competence to declare war; private individuals cannot make wars. Second, there must be a just cause; those attacked must deserve it. Third, there must be a right intention to achieve a good or avoid an evil. The first condition is straightforward. The third can cause difficulties because aims can change during a war, but the general idea is that a country cannot use some wrong as a pretext for acquiring territory and so forth. It is the second condition that is most troublesome.

Today, many people think of a justifiable war as one in response to aggression, and the Nuremberg crime against peace clearly supports the claim that wars of aggression are not justifiable. In effect, there are two claims.

1. Defense against aggression is always justifiable.

2. Aggression is never justifiable.

Whether these claims are correct partly depends on how one conceives of aggression. One must determine who is the object of aggression. International law treats war as a relation between states, so aggression is against states. However, aggression against states need not significantly harm persons in them. For example, sending war or even fishing ships within territorial limits might be considered aggression against a state, but it need not harm its citizens. So construed, it seems doubtful that a victim state would always be justified in going to war. If so, the first claim is probably not correct. Some theorists support this point by holding that the good to be achieved, even in defense against aggression, must outweigh the evil of war.[6]

To support the second claim, one might construe aggression as initiating hostilities—firing the first shot or sending troops into another country's territory. At first blush, it seems plausible that such aggression is never justifiable. A moment's reflection casts doubt on this claim. No less a thinker than Immanuel Kant distinguished aggression from first hostilities and thought war justified in response to aggressive threats.[7] An example would be Israel's 1967 first strike on the basis of reliable intelligence that other countries would soon attack. Consequently, the second claim, that aggression is always wrong, also seems incorrect. Nevertheless, war in defense against aggression endangering the lives and well-being of citizens, such as Nazi Germany's invasion of Poland in 1939, is a widely accepted justification for war.

Another often defended justification for war is to eliminate injustice in another country. Historically and in international law, it is claimed that countries ought not intervene in the internal affairs of others. However, there are extremes of injustice that people using various theories believe can justify a war to "liberate" foreign citizens.[8] Possible examples would be the invasion of Cambodia to save the people from the Khmer Rouge regime that executed up to one third of the population, or against Nazi Germany had Hitler not invaded other countries but still run extermination camps inside Germany. However, not all theorists agree with this view.[9]

In sum, then, there is fairly widespread agreement that war in response to aggression seriously endangering the lives and well-being of citizens is justifiable. A preemptive first strike against imminent aggression of this sort is also justifiable. Although more controversial and not accepted in international law, many theorists believe war to stop gross injustice in another country is justified. Apparently all agree that proportionality in doing more good than evil is always required, although different theories determine the good and evil differently, that is, in terms of rights, utilities, and so on.

Morality in War It is tempting to believe that anything is fair in war if not in love. War is hellish, and if the very survival of one's country or way of life is at stake, then surely anything goes. On reflection, however, this view is implausible. Would a country be justified in amputating the legs of all prisoners so they could not escape, and then castrating them so that after the war they would not be able to produce a new generation capable of war? Or, to take an historical example, is it justifiable to destroy a conquered city totally and literally plow it under as the Romans did to Carthage? All ethical theories place limits on the type of conduct that is permissible in prosecuting a war.

Another initially tempting but ultimately unsatisfactory view is that if a country is not justified in going to war, then all acts of combat by its individual soldiers are wrong. The difficulty is that one cannot simply transfer the wrongness of the acts of the leaders of a country to those of individuals in it. A soldier, for example, might be conscripted and have little choice in fighting. Moreover, it is often unclear whether or not the war is unjustified. There was much disagreement over the justifiability of the United States fighting in Vietnam and even greater disagreement over the Civil War. The principles of right conduct in war apply to all soldiers, whether or not their cause is just.

Natural-law theory has two basic principles regarding the morality of conduct in war—those of proportionality and discrimination. The principle of proportionality states that the force used must be proportional to the end sought. The end is both the immediate military end and the general political end of the war.[10] As an example of a political end, one might say that the use of a nuclear bomb on North Korea during the Korean War would have been disproportionate to the political end of stopping the invasion of South Korea. The military end, however, is the one more usually in question. Some weapons are thought to inflict greater casualties than militarily necessary. For example, dumdum bullets, which splinter and send fragments throughout the bodily area where a person is hit, produce excessive long-term damage not necessary for rendering a person *hors de combat*. Although a variety of military weapons are completely banned by international agreements, the weakness of the principle of proportionality is military necessity or effectiveness. No weapon that is highly effective is likely to be found disproportionate to the end sought. Thus, considerable debate has surrounded the use of flame throwers and napalm bombs, but they have not been banned.

The principle of discrimination primarily pertains to who can be a legitimate target of military action. The principle is often stated as prohibiting intentional attack on noncombatants, but it might better be stated as prohibiting intentional attack on nonmilitary targets. Who exactly is a noncombatant is highly debatable, and usually some nonuniformed personnel, such as munitions workers at work, are considered legitimate targets of attack. It is important that the natural-law principle prohibits intentional attack. Many theorists use the doctrine of double effect, which states that killing can be justified as a known side effect, provided it is not intended as a means or end and the good sought outweighs the evil done. For example, it would be permissible to bomb Gestapo headquarters in Copenhagen although innocent prisoners held in cells below and other Danes might be killed or injured.[11] Yet, area bombing of civilian population centers cannot be justified by this doctrine, in part because the intention is to kill noncombatants and the policy was not successful, that is, did not produce a proportionate good.[12]

On a *natural-rights* view, the fundamental principle is that a permissible act does "not violate the rights of the people against whom it is directed."[13] As everyone has a natural right to life, it seems that any killing in war would violate natural rights. There are two possible ways to avoid this conclusion. One is to use the right of self-defense as derived from soldiers' rights to life. On this approach, soldiers have a right to kill attackers to defend their own right to life. However, this approach faces a difficulty with the use of missiles, bombs, and artillery killing at a distance. Often those attacked pose no immediate threat to a soldier's life. One must, then, expand the notion of those threatening one to include all persons significantly participating in the war effort. Alternatively, one can take the view that combatants give up or forfeit their right to life. Again, one will need to take a broad view of what acts forfeit the right to life, for example, delivering military supplies.

A coordinate restriction would be to prohibit some means of attack as unnecessary to defend oneself or violating rights not forfeited. Soldiers do not forfeit rights to live without unnecessary injuries, as might be caused by dumdum bullets, after the war. The extent of injury caused by such bullets is also unnecessary for self-defense. The application of a natural rights view to weapons and means of attack requires considerable analysis.

On a *Kantian* view, one must ask what methods of war one could not will as a universal law. Kant himself had a very limited view about what is forbidden in war. His primary principle is that war must be conducted so as not to preclude a future peace.[14] Among the actions he thought prohibited were the use of assassins, poisoners, killing by ambush, and even spies. Charitably, one must recognize that he was writing at a time when wars were usually conducted by formal armies confronting each other on a clear field of battle, as during the Napoleonic Wars.

One could also use Kant's formula of humanity as an end—that people must be treated as ends and not as mere means. On this formula, one might hold that combatants have accepted the risk of death. Therefore, killing them is permissible for it stems from an activity they have chosen. (Of course, a conscript has not made a fully voluntary choice.) Noncombatants are not engaged in military activity and so have not accepted the risk of death.[15] Similarly, weapons causing unnecessary suffering go beyond what enemy combatants could will and thus fail to respect them as ends.

A *contractarian* account of morality in war requires a significant modification of Rawls's view. He restricts his contractors and principles to those for a single state, but war is between states. Hence, one must conceive of a contract between persons from various states who do not know to which state they belong. Given the maximin strategy of choosing to make the worst-off persons as well off as possible and/or the principle of greatest equal liberties, contractors would adopt principles limiting killing and injury so far as possible to combatants.[16] They would also agree to limit death and destruction as much as possible, and this would presumably include weapons that cause unnecessary suffering.

General *utilitarian* guidelines to morality in war were formulated a century ago by Henry Sidgwick.[17] He gave two main principles governing moral combat. First, any harm that does not materially contribute to the ends of the disabling or the submitting of the enemy is wrong. Second, acts that contribute only slightly to these ends in comparison to the amount of harm they cause are wrong. Both of these principles are straightforward applications of the principle of utility. In the first, one causes harm but does not produce any good, so the conduct cannot be useful. In the second, the harm caused is greater than the good promoted. Unlike natural-law theorists, utilitarians would not be concerned with whether one intentionally or only foreseeably kills noncombatants. The general goal is to avoid killing them, but it makes no difference whether, in particular circumstances, their deaths are intended or merely foreseen.

An *act utilitarian* would apply these principles to particular situations. Thus, there would not be any absolute prohibitions. Each particular situation would have to be evaluated on its own. To take a classical situation, a patrol behind enemy lines that captures prisoners it cannot care for and whose release might endanger an important mission might find the greatest net utility in killing them. Considerations of long-run utility might alter this judgment. If one's side kills prisoners, even in such situations, the other side is likely to do so as well. In the long run, this could create less utility than if both sides refrained from killing prisoners. In particular, if there are generally accepted conventions about treatment of prisoners or noncombatants that produce long-run utility, an act utilitarian would have good reason to comply with the convention.[18] However, an act utilitarian would always permit an exception to such rules or conventions if, in a particular situation and taking into account effects on long-run utility, more net utility would be gained by breaking them.

Rule utilitarians stick by their rules. However, a major issue is whether all the rules would have an exception for military necessity. If one is engaged in a war and believes that victory for one's side is a great good, then any rule that significantly decreases the chances for victory would not promote the greatest net utility. For any major war, one should believe victory to be a great good, otherwise the massive destruction and many deaths cannot be thought justified. Consequently, rules would probably contain an exception for military necessity. This does not mean some military advantage but when compliance with the rule would probably lead to the loss of the war. Consequently, although rule utilitarians will have rules protecting noncombatants and prohibiting the use of weapons causing unnecessary harm, many if not all of these rules will have exceptions.

Responsibility for War Crimes Even if an act contrary to rules of war has been committed, the actor might not be responsible for it. Generally, this issue should be settled on the basis of the usual principles of criminal responsibility. The chief issue that is different is the defense of superior orders, that is, the claim that one is not responsible or did not commit a wrong act because one was obeying orders. The standard view, expressed by the Nuremberg Tribunal, is that superior orders do not constitute a defense for illegal conduct.[19] Nevertheless, as applied at Nuremberg the question was whether a person had a "moral choice."[20] Unfortunately, the expression moral choice is not clear. The general idea is that when the punishment for disobedience is great and immediate, especially the possible loss of one's life, persons are not to be blamed for choosing their own lives over those of others.[21] Other reasons exist why low-ranking soldiers might not be responsible. They are trained to obey instantly; the wrongfulness of an order is not always apparent; and in the midst of combat with one's life at stake, it is not possible to exercise calm deliberation and fully voluntary choice.

Matters are generally deemed to be otherwise with high-ranking military officers and political officials. They have more time to reflect on the justifiability of policies and orders; their lives are not usually in immediate danger. However, at least two issues arise even for military leaders. First, are they responsible for the conduct of their troops even if they have no effective control over their conduct and have not given orders or adopted policies supporting war crimes? The U.S. Supreme Court has held that they are,[22] but many people question the fairness and justice of that view. Second, are leaders responsible if they adopt policies that do not explicitly order or require war crimes but that are likely to lead to their commission?

Readings   In the first selection, Robert L. Phillips offers a contemporary natural-law argument for the justifiability of killing in war. He presents the principle of proportionality. He then uses the doctrine of double effect to distinguish between murder and killing a combatant. Killing a combatant is justifiable if one intends only to kill the combatant in the person, that is, stop the person being a threat. If one directly intends the person's death, then the killing is wrong and murder. The selection ends with a brief excerpt of his application of the doctrine to killing noncombatants.

Anthony E. Hartle, in the second selection, analyzes two humanitarian principles underlying the laws of war. He argues that the first, that "individual persons deserve respect as such," has priority over the second concerned with minimizing suffering. The first principle is closely analogous to Kant's formula of treating persons as ends, never merely as means. Thus, Hartle's argument can be construed as one for the priority of a Kantian principle over utilitarian concerns.

In the final selection, Richard Brandt provides a utilitarian basis for rules of war. He begins by restricting the rules to those that would not prevent a country using all necessary power to win. Given this major restriction, he then analyzes rules not imposing any cost on military success, rules that would possibly limit military success, and finally rules that would require military losses. A major consideration that he invokes is the long-run utility of rules for future wars.

Notes

[1]Thomas Hobbes, *Leviathan*, ed. Michael Oakeshott (Oxford: Basil Blackwell, n.d.), Chapter 13, p. 82; Immanuel Kant, *The Metaphysical Elements of Justice*, trans. John Ladd (Indianapolis, Ind.: Bobbs-Merrill, 1965), p. 116, Akademie, p. 344; Immanuel Kant, *Eternal Peace*, trans. Carl J. Friedrich, in *The Philosophy of Kant*, ed. Carl J. Friedrich (New York: Modern Library, 1949), p. 436.

[2]International Tribunal at Nuremberg, "Judgment and Opinion," in *War and Morality,* ed. Richard A. Wasserstrom (Belmont, Calif.: Wadsworth, 1970), p. 102.

[3]See T. R. Miles, "On the Limits to the Use of Force," *Religious Studies* 20 (1984): 113–120; Jenny Teichman, *Pacifism and the Just War* (New York: Basil Blackwell, 1986), Chapter 5.

[4]*Gillette* v. *United States,* 401 U.S. 437 (1971).

[5]*Summa Theologica,* II–II, Q. 40, a. 1.

[6]See William V. O'Brien, *The Conduct of Just and Limited War* (New York: Praeger, 1981), p. 28.

[7]*Metaphysical Elements of Justice,* p. 119, Akademie, p. 346. See also Nicholas Fotion and Gerard Elfstrom, *Military Ethics* (Boston: Routledge & Kegan Paul, 1986), p. 114.

[8]See Fotion and Elfstrom, *Military Ethics,* p. 115 (utilitarian); David A. J. Richards, *A Theory of Reasons for Action* (Oxford: Clarendon Press, 1971), pp. 137–138 (contractarian); David Luban, "Just War and Human Rights," *Philosophy and Public Affairs* 9 (1980): 175 (natural rights); Daniel F. Montaldi, "Toward a Human Rights Based Account of the Just War," *Social Theory and Practice* 11 (1985): 145 (Kantian rights); and Robert L. Phillips, *War and Justice* (Norman: University of Oklahoma Press, 1984), pp. 20–21 (natural law).

[9]O'Brien, *Conduct of Just and Limited War,* p. 23 (natural law).

[10]O'Brien, *Conduct of Just and Limited War,* p. 40.

[11]Phillips, *War and Justice,* pp. 48–50.

[12]Phillips, *War and Justice,* pp. 51–55; John C. Ford, S.J., "The Morality of Obliteration Bombing," in *Morality and War,* ed. Richard A. Wasserstrom (Belmont, Calif.: Wadsworth, 1970), pp. 15–41.

[13]Michael Walzer, *Just and Unjust Wars* (New York: Basic Books, 1977), p. 135.

[14]Kant, *Eternal Peace,* p. 434; Kant, *Metaphysical Elements of Justice,* p. 120, Akademie p. 347.

[15]For an interesting variant of the Kantian position, see Barrie Paskins and Michael Dockrill, *The Ethics of War* (Minneapolis: University of Minnesota Press, 1979), pp. 221–236.

[16]See also Richards, *A Theory of Reasons for Action,* pp. 143–144.

[17]*The Elements of Politics* (London: Macmillan, 1891), p. 254.

[18]See also George I. Mavrodes, "Conventions and the Morality of War," *Philosophy and Public Affairs* 4 (1975): 117–131.

[19]"Judgment and Opinion," p. 109.

[20]Guentér Lewy, "Superior Orders, Nuclear Warfare, and the Dictates of Conscience," in *War and Morality,* ed. Richard A. Wasserstrom (Belmont, Calif.: Wadsworth, 1970), p. 119.

[21]Richard Wasserstrom, "The Responsibility of the Individual for War Crimes," in *Philosophy, Morality, and International Affairs,* ed. Virginia Held, Sidney Morgenbesser, and Thomas Nagel (New York: Oxford University Press, 1974), pp. 57–58.

[22]*In re Yamashita,* 327 U.S. 1 (1945).

Bibliography on Morality in War

Bailey, Sidney. *Prohibitions and Restraints in War.* London: Oxford University Press, 1972.

Childress, James F. *Moral Responsibility in Conflicts: Essays on Nonviolence, War, and Conscience.* Baton Rouge: Louisiana State University Press, 1982.

Cohen, Marshall, Nagel, Thomas, and Scanlon, Thomas, eds. *War and Moral Responsibility.* Princeton, N.J.: Princeton University Press, 1974.

Falk, Richard A., Kolko, Gabriel, and Lifton, Robert Jay, eds. *Crimes of War.* New York: Random House, 1971.

Fotion, Nicholas, and Elfstrom, Gerard. *Military Ethics: Guidelines for Peace and War.* Boston: Routledge & Kegan Paul, 1986.

Held, Virginia, Morgenbesser, Sidney, and Nagel, Thomas, eds. *Philosophy, Morality and International Affairs.* New York: Oxford University Press, 1974.

Luban, David. "Just War and Human Rights." *Philosophy and Public Affairs* 9 (1980): 160–181.

Montaldi, Daniel F. "Toward a Human Rights Based Account of the Just War." *Social Theory and Practice* 11 (1985): 123–161.

O'Brien, William Vincent. *The Conduct of Just and Limited War.* New York: Praeger, 1981.

Paskins, Barrie, and Dockrill, Michael. *The Ethics of War.* Minneapolis: University of Minnesota Press, 1979.

Phillips, Robert L. *War and Justice.* Norman: University of Oklahoma Press, 1984.

Ramsey, Paul. *The Just War: Force and Political Responsibility.* New York: Charles Scribner's Sons, 1968.

Taylor, Telford. *Nuremberg and Vietnam: An American Tragedy.* New York: Quadrangle, 1970.

Wakin, Malham M., ed. *War, Morality, and the Military Profession.* 2d ed. Boulder, Colo.: Westview Press, 1986.

Walzer, Michael. *Just and Unjust Wars: A Moral Argument with Historical Illustrations.* New York: Basic Books, 1977.

Wasserstrom, Richard A., ed. *War and Morality.* Belmont, Calif.: Wadsworth, 1970.

Problem Case
Taking a Village

Lt. Carl's patrol moved along the small dirt road through the jungle. Presently, it came within sight of a small village across an open space of about 100 yards. Enemy troops had been reported in the village, and Lt. Carl's orders were to remove them.

Two days earlier, leaflets had been dropped on the villages in this area warning them that attack might be forthcoming. Headquarters assumed that innocent civilians would evacuate the villages and that those who remained were enemy soldiers or their supporters. However, Lt. Carl believed that unlikely. Minelets had been dropped along and around all the jungle trails and roads in the area, making it unlikely civilians would risk leaving their villages.

As he watched, Lt. Carl saw two enemy troops with military pants and rifles, but wearing peasant shirts, cross between houses. He also saw a couple of women, one with a small child, go down a street. He had his men spread out around the edge of the clearing, then called in artillery fire on the village. After a short barrage, he and his men attacked.

After the village was taken, eight enemy dead were found. The rest had probably escaped into the jungle. Two civilians and one child had been killed by the artillery fire, and two apparently unarmed teenagers had been killed by his men while attacking. Lt. Carl had lost one man killed, and three wounded—one by a mine in crossing the clearing to the village and another by a booby-trap in the village.

Is it permissible to drop minelets (small plastic mines) on jungle paths and roads heavily used by civilians as well as enemy? Should Lt. Carl have attacked without the artillery barrage, even though he might have lost more men, to avoid casualties to civilians in the village? Are combat soldiers attacking such a village guilty of war crimes if they shoot young men without first checking to see if they are armed enemy?

ROBERT L. PHILLIPS
JUS IN BELLO

I outline below, in point form, the doctrine of the just war. . . .

BELLUM JUSTUM

Jus ad Bellum

   I. Last resort.
  II. Declared by legitimate authority.
 III. Morally justifiable:
    A. Defense against aggression.
    B. Correction of an injustice that has gone uncorrected by legitimate authority "in another place."
    C. Reestablishment of a social order which will distribute justice.
    D. Undertaken with the intention of bringing about peace.

Jus in Bello

   I. Proportionality: The quantity of force employed or threatened must always be morally proportionate to the end being sought in war.
  II. Discrimination: Force must never be applied in such a way as to make noncombatants and innocent persons the intentional objects of attack. The only appropriate targets in war are combatants.
    A. The Principle of Double Effect: In a situation where the use of force can be foreseen to have actual or probable multiple

From *War and Justice,* by Robert L. Phillips. Copyright © 1984 by the University of Oklahoma Press.

effects, some of which are evil, culpability does not attach to the agent if the following conditions are met:

1. The action must carry the intention to produce morally good consequences.
2. The evil effects are not *intended* as ends in themselves or as means to other ends, good or evil.
3. The permission of collateral evil must be justified by considerations of proportionate moral weight. . . .

The "other half" of *bellum justum* is *jus in bello,* or the doctrine of just behavior in combat. . . .

I. *Proportionality.* The principle of proportionality holds that in cases where the use of force is justified it cannot be employed in absolutely any measure. Obviously, if the aim of war is the correction of injustice, then the level of force must not be such as to create new and greater injustices. This principle is sometimes confused with the doctrine of "minimal force," which holds that the least amount of force consistent with effecting the desired ends ought to be our goal. While minimal force should always be used, we also have to consider the *degree* of violence, for some military tasks might very well require a minimum of force which would be disproportionate. That is, our calculations must include not only a forecast of necessary minimal means but also of consequences.

This distinction is of crucial importance because it directs our attention to the means of waging war and thus to the moral questions provoked by certain types of weaponry. In effect, proportionality is not to be calculated relative to a weapons system taken as a "given" but, rather, in terms of a calculus which will include the weapons themselves. So, for example, it may not be morally acceptable to say the following sort of thing: Given the fact of nuclear weapons deployed for massive retaliation, what casualty level is acceptable within the possibilities of these devices? Now this is precisely what some military thinkers have attempted to do . . . , but my contention here is that this move renders the whole conception of proportionality vacuous by making its significance dependent upon whatever weapons happen to exist at a given time. It is, of course, extremely difficult to counter in any meaningful way the onrush of weapons technology. The operative principle of the technocrat is: "If x is possible, then x ought to be"; but the alternative to not doing this is making morality completely subordinate to whatever technological development happens to be occurring at the moment.

I hasten to add that the motivation of those who argue that proportionality is relative to conditions is not simply self-serving. If one knows that certain sorts of weapons will be used which one also knows will cause casualties that are disproportionate on any objective basis, it is obviously morally preferable to attempt to obtain whatever proportionality is possible relative to the system—even in the case of massive retaliation with nuclear weapons. The danger here is that we will fall into the habit of doing no more than this. I suggest that modern history reveals just this pattern of thinking by just-war theorists. A weapon is invented and employed, and suddenly it is a fait accompli. Morality then tags along with a "justification" based ultimately on the principle that even if the means are disproportionate in themselves it is better to try to limit their use than to permit unrestrained employment. This is a principle with which one cannot disagree, but it must not be our guiding principle in thinking about means. Rather, we must evolve some conception of proportion which will allow us to include weapons and modes of warfare *as such* in our prohibitions. It is not, of course, the province of *bellum justum* to provide a criterion of nonrelative proportionality but only to establish that the principles of justice do in fact require such a standard.

II. *Discrimination.* What is true for proportionality is a fortiori true for the principle of discrimination. The notion that force ought to be morally justified only if it can be employed in a discriminate manner lies at the heart of *jus in bello.* The principle of double effect is, in turn, at the heart of discrimination.

(A) Put as simply as possible, by emphasizing intention as the defining feature of moral actions, the supporters of *bellum justum* attempt to mark a difference between killing in war and murder in two different cases. First, the killing of enemy combatants in a justified war may be morally acceptable under some circumstances. Second, the killing of noncombatants incidental to the prosecution of a necessary military operation in a justified war may also be morally acceptable under some circumstances. . . .

The principle of double effect is a refinement of a more general set of considerations having to do with the discriminating use of force. If the use of force by legitimate authority is to be justified, then obviously it cannot be administered in any quantity nor can it be directed at any and every target. This is "obvious" because we are assuming that if anything can be said to be evil it is direct acts of violence upon other people. If there is to be a distinction between killing in war and murder, there must also be a prior conception of relevant differences in potential targets. The most widely discussed aspect of double effect has been noncombatant immunity, and one of the key issues raised here is how to make such immunity compatible with the foreknowledge which we will normally possess of the certain death of noncombatants incidental to military operations.

Double effect is derived from a quite general criterion of moral judgment enunciated succinctly but clearly by Aquinas: "now moral acts take their species according to what is intended and not according to what is beside the intention, since this is accidental" (*Summa* 2.2, q. 64, art. 7).

Aquinas, I take it, is arguing not that the consequences of actions are morally irrelevant but, rather, that when one raises questions about the morality of a particular action (as opposed to its utility, its beauty, and so on) one is inevitably making reference to the agent's intentions. "Accidental" is used here not exclusively to mean the unforeseen but to include the foreseen but undesired consequences of the action. "Accidental" may be understood as "collateral."

Following this line, we may summarize the principle in the following way: In a situation where the use of force can be seen to have actual or probable multiple effects, some of which are evil, culpability does not attach to the agent if the following conditions are met: (1) the action is intended to produce morally good consequences; (2) the evil effects are not intended as ends in themselves or as means to other ends, good or evil; and (3) the permission of collateral evil must be justified by considerations of proportionate moral weight.

How do these considerations apply to the combat situation? There are at least two senses in which it is sometimes claimed that there is no relevant distinction between killing in war and murder. First is the view that all killing is murder, that it is always wrong deliberately to take another human life. This would mean that in the combat situation it would be wrong to kill both combatants *and* noncombatants and, indeed, that there is really no moral difference between these classes. This is clearly a version of pacifism. . . . This view holds that under no circumstances may the death of another human being be directly willed; killing is wrong even if one's own life is placed in grave risk and even if the other person is the aggressor.

According to the second view, the killing of noncombatants is murder, while the death of an aggressor combatant in wartime is morally acceptable. Thus if a war could be fought entirely between combatants, it would be, in principle, possible to avoid committing murder. It is further argued, however, that in an actual combat situation where there is foreknowledge that operations will cause the death of noncombatants, there is no relevant difference between killing and murder. This view has generated two rather strikingly different conclusions with respect to what a moral agent ought to do faced with the possibility of combat.

On the one hand, since modern weaponry is by its very nature indiscriminate, and since foreknowledge of the death of noncombatants cancels whatever good intentions we may offer by way of exculpation, we end up as pacifists by default. While admitting the theoretical possibility of a just war, the indiscriminate use of force which must necessarily be a feature of contemporary warfare makes us pacifists, as it were, "war by war."

On the other hand, starting from the same premises, it has sometimes been argued that since there are no relevant differences between killing and murder with respect to noncombatants, war may be fought without any restraint at all. That is, if a war is justified then the absence of criteria for distinguishing between killing and murder is a permission to employ any means whatever to bring about victory. This argument is frequently found embedded in a larger utilitarian framework which, in extreme cases, would permit the killing of noncombatants as a means of securing peace. This seems to have been the line taken by Sir Arthur Harris over the British terror bombing of German cities in the Second World War. When reproached with the indiscriminate character of carpet bombing Harris replied, "It is war itself which is evil," thus implying the pointlessness of attempting to make distinctions (at least for the purposes of bombing) between combatants and noncombatants.

These then are the two main lines of criticism directed against the moral significance of the principle of double effect and, consequently, of the distinction between killing in war and murder.

Let us turn first to the question: How can we escape the charge that killing an enemy combatant is murder? If force is ever to be morally justified, its employment must be against a target other than a person as such. One must not be directly seeking the death of another human being either as such or as a means to some further end. Therefore, the intention or purpose of the act of force must be toward *restraint* of the aggressor. This is the beginning of an answer to the pacifist. For he and the defender of *bellum justum* are surely in agreement, and correctly so, that the death of another human being ought never to be directly willed if the target is the man himself in his humanity or the man who represents the values of the enemy in a particular historical situation (this prohibition must imply the intrinsic value of other persons). Yet, if force may be justified, then what is the target? The answer must be that the proper target of the discriminate use of force is not the man himself but the combatant *in* the man.

It may be objected that it is a logical impossibility to separate out the totality of actions plus the underlying rationale for such behavior which together constitute the combatant in the man. That is, to speak of a particular man or of "man" in general apart from particular behavior patterns is to speak of a nonentity. Hence, the combatant in the man is not a possible target. Furthermore, it may be urged that even if some such distinction is possible, to kill one is to kill the other. A soldier going into combat with the intention of restraining or incapacitating combatants must know before he ever lifts a weapon that combat will result in the death of a great many persons.

A utilitarian might put the objection in the following way: Jones and Smith both go into combat armed with machine guns. Jones, a supporter of the traditional view, carries with him the intention to incapacitate or restrain the aggressor, whereas Smith intends merely to kill as many of the enemy as he can in order to avoid being killed himself. On meeting the enemy they both open fire, and they both kill one enemy each. What difference does "intention" make from the moral point of view? In both cases an act of extreme violence, the unleashing of a stream of bullets, has resulted in the death of a person. A corpse lies before both Smith and Jones—this is the brute, ultimate fact which no amount of "intentional" redescription can alter. Thus, there is only *one* action here, the killing (possibly murder) of a human being.

In trying to answer this there are two things that have to be said about intention. The first has to do with the way in which awareness of an agent's intentions is crucial in understanding the meaning of an action and consequently in knowing how correctly to describe it. If one were to universalize the utilitarian's position on the irrelevance of intention, the results would be quite disastrous for any attempt to understand human action. Setting the moral question entirely aside, we would be unable to make intelligible whole classes of human behavior if we supposed that such behavior could even be described as human action without making intention central. That is, there are cases where two quite different actions are identical with respect to result, observable behavior, and foreknowledge of the result; and the *only* way to distinguish the two is by reference to intention. As an example, take the case of self-killing. If we follow the critic's suggestion and consider as relevant only foreknowledge of result, behavior patterns, and end result (a corpse), then suicide would be effectively defined as *any* action which the agent knew would bring about his own death. This is clearly absurd, for it would not permit us to distinguish between an officer who shoots himself in order to avoid a court-martial and an officer of the same regiment who courageously fights a rear-guard action in such a way that he knows he will not survive. In both cases there is foreknowledge of one's own death, there are objective behavior patterns leading to that result, and there is the result itself. They differ importantly only with respect to intention. Intention is what makes them different actions. To put the point in a general way, failure to take account of intention means that we are unable to make the difference between doing x in order that y shall result and doing x knowing that y will result.[1]

Smith and Jones both have foreknowledge of the impending death of the enemy, they both take identical action, and the result is the same—the enemy soldier is dead. And yet there are two different actions here: Jones does x knowing that y will result; Smith does x in order that y shall result. Well, the critic might reply, there certainly is a difference in intention here, and, thus a description of what is happening will have to make reference to all the facts. Granted, if we want to understand thoroughly what is going on here, then we must take account not only of what the agent knows and foreknows, of behavior and results, but also of what the agent supposes himself to be doing; and that will involve us in including the element of intention in our explanation of his behavior. Having granted this, one has not shown that intention makes any *moral* difference.

The critic is correct. What has been established so far is that intention is a criterion for distinguishing *different* human actions. The importance of this is that in order to show that different moral verdicts are to be applied to Smith and Jones, we first have to show that there were two separate actions involved. The *moral* difference between their actions is, of course, a different matter. What is the difference? Let us recall the objection: The critic will say that it is sophistry to suppose any moral significance in directing force toward the restraint or incapacitation of the combatant while at the same time using means which we know will result in his death. The end result is the same and will be foreknown to be the same, whether or not we "directly" attack the man.

The crucial difference between Smith and Jones is that the latter is logically committed to behaving differently toward those enemy soldiers who have removed themselves from the role of combatant than is his companion Smith. The belief that force must be directed against the combatant and not against the man is the only presupposition which could provide a moral basis for taking prisoners. Smith would have no reason to observe this distinction. He might, on a whim or for immediate prudential reasons, decide to spare the life of the enemy, but he is not logically committed by his beliefs to doing so. The almost universal belief that a man who voluntarily restrains himself or who is restrained by being wounded ought to be immune from attack is only intelligible on the basis of the distinction between the man and the combatant in the man. The moral principle that prisoners ought to be taken and well treated will itself be justified by showing that it is impossible, except in some wholly imprudent fashion, to universalize the killing of those who have surrendered. That is, no rational being could consistently will the killing of all prisoners and include himself in his own prescription. Thus while Jones will have foreknowledge of the death of the aggressor (an admitted evil) the thrust of his actions will be against the combatant and not the man, and the moral payoff of this is that only he is logically committed to observe the moral principle concerning prisoner immunity. To summarize: To those who argue that there is no relevant difference between killing in war and murder in the case of one combatant killing another, we may reply that it is possible, given a well-thought-out doctrine for the justification of the use of force, to direct forceful actions in such a way that while the death of the enemy may be foreknown it is not willed. The purpose of combats as expressed in the actions of individual soldiers is the incapacitation or restraint of an enemy combatant from doing what he is doing as a soldier in a particular historical situation; it is not the killing of a man. This is the essence of the distinction between killing in war and murder in the case of combatants, and the moral relevance of the premise is exhibited in the obligation to acknowledge prisoner immunity, an obligation not incumbent upon someone who fails to observe the central distinction between the man and the combatant in the man.[2] . . .

So far we have been discussing double effect exclusively in connection with the killing of enemy combatants in an attempt to deal with the criticism that all killing in war is murder. We must now tackle the "other half" of that criticism, namely, that the killing of noncombatants in war is murder. This is obviously a more difficult problem to come to grips with than the question of combatant deaths. For in the latter case the enemy soldier is armed and is personally directing acts of force against others. Although, as we have argued, in directing an act of force against an enemy combatant there should be no intention to kill the person, yet in the case of the aggressor there is an important sense in which he may be said to bring his own death upon himself, particularly in those cases where surrender is possible. A soldier fighting in a just cause may be forced to use weapons which will result in the death of the aggressor, but the aggressor will have participated directly in this outcome. A combatant may change his status by reverting to a noncombatant role; but if he refuses to do so, then much of the responsibility for what happens rests with him.

The problem of noncombatant immunity is frequently thought to center upon the difficulty of distinguishing a separate class of noncombatants, particularly in modern warfare. This is, I think, a large mistake, and it arises in part from an excessively literal reading of war solidarity propaganda. In fact, it is relatively easy to distinguish, in any historical war, whole classes of people who cannot, save in the inflamed world of the propagandist, be said to be combatants in any sense which would make them the object of attack. There will, as with every interesting distinction, be borderline cases. The criterion will be something like this: Generally speaking, classes of people engaged in occupations which they would perform whether or not a war were taking place, or services rendered to combatants both in war and out, are considered immune. This would exempt, for example, farmers and teachers (since education and food are necessities in and out of war) but not merchant sailors transporting war materiel or railway drivers in charge of munitions trains. In other words, the soldiers who are now eating and studying would have to do these things even if they were not soldiers, so that classes of people supplying those sorts of goods and services may be said to be immune from attack, whereas those who are engaged in the production and supply of goods used only in war are not immune. And, of course, certain classes of people may be said to be permanently noncombatant—young children, the mentally defective, and those who are in various ways physically incapacitated. Again, some "hard" or limiting cases will arise, particularly in guerrilla war, but they are less numerous than is sometimes supposed.

The *real* difficulty is not in delineating classes of individuals who merit immunity but in deciding what constitutes a direct attack upon them, for it is plausible to suppose that the deaths of noncombatants can be excused only if their deaths can be construed as collateral or beside the intention of the perpetrators. . . .

Two conclusions can be reached from all of this. To begin with, in a justified war combatants are the objects of attack by other combatants. In this context the use of force is directed toward incapacitation and not toward killing. Combatant deaths may be foreseen, but this is compatible with the intention to incapacitate. Second, noncombatant immunity is presupposed and will be stated in absolute terms. Noncombatant deaths may be foreseen but may also be regarded as collateral damage if they occur in the context of a justified war. . . . The critic's error in both cases is to run together intention and foreknowledge or expectation.

Notes

[1] This is a modification of an example in A. MacIntyre, "The Idea of a Social Science," in *Against the Self-Images of the Age* (London: Duckworth, 1971), pp. 211–229.

[2] There are many excellent discussions of the problem of prisoner immunity. The best is in P. Ramsey, *The Just War*.

ANTHONY E. HARTLE
HUMANITARIANISM AND THE LAWS OF WAR

That moral principles underlie and constrain the activity of members of professions such as medicine and law is generally acknowledged. Whether the same can be said of the military profession is a question likely to generate considerable uncertainty. In this paper I shall show that, like other professions, the military profession is informed by a moral teleology. The source of this teleology, for the profession of arms, is manifested in the laws of war. The laws of war, in turn, reflect two humanitarian principles:

1. Individual persons deserve respect as such (HP1).

2. Human suffering ought to be minimized (HP2).

These two principles differ in terms of schemes of justification; the first is non-consequentialist and appeals to human rights, while the second is consequentialist and is based on utilitarian considerations. My argument will conclude that HP1 has priority over HP2 in the formulation of the laws of war.

I

While there are few instances of provisions of the laws of war that are obviously attributable to one and only one of the two humanitarian

From Anthony E. Hartle, "Humanitarianism and the Laws of War," *Philosophy* 61 (1986): 109–115. © Royal Institute of Philosophy; reprinted with the permission of Cambridge University Press, the publisher.

principles, it also appears that HP1 and HP2 are none the less distinctly different principles that can conceivably come into conflict. A classical combat situation presenting problems of moral choice is that in which enemy soldiers are taken prisoner by a small force carrying out a critical mission behind enemy lines. By examining this type of situation carefully with respect to the two humanitarian principles, we can clarify the moral nature of the laws of war.

Consider the often discussed prisoner case filled out as follows. The success of the small force in carrying out its mission will allow the seizure of a major transportation centre without a significant battle which would affect a sizeable civilian population. If the battle does not occur, many combatant and non-combatant casualties will be avoided as well as extensive destruction of civilian property. The force carrying out the mission, however, takes several wounded enemy soldiers prisoner. The mission is such that accomplishment is not possible if the force keeps its prisoners in custody. If the prisoners are released, it is highly likely that the force will be compromised and that the mission will fail. Under the circumstances, the commander of the force must decide whether to kill the prisoners and whether such execution can be justified.

We are particularly concerned not with his decision, but with the laws of war that apply to such a situation. In the discussion that follows, the two humanitarian principles will be applied directly to situations involving choice among specific alternative actions. With respect to the laws of war as they exist, however, these two principles are the basis for *formulating* the laws. Only in situations for which there is no applicable law or in situations in which the justifiability of a particular law is being questioned would the principles be applied directly in determining appropriate choices of action.

Before examining the existing laws of war on the subject of the treatment of prisoners, we should recognize that there can be a conflict between HP1 and HP2 if we apply these humanitarian principles directly in attempting to decide what to do in a given situation. In our hypothetical example, consideration of the question under HP2 indicates that the answer is 'kill the prisoners', for in the short term this action will cause considerably less suffering than not killing them. Unless we assume some condition such that the warring party to which the capturing force belongs would inevitably lose the war and that capturing the transportation centre would only prolong the war with the result of increased suffering, the logical action under HP2 will be to execute the prisoners and carry on with the mission.

One might object by saying that allowing the execution of prisoners will in the long run be counterproductive, that suffering will thereby be increased by heightening determination not to surrender and by encouraging battles and wars of annihilation, but if the prisoners are executed only in highly exceptional circumstances such as those presented in the hypothetical case above, the objection in terms of long-term effects is not persuasive.

Under HP1, however, the decision to execute the prisoners cannot be justified. If the leader of the capturing force is to respect his prisoners as individual persons, he cannot eliminate them solely as a means of expediting his mission, which he would be doing if he executed them. The prisoners, under HP1, have a basic right not to be treated cruelly or inhumanely. Both descriptions apply to summary execution.

The two humanitarian principles appear to call for opposite courses of action in the prisoner example, a situation which indicates that different laws would be produced if one or the other of the principles were considered in framing laws concerning the treatment of prisoners. There are similar situations that can arise if the two principles are applied directly. Some of the most obvious are those involving deliberate attacks on groups of civilians, use of weapons that are considered inhumane, and resettlement of civilians in occupied territories. We can hypothesize situations in which one course of action appears to be the logical choice if we desire to minimize suffering, while a different course of action is preferable if we are to respect individual persons as such. Our concern with the prisoner example and others like it, however, is that of first determining what the actual laws of war require and then identifying which of the two foundational moral principles underlies the existing law. The answers to two questions will thus clarify the issue. First, what do the laws of war permit or prohibit? Second, from what moral principle is the applicable law of war derived?

With respect to our prisoner example, clear evidence can be found in specific national regulations which are derived from the codified laws of war. Although the American manual, *The Law of Land Warfare*, written in 1956, does not specifically prohibit killing prisoners under any and all circumstances, the wording suggests that intention:

> A commander may not put his prisoners to death because their presence retards his movements or diminishes his power of resistance. . . . It is likewise unlawful for a commander to kill his prisoners on grounds of self-preservation, even in the case of airborne or commando operations . . . (para. 85, p. 35).

The United States Air Force pamphlet, *International Law—The Conduct of Armed Conflict and Air Operations,* reflects the same position in referring to Articles 12–16 of the 1949 Geneva Convention Relative to the Treatment of Prisoners of War, but in more unequivocal terms: 'These provisions prohibit killing or mistreatment of PWs whatever the military reasons . . .' (para. 13-2, p. 13-1). The laws of war, as construed by the United States, prohibit the killing of prisoners. This interpretation of the laws of war appears warranted and is shared by Geneva signatories. Thus, the laws of war that apply in the case of the captured prisoners are derived from HP1 rather than from HP2, for by applying HP2 directly, we found that killing of prisoners of war could be justified in some circumstances. We must conclude, then, that HP1 has priority over HP2 in framing the laws of war in this instance. In fact, such appears to be the case in all situations in which specific rights recognized in the laws of war are involved. In the three additional circumstances suggested above (attacks on civilians, use of inhumane weapons, and resettlement), the applicable laws of war are based upon recognition of the rights of persons and thus derive from HP1. This suggests strongly that, with respect to formulating laws of war in general, HP1 has priority over HP2. If we turn now to the fundamental documents of the codified laws of war, we will find the same moral point of view embodied there.

II

An examination of the current laws of war reveals the humanitarian concern that pervades the requirements and limitations established in their provisions. The 'Martens Clause'[1] found in the preamble to both the 1899 and 1907 Hague Conventions indicates the spirit in which those two sets of constraints on warfare were promulgated:

> Until a more complete code of the laws of war can be issued, the High Contracting parties think it expedient to declare that in cases not included in the Regulations adopted by them, populations and belligerents remain under the protection and the rule of the principles of the laws of nations, as they result from the usages established between civilized nations, from the laws of humanity, and the requirements of the public conscience. . . .[2]

The United States Air Force manual concerning the conduct of armed conflict under the laws of war refers specifically to 'the principle of humanity, which forbids the infliction of suffering, injury or destruction not actually necessary for the accomplishment of legitimate military purposes'.[3] A subsequent passage states: 'The principle of humanity also confirms the basic immunity of civilian populations and civilians from being objects of attack during armed conflict'.[4]

Through the Martens Clause, the Hague Conventions are set upon the foundation of the 'laws of humanity and the requirements of public conscience'. As the United States Air Force manual further points out, the Geneva Conventions in turn

> safeguard such fundamental rights as freedom from torture or cruel and inhuman punishment; freedom from arbitrary exile; freedom from arbitrarily imposed punishment; and right to legal remedy for any abuse; right to minimum standards of respect for human rights at all times; and right to health, family sanctity and non-abuse.[5]

The four Geneva Conventions were produced at the Diplomatic Conference of 1949, and those at the Conference affirmed that their work was 'inspired solely by humanitarian aims'.[6] The law of Geneva is specifically concerned with four primary areas under the heading of humane treatment for 'protected persons':

1. Care of the wounded, sick and shipwrecked.
2. Treatment of prisoners of war.
3. Immunity of non-combatants.
4. Treatment of the population of occupied territory.

All of the prohibitions and requirements in the Conventions can be directly related to the protection of the rights of individual persons.

The Geneva Conventions thus specify measures required by the concept of human rights, which today is the dominant manifestation of the concept of respect for persons. Respect for persons entails the ideas of equality of consideration and human dignity. Individual persons cannot be treated with respect for what they are unless they are considered equally as persons (though that consideration obviously does not further entail equal treatment). To give preferential treatment is to deny the individual discriminated against the full status of a person—a rational being capable of independent choice and thus deserving of respect from other rational beings solely on the basis of that status. Human dignity is inherent in such a concept. In terms of modern ethical theory, the preferred means of establishing a framework for assessing the actions required in order to respect the status of individual persons is the delineation of fundamental human rights.

The principle thrust of the Geneva Conventions of 1949 is the attempt to specify the rights of non-combatants. The primary categories of non-combatants are (loosely) those disabled from fighting and those not directly participating in combat. Honouring their rights as required by the Conventions is a moral and legal obligation placed upon all signatory parties.

An examination of the Hague Conventions shows that they are logically consistent with the second humanitarian principle (HP2). They are specifically concerned with the way in which war is to be waged. Article 23e, which prohibits the employment of weapons or material calculated to cause unnecessary suffering, and the Hague Regulations concerning the protection of prisoners of war and civilians were framed with the intent of ameliorating the evils of war.[7] The articles prohibiting treacherous or perfidious actions were framed to achieve the same end by avoiding the prolongation of war, which would probably occur if such actions were taken. Unless some minimal standards of conduct are mutually recognized, there will be no basis for settlement of the conflict other than the virtual annihilation of one of the warring parties. Almost every provision of the Hague Convention can be seen as a direct means of minimizing human suffering, even though the motivation for establishing the conventions of war codified at The Hague may have been largely prudential.

Observance of the law of The Hague will in most cases cause less human suffering than would be caused by its non-observance. That the law of The Hague manifests the first humanitarian principle (HP1), however, is not as clear. Whether one shoots and kills an enemy soldier with a standard 0·45 calibre round or whether one shoots and kills an enemy with a 0·45 calibre round with a notched bullet appears to have little to do with respecting his status as a person. Such a constraint does, however, clearly have to do with minimizing human suffering.

III

The foregoing discussion shows that the laws of war govern practice under moral principles; accordingly, the legal rights established in the laws of war should reflect moral rights. It is clear that such rights derive from HP1. Since the laws of war do prohibit the killing of prisoners, which is consistent with HP1, one could again conclude that the two humanitarian principles, HP1 and HP2, have a priority relationship in which HP2 is subordinate to HP1. Further, as other examples of potential conflict between the principles indicate, it appears that HP1 will have priority in all cases in which recognized rights are involved. The laws of war specifically recognize that prisoners of war have a right to be treated humanely and with respect for their persons, which must certainly include the right not to be murdered. Accordingly, the right of the prisoners not to be killed would have to be satisfied before the criterion of minimizing suffering is applied. Once the non-consequentialist principle is satisfied, if more than one alternative law remains under consideration, one turns to HP2 for further discrimination among possible laws.

HP2, applied directly to actions, functions just as the Happiness Principle (or Pleasure Principle) functions in act-utilitarian theory. Minimizing suffering is merely the converse of maximizing happiness, so that if HP2 were the sole basis for deciding what to do in situations involving moral choice in warfare, we would be concerned with a particular application of utilitarianism. Our discussion has shown this not to be the case. Further, if HP2 were the principle from which all the laws of war were derived, we would be concerned with a form of rule utilitarianism, with the laws of war being the rules which, all things considered, best served HP2 (such a situation would be the ideal, that is, though it certainly has not been achieved in practice). This, however, is not the case, for HP1 appears to have priority over HP2 in important instances, namely, those in which the two principles conflict. While we have not examined all such cases (nor would it be possible to do so), the representative cases make this a reasonable conclusion. The point argued here is that analysis of the current laws of war reveals that HP1 has priority over HP2 in the formulation of such laws.

In sum, the moral character of the laws of war is articulated by the two humanitarian principles that separately or jointly provide the moral basis for determining specific rules of conduct. The principle that individual persons should be respected as such can, however, come in conflict with the principle that human suffering ought to be minimized. When that occurs, it appears there is a plausible argument for holding that the first principle (HP1) has priority. If HP1 provides the basis for justified participation in war, then HP1 is more fundamental than HP2. And if that is the case, only when the first is satisfied will the second principle be applied. Because the laws of war are incomplete, and will probably remain so, it is important to establish these principles and their relationship. Lastly, though some commentators such as Richard B. Brandt consider a form of utilitarian theory to be the appropriate interpretation of the moral basis of the laws of war,[8] we have seen that HP2, which in itself can be considered a limited utilitarian principle, is more appropriately viewed as subordinate to HP1, which in turn is most plausibly seen as non-consequentialist and thus not a utilitarian principle.

Notes

[1]So called in recognition of the Russian jurist, F. F. Martens, President of the 1899 Hague Conventions (see Sidney Bailey, *Prohibitions and Restraints in War* [Oxford, 1972]).

[2]Leon Friedman (ed.), *The Law of War: A Documentary History* (New York: Random House, 1972), Vol. 1. 309.

[3]Department of the Air Force, *International Law—The Conduct of Armed Conflict and Air Operations,* AF Pamphlet 110-31 (Washington, DC, 19 November 1976), 1–6.

[4]AFP 110-31, p. 1–6.

[5]AFP 110-31, p. 11–4.

[6]Morris Greenspan, *The Modern Law of Land Warfare* (Berkeley: University of California Press, 1959), 22.

[7]This point is presented clearly in the Preamble to Hague Convention No. IV (1907).

[8]Richard B. Brandt, 'Utilitarianism and the Rules of War', *Philosophy and Public Affairs* 1 (Winter 1972), 145–165. [Partially reprinted below.]

R. B. BRANDT
UTILITARIANISM AND THE RULES OF WAR

I wish now to explain in a few words why I think rational, impartial persons would choose rules of war that would maximize expectable utility. Then . . . I shall classify the rules of war into several types, and

From R. B. Brandt, "Utilitarianism and the Rules of War," *Philosophy & Public Affairs* 1. no. 2 (Winter 1972). Copyright © 1972 by Princeton University Press. Excerpt, pp. 152–161 reprinted with permission of Princeton University Press.

try to show that representative rules of each type would be utility-maximizing and therefore chosen. I shall hope (although I shall not say anything explicitly about this) that the ideal rules of war, identified in this way, will coincide with the reflective intuitions of the reader. If so, I assume that this fact will commend to him the whole of what I am arguing.

I have suggested that rational persons . . . believing that their country may well be involved in a war at some time, would prefer rules of war that would maximize expectable utility, *in the circumstance that two nations are at war.* Why would they prefer such rules? About this I shall say only that if they are self-interested they will choose rules which will maximize expectable utility generally, for then their chance of coming out best will be greatest (and they do not know how especially to favor themselves); and that if they are altruistic they will again choose that set of rules, for they will want to choose rules which will maximize expectable utility generally. The rules of war, then, subject to the restriction that the rules of war may not prevent a belligerent from using all the power necessary to overcome the enemy, will be ones whose authorization will serve to maximize welfare.

It is worth noting that a preamble to the U.S. Army Manual[1] offers an at least partially utilitarian theory of the rules of war (I say "at least partially" because of doubts about the interpretation of clause *b*). This preamble states that the law of land warfare "is inspired by the desire to diminish the evils of war by: *a.* Protecting both combatants and noncombatants from unnecessary suffering; *b.* Safeguarding certain fundamental human rights of persons who fall into the hands of the enemy, particularly prisoners of war, the wounded and sick, and civilians; and *c.* Facilitating the restoration of peace" (p. 3).

Which rules, then, would maximize expectable utility for nations at war? . . .

First, however, we must understand why the above-mentioned restriction, guaranteeing that the rules of war will not prevent a belligerent from using all the force necessary to overcome the enemy, must be placed on the utility-maximizing rules of war. The reason for this restriction is to be found in the nature of a serious war. There are, of course, many different kinds of war. Wars differ in magnitude, in the technologies they employ, in the degree to which they mobilize resources, in the type of issue the belligerents believe to be at stake, and in many other ways as well. . . .

It is possible that the rules which would maximize expectable utility might vary from one type of war to another. I shall ignore this possibility for the most part, and merely note that practical difficulties are involved in equipping military handbooks with different sets of rules and establishing judicial bodies to identify the proper classification of a given war. I shall take the position of Britain in World War II as typical of that of a belligerent in a serious war.

The position of a nation in a serious war is such, then, that it considers overpowering the enemy to be absolutely vital to its interests (and possibly to those of civilized society generally)—so vital, indeed, that it is willing to risk its very existence to that end. It is doubtful that both sides can be well justified in such an appraisal of the state of affairs. But we may assume that in fact they do make this appraisal. In this situation, we must simply take as a fact that neither side will consent to or follow rules of war which seriously impair the possibility of bringing the war to a victorious conclusion. This fact accounts for the restriction within which I suggested a choice of the rules of war must take place. We may notice that the recognized rules of war do observe this limitation: they are framed in such a way as not to place any serious obstacle in the way of a nation's using any available force, if necessary, to destroy the ability of another to resist. As Oppenheim has observed, one of the assumptions underlying the recognized rules of war is that "a belligerent is justified in applying any amount and any kind of force which is necessary for . . . the overpowering of the opponent."[2] This limitation, however, leaves a good deal of room for rules of war which will maximize expectable long-range utility for all parties.

This restriction, incidentally, itself manifests utilitarian considerations, for a nation is limited to the use of means *necessary* to overcome an opponent. Clearly it is contrary to the general utility that any amount or manner of force be employed when it is *not* necessary for victory.

It will be convenient to divide the rules restricting military operation, especially the targets and weapons of attack, into three types. (I do not claim that these are exhaustive.)

1. *Humanitarian restrictions of no cost to military operation.* There are some things that troops may be tempted to do which are at best of negligible utility to their nation but which cause serious loss to enemy civilians, although not affecting the enemy's power to win the war. Such behavior will naturally be forbidden by rules designed to maximize expectable utility within the understood restriction. Consider, for example, rules against the murder or ill-treatment of prisoners of war. A rule forbidding wanton murder of prisoners hardly needs discussion. Such murder does not advance the war effort of the captors; indeed, news of its occurrence only stiffens resistance and invites retaliation. Moreover, there is an advantage in returning troops having been encouraged to respect the lives of others. A strict prohibition of wanton murder of prisoners therefore has the clear support of utilitarian considerations. Much the same may be said for a rule forbidding ill-treatment of prisoners. There can, of course, be disagreement about what constitutes ill-treatment—for instance, whether a prisoner is entitled to a diet of the quality to which he is accustomed if it is more expensive than that available to troops of the captor army. It is clear, however, that in a war between affluent nations prisoners can generally be well-housed and well-fed and receive adequate medical care without cost to the war effort

of the captors. And if they receive such treatment, of course the captives gain. Thus a policy of good treatment of prisoners may be expected to make many nationals of both sides better off, and at a cost which in no way impairs the ability of either to wage the war.

Again, much the same may be said of the treatment of civilians and of civilian property in occupied territories. There is no military advantage, at least for an affluent nation, in the plunder of private or public property. And the rape of women or the ill-treatment of populations of occupied countries serves no military purpose. On the contrary, such behavior arouses hatred and resentment and constitutes a military liability. So utility is maximized, within our indicated basic limitations, by a strict rule calling for good treatment of the civilian population of an occupied territory. And the same can be said more generally for the condemnation of the wanton destruction of cities, towns, or villages, or devastation not justified by military necessity, set forth in the Charter of the Nuremberg Tribunal.

Obviously these rules, which the maximization of expectable utility calls for, are rules that command our intuitive assent.

2. Humanitarian restrictions possibly costly to military victory. Let us turn now to rules pertaining to actions in somewhat more complex situations. There are some actions which fall into neither of the classes so far discussed. They are not actions which must be permitted because they are judged necessary or sufficient for victory, and hence actions on which no party to a major war would accept restrictions. Nor are they actions which morally justified rules of war definitely prohibit, as being actions which cause injury to enemy nationals but serve no military purpose. It is this large class of actions neither clearly permitted nor definitely prohibited, for reasons already discussed, that I wish now to consider. I want to ask which rules of war are morally justified, because utility-maximizing, for actions of this kind. In what follows I shall be distinguishing several kinds of action and suggesting appropriate rules for them. The first type is this: doing something which will result in widespread destruction of civilian life and property and at the same time will add (possibly by that very destruction) to the *probability* of victory but will not definitely decide the war. Some uses of atomic weapons, and area bombing of the kind practiced at Hamburg, illustrate this sort of case.

A proper (not ideally precise) rule for such operations might be: substantial destruction of lives and property of enemy civilians is permissible only when there is good evidence that it will significantly enhance the prospect of victory. Application of the terms "good evidence" and "significantly enhance" requires judgment, but the rule could be a useful guideline all the same. For instance, we now know that the destruction of Hamburg did not significantly enhance the prospect of victory; in fact, it worked in the wrong direction, since it both outraged the population and freed workers formerly in non-war-supporting industries to be moved into industry directly contributing to the German war effort. The generals surely did not have good evidence that this bombing would significantly enhance the prospect of victory.

This rule is one which parties to a war might be expected to accept in advance, since following it could be expected to minimize the human cost of war on both sides, and since it does not involve a significant compromise of the goal of victory. The proposed rule, incidentally, has some similarities to the accepted rule . . . from the U.S. Army Manual, that "loss of life and damage to property must not be out of proportion to the military advantage to be gained" [p. 19].

This rule, which I am suggesting only for wars like World War II, where the stakes are very high, may become clearer if seen in the perspective of a more general rule that would also be suitable for wars in which the stakes are much lower. I pointed out above that what is at stake in a war may be no more than a tiny strip of land or national prestige. (The utility of these, may, however, be considered very great by a nation.) Now, it is clear that a risk of defeat which may properly be taken when the stakes are small may not be a proper risk when the stakes are virtually infinite; and a risk that could not properly be run when the stakes are enormous might quite properly be run when the stakes are small. So if the above-suggested rule is plausible for serious wars, in which the stakes are great, a somewhat different rule will be plausible in the case of wars of lesser importance—one that will require more in the way of "good evidence" and will require that the actions more "significantly enhance" the prospect of victory than is necessary when the stakes are much higher. These thoughts suggest the following general principle, applicable to all types of war: a military action (e.g., a bombing raid) is permissible only if the utility (broadly conceived, so that the maintenance of treaty obligations of international law could count as a utility) of victory to all concerned, multiplied by the increase in its probability if the action is executed, on the evidence (when the evidence is reasonably solid, considering the stakes), is greater than the possible disutility of the action to both sides multiplied by its probability. The rule for serious wars suggested above could then be regarded as a special case, one in which the utility of victory is virtually set at infinity—so that the only question is whether there is reasonably solid evidence that the action will increase the probability of victory. The more general rule obviously involves difficult judgments; there is a question, therefore, as to how it could be applied. It is conceivable that tough-minded civilian review boards would be beneficial, but we can hardly expect very reliable judgments even from them.[3]

These rules are at least very different from a blanket permission for anything the military thinks might conceivably improve the chances of victory, irrespective of any human cost to the enemy. In practice, it must be expected that each party to a war is likely to estimate the stakes of victory quite high, so that the rule which has the best chance of being respected is probably the first one mentioned, and not any modification of it that would be suggested to an impartial observer by the second, more general principle.

The reader may have been struck by the fact that these suggested rules are essentially institutionalized applications of a kind of act-utilitarian principle for certain contexts. This may seem inconsistent with the notion of a system of absolute rules themselves justified by long-range utilitarian considerations. But there is nothing inconsistent in the suggestion that some of the "absolute" rules should require that in certain situations an action be undertaken if and only if it will maximize expectable utility.

It may be objected that the rules suggested are far too imprecise to be of practical utility. To this I would reply that there is no reason why judgment may not be required in staff decisions about major operations. Furthermore, the U.S. Army Manual already contains several rules the application of which requires judgment. For example:

> Absolute good faith with the enemy must be observed as a rule of conduct. . . . In general, a belligerent may resort to those measures for mystifying or misleading the enemy against which the enemy ought to take measures to protect himself.

> The measure of permissible devastation is found in the strict necessities of war. Devastation as an end in itself or as a separate measure of war is not sanctioned by the law of war. There must be some reasonably close connection between the destruction of property and the overcoming of the enemy's army. . . .

> The punishment imposed for a violation of the law of war must be proportionate to the gravity of the offense. The death penalty may be imposed for grave breaches of the law. . . . Punishments should be deterrent . . . (pp. 22, 23–24, 182).

It has sometimes been argued, for instance by Winston Churchill, that obliteration bombing is justified as retaliation. It has been said that since the Germans destroyed Amsterdam and Coventry, the British had a right to destroy Hamburg. And it is true that the Hague Conventions are sometimes regarded as a contract, breach of which by one side releases the other from its obligations. It is also true that a government which has itself ordered obliteration bombing is hardly in a position to complain if the same tactic is employed by the enemy. But maximizing utility permits obliteration bombing only as a measure of deterrence or deterrent reprisal. This rule, incidentally, is recognized by the Army Manual as a principle governing all reprisals: "Reprisals are acts of retaliation . . . for the purpose of enforcing future compliance with the recognized rules of civilized warfare. . . . Other means of securing compliance with the law of war should normally be exhausted before resort is had to reprisals. . . . Even when appeal to the enemy for redress has failed, it may be a matter of policy to consider, before resorting to reprisals, whether the opposing forces are not more likely to be influenced by a steady adherence to the law of war on the part of the adversary" (p. 177). Purposes of retaliation, then, do not permit bombing in contravention of the suggested general principles.

Special notice should be taken that widespread civilian bombing might be defended by arguing that a significant deterioration in civilian morale could bring an end to a war by producing internal revolution. Our principle does not exclude the possibility of such reasoning, in the presence of serious evidence about civilian morale, when the stakes of victory are high. But we know enough about how bombing affects civilian morale to know that such bombing could be justified only rarely, if at all. The U.S. Army seems to go further than this; its rule asserts that any attack on civilians "for the sole purpose of terrorizing the civilian population is also forbidden."[4] It may be, however, that in actual practice this rule is interpreted in such a way that it is identical with the less stringent rule which is as much as utilitarian considerations can justify; if not, I fear we have to say that at this point the Army's theory has gone somewhat too far.

3. *Acceptance of military losses for humanitarian reasons.* Let us now turn to some rules which have to do with what we might call the *economics* of warfare, when the ultimate outcome is not involved, either because the outcome is already clear or because the action is fairly local and its outcome will not have significant repercussions. What damage may one inflict on the enemy in order to cut one's own losses? For instance, may one destroy a city in order to relieve a besieged platoon, or in order to avoid prolonging a war with consequent casualties? (The use of atom bombs in Japan may be an instance of this type of situation.) It is convenient to deal with two types of cases separately.

First, when may one inflict large losses on the enemy in order to avoid smaller losses for oneself, given that the issue of the war is not in doubt? A complicating fact is that when the issue is no longer in doubt it would seem that the enemy ought to concede, thereby avoiding losses to both sides. Why fight on when victory is impossible? (Perhaps to get better terms of peace.) But suppose the prospective loser is recalcitrant. May the prospective victor then unleash any horrors whatever in order to terminate the war quickly or reduce his losses? It is clear that the superior power should show utmost patience and not make the terms of peace so severe as to encourage further resistance. On the other hand, long-range utility is not served if the rules of war are framed in such a way as to provide an umbrella for the indefinite continuation of a struggle by an inferior power. So it must be possible to inflict losses heavy enough to produce capitulation but not so heavy as to be out of proportion to the estimated cost of further struggle to both sides. This condition is especially important in view of the fact that in practice there will almost always be other pressures that can be brought to bear. The application of such a rule requires difficult judgments, but some such rule appears called for by long-range utilitarian considerations.

The second question is: Should there be restrictions on the treatment of an enemy in the case of local actions which could hardly affect the outcome of the war, when these may cause significant losses? Rules of this sort are in fact already in force. For instance, . . . the Army Manual forbids killing of prisoners when their presence retards one's movements, reduces the number of men available for combat, uses up the food supply, and in general is inimical to the integrity of one's troops [p. 35]. Again, the Second Hague Convention forbids forcing civilians in occupied territory to give information about the enemy, and it forbids reprisals against the general civilian population "on account of the acts of individuals for which they cannot be regarded as jointly and severally responsible."[5] The taking of hostages is prohibited (Army Manual, p. 107).

All these rules prescribe that a belligerent be prepared to accept certain military disadvantages for the sake of the lives and welfare of civilians and prisoners. The disadvantages in question are not, however, losses that could be so serious as to affect the outcome of a war. Furthermore, the military gains and losses are ones which are likely to be evenly distributed, so that neither side stands to gain a long-term advantage if the rules are observed by both. So, without affecting the outcome of the war and without giving either side an unfair advantage, a considerable benefit can come to both belligerents in the form of the welfare of their imprisoned and occupied populations. Thus the long-run advantage of both parties is most probably served if they accept forms of self-restraint which can work out to be costly in occasional instances. Such rules will naturally be accepted by rational, impartial people in view of their long-range benefits.

Notes

[¹Department of the Army Field Manual PM 27-10, *The Law of Land Warfare* (Department of the Army, July 1956).—Ed.]

²[L. Oppenheim,] *International Law,* [ed. H. Lauterpacht, 7th ed. (New York, 1952),] p. 226.

³If we assume that both sides in a major struggle somehow manage to be persuaded that their cause is just, we shall have to expect that each will assign a net positive utility to its being the victor. For this reason it makes very little difference whether the more general principle uses the concept of the utility of victory by one side for everyone concerned, or the utility for that side only.

One might propose that the general restriction on rules of war, to the effect that in a serious war the use of any force necessary or sufficient for victory must be permitted, might be derived from the above principle if the utility of victory is set virtually at infinity and the probability of a certain action affecting the outcome is set near one. I believe this is correct, if we assume, as just suggested, that each side in a serious war will set a very high positive utility on *its* being the victor, despite the fact that both sides cannot possibly be correct in such an assessment. The reason for this principle as stated in the text, however, seems to me more realistic and simple. There is no reason, as far as I can see, why *both* lines of reasoning may not be used in support of the claim that the principle (or restriction) in question is part of a morally justifiable system of rules of war.

⁴[Marjorie M.] Whiteman, *Digest of International Law,* [(U.S. Department of State, 1963),] X, 135.

⁵Article L.

About the Editors

Michael D. Bayles is professor in the Department of Philosophy at Florida State University. He has previously taught at the University of Idaho, Brooklyn College, the University of Kentucky, the University of Western Ontario, and the University of Florida. He has also been director of the Westminster Institute for Ethics and Human Values in London, Canada, and a fellow at Harvard Law School, the Hastings Center, and the National Humanities Center. His books include *Reproductive Ethics* (1984), *Principles of Law* (1987), and *Professional Ethics* (2nd ed., 1988).

Kenneth Henley is associate professor in the Department of Philosophy and Religion at Florida International University (The State University of Florida at Miami). He has previously taught at the University of Kentucky and the University of Hull. He received his B.A. in English from the University of Virginia, and then turned to philosophy for his Ph.D., also at Virginia. He has published articles in ethical theory, applied ethics, social philosophy, and philosophy of law. His most recent article is "Constitutional Integrity and Compromise" in the anthology *Philosophical Dimensions of the Constitution*. He is currently working on the topic of legal determinacy and the rule of law as a distinct political ideal.